LONDON BOOKSELLERS AND AMERICAN CUSTOMERS

THE CAROLINA LOWCOUNTRY AND THE ATLANTIC WORLD
Sponsored by the Lowcountry and
Atlantic Studies Program of the College of Charleston

Money, Trade, and Power:
The Evolution of Colonial South Carolina's Plantation Society
Edited by Jack P. Greene, Rosemary Brana-Shute, and Randy J. Sparks

The Impact of the Haitian Revolution in the Atlantic World
Edited by David P. Geggus

London Booksellers and American Customers: Transatlantic Literary
Community and the Charleston Library Society, 1748–1811
James Raven

LONDON BOOKSELLERS AND
AMERICAN CUSTOMERS

*Transatlantic Literary Community and
the Charleston Library Society, 1748–1811*

JAMES RAVEN

University of South Carolina Press

© 2002 University of South Carolina

Published in Columbia, South Carolina, by the
University of South Carolina Press

Manufactured in the United States of America

06 05 04 03 02   5 4 3 2 1

Library of Congress Cataloging-in-Publication Data

Raven, James, 1959-
  London booksellers and American customers : transatlantic literary
community and the Charleston Library Society, 1748–1811 / James Raven.
    p. cm.
  Includes bibliographical references (p.) and index.
  ISBN 1-57003-406-0 (alk. paper)
    1. Charleston Library Society (S.C.)—History—18th century.
  2. Prorietary libraries—South Carolina—Charleston—History—18th century.
  3. Subscription libraries—South Carolina—Charleston—History—18th
  century. 4. Charleston (S.C.)—Intellectual life—18th century.
  5. Book industries and trade—England—London—History—18th century.
  6. Book industries and trade—South Carolina—Charleston—History—18th
  century. 7. Charleston (S.C.)—Commerce—England—London—History—18th
  century. 8. London (England)—Commerce—South Carolina—Charleston—
  History—18th century. 9. Charleston Library Society (S.C.)—Records
  and correspondence. I. Title.
  Z733.C4773 R39 2001
  027'.2757'915—dc21

                                                    2001003345

For Jinny Crum-Jones and Ian Jones

Caelum, non animum mutant qui trans mare currunt

Epistles of Horace, 1.2.27

CONTENTS

List of Tables   *ix*

List of Figures   *xi*

List of Illustrations   *xiii*

List of Abbreviations   *xv*

Preface   *xvii*

Acknowledgments   *xxi*

PART ONE

1   Introduction: Colonial Book Traffic and Transatlantic Community   *3*

2   The Enrichment of Charleston and Literature in South Carolina   *19*

3   The Early Membership and Mission of the Library Society   *37*

4   Organization and Sociability   *53*

5   New Members and the Desire for Grandeur   *67*

6   The Booksellers   *84*

7   Ordering the Books   *102*

8   Financing the Orders   *115*

9   Getting the Books Across   *133*

10   Literary Priorities   *150*

11   Learned and Scientific Community   *166*

12   Fiction, Prints, and Changing Attractions   *184*

13   Pirates, Reprints, and the Final Letters   *204*

14   Epilogue   *218*

PART TWO

The Letter Book   *233*

Charles Town Library Society "Copy Book of Letters," 1758–1811   *237*

APPENDIX 1
Members of the Charleston Library Society before 1779 *343*

APPENDIX 2
Chronological List (by Date of Admission, 1759–1779) of New Members
Purchasing New Shares *353*

APPENDIX 3
Reconstruction of the Foundation Collection of the Charleston Library Society
during Its First Twenty Years, 1748–c.1769 *357*

Notes *375*
Bibliography *453*
Index *473*

TABLES

1. Published Styles and Occupations of Members of the Charleston Library Society in 1750   *40*
2. Presidents of the Charleston Library Society, 1749–1811   *73*
3. Librarians of the Charleston Library Society, 1749–1811   *74*
4. Secretaries and Correspondents of the Charleston Library Society, 1749–1811   *74*
5. Booksellers to the Charleston Library Society, c. 1756–1811   *86*
6. Monies Sent to London and Debts Recorded by the Charleston Library Society, 1759–1811   *122*
7. Charleston Library Society Book Orders and Shipments: Identifiable Transatlantic Passages, 1758–1810   *138*
8. Comparative Passages of Transatlantic Book Orders and Shipments, 1728–1774   *142*
9. The 1806 and 1811 *Catalogues:* Division of Charleston Library Society Holdings by Subject and Size   *187*

FIGURES

1. Publication of Printed Items in Charleston, by Title,
   to 1811   *29*
2. Titles Listed in the Charleston Library Society *Catalogue* of 1770,
   by Subject   *185*
3. Titles Listed in the Charleston Library Society *Catalogue* of 1811,
   by Subject   *185*

ILLUSTRATIONS

following page 114
 1. 1704 bookplate of the Society for the Propagation of the Gospel in
    Foreign Parts
 2. Library membership certificate of Charles Cotesworth Pinckney, 1769
 3. Frontispiece to the first volume of the *Universal Magazine* (1747)
 4. The Charleston Courthouse, designed in 1792
 5. Map of the sites of the London booksellers, book agents, instrument makers,
    and merchant-brokers to the Charleston Library Society, 1758–1811 (with
    inset)
 6. Portrait of William Strahan (1715–1785) by Sir Joshua Reynolds, c. 1780
 7. Portrait of James Rivington (1724–1802) from a New York engraving by
    A. H. Petchie
 8. "John Stockdale, the Bookselling Blacksmith," c. 1781
 9. Exterior view of Lackington's Temple of the Muses, Finsbury Square, c. 1829
10. Interior view of Lackington, Allen, and Co., 1801
11. Advertising woodcut of the ship *Mermaid, South Carolina Gazette,*
    14 Sept. 1769
12. Demonstration of electrical experiments, frontispiece to George Adams, *An
    Essay on Electricity,* 4th ed. (London, 1792)
13. Detail of electrical experiments, plate 4 in Edward Nairne, *The Description
    and Use of Nairne's Patent Electrical Machine,* 8th ed. (London, 1796)
14. The solar microscope, fig. 4 in George Adams, *Micrographia Illustrata; or, the
    Knowledge of the Microscope Explain'd* (London, 1746)
15. Portrait of Jesse Ramsden (1735–1800)
16. The Boydells' *Shakespeare Prints: The Merry Wives of Windsor,* c. 1803

ABBREVIATIONS

AAS   American Antiquarian Society, Worcester, Massachusetts
AM   Anniversary Meeting (the Annual General Meeting of the
           Charleston Library Society held the 2nd Tuesday of January each
           year)
APS   American Philosophical Society, Philadelphia
BL   British Library, London
Bristol   Roger P. Bristol, *Supplement to Charles Evans' American Bibliography*
           (Charlottesville: Bibliographical Society of America and Bibliograph-
           cal Society of Virginia, 1970)
C   Charleston Library Society Committee Minute-Book, 1759–80
           [Apr. 1759–Feb. 1760, Jan 1761–Dec. 1762, Feb. 1764–Dec. 1777,
           Jan. 1778, Jan. 1780] and May 1783– Jan. 1791.
CAB   [Jeremy] Condy Account Book, American Antiquarian Society,
           Worcester, Massachusetts
CC   *Charleston Courier*
CG   *City Gazette,* Charleston
CGDA   *Charleston Gazette and Daily Advertiser*
CLS   Charlesto(w)n Library Society
CM   Charleston Library Society Committee Meeting
CUL   Cambridge University Library
DLC   Library of Congress, Washington, D.C.
DNB   *Dictionary of National Biography*
ESTC   *English Short-Title Catalogue* (subsuming the *Eighteenth-Century
           Short-Title Catalogue*)
FRS   Fellow of the Royal Society, London
HKP   Henry Knox Papers, 1719–1825 (56 MSS vols.), Massachusetts His-
           torical Society, Boston
HSP   Historical Society of Pennsylvania, Philadelphia
HP   [David] Hall papers and letterbook, American Philosophical Society,
           Philadelphia
IHR   Institute of Historical Research, London University
J   Charleston Library Society Journal-Book, 1759–80 and 1783–90
           ("Journall of the Proceedings of the Charles Town Library Society
           1759")

JMAL   John Murray Archives, Albemarle St., London, John Murray I
        Account Ledger 1768–80

JMDB   John Murray Archives, Albemarle St., London, John Murray I Day
        Books 1768–73, 1774–76, 1795–97

MLB   John Murray Archives, Albemarle St., London, John Murray I Letter
        Books (10 MSS vols.) 1765–93

LCP   Library Company of Philadelphia

MHS   Massachusetts Historical Society, Boston

NYPL   New York Public Library

NYSL   New York Society Library

PEM   James Duncan and Stephen Phillips Libraries, Peabody Essex
        Museum, Salem, Massachusetts

PHL   Philip M. Hamer et al., ed., *The Papers of Henry Laurens,* 13 vols.
        (Columbia, S.C.: University of South Carolina Press, 1968–)

PRO   Public Record Office, Kew, London

QM   General Meeting of the Charleston Library Society (from 1761
        known as the Quarterly Meeting)

Rules and   *The Rules and By-Laws of the Charlestown Library Society...*
By-Laws   followed by edition date, as separately printed and published from
              1750, and including *South Carolina Gazette* advertisements of
              26 Apr. 1748 and 23 Apr. 1750.

SCHM   *South Carolina Historical and Genealogical Magazine*

SCG   *South Carolina Gazette*

SCSG   *South Carolina State Gazette and General Advertiser*

SPCK   Society for Promoting Christian Knowledge

SPG   Society for the Propagation of the Gospel in Foreign Parts

STCi   *Short-Title Catalogue, 1475–1640* (Pollard and Redgrave)

STCii *Short-Title Catalogue, 1641–1700* (Wing)

8vo–   "Octavo et Infra" cataloguing division in Charleston Library Society
        Catalogues (that is, volumes of octavo size and smaller)

PREFACE

ISSUES CONFRONTED BY THIS VOLUME are currently being investigated by historians of the book, of empire, and of the colonial problem. These challenges were only hazily appreciated when I first came upon the letter book of the Charleston Library Society in the summer of 1994 and began to think of preparing an edition of the correspondence. To a historian researching the British book trade in the eighteenth century, the value of the fragile volume handed to me by Catherine Sadler, librarian of the Charleston Library Society, was immediately apparent. For students of literary London and its book trade in the eighteenth and early nineteenth centuries, the Charleston records offer unique and valuable evidence. Here are copies of letters sent to and from leading London booksellers for whom very little (and in some cases no other) extant correspondence survives. Moreover, the letters explain in unrivaled detail aspects of colonial book ordering and the process of transmission across the Atlantic. It quickly became clear that a fully annotated edition of the letters would assist new understanding of the book and print export trade from London to the American colonies (the subject of an essay that I was then writing for the new multivolume *History of the Book in America*).

That was the extent of the original ambition. As the edition took shape, however, the scope of the study extended. Discussion of the ordering institution and of the resulting literary profile of the library encountered further questions currently raised by scholars illuminating the social, cultural, and literary history of the eighteenth and early nineteenth centuries on both sides of the Atlantic. As I quickly discovered, the letters invited fuller investigation of the literary underpinnings of both the practice and perception of civic and transatlantic community during a period of fundamental transformation.

In itself, this investigative journey offered further insight into the developing history of the book. As with so many recent "book histories," the focus is upon material culture—printed books and prints, and their origins, dissemination, and effect. Discovery of letters such as those at Charleston are of obvious value in the pursuit of established questions about changes in eighteenth-century publishing and communications. In particular, the letters urged the extension of research strategies, including comparative use of the ship entry and departure notices in newspapers and of the business records of transaction agents. Exploration of such a range of sources underlined differences between histories of the book (or parts of those histories) starting with an event and asking how print affected this event or was changed by it, and those starting with the material artifact and asking questions primarily to illuminate the broader literary history of the origin and reception of that text. As is the case with the Charleston letters, vividly detailing the London and export book trade of the eighteenth century, any categorization of the resulting study as "book history" must be sufficiently broad to allow a history of communication and of social and political transformation that goes beyond the immediate inception and reception issues of books. As a historian grateful for and admiring of bibliographical research on so many aspects of the material text, I am nevertheless unsympathetic to those who would then establish "book history" as a bounded (and thereby conservative) discipline. For this writer, a meaningful history of books cannot exist without people or without changing causal agencies—the "history" is one of the involvement of books and print in human activity, not simply a history of books that adheres only to questions of material production or physical description (a proper domain of descriptive or analytical bibliography).

One aim of this study, therefore, is to contribute to opening up the so-called "history of the book" to engagement with broader historical concerns. This necessarily involves perilous (some might say foolhardy) interaction with a forbidding range of scholarship in intellectual, social, political, religious, and economic history, and it pursues a conception of cultural history as a sum total of past ideas and practice rather than as a residual category of social history. In Clifford Geertz's influential formulation, culture might be regarded as "webs of significance" in which subjective social interaction is constantly recreated. "Culture" is no mere imposition from on high but the sum of individual interpretations in which identified threads of commonality are still capable of different meanings for different observers and practitioners.[1] That perspective remains a crucial determinant in the argument of the following chapters, each attempting to contribute detailed components to the understanding of the mental constructions of "community." As others have insisted, a transition from the classically posited mechanical solidarity (*gemeinschaft*) to a more organic solidarity (*gesselschaft*), can be reinterpreted, within one specific society, as the evolution of different cultural modalities and of appropriated and self-identifying ideas and emblems of community. In the conclusion of Anthony P. Cohen: "people construct community symbolically, making it a resource and repository of meaning, and a referent of their identity."[2]

The following will not engage with the broader theoretical investigations of these issues, but it does aim to provide well-grounded insights into aspects of community and its transatlantic perspectives that were clearly more than just composites of social structure. In particular, by specific histories of an institution, its members, its material collection, and its usage, the study attempts to investigate the relationship between print and the different appearances, understandings, and expressions of "community." It aims to recover different ideas of attachment and the construction of boundaries, established from various and changing perceptions, including those of defensiveness and a fear of loss. Even within groups apparently bonded by similarities in wealth and status, ideas of association and relationship can differ between individuals and between self-constructed associations. The result might be more an accretion of perceived connections and boundaries than a force for integration and inclusive social bonding. In the words of Cohen, "the '*com-monality*' which is found in community need not be a uniformity. It does not clone behaviour or ideas. It is a commonality of *forms* (ways of behaving) whose content (meanings) may vary considerably among its members. The triumph of community is to so contain this variety that its inherent discordance does not subvert the apparent coherence which is expressed by its boundaries."[3]

The following book remains a staging post towards a planned study of transatlantic community in the eighteenth century. The book and print traffic across the Atlantic maintained links not just between two contemporary societies (and the difficult, complex, and changing relationship between them), but textual connections over space and time (both easily underestimated and undervalued). My attempts to reconstruct a changing colonial psychology of literary belonging is grounded in an analysis of the spatial and temporal contortions created by the importation of ancient and modern literature, whose antiquity and currency were not simply distinguishable to their recipients and producers. Readers constructed their imaginary community from an eclectic provision. A key issue concerns the processes by which libraries that were founded to overcome a perceived knowledge deficit and to crusade for very particular home-country values, were transformed into institutions that reproduced learning, contributed to new discovery and debate, and configured colonial knowledge. The following aims to provide a fresh analysis of the early history of the Charleston Library Society, informed by its transatlantic correspondence, and attempts to reevaluate the framework in which cultural identities were forged, promulgated—and contained.

---

1. Clifford Geertz, *The Interpretation of Cultures* (London: Hutchinson, 1975), pp. 3–30.
2. Anthony P. Cohen, *The Symbolic Construction of Community* (London and New York: Routledge, 1985), p. 118.
3. Cohen, *Symbolic Construction of Community,* p. 20.

ACKNOWLEDGMENTS

I ACKNOWLEDGE WITH GRATITUDE the permission of the Charleston Library Society to reproduce letters and documents in their possession. The library on King Street has offered me every assistance in my research, and the generosity of Catherine Sadler (Librarian), Patricia Glass-Bennett, and their colleagues, ensured that my various visits were both productive and a very great pleasure. The South Carolina Historical Society in Charleston was similarly hospitable, and I am particularly grateful to John H. Wilson of Charleston, for his indefatigable checking of newspaper notices. I also wish to acknowledge the ready assistance given to me by librarians, archivists, and staff at the Lambeth Palace Library, London; the Cambridge University Library; the Boston Public Library; the Southern Historical Collection and the North Carolina Library, Wilson Library, University of North Carolina, Chapel Hill; the South Caroliniana Library and Archives Department, University of South Carolina, Columbia; the Rare Book, Manuscript, and Special Collections Library, Duke University; and the South Carolina Historical Society, Charleston. Donna Andrew, Joshua Civin, Timothy Clayton, Walter Edgar, Antonia Forster, John Gilmore, Neil Hitchin, Mark Kaplanoff, Robert Leath, Warren McDougall, David Moltke-Hansen, David Money, Alison Morrison-Low, Michael O'Brien, Edward Pearson, Kathryn Preyer, Liba Taub, Calhoun Winton, and Betty Wood offered generous comment, provided many additional references, and eliminated numerous errors. I also benefited greatly from the criticism and advice given in seminars at the American Antiquarian Society; Brasenose College, Oxford; St. Cross College, Oxford; Sidney Sussex College, Cambridge; and the Cambridge Bibliographical Society. I am also very much indebted to Randy Sparks, then of the College of Charleston, for arranging both hospitality and a further presentation of my work. Rebecca Starr read the entire typescript with enviable critical acumen and I have tried my best to correct and respond accordingly. Appendix 3 was very kindly completed by Patricia Aske, with the assistance of Nigel Hall, who also produced plate 5 and refined the bibliography and other sections of this work. Alex Moore, first as director of the South Carolina Historical Society, and then as editor at the University of South Carolina Press, has offered generous and supportive advice, in tandem with the invaluable suggestions of my press readers. I also wish to pay tribute to managing editor Barbara Brannon and copyeditor Noel Kinnamon, whose magnificent editorial work has rescued me from many errors.

The study could not have been completed without generous grants from the Bibliographical Society and the Bibliographical Society of America (the Fredson

Bowers Award, 1995). These secured research visits to Charleston and several other archival expeditions in the United States and Britain. Much of the writing was completed during tenure of a visiting fellowship at the American Antiquarian Society in the summer of 1995. Ellen Dunlap, John Hench, Tom Knoles, Marie Lamoureux, Marcus McCorison, Russell Martin, Caroline Sloat, and all my friends at the American Antiquarian Society offered their usual expert and impeccably tolerant assistance. In particular, Alan Degutis transformed this study by new trawls through the North American Imprints Program. Further writing was completed during a Maclean Contributionship Fellowship at the Library Company of Philadelphia in the spring of 1996, and I am very grateful for the advice and encouragement of James Green and his colleagues at the library company. A condensed account of the capture of a Charleston Library Society book shipment by privateers was published in Arnold Hunt, Giles Mandelbrote, and Alison Shell, eds., *The Booktrade and Its Customers 1450–1900: Historical Essays for Robin Myers* (Winchester and Newcastle, Del.: St. Paul's Bibliographies, 1997).

Many American friends ensured that suitcase life was neither difficult nor dull. As always, Elizabeth Durkee banished the stress of travel by sharing with me her wonderful home, garden, and conversation. For more than a decade now this has been a much loved and much appreciated delight. Patricia and Alan Clark (who also generously rechecked some local publications) welcomed me, once again, to Atlanta and enabled me to work at the Woodruff Library, Emory University. When my good friends, Jinny Crum-Jones and Ian Jones, suddenly left for the New World, non-Puritan Cambridge went into mourning. Without their subsequent invitations to share the pleasures of Charleston and the Carolinas, however, this book would not have been born.

PART ONE

Chapter One

INTRODUCTION: COLONIAL BOOK TRAFFIC AND TRANSATLANTIC COMMUNITY

THE CHARLES TOWN LIBRARY SOCIETY was founded in 1748, three years before the British Museum and ten years before the first major proprietary subscription library in Britain. The Charleston library was at least the sixth such institution to be established in North America, after the Library Company of Philadelphia in 1731; the Philogrammatican Library at Lebanon, Connecticut, in 1739; the Library Company of Darby, Pennsylvania, in 1743; the Union Library Company of Philadelphia in 1746; and the Redwood Library Company, Newport, Rhode Island, in 1747.[1] The Charleston library's eighteenth- and early-nineteenth-century correspondence is an extraordinary survival. The letters of the Charleston Library Society offer a uniquely vivid portrait of a transatlantic traffic in intellectual commodities. The letters record changes in the conduct of the book trade between North America and Britain before and after the American Revolution, and they open a window on the practices of transatlantic literary exchange and dependency, improving our understanding of the meaning of cultural community, civic identity, and the cosmopolitan aspirations of British Americans.

In all, there survive copies of 120 letters, the first written and dispatched in August 1758 and the last in January 1811. All but one of the letters were entered in the "Copy-Book of Letters." The preparation and custody of this, together with the "Committee's Minute-Book" and the "Journal-Book" for minuting proceedings of anniversary and quarterly meetings, were the responsibility of an elected secretary of the society.[2]

The letters were sent to and received from London booksellers, agents, and intermediaries. The ranks of those involved in executing the Charleston book demands included the most esteemed and active of London booksellers of the period (as well as a few rogues), leading London Carolina merchants, and general mercantile firms.

In the absence of any kind of cumulative stock list, analysis of the purchasing patterns of the Charleston Library Society is reliant upon the infrequently issued catalogues of the library. Those for 1750 and 1770–1772 are rare but invaluable guides to the holdings of a large institutional colonial library. After a problematic gap, during which the library rules were reprinted (1785), new catalogues were issued in 1806 and 1811. The letters can supplement these infrequent stock lists and suggest with new clarity the depth of scientific enthusiasms, the particular distinctions between practical and more philosophical interests in legal and political literature, and the extent to which library members were superficial if well-meaning followers of literary fashion and trends.

The earliest letters date from the decade when Charleston, importing thousands more slaves than books, became one of the richest communities in North America. The letters therefore not only provide a rare glimpse of overseas literary commerce from the mid-eighteenth century to the War of 1812, but they also chart the course of an exacting cultural connection between the capital of the British empire and one of its fastest growing and most prosperous colonial outposts. The exchanges between the Library Society and its London booksellers continued as the affluent and diverse society of Charleston claimed new domestic and international influence. The literature demanded by Charlestonians had to be acknowledged as important and fashionable as well as practical and instructive. A mixture of self-confidence and social anxiety surfaces in the grand letters dispatched to London. Many of them lambast the traders for their ignorance, delay, or failure in recognizing the value of serving the merchants of Charleston. It is a remarkably lively correspondence, for which an alternative title might be "reprimanding the bookseller."

The surviving records of the other major early American library foundations provide valuable comparisons with the Charleston library, although all are fragmentary. The minute books and some separate letters and invoices of the Library Company of Philadelphia remain at that library and in the neighboring collections of the Historical Society of Pennsylvania, but the minutes are often summary in respect of book orders and literary debate. Although fine drafts and copies of letters to and from the Library Company's first book agent in London, Peter Collinson, do survive, along with the first and other early orders for books, many of the later book requests, or "catalogues" as these lists were called, do not. Collinson was entrusted to execute the Library Company's wishes as he believed best, but most details of his decisions and difficulties are unrecorded. Accounts of the book-ordering methods undertaken by Collinson's successor, Benjamin Franklin, when resident in London in the 1760s, are unsurprisingly sketchy. Only when the merchants Woods and Dillwyn were employed as agents to the Library Company later in the century is more precision offered by the minutes, together with invoices of book orders, surviving serially from the late 1780s.[3] Unlike the Charleston Library Society, the Library Company employed loyal Quaker agents and general merchants to send over its books and did not correspond directly with London booksellers (although the agent was asked to pass on motions of censure to particular stationers and booksellers).

Surviving records from other early American library societies are even less informative. In Rhode Island, the Redwood Library Company minutes detailing orders for shipment from London do not supply the names of booksellers or agents, and no correspondence relating to them survives. All that is known from the Redwood Library's minutes is that 751 titles in 1,338 volumes and costing over £9,600 in New England currency were bought in London by John Thomlinson, the merchant son of a wealthy Antigua planter. The consignment probably arrived in the summer of 1749.[4] The New York Society Library, founded in 1754, preserves valuable but interrupted and brief minute books and no extant early correspondence. Details of book orders and receipts are fragmentary.[5]

As well as detailing the mechanics of setting up and extending a library society, the Charleston letters chronicle the library as a social institution and the changing cultural identities fostered by the members. The correspondence, together with the other records of the library, contribute to our understanding of the genesis of the distinctive culture—in its broadest sense—of the southern plantocracy and mercantile elite. It is the one register from the colonial south displaying the interests of a literary elite in communal rather than individual aspect. The history of what was in effect an aggressive civilizing offensive offers further perspectives on the colonial situation and the relationship between colony and metropole. Claims for inclusivist citizenship invited discussion of what counted as knowledge and, indeed, as ideological tools to ensure commonly shared distinctions of dependency and independence.

For the literary historian in particular, the Charleston Library Society letters reveal fresh detail about the overseas activities of the eighteenth- and early-nineteenth-century London book trade, the mechanics of transatlantic ordering, financing, and transporting of books, periodicals, prints, and library accessories. The letters record the type of literature requested, the time that orders took to arrive, the manner of their journey, and the developing tensions between loyal colonial customers and a rapidly changing book trade at the heart of the empire. The trade and correspondence are not continuous and the gaps are significant. Most of the early incoming letters are lost, but full copies of outgoing letters, together with some drafts, and the complete supporting evidence of the journal of quarterly meetings of the society and its library committee minute books, enable an extensive reconstruction of both correspondence and transactions. Occasionally, reference is made to some remonstrance or request by a bookseller where the absence of the original is frustrating,[6] but during the final thirty years of the correspondence incoming letters were also copied into the letter books. In particular, the letters from London booksellers such as John Stockdale and the firm of Lackington, Allen, and Co. offer striking detail about the operation of transatlantic book commerce. None of the overseas letters of these businesses survive in London. Moreover, the Library Society correspondence complements the relatively few extant letters upon which to base an analysis of the eighteenth- and early-nineteenth-century London book trade, such as those of Robert Dodsley, John Murray I and II, and the fragmentary letters of the Dilly brothers, Joseph Johnson, and John Stockdale.[7]

The letters further illuminate from the American perspective the efforts and frustrations of gaining access to new or rare literature in the late colonial and early national periods. Against formidable obstacles of cost, risk, and time, the transatlantic book trade hugely increased during the second half of the eighteenth century. This expansion was partly a result of the limited and unbalanced development of colonial printing, but partly also a result of the strength of the cultural and social bonds of empire. In addition to early supply constraints and direct political prohibitions, American publishing was frustrated by the tenacity and adaptability of British mercantile and monopolistic trade practices. North American newspaper advertising and colonial booksellers' catalogues were used to retail London wares in a manner similar to provincial English practice (where local book printing was similarly handicapped by the dominance of the London trade system).

Throughout most of the colonial period most books had to be shipped in, whatever the capabilities of publishing and reprinting in North America. British legal publishing monopolies and patents reserved printing rights to Bibles, prayer books, psalters, almanacs, and certain law books. Further political and legal impediments were in force within the colonies. In 1671 Sir William Berkeley, governor of Virginia, offered public prayer to keep the colony free from schools and printing.[8] Edicts against presses were imposed by the governor of New York in the 1680s and reinforced by royal proclamation. In other colonies restrictive local licensing remained in force until 1730. Beyond this, basic economic considerations of paper, printing equipment, and labor costs also figured largely. Paper manufacture commenced only in 1690, near to Philadelphia. The first paper mill in Massachusetts opened in 1717. Total output remained slight until the final third of the eighteenth century and was generally of very low quality. The expense of importing fine paper contributed directly to the relatively high costs of American printing. Most equipment was also unavailable locally. Together, printing press and type might comprise 90 percent of start-up capital costs. No presses were manufactured in the colonies until the 1760s, and even then printing presses were imported right up until the end of the century. In 1766 an Edinburgh press and accompanying materials from Alexander Donaldson were shipped from Leith to Charleston, and as late as 1793 Isaiah Thomas in Massachusetts ordered his new press from London.[9]

The confident expansion of the transatlantic book trade was boosted also by changes to the types of literature imported. The slowly developing North American domestic book printing led off with the production of almanacs and other small practical books, but this tended to exaggerate further the need to ship in other literature. At the same time, economics continued to count. Throughout the century the relatively cheap price of many imported English novels could not be matched by locally reprinted editions.[10] Periodical publications were especially popular British imports, even if they were to become increasingly problematic. A related change concerned the condition of the books ordered, where the increase in the number of skilled American binders reduced the demand for British and European publications to be sent across already bound in quality coverings.[11] The other issue central to changes to the kinds of book imported—and one often related to arguments about the later decline in foreign imports—is the allegation that London booksellers used the colonies as a dumping ground for unwanted remainders and poor sellers. In a study of the eighteenth-century transatlantic trade, Stephen Botein made much of the consignments of unsalable titles or "rum books" sent out first from London by the likes of Robert Boulter and Richard Chiswell in the late seventeenth century, and later, in much larger quantities, by Thomas Osborne, William Strahan, and James Rivington, among others.[12]

To understand the relative impact of such London promotions and off-loadings, we need to examine carefully the strength and specificity of demand in North America and the ways in which it could be satisfied, further encouraged, and refined. Put simply, the dynamics of book importation rested with three groups: London traders, colonial traders, and colonial customers. London booksellers and merchants, already exploring new business methods at home, undertook many greater risks in the book market from the mid-eighteenth century. At the same time, colonial importers, merchants, and booksellers developed more specialized trade and trading practice. Against the Botein argument we should compare the careful ordering of eighteenth-century colonial booksellers such as Henry Knox (who opened his London Book-Store in Boston in 1770) and Jeremiah (Jeremy) Condy, Baptist minster and bookseller of Boston from 1754 to 1768.[13] Where dumping was attempted it might have been allied to the wholesale auctions of books, about which we still know far too little. What remains remarkable is not only that demand soared in the second half of the eighteenth century but that the attraction of transatlantic imports for colonial traders and customers was sustained despite the many costs, risks, and inconveniences involved.

It is clearly important to consider the exact identity of the customers—and especially the high-spending customers. Social imperatives loomed large in maintaining the attraction of imported books. American book imports were lifelines of identity, and they were direct material links to a present and past European culture. The bookseller David Hall's midcentury analysis of a declining religious market in Pennsylvania was an accurate one. Increasingly, literary fashion—and fashion of a secular kind—played a prominent part in growing demand. It was also part of a broader commerce in which London booksellers were supplying a market society straddling the Atlantic.

Despite calculations of lower per capita consumption between about 1720 and 1750, in absolute terms (and with corresponding changes in the social profile of consumption) the colonies imported three times as many goods in 1750 as in 1700. From the late 1740s a major increase in per capita consumption also began. The practice of purchases supported by current financing was increasingly replaced by use of credit advanced by British merchants.[14] As John Clive and Bernard Bailyn have noted, the thirteen colonies were in many respects "cultural provinces" of the mother country, attempting to adopt cosmopolitan standards of taste. Books were notable luxury goods—totems of respectability and conveyers of metropolitan thought.[15] "In the last ships" became the familiar boast of booksellers' newspaper advertisements listing imported titles. In fast-growing cities in particular, the import of books as status-bearing luxuries was pronounced. This appetite for literary commodities has even been seen as revolutionizing political discourse and creating "an indispensable foundation for the later political mobilization of the American people."[16] If there was a strong link between newly imported material culture and new nationalism, however, political independence brought no less and in certain areas even more clamor for things European. In the Federalist period, in the words of one of its historians, "peace brought a riot of luxury," and a New England "codfish aristocracy" was both envied and mocked for pursuit of a new cosmopolitanism.[17]

In the early eighteenth century individual customers like James Logan (1674–1751), the great bibliophile of Philadelphia,[18] ordered increasing numbers of books through London, but it was the development of institutional demand that was to have particular significance both for North American access to new literature and for the responses of British booksellers and agents. In Britain also, an increase in new customers and readers and an increased propensity for book-buying individuals to buy more cannot entirely account for the sharp upswing in the production of books and periodicals: domestic demand from libraries and other institutions was a particular feature of the late-eighteenth-century trade.[19] Commercial circulating libraries developed from the lending services of booksellers, with notable pioneers established in the 1740s. By 1800 more than 200 such libraries operated in Britain, more than double the number of private proprietary or subscription libraries, the earliest including the 1731 Library Company of Philadelphia and the Liverpool Library founded in 1758.[20] The proprietary libraries, however, commanded much grander literature, membership, and intentions than their cheaper cousins. The Liverpool Library typically advertised assistance to "Gentlemen and Ladies who wish to promote the Advantage of Knowledge." Such institutions embraced social ambition, as well as offering the obvious benefits of shared literary knowledge and financial resources to access expensive, luxury items.

Many of these libraries generated a strong sense not only of pioneering a service but also of a moral imperative for so doing. This was especially true in the remote and isolated towns of the colonies. In a letter of 1732 sent by the founders of the Library Company of Philadelphia to their London book agent, it was noted that "an undertaking like ours was as necessary here, as we hope it will be useful; there being no manner of Provision made by the Government for public Education, either in this or the neighbouring Provinces, nor so much as a good Book-Sellers Shop nearer than Boston."[21] It was for the same reason that the Charleston Library Society, founded sixteen years later, negotiated directly with a London bookseller. Like the Philadelphia and New York libraries it also maintained direct London connections even when late-eighteenth-century colonial booksellers also offered their services to supply large quantities of European books.

Nevertheless, for the colonial customer, the bookseller-merchant, and the Library Society decisions to buy from London were far from straightforward. At the beginning of the eighteenth century, the immediate obstacle to purchasing books from Europe was the far from simple question of acquiring precise information about publication and availability; the next task was to set about securing a resident agent to manage the affair on the other side of the Atlantic. Both problems were generally faced by all the commercial customer groups: wealthy or well-connected individuals; colonial booksellers and general merchants; and institutional customers including libraries, churches, colleges, and gentlemen's societies.

The provision of information was transformed during the eighteenth century, ultimately perhaps at the cost of lifting expectations to unattainable levels. From the mid-seventeenth century prospectuses like those preserved in the Winthrop papers detailed "new bookes that are lately come out," together with booksellers' catalogues, including those from the great fairs of Frankfurt.[22] A century later, almost all the leading London booksellers printed catalogues of new or in-stock titles. William Strahan sent catalogues to David Hall, his bookselling protégé in Philadelphia, Thomas Longman did the same for Henry Knox in Boston,[23] and John Murray sent catalogues to Robert Miller, merchant in Williamsburg, "which I beg of you to shew your Friends who may perhaps order some Books from it."[24] Colonial traders then advertised imports in newspapers. From the mid-eighteenth century the individual or institutional customer enjoyed more opportunities to read of new publications in London newspapers and periodicals. The periodical journals in particular, popular imports in their own right but also attempting comprehensive reviewing of new publications together with extracts and criticisms, led to exacting orders sent either to the colonial bookseller or directly to the London wholesaler or agent.

Contacts were nurtured to help solve logistical difficulties, notably the location of specific booksellers, the securing of credit, finance and transit arrangements, and in some cases, the dilution of a sense of inferiority to which certain colonial customers were prone. Individual purchasers in particular often depended upon family and friends in London, or made strategic use of journeys there to establish or revive contacts with booksellers or fellow bibliophiles. Increase Mather was supplied with books via, among others, the professor of Hebrew at Utrecht. Cotton Mather's great library was fed by widely dispersed agents and contacts, including one in Tranquebar in the East-Indies sending "the first things that ever were printed in those parts of the world."[25] Some of the earliest importers like the troublesome Benjamin Harris of Boston, driven out of London in 1686 for his over-ardent Protestantism, set up shop and then revisited London (some, like Harris, more than once), before returning permanently to North America. Among other venturers, Samuel Sewall ordered books from London booksellers and also from Amsterdam.[26] The Philadelphia library of James Logan, open to the public in 1760, and probably the finest library anywhere in the colonies in the first half of the eighteenth century, developed from Logan's 1710 and 1723 journeys to London.

Perched on the edge of the world, colonial book collectors needed book scouts, especially if, like Logan, they regarded booksellers as cheats and profiteers. Agents like Logan's friend John Askew coordinated the financing, assembly, and dispatch of the books ordered. To make London purchases for the Winthrops, Edward Howes was sent money by their various City acquaintances. All the shipments sent out by Richard Chiswell to John Usher from at least 1679 to 1685 were arranged through John Ive who also managed the account of Sewall.[27] Clients sent agents long letters of instruction detailing destinations, requirements, and total budgets. Logan, like many other merchant bibliophiles, was able to exploit his commercial and political network to locate and retrieve the books he wanted. From 1718 Logan's main agent was the Quaker writer Josiah Martin, and a twenty-five-year series of book letters records the ups and downs of this personal transatlantic commerce. From 1727 Logan also employed on "a reasonable Commission" William Reading, librarian of Sion College.[28]

As already noted, the Library Company of Philadelphia depended upon the London merchant (and esteemed patron of botanical and scientific endeavor) Peter Collinson, to liaise with Meadows, Innys, Osborne, and other booksellers. Collinson was also asked to reprimand and dismiss booksellers, until he too lost patience with the Library Company and despite some later attempts at reconciliation, was replaced as agent in 1760.[29] At midcentury, the New York Society Library engaged John Ward as its London agent-bookseller,[30] but in 1771, faced by silence from his successors, the Society resolved "to find out and settle a Correspondence with some Bookseller in London who will supply the Library with such books as may be ordered from Time to Time upon the best Terms." The last condition was no small matter; breakdowns between customer, agent, and bookseller were common. As Logan reminded one supplier at the end of the 1740s: "Thou may therefore well excuse me for finding fault with thee as I do when thy prices are unreasonable, who have been a buyer of Books above these 50 years and am not to be put off as a common American, as thou hast divers times served me, for I know a book well."[31]

A surprising number of colonial customers, merchants, and booksellers made at least one visit to London themselves, and many recent immigrants were able to exploit active connections. Condy of Boston had been in England in 1735–1738, and in May 1771 Joseph Cabot, merchant of Salem, then in London, bought various books and periodicals including the last four volumes of the *Town and Country Magazine* and the *London Magazine,* a large quarto Bible and Malachy Postlethwayt's magnificent (and expensive) *Dictionary of Trade and Commerce.* Before returning, though, he also appears to have left a shopping list for his bookseller George Pearch.[32] The London merchant John Thomlinson, whose books bought in London in 1747 set up Redwood's Rhode Island library, originated from Antigua, where Redwood was born and had inherited a large plantation. Thomlinson was also the British agent for the Assembly of New Hampshire and a proven and trusted correspondent of New England merchants.[33] Library societies, indeed, were supremely well placed to develop connections, given the normal range of members' contacts with London.

Not least of the difficulties in both ordering and receiving books, however, was the time required to complete the transaction. The months taken to cross and recross the Atlantic added to credit difficulties and interest charges, and a lengthy journey was a major handicap to receiving new publications and up-to-date trade information. In 1708 Wait Winthrop was informed by Samuel Reade in London that "ye person you mention that did collect those bookes hath been dead many yeares, & none hath succeeded him in that curiosity; ye bookes almost out of printe, & upon inquiry of severall booksellers cannot heare of but very few."[34] Even for those engaged in regular book traffic, transatlantic letters typically took more than two months for delivery, and news of safe arrivals often more than twice as long.

The ships taking books from Britain and payment and orders back were powered by the northeast trade winds and the difficult westerlies. The circuit averaged about nine months. In any season, ships crossed the Atlantic by several different routes. Those on the "sugar route" made their way south to Madeira or the Canary Islands and then sailed to the Caribbean on the trades. Outgoing vessels to the Chesapeake or ports further north followed either a course known as the "bow," passing near to the Azores, the more northerly "string," or, from Glasgow, crossed north of Ireland towards the southern point of Newfoundland. To reach further destinations, but also to return, ships leaving southern colonial ports had to work their way up the North American coast to a latitude of about forty degrees north, where the westerlies filled the sails back to England. In addition to the crucial wind belts, the Gulf Stream added up to 130 miles a day to the speed of a Britain-bound ship, although favorable winds were ultimately much more important and less predictable than ocean currents. There was, however, great seasonal variation. Strong east or west adverse winds off Britain delayed ships clearing port in late winter and early spring, while Atlantic gales made winter crossings perilous. In August and September hurricanes affected the Caribbean and the southeastern American coast. Winter ice also closed harbors north of the Chesapeake for weeks or even months. Philadelphia, further south than New York and Boston, but served by rivers, was the more vulnerable. Really severe winters blocked all ports. That of 1732–33 closed New York for some days, Boston for three weeks, and Philadelphia for more than three months. The result was that although ships left from English harbors throughout the year, relatively few set off in April or June. The return passage was far more seasonal, with ships from the American colonies seldom arriving in spring and most likely to dock between midsummer and late autumn. With few exceptions, the only transatlantic vessels arriving in England in late winter were sugar and tobacco ships from the south.[35]

There was one further handicap for English shipping to the Atlantic—the English Channel. It was not only a tempting occasional run for privateers, but also a permanent impediment to picking up the trade winds. The westerlies launched English Bibles on the Thames and then arrested their journey by becalming the Downs. By contrast, Spanish psalters bound for Mexico gained almost immediate access to the trades from Cadiz. The cargoes, including trunks and parcels of books, were loaded at the London docks, but in order to avoid the possible delays in the Downs, letters, small packages, and elite passengers often joined the London ships at Portsmouth. News for the colonies was often sent to Plymouth or Falmouth by outrider. This explains how many London booksellers, using the mail service to the southwest, were able to warn colonial customers by an advance ship that their order was windbound (or worse). It probably also explains the decision, not always understood by American booksellers and customers, to send on invoices and letters of explanation separately from the books themselves. It was the result not just of security concerns, but also of shipping speeds and overland mail and transit arrangements.

Bristol remained the premier English outport, although its shipping also had to fight the westerlies. In addition, Liverpool, Glasgow, the Irish ports, and Plymouth developed as major transatlantic ports. Others, like Southampton and its rice cargoes, profited from particular trades. For London booksellers, however, the transport of books to the outports was financially impractical; it was also usually not at all clear that carriage for large orders would be any faster than letting the shipment take its chance on the conditions in the English Channel. There were certain exceptions. Later in the century and particularly during periods of war with France, London booksellers did use ships leaving western ports for the southern American ports. Similarly, it is likely that some of the requests by colonial customers for their orders of parcels of magazines, pamphlets, and the like to be placed in the captain's cabin rather than in the hold (to speed unloading times), ensured that some packages were sent ahead with the mail to reach ships already past the Channel. Another exception was in Scotland where many orders sent to Edinburgh were collected and then sent to Port Glasgow for shipment to the colonies.[36]

The traffic in books to America was certainly advanced by improvement in these shipping services. During the first half of the century the Atlantic was shrunk, although this was more a result of more frequent sailings than by any improvement in speed or predictability of passage. Increasing knowledge of the oceans did reduce risks, however, as did improvements in navigational aids and the construction of offshore warning lights. By 1740 there were forty lighthouses around the British Isles and early colonial lighthouses included those at Boston, built in 1716, and Tybee Island, Georgia, built in 1740.[37] It now seems that New England shipping routes at least also became more regularized despite the emphasis in many histories on the frequency of route changes.[38] With renewed confidence, the American packet boat service was reestablished in 1755 after earlier brief experiments in the 1710s and now aimed at achieving a monthly correspondence. The British Post Office established regular Charleston-bound packet ships from the 1760s, leaving Falmouth for Barbados, Jamaica, Pensacola, St. Augustine, and thence to Charleston before returning home. On the eve of the Revolution five vessels sailed this route, each completing two circuits annually and with the swiftest (but very unusual) packet boat sailing on the return leg taking three weeks.[39] Over the course of the eighteenth century, not only was a previously Mediterranean-focused "first Atlantic"[40] succeeded by a second, predominantly British Atlantic, but exceptional enterprise also advanced the flow of traffic across it. Charleston and South Carolina were prominent beneficiaries of these developments—in which distance was less important than the direction of routes and ports of contact.

In such ways, both the letters and the history of the Charleston Library Society embody the imaginary participative space of empire. Our recovery of evolving disputes and redefinitions contributes to an understanding of how, in the words of one historian, "a grammar of difference was continuously and vigilantly crafted as people in colonies refashioned and contested European claims to superiority."[41] The still broader question concerns an exploration of cultural history in the problematic of "Atlantic history," where different approaches have suggested its conceptualization as the study of an "inland sea of western civilization" or of an interior ocean, or more recently (and imaginatively) of a variable perspective capable of recasting national and regional histories on either side of the Atlantic. To put this another way, the Atlantic might be examined as a zone of circulation and exchange, as the fulcrum of connections between four continents, or as a perspective that recasts national histories (many boasting an exceptionalism that can be much refined by transatlantic comparisons).[42]

Within this Atlantic context, the Library Society was a locus for the expression of social and political community, most obviously in its promotion of notions of civility. Quite apart from showing exactly how books were acquired, the Charleston library letters provide fresh insight into the social and intellectual history of the southern colonies in the eighteenth and early nineteenth centuries. By a wide-angle approach to the institutional history of the library one might identify key changes to the cultural history of the whole region. In particular, this gives prominence to the relationship between the cultural life of South Carolina and the development of political thought in the immediate pre- and postrevolutionary eras, and it also contributes to current Anglo-American research interest in the social and political history of consumption in the eighteenth century. The extent to which consumption and cultural capital (*pace* Pierre Bourdieu) established and stabilized social identities and relationships is inexorably political, and power was exerted by means of symbolic forms as well as resulting from the grounding economic conditions of empire. In the colonial situation, where local political authority might be weakened by the absence or lack of confidence in a traditional, familiar structure, this fashioning of symbolic power was largely enabled by forms of material consumption (and hence energetic importation) that forged new knowledge, differences, and values.[43]

Studies of the use of public information by colonial elite groups to consolidate political power[44] contribute substantially to historical debate about the political effects of print-led public discourse.[45] In the wake of Jurgen Habermas, print has frequently been characterized as midwife to a politicized public sphere, animated during the eighteenth century by an increasingly democratic rationality. Particular attention has been given to the role of print as a contested medium, but one in which the quality of what might be called "printedness" was also valued by recipients for its ability to transmit ideas in an impersonal way.[46] This construct has been especially attractive when transferred to study of the development and consequences of a "print culture" in eighteenth-century North America. The beguiling impersonality of books and prints is claimed to have enhanced the "civic and emancipatory" characteristics that underpinned American political transformation.[47] Critics, reminding us of the continuation of the "grain of the voice in addition to, or instead of, the silence of print"[48] and of the importance of rhetoric in practice,[49] nonetheless invite further consideration of print in action and of changing forms for literary usage and performance. Nowhere is this more important than where the discussion and sociability encouraged by literature and print found immediate political influence. The continuing debate about the relationship between the spoken word and print culture in North America encourages new research to test ideas about the creation of a public sphere distanced from and critical of the sphere of the state in the colonial and early national periods.[50]

Another specific interest of this study is therefore the broader cultural development of new forms of sociability and its consequences in a community marked both by the radicalism and, at least before the Revolution, by the unity of the elite. The Library Society fostered a sociability that was fed by texts and London connections, but supported and encouraged by the institution of the library itself. It served as an intellectual and civic forum, a promoter of both formal and informal meetings and discussion (if not at a permanent site until late in the period), and the hosting of social and political events and of scientific, natural history, and astronomical observations and experiments. The promise of an associated college was held out to members and citizens. With its regular dinners and the development of the library collection, establishing, eventually, a repository where books, instruments, and curios could be consulted, the Charleston Library Society was *the* center for cultivation in the region. It provides an archetype for what Richard L. Bushman has proposed as the three interrelated aspects of the idea of "cultivation"—personal refinement, the assemblage of individuals, and the preparation of fitting environments for such assemblies.[51]

In this respect, the history of the library offers further investigation into the nature and boundaries of a created sense of community. In their broader context such institutions offered more than an intellectually and politically sensitized "community of conscience" (in the influential formulation of Habermas). The history of the library society contributes to a wider understanding of the evolution and transformation of voluntary associations to advance both notions of purposeful sociability and particular political programs. The relationship between the library and the public and public opinion becomes a key issue, in much the same way that the relationship between particular, often formalized private societies and an increasingly turbulent public opinion and politics has been central to cultural and political histories of the French revolution. Approaches to understanding the intellectual and cultural history of British American colonial society in the decades leading to independence have been much influenced by studies of the manner in which existing French private societies, in the form of salons, were challenged by new musées, voluntary clubs, and associations that produced fresh political agendas out of intellectual sociability.[52]

Intentionality can always be questioned here, and it is certainly the case that these "discursive institutions" were directed to pleasure and play as much as to scripted philosophies. In parallel studies of the American revolutionary decades,

Habermas's definition of communities of conscience has been rightly qualified and refined.[53] Nevertheless, apparently politically innocent activities are rarely value-free. The appetite for social interaction was often fueled by practical wants and ambitions, not least by the empowerment and enrichment by advantageous marriage and family alliances. With similar complexity, the envisaging of class and social exclusivity might have been as much culturally and ideologically driven as it was grounded in economically determined relationships. The interplay between social reality and its representation, always historically problematic, is at least partly observable in the empowerment enabled by the literature and debates of a library society.

Other problems and questions remain. Reappraisal of notions of sociability has also tended to neglect questions of the hierarchies and exclusions established by these public discursive institutions. Written (and often printed) objectives were professedly universal, but sociability, as fostered by early American library societies, was manifestly exclusive. As has also been observed about French literary societies of the period, such institutions also constructed a largely masculine space in which women were publicly marginalized. Even when— eventually—some women were admitted or, as at the Charleston library in its early days, associated with these societies as borrowers of books under their husband's or father's authority, they acted as adjuncts to male leadership, observing or conforming to male behavior in an overwhelmingly male social institution.

The ambition to advance sociability and cultivation in Charleston and North America was as much mimetic as homegrown. Even when projected as the independent action of colonial associations, their aims and ideals remained rooted in the colonial situation and in effective, if necessarily selective, cosmopolitanism. As Bushman puts it, "America enjoyed bits and pieces of London."[54] Library development hinged upon the social, political, and business worlds constructed by the different trades across the Atlantic—relationships perhaps most effectively studied to date by economic historians.[55] This commercial-political network underpinned the development of the early American library society and certainly delayed the fragmentation and ultimate dissolution of its transatlantic business and literary relationships.

As part of this interaction between trading and cultural diasporas, study of the Charleston Library Society assists in recovering the constructions of a Carolinian sense of self and of the objectives of members of its apparently homogenous pre-Revolution elite in relation to their neighbors and imperial governors. The library letters sent to London boast self-importance and ambition, but also detail a library operating despite its many problems. The sense of achievement contributed to a self-mythologizing, constructing a particular sense of identity. In part, this was defensive, in relation not only to the cultural domination of London and an idealization of their British past and present, but also to literary self-projections of the northern British American colonies. Contemporary eighteenth-century representations of a logocentric New England culture contrasted with the continued portrayal of an unlettered south—and of the Carolinas in particular. The Charleston library helped promulgate a counter-myth for both export and local consumption. Its activities constructed a sense of resistance to common report and to the many unhelpful commentaries from diarizing visitors.

The distinctive regional identity of the Carolinas backlights this history. Colonial Charleston rarely looked north on its own continent. Links with Philadelphia, New York, and Boston were restricted to specific trades, with social intercourse often limited to health trips. Commercial and social affiliation was remarkably weak when compared to the strong and flourishing connections with Britain and the Caribbean islands. The self-depiction by these southern provinces as part of the British family was also mirrored by many real family bonds, particularly among leading merchant firms. This Atlantic-wards outlook, together with disdain for both the immediate north and the Carolina backcountry, endured through the early years of the Republic. Loyalists returned to a state and to a city retaining strong British links, from the practical conduits of communication to more philosophical and cultural identifications. It contributes largely to explaining how the fervent nationalism, historically grounded in the British past and so evident in Charleston society in the years leading up to the Revolution, harbored later sectionalism.[56] Particularly after the slave revolt in Sainte Domingue and the disillusionment with French politics in the 1790s, admiration for British liberty and its protection of property and rank flourished anew. The cultural history of the Charleston library has to take account of the particular distinctiveness of the city and its inheritance—a tradition incorporating British historical perspectives and particular contemporary transatlantic links.

Both the stability and the peculiarity of the social and political elite of South Carolina are never far from this account. The leadership of the colony took pleasure and pride in punching above its weight; merchants and planters put their commercial and often legal skills to good use in aggressive lobbying notable for radical assertiveness and for a unity rare in colonial politics. The exposition of this communal zeal, consciously placed above private interest, appeared in consensual, public rhetoric, or what has been called a "conception of enlightened group interest."[57] The lowcountry's much intermarried families, sharing legislative, legal, and administrative offices between them, pointedly disapproved of public political argument, seeking instead (if not always attaining) an idealized civic discourse. Although this conduct often appeared as a radical country ideology, it was articulated from a society in which status derived from land, slaves, and commerce, and where the elite was, certainly in comparison with the Virginian tobacco aristocracy, absentee, residing for the most part in their Charleston houses and mansions and oriented to London and to the cosmopolitan world.[58]

Popular intellectual history and wide-ranging social and political history thus converge in any account of the Library Society and must also command an extensive geographical sweep. As with all books and prints, those collected in Charleston were not neutral or passive, nor were they static objects confined to ordained spaces and communities. Paternoster Row, Fleet Street, and the other sites of the London book trades comprised the center of a spreading web. The communication complex spread thousands of miles, based on the basic transportability of printed texts. For three hundred years the printing press had ensured the availability of replicated texts in uniform editions, enabling common standards and expectations, even if the use and reading of texts remained highly culturally conditioned and contingent upon immediate experience and aptitude.[59] The Atlantic world supported a diffusion of print hugely expanded both geographically and temporally—in terms, that is, of the lag between publication and reception. This study explores aspects of that structure and looks at the mechanics of the cultural transaction it supported.

The main motif in all this concerns the particularity of colonial literary demands. London booksellers received requests for texts to support academic enquiry and to enable scientific discovery and botanical evaluation; the same booksellers were asked to supply texts to endorse notions of English liberty and of polite behavior. When Governor Boone refused to allow Christopher Gadsden to take his seat in the South Carolina colonial assembly in 1764, and the Carolina Commons insisted on legislative rights based on the "ancient constitution of our Mother Country," the texts sent over from London supplied Gadsden's intellectual armory and influenced his audience. Literary sources informed both the boasts of harmony and the cultivation of a country ideology that contradicted the realities of almost constant conflict either in the backcountry or with colonial and foreign powers. When Alexander Garden and Lionel Chalmers sought out plants or wrote about disease and climate, they relied heavily on imported texts to support their European correspondence, observations, and specimen-hunting expeditions. Later, the advances of both the Anglican episcopal church and evangelicalism were sustained by the literary and institutional zeal of the Charleston library, an institution at first wary of "polemical divinity," but within two generations of its founding drawn into violent political and sectarian controversy.

Chapter Two

THE ENRICHMENT OF CHARLESTON AND LITERATURE IN SOUTH CAROLINA

FROM THE EARLY EIGHTEENTH CENTURY Charles Town, South Carolina, was an ambitious community of sharp contradictions. Excepting, perhaps, smaller settlements in the West Indies, no other British town of the period could match its combination of social and natural extremes. First settled in 1670, Charleston was the center of a plantation society that was prosperous but ever fearful of dissolution. The town came to boast elegant architecture and a confident, complex society, but one also visited by hurricane, plague, fever, war, and riot. As Charleston grew it was divided by social rivalries as well as by sporadic outbreaks of religious and communal hostilities despite many contemporary boasts of the harmonious coexistence of its immigrant European inhabitants and different sectarian groupings.[1]

Economically and politically these were tumultuous years. A plantation economy, supporting a society of a handful of super-wealthy families, a few hundred professional and lesser trading families, and tens of thousands of slaves, underwent political turmoil in the years before and immediately after independence. In fact, the colony was rarely at peace in its first century, and from the 1760s, was riven by both revolutionary and Loyalist zeal. Although Charleston was later distinguished both by its Federalist leadership and as a nationalist center, pragmatic politics and economic imperatives constrained the more abstract political ideas and philosophies of Carolinians. Despite bitter divisions over imperial legislation and postwar politics, neighbors and families largely maintained a customary restraint that left violence to the debating chamber and the written page. Permanent expulsions were few and compensation eventually followed the revolutionary and immediate postwar appropriation of Loyalist property.

Charleston's prosperity and new-wealth social mobility derived from the cultivation of rice, indigo, and much later, cotton. Overlooked by many accounts, the colony's earliest "cash crops" were the tar, pitch, and turpentine that comprised the naval stores exported to Britain and for which slave labor was first developed.[2] Rice, however, dominated the region's economy by about 1720, indigo was produced in quantity from the late 1740s, and both staples were exchanged for textiles and other manufactured products from Britain. Rum and sugar came from the West Indies and flour and other provisions from the northern colonies.

Rice and indigo production also propelled the startlingly successful traffic in Africans. Most arrived directly from their native lands, others from the West Indies. According to contemporary estimates some 37,000 slaves were imported to the colonies between 1706 and 1739, and more slaves entered through the port of Charleston than by way of any other town in mainland North America.[3] After a brief slough following the Revolution, the slave trade resumed in 1803. Some 39,000 Africans were imported in 1807, a year before an act of Congress with general powers to regulate foreign commerce finally served to ban the slave importation trade (but not, of course, slaveholding itself).[4] In eighteenth-century Carolina, flourishing from its plantation returns, few championed the abolition of slavery. Henry Laurens's son John (who died prematurely at 27) and David Ramsay, historian and scholar, were rare critics of the trade, but also advocates of improvements to the existing slaveholding structure and apologists for those identified as kindly slaveholders.[5] Cotton production advanced swiftly from the late 1780s, also following a dramatic collapse in the export of indigo. Cotton enabled the great planter families of the Carolinas not only to survive but to consolidate their position. By 1810 the open society was closing, while slavery, in most quarters, was redefined as a natural extension of familial inequality.[6]

The expansion of Charleston was rapid. The town boundaries were enlarged in 1743, with new fortifications built against the Indians. An original seventeenth-century community of about thirty wooden houses had increased to over 1,200 dwellings by 1765. Wealth from the Carolina crops and slave trade also sustained a cluster of fine houses, churches, and, eventually, civic buildings. Nevertheless, as one historian has put it, in 1756, when its first state house was completed (after four years in the building), Charleston still "did not look like a capital city."[7] In many ways, the prodigious growth of the colony as a whole was the most outstanding feature of the second third of the century. By various contemporary estimates, a population in South Carolina of some 64,000 in 1750 had doubled to 140,000 by 1775, and other observers calculated that a 40,000 white and 40,000 black population in 1754 had increased to 45,000 whites and 80,000 blacks by 1769.[8]

The exact population of Charleston itself at this time is unrecorded, but it is at least clear that the town underwent rapid development and infilling of central plots of land. It is also evident that the extraordinary growth of the colony forced sudden reassessment within Charleston of its own role and aspirations (of which the Charleston Library Society was one exemplar). In 1770 William Bull calculated that Charleston held 5,030 whites, 5,833 blacks, and 24 free Negroes and mulattos.[9] George Milligen-Johnston appears to have estimated that Charleston's white population had reached 12,000 by 1775.[10] At the first reliable census, that of 1790, the total population of Charleston and its outlying parishes had reached 67,000 of whom 50,000 were slaves. The two parishes in the town proper then comprised some 16,400 inhabitants of whom 7,700 were slaves.[11] Until the ascent of Baltimore, Charleston remained the fourth largest city in British and revolutionary America. In 1800 it was the fifth largest urban center in the United States (after New York, Philadelphia, Baltimore, and Boston), but Charleston then advanced to third ranking by about 1815 after the remarkable early-nineteenth-century increase in cotton production. Throughout much of this period, moreover, the port of Charleston both imported and exported more goods than Boston, New York, and Philadelphia combined.[12]

Hasty evacuation and rebuilding contributed notably to this transformation. Natural disasters, like the hurricane of 1752, were frequent, and great fires, like those of 1740, 1778, and 1787, a common tragedy. To these was added the rage of epidemic. The luxurious flora and fauna, fascinating to local scholars, flourished in a climate oppressive for much of the year and nurturing disease all the time. In the severe summer months the great planters lived in the city to escape malaria, but yellow fever and other diseases struck indiscriminately, adding to the perception of Charleston as a place at the edge of the world.[13] In 1699 a survivor of the yellow fever epidemic wrote that "the Distemper raged, and the destroying Angel slaughtered so furiously with his revenging Sword of Pestilence . . . that the dead were carried in carts, being heaped up one upon another. Worse by far than the great Plague of London, considering the smallness of the Town. Shops shut up for 6 weeks; nothing but carrying Medicines, digging graves, carting the dead; to the great astonishment of all beholders."[14] Major outbreaks of the fever followed in 1745, 1748, and 1799. The disasters encouraged prophets of doom. After a fire in 1740 one of the preachers concluded, "Yes: Charlestown is fallen, is fallen, because their Tongue, and their Doings are against the LORD, to provoke the Eyes of his Glory—Wo unto their Soul, for they have rewarded Evil unto themselves."[15]

Both the dismay and enthusiasm were echoed in recurrent religious controversy, prominently in the final decade of proprietary rule but also in the 1740s. The divisive potential of religion was manifest in various conflicts between the Anglicans and Presbyterians. It underpinned Charles Pinckney's support of the separation of church and state in the colony. At the same time, however, South Carolina, and Charleston in particular, attracted an increasing (if questionable) reputation for sectarian harmony.[16] A refuge for Huguenots and assorted religious exiles, Charleston was deemed notable for the relative ease with which Nonconformists and Episcopalians lived and worked together. During the century two great Episcopal churches were built, in addition to Presbyterian, Congregationalist, Baptist, and Catholic churches. Wealthy planters included both Baptists and Presbyterians. Immigrants and long-term visitors arrived from and maintained business and familial contact with different parts of Britain and Europe. Jews enjoyed a greater liberty of worship and civic participation in Charleston than elsewhere in the colonies. The Scots were also especially prominent, while the establishment of civic societies such as the Caledonian and Hibernian societies of St. Andrew and St. Patrick, appeared not to exacerbate existing tensions.

In other ways, however, the city was rarely at peace. Successive Indian wars and incursions predated and then continued during the Seven Years War from 1756. Within a decade of the end of that war, Charleston was engulfed by the War of Independence, preceded by the turbulence of political rivalry—the controversy surrounding the election of Christopher Gadsden to the assembly in 1762 and the refusal of the governor, Thomas Boone, to administer the oath after what he alleged was a violation of election law. Gadsden, reciting ancient constitutional rights, won in 1764 and the defeated but unapologetic Boone returned to London. Further antagonism between the lower house and the council and the governor from 1769 brought legislative shutdown from 1772.[17] Four years later the declaration of war with the mother country sent many Loyalist citizens into temporary exile to St. Augustine, until British reoccupation of South Carolina from early 1780 and the surrender of the Charleston garrison in May. Charleston remained in British hands until mid December 1782, two months after the Yorktown surrender. Thereafter, banishment and property redistribution fractured the community still further. The most ardent or despised Loyalists began longer and often permanent exile to Britain, although certain attempts to restore property and to place clear time limits to disqualification from office were made in the years after 1784.

The European conflicts of the turn of the nineteenth century caused further disruption to trade and communications. In addition, Barbary pirates, operating in the Mediterranean in the early years of the nineteenth century, continued as a persistent nuisance until Jefferson dispatched armed ships and enforced a favorable trading treaty with Tripoli. Government responses to British and French hostilities enjoyed less approval in Charleston. American vessels were especially disrupted by the Berlin Decree and the retaliatory orders-in-council of 1806. A year later Jefferson's proclamation closed all ports to all armed British ships. The nonimportation act against Britain and then the embargo act of December 1807 halted all foreign commerce in response to British and French claims to seize American trading vessels bound for enemy ports. Under the "dambargo" American shipping was confined to home ports, undermining American currency and obliging Charleston merchants to ship their goods to Amelia Island (British East Florida) for transport at exorbitant rates to overseas markets. On 24 June 1812 news reached Charleston of the declaration of war on England,[18] but in fact the embargo of four years earlier marks, in retrospect, the crucial divide in the long-term economic history of the Carolinas. New England merchants, seizing their opportunity, developed a cotton manufacturing industry that placed northern agents in the south, redirected the flow of Charleston trade to New York, Newport, and Boston, and ensured that in South Carolina an age of commerce was replaced not by an age of industry, but by an age of agriculture. In George Rogers's words, "this shift in lines of communication was to relegate the state to a backwater."[19]

Nevertheless, as its library society celebrated its fiftieth anniversary in 1798, Charleston was a burgeoning and ambitious city with rapid economic growth. Although no longer the seat of South Carolina government, the city's political primacy in the state and the lower south was unquestioned. The political consolidation and expanding influence of its planter aristocracy were linked to a vibrant social season and nationally directed perspectives. Only later did the defense of slavery make Charleston the aggressive champion of southern rather than nationalist rights; only later was early Charleston society to be characterized as narrow and superficial. Instead, the region's grandees (several, members of the American Philosophical Society) were deeply influenced by and contributed to broad debates about civic rights, religious observance, parliamentary representation, and the benefits of trade and agrarianism. Many explored native natural history and scientific experiment.

Both social season and science were funded by the extraordinary and rapidly accumulated riches of the colony and its lowcountry elite. Together with other cash crops, rice created vast fortunes and inaugurated an economic boom that transformed South Carolina in the second half of the eighteenth century. It has been calculated that in Charleston in the forty years after 1722 mean personal wealth increased by an annual compound growth rate of more than 2 percent. By the mid-1770s the inventoried wealth-holders of Charleston were by very far the richest in North America. The propertied of Charleston, indeed, were nearly four times as rich as those of the next wealthiest district in all the colonies, Annapolis County, Maryland.[20] Such astonishing prosperity was shared, if unequally, among an elite fortified by remarkable familial and commercial interconnections until long after the Revolution. Despite increasing backcountry challenges, members of the vastly wealthy lowcountry elite consolidated their resources. They largely countered and neutralized the political and social stresses of the 1790s and early 1800s by championing a pragmatic and broadly shared exposition of public interest. Buttressed by rice, indigo, and then cotton wealth, and deftly commanding and adapting governmental institutions, the planter-merchant aristocracy, with its Caribbean outreaches, maintained its influence many decades beyond independence.[21]

No one can dispute the accumulation of wealth driving consumption and the negative verdicts on the colony. The startlingly narrow distribution of this wealth encouraged contemporary indictments, led by Puritan New England condemnation of a gorging opulence and "corpulent and lordly planters."[22] The Manigaults and the Pinckneys were most conspicuous, but other families gained massive fortunes. James Crokatt, a key figure in the history of the Charleston library, died in 1765 worth nearly £47,000, including 55 slaves as well as an estate at Luxborough in England worth £30,000.[23] The elite was also closely entwined by marriage as well as by the social and political association evident in the colonial assembly. No opposition group formed in the lower house in the early years. Even more significant was the growing wealth of the middling and aspiring citizens. Modern calculations based on an analysis of probate records from 1760 to 1789 suggest that 30 percent of all free men in Charleston left estates worth more than £1,000 sterling, compared with 20 percent of all men in Boston leaving the same amount.[24] In slaveholding Carolina, moreover, the narrowness and isolation of this broader elite remained still more extraordinary. On the eve of the Revolution St. Stephen's parish was populated by 126 white men and about 5,000 blacks.[25]

To this must be added consideration of changes to the social structure and to the exercise of power by the elite between the mid-eighteenth and the early nineteenth centuries. One aspect of this development was increased regional division in which the dominant political influence and social snobbery of the lowcountry planter and merchant elite bred much resentment among the rival upcountry elite. Even more prominent was the transformation of the planter elite from what has been characterized as a would-be aristocracy to an extraordinarily prosperous squirearchy. The European aspirations of the social leaders of the 1750s were replaced by the more domestic focus of the great planter-squires of the early nineteenth century.[26] In this, the "sprawling cousinage" of kinship relations was undiminished, but generational differences were also apparent. The undoubted success story for the planters during the first three decades after the Revolution—the period when their power base was apparently most threatened by democratic impulses—involved a changing social role that also affected the nature of the planters' cultural leadership. In the colonial era the Carolina gentry adopted both elegance and loftiness to fend off charges of provincialism. Grafted on to their economic power was a developing cultural authority of gentility and practiced refinement that dominated the lowcountry's social order.[27] As the narrow, intermarried planter elite consolidated its power, its greater self-confidence fostered greater exclusiveness. This became more stark, at least in social and cultural terms, with the challenges from new gentry-planters, beneficiaries of the cotton boom. These maintained the dominance of the planter elite but in so doing modified social customs and lifestyle. One early-nineteenth-century observer, contrasting the old and new plantocracies, identified "the remnant of a peculiar race of people . . . characterised by a high and gentlemanly bearing."[28]

If the result was a more isolated caste, the more squirarchical model offered a leadership that adopted new cultural referents. As Mark Kaplanoff argues, the great planters continued to see themselves as builders, and in this, adaptability was paramount. How this consolidation of power and changing social structure affected cultural life in Charleston and the surrounding region continues to be problematic. The generational differences within the elite were certainly reflected in different intellectual and literary attachments. Like the surviving gentlemen of colonial Charleston, a distinctive literary pedigree and influence was apparent in the early nineteenth century.

Eighteenth- and early-nineteenth-century Charleston, then, was hardly dull; its wealthier citizens attempted to promote elegance and civility, while the town remained on the brink of disaster from hurricanes and fevers, Indians and priva- teers, and the uprisings of slaves. Various small-scale insurrections were common from the 1720s, all easily put down. In 1738, however, a Spanish edict granting lib- erty to slaves fleeing British colonies destabilized an already volatile situation. The Stono slave rebellion, which followed in September 1739, became the largest such revolt on the North American mainland during the colonial period. It was brutally put down, but not before almost taking the life of the lieutenant governor, William Bull.[29]

Maintaining order in this society was an attendant ordeal, but for the intellec- tual elite and much of the planter and merchant aristocracy the terror of dullness rested mainly with the specter of cultural and literary isolation. Here, as noted above, the historical debate is a lively one. Some historians, accepting the extraor- dinary gulf between a rich planter and merchant elite sending sons to be educated in Britain and a middling sort of lesser tradesmen reliant on very poorly supported schools, argue nonetheless that a literary culture of Charleston and the Carolinas was dawning by 1750. It embraced home-produced drama, satires, and mock-hero- ics, and it encouraged inquiring citizens such as Rev. Thomas Morritt, a mission- ary and a pioneer of advanced learning in the colonies, the commissary Rev. Alexander Garden, and, a decade later, scientific and medical investigators includ- ing Drs. John Lining, John Moultrie, and Alexander Garden. In Charleston "the fine arts . . . were as definitely and frequently a part of southern provincial life as were science and education and religion."[30] A firm, if minority, voice among con- temporary commentators also commends the politeness found among aspirant gentry in this part of the British realm. A visitor in 1745 to the plantation of the merchants and slave traders, the Wraggs, decided that "the people live in the Gen- teelest manner."[31]

For other scholars, the verdict is much like an extension of the critique of the dangers of luxury and moral corruption evident at the time. Governor James Glen of South Carolina, in a report to the Board of Trade and Plantations, was concerned that wealth was leading to great luxury in Charleston,[32] and as summarized by a modern historian, the town and colony were "characterized by a whole-hearted devotion to amusement and the neglect of religion and intellectual pursuits. . . . While colonies like Massachusetts and Pennsylvania had produced socially dull but mentally stimulating societies, South Carolina had developed in just the opposite direction."[33] A more nuanced account suggests that a somewhat misproportioned cult of virtue was forged exactly against the perceived perils of materialism and corruption and did at least result in a tangible cultural and literary response.[34]

All of this has focused attention upon the political and ideological culture of South Carolina, although the means by which education, discussion and involvement actually operated have been little considered. The Charleston Library Society is the obvious candidate for reexamination. It acted as both an intellectual and social center. In the parlance of modern cultural studies, the Charleston library became a real "discursive institution," a private society bounded by distinctive discourse and practice. Here was a library grandly projected, ambitious for improvement, and confident, from its privileged perspective, of refining intellects and changing public culture.

Of the effects of such institutions, their most prominent contemporary advocate had no doubts. Benjamin Franklin, founder of the Library Company of Philadelphia, believed that these libraries "improved the general Conversation of Americans, made the common Tradesmen and Farmers as intelligent as most Gentlemen from other Countries, and perhaps have contributed in some Degree to the Stand so generally made throughout the Colonies in Defence of their Priviledges."[35] The influence of the library in Pennsylvania was avowedly social, intellectual, and political. The aim was principled, idealized improvement, in line with both British and classical heritage, and for the library enthusiasts, evident in the progress of the modern age.

The cultural history of early Charleston has been subject to more troubled debate than that of Philadelphia, however. Franklin's assessment rests uneasily with both contemporary and modern accounts of more-money-than-sense vulgarity in the Carolinas. Even though historical—as opposed to antiquarian—study of the civic and community history of early Charleston is less advanced than for many other early North American cities, new studies have offered much more refined analyses of cultural development that use examples from Charleston, including the "discursive institutions" of coffeehouses, clubs, salons, and the like.[36] We can no longer accept unquestioningly the Massachusetts perspective of Josiah Quincy, Jr., visiting South Carolina in 1773 and reporting that "cards, dice, the bottle and horses engross prodigious portions of time and attention: the gentlemen (planters and merchants) are mostly men of the turf and gamesters. Political inquiries and philosophic disquisitions are too laborious for them."[37]

Other assessments that Charleston and South Carolina existed in what was virtually a religious and intellectual vacuum[38] are also no longer sustainable given new studies of both anglicanization and evangelicalism that identify resurgent sectarian activity and conflict in the region.[39] The same historian who claims that "pleasure became the goal of social life" and that "the religious indifference of South Carolina was matched by a pervasive intellectual indifference," also admits that Carolina pioneers in botany and zoology like Alexander Garden won international reputations and that the Charleston Library Society, if exceptional, did promote interest in learning and debate.[40] For another historian, more persuaded by Charlestonians' religious and intellectual interests, the frictions between the elite's emulation of all things British, their materialism, and allegations of their lazy and dissipated behavior are simply part of an involved tapestry in which "reconciling these conflicting reports and opinions presents a difficult problem because none was without foundation."[41] Another historian of the south has linked reassessment of Charleston as "a molder of literary and political ideology" to wider definitions of the city as "the place of intellect."[42] In similar vein, a broad-ranging study of the urban context of British American belles lettres includes lively examples from eighteenth-century Charleston to illustrate the relationship of literary institutions and private associations to sociability and "complaisance."[43]

A library and its material collection—books, prints, scientific instruments, statues, paintings, and other artifacts—offered working, tangible sustenance for cosmopolitan and polite discourse (if difficult for the historian to retrieve). This collection might be a private one, such as that of the Manigaults, giving individual and familial benefit, but the collection might also be more broadly social, most notably as a shared community library or library society. Important distinctions developed between the aims, the ambitions, and the language expressing the sociability and the practice of what was often a highly exclusive institution. In qualification of interpretations of sociable sodalities that assume open, almost protodemocratic models of operation for voluntary societies in colonial America, access to and the operation of library societies were hugely contained—bounded by rules, formal and informal, by physical enclosure, and by formidable efforts of self-projection.

The colonial extension of London society remains a key issue. The promotion of civility and the advance of particular modes of sociability and cultural practice very largely derived from Charlestonian cosmopolitan ambition. The metropolis and the outpost were to be linked by specific cultural conduits—personal voyages, letters, books, and other cultural traffic. The material imports of print and books attested, in fact, to the particular signification of the London-Charleston relationship. Many of these connections were personal and regularly refreshed. As late as the 1770s up to fifty absentee South Carolina proprietors were living in

England, and both British cultural influence and the prestige of the Anglican Church increased rather than diminished in the south in the early decades of the Republic.[44] In the colonial extension of British and London society in the Carolinas the Library Society proved a guiding beacon.

In the southern colonies, with their dispersed rural settlements, literature had at first been a scattered and relatively rare commodity. By 1700 the white population of Virginia surpassed 64,000 and reached about 140,000 by 1740 (compared to a New England population of about 90,000 in 1700 and over 281,000 in 1740[45]), but bookselling in the colony developed slowly, certainly in comparison with New England, New York, and Pennsylvania. William Parks, then of Annapolis, was asked to set up a press in Williamsburg in 1730. He moved there in 1731 and although he sold books from his printing office, he did not establish a designated bookshop until 1742.[46] It is now impossible to gauge in these early years how much printing was carried on, but we can be sure that most was jobbing work, with financing and very often the paper used supplied by the customer directly. Local government was the greatest early customer, but even this seems surprisingly modest in early-eighteenth-century Virginia.

Further south, the prospects seemed brighter. Three competing printers arrived in South Carolina in 1731, all enticed by an offer of a thousand pounds in local currency from the Commons House of Assembly. One of the three, George Webb, proved no more than a two-imprint man, and another, bookseller Eleazer Phillips, lost his son and printer, Eleazer junior, within a year of their arrival. Phillips returned to New England in 1750, and the shop continued printing under Jacob Viart.[47] The third of the early printers, Thomas Whitmarsh, printed various jobbing pieces for the assembly from 1731.[48] He began publication of the *South Carolina Gazette* in January 1732, four months after signing an agreement with his former Philadelphia associate, Benjamin Franklin, for "copartnership for the carrying on of the business of printing in Charlestown."[49] Franklin sent on a printing press, "400 weight of letters," and a supply of books. Whitmarsh, however, died in late 1733, having printed the *Gazette* until September of that year.[50] His successor was another employee of Franklin, Louis Timothée, or Lewis Timothy as he was known, a native of the Netherlands, who had arrived in Philadelphia in 1731. After his death in 1738 Timothy was succeeded by his wife Elizabeth and then by his son Peter from 1746 until his own death in 1783.[51]

Such competitive but stuttering beginnings set the course for South Carolina printing, publishing, and bookselling for the rest of the century. No single printer or bookseller was to command the supremacy of Parks in Virginia and James Davis in North Carolina. If any printers and booksellers had claims to preeminence in Charleston, it was first the Timothys and later Robert Wells (of whom more below). Unsurprisingly for the early years, Lewis Timothy printed very little besides

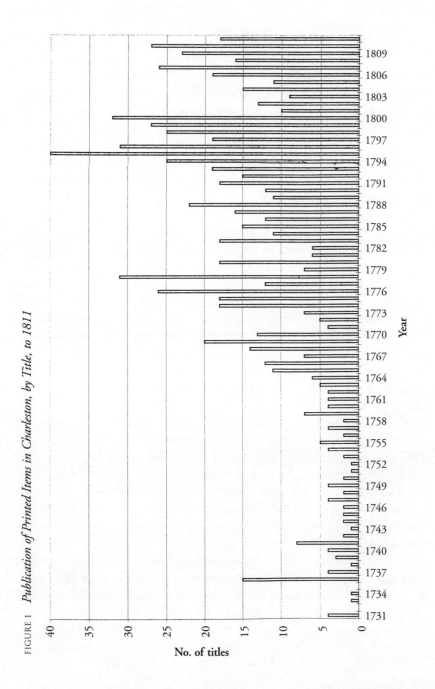

FIGURE 1   *Publication of Printed Items in Charleston, by Title, to 1811*

his newspaper although he did issue Nicholas Trott's *Laws of the Province of South-Carolina* in 1736.[52] Figure 1 charts the publication of printed items in the eighty years before 1811. Most of these items are simple broadsides or proclamations, and very few are volumes of more than 20 pages. They include a few important works, but the striking variation in totals reflects more the political excitements of the late 1760s and mid-1770s. An upsurge in the late 1790s apparently responded to growing Charleston demand, but it is striking how the local imprints do not hugely increase in the first decade of the nineteenth century. If consumption of American publications did rise in these years, it was supplied from the north and not from the locality. Printed output from Charleston between 1801 and 1806, at least in terms of different titles, was not equal to that of the mid-1770s or the late 1780s. The profile is therefore very different from that recovered for early national Philadelphia where the rapid increase in printing also stimulated the development of publishing.[53]

For most of the period, printing in Charleston was no easy business. Like most local firms, the print shop was frequently laid low by scarcity of local money and by problems in securing adequate supplies of paper, type, and other materials from Britain. Striking early examples of local Carolina printing did include Lewis's 1737 edition of John and Charles Wesley's *Collection of Psalms and Hymns* that predates the earliest London printing, but this was a very rare endeavor.[54] The expense of local printing and the relatively limited demand for Charleston publication persisted for the rest of the century. According to Ramsay's contemporary, John Shecut, "Doctor Ramsay's History of the Revolution, his History of South-Carolina; and governor Drayton's View of South-Carolina, with many other publications that might be named; although works of acknowledged superior merit, have scarce cleared the expenses of the paper, the printing and the binding."[55] More typical were instructive or useful ephemera, cheaply produced, such as the early 1737 print of the "West Prospect of St. Phillips Church," or the standard almanacs, that for 1737 offering "a particular Description of the Herb which the Indians use to cure the Bite of that venomous Reptile a Rattle Snake, an exact Print of the Leaf of the Plant, an Account of the Places it grows in, and the Manner of using it, &c made publick for the general Good."[56] Among various local religious publications was *The Real Christian's Hope in Death: or, Accounts of the Comfortable Dying Beds of Several Persons of Piety.*[57]

The only other outlet for locally (or part-locally) financed publication was by subscription. Some of these editions were printed in Charleston, but most, at least in the early and middle decades of the century, entailed transatlantic endeavor.[58] The latter ranged from the 1749 "Proposals for publishing by Subscription, for the Benefit of the Author, A New and most concise Method (hitherto unknown) of

Multiplication and Division, by which any Number or Quantity of Figures may be instantly multiplied and divided" to the self-congratulatory *Memoirs of Major Robert Rogers* and the ostentatious proposals of booksellers Fletcher and Rivington.[59] Less successful was James Adair's putative "Treatise of the Indian Americans" noted as "being no fiction, but drawn from the very Life of the Indian, after 14 Years Observation and Experience in all our southern Nations." Together with his later "Essays on the Origin, History, Language, Religion and Religious Rites . . . particularly of the several Nations or Tribes of the Catawbas, Cherokees, Creeks . . . ," it was advertised in the *South Carolina Gazette* to "be put to Press in London, as soon as a sufficient Number of Subscriptions are obtained."[60]

It was therefore against the dearth of local publication and reprinting in Charleston, that book importation assumed increasing importance. Midcentury newspaper advertisements do chronicle a small but fast-developing local market in old and secondhand books and collections by auction and "vendue" as well as by later fixed-site traders. "A choice Collection of Books to be sold, among which are, a compleat Sett of Magazines to 1743" was typical of notices offered by Elizabeth Timothy, who also acted as selling agent.[61] Yet this trade always remained limited, still dependent on replenished supply from abroad (or eventually from the northern cities), and never able to satisfy demand for the latest literature from Europe. This arrived either by direct importation by individual customers or by general supply and specific order through local general merchants and booksellers such as Eleazer Phillips and the Timothys. From the first decades of the century many general merchants offered books for sale as the occasion arose. Auctions by public outcry also included new books and print.

From the 1730s increasing numbers of importers advertised books, including Henry and Alexander Peronneau, Edward Wigg, Peter Horry, and Robert Raper.[62] As well as printing annual accounts of goods imported and exported, Raper, like Timothy, advertised "Bibles, Testaments, Common Prayer Books with Cutts and Dyche's Spelling Books."[63] Exceptional titles were given special treatment. Rapin's *History of England* (one of the most popularly advertised titles) was listed alongside "brass candlesticks," "trooping saddles," and "fine Florence oyl" in a typical advertisement by Peter Horry in 1738.[64] Among others, John Sinclair, later to be first librarian of the Charleston Library Society, was advertising "curious collections" of books by the late 1740s. He boasted of "the latest and best Editions, and neatly bound, gilt and letter'd, consisting of several Hundred Volumes . . . a Catalogue of which may be seen with the lowest Prices affix'd."[65] By midcentury, auction advertisements appeared on behalf of Samuel Peronneau, Peter Horry, Samuel Carne, and Samuel Kynaston.[66] Carne, a frequent importer of drugs and medicines, marketed an impressive range of medical books by the mid-1750s.[67]

It is difficult to gauge the range of imported print, although the fact that particular titles are given in the newspaper advertisements suggests the singularity of these arrivals, many of which do indeed appear to be single (or at least one of very few) copies within a mixed consignment. Besides Bibles, prayer-books, spelling books, and cheap print, individually listed titles were usually a motley. Not all of them, despite the announcements, were fresh off the press. Rapin still headed the list in 1752 import notices by Charles Woodmason. In the same advertisements, alongside Tillotson and Watt, "Newton's philosophy explain'd for the use of the ladies" is a singular title explicitly for female readers.[68] Certain books drew large, grand advertisements, such as the notice for the single work *Architecture* by Leon Baptista Alberti "with curious copper Plates," given prominence in the *Gazette* in 1761 for a sale at public vendue.[69] In these early years, novels were not conspicuous although they did feature in a few traders' advertisements. The stock of the lately deceased Isaac de Costa was auctioned with a *Catalogue of Books* "just imported in the last Vessels" printed in February 1753. As advertised in the newspaper, this catalogue ranged from the *Universal History,* Tillotson, and Josephus, to modern fiction, including Fielding's *Amelia,* Hayward's *Betsy Thoughtless,* Coventry's *Pompey the Little,* Smollett's *Peregrine Pickle,* and several lesser-known novels. Beneath was an avowal that "The Undertaker flatters himself, that, as this Collection will afford equal Entertainment for the *Religious,* the *Learned,* the FAIR, the *Gay,* and the *Young,* they will favour him with their Presence and Encouragement. The Ladies can no where else furnish themselves so well, and at so easy Rates, with the newest, best, and most Entertaining Books."[70] In another advertisement of 1753, from Thomas and William Ellis, novels again dominate.[71]

Book supply to the southern settlements also became more regularized. The Edinburgh merchants Hugh and Robert Clerk, for example, exported many book consignments on successive voyages to Charleston from the late 1740s. Many were shipped by Andrew Cowan sailing to Charleston from Leith twice a year, carrying books among a huge assortment of goods and taking back rice and other Carolina produce to Scotland in return.[72] In 1749, to take one year, Cowan arrived at Charleston 27 March, returning for Scotland 29 May, and leaving Leith for Charleston again 12 October. The October shipment included four boxes and six hundredweight of books for the Clerks, which arrived 8 January 1750, along with goods to be sold "by the said master [Cowan] at his store on Bedan's wharf."[73] Among other Cowan cargoes were 134 Bibles, "a neat desk and book case with glass doors, a Collection of entertaining books," and, advertised as among a wide-ranging consignment, "a small collection of books on various subjects . . . to be sold by [Andrew Cowan] at one of Mr. Motte's back stores."[74] It was also about this time that book supply from Scotland began to strengthen. In early 1747 Eleazer Phillips was advertising Scots Psalms and "the larger confession of faith in the church of Scotland" and appears to have commenced the sort of buying in of stock from Edinburgh and Glasgow that has been identified from the surviving Scottish customs records.[75] In 1751 Francis Bremar similarly advertised "Scotch psalm books" just imported from London and Bristol.[76]

By the 1760s book-trade competition quickened in Charleston with the opening of new shops by Nicholas Langford and Peter Timothy's brother-in-law Charles Crouch. Over the decade grand lists of books such as those "just imported from London and Chester" by John Edwards and Co., and those "just imported . . . from London" by Langford filled columns of the *South Carolina Gazette.*[77] In the same years James Rivington, now of New York, and an increasingly notorious book-trade operator, was advertising in the *Gazette.*[78] Among others, in May 1761 John Scott had "just imported" Dyche's spelling books and New Testaments, Richard King offered book imports in June 1763, and in September of that year Atkins and Weston also brought over books and prints from England.[79] The King advertisements listed an impressive range of titles, from popular sermons, poetry, and practical manuals to periodicals, including the seven volumes to date of the *Critical Review.* Although we cannot be certain (and it might have been a canny commercial ploy) the listing of individual titles with the number of volumes to each set implies that these booksellers imported one copy only in each consignment. This, in an uncertain market, was certainly the low risk strategy for both retailer and supplying wholesaler. Samuel Carne, now in partnership with Wilson, seems to have lost out in the new market, selling off his plate and furniture and "about 400 volumes of books, the remains of his library" according to the *Gazette* advertisement of late 1763.[80]

The importation of books and periodicals was to create further local binding demand. Wells, at least, established his own bindery and Isaiah Thomas recalled that two Scottish binders, George Wood and James Taylor (also "an inconsiderable dealer in books"), were at work during his time in South Carolina.[81] By the early 1760s, Wood publicly announced that "he continues to bind books of all kinds, in the neatest and strongest manner, either plain, gilt, or lettered, to any gentleman's fancy or taste."[82]

Nevertheless, trade in dry goods (of which books formed a small part) was volatile,[83] and as book imports increased, so expectations in the southern colonies also rose higher. At midcentury local booksellers were accused of failing to meet the literary needs of the town and of allowing it to falter in its pursuit of cosmopolitan standards of learning and taste. Leading critics included many notables of the planter aristocracy and merchant citizens of South Carolina. In Charleston the wealthy nurtured the link to London and Britain and were especially anxious to gain access to the latest reading. Problems were evident in the early years of importing—

with accompanying confirmation of the value placed on literary goods. An anguished advertisement by the general merchant, John Dart, in 1738 offered the extraordinary reward of thirty shillings per volume, for the "lost or stolen one vol. of Shakespear's Plays, one vol. of Plutarch's Lifes, and a small collection of Poesies printed in Dublin." All were odd volumes needed to make up sets but all had failed to arrive off the ship to Dart's store in Tradd Street.[84]

Access to the books arriving in Charleston could obviously be much improved and, if thought appropriate, widened by the shared convenience of a library. The beginnings were not auspicious, but the first library was also a very particular gift. Thomas Bray, who set up the Society for Promoting Christian Knowledge (SPCK) in 1699, with the Society for the Propagation of the Gospel in Foreign Parts (SPG) following in 1701, founded a library in Charleston in 1698.[85] Bray sent over more than two hundred books in 1700 and on 6 November the South Carolina Assembly ratified an act for establishing the "Provincial Library at Charles-Town."[86] The books were mostly religious but also practical guides and grammars.[87] The Carolina assembly contributed £225 towards buying the books, and the law passed in 1700 specified conditions under which the inhabitants might borrow.[88]

The assembly also provided for cataloguing the parochial libraries, but the fate of these and the books of the first public library is unclear. Some have blamed its demise on sectarian narrowness. Entrusted to the care of the Episcopal minister of Charleston, it has been claimed that little attempt was made to broaden the library's appeal to other communities in the town.[89] According to Edward Marston, writing in the year of its foundation, and much cited since, "the Dissenters, from the choice of books, most of which were wrote by Episcopal Divines, and in the defence of the doctrine, discipline and worship of the Church of England, soon perceived the intention of the society; and a library, framed on such a narrow foundation, was treated with neglect, and proved utterly ineffectual for promoting the desired end."[90] We do at least know that in 1707 the SPG was sent a list of twenty-two religious volumes (with two titles marked as "stole away"), bearing the society's seal and recovered from the estate of the late Rev. Samuel Thomas of Charleston.[91] What happened to these books is not known, although three years later an SPG plan to establish a school at Charleston included a proposal to oblige three clergymen to make a public declaration of books lent, and to whom, "for the recovery of such Books as are wanting."[92] The scheme, objecting to the apparently free access to these books and blaming their loss on "embezlement," seems not to have brought about their return. It is at least certain that in 1724 the headmaster of the Free School, Rev. Thomas Morritt complained there was now no library in the town.[93]

However dismal the early history of a public library in Charleston, it does underscore the importance of private libraries. Although most were very modest, domestic libraries were numerous. The 438 South Carolina libraries listed in inventories in wills proved between 1670 and 1775 by no means comprised all the private book collections in South Carolina of the period.[94] Many were clerical. The Rev. Richard Ludlam, rector of St. James, Goose Creek, left behind a library of more than 250 volumes at his death in 1728.[95] Gentlemen collectors included Thomas Gadsden who left a library inventoried in 1741 with 135 volumes.[96] At his early death, Peter Manigault's library was valued at £3,000; among those with libraries valued at more than £1,000 were the Independent minister John Thomas, the lawyers James Michie and John Rattray, the Goose Creek planter and patriot leader John Mackenzie, and Sarah, the widow of Nicholas Trott.[97] Almost nothing is known of the manner in which they accumulated their collection. Most attempting to build a library probably asked friends and family to bring back books with them from London or applied to the increasing number of local booksellers and general merchants trading in books. The wealthiest bibliophiles, Peter Manigault (collecting for himself and his father Gabriel), Henry Laurens, and probably Ralph Izard, engaged London agents.[98]

The local book dealers also started lending services, much as booksellers in Europe pioneered commercial circulating libraries at this period. The Charleston merchants emulated in some respects the expanded private collection, where a gentleman might regularly lend books to friends and neighbors. In the close and relatively small community of Charleston the development of this is easily explained—as are the inevitable problems. James Bulloch published a list of books "borrowed of the Subscriber, and never returned . . . most of which Books have been out several Years" in the *South Carolina Gazette* in December 1737. Titles included Salmon's *Review of the History of England,* Cato's *Political Letters,* and the *Guardian.*[99] One Charleston bookseller took out an advertisement in the *Gazette* in 1748: "Thomas Tew desires all Persons that have borrowed any of his Books, (particularly the 3 Vols. of Warburton's divine Legation of Moses, and the 6th Vol. of Rollin's ancient History) to be so kind as to return them immediately."[100]

As access to these limited supplies improved, a further difficulty for the serious student of London literature—religious, academic, or simply fashionable— remained in the securing of regular, efficient service. This provision was earnestly sought. As an early piece in the *Gazette* had declared, without the requisite "Judgement, Wit, Vivacity . . . and Knowledge of Books" a man might be dismissed as a "Molatto gentleman."[101] Frustration with failures in book supply was also coupled with fears about civic and political loss to the community and repeated emphasis upon the needs of attachment to Britain. More dependable and informed acquisition of London material required new undertakings and ventures that made direct contact with London. For many, Charleston traders were simply not up to the mark. Also in 1748, just as Tew sought to locate his lost books, the Charleston schoolmaster Hugh Anderson complained in a public letter to the newspaper, "there is no Bookseller in this Province who can supply a necessary Variety of Books, or take in for Sale such Books as the Owners may incline to sell."[102] Within months a plan for a library society was launched.

Chapter Three

THE EARLY MEMBERSHIP AND
MISSION OF THE LIBRARY SOCIETY

THE CHARLES TOWN LIBRARY SOCIETY was founded by seventeen young merchants, planters, lawyers, and physicians in the spring of 1748. Together with two
further recruits they signed a roll of subscription on 13 June. Rules for the organization of the society were published in draft in the *Gazette* on 26 April and agreed
on 28 December 1748.[1] From the outset, however, communications failed. The
original act of incorporation obtained in 1754 and ratified by the Lords Justice in
Council on 24 June 1755 was captured by the French during its transatlantic passage. A replacement did not arrive until 1757.[2]

The founders, of different resources and professions, shared youth and ambition. Prominent among them were the wealthy planter Thomas Middleton (aged
29), the merchant Robert Brisbane (one of the oldest founders at 41), the lawyer
William Burrows (aged 22), the merchants Joseph Wragg and Samuel Wragg, Jr.
(both in their 20s),[3] and the printer Peter Timothy (aged about 23). The Wraggs,
Middleton, and another planter founder-member Thomas Sacheverell were already
very wealthy men; their co-pioneers the printer Timothy and the peruke maker
Alexander McCauley enjoyed far humbler incomes.

On 1 April 1749 the first officers were elected. John Cooper, a merchant and
distiller, was chosen president. His annual term of office set the model for the opening years of the society. This was either because of an original intention that presidents should serve an annual term only or because some sort of compromise was
extracted from rival claimants. Whatever the cause, the tenure of the library's leadership by Cooper, as well as by his immediate successors, typified the social background of the early membership. The first librarian, John Sinclair, traded in food
and dry goods imported from London. Paul Douxsaint and John Neufville traded
as dry goods merchants, as did William Logan, the youngest of the founding members (he was 22 in December 1748). Samuel Brailsford, first secretary, together with
his brother Morton, were merchants and slave traders. The first library officers and
members must have almost daily encountered one another at the wharves and merchants' meeting places.

The founding group also reflected Charleston's religious and ethnic diversity.
Sinclair was a Quaker. Douxsaint and Neufville were both of French Huguenot

extraction.[4] The father of the Brailsfords, Edward, had arrived from London in the 1720s. Logan descended from a long established Carolina family; his grandfather Colonel George Logan of Aberdeen sailed to the colony in 1690. At least five other of the founder members were of Scots (or what was often called "North British") origin and maintained active Scottish links. In addition to Brisbane, Glasgow merchant in partnership with his brother,[5] the Scots included Alexander Baron, a schoolmaster; James Grindlay, a lawyer; McCauley, the peruke maker; and Patrick McKie, physician and keeper of a hospital for sick Negroes. Another Scot, James Crokatt, Indian trader, colony agent, London merchant, and a prime mover in establishing the Masons in Charleston, was to do much to assist in the foundation of the library by securing the 1754 charter. His "care & diligence" are applauded in the printed rules.[6]

The subsequent membership of the Charleston Library Society is not fully recorded, unlike that of the Library Company of Philadelphia, with its carefully preserved share-book.[7] The only reliable indication of those admitted to join the nineteen founders in the early years is a list of members published in the *Gazette* on 23 April 1750. The 129 names listed confirm the extraordinary enthusiasm for the project in its earliest years. Thereafter, however, we have no record of admission to membership of the Library Society until the journal records of general meetings from 1759.[8] Proposals for membership, many of which were requests from the applicants themselves, are recorded in entries for all subsequent meetings after 1759. It is also possible to reconstruct at least some of the membership admitted between 1750 and 1759 from the minutes of later meetings that record the names of members in attendance, or from the names of committee members listed when elected at meetings after 1759. A reconstruction of this membership to 1770 is given in appendix 1, but some members elected 1750–1759 might be missing if they died or moved away before 1759 or were elected or converted to "country" membership (that is, excused attendance at meetings and committee membership because of their distance from Charleston). These exclusions might be significant. Were it not for a later reference in the minutes to Alexander Garden, then exiled in London, as "our country member," his name would not appear in these lists.[9]

Many of the early members can be identified as merchants, including some also acting as physicians or bearing the title of gentleman. Of the 129 members recorded in the 1750 advertisement, 38 were styled "Esqs.," (with 7 suffixed by "Hon."), 16 were styled "Doctor," 2 "Capt.," 3 "Rev.," and 68 grouped as "Messrs." (including 4 of the named library officers). Not unexpectedly, many of these members were also related to each other—brothers, brothers-in-law, fathers and sons, uncles and nephews, cousins—but the range of professions was no less varied. Members included wealthy planters, a very broad range of merchants, various professional men of the town, clerics, and some masters of ships. From the elections and committee membership recorded in the minute books and journal it is also clear that this elite was not closed in the sense of being restricted to a landed aristocracy. Local society was relatively fluid; trade and the learned professions supplied entrants to the patriciate, and boundaries between merchant and planter identities often blurred.

Table 1 lists members of the Library Society in 1750 together with known trades and professions (in part from their advertisements in the *South Carolina Gazette*), but the list is more an indication of the profile of membership than an attempt at an exhaustive survey. Many more library members than those with trades specified in table 1 were involved in commerce. The mercantile occupation was a flexible one. Some were occupied full time with an importing and exporting business, in general or specific goods, with fixed-site warehousing and other premises, often on a very large scale. Others were occasional traders, like most property owners in Charleston, venturing capital in specific commercial endeavor when the opportunity or necessity arose. Between 1750 and 1755 some 174 merchants and 68 craftsmen advertised in the *Gazette*.[10] Craftsmen, including slaughtermen, soap makers, tallow chandlers, coopers, sail makers, and the like, are not represented among the library membership, as might well be expected, but some of those merchants dealing in soap or basic goods were clearly relatively humble traders compared to the established general merchants and major importers and exporters. At the same time, many of those marked down as "Messr."—and notably Laurens and Wragg—were advancing as planters and leading merchants of the town. The father of the library founder members, Samuel and Joseph Wragg, had broken the monopoly of the Royal African Company to bring in record numbers of Negroes in the 1730s. In 1740 the Wragg plantation spread over 14,000 acres. The earliest recorded library member who was a sea captain, Peter Bostock, was master of a slaving ship and also a custodian of Garden's specimen shipments to England. In 1756 Garden removed certain consignments of trees and plants from the ship of Samuel Ball to the greater below-deck stowage offered by Bostock, who might—it is possible to suggest—have had more sympathy for the scientific work of the doctor.[11]

It is also notable that two book-importing merchants were among prominent early members of the Charleston library. John McCall, Jr., librarian from July 1783, and secretary of the Library Society until at least the last general meeting of 1787, was the son of John McCall (d. 1773) a leading Charleston importer, whose business he managed from the mid-1760s.[12] Also city treasurer and clerk to the South Carolina Society,[13] McCall, Jr., was typical of the general merchant, importing (among many other goods) cloth, silk, laces, cheese, china, hats, and books.[14] In October 1764, for example, the *Gazette* announced that "John McCall Junior, Has just imported . . . A well chosen Assortment of European and East-India Goods, suitable for this Province" and including "Best ink-powder, Dutch and common

TABLE 1   *Published Styles and Occupations of Members of the Charleston Library Society in 1750*

The full list of 129 names of 1750 is included in the 273 (and 2 honorary) known members, 1748–1779, given in appendix 1. Trades as listed publicly in 1750 are added in brackets.[12]

7   Honorable Gentlemen
("The Hon. . . . Esq.")

Hector Berenger de Beaufain
Joseph Blake
William Bull
John Cleland
William Middleton
Charles Pinckney
Andrew Rutledge

31   Gentlemen ("Esqrs.")

including:

David Deas (dry goods, slave trader)
Gabriel Manigault (sugar, oil)
Henry Middleton (dry goods)

1   Military

Lieut. Colonel Alexander Heron

3   Clerics

Rev. John Baxter
Rev. Levi Durand (missionary to Christ Church)
Rev. Alexander Keith (St. George's Parish, Winyah)

2   Captains

Peter Bostock
Joseph Hatton

16   Doctors

including:

Samuel Carne (dry goods)
David Caw (parish doctor of St. Phillip's)
Lionel Chalmers
Thomas Dale
James Irving (dry goods)
John Lining, Library president (spirits and cordial waters)
George Milligen (drugs)
David Oliphant (or Olyphant) (dry goods, salt, medicines; medical partner of Lining)

68   "Messrs."

including:

Morton Brailsford (dry goods)
Robert Brisbane (medicines)
Francis Browne (medicines, dry goods)
Alexander Chisholme (orange trees, seeds, vinegar)
John Crokatt (hemp seed)
Benjamin Dart (dry goods)
Paul Douxsaint (dry goods)
Bransill Evance (dry goods)
Christopher Gadsden (dry goods)
Samuel Hurst (dry goods)
Henry Keenan (foodstuffs)
Henry Laurens (dry goods)
Richard Martson (dry goods)
George Murray (misc. goods)
John Neufville (dry goods)
John Parnham (dry goods)
Joseph Pickering (Philadelphia goods)
Rice Price (vinegar, wine, dry goods)
John Raven Bedon (foodstuffs, beer)
Patrick Reid (miscellaneous goods, dry goods)
John Scott, "Merchant" (Philadelphia flour, soap, dry goods)
William Scott (dry goods)
John Sinclair, librarian (food, dry goods)
Charles Stevenson (madeira, dry goods)
Ralph Taylor (rum, sugar, dry goods)
John Wragg (planter, dry goods)
Joseph Wragg (planter, dry goods)
Samuel Wragg (planter, dry goods)

1   without title

Peter Timothy (silkworms, seeds, stationery wares)

129   Total

quills; royal, post, fool's-cap, pot and other writing-paper; all sizes of blank books; bibles, testaments, common prayers, psalters, spelling, and other schoolbooks, &c." Nearly a decade later similar notices declared that "J. McCall Has just imported New-England primers, horn, spelling, picture, jest, drawing and writing books."[15]

The other book-trading member of the Library Society commands more attention. Robert Wells revolutionized local book supply in Charleston during the third quarter of the century. Arriving in Charleston from Britain in 1752, Wells acquired a printing house in 1755 and by 1764 ran his own newspaper, the *South Carolina and American General Gazette*.[16] In a colorful vignette in his early-nineteenth-century history of printing, Isaiah Thomas famously accused Wells of having employed heavy-drinking Negro slaves as his pressmen,[17] but his letters and business profile suggests a careful worker (even if it was unfortunate that his printing of the 1770 Library Society *Rules* opened with an announcement about the educational advantages for "Making" rather than for "Mankind").[18] As long as he published his own newspaper, Wells regularly advertised his wares as at "the Great Stationery and Book-Store, on the Bay."

Situated on the harbor near the Cooper River end of Tradd Street, the shop was the great center for book imports for three decades. In addition to his newspaper advertisements for imported books, Wells placed bold puffs in his own publications. In 1771 he typically described his shop as boasting "the LARGEST STOCK and greatest VARIETY of BOOKS to be met with in all America, consisting of many THOUSAND Volumes."[19] Notably approving of the Stamp Act despite its imposition of tax on American newspapers, Wells acquired various official positions and the patronage of royal officials. In addition to acting as marshal of the local vice admiralty and as public auctioneer, he became a close friend of John Stuart, superintendent of Indian affairs for the southern parts of British North America.[20] In Charleston, Wells, like McCall, acted also as a general trader and from time to time also included the auction of African slaves among his goods as leading vendue master. In February 1768, for example, he sold some seventy Negroes in one day.[21] As a notable Loyalist, Wells returned to London during the Revolution, when his business was continued in Charleston by his sons John and William Charles. British withdrawal from Charleston in December 1782 finally brought the end of the Wells firm, but as the Library Society letters confirm, Robert Wells, appointed Library Society bookseller from April 1787, was to act as a much needed agent and go-between for the society in London to the end of 1789 (see below, letters 40 and 41).

In summary, therefore, the early membership of the Library Society was relatively small but represented a broad cross-section of the propertied and professional of Charleston, all profoundly aware of the isolation of their town. In 1748, the gentlemen setting up the library certainly proclaimed grandiose designs. Compared to the "Articles of Agreement" to establish the Library Company of

Philadelphia in 1731 and certainly compared to the simpler "Articles of the Sub-scription Roll" of the later New York Society Library in 1754, the Charleston founders offered an elaborate vision. For the founders of the New York institution, a public library was to be "very useful, as well as ornamental to this city" and "advantageous to our intended college." The Philadelphia library motto declared *Communiter Bona profundere Deum est* (To pour forth benefits for the common good is divine).[22]

According to its printed apologia, the aim of the Charleston Library Society was to advance civilization *trans mare* and to extend the legacy of the ancients and of modern European culture. The *Rules of the Library,* when printed in 1762, opened with the "Advertisement" subtitled *Et Artes trans Mare Currunt* and began, "The advantages arising to mankind from learning are so evident, that all civilized soci-eties, both ancient and modern, have ever given the greatest encouragement to the promotion of it, and ever held it in the highest veneration and esteem. . . . Let any person of common consideration and humanity, take a serious view of the Indian-inhabitants of this extensive continent, and it will be impossible for him to reflect without very mortifying sentiments, how little human nature uncultivated differs from the brute; on the other hand with what exalted pleasure will he contemplate the splendid figure which Great-Britain, the admiration and envy of the world, at present makes when compared with its rude and savage state in the days of Julius Caesar."[23]

This was the manifesto of an overt and civilizing mission, but the key question concerns its object. The charge of many other society libraries, notably that of New York, and of proselytizing library institutions such as those of Bray and the SPG and SPCK, also invoked images of native American peoples. In Charleston the call appears less to discipline natives than to attend to the maintenance of the colonizers' own cultivation, and, by implication, to that of inadequate immigrants joining them. The sentiments expressed broadcast the identity of the new leaders of civi-lized society in the Carolinas.

The contrast to other mission statements needs emphasis. Elsewhere, the library charters of Bray and in New York were the product of a colonial encounter in which print acted as an agent of empire, unpure but simple. The quest to promote learn-ing became a straightforward extension of the giving of the Book, of the Bible. It was the further pursuit of the "literall advantage" identified by Samuel Purchas in the early seventeenth century as the European confidence in the superiority in writing, reading, and knowledge. In Purchas's words, "God hath added herein a further grace, that as Men by the former exceed Beasts . . . and amongst Men, some are accounted Civill, and more both Sociable and Religious, by the Use of letters and Writing, which others wanting are esteemed Brutish, Savage, Barbarous."[24] Such was the ambition represented by the 1704 bookplate of the Society for the

Propagation of the Gospel in Foreign Parts (plate 1). The bookplate can be found among various collections in North America, including in some volumes given to King's College, New York (now in Columbia University Library). In the engraving the holy book is held aloft from the prow of the ship to the apparent acclamation of clapping and waving natives ashore.[25]

The bookplates of the New York Society Library, founded a few years after the Charleston library, offered visual manifestoes of the idealized process. In the imaginary scenario, an Indian brave knelt on the floor of a library, tomahawk discarded and receiving a book from Minerva, goddess of wisdom and knowledge. The primitive appeared as the abased convert to knowledge.[26]

The Charleston Library Society stopped well short of the New York parable, however. In the words of the preamble to the Charleston library *Rules:* "As the gross ignorance of the naked Indian must raise our pity, and his savage disposition our horrour and detestation, it is our duty as men, our interest as members of a community, to prevent our descendants from sinking into a similar situation. To obviate this possible evil, and to obtain the desirable end of handing down the European arts and manners to the latest times is the great aim of the members of this Society, who are ambitious of approving themselves worthy of their mother country, by imitating her humanity, as well as her industry, and by transporting from her the improvements in the finer as well as the inferiour arts."[27] The key emphasis here is upon the need to prevent the descendants of current Carolinians from sinking to the level of the brute Indian. In South Carolina the proclaimed challenge was to extend European civilization to the present and future citizens within Charleston and other outposts, not to those living in the woods. Bridging the two worlds, of course, was the problem of the quality of learning among colonists who did spread out into the new lands. Charleston's great wealth might support a new center of learning, albeit one created in unseemly haste, but the cultural poverty of the backcountry could not be treated quickly. At the same time as the library's *Rules* were being printed, the visiting Anglican minister Charles Woodmason wrote despairingly of the Carolinas: "few or no Books are to be found in this vast Country, beside the Assembly, Catechism, Watts Hymns, Bunyans Pilgrims Progress—Russells—Whitefields and Erskines Sermons. Nor do they delight in Historical Books or in having them read to them, as do our Vulgar in England, for these People despise Knowledge, and instead of honouring a Learned Person, or any one of Wit or Knowledge, be it in Arts, Sciences, or Languages, they despise and Ill treat them—And this Spirit prevails even among the Principals of this Province."[28] For the library pioneers, acutely aware of isolation and of touching the boundary of civilization, the retention (rather than the diffusion) of Purchas's "advantage," required a resounding expression.

The oldest surviving seal of the Library Society, engraved by Thomas Coram, a native of Bristol who arrived in Charleston in 1769, was based on the library's first seal, lost in the fire of 1778. The seal depicts the goddess of reason who is probably also to be taken as Minerva, although no owl or helmet was included. Under rule 7 (1750) of the Library Society the common seal was to be "engraven [with] the Emblem or Heiroglyphic [*sic*] of Learning." In classical dress, encircled by a banner, and with an open book resting on her lap, the presiding goddess sits on a throne of books and scrolls, and carries a scepter with a shining eye in the finial. The eye, representing the light of reason, was commonly associated with ancient Egyptian hieroglyphs. This was largely owing to the influence of the *Treatise on Hieroglyphics* of Horapollo Nilous, claiming to date entirely from later antiquity and popularized by various early-sixteenth-century editions and compilations.[29]

The other visual manifesto for the Library Society was created by the membership certificates, where at least one survival predates the 1778 fire (plate 2, the certificate of Charles Cotesworth Pinckney). Engraved by James Mynde of London, the text is framed by the apparatus of learning, arts, and sciences, including a telescope, a microscope, an artist's palate, a sun dial, a globe, books, a quadrant, hygrometers, callipers, and an inkwell. The lower frame is broken by the surround for an impression from the seal. Above the top frame shines the benign, garlanded head of the goddess with the light of reason radiating from behind.

The emblems of both seal and certificate echoed the enlightenment iconography adopted by many gentlemen's societies, edifying publications, and even official and civic institutions. Minerva became perhaps the most replicated classical image, and the shining eye featured very widely in the mid-eighteenth century atop representations of pyramids and in various masonic symbols and devices. Most strikingly, the eye was to feature in the great seal of the United States. Among the library societies, the seal of the Library Company of Philadelphia was also designed with a device of "Two Books open, Each encompass'd with Glory, or Beams of Light, between which water streaming from above into an Urn below, thence issues at many Vents into lesser Urns, and Motto, circumscribing the whole."[30]

The new Charleston library, then, was intended as a beacon of civilization to inspire future generations of British Americans. More troublesome was how to determine the translation of such high-sounding ambitions into practical effect. For some of the early library members this required a quality collection rather than a large one. The Rev. Alexander Keith, rector of Prince George, Winyah, and assistant rector at St. Philip's, 1749–1755, opened his commonplace book with the words, "Much knowledge is not always obtained by reading many Authors, but by Reading the best in a Regular Method. As Life is short, Time is precious . . . therefore We ought to study that work which will be most useful in our proper Station."[31] Other members of the library proposed the advance of formal education and entertained a project of setting up an academy with salaried professors and buildings. The original printed rules made clear that capital stock accumulated from contributions, admission fees, membership monies, fines, forfeits, donations, and interest (detailed further below), and that this was to be invested by being "let out at interest and continued at interest until a fund is raised" or in the version of 1762, "put out at interest on good and sufficient security, in order to raise a fund for endowing and supporting a future Academy."[32]

Progress was slow. After a poor response to the advertisement of April 1750 announcing the plan for a society not just "for Erecting a Library" but also for "raising a Fund for an Academy at Charles Town," the college proposals were reviewed by the Library Society committee in 1762 and again in 1772. The 1762 report estimated the requirement to be £24,500. At seven times the annual income of the library at the time, it was a sum beyond available resources. The 1772 project was backed by a bill in the legislature and an initially promising range of subscriptions, but again it failed. The eventual College of Charleston was a product of broader endeavors, following a series of bequests in the 1770s. Even so, the first meeting of the trustees of the college did not take place until August 1785.[33] Before then, in the absence of a college and of more basic schools, the mid-century civilizing aspirations of the new library could, it seems, be effected only by some sort of civic osmosis.

The distance of two and a half centuries makes many exclusivist claims seem both preposterous and shameful in retrospect. But this should not deter attempts at an understanding of the subtleties of the project and the social and political relationships implicated in a society that upheld high codes of honor and enlightened ambitions, while its founders and early members included most of the leading slave importers of the century and others whose ethical perspectives now appear contorted and bounded by self-interest. The expectation, quite obviously, was that only certain orders of humanity would appreciate the new foundation.

Across their full range, the library manifestoes of colonial British America asserted that some human beings might be able to read the book, others might have to be taught to do so, and yet others had to be content to see the book and only listen to its words. Some stood to receive books, some knelt, others—who might not, indeed, fully qualify as mankind—did not receive the book at all. This was quite obvious in a Charleston where a manifest brutality, embracing burnings, brandings, and other violent punishments, encircled all sites of civility.[34] The library, indeed, was to operate against the leveling principle. It was to promote enlightenment but uphold distinction. Although the collection was a gift for education and illumination, strict rules were to guarantee both preservation and exclusion.

At this very time, however, certain other voices urged clarification in respect of Carolinian attitudes both to colonization and the potentialities of man. A broadside from the Bishop of London, for example, insisted that Charlestonians must not "consider a Being that is endow'd with Reason, upon a Level with Brutes."[35] Just as the Library Society was founded, the commissary in Charleston, Rev. Alexander Garden, set up his school for slave children, George Whitefield was urging the Christian conversion of the Negro, and lively debates (almost all instigated from without the colony) were conducted in the *South Carolina Gazette* about the efficacy of baptizing slaves and teaching them to read and write. Even more widely, Linnaeus's much discussed *Systema naturae* of 1758,[36] listing both "American" and "African" in its categories of "Homo," reaffirmed earlier inclusivist descriptions of the types of man, such as those by Sir William Petty in the late seventeenth century.

If, however, the Charleston library was never intended to redeem the brother Indian from being "savage" and "brute," then missionary-like advances towards the Negro African were unthinkable. The common view was that described by the "Itinerant Observations in America" carried by the successive issues of the 1745 and 1746 *London Magazine*. Negroes were claimed as "people," but, because of their physiognomy, including what was thought to be their hardiness under the lash, as well as their alleged mental incapacities, they were regarded as a very different kind of people.[37] Such a view was not to be challenged by leading library members like the Wraggs, the Brailsfords, Wells, or the Deas brothers, then advertising weekly cargoes of "prime, healthy Negroes . . . just arrived."[38] However grandiose and benevolent the language of the founding instrument of the Charleston Library Society, the practical intent was clearly limited. Perhaps the most famous confrontation within the colony resulted from the Whitefield-inspired enthusiasm of the brothers Hugh and Jonathan Bryan in 1742 (less than three years after the Stono rebellion) to gather together Negroes to teach them Christianity. The immediate curtailment of Hugh Bryan's incendiarism was to serve, in Eliza Pinckney's words, "as a warning to all pious minds not to reject reason and revelation and set up in their stead their own wild notions."[39] Neither Bryan appears to have been a member of the Library Society.

The printed aims of the library responded, in fact, to new convictions evident by the mid-eighteenth century and quite beyond the colonial situation. Within contemporary European society the question of who was included and who was excluded from the proper ambit of literature was complicated by the responses to both the expansion of book production and the increasing prosperity of the middle ranks of society. What Leibniz described as the "deluge of print" was thought to threaten serious social consequences. Hostile critics of an apparently new consumerism were quick to include misplaced literary enthusiasms in their dystopias. From some local quarters, commentary on the literary aspirations of Charleston reflected acute awareness of the town's perilous position in the moral geography of the empire. In the mid-1730s the *Gazette* remarked that the "new Gentleman, or rather half Gentleman," who had acquired money but no "experience of Men or

Knowledge of Books" cut a ridiculous figure, a "Molatto Gentleman."[40] A more robust response questioned the literary learning most appropriate for a great colonial trading center. More than thirty years later—and just after the debate between library members about ordering editions of Greek and Roman literature from London[41]—Henry Laurens seriously doubted the value of the classics in a "commercial Country." As he wrote, "hundreds of Men have their Mouths fill'd with jabbering Latin, while their Bellies are empty."[42] The most obvious contribution that the classics made, indeed, was to provide names for slaves—Caesar, Polydore, Scipio, and the like.

Whether in representation or reality, lofty ambition was thus problematically situated against the new advocacy of "public use" and "useful knowledge." The rejection of the erudite for the selection of knowledge most applicable to the common good, and much in the spirit of the *Encyclopédie,* encouraged the establishment of new libraries, but also complicated decisions about the selection and arrangement of books and even about the expression of purpose. Late-eighteenth-century concern about many libraries reflected conflict between increased print circulation and the exclusivity of book reading and collection. Although knowledge was a commercial artifact that one might buy—and to distribute it could be charitable and philanthropic—to distribute it indiscriminately could be dangerous. In many ways, collecting, library building, and book arranging illustrated these new perceptions of what a book should be for. From at least the mid-eighteenth century the book in Britain became the focus of broader industry, focusing on the social accoutrements of print, and ranging from house design and furniture to grandiose representations in painting. The book trades encouraged fashion, emulative buying, and often provocatively, the extension of reading. It is this tension—between promotion and guardedness, between commercialization and exclusivity—that became a recurrent theme in statements—physical as well as literary—about the use of books. And it was this tension that underpinned any effective expression of the "public use" of the Charleston Library Society—a society typical of its time (if in untypical surroundings) as being committed to protect civilization as much as to promote it, and in which benevolence might translate as preservation, and promulgation as defense.

Set against the exceptional social structure of the Carolinas, the visions that were offered of what the library might become were all the more striking. From where, then, did the Charleston gentlemen derive their inspiration and the formal and visual language by which they set out their ambition?[43] Of limited influence on the founders of the Charleston library was the practical development of colonial libraries. There were few civic models to consider, with the Library Company of Philadelphia the earliest and greatest exemplar, founded in 1731.[44] Some connections were evident—Lewis Timothy had not only been employed by Franklin, moving spirit of the Philadelphia library, but had served briefly as its first librarian. There are, however, no direct references to the Library Company or other later institutions in the early records of the Charleston library.

The more obvious British and European models were unlikely to have deterred emulation because of their grandeur. Many Charleston library members, British born, British educated, or visitors to Britain, continued to be more familiar with London, British, and European archetypes than with any such public institutions in colonial towns. Late-seventeenth- and early-eighteenth-century foundations from the Royal Society to the Society of Antiquaries established both correspondence communities and homes for meetings, debates, and collections. In various ways modest, often short-lived, literary and scientific groups emulated the major London and European institutions, including the prestigious royal and national academies of science. Most included a library (and often a scientific collection and curiosity cabinet). The number of such establishments was modest by the mid-eighteenth century, although one survey lists more than 3,000 libraries established at some time between 1700 and 1799, with 923 society libraries and 1,005 subscription libraries operating in Britain at some point before 1850.[45]

More local encouragement was provided by country-house book collectors, themselves imitating the activities of the British gentry and nobility. The domestic library and its extension into something to be shared by friends and neighbors was, after all, emulated by numerous Charleston landowners and professionals. By the mid-eighteenth century many English gentlemen were regular book purchasers and bought and arranged books with increasing concern to display their trophies to others. A boom in the fashioning and equipping of domestic libraries paralleled the commercial restructuring of bookselling. Modest ventures of provincial gentlefolk and well-to-do tradesmen emulated the palatial attempts of great and often new wealth.

While demonstrably not fully public or open, a gentleman's library offered an example of a collection in use and a respect for the privilege of access. Informal membership of such circles as much as the formal membership of a proprietary library remained carefully guarded, and the honor required appropriate recognition. An appreciation of literary and classical traditions and allusions, even of a particular architectural vocabulary, certainly extended to the design of the library or book parlor, to its cases, ornaments, furniture, and even ceiling designs. Allegorical library fitments were suitably designed to impress and reassure.[46]

In South Carolina, as in country towns up and down Britain, small yet distinguished collections were painstakingly amassed quite in addition to the projects of the major bibliophiles. The libraries evidenced by probate records and inventories (mentioned above) included many of those who founded the Charleston Library Society or served as its early presidents and officers. Dr. John Lining (1708–1760), physician, distinguished medical author, and second president of the Library Society, had himself been bequeathed classical lexicons and dictionaries and mathematical volumes. Far larger was the library left by the lawyer James Michie, fourth president of the Library Society, at his death in 1761. Valued at some £1,750 the bulk of the collection was of law books, but also included poetry and history, and all, according to the newspaper sale advertisement, "in very good condition, many of them in elegant bindings." Not as valuable but more intellectually wide ranging was the personal library of the Library Society's sixth president, the merchant Daniel Crawford. At his death in 1760 it comprised well over 350 volumes including works in French, Latin, Greek, and Hebrew, but also numerous religious works from Hooker to Whitefield, political and educational treatises, and romances and belles lettres. Of other library members, Andrew Rutledge left a library of 340 volumes valued at £340, John Cleland left 32 titles in 89 volumes, Thomas Dale a very large library valued at £880, the Crown official Hector Berenger de Beaufain left 359 volumes (including works in Greek, Latin, French, and Italian), and George Seaman left over 120 volumes and three dozen pamphlets valued at over £100.[47]

Other influences helped bridge these practical interests in book collection and the grander vision of the Library Society. To some extent models were available as much from symbolic representations as from existing buildings and practice. One obvious source was illustrations in books on the shelves of the libraries themselves. Much of the print ordered and sent from England offered successive lessons in the relationship among books, civility, and useful knowledge. In particular, many authors (some, of course, known from reading and conversation in visits to London) advanced direct instruction in literary respectability, taxonomies of the branches of learning, and even shelf arrangement. The frontispieces to the most popular periodicals ordered for the American libraries exemplify such visual inspiration. The frontispiece to the 1747 first volume of the *Universal Magazine* (plate 3) sets out the library, open to the world, with the ships setting out from harbor, all beneath the banner flown from Mercury's caduceus. An extraordinary parable was extended by these illustrations, one calling upon a flexible and often jumbled repertoire of classical emblems. Many were based on engravings in Pierce Tempest's 1709 reprint of Caesar Ripa's *Iconologia*. As Tempest introduces Ripa, "these images are the Representatives of our Notions; they properly belong to Painters, who by Colours and Shadowing, have invented the admirable Secret to give Body to our Thoughts, thereby to render them visible."[48] In successive frontispieces, Minerva, goddess of wisdom and learning, alluded to in the Charleston library seal, and the vehicle of the book transaction in the New York Society Library bookplates, is once again the crucial emblem of bibliographical benevolence.[49]

It would nevertheless be a mistake to confine the search for influences either to functioning or to virtually represented libraries and book collections. The public ambition of the Charleston library was more broadly derived. The elaborate preamble and articles of its printed rules suggest that members were modeling their library society upon a commonly shared notion of the social and publicly useful institution. These proliferated in Charleston. The St. Andrew's Society was founded in 1729, and the St. George's Society in 1733. The first Freemasons' lodge in Charleston was opened in October 1736, and at a celebration there in June 1738 the South Carolina grandmaster discoursed "on the Usefulness of Societies, and the benefits arising therefore to Mankind."[50] The South Carolina Society, largely French Protestant, was established in 1737, and the Amicable Society and the St. Cecilia Society, apparently the first civic musical society organized in America, both in 1766.[51] Later societies included those to rival Andrew of Scotland and George of England, namely the St. David's Society (1778) and the Friendly Sons of St. Patrick (1773), successor to the Irish Society (1749) and forerunner to the Friendly Brothers of Ireland (1786) and the distinguished Hibernian Society (1801). Besides these were the Fellowship Society (1762), the German Friendly Society (1766), the Mount Sion Society (1777), and the Hebrew Orphan Society (1791). More exotic sodalities included the Select Batchelors' Society, advertised as meeting quarterly at a house in King Street in 1770.[52]

A multiple overlap in membership of the different groups reinforced the relationship between the Library Society and the succession of local societies. By 1775 many members of the German Friendly Society were not of German ancestry, and other apparently ethnic fraternities were opened to others.[53] The first Charleston masonic lodge was augmented in 1754 by the establishment of the Grand Lodge of Freemasons. Grandmaster Peter Leigh was supported by stewards, Egerton Leigh, Samuel Perkins, John Stuart, Henry Laurens, Charles Pinckney, and Robert Wells, most of whom were prominent library members.[54] Dr. John Lining, second president of the Library Society, was also senior warden of Solomon's Lodge of Masons.[55] In 1741 the Ubiquarians, determined to follow the "Virtue and Morality of the Ancient Romans," set up a local convention in which Charles Pinckney, chief justice of the colony, was elected as praetor and William Bull, Gabriel Manigault, Isaac Mazyck, William Elliott, and Jacob Motte, as senators.[56] Few Library Society members were not also members of at least one of the purportedly national societies such as the St. Andrew's and St. George's, or other polite organizations such as the St. Cecilia's.

Many articles and phrasings from the surviving printed rules of these other Charleston societies are echoed by the Library Society proclamation. The preamble to the printed rules of the St. Andrew's Society announced that "the Principal Design of a Society is to promote some Publick Good, by the joint Endeavours of a Number of People."[57] The Charleston Fellowship Society, founded in 1762 to raise funds for a hospital, and incorporated in 1770, printed *Rules* with a grandiose preamble setting out the society's aims together with a constitutional model of officer elections and annual and quarterly meetings (and in this case weekly meetings also) much resembling that of the Library Society. The 1774 *Rules of the St. Cæcilia Society* has no preamble, but the constitutional model is again similar. The preamble to the *Rules of the Charleston Chamber of Commerce,* also printed in 1774, is more strikingly close to the language of the Library Society apologia, asserting in commanding tones that the "advantages arising are so clear." These other societies postdated the Library Society and many gentlemen were members of more than one of them, but the formulaic exposition of the preambles and the similarity between the constitutional provisions suggest a broader pre-existing model.

In part, of course, the grandiose language of the governing document reflects the social profile of the founders and early members of the Charleston Library Society. Within about a decade of its establishment the Library Society boasted the membership and patronage of the most distinguished of all Carolinians, even if the founders were second ranking members of the elite—most of them merchants and professional men. Thomas Middleton was the only founder who was also a member of the assembly and none of the founders were members of the council. The intellectual slant of the Library Society membership, illustrated, for example, by the admission of twenty-three of the thirty physicians who practiced in the colony before 1770,[58] probably heightened the rhetorical fervor. Alternatively, the same sort of language could just as well be adopted in an attempt to impress the colonial authorities, the governor, and the friends of Carolina in Britain.

Such expression was one further aspect of the particular social objectives, evident from the foundation of the Library Society. The special sociability that focused on literature and libraries was widely demonstrated in British America. Boston, Philadelphia, and New York boasted popular literary clubs, and in smaller settlements, similar ventures thrived. Typically, at Salem in 1760 a social library was founded by members of a "Monday Evening Club," most of whom were young merchants and clergymen. Shares cost $11, with the library originally housed in a brick schoolhouse.[59] The Library Company of Bridgetown at Mount Holly, New Jersey, was founded in 1768 and published a catalogue of 162 entries with twenty pages of governing "articles" and a list of members.[60] Crokatt and others who promoted the Charleston Library Society remained active in the establishment and extension of various other societies and masonic lodges, many apparently taking inspiration from London literary establishments of the Kit-Cat Club as well as the virtual community of the *Spectator.*

The sociable cast of this history can indeed be set in broader perspectives. David Shields has modified the influential and general evaluations of Habermas, rightly emphasizing his uninterest in the nonpolitical and at least superficially, nonideo-logical inducement to the formation of private societies. Not all of these societies were communities of conscience and many "projected" the welfare of others beyond their membership. In Shields's words, "many of these groups confessed wit, affection, or appetite as the grounds of community, not conscience."[61] Of like-minded spirit, the Independent Meeting House of Charleston has been described as "a Circle of intellectuals that was perhaps the most important in the city during the years immediately before the Revolution."[62]

Similar observations can be made about the Charleston Library Society (espe-cially concerning its later development as will be suggested in the next chapter), but the cast of such a society also remained exclusive. When aiming to help others, the society did so from the vantage point of propertied privilege. In this respect, inter-pretation of the motives and ideals behind the carefully crafted founding docu-ments and pronouncements of the various elite Charleston societies with their written rules and behavioral precepts resemble "public transcripts" offered to encode and signal hidden agendas. Cultural symbols of domination, from open parades to closed meetings, served to clarify and reinforce hierarchies.[63] Enlighten-ment again represented protectionism; the advance of learning was to extend down the generations of the colonial elite, not down the social ranks or across the broader ranks of all mankind.

It follows, then, that both the overt and the implied emphasis on exclusivity refines interpretations of the Library Society and similar sodalities as accessible communities of interest and fellow feeling.[64] Many societies, and most especially the masonic lodges, combined civility with exclusivity. Both the material and the discursive institution appropriated rigid protocols and arrangements in pursuit of specific ideals of polite sociability.[65] Although after the Revolution masonic and much other society membership seems to have been less concerned with fortune, rank, and hierarchy, in the colonial period at least, the associations espoused elit-ism. The influence of these exclusive and almost entirely male formations turns on the extent to which secrecy and ritual were transposed into events and occasions at which ceremony was more sociable and overt. The civic presence of the Charleston clubs and fraternal orders was not a reserved one. The *Gazette* of 9 January 1755 described a procession of more than one hundred Charleston gentlemen to St. Philip's Church on St. John the Evangelist's Day. Those gathered included the Ubi-quarians and the Freemasons, and after church all adjourned to the Corner Tavern where with "Harmony and Regularity" they dined and spend the rest of the day and evening together. Such events contributed to a rapidly developing civic culture, if socially narrow and open to the representation of extravagant living. And the Library Society had a more obvious claim than any of these societies to an elevated pursuit of civilization through the stock of the printed page.

Chapter Four

ORGANIZATION
AND SOCIABILITY

LIKE ALL THE NEW COLONIAL social libraries, the Charleston Library Society was governed by precise regulations. Formal revision of the 1748 constitution continued throughout the early years. Following the 1750 publication of the rules, new rules were debated and ratified at the April general meeting of 1759. These, together with a "proper Introduction" (which became the "Brief historical introduction" or "Advertisement" devised and revised by committee), were apparently approved at a general meeting of October 1759, but then debated again "paragraph by paragraph" at the anniversary meeting of January 1761. The final version was printed by Robert Wells in 1762.[1] The rules continued to be updated, with major revision and reprinting in 1769, specific modifications in 1771, 1772, 1777, and 1783, and a further reprinting in 1785.[2]

Under the foundation rules of the Charleston library four general meetings were convened each year. The first, deemed the anniversary meeting, took place on the second Tuesday of every January, followed by further general meetings (usually called "quarterly meetings" after 1761) on the first Wednesday in April, June, and October. At each anniversary meeting the members elected (or reelected) a president, vice president, treasurer, librarian, steward, and a secretary and correspondent (this last was originally envisioned as a combined post; the post of bookseller was also added later).[3] Under the third rule of the society, as reformulated in 1762, the president (or in his absence, the vice president) chaired all meetings to "keep regularity and decency, sum up all debates and put questions, call for all reports of committees, and accounts from the Treasurer and others." Additional extraordinary meetings were permitted, and all meetings were to be advertised publicly by the secretary-correspondent, who was to receive a stipend for his labors. The librarian was also to receive separate remuneration.

Formality bound proceedings. It was always intended that the thorough and lengthy rules were to be read out by the president at the beginning of every general meeting—by 1770 all fourteen closely printed pages of them.[4] With equal punctiliousness, each quarterly general meeting of all members appointed a quarterly committee. This committee comprised twelve members with a quorum of five and with six retiring each quarter; members were appointed by the president and ratified by the general meeting. Different members' houses seem to have hosted the committee. In 1759, for example, it met at John Gordon's house. "Lists of all Committees, the times of their meetings and adjournment" were to be "constantly hung up in the Library," and any member of the society was allowed to attend a committee meeting—although it was soon obvious that attaining a quorum was a greater problem than unacceptably large attendance. This was despite the fines of up to £3 for a committee member's absence at a meeting, later accompanied by a fine of ten shillings for all members of the society resident in Charleston not attending a quarterly meeting. It would suggest that such fines were less a threat than an integral revenue raising scheme.

Equally regulated were the conditions for the safekeeping and borrowing of the books and other property of the society. The librarian, salaried at a rate determined by the anniversary meeting, was by 1755 to open the library from noon to 1 pm daily except on Thursday when the hours were 3 to 5 pm.[5] By 1762, however, he was required "by himself or deputy, [to] give punctual attendance in the Library six days in the week, from the hour of nine till twelve in the forenoon, to deliver out books to the members," a period extended by 1770 to include from 3 to 5 pm in the winter and from 4 to 6 pm in the summer, "Sunday and the afternoon of Saturday excepted."[6] This was changed in 1785 to 9 am to 1 pm, Sundays and holidays remained excepted, but Saturday now seems to have been treated as any other work day. Sometime after 1785 it was changed to 10 am to 2 pm, and was certainly stated as such in the 1804 rules.[7] These hours, apparently so limited, were generous compared to the New York Society Library, open for one hour, 11 to 12 am, Tuesdays and Fridays only, until 1757 when opening was extended to between 2 pm and 4 pm on Wednesdays, and then after further extensions in 1789, to between 10 am and 2 pm daily from 1793. In the early years, the concentrated opening hours of the society libraries, if inconvenient for use of the library as a reference resource, did at least result in the more frequent meetings of members.

Members recognized from the beginning that there might be a problem in ensuring that all members were aware of what the library held and of what, therefore, they might borrow. Originally, under the 1750 rule 12 "two hundred or more Catalogues, as occasion shall require, of every parcel of Books sent over to the Society, shall be printed in London, and distributed here among the Members." From these catalogues members could order books from the librarian. William Strahan, the London bookseller, was duly asked to print a catalogue of holdings from a manuscript list sent over to London. It was of elementary design, with books and pamphlets listed and given a successive number within format categories (folio, octavo, quarto and "twelves"), but without any alphabetical subdivision (so finding a work entailed knowing its size and then looking down the entire list). The number of volumes to each work was listed, but no indication of the year or place of publication of the edition was included. The lists were printed on one side of the page only, leaving blank interleaving for the marking of additions and corrections, or even, perhaps, to assist in ordering by dispatch and return of the catalogue itself.

Despite the discreet silence of the library records, it is now apparent, however, that the first printing of this catalogue was a disaster. Simple though the original plan might have seemed, Strahan's resulting work was strewn with errors. The octavos and twelves were printed on both sides of the page and the entire order of the format subdivisions was muddled. The opening page of pamphlets was followed by folios, numbers 1–56, quartos from number 14, octavos from number 135, twelves from number 44, then twelves from number 1, quartos 1–13, and octavos 1–134. Alphabetically rearranged and refined by much bibliographical research to identify titles and editions, the listings are reproduced in appendix 3, together with subsequent library orders from the letters sent before 1770 (the holdings will be discussed in more detail in the following chapters). Tellingly, only a single copy of this Strahan catalogue now survives (at the Library of Congress, where it arrived some time in the 1880s). Most copies were probably destroyed as unusable. Certainly, by 1762 the Charleston librarian was further charged with keeping "an exact catalogue of every book and instrument,"[8] and the later catalogues were printed in Charleston. New editions of these printed catalogues and rules were duly distributed to members. The annotated copy of the 1770 edition of the *Rules* belonging to Robert Rowand (admitted member 1763), survives at the Library Society today.

Under the rules only a single work (although one that might comprise multiple volumes) was allowed to be borrowed on each occasion (left open in rule 12 as printed in the 1748 newspaper advertisement, but specified from 1762, rule 20), and members were clearly expected to read promptly. Loans were limited to four days for pamphlets, twelve days for duodecimos and octavos, sixteen days for quartos, and twenty-four days for folios. Members living outside Charleston, however, were granted time extensions engagingly calculated at twelve hours for every six miles' distance. Under the rules a five-shilling fine was imposed for every twelve hours overdue (1750, rule 12; 1762, rule 20; 1770, rule 22).

These were exacting conditions, established with a certain confidence that members were so heedful of each other's good opinions that the system would not break down through abuse, but also that members might be indulged in longer loans at a clear financial advantage to the society. Members were indeed increasingly scattered as the estates accumulated. Headrights of 50 acres for each imported slave sanctioned the expansion of plantations so that settlements such as Goose Creek, eighteen miles up the peninsula from Charleston, soon served as satellite communities outside the capital. As has often been pointed out, planters and merchants of Goose Creek, the first important settlement outside Charleston, acted as though it was a Carolina Hampstead or Newington Green. Here, in St. James's Parish, Goose Creek, Alexander Garden established his "Otranto" estate, with the Deas and the Izard families as neighbors.[9] Many other library members, at least when not in their Charleston houses, must also have sought longer-term loans for their books, just as they extended their plantations or acquired new ones, like the Brisbanes, magnificently established on the Ashley River. Not that this scattering of library members, which would have seemed extraordinarily far-flung in Britain, was unusual in eighteenth-century North America. Similar lending allowances are evident elsewhere. In Baltimore, according to the 1797 library rules, "persons at the distance of five miles and upwards from town, may keep the books, which they keep, one-third of time longer than others."[10] At the April quarterly meeting in Charleston in 1762 Dr. Deas moved "that oyl cloth be provided for the packing up Books that Country members may send for."[11]

A certain anxiety about possible inaction was evident from the outset, with forfeits to discourage unfilled offices and poor attendance at meetings. All library members were under the obligation of serving as an officer once in seven years, and any member refusing to comply was fined £5, although members were excused if deemed "country members," that is living at a distance from Charleston. This was usually allowed on application, but several high-profile requests were thrown out by general meetings, including one from William Hopton in 1775, which "after some debate was rejected."[12] The library committee also repeatedly acted on defaulters. It was suggested at the anniversary meeting of 1768 that members late for meetings should be fined.[13] This was referred to the committee revising the rules and then translated into a toughening of the first rule for strict attendance at the publicly requested hour (noting, then, that the presiding chairman was to open the meeting at 11 am). In addition, in 1770 the secretary was charged with reading out the names of any committee members "neglecting to attend at their stated times of meeting."[14] Further rules debarred members from voting or attending a committee meeting once they were six months in arrears with subscriptions or fines. The same rules stipulated that "the name of every member dismissed [from] the society shall be hung up in the library, with an account of the sum due by him to the society; and also the name of every member who is indebted for six months subscription."[15]

The rules, indeed, as printed in successive versions with additions and amendments, partly reflected the unsettled history of the library in its first decades. By the mid-1750s many weekly contributions lapsed and overdue books accumulated. A long list of such books was advertised in the *Gazette* over a period of three months, suggesting to a later custodian of the collection that "the spirit of the Society flagged, and was on the brink of dissolution."[16] Although a visitor in 1763 described the society as "at present in a flourishing State,"[17] suggesting some sort of revival, in the same year it was reported at the anniversary meeting that "the Spirit of this Society is much lessen'd & the Vigor it first set out with almost annihilated."[18] In response, members proposed meeting together every Wednesday at Dillon's tavern (at 6 pm in winter and 7 pm in summer) to "associate together . . . in order to converse freely on such matters as may ocurr & they conceive may be of utility to be offer'd to the monthly Committee."[19] The proposal, "taken into consideration," does not seem to have been acted upon, or if it was, it does not seem to have proved helpful.

During the mid-1760s, canceled or inquorate meetings again became a serious problem. In response, heavy fines, such as those approved at the quarterly meeting of 1 April 1767, were imposed for nonattendance at committee meetings.[20] At a committee meeting of June that year printed notices were ordered to remind members of the dates of meetings and to facilitate the levying of fines.[21] There seems to have been no immediate response, however, with several inquorate meetings during 1768.[22] At the same period there is evidence that potential library committee members were identified from among the citizenry of Charleston whether or not they were already Library Society members. John Hume, for example, was admitted member in July 1759 and was then elected to the committee at the next general meeting in October. William Mason was admitted member in June 1764 and put on the committee and elected secretary all at the same meeting.

Other regulations policed the conduct of the formal meetings. Procedure resembled that of a debating society. The original rule 22 of the Library Society (rule 34 by 1762, rule 3 in 1772) decreed that any member speaking must address his remarks to the president, who also determined who might speak. Similar practices were later confirmed by associations such as the Medical Society of South Carolina (almost all of whose members also belonged to the Library Society). Rules here stated that "members shall address the President standing; and no member shall be interrupted whilst he is speaking, unless he be called to order by the President."[23] Meetings, as reflected in the journal of the Library Society, adopted debating manners similar to those of the Westminster Commons and the colonial assemblies—and, like the latter, at least, were probably observed more in the breach than in the minimally constructed formal record. More importantly, all meetings, convened under an increasingly august presidency (see below, ch. 5) and adhering to rigid etiquette, adjourned to the distinctive sociability of the after-meeting dinner.

The dinners following the meetings, and as included in the original design of the society, enticed the more remote members to meetings, but also provided a forum for discussion and sociableness, complementary to the formal meeting. It was a practice common to many Charleston societies, the German Friendly Society, for example, following all its quarterly meetings with dinners. They were gracious affairs. Under the original rule 20 of the Library Society (brought forward to rule 7 in 1762) it was decreed that for the anniversary meeting the steward was to provide "a sufficient dinner" for which each member was to pay forty shillings one week in advance. Entertainment was appropriately lavish, and it is not at all clear that the £2 up front was ever followed by the sort of payment necessary to cover the far greater costs of these events. A surviving bill to the library treasurer for the 1778 dinner amounted to £432 for thirty-five gentlemen, or £12.6s per head.[24] These were what has been called elsewhere "decorous dining,"[25] a practice confirming a centerpiece of public and political sociability, a confirmatory unity, whatever other divisions, of the elite.[26] With some exceptions (the 1755 anniversary meeting commenced at 9 am, with the offer to all members of an audience with the president at 3 pm the previous Wednesday[27]), the earliest dinners were held at times varying from 11 am to the early afternoon. At the anniversary meeting of 1765, apparently in response to some demand for standard times, it was resolved that the next quarterly meeting, and those thereafter, should begin at 11 am and that "the members of the said Society do then dine together."[28] Times remained variable, however, perhaps according to the style of the formal meeting and ensuing sociability that was planned. In 1767 William Mason advertised the quarterly meeting of October as meeting at 10 am.[29] In the early nineteenth century the society advertised its anniversary meetings with later dinners. In January 1804 it was provided at 3:30 pm, following a meeting in the library room of the Courthouse at noon, with the quarterly meeting of June that year starting at 1 pm.[30]

In this way, therefore, the Charleston Library Society, formally established with its elegant statement of mission and proclaiming public and beneficent intent, also served as a private club, reminiscent of other societies of the town. The division is not simple or absolute, however. This was a social institution characterized by its discursive functions, a private society soon exerting a more formative influence in the civilizing mission than any other local club. The Charleston Library Society acted as a philanthropic but exclusive institution, while adopting current notions of a "social library" as one providing a circulating collection of materials (and usually a reading room), assembled, preserved, and issued for loan under detailed rules, and maintained for members by fee, subscription, or payment into joint stock.[31]

The accumulation of capital stock from members' initial and then five-shilling weekly contributions and fines also enabled the society to act as a bank. The Library Society lent out sums at interest with the intention of augmenting the endowment designed to buy books and instruments and to build and staff a college. Under the earliest rules of the society, members were to set aside an initial £1,600 sterling and £100 each year thereafter to buy books. The remainder of the monies accruing from weekly dues, donations, fines, and forfeitures, were to be "let out at Interest on good Personal Security, that Funds may be raised" (1750, rule 11). By April

1767 the total sums lent in bonds was £8,500 currency (with cash in hand of just over £528), and by July 1768 the total was £10,500 comprising 8 separate bonds (1 of £3,500, 1 of £1,500, 2 of £1,000, and 4 of £500). In March 1769 total funds reached more than £11,100, and in January 1772 the society claimed £14,500 in bonds, increasing by a further £1,000 by July.[32] Library Society members were explicitly precluded (1762, rule 27) from borrowing or standing as security for other borrowers, but some of those lent money were later elected or were related to existing members. The bond holders included the firm of McLeod, Donnom, and Mazyck, that of Livingston, Freer, and Legare, and that of Middleton, Lorton, and Hope.[33]

This policy of letting out sums was a normal practice for institutions such as friendly gentlemen's societies and churches. It also helps explain why interest in committee membership increased in the 1770s. As the Charleston Library Society became richer, committee membership offered greater attraction. Although as the constitution insisted, none of the debtors or guarantors could be society members, its rotating committee, appointed by each quarterly general meeting, decided between the different applications for loans following public advertisement placed by the society in the *Gazette*. In June 1773, for example, the committee considered "several applications" and after balloting, Philip Meyer was lent £1,000 currency, with John Wagner acting as security. This was about the average sum lent at any one time, with some larger and some smaller offers according to society funds and inclination. Following its November 1774 public advertisement for lending £1,500 currency, the committee met in January to consider various applications and "after some deliberation" offered it to David Oliphant, with John Walter as security.[34] More typically, Samuel Hopkins in June 1792 was lent at interest the standard £1,000.[35]

The provision of security remained crucial to applications for Library Society loans and also to the continuing loan arrangement. The high-risk option of acting as a lending institution in order to generate more income proved a constant source of anxiety, given the vulnerable state of financial markets. Sometimes the library committee deemed that a single name was adequate security but on several occasions a number of guarantors were supplied, and the quality of warranty must obviously have contributed to the committee's decision. In November 1771, for example, in competition with several other applicants, James Wilson was lent £1,000 after naming six gentlemen "obligers."[36] With less deliberation, William Hall was lent £500 currency in May 1767 with his brother Hercules Hall as sole security.[37] This allotment appears to have been unproblematic, but many of the loans did cause great disquiet. In 1762 Percival and George Pawley's bond was called in for the next year, the library committee having already demanded additional security.[38] A further crisis developed in late 1764 when the committee discovered that the firm of Bosomworth, Harvey, and Smith were late in paying the interest due on their bonds. The members decided to take legal action in the event of payment not received by the January anniversary meeting (and the threat appears to have worked).[39] Again, in July 1774 one of the guarantors of a loan to a Mr. Hopkins became bankrupt, and the July general meeting decided to call in the bond (which remained an ultimate although obviously not always redeemable sanction). In fact, shortly afterwards Hopkins offered new security and "after some debate" the next general meeting decided to honor the existing agreement.[40]

Even riskier, perhaps, were the sums from the Library Society's capital lent to the colonial treasury in the revolutionary years. Although interest bearing and supported by the like-minded actions of scores of other individuals and institutions, the society became a major subscriber to the bonds. Through the agency of Thomas Grimball, member since 1766, the society agreed eleven separate loans to the South Carolina Treasury between December 1776 and December 1779. By May 1780 the net loan outstanding came to £19,954 currency (from a total gross loan of £35,500 currency). The total state debt of over £8.6 million currency derived from dozens of separate loans from individuals (headed by Gabriel Manigault, the largest individual bondholder in 1779) and many library members such as Middleton, Grimké, Izard, and Brailsford, but also from religious and fraternal institutions. Of these the Library Society was the third largest donor, after the parish of St. James, Goose Creek (£40,000), and the Fellowship Society (£24,000). To a lesser degree other Charleston societies, including the German Friendly Society, the St. Cecilia Society, St. George's Society, and the Winyah (or Winyaw) Indico Society, as well as the Society for the Propagation of Christian Knowledge, also bought state bonds.[41] The investment of the endowment in interest-bearing notes might in part have been a political statement, but it was also a high-risk financial strategy that ultimately contributed to the postwar uncertainties. At the anniversary meeting audit of 1784 the treasurer was "directed to exchange the Indents belonging to the Society for Money deposited in the Public Treasury of this State, the New Indents in Sterling," and in 1788 the treasurer, Joshua Ward, reported on the "considerable sum of money due the Society on Bonds together with the Interest" about which the meeting unanimously agreed to sue and to recover.[42] Finally, in July 1790 all existing bonds and notes were immediately called in (with no reason given).[43]

Of all the organizational features of the Charleston Library Society, however, none was more problematic, at least in the early years, than the provision of a site for meetings and for the library collection itself. Neither a library building nor a reading room was properly provided until 1768, no purpose-built library existed until well into the nineteenth century, and even the quarterly general meetings moved between different houses and taverns until the late eighteenth century. On the last day of July 1749 secretary Samuel Brailsford advertised a meeting of the society to take place "at the usual hour" at Thomas Blythe's tavern in Broad Street. Early next year the "Annual meeting," as it was styled, was also held at Blythe's establishment. The anniversary meetings continued at the tavern (presumably in a large back room) for the next four years. The tavern was now maintained by John Gordon.[44] Although not formally recorded, the library's receipt books strongly suggest that the after-meeting dinners took place in Dillon's tavern in the 1760s and early 1770s and by at least 1775 at Ramage's tavern (both usually styled "houses").

Storage for the books and, ideally, the sort of reading room then being built in great European houses and libraries, were even more problematic. According to the *Gazette,* it was agreed at the 1756 meeting "that a committee be appointed, to consider of Ways and Means to procure a proper Place for depositing the library in."[45] Until 1755 when John Sinclair left South Carolina in failing health, the collection of books and instruments was almost certainly housed first in his store or house in Broad Street and then (from late 1749) at his new residence in the Bay. From February 1755 the library resided in the Broad Street home of the new librarian, William Henderson, master of the Free School, and then in the home of his successor from September 1756, William Carwithen. On Elliot Street, Carwithen's house was well situated in "a central part of the town very convenient to members."[46] In 1764, in response to a request from library president Bull, Thomas Boone, the governor of the colony, offered the former council chamber for the library, but members decided that the move could not be justified given the uncertainty about the conditions of tenure. John Cooper urged the society to accept the offer, informing the meeting that an order of council had decreed that unless the society accepted the offer of the old council chamber within six months it was to be offered to the clerk of common pleas as an office. Gabriel Manigault, the library's vice president, however, gave his opinion that as the chamber had been built at public expense it was not in the gift of Governor Boone at all, and he was concerned that even with the sanction of all three branches of the legislature and of royal confirmation, a room that "had cost the publick a very considerable sum of money" might not with propriety be given over "to the use of any private community."[47] Permanency was essential if, as members argued, they were to create "not only an useful but ornamental Repository for their Books and future Apparatus for experimental Philosophy."[48] Nor was Boone the most popular man in town. Having intervened in the election of Christopher Gadsden to the Carolina Commons, then precipitously dissolving the chamber and warning the press to observe good behavior, Boone set off a public brawl that resulted in new confidence within the Commons and his own departure for England the same year.[49]

At the same contentious meeting of October 1764, however, Manigault offered the Library Society "a very large & convenient room," in a building he owned in or near the corner of Kinloch Court, off State Street. The lease was for twenty-one years and Manigault proposed paying for the new fitments himself. The proposal was keenly accepted by the library committee, and the new room was fitted up and completed in January 1765, and it hosted a committee meeting on 6 February.[50] We know little of the subsequent furnishing of this room, save for an order of the committee to "recommend that proper shelves [for the Mackenzie book bequest] be erected on the whole breadth of the West end of the Library Room . . . to correspond with the rest."[51] When shown around by Charles Cotesworth Pinckney and Rutledge in 1773, the New England visitor, Josiah Quincy, described this "public library" as "a handsome, square, spacious room, containing a large collection of very valuable books, cuts, globes, etc."[52] With the anticipation of hostilities various preparations were made to pack or even move the books to safer quarters but little appears to have been done. Then, in 1778, as already noted, the building was consumed in the disastrous fire that destroyed most of the neighborhood and almost half the town.[53] All but 185 volumes were lost.

Thereafter the Library Society's book collection moved frequently up to 1792. When in late 1779 a Mr. Simons bought the land "whereon the House occupied as the Library Room now is," he asked that the books be moved out.[54] William Gibbes offered part of his office in January 1780, but after the British seizure of Charleston that spring, the recently elected librarian, Francis Fariau, apparently transported the remnants of the library with him as he moved from house to house during the two years of military occupation.[55] The books were cased up and a committee was appointed in April 1783 to consider new quarters. The Queen Street office of Daniel Cannon was very briefly home to the small collection, before the appointment of John McCall as librarian in July 1783 when the books were taken to his office. Next April, however, the books moved to a room in the Exchange, by agreement of the intendant and wardens of the city. This arrangement lasted some three years. The Charleston Council repossessed the room in October 1787, and the library, now attempting to rebuild its stock despite the depletion of its funds, was rehoused in rooms, first at the corner of Bay and Broad Streets (in a house noted as "no. 132" where the Library Society also met for its anniversary meeting in 1788), and then in 1788 at the corner of Tradd and Bay Streets ("no. 1"). In 1789 a room over the new market in Meeting Street was rented and the librarian ordered to provide fourteen green chairs and two large tables, one to be covered with green cloth, but the new room was rejected at the next July meeting as not being in a proper state, especially for the society's meetings.[56] Instead, at £60 pounds a year the society hired two rooms on the second floor of another house on the south corner of Tradd and Bay Streets, which also offered a couple to furnish the entertainments in exchange for living there.[57] In 1791 the library was again moved to the corner of Broad and Church Streets, but at last in 1792 it was more permanently sited in rooms on the upper floor of the newly completed Courthouse.

The courthouse building was originally intended as a replacement, on the same site, for the first colonial statehouse gutted by fire in February 1788, but the new design for rebuilding by Judge William Drayton had quickly to be modified. Earlier that year the assembly had in fact already begun discussion about its future, and in 1790 it moved to the new state capital of Columbia.[58] As a result, the court and public offices extended their occupancy of the rebuilt Charleston premises. A third floor was added to the original rebuilding plan, based around the surviving burned-out shell of the old statehouse. What was then restyled the "Courthouse" was funded by subscription, with many Library Society members giving generously. There was apparently an early understanding that the Library Society was to be granted space in the new building. It was the prime location. Constructed of brick cased by plaster, the new courthouse stood at a corner of the intersection of Broad and Meeting Streets, at the very heart of Charleston (plate 4). Another corner boasted the magnificent Episcopal Church of St. Michael, another was taken up by the jail, and another was eventually to house the Bank of the United States.

The Courthouse, with its principal entrance on Broad Street, comprised the law courts on the ground floor, civic offices above, and a third-floor upper storey containing jury rooms to serve the three courtrooms, the offices of the state treasurer and comptroller, and from 1806, a southwestern corner room fitted out for the library and meetings of the Medical Society of South Carolina. The rooms housing the Library Society and its natural history museum occupied the eastern part of the third floor. This comprised more than one third of the total floor space of the upper storey (excluding the grand stairway) and was served by a total of ten windows, two to the south, five to the east, and three to the north. The main room comprised five or six "apartments" separated by ceilings and bookcases, and with desks and chairs provided for visitors and readers.[59]

The Charleston Library Society remained in the Courthouse until 1835 when it purchased and moved into the South Carolina Bank building at the corner of Church and Broad Streets. By 1817, however, when visited by Ebenezer Kellogg, a New England school teacher (and not perhaps the most impartial observer), the Courthouse lodgings were already showing signs of wear and even a certain neglect: "The room is divided into five or six apartments, not in the manner of alcoves like Harvard and Yale libraries, but by ceilings which have openings little wider than are required for doors. In one apartment we find theological, in another historical works; and so of the other rooms. All the more expensive works I could think of were found there. . . . The room is always open and a librarian present who directs to any book called for. . . . [The library] is kept less neatly than it should be. In one of the recesses stands a full length cast of the Apollo Belvidere. You see in it the beauty which has made it the admiration of the world. . . . It is too much covered with dust."[60]

We know little of how the Charleston library actually operated from its shifting residences in the early decades, but at least from the time of its permanent room, 1765–1778, and then after 1792 in the Courthouse, communal use must have been frequent. The enthusiasm (to be discussed below) to own scientific apparatus that could be used and appreciated by many persons at once, is another clue. Nor do the library rules include commandments such as that from the Savannah Library Society (founded 1809) that smoking and "audible conversation is at all times prohibited."[61] The library room would seem an obvious meeting place for like-minded members, with the quarterly meetings providing a more formalized framework, if at different locations.

In fact, despite the obvious weakening of visions of a permanent, grand library room, frequent moves and confined accommodation were quite typical of many early library societies. The Library Company of Philadelphia was first housed in the librarian's lodgings and then moved to the new west wing of the Statehouse some time before 1742, fifty years before the erection of a proper building in 1789 (opening in 1791). When the New York Society Library was established in 1754 its first books were "placed for the present, by Leave of the Corporation, in their Library Room in City-Hall."[62] The room was maintained in the reconstructed hall, now named Federal Hall, from 1789 until a purpose-built library was finally opened in 1795.

The absence of permanent library rooms, if common to the American cities, must have been the more frustrating given the ostentation of many such buildings in Europe and the many reports of them brought back by American travelers. John Rutledge, Jr., for example, making his Grand European Tour in 1788, visited the 40,000–book collection at the palace at Mannheim: "a very large Library handsomely arranged—a cabinet of paintings, one of natural history, another of medals—galleries of sculpture— engravings etc. . . . The Library room is much admired for its size, architecture, and decorations, but most particularly for the painting of the ceiling—the execution of which is truly great—the design is a representation of the virtues, sciences, and arts which (aided by time) discover the truth; their goddess Minerva, placed near the throne of truth points out (to them) the road to it. At their feet, Ignorance with the vices are falling headlong into the abyss."[63]

The need for space to display acquisitions to their greatest advantage was even more acute with the development of collections other than books. In common with European counterparts, the early American society libraries came to take particular interest in scientific and natural history collections. In addition to its scientific instruments, the Library Company of Philadelphia acquired an extraordinary and miscellaneous collection of "curiosities," largely by gift and bequest. Its collection of Roman coins came from Charles Gray, MP, in 1752; other curios that soon exceeded all available storage space included Eskimo parkas, the hand of a mummified Egyptian princess (sent by Benjamin West), and dozens of other exotic, and often rotting, specimens. The earliest years of the Charleston Museum, founded in 1773, have left relatively few historical traces, but the collection appears to have been supported by men with a variety of interests.

Some thirty years after the first curios arrived at the Philadelphia library, William Bull, presiding at the January 1773 anniversary meeting of the Charleston Library Society, proposed that "a special Committee should be appointed for collecting materials for promoting a Natural History of this Province." The committee was duly established, comprising at the outset Dr. Alexander Baron, Dr. Lionel Chalmers, John Colcock, Charles Cosslett, Dr. Peter Fayssoux, Thomas Grimball, and fifteen other members. In March and April the committee placed a large advertisement in the *Gazette* inviting Charlestonians to "procure and send to them, all the natural Productions, either Animal, Vegetable, or Mineral, that can be had in their several bounds. . . . Of the Animal Tribe they would wish to have every Species, whether Terrestrial or Aquatic, *viz.* Quadrupedes, Birds, Fishes, Reptiles, Insects, Worms, &c. . . . Of Vegetables they will thankfully receive every Kind, from the loftiest Tree in the Forest, to the smallest Plant of the Fields. — A complete specimen of any Tree or Plant, will be two small Branches of each, one having the Flower in full Blossom, and the other the ripe Fruit."[64]

The initial enthusiasm is revealed by a succession of recorded gifts—ones, which if they survived in any state at all, were to leave the library forty years later to augment the museum of the Literary and Philosophical Society, founded in the town in 1813. If, as is so often claimed, the original collection constituted the oldest such museum in North America, its contents seem to have been modest, although typically eclectic.[65] In July 1773, for example, the president presented the library, in the name of William Williamson, with "the Head and Neck of an uncommon Bird, killed at a place called Stephens's Creek." The general meeting "order'd that it be recommended to the select Committee to take some Method for preserving it in good Order."[66] The Library Society was hardly in a position to decline this august gift, but of the fate of the bird and the progress of its pickling, the Library Society records are silent. The same meeting, however, "ordered that the special committee for promoting the Natural History of the Province have been at their discretion to cause proper places to be erected for keeping any Curiosities they may receive from time to time & to employ some proper Person to draw representations of such of them as are perishable." The treasurer was ordered to pay the artist accordingly.[67] At the next meeting in October 1773, a painting of the head and neck of the bird was presented, drawn by the fifteen-year-old son of the founder member and lawyer William Burrows. The meeting ordered that the drawing be varnished, framed, and glazed, and thanks sent to the artist. No payment was mentioned, and no further action on commissioning or receiving sketches of items presented for the museum is recorded.[68]

Silence, indeed, accompanies the development—if any—of the natural history collection, until late in the century. At the back of the surviving 1798 accessions book is a list of "Articles for the Museum." These include a case presented by Capt. William Hall containing a collection of insects from Surinam, together with an apron worn by Surinam natives, arrows, the head of a bird called the Bannana [*sic*] Beak, a wasps' nest, and an ostrich egg. Also that year, Thomas Branford Smith, son of the 1750 vice president, donated "a beautiful species of spider, caught in his Piazza," and Nathaniel Russell gave "a humming bird & old wife Fish & young alligator." Gifts of other members included many beaks, tusks and teeth, an Indian helmet, "a human thigh bone with oysters growing out of it," the head of a turtle from Calcutta, "a caterpillar taken from an apple-tree at Newport Rhode Island," the skin of a rattlesnake, a pair of chop sticks, "2 Scotch pebbles from Fifeshire," a chicken with six legs, and another with two heads, a pair of east Indian slippers, and a Calcutta turtle that died within three days' sail of Charleston.

Chapter Five

NEW MEMBERS AND
THE DESIRE FOR GRANDEUR

MUCH OF THE SURVIVING EVIDENCE suggests the increasing exclusiveness of the Charleston Library Society. In part, this is because many of those who joined the library in its first two decades became the establishment of the town and included many of the famously wealthy political and social leaders of the colony. Henry Laurens, vice president of the Library Society from 1767, was by the early 1770s one of the wealthiest men in North America and the owner of at least eight plantations. Of the thirty-eight men defined as leaders in the assembly between 1748 and 1770, twenty-five, or two-thirds, were members of the Library Society. These included thirteen merchants, five lawyers, four planters, two physicians and a placeman.[1]

The main indication that the Library Society became increasingly restrictive and closed results from the journal record of membership elections. The journal, however, offers no certain register of all deaths, absences from Charleston, or conversions to the relatively inactive "country" membership, and it is therefore impossible to gauge the full, changing profile of membership between 1750 and 1819. Compared to our one figure of existing membership in the early period (129 in 1750), at least a further 144 members, and 2 honorary members were admitted before 1779 (as detailed by appendix 1), of which 92 were new share holders (see appendix 2). Admission rates were far from even, and as Waterhouse's study of the Charleston gentry pointed out, Library Society expansion stalled in the 1760s. As appendix 1 reveals, 40 new members were admitted between 1761 and 1770, with 20 of these purchasing new shares (appendix 2). This compares to 159 men admitted to the St. Andrew's Society in the same period.[2]

In Charleston, a library society founded by young men keen to make their mark soon became an affirmation of distinction achieved. To bolster its authority and to secure establishment endorsement the Library Society ceased to elect members as president in one-year rotation and now elected as president the colony's governor or his deputy. This accords with the evolution of the lowcountry elite by the end of the eighteenth century into a narrow interlocking caste.

If the leadership and general tone of the Library Society was more select, however, this also attracted dozens of up-and-coming merchants, lawyers, clerics and physicians who wanted to join the upper elite. By the late 1770s the quarterly general meetings considered and voted upon blocks of names. Partly, this is a consequence of the death or resignation of some of the first generation of library members, but the creation of entirely new shares was also very brisk. Between 1771 and 1778 at least 18 men bought or inherited the existing shares of former members, compared to 69 completely new shares instituted during the same eight years (appendix 2). These new members are included in appendices 1 and 2, surveying known membership of the first thirty years of the library, but journal entries continue (after the 1780–1783 break) through the late 1780s, when up to a dozen new members were admitted each year.

Even so, in the broader context, the Library Society became more exclusive. The membership of 280 claimed by the library in 1819,[3] was more than twice that of 1750, but over the same period the white population of Charleston probably increased fourfold or more.[4] For the early national period, the identity of library membership remains at its most problematic owing to the loss of relevant records. From newspaper advertisements and fragmentary reports of meetings it is nevertheless clear that membership for at least the first decade of the nineteenth century retained protected status. Comparisons with other American cities confirm the narrowness of the membership. In 1798 the rapidly growing city of Baltimore, earlier harboring aspirations as Federal capital, boasted more members in its library company (founded in 1795 by 59 initial subscribers) than there were in the Charleston library. Despite the requirement to purchase a share at $20 and pay $4 annually thereafter, the Baltimore library comprised 226 members by 1798 and 346 by 1799.[5] Some 404 members were listed by the Baltimore Library Company as early as 1804, just ten years after its foundation.[6] Down the coast from Charleston, another new library attracted immediate support. The Savannah Library Society was founded in 1809 with 81 in attendance at the inaugural meeting.[7] By comparison, expansion in Charleston was guarded. Although visitors were accorded proper respect, especially when they were from afar, admission policy to the Charleston library rooms appears to have contrasted, for example, with developments at the Baltimore Library Company, where nonmembers were allowed access under the general assembly's act of incorporation. The act proclaimed a desire for improvement akin to the founding document of the Charleston Library Society, but its apparent democratic spirit was addressed from the opening words: "Whereas the establishment of public libraries under judicious regulations, cannot fail to promote the diffusion of useful knowledge, and the interests of virtue, and to grow greatly beneficial to society."

The Revolutionary War interrupted the election of new members to the Charleston library but it also revealed the diversity of view among the existing membership. Most significantly, however, formal disputes did not apparently arise in library meetings or committees, even though other sources make plain the ideological divisions. In December 1781 a long list of men and women banished by the British included at least 26 library members including Richard Beresford, Aedanus Burke (later South Carolina representative in the First Congress and distinguished judge), Bellamy Crawford, Robert Dewar, Christopher Gadsden, Benjamin Legare, David Oliphant, David Ramsay, Samuel Prioleau, Philip Prioleau, Thomas Pinckney, Charles Cotesworth Pinckney, and Charles Pinckney. Then, a few years later the estates of the Crokatts, Robert Wells, and George Saxby were among confiscations of nonresident Loyalists, while 12 of the 25 of those first banished from the state, with their estates also confiscated, were also library members, including Charles Atkins, John Hopton, Robert Johnston, Thomas Phepoe, Robert Phelp, John Wragg, and Alexander Wright. The several banishment and confiscation lists that followed contained many more library members' names including James Brisbane, Samuel Carne, Alexander Garden, and Alexander Rose.[8] Given that the various confiscations applied to leading property holders and members of the elite, it is hardly surprising that library members counted among them; the striking feature is that large numbers appeared in each of the rosters, Patriot and Loyalist.

Other exclusions are more conspicuous. All seems, at least formally, to have been a strictly male affair. Although women were not explicitly banned from membership of the Library Society (unlike in the rules of the St. Cecilia Society and many other Charleston associations), it seems that the society assumed that there would be no such application. Conventional restriction of library membership to one per household might also have played its part. One specific section of the rules[9] permitted the disposal of stock to anyone including those not members if sanctioned by the general meeting, but no member was allowed to dispose of his share to any other member "and if any member, as heir, executor or administrator of another, or by any means whatever shall have a plurality of shares, he shall not have any greater privileges in voting or taking out books than any other member who hath but one share." Effectively, this appears to have been a disincentive to have more stock owned or membership taken by more than one person in each household (although, again, this was not formally forbidden in the early rules).[10] When Charles Pinckney, Jr., was admitted member in April 1778, for example, in the place of Miles Brewton who had recently died, Brewton's legatees were Pinckney's mother and his aunt Mrs. Motte, but both "resigned their right."[11] This certainly suggests that they might have taken up Brewton's shares had they so wished.

As will be discussed below, the library collection overwhelmingly reflected masculine interests, but it seems likely that many women did read the books and magazines borrowed from the library by male members of their household. This was certainly what happened at the Philadelphia Library Company in the decades before the first official female shareholders are recorded in 1769, with various women writing of their use of the library.[12] It was also the practice at the Union Library of Hatboro, Pennsylvania, where borrowing records between 1762 and 1774 suggest that many men borrowed on behalf of women.[13] In Charleston there is no shortage of similar candidates. Many women appear in the known mercantile community of mid-eighteenth-century Charleston, most of them widows carrying on the business of their late husbands. Several Charleston women were more than capable of holding their own in learned elite circles.

Notable in Carolina society was Eliza Lucas Pinckney, the indigo experimenter, wife of library member Charles Pinckney (d. 1758), and mother of the fifteenth president of the library, Charles Cotesworth Pinckney.[14] In 1740 Eliza reported, "I have a little library well-furnished (for my papa has left me most of his books)." She asked her father to order music books from London, and her future husband lent her Virgil, allegedly providing the inspiration for her own cedar grove. Of Virgil, she decided, "tho' he wrote in and for Italy, it will in many instances suit Carolina."[15] Charles Pinckney also set her off reading Locke. As she wrote to a friend, "I don't affect to appear learned by quoting Mr Lock, but would let you see what regard I pay to Mr Pinckney's recommendations of Authors."[16] Eliza Pinckney then read Richardson's *Pamela* and discussed both it and Locke with her friends in letters. She found fault with Locke and thought *Pamela* exhibited "that disgusting liberty of praising her self."[17] Notably, Eliza had requested the loan of Virgil despite the warnings of "an old lady in our Neighbourhood" who "has a great spite at my books and had like to have thrown a volume of my Plutarchs lives into the fire the other day. . . and begs most seriously I will never read father Malbrauch [Nicolas Malebranche]."[18] In 1754 she received the play *Boadicia,* written in the previous year by Richard Glover, and Richardson's *Charles Grandison,* also of 1753.[19]

It is true, of course, that this remarkable and well-read woman was hardly typical of the wives of most members of the library (George Washington, as United States president, was a pallbearer at her funeral). The correspondence and wills of a few other women readers do survive, however. Mrs. Jean DuPre of St. James, Goose Creek, owned numerous religious books and twenty-one history books at her death in the late 1740s.[20] Martha Laurens Ramsay was a noted book lover who from an early age requested globes and scientific tuition.[21] Another of Eliza Pinckney's early companions was Mary Perrie, wife of the library member and Georgetown Winyah planter-merchant John Cleland. The London-born Cleland left a small but significant library (see below).[22]

By contrast, Ann, the wife of Gabriel Manigault, library president and vice president and perhaps the wealthiest man in the colony, used her diary to record social news and the state of her own health rather than notes on any reading. An occasional playgoer, the only literary reference in Ann Manigault's diary is to the theater. More generally, several visitors' disparaging remarks about Charleston in the eighteenth century included observations about women's learning that were not encouraging. In 1778, for example, Ebenezer Hazard wrote that "the people of Charleston possess liberal sentiments and polite manners. A learned education has been neglected among them. . . . The young ladies are generally kept in the country till they are 15 or 16 years old, and then brought to town and put to a boarding school for a year. I am told *their* education in particular is scandalously neglected."[23] A rare external reference to women borrowing books from the early Library Society comes from Mary Stead Pinckney, writing from Paris in 1797 where her husband, Charles Cotesworth (and most recent library president), was about to be spurned on his official embassy to France. Writing to Rebecca Izard, daughter of her sister, Elizabeth Stead Izard, Mary Pinckney described a visit to the Angoulême china factory, adding, "if you wish to read a particular account of what we saw, send to the Library for the works of the Abbé Raynal, where your uncle says it is very accurately described. I read it many years ago & do not recollect it."[24] Rebecca Izard's father, Ralph, had succeeded her uncle as library president that year; the household membership (if the grandest possible) was, without equivocation, sufficient to allow the young Elizabeth access to reading.

At the very end of the period considered here, the earliest surviving book circulation records (from 1811) also confirm that women regularly borrowed books by use of the membership held in the household. Moreover, books were now signed out under their own names. Juliet Elliott, for example, borrowed Maria Edgeworth's *Tales* and her novel *Ellen* (6 volumes in all) in July 1811, returning one set nine days later and the other two days after that. Mrs Elliott, probably the wife of Barnard Elliott, and then aged 33, was one of 26 borrowers on the day in which she visited the library (or had her books collected from there by a servant). Few indeed, appeared to have visited the library in person at this time. Of the 24 separate loans made on a typical day in July 1811, for example, 19 were "by order," 2 were collected by the son of the member, and only 3 were by "self."[25]

In social terms all continued to be very narrowly based. Membership of the Charleston library was kept exclusive by election and by entry fee. Unlike the St. Cecilia Society, never to be composed of more than 120 members at any one time, there was no prescribed limit to membership. Under the printed 1750 rules those wishing to become members were to write to the secretary who was then to display a public advertisement at the Exchange for three days giving notice of a special meeting for members to ballot on the application (rule 6). Later, applicants were obliged to write to the president of the Library Society, through the offices of the secretary. If sanctioned by the president the application was then put to the ballot of members at a meeting (itself, of course, advertised at least three days in advance).[26]

In practice, Charleston library membership votes were almost always taken at the regular quarterly meetings. It remained, however, an ordeal that was not only public but expensive. Under the original rules, each successfully elected member was required to pay a fee of five shillings currency each week (1750, rule 9), but by 1762 (rule 15; 1770, rule 17) each member was liable to a lump sum entry fee of £50 currency in addition to the further five shillings every week until his total contribution to the library stock amounted to £200 (rule 17; 1770, rule 19). Such payment, including the admission fee, comprised 150 months or just over 12 years of weekly fees. After this the member was still required to pay, but then at a weekly rate of two shillings and sixpence. This compares to the initial share in local currency of forty shillings and ten shillings per annum thereafter for members of the Library Company of Philadelphia and the five pounds original subscription money and ten shillings annual charge (again in local currency) of the New York Society Library. By sanction of a Charleston Library Society quarterly meeting any member could leave or otherwise dispose of his share in the society's stock to another person even if the beneficiary was not a member of the library.[27]

Denial of admission to the Library Society appears to have been very rare, although we cannot know, of course, how many were dissuaded from putting their name forward at all. The first recorded instance of rejection was that of the merchant and tavern keeper Daniel Dott, who was turned down by a majority of votes at the general meeting of April 1772. The rejection was the more emphatic in following upon his unsuccessful application to be librarian of the society.[28] Blythe, Gordon, Dillon, and Ramage were all paid for putting their taverns or "houses" at the disposal of the Library Society for its meetings and dinners; perhaps Dott, as a fellow tavern proprietor, was unacceptable as a full member of the society. Less arbitrary was the enforcement of the rules relating to nonpayment of dues. As noted already, the rules dictated that after warning letters, names were to be publicly displayed when six months in arrears, eventually leading to dismissal and the further public display of the full amount owed.[29] In 1777 it was ordered that the name of Dr. Fayssoux (then several years in arrears) "be struck out of this list of members & be hung up in the Library room with the amount of arrears due by him." A year later, John Dart's name was similarly excised and displayed.[30]

Library Society share transactions ensured further proscription and control. Existing shares were, with permission, bequeathed by members or assigned to others then not members, but shares were also created anew. It also becomes evident from the records that shares were bought in commercial transaction and even by public auction (as by Robert Philip in 1774, for example; see appendix 1), although purchasers of new shares technically had to be approved by a majority vote at a general meeting. As appendices 1 and 2 demonstrate, many of those later admitted to the library inherited shares and library memberships. Heirs to shareholders were deemed rightful successors even in the absence of precise bequest. In 1770 Jacob Motte succeeded to his late father's share as heir-at-law even though the transfer was not specified in his father's will.[31] Transfer of Library Society shares by bequest or designation was relatively simple, but the distinction between inheriting or buying a share in library stock and being admitted a full member of the society remained critical. In January 1763 the anniversary meeting learned from a letter to the president from Mrs. McCauley that she had disposed of her husband's founding share to William Scott.[32] This seems to have been accepted without demur, but in January 1771 when William Mazyck was admitted to the Library Society, he was forced to buy a new share with his own money when refused admission earlier at the same meeting to the share left by the late William Carwithen. A letter was read out from Carwithen's widow, proposing Mazyck's admission to the Carwithen share, but the members judged that Mazyck "could not be admitted upon the application of Mrs. Carwithin, she having no interest in the Society."[33]

The acquisition or purchase of a share, however, did not bring automatic entitlement to Library Society membership. In late 1777 Jacob Valk bought the share of John Dart, but at the subsequent anniversary meeting Valk's membership application was balloted and rejected.[34] Jacob Valk was a broker of King Street, as listed in the 1782 directory, but had left by at least 1790. We simply do not know why Valk was spurned by the Library Society. He maintained a long room as a venue for meetings and entertainments, and perhaps, like Dott, he was rejected because of his financial association with providing venues for meetings. Valk was also, however, a

---

TABLE 2 *Presidents of the Charleston Library Society, 1749–1811*

John Cooper	1749
John Lining	1750
Charles Pinckney	1751
James Michie	1752
Gabriel Manigault	1753–1756
Thomas Smith	1756
Daniel Crawford	1757
[Gov.] William Henry Lyttelton	1758–1761
[Lt. Gov.] William Bull	1761–1767
[Gov.] Lord Charles Greville Montagu	1767–1769
[Lt. Gov.] William Bull	1769–1778
Gabriel Manigault	1778
Col. Charles Pinckney	1779–1780
Thomas Bee	1783–1792
Gen. Charles Cotesworth Pinckney	1792–1796
Ralph Izard	1797
Gen. Charles Cotesworth Pinckney	1798–1807
Henry William DeSaussure	1807–1812

renowned money lender, whose undertakings helped to purchase his Fairlawn plantation on the Ashley River. Grudges, specific or general, against his activities might have played a part in his rejection. It is also just possible that, despite the apparent political balances of the library, Valk upset sensitivities at a key time. In September 1778 he was "summoned for neglect of duty" on the muster roll. Like many library members he was soon expelled from Charleston as a Loyalist and his estates confiscated, but his muster roll failure possibly marks him out as someone whose commitments changed.[35]

Through all of this, the Charleston Library Society remained a rich man's club, uninterested in any social extension of "the desirable end of handing down the

TABLE 3 *Librarians of the Charleston Library Society, 1749–1811*[43]

John Sinclair	1749–1755
William Henderson	1755–1756
William Carwithen	1756–1770
William Hort	1770–1771
Thomas Powell	1771–1772
Samuel Price	1772–1778
Francis J. Fariau	1779–1783
John McCall, Jr.	1783–1787
Philip Prioleau	1787–1790
William Blamyer	1790–1797
John Davidson	1797–1813

TABLE 4 *Secretaries and Correspondents of the Charleston Library Society, 1749–1811*

Samuel Brailsford, secretary	1749–1750
John Sinclair, correspondent	?1749–1755
John Remington, secretary	1751–1759
Robert Brisbane, correspondent	1756–1759
John Butler, secretary	1759
William Michie, secretary and correspondent	1760
John Remington, " "	1761–1764
William Mason, " "	1764–1767
John Colcock, " "	1768–1780
John McCall, Jr., " "	1780–1787
William Blamyer, " "	c.1791–?1792
[Charles Cotesworth Pinckney, president, often acted as secretary 1792–1796 and 1798–1801]	
[John Davidson, librarian and treasurer, often acted as secretary 1801–1811]	

European arts and manners to the latest times." Whatever the New York tableau might suggest, no Indian brave, however fully converted and submissive, was going to kneel on the floor of this society library room. Indeed, at the anniversary meeting of 8 January 1760, presumably just after a rereading of the society's grand enlightenment aims, congratulations were given to the its former president, Gabriel Manigault (1704–1781), on his successful return from slaughtering the "brute" Cherokee in battle.[36]

The victor of the Indian wars was a typical figurehead for the society after its first decades. The library became a bastion of respectability headed by Charleston's greatest citizens. The early presidents included the physician and intellectual John Lining, the self-made merchant Charles Pinckney, and the bibliophile merchant Daniel Crawford. Manigault, planter-merchant, a notably honest public treasurer, 1735–1743, and probably the richest man in South Carolina, served as president of the Library Society between 1753 and 1756 and again in 1778. At other times—and as part of the increased grandeur of the library from its second decade onwards—the colony's governors (or acting governors) were usually invited to accept election as Library Society president (see table 2). Balancing this appointment, six of the seven Library Society vice presidents serving between 1750 and 1770 were leading Charleston merchants. William Henry Lyttelton, governor of the colony, was elected president in 1758 and appears to have been a relatively conscientious functionary for two years. In succession, Lieutenant and Acting Governor William Bull (1710–1791), served as president for six years from January 1761 (having been chairman of the July 1760 meeting in the absence of both president and vice president). At the anniversary meeting of January 1767 Bull resigned to give the place of honor to the newly arrived governor, Lord Charles Greville Montagu, second son of the Duke of Manchester. Gabriel Manigault also resigned as vice president in January 1767, but both Bull and Manigault returned to their positions within three years when, in October 1769, Montagu, now deeply unpopular in Carolina, was "unceremoniously dumped as head of the Society."[37]

From 1779 the Pinckney family involved themselves still more with the library. Charles Pinckney had been third president in 1751, and Colonel Charles Pinckney (1731–1782) a wealthy lawyer and planter, joined the library committee appointed at the July 1770 meeting.[38] He became president, 1779–1780. His son, Charles Pinckney (1757–1824) was governor of South Carolina 1789–1791, 1796–1798, and 1806–1808, and a key player in the nationalist cause.[39] He was also second cousin to Charles Cotesworth Pinckney, member in 1769 (see plate 2), and later Federalist vice presidential candidate in 1800 and the party's presidential candidate in 1804 and 1808. Charles Cotesworth Pinckney, educated in London and Christ Church, Oxford, was president of the Library Society from 1792 to the end of

1796, when he left for Paris as United States minister to France. When this embassy was famously rebuffed, and following his nine months' retreat to the Netherlands, Pinckney returned to America, resuming the library presidency from 1798 until 1807.[40] The intervening president, Ralph Izard (1741/2–1804), a wealthy planter, was one of the state's first two federal senators and a leading bibliophile.[41] A keen supporter of the development of the South Carolina College, Pinckney also appears to have been a remarkably proactive president of the library. Like his successor, Henry William DeSaussure, he shared with the long-serving librarian John Davidson[42] in the sort of library book ordering and business correspondence that had formerly been the almost exclusive responsibility of the elected secretary and correspondent. Pinckney, active in the Agricultural Society (founded in 1785), the Society of Cincinnati (founded 1783), and the Charleston Museum (from 1773), was also involved in the foundation of the Bible Society of Charleston in 1810. The Library Society remained a leader in this high-minded reshaping of Charleston's public life.

The secretary-correspondents of the Library Society comprised merchants and prominent Charleston citizens. They were more representative of the monied members of the society, perhaps, than the librarians, although the secretary was also generously remunerated. Remington was awarded £70 as a "salary" for acting as secretary in April 1762, and in 1775 Colcock received £50 a quarter as secretary.[44] The salaried librarians (listed in table 3) were more humble individuals. Charged with the duties of attendance at the library and cataloguing the collection, eleven librarians were elected by the Library Society between 1749 and 1813 (see table 3). Elections in the early 1770s were especially contentious. In 1770 both William Hort and John Parnham wrote to propose themselves as librarian, but as neither was then a member neither was deemed eligible at the September general meeting. Later in the discussion, however, following a separate written request, Hort was elected a member and librarian.[45] Hort lasted only some months, and in the contest to succeed him as librarian Thomas Powell gained 17 votes and Brisbane 15, and yet Powell too resigned his post within a year.[46] Dott, rejected for membership, was a candidate alongside John Parnham and Samuel Price to succeed Powell, but Price was elected unanimously, ending the turbulent months.[47] The salary was handsome. For keeping the hours prescribed by the rules,[48] the long-serving William Carwithen was paid £300 per annum in 1762.

Broader assessment of Library Society development proves difficult, given its different features and a fitful history so often at variance with its proud claims. By the late eighteenth century, although the Library Society remained preeminent in the literary and social life of Charleston, those seeking reading and enlightenment enjoyed new resources and greater choice. In 1763 George Wood had announced his intention of starting a circulating library and a further commercial lending library was opened by Samuel Gifford in 1772.[49] Neither appeared large or long-lived, but they represented new opportunities for booksellers and importers to widen their stock and extend their services. At the same time, many gentlemen enlarged their private libraries, and an increasing number of libraries and collections of better quality were offered for sale. As early as 1756 Robert Wells had advertised in the *Gazette* "a choice assortment of Modern Books, ordered by the late Mr. John Sinclair [first librarian of the Library Society], just before his death," along with the library of the recently deceased Rev. Alexander Garden.[50] In 1761 Wells proudly advertised the library of James Michie, early president of the Charleston Library Society. Michie's library was to be auctioned and ranged over law books, classics, epic poets, and histories "in general in very good condition, many of them in elegant bindings."[51] Among the finest of these libraries in transit was that bequeathed to the Library Society by John Mackenzie, radical Patriot of Broom Hall, Goose Creek, "for the use of a college when erected."[52] When printed in 1772 the *Catalogue* of the bequest included 861 volumes including some 125 folio editions. Notable among this magnificent collection were a volume of Hogarth prints and various admired classical, historical, and legal texts. The Mackenzie bequest was separately stored and lettered separately ("JM") in readiness for use in the proposed college.[53] Until recently it was assumed that all but a handful of the Mackenzie volumes were lost in the 1778 fire;[54] at least thirty books survived, however (possibly because not all the volumes had been transferred to the Library Society before 1778), and these are now shelved at the College of Charleston.[55]

By the early nineteenth century, Charleston boasted still broader achievement. In 1800 Henry Adams wrote in his history: "The small society of rice and cotton planters at Charleston, with their cultivated tastes and hospitable habits, delighted in whatever reminded them of European civilization."[56] The Library Society's museum was transferred to the Museum of the Literary and Philosophical Society of South-Carolina in 1814. The Philosophical Society had been founded in 1809, followed by the Antiquarian Society of Charleston in May 1813. These were combined under a new incorporated name of the Literary and Philosophical Society of South-Carolina, in 1814.[57] In November 1806 a second Charleston library society was also mooted and in pursuance of this, twenty-one members met on 2 February 1807. The rival library was finally incorporated in 1813 under the name Franklin Library of Charleston, but was no challenge for the existing Library Society. Six years later the Franklin Library comprised 1,364 volumes and claimed "upwards of 151 members."[58]

Whether all this added up to a flourishing cultural life was and is debatable, however. The Charleston Library Society did become an attraction for visitors, established during the second half of the century as a pivot in a broader network of fellowship and sociability. Visitors like Quincy were offered generous and solicitous hospitality, visitors' interest or membership in other libraries acting as passports to book-led civility. The maintenance of this cultural highroad was clearly important to the Library Society. In 1765 Pelatiah Webster visited the city and on 6 June "spent the forenoon very agreeably in the Library with the Librarian Mr. Carwithen" and he returned the next day to attend at the library even though it was "very sultry" and again on six days later.[59] For all the snootiness of later visitors, this was a place to visit.

The impressions of early-nineteenth-century tourists were more ambiguous. In 1810 John Lambert traveled through South Carolina and in Charleston was introduced to Davidson the librarian. Like Kellogg in 1817, Lambert was taken to the library in its Courthouse rooms and "spent many an hour in it very agreeably." He made particular note of the library's imported "Boydell Shakspeare" series,[60] but went on to describe a library, ostentatious, curiously Loyalist, and set in a town where the arts were still unappreciated:

> The large prints are framed, and hung around the room. The portraits of the king and queen, belonging to that [Boydell Shakspeare] edition, are placed on either side the door-way leading to the inner room. I was not surprized at the obscurity of their situation, but was astonished to find them exhibited at all; and it is said that some opposition was made to their being put up. There is a large painting, executed by a Mr. White, of Charleston, exhibited in the library, and is considered a very favourable effort for a young artist. The subject is the murder of Prince Arthur. The countenances of the ruffians are scarcely harsh enough, and their figures are not well proportioned. It is, however, a more successful specimen than could possibly be expected in a place where the arts meet with no encouragement, and where *genius* must resort to agriculture or commerce; to law or physic, if it wishes *to avoid starvation!* some new casts from the Apollo Belvidere, Venus de Medicis, Venus rising from the sea, &c. were deposited in the Library to be exhibited for a short time. . . . The library also contains a few natural curiosities, such as fossils, minerals, mammoth bones, snakes, armadilloes, poisonous insects in spirits, &c. and two remarkable deer's horns which were found locked in each other. . . . A Museum has been lately established by a gentleman,[61] who occupies a room adjoining the library. His collection at present consists chiefly of birds; and I doubt whether the liberality of the inhabitants will enable him to increase it.[62]

In the same year, another visitor to Charleston, the Scotsman J. B. Dunlop, also praised the library —"tho it cannot boast of Superior excellence"—and the two statues within—"tolerably handsome ones."[63]

Long after the Revolution, contemporary observations continued to suggest that the literary culture of the town was not deep. An account of 1797 reported that there were no booksellers of consequence in Charleston, "the liveliest city in all America,"[64] and that London and the northern American cities were apparently indispensable to book supply. Even by 1819 the final part of Shecut's historical essay concluded that "notwithstanding these energetic attempts of numerous individuals, to establish the literary character of South-Carolina, and to prove to the old world, that her soil is by no means unfavourable to the generation or cultivation of the arts and sciences, and that her sons want but appropriate stimulus to their labours, that of public patronage, to shield them from loss, while endeavouring to raise her literary fame to a level with that of the most favoured nations, examples are yet to be seen of the most unpardonable apathy and shameful neglect of her citizens."[65]

Adding to this perceived problem of a vulgar, lavish town, were reports of the narrowness of the elite. Other questions continued about the successes of the Library Society. The library instilled new cultural ambition and clearly improved access to a broad and modern range of literature, but membership remained limited and the aims of the founders remained far-fetched. There is some evidence that the library did extend access by the early nineteenth century, with Dunlap reporting on his visit in 1810 that "the Library is private but any Stranger is at Liberty to visit it during his residence in the City by being introduced to the Librarian by one of the Subscribers."[66] Courtesy to gentlemen from foreign parts, however, was very different from opening up the private club. This was not the sort of broader public access being offered by the new library companies in Baltimore and elsewhere. Even the Charleston library eventually recognized this. In 1853 a radical report of the library committee concluded, "our position at present is one of exclusiveism [*sic*] and privilege. To acquire new activity, we must reject these, and appeal to popular sentiment."[67]

These equivocal verdicts are mirrored by social histories offering conflicting conclusions about the wider picture. Carl Bridenbaugh portrayed the town as elegant but lacking cultural discipline. By contrast, Frederick Bowes offered more sustained praise of Charleston's art and literature. More recently, Richard Waterhouse has challenged Jack P. Greene's analysis of colonial cultural values. Greene holds that South Carolinians were very different from other British North American colonists because very largely they did not construct beliefs around idealized concepts of the colonial past and the British present. By contrast, Waterhouse suggests that Carolina's elite developed a value structure based precisely on a contemporary English cultural model.[68] Only Virginia sent more students to Oxford and Cambridge in the years before 1763, but thereafter—and in a way that helps explain the failure to support a local college—South Carolina Oxbridge students were three times as numerous as Virginians before the Revolution. During the same twenty-six years there were more South Carolinians at the Inns of Court than from all the rest of the southern colonies combined.

Although the organization and ideals of the Charleston Library Society would seem to support this interpretation, its development also offers reservations. The Library Society faced up to charges leveled repeatedly against Charleston that new-rich decadence and materialism suffocated good taste and intellectual curiosity. It was an enterprise founded by younger and second-ranking members of the elite but then adopted by the greatest in the colony. As a result, its public role was limited. The exclusiveness and guardedness of Charleston's public culture—even if the processions were public events—has also been noted. Sociability was centered on the formal societies; there were few public social performances; theater and opera were infrequent and almost always by subscription. Even the sympathetic Waterhouse concludes that this amounted to hobbled civilization—whereas Shakespeare was the most popular playwright in other colonies "it is perhaps indicative of the shallowness of the Carolinians' taste that few Shakespearean plays were put on in the period before 1770."[69]

Another analysis, emphasizing the exceptionalism of South Carolina's elite in the early Republic as being able to admit to their disinterestedness—to "a wisdom learned through experience in the school of commercial lobbying"—supports rather than undermines suggestions of a harmonious but primarily commercially orientated political and social leadership.[70] According to Rebecca Starr's persuasive analysis, the commercial lobbying of Carolina elites supplied a set of pragmatic, rational values embracing the naturalness as well as the beneficial utility of dispassionate regard for legitimate claims of interest. This outlook enabled the Carolina leadership to avow that although they were not (as they argued no one could be), "disinterested," they were "dispassionate." By such argument, Carolinians attempted to sustain working political relations with those of differing or even opposing interests. Such sociability, according to Starr, worked to knit together elites, however much this sociability might have been pragmatic and superficial. Clearly, adherence to this conviction varied between individuals, with some far more offended than others by vulgarity of mind or by inappropriate behavior. The importance was political, however, inasmuch as the defacto and utilitarian philosophy of enlightenedness created a working harmony with the largely agrarian backcountry.[71]

Evidence from the surviving letter book of the Charleston Library Society will not finally settle debate, but the correspondence does offer extraordinary details of the library's activities, and it contributes to the continuing reevaluation of Charleston's intellectual and social life in this energetic, often chaotic, period. Above all, it provides commentary and staging posts (in otherwise uncharted territory) to explain the one other major achievement of the Library Society—the realization of the collection.

The growth in the Library Society collection, despite the periodic lulls and catastrophes, extended to a very broad range of literature. Strahan's strangulated

1750 *Catalogue* listed 56 folio titles, 27 quartos, 189 octavos, 74 duodecimos, and 21 "pamphlets."[72] The 1770 *Catalogue,* printed by Wells in Charleston, listed 172 folios, 106 quartos, and 506 octavos and smaller volumes.[73] Wells's 1772 *Catalogue* listed 184 folios, 115 quartos, 555 octavos and smaller volumes, and an additional 135 classical titles. Although disaster hit in 1778 when the then collection of 6–7,000 volumes, paintings, prints, globes, instruments, and natural history specimens were almost all destroyed by fire,[74] the Library Society quickly recovered and continued its swift accumulation of both members and volumes. Insurance, indeed, had been taken out in London on the whole collection in 1773 (letters 29, 31).

After the War of Independence and the British occupation of Charleston, many library members had left the colony, others were obliged to rebuild their fortunes, and the society found great difficulty in collecting either the principal or interest on its bonds. The hiatus in its progress was relatively brief, however. A manuscript catalogue of 3 November 1790 listed 342 volumes, with the McKenzie collection reduced to 403 volumes. From late 1791 new book orders were sent to London, the meetings and dinners were regularly and confidently advertised, and the intellectual and social prestige of the institution seemed fully restored (even if the continued failure to attract large donations and bequests was criticized in the 1826 *Catalogue*). In 1806 the Charleston library *Catalogue* boasted 5,084 volumes, and 7,067 were listed in the *Catalogue* of 1811.[75] The Bristol Library Society, which in many ways might be regarded as an exemplar of the merchant-led, exclusive proprietary library of these years, listed in its first catalogue of 1790, a mere 1,417 titles.[76] By 1819 the Charleston library commanded, in addition to its 280 members, a capital in funded debt of $10,000 and a yearly income of $3,000.[77] The 13,000 volumes in the library at this date compare to estimates for the New York Society Library in 1813 of between 12,000 and 13,000 volumes, while the Library Company of Philadelphia held over 14,000 titles. The fast growing Library Company of Baltimore, founded only in 1795, commanded more than 7,200 volumes in 1809 and more than 10,400 volumes in 1827.[78] As recorded in its correspondence, the Charleston Library Society spent a total sum on book purchases from London, 1759–1811, that was a few shillings short of £4,870.[79]

Almost all the books and materials of the Library Society were bought from London. The library committee did receive a gift from the Quakers of London[80] and also accepted a few local large donations. Notable were bequests of $600 from Benjamin Smith in 1770 and a year later, that of the splendid library of John Mackenzie. Judge John Faucheraud Grimké also offered at cost price his library to reestablish the society's collection after the War of Independence. The Charleston Library Society was largely not, however, an object for the philanthropy of others. It was neither heir to nor beneficiary of the enterprise of Thomas Bray and the later Bray Associates in London who packed off libraries to Charleston, Annapolis, and dozens of other colonial destinations. Without a college, books did not arrive in Charleston in the manner that the Earl of Burlington sent learned publications to the College of William and Mary, Jeremiah Dummer, George Berkeley, and Isaac Watts to Yale, and Samuel Holden and Thomas Hollis (after the disastrous 1764 fire) to Harvard.[81]

In the first decades of the Charleston Library Society, other acquisitions not specifically ordered from London were very few. Stephen Hales is known to have sent a thousand copies of his 1743 book on ventilators to the American colonies, and in 1758 he presented Alexander Garden with twenty-five copies of the second volume. Garden was asked to distribute the books to all "such persons as had opportunity, power, or influence, to put his many good advices in execution."[82] The Library Society possessed one of these. In 1760 Governor Lyttleton made a gift of Guicciardini's two-volume folio *History of the Wars in Italy.*[83] David Barclay, Jr., and Daniel Mildred presented several volumes on behalf of the Society of Friends in the autumn of 1766, as reported at the April 1768 general meeting.[84] In July 1767 Lord Hope gave "sundry books" to George Milligen for the library, noted as being "a little out of repair." Later that year a volume containing six books "supposed to be Chinese Characters" was presented by the former library member William Henderson, then in England, together with four volumes of Reform theology presented by Samuel Prioleau.[85] Among other small individual gifts to the society was a copy of Jean André Deluc's *Recherches sur les modifications de l'atmosphère,* published in Geneva in 1772. The book had been bought by John Laurens when in England in 1772 as a thank-you present for Garden. It was sent via Laurens's father, Henry, longtime library member and its vice president since 1767. He was so impressed by it that he bought a further copy to send to his brother James to present to the library.[86]

Acquisitions from local book suppliers remained extremely rare. In late 1776 the bookseller Nicholas Langford wrote to the Charleston Library Society to announce his holding of Belidor's four-volume folio *Architecture hydraulique.*[87] Purchase of this was approved at the next meeting in April, provided that Langford was able to letter the volumes with the library's initials.[88] At the same April meeting Thomas Bee announced that he had purchased 31 folio volumes of an encyclopedia at an auction, together with 9 similar volumes, and these the library also bought. The suspicion remains that only someone with the authority of Bee could have bought volumes in advance of approval. He repeated his action in 1784, apparently to assist in the library's postwar recovery,[89] but no similar instances occur in the surviving early records of the society.

The extent, indeed, to which the Library Society's collection was augmented by the donations of members, well-wishers and would-be members is relatively obscure. The early committee minutes and records of general meetings do refer to a few benefactions, but these are often more notable for the benefactor than for the books. In a section of the surviving accessions book dated (but probably not confined to) "1798" a total of 69 titles were presented to the library including Lewis's controversial novel *The Monk,* presented by T. B. Bowen, and John Moore's much more respectable and earlier novel *Zeluco,* presented by William Drayton, who also gave the library a copy of the *History of South Carolina.*

The experience of other society libraries of the period suggests that donations were a natural extension of the private book and pamphlet lending activities among family, friends, and like-minded associates. Yet the emphasis in the Charleston library's rules upon the accumulation of monies to provide an annual purchase fund lends further weight to the notion that this was a library developed in distinction from the private book buying of local gentlemen. We know that some £500 was spent on books between 1759 and 1770 (see table 6 below) and that the 1770 *Catalogue* listed 419 more entries than the 1750 *Catalogue.* This apparently lavish expenditure of an average of more than £1 per title might suggest that almost every addition to the library did indeed arrive from London, especially when even this estimate excludes any additional payments that might have been made to booksellers between 1750 and 1759.

As noted, the book-purchasing capital raised by members' subscription of an initial £1,600 sterling and £100 each year thereafter, was to be supplemented by monies accruing from weekly dues, donations, fines, and forfeitures all let out at interest (1750, rule 11). In her summary of the Charleston library's history, Anne King Gregorie concludes that £1,600 had indeed been spent on books before the annual expenditure for such purchases was restricted to £100, the surplus then being applied to scientific apparatus and the fund for a professorship of mathematical and natural philosophy.[90] It would seem, however, that this is a rehearsal of the intentions as declared in the early years and repeated in the rules (1750, rule 11), rather than what certainly happened. Again, as planned, when the fund reached £800 or £900 sterling, scientific instruments were to be bought, together with more instruments when annual interest receipts reached £300 (with even more ambitious plans for a salary for a professor of mathematics in the event of still larger annual returns on the money put out to loan). Later this ambition was simplified to £100 each year for "books and such mathematical or philosophical instruments as the Society shall judge proper" (1762, rule 24). The committee retained responsibility for gathering members' suggestions for books and placing these before the quarterly meetings. Each proposed title had to be agreed at two meetings before it was sent for. The secretary-correspondent then prepared the letters for orders to the Library Society's bookseller, elected annually at the anniversary meetings, although technically it remained the responsibility of the committee to compose "answers to all letters sent to the Society by any foreign correspondents" (1762, rule 10).

Chapter Six

THE BOOKSELLERS

ALL THESE BOOKS AND PAMPHLETS came from London, but with the remarkable distinction that they were supplied directly, with very few exceptions, throughout the period. Given the rapid development of local Charleston bookselling, by the late 1760s, at the very least, the Library Society could have used local booksellers or general merchants to supply some of its books from Britain. Indeed, by early 1764, and following the bold advertisements of Crouch, King, Langford, Scott, Wood, and others, library members seriously discussed the possibility of employing local booksellers. At the anniversary meeting of that year it was resolved that in future books would be bought locally "if they can be bought here at near the Sterling Cost, or not exceeding ten Pr Cent Advance, on the first Cost."[1] Even with this incentive of a 10 percent premium, no local supplier seems to have been capable of securing a long-term association with the society. On the eve of the Revolution, when also beginning a reprint business, Robert Wells claimed to command the largest stock of books for sale in British America, but his prices were high. If, as has been suggested,[2] the 10 percent offer was an open invitation for him and other local bookmen to supply the library, none apparently could afford to take it up.

Apart from the 1764 suggestion and the 1776 Langford approach,[3] the minutes of the committee and the records of the meetings contain no reference to local booksellers before a probable short-lived approach to a bookseller in Philadelphia in 1792. The 1798 accessions book does list certain Charleston transactions, as will be detailed below, and a certain if limited trade from Philadelphia is recorded by letter in 1809–1810 and 1813. It is of course quite probable that a few books were secured for the Charleston library by local suppliers, even though no record of this is given in the journal or in a correspondence almost exclusively overseas. The failure to mention any previous help by Wells, leading local bookseller, when the society contacted him later might be significant, however, and the match between the London orders and the 1770 and 1772 published catalogues is remarkable. Certainly, the great majority of books is accounted for in the London orders. Although a few other supply routes have been suggested, most cannot be verified. The biographer of Charles Cotesworth Pinckney wrote that he "undoubtedly ordered books for the Society while he was in France and the Netherlands," but no evidence for this is offered.[4]

Later, any suggestion that the Library Society failed to secure a local supplier because Charleston bookselling was inadequate becomes even more problematic. By the final third of the century the Library Society might easily have placed orders with local booksellers. Nicholas Langford went to London himself to replenish his stock in 1771,[5] and there were, for example, front-page advertisements for large shipments of books imported by John Miller and C. Say even in the difficult year of 1783.[6] Robert Wells imported books from London; others imported from Scotland. After the war, various booksellers resumed the import of new literature from London and other British ports.[7] By the early years of the next century bookselling and book auctions markedly increased in Charleston. Prominent among the booksellers, Samuel Hueston (a naturalized citizen in 1802) advertised in the newspapers in May 1803 that "at the request of his friends [he] will continue the Book Auctions every Saturday evening."[8] One other objection to local dealing was also developing. Given the very high proportion of requests for London publications, it was easier to send for all members' suggestions at once rather than rely on piecemeal and unpredictable local suppliers for one or two of the titles (the condition of which might be unpredictable and which would also require local binding or labeling). By the early nineteenth century Charleston booksellers such as Ebenezer Thomas and William Price Young were, despite recurrent long-distance credit difficulties, surely capable of undertaking large imports to order. Young was even a member of the Library Society.

That the Library Society chose not to buy books from such importers but to deal directly with London firms appears a signal affirmation of their determination to maintain direct contact with the literary and political center. It offers a stark contrast with the ordering procedures of more northerly and more humble library societies. When the library at Salem, for example, requested London books they were not ordered directly from London but through Jeremiah Condy, an established bookseller of Boston, as well as from local suppliers.[9] The comparable society libraries, the Library Company of Philadelphia and the New York Society Library, did, with varying success, maintain agents in London. For both it was an essential means to acquire books otherwise unobtainable or at very high risk of delay, but the Philadelphia library's connections, first with the bookseller to the Society of Friends, and then with the Quaker merchants Woods and Dillwyn were very particular relationships, and both the New York and Philadelphia libraries were quick to find alternative, local suppliers for the more easily obtainable books. Both libraries were also purchasing American publications and editions as a matter of course— but a course apparently rejected by the Charleston library much before 1820.

In this respect, quite obviously, London was more important to Charleston than Charleston to London, and the example of the Library Society's direct connections with the London trade is illuminating, but clearly not of major significance in terms of the overall volume of traffic in books in and from Britain. What makes the Charleston outpost the more outstanding today is that because so very few business records and correspondence of eighteenth-century London booksellers survive, the Library Society letters provide unique insights into the conduct of trade and relationships between purchaser and supplier. They also greatly supplement the very few surviving sources for understanding the mechanics of the transatlantic book trade.

The two other most helpful survivals here are the well-known correspondence between William Strahan and "Davie" Hall in Philadelphia, and the business letters of John Murray I.[10] Murray, himself a former sea captain, maintained various far-flung customers and contacts, with a notable network of Scots customers overseas. Strahan, as we shall see, was an early bookseller to the Charleston Library Society, but, a generation later, Murray had very mixed success with Charleston customers and was not a Library Society bookseller. After the War of Independence, Murray did try to sell some books in Charleston through an apparently keen agent, James Scott, vendue master of Champney's Street, but after two years of silence had to write to demand "an immediate and ample remittance."[11] The letter had no effect. More rewarding was the recommendation given by an existing customer, Rev. Dr. Gates, in 1792 for Murray to become bookseller to Dr. Robert Smith, first principal of Charleston College, and a member of the library since 1763.[12] By then, however, the Library Society had engaged the London Carolina merchants Bird, Savage, and Bird to supply them and there was never to be the sort of connection between the society and Murray as there had been with Strahan, the other major surviving commentator of the overseas trade as viewed from London.

TABLE 5   *Booksellers to the Charleston Library Society, c.1756–1811*

William Strahan	before Jan. 1756
John and James Rivington	1756
James Rivington	1756–1759
Thomas Durham and David Wilson	1760–1764
(Robert Dodsley, who was deceased	1764)
James Dodsley	1765–1766
James Fletcher	1766–1769
William Nicoll	1769–1775, 1783–1785
(Charles Dilly, who declined	1786)
Robert Wells	1787–1789
John Stockdale	1791
Bird, Savage, and Bird	1792–1801
Lackington, Allen, and Co.	1801–1809

From the London perspective, the commercial potential of the overseas, and particularly the North American market, was increasingly apparent by the 1740s. By then at least a dozen London booksellers were dispatching major book cargoes to colonial traders and a few major individual customers, a development well documented by the evidence for book sale and auction catalogues and by certain surviving correspondence. Robert Winans identifies the printing of 9 colonial importing booksellers' and auction catalogues between 1693 and 1730, 1 between 1731 and 1740, 13 between 1751 and 1760, 19 between 1761 and 1770, 15 between 1771 and 1780, 32 between 1781 and 1790, and 72 between 1791 and 1800. The earliest surviving catalogue, that of Samuel Gerrish of Boston issued in 1717, advertised 1,000 entries in 45 lots.[13] In addition to traders whose business was wholly or largely in books were numerous small merchants such as John Barkley or Thomas White in Philadelphia in the 1730s, bringing in books as part of their general business.[14] During the third quarter of the century, London wholesaling booksellers pursued the American market with great zeal. As research continues on both London booksellers and American traders and customers of the period, evidence is accumulating (from usually very fragmentary sources) that a very large number of the wholesale publisher-booksellers—and almost all the familiar names—were at one time or another engaged in colonial trade. Such booksellers include the Dodsleys, the Longmans, the Rivingtons, Cadell, Millar, Nicoll, Wilson and Durham, Richardson, the Dillys, and dozens more. Best known, because of the survival of their correspondence and business papers, are the initiatives of William Strahan and his dispatch of £18,000 worth of books and printing material to David Hall in Philadelphia between 1760 and 1772.[15] Typical of more modest operations were those of Thomas Osborne, who entered the colonial book trade in about 1748 and sent one of his first ships to William Parks in Williamsburg.[16] Osborne continued to receive orders from William Hunter of Williamsburg, who from the 1750s, also bought Bibles, law manuals, and other books on commission from the London booksellers Samuel Birt and Thomas Waller.[17] Birt also supplied Henry Laurens in Charleston in the 1740s, as the Corbetts later supplied Peter Manigault in the 1750s.[18] Later evidence of the Boston trade highlights the ambition of Longman and Gill and Wright to dispatch more, and as a result, many more books were marked by the colonial booksellers as "sent without order."[19] Even the relatively modest trader Jeremy Condy had to return unordered books to his supplier Joseph Richardson—and including some shown to have been London unsalables.[20]

Appointments as bookseller to the Charleston Library Society included some of the most distinguished London booksellers of the age, even though they rarely enjoyed for long the favor of the society (see table 5). From the foundation of their library in 1748, the gentlemen members elected and then sacked their booksellers with great gravity and regularity. William Strahan, John and James Rivington,

Thomas Durham, David Wilson, James Dodsley, James Fletcher, William Nicoll, and John Stockdale were all successively elected and dismissed as bookseller to the society. Charles Dilly, simply ducked and refused appointment. As it attempted to rebuild its stock after the 1778 fire and the disasters of the war and the occupation, the society relied briefly on the exiled Charleston bookseller (and former Library Society committee member) Robert Wells. Then the society turned to, but quickly away from, the pro-American John Stockdale for the year 1791–1792.[21] His dismissal for incompetence—against which Stockdale sent an aggrieved rebuke to the society (the remarkable letter 53)—was followed by a new policy of employing general merchants Bird, Savage, and Bird to collect orders from the supplier booksellers. For ten years the firm, based at Bury Court close to St. Mary Axe, served the society well, despite the occasional blunder of addressing its letters to the South Carolina Library Society (letters 63, 72). In the early months of 1801, however, Bird, Savage, and Bird encountered business difficulties and declined trade. From late 1801 until 1809 the Library Society employed Lackington, Allen, and Co. The location of these bookshops and other suppliers and agents of the Charleston Library Society is shown in plate 5.

One of the most revealing features of the Charleston library letters are the terms in which the elected booksellers were informed of their appointment and the conditions under which they were to accept the honor. Elections to serve as bookseller were made, along with the those of other officers, each January at the anniversary meeting open to all members. The outcome was solemnly recorded in the journal. Names of "respectable booksellers" were put forward by members, some of whom claimed a knowledge of the London book trade from contacts made when in Britain. Majestic letters were then sent across the Atlantic informing a usually unprepared bookseller of his appointment (and sometimes reappointment). The instructions (and these were formally so called) detailed not only the society's orders, but also binding, labeling, shipping, and packing requirements. Rule 14 of the Library Society demanded that all books be labeled "Charles Town Library Society" on the front cover (and additionally from rule 32 in 1762, and on the spine (called the "back") "C.T.L.S.," echoing the insistence by the SPG in the 1690s that all books destined for North America, including Charleston, be lettered with the name of the holding parish "to preserve them from Loss and Imbezell-ment."[22] The Library Society designed the measure both for security and to add a certain grandeur and uniformity to the collection.[23] The society did not simply appropriate the title "Bookseller" for its appointee—a fair enough shorthand—but also used it to withering effect in such post-dismissal references as "Mr. David Wilson formerly a Bookseller."[24]

The letters chronicle a turbulent business history. The bookseller was often placed in an impossible position, faced by orders containing conflicting or incomplete information, cancellations of previous requests already packed and shipped, and invitations to use careful judgment to order additional new works of good taste and importance. A request to William Strahan, for example, to purchase "any pamphlets or papers of Character useful or entertaining" was, several booksellers later, qualified to mean that "no Subject is excluded, which is either usefull or entertaining, at all times avoiding polemical Divinity in every shape, unless, particularly Ordered" (letters 1, 17). Such matters were, of course, no new source of dispute in long-distance book ordering. The Library Company of Philadelphia and bibliophiles like James Logan of the same city, employed book agents to avoid anticipated enslavement to a bookseller's ignorance or deceits.[25]

The Charleston library's secretary was always ready to convey the belief of members that the bookseller was lazy, exercising bad judgment, or unloading unsalable books. James Fletcher narrowly escaped dismissal in the January 1768 vote, after which he was informed that members "were highly Offended at your remissness in Several Particulars (especially in sending out the Classics unlettered contrary to the full and clear Instructions given you by their late Secretary)." When the next year's anniversary meeting did indeed sack Fletcher and appointed Nicoll in his stead, the secretary warned the new supplier: "the late Bookseller not attending to the spirit of the above General Instructions, supplied the Society not only with all the unsaleable hawk of his Shop, but with many books about the size of Plays & Pamphlets & which being Sewed in Boards too were often doubly unfit to have places in our Library" (letter 21). Nicoll tried his best, before the long disruption caused by the War of Independence. In 1785, however, within a year of trade resumption, the bookseller was told, "if you wish to continue in your present Connection with the Society, it will be necessary to be more attentive to Directions." The next letter to Nicoll summarily dismissed him because of "the backwardness you seem to shew in serving" (letters 37, 39). Failure to understand a commission or to prevent a slow sea passage usually brought a termination of business—and quite possibly some relief in London.

What then did the members require in their bookseller, in one "properly qualified to serve" (letter 6)? The key word used to describe his qualities was "respectable," but what did this mean? In the first half of the eighteenth century several London book merchants had ranked among the most distinguished citizens of their day, including Bernard Lintot, Thomas Guy, the Knapton brothers, and the greatest of them all, Jacob Tonson. Yet the full cast of booksellers was extremely diverse, from roguish entrepreneurs like Edmund Curll to hardworking popular trade publishers like Thomas and Mary Cooper. Many were unsettling to those who attempted to classify them. All booksellers were traders, but many were also the manufacturers and purveyors of hallowed literature and the conduits of intellectual debate. The ranks of the bookseller-publishers, moreover, included not only hardworking apprentices who became partners and proprietors, but former stewards, curates, and even sea captains. The most successful were invited to court; others were sent to King's Bench. Some bought magnificent villas and estates; some died penniless; a few managed to do both. Many were praised for their sobriety and devoted family lives; many were depicted as drunkards and *bons viveurs*. Within the profession there was much snobbery, conflict, and vindictiveness, but also respect, compassion, and attempts to support fellow booksellers in times of financial or political difficulty.

The perspective from Charleston must have been problematic. Presumably a reputation for dependability as well as for an informed knowledge of the trade and of literature was a determining quality in bookselling respectability. The social dimension was of lesser concern, particularly perhaps in the view of Charleston customers. As it was, in the cast lists of the eighteenth-century book trade, arriviste booksellers were among the most successful and well known: William Lane the poultryman's son, Thomas and James Harrison the sons of a Reading basket weaver, Thomas Wright the son of a Wolverhampton buckle maker, Ralph Griffiths the former watchmaker, and, to figure dramatically in the Library Society's business, Robert Dodsley, the former footman from Mansfield, and John Stockdale, the former blacksmith from Cumberland. Dodsley even marketed himself on the fetching conceit of his social mobility.

In terms of reputation within the trade, in fact, the Library Society's first choices of bookseller were rather hit and miss. We know from the letters and their detailing of monies owed that William Strahan had served as bookseller at some time in the society's first years—and also that he was no longer in service by 1756. Of William Strahan (1715–1785), confidante of Benjamin Franklin, there was no question of his respectability and success in the London trade. He is perhaps best known as the printer of Johnson's *Dictionary* and Gibbon's *Decline and Fall*. To historians of print and publishing of the period he is also celebrated for the survival of many of his business records and letters.[26] After those of Ackers and Bowyer, Strahan's ledgers comprise only the third substantial surviving printing business record of this period, while just as valuable are Strahan's transatlantic letters to David Hall in Philadelphia.[27] To the Charleston Library Society, Strahan was a leading London book supplier and friend of American booksellers, and, as likely to be welcomed by members like the Brisbanes and Alexander Garden senior, a native Scot.

In Strahan, the Library Society elected a powerful and versatile agent in London. Strahan amassed great wealth, largely from investment in book copy, all underwritten by the expanding demand for his presswork. Until 1748, the year of the foundation of the Charleston Library Society, Strahan maintained a printing office at Wine Office Court, off Fleet Street. In 1748 he moved to Little New Street, but in 1753 this shop was rebuilt and extended by demolishing six adjoining houses.

He proudly proclaimed the new premises to be "the largest and best Printing-house in Britain."[28] Later, a second office (the King's Printing Office) was opened in East Harding Street. In their search for a "respectable bookseller" the library members could hardly have done better. At the end of his career Strahan's position as one of a handful of eminent London bookseller-citizens was crowned by his service as an MP from 1774 to 1784. In his portrait by Sir Joshua Reynolds, Strahan determinedly personates the prosperous gentleman (plate 6).

Notwithstanding his celebrity, William Strahan's service to the Charleston Library Society was relatively brief. The exact reason for the break in relations is not known, but the extraordinary debacle of the misprinted 1750 library *Catalogue*[29] must have shaken members' confidence in his abilities. A further clue might lie in the identity of Strahan's eventual successor as society bookseller. That choice was also to prove more problematic. In January of 1756 a notice of the new officers advertised in the *Gazette* included John and James Rivington as booksellers. The Rivingtons were a prolific trading family. John (1720–1792) traded with his brother James (1724–1802) from 1742 to 1756 at the Bible and Crown, no. 62, just east of Canon Alley on the northern side of St. Paul's Churchyard, while another brother, Charles II (d. 1790), was printer in White Lyon Court and later in Steyning Lane. The brothers' father, Charles Rivington, had published at the Churchyard shop between 1711 and his death in 1742, and their descendants continued in the trade to this century.[30] The total number of eighteenth-century imprints bearing the name of Rivington or Rivingtons and currently recorded by the *ESTC* is a remarkable 5,908. Many were titles published by large associations of booksellers. As far as respectability was concerned, John Rivington in particular worked to extend both the wealth and the pious reputation of his family. The total value of Rivington's share in trade books was some £3,906 by 1760 and £5,324 by 1772.[31] In John Nichols's words, the younger Rivington was "universally esteemed" and enjoyed "the especial patronage of the Clergy, particularly those of the higher order."[32] John Rivington was reportedly rarely absent from prayers in St. Paul's at six or seven in the morning, even if this meant dressing in the cathedral.[33] Such piety made him an easy target, and the bookseller Henry Dell, for one, lampooned Rivington as a great hypocrite with "a weak dishonest rotten heart."[34] Like Strahan, however, the Rivingtons acquired great civic distinction. In 1760 John Rivington was elected bookseller to the Society for Promoting Christian Knowledge, he was to become a member of the Court of Lieutenancy, and both he and his younger brother, Charles, the printer of Steyning Lane, served as members of the Common Council.

The extent of the Library Society's actual dealings with the full Rivington enterprise is somewhat muddled, however. Although John was cited as bookseller, the society's letters were sent to his brother James. James Rivington was the black sheep of the family (plate 7). An enigmatic character, he broke with his brother in 1756—exactly at the time that they were jointly elected as the society's book-sellers.[35] It was to James alone (or as "Rivington and Fletcher") that Brisbane and Butler wrote from at least 1758 on behalf of the library committee. It is at least pos-sible that the society had been persuaded by James Rivington's flamboyant assault on the American market which he launched in series of public advertisements designed to undercut the London trade. Both Rivington brothers had been dealing with America—John had a correspondence with William Bradford III in Philadel-phia[36]—but from the mid-1750s James Rivington independently offered colonial merchants a discount of 16 percent on exported bound books, together with one year's credit (as against the usual three to six months) and an offer of the return of unsold items.

After the split with his brother John, James Rivington formed a partnership with James Fletcher (to feature as a future Library Society bookseller in his own right) and now offered major shipments of books. These were largely "rum books" or dull, unsalable titles that needed off-loading, but spiced up by a few loss leaders to attract clients. In October 1756 Rivington and Fletcher advertised their forth-coming publication of two books of divinity in "beautiful editions" in the *South Carolina Gazette.*[37] The books were to be available from Wells. The Library Soci-ety's new choice would certainly have widened any breach with Strahan, whose let-ters to Hall in Philadelphia have been a leading source for James Rivington's bad press. In the Hall correspondence Strahan depicted Rivington as an overambitious rogue, but this was often exactly because Rivington succeeded in wooing away cus-tomers by offers of cheap goods and easy credit.

There is no doubting Rivington's challenge to the London book trade, and per-haps it is the case that for all their grand statements, Charleston library members were indeed tempted by his discounts.[38] His advertised job lots must have had no appeal, however, and it is more probable that the name Rivington commanded respect in its own right, without the society's being fully informed of recent devel-opments. Conversely, it is not clear that the Charleston Library Society was the sort of customer Rivington courted. The first recorded business letter is typically per-nickety in its instructions about periodicals, choice of pamphlets, price of books, and labeling and binding. A later letter sent to Rivington in August 1759 (letter 5) is a classic reprimand from the society, charging him with ignoring their letters and further orders and of misdirecting packages to other merchants' houses in Charleston with the result that the precious reviews and magazines were received late. According to the secretary, the members "think themselves much slighted," and his letter demanded an exact statement of account as it built to a crescendo of indignation. In fact, what the Library Society did not then know was that Riving-ton, after a particularly bad day at the Newmarket races, had gone bankrupt.

Following his disaster, Rivington emigrated to New York in 1760 where he set up shop and recommenced his undercutting activities to the fury of Strahan and others. The Library Society, however, was to be no customer of his again.

In July 1760 the society elected the firm of Durham and Wilson as its bookseller, although John Rivington had also in the meantime supplied the library with some pamphlets (and, presumably, monthly periodicals) after James's failure (letter 6). Thomas Durham and David Wilson had been in partnership at Plato's Head near Round Court in the Strand since 1753. They published a variety of learned and popular titles, but appear to have been adept as agents for other wholesale booksellers. Gathering the ordered publications from a diversity of bookseller-publishers was, after all, a key task in supplying the Charleston members. The firm served the Library Society for three and a half years, although from the 1761 anniversary meeting the elected bookseller was Wilson alone, to whom the secretary wrote. It was then, in early 1764, after two difficult years for the library (committees were poorly attended and one decided to debate the "poor spirit" of the society), that some thought was given to buying locally. It appears that this did not come to much, or at the very least was a temporary measure while problems with London were sorted out. Wilson was apparently not reelected at the January 1764 meeting, but it was not until October that a letter was sent to a successor, the letter blaming the previous secretary, Remington, "for having neglected to comply with the directions given him by the Society" (letter 13).

The newly elected bookseller was Robert Dodsley. It proved a somewhat unfortunate choice: by the time the letter of appointment arrived in London, he was dead. The selection of Dodsley was nevertheless a striking one. His career as bookseller, author, and encourager of literary genius has claims to be one of the most astonishing in a century of remarkable "rises." Born in Mansfield in 1704, he arrived in London as a footman. He published his morality poem, *Servitude,* sometime before his twenty-fifth birthday, *A Muse in Livery* followed in 1732, and with help from Pope he set up his Tully's Head bookshop in Pall Mall in 1735. This was probably set up outside the city walls in order to avoid confrontation with corporation trading formalities, but it was to become one of the most distinguished bookshops of the century. Admired and sponsored by Pope, and a successful playwright and author in his early years, Dodsley was publisher of at least 603 different works, and he first published Gray, Burke, and Dr. Johnson, among others. He served as Pope's primary publisher and later published both Johnson's *Dictionary* and Lowth's *English Grammar.* The landmark *Collection of Poems by Several Hands* was issued between 1748 and 1758. At the same time, experiments in periodical papers included the *World* and the *London Chronicle,* before the enduring success of the *Annual Register,* founded in 1758.[39] Unlike John Almon or his brother James, and more like James Lackington at the end of the century, Dodsley apparently exploited rather than recoiled from the charge of being among "base-born book-sellers." In advertising his literature and services he issued long-list notices, retained almost throughout the year in numerous newspapers and announcing a set season's stock. He also became renowned for the poetical publications and verse satires advertised separately from his main listings. In 1764 Robert Dodsley's fame was unavoidable to those seeking a new bookseller, and the Library Society wrote to inform him of his election because of his "Established Character" (letter 13).

William Mason's letter of appointment was received instead by Dodsley's suc-cessor, his much younger brother James, who had been taken into partnership by Robert in 1750 and who had been running the shop alone since 1759. Formally elected bookseller at the anniversary meeting of 1765, his tenure of office was brief. Whether or not he pleased the Charleston library members, James Dodsley is a much neglected figure. A revisionist biography of Robert Dodsley corrects certain confusions between the two brothers, but appears resigned to the neglect of James (who is to blame for burning most of his brother's business and personal letters).[40] James Dodsley continued the Pall Mall business until his death in 1797. In total, the Dodsley bookshop was involved in the publication of more than 600 separate works and some 2,800 editions between 1735 and 1800. James Dodsley left over £70,000 and a landed estate near Chislehurst.[41] There is an important story in the extension of the business after Robert's retirement in 1759, and until his own death in 1797, but when it is written, the part played by the Charleston Library Society will be as inglorious as it is instructive. Few if any of the society's booksellers had sought election, but in James Dodsley's case the appointment was a hand-me-on that the anniversary meeting probably felt obliged to confirm. When the bookseller appeared to be nonchalant about serving the Charleston library, the committee was even quicker to protest than normal.

The next anniversary meeting dumped James Dodsley as bookseller, and the secretary, William Mason, wrote instead to James Fletcher with the news of his unanimous election. Even before his letter announced this, Mason explained to Fletcher that Dodsley "had not served them with that punctuality which the Spirit of their Society required." It does not seem to have occurred to the society that the fulsome expression of such complaints did not necessarily serve the library's best interests given the close network of London booksellers. Fletcher had been partner of James Rivington and was not far from the Rivingtons on the north side of St. Paul's Churchyard (see plate 5). Communication between members of the trade was essential to the completion of customers' orders when this involved acquiring each other's publications, as well, of course, to continuing collaboration in joint publications and copy ownership. Two James Fletchers, father and son, were book-sellers at Oxford and London. James Fletcher senior was bookseller of St. Paul's Churchyard (1710–1795), and the Turl, Oxford, from 1730 and at Westminster

Hall, but the society was almost certainly writing to his son James. James junior was not formally taken into the family business in 1769, but he had already partnered James Rivington. As noted above, the three-year tenure of the Charleston "book-sellership" proved, after a generally happy beginning and flurry of business for Fletcher, a grisly affair. His "extraordinary neglect" is already the subject of a motion at the meeting of July 1767 after which a letter (17a) was drafted to complain that not even "any private person much less a Society will put up with such remissness." Fletcher's bare survival at the January 1768 vote (letter 18) also hinted at a certain factionalism in the society, with some body of support for retaining him.

When the inevitable happened, and Fletcher was replaced as bookseller by William Nicoll[42] at the 1769 anniversary meeting, the late bookseller was soon coupled with James Dodsley as an example of the lax and feckless tradesman. Library Society secretary John Colcock pointed out that Fletcher had not even yet, after three years and constant reminders, obtained and settled a full account on behalf of the library with Dodsley (letter 21). By contrast William Nicoll was in certain ways the most successful of the society's booksellers, possibly because he indulged the secretary with confirmatory complaints that Fletcher was also unhelpful to him (letter 23). A society letter of early 1770 even lavishes rare praise on the bookseller (letter 24).

William Nicoll was bookseller at the Paper Mill and then no. 51, St. Paul's Churchyard, trading 1761–1775, and a publisher of political pamphlets, many printed by Strahan. He died in 1778. Relatively little is known about his business, and the letters to Nicoll are particularly helpful in suggesting the sort of workaday affairs he managed. His long tenure of the office of bookseller to the Library Society, 1769–1785, was, however, broken by the war, 1775–1783, and the interval probably staved off the decline in relations already evident by the early 1770s ("not sufficiently careful," warned letter 27; "the Society take greatly amiss," declared letter 29). The period of Nicoll's association with the library also spanned the destruction of the collection by fire in 1778, and although some proposal from Nicoll of March 1779 almost certainly related to plans to restock, it did not arrive with Secretary Colcock until early 1780 when it was presented to the anniversary meeting (letter 32).

In May 1780 the garrison of Charleston surrendered to the British, and no further Library Society meeting was held until February 1783. Charles Morgan, a stationer and bookbinder on Broad Street, continued to run a circulating library in 1782,[43] but this was no substitute for the Library Society. Rebuilding the society's collection was the members' paramount concern on the resumption of peace, and some modest book-buying activity on the part of individual members is hinted at in the surviving records. In October 1784, for example, the treasurer reimbursed the president, Thomas Bee, for buying three volumes of "Gibbon's Roman History."[44]

Given the task ahead, however, the restoration of the services of a London book-seller was essential. The former bookseller's earlier offer was still on the table, and the friendly tone of the letters between Colcock and Nicoll was continued by the new secretary John McCall, Jr.—for a while. In the summer of 1785 the commit-tee complained about the quality of the books received, and he was summarily warned, "if you wish to continue in your present Connection with the Society, it will be necessary to be more attentive to Directions" (letter 37). Nicoll did not sur-vive the next anniversary meeting vote, when his unpunctuality was marked down as his principal crime.

Some of the letters from Colcock to Nicoll do indicate that the society should have been grateful to the bookseller for maintaining the business, and in this Col-cock was to be proved correct. In January 1786 the normal commanding appoint-ment letter was dispatched to a new bookseller and, also as usual, carried damning accusations against the previous bookseller. As recommended by the rector of St. Philip's, Charleston, the recipient of this letter was Charles Dilly to whom McCall also enclosed "a Copy of our Rules for your Government" (letter 38). Nicoll was also informed (letter 39) that he had been replaced by Dilly, "from the backward-ness you seem to shew in serving [the society]." Charles Dilly (b. 1739) was the sur-viving brother of a renowned City firm. Edward Dilly (b. 1732) traded at the Rose and Crown, 22, the Poultry, from 1755, and eleven years later entered into part-nership with his brother, who maintained the shop after Edward's death in 1779 and traded until 1800. During the partnership at least 898 publications were issued wholly or partly under their names, with a further 1,621 books published by Charles Dilly between 1779 and his retirement. In total, the Dillys were formally associated with nearly 3,000 books between 1749 and 1800, most of them religious essays, sermons, or improving works. The brothers were acclaimed for their literary gatherings and dinners, and according to John Nichols, the genial Edward "almost literally talked himself to death."[45] Edward had been among those publishing John-son's *Lives of the Poets,* 1779–1781, and Charles was to publish Boswell's *Life of Johnson* in 1791. At his death in 1807 Charles Dilly bequeathed over £80,000 to his heirs.[46] The shock in Charleston, then, must have been considerable when Dilly declined to accept the Library Society's business without better security for his credit. The blow was the harder given that the Dilly brothers were well known as friends of America. In 1764 Charles had even made a business trip to America and expressed eagerness to meet American authors.[47] Dilly, however, was only too well acquainted with the credit risks in taking on American customers in the aftermath of the war.

In the wake of this embarrassment, Library Society members turned in April 1787 to Robert Wells. The former bookseller of Charleston, a fervent Loyalist, was now in exile in London, but the committee's approach to him seems to have been a reluctant and an interim decision. Wells was a former member and committee member of the society and had already volunteered to serve as its London bookseller. The implication of the letter sent to him on his appointment is that members believed he had abandoned the trade for good or even were uncertain of what his business now consisted (letter 40). The exact course of dealings with Wells, beyond one full report of 1789 (letter 41), is now obscure, but in 1791 the society appointed John Stockdale of Piccadilly as its new bookseller. John Stockdale, originally a blacksmith of Cumberland (plate 8), was a former shopman of John Almon, the friend of Wilkes who had set up at 178 Piccadilly in 1763.[48] Almon's business was turned over to one of his later partners, Debrett, but some of his trade was also captured by Stockdale, trading on his own from 1781, three doors down from Almon, opposite Burlington House. Stockdale published at least 1,236 books and pamphlets between 1780 and 1800, with his bookselling career continuing for a further fourteen years. John Stockdale died bankrupt in 1814, although nothing seems to be known about the circumstances of his failure. Stockdale's pro-American sympathies, inherited from Almon and his associates, almost certainly figured in the society's decision to use him, anxious as the committee members were about their credit-worthiness in London after the war.

The correspondence between the Library Society and Stockdale reveals valuable insights into the way in which a London bookseller attempted to collect and dispatch an overseas order (and will be discussed further below), but the outcome of the appointment was a dismal one. The new bookseller lasted only one year, despite his determined protest (letter 53), and in January 1792 the president, Charles Cotesworth Pinckney, wrote to the general mercantile firm Bird, Savage, and Bird to settle the account with Stockdale. The former bookseller probably had good reason to feel aggrieved, given the rarity of some of the books ordered, and Bird, Savage, and Bird admitted that he had eventually been able to put together what was a difficult shipment (letter 52). Stockdale might also have felt that he had been given a certain freedom in being told that he could send out either part or whole of the order (letter 43), but his failure to acknowledge that he was at least embarking on collecting the books, together with the society's growing anxiety and Stockdale's own attempts to include some additional items, ensured that letters were soon dispatched from Charleston to take the business out of his hands.

It was also the beginning of an entirely new course in the history of the Library Society's London orders, with the new merchants appointed used as general agents to assemble and process each shipment. Henry M. Bird, his brother Robert, and Benjamin Savage comprised a leading firm in the Anglo-Carolina trade. Henry Bird had been trained by his father-in-law, William Manning, one of the leading Carolina and West Indian merchants of the second half of the century. Benjamin Savage was the son of John Savage, a Jew born in Bermuda and a leading merchant of Charleston, who had accumulated one of the largest fortunes in the Carolinas in partnership with Gabriel Manigault, former president of the Library Society. Savage organized the Charles Town Chamber of Commerce to "adjust disputes relating to trade and navigation"[49] and in 1773 was its first president, before his flight to a Loyalist London exile. Here young Benjamin was placed in the commercial house of Manning. The firm of Bird, Savage, and Bird continued to write to Gabriel Manigault with family news and political news, quite besides business affairs. Letters written in 1785 under the firm's name, for example, kept Gabriel informed of the illness and then slow recovery of his brother Joseph in London.[50]

Bird, Savage, and Bird, who, according to Rogers, "represented a new generation of Carolina merchants in London" and were highly esteemed as the protégés of Manning and Savage, were "the best example of the immediate re-establishment of commercial ties after the Revolution."[51] The partners were major subscribers to the South Carolina state debt in 1790, and DeSaussure did business with Bird, Savage, and Bird for thirty years. The firm also enthusiastically promoted Anglo-American trade from the mid-1790s, when war in Europe offered the prospect of importation of rice to meet food shortages and army provisioning. In the ensuing trade boom—during which British duties on grain and rice importation were lifted—many of the firm's clients, including DeSaussure, grew extremely rich.[52]

Nonetheless, the continued appointment of Bird, Savage, and Bird by the Library Society seems to have been by default, the library president believing at first that the firm was to act as a go-between to secure the services of another "Bookseller of Reputation and punctuallity" (letter 51). The merchants, however, were swift to recognize an opportunity for longer employment, and for levying a 2½ percent commission on their service of sending on book orders to various London booksellers, coordinating payment, packing, insurance and freight charges, and arranging dispatch. No single bookseller could be as efficient, the merchants assured the Library Society. The results, they insisted, were cheaper books, even allowing for commission charges (letter 52). Letters from Bird, Savage, and Bird did not itemize the booksellers with whom they did business, but the first two major shipments contained books from Ogilvy and Speare of High Holborn (letters 69, 75). David Ogilvy had opened as a bookseller and circulating librarian in Middle Row, Holborn, in about 1783, publishing a sale catalogue "of several libraries of books, comprehending a capital variety in all languages" early in 1784. Between about 1787 and 1797 Ogilvy was partnered by Speare. Together they ran the "London and Westminster Circulating Library" and issued eight-page catalogues for "books beautifully printed on writing paper, in a superior stile of elegance." Ogilvy died in 1812 aged 70. Very little is known of the Ogilvy and Speare business, except that it was replaced by David Ogilvy and Sons from 1797 until 1807 (when the bookstock and library were sold off). It might well be significant that copies of the various Ogilvy and Speare 1793 and 1794 catalogues survive in American libraries.[53]

Other booksellers and client traders used by Bird, Savage, and Bird are unnamed, save for the Boydell firm, supplying the Shakespeare prints, and an intriguing hint from Bird, Savage, and Bird, after settling Stockdale's bill, that they might have future reliance upon him (letter 52). Equally uncertain is the perception of change—if any—in entrusting the selection and dispatch of books to a general merchant firm. The arrangement had come about unexpectedly, but the result might not have seemed unusual. The Library Company of Philadelphia engaged the Quaker general merchants Woods and Dillwyn, and then Samuel Woods from 1783 until at least 1824. Orders from the Lloyds, founders of the largest book collection in Maryland by the end of the eighteenth century, were sent to the merchants Thomas Eden and Co.[54] Of the 2,000–volume foundation collection of the Baltimore Library Company in 1797, some 1,300 volumes were ordered from London with a $1,200 bill of exchange. This together with the next (1797) order for a further £300 worth of books, was arranged through the agency of William Murdock, a London general merchant.[55]

For some eight years Bird, Savage, and Bird managed the Charleston library's book orders, handled the bills of transfer for payment, and dealt with the London booksellers. After the Peace of Amiens in March 1802, the partners failed, stopped payments in February 1803, and were finally declared bankrupt five months later.[56] The last surviving correspondence between Bird, Savage, and Bird and the Library Society, however, is dated 1799, and it is possible that the firm's difficulties were evident by the turn of the century. Certainly, in September 1801 the society reverted to direct correspondence with a bookshop and elected Lackington, Allen, and Company its bookseller.

The new appointment lasted eight years. Again, this was well beyond the average term, but, predictably, it ended in acrimony and confusion. Lackington, Allen was successor to the extraordinary enterprise of James Lackington who had first set up shop in London in 1774. For Henry Curwen, the nineteenth-century book-trade memorialist, Lackington was "an eminent example of how a man of no attainments or advantages can conquer success by sheer hard work and perseverance."[57] Lackington's lively early career, notorious in his own day and much remarked upon since,[58] has overshadowed the later years of Lackington, Allen. The empire was built from remaindered books sold at discount, from large and rapid turnover and originally from the controversial refusal of credit. In 1793 Lackington sold a quarter of his business to his former apprentice Robert Allen, before opening his "Temple of the Muses" a year later in a block of houses converted to a great shop and warehouse in Finsbury Square (plate 9). Lackington finally retired in 1798, disposing of the remaining three-quarter shares to his cousin and also one-time apprentice George Lackington. The firm survived until fire gutted its then Piccadilly premises in 1841.[59]

The bookshop was then in its prime, celebrated in an Ackermann print and numerous derivative engravings (plate 10). In 1801, the year in which the Library Society first addressed the firm, the ten-year-old Charles Knight was taken by his bookseller father to this great mecca of literature:

> We enter the vast area, whose dimensions are to be measured by the assertion that a coach and six might be driven round it. In the centre is an enormous cir-cular counter, within which stand the dispensers of knowledge, ready to wait upon the country clergyman in his wig and shovel-hat; upon the fine ladies in feathers and trains; or upon the bookseller's collector, with his dirty bag. . . . We ascend a broad staircase, which leads to 'The Lounging Rooms,' and to the first of a series of circular galleries, lighted from the lantern of the dome, which also lights the ground floor. Hundreds, even thousands, of volumes are displayed on the shelves running round their walls. As we mount higher and higher, we find commoner books in shabbier bindings; but there is still the same order preserved, each book being numbered according to a printed catalogue. This is larger than that of any other bookseller's, and it comes out yearly.[60]

Most of these annual catalogues survive for the years 1787–1820 and chronicle the expanding business.[61] Copies of the 1787 catalogue could be bought at six other bookshops in London and Westminster, but also at Vowell's in Cambridge and Palmer's and Merrick's in Oxford.[62] By 1792 the catalogue claimed four London outlets and bookseller-agents at Cambridge, Oxford, Sherborne, Bath, Coventry, Bury, Plymouth, Norwich, Bristol, Newcastle, and Edinburgh. The firm gained increasing respect, not least because of its width of stock. It also appears to have anticipated foreign markets ever since Lackington's audacious declaration in 1780 that "not an hour's credit will be given to any person, nor any books sent on board ships, or into the country before they are paid for."[63] In 1801 the business was still growing with 800,000 volumes in 21,868 entries in an annual catalogue now 516 pages long.

It is nonetheless remarkable that in succession to more conventional booksellers, the Charleston Library Society should have approached the firm of Lackington, Allen early in the new century. James Lackington, who died only in 1814, remained a favorite of public gossip and hostile satirical prints. Sketches mocked the firm's cheapness and ostentation. Peter Pindar was moved to produce an *Ode to the Hero of Finsbury Square*. Lackington's notorious autobiographical *Memoirs* went through many editions—one of which rests in the collection of the Library Society—and in 1804 the "cobbler-turned-tycoon,"[64] published his extraordinary *Confessions*.[65]

The choice of Lackington can be explained in several ways. First, the Library Society had moderated many—although, as we shall see, far from all—of its exacting demands. The stentorian tone of the society's early letters weakened. The enforced use of Robert Wells, when relocated to London, and the subsequent debacle with Stockdale proved a watershed. Reports by Wells—former society committee member—and by the Carolinaphile Bird, Savage, and Bird offered a sympathetic appreciation of the difficulties faced by London suppliers. At the same time, the London book trade now included businesses capable of dealing more efficiently with the book-search demands of overseas literary societies and libraries. Lackington, Allen presented itself as such a firm, and clearly the finely catalogued breadth of its stock was telling. Booksellers elected by the Charleston Library Society were always required to collect books from other wholesalers and very often from antiquarian dealers to complete orders. This, as Bird, Savage, and Bird explained, had become very difficult and time-consuming for a single bookseller like Stockdale (letter 52). Lackington, Allen's Emporium was a different matter.

Chapter Seven

ORDERING THE BOOKS

Good relationships with booksellers, as charted by the surviving Charleston Library Society letters, depended upon the effective execution of the society's orders. This was not as simple as it might have first appeared, and the correspondence detailing the various disasters—and a few successes—offers an extensive account of the transatlantic book ordering procedure of the time. The following discussion provides an introduction to this, but many more specific examples of what was deemed good or bad practice can be gained from studying the letters themselves as reproduced and annotated below.

There is, of course, a natural bias in the letters from Charleston toward highlighting misunderstandings, delays, and failures. That is what many business letters were for. As a result, the accomplishment of the society's various dealings with the London trade is not given equal attention. Even at the time that they were written, however, the letters' relentless cataloguing of error, with little acknowledgment of success, clearly frustrated the development of cordial business relationships between bookseller and library, and there is no doubting the intemperate tone often adopted by the society's correspondent.

This crisp, sometimes accusatory language of the letters was the more problematic given that only sustained understanding between the parties secured the smooth operation of such a trade. The most successful transatlantic commercial ventures and certainly the continuation of them were the result of sound communication. Given the distances and obstacles involved and in the absence of the financial institutions taken for granted in later years, carefully nurtured trust between partners—as well as tolerance during financial sloughs—was essential to the conduct of business. Given the relative frequency with which members of Charleston's elite resided in London, where they made direct contact with booksellers and other tradesmen, personal relationships were also developed and nurtured. In 1755 for example, Thomas Corbett, Library Society member, then in London, sent to Peter Manigault two sets of Strange's *Reports* (one destined for another friend), taking credit from Gabriel Manigault's account and arranging for carriage—all of which involved contacts with particular London tradesmen.[1]

The strongest bonds between business partners were familial, a characteristic common to many early modern trades, including those of printing and publishing.

The transatlantic book trade was certainly no exception to this. As pronounced as kinship between book merchants, were family ties among those supporting their trade, between colonial traders, sea captains, and those offering bill-brokering and insurance. According to one estimate, in the first decade of the eighteenth century about one in three of every adult males living in Boston and one in four living in Charleston had at least some part in the ownership of a seagoing vessel.[2] The Charleston Library Society letters offer a further demonstration of the intimacy of commercial, seafaring, and—in this case—literary and scientific communities. Their closeness ensured not only confidence but a rapid and accurate exchange of information. Most of the orders sent out by the society, for example, were appended to letters written either on the day or on the day before the ship cleared out from port. Captains like Ball, Cheesman, Kerr, and Kennedy, making regular transatlantic passages, were frequent carriers, and ships' masters were apparently well known and trusted associates. More direct, family associations between merchants, brokers, and other agents also appear in the letters, and these must have eased transactions.

A network much noted in studies of overseas commerce of the period involved a Scottish diaspora. Scottish interest in the mid-eighteenth-century transatlantic book trade was headed by Strahan and David Hall, but included many other Scots booksellers, agents, and customers. James Rivington's "branch" shop, opening in Boston in 1762, was kept by his Scots partner William Miller. From the commencement of his trade in 1768, John Murray's transatlantic customers included a large number of Scots, most notably, Robert Miller, general merchant of Williamsburg, whose sisters lived in London and delivered both his orders and payment to the London bookseller.[3] Writing to Miller, Murray hoped such loyalties would excuse a certain commercial impertinence: "I have transmitted without order 2 Copies of the Edinb. Magazine not denoting but your regard for Scotland will make you procure orders for many of them."[4] In Charleston, with its large and proud Scots community and connections, the Library Society included the Scotsmen James Scott, Robert Wells, and the Brisbanes, and the ordering process was aided by a sense of kinship, if not with the booksellers, then with some of the intermediaries. Not the least of these was James Crokatt, the sometime agent of the colony and key founder member of the library, who maintained commercial and social bonds with brothers, sisters, and other kin in Charleston, London, and Edinburgh.[5] The evidence, indeed, suggests a certain mitigation of the hostility shown to prominent Scots in the period. Denunciation of the "Scotch Jews" was rife in London, particularly in the years of Bute's influence in the early 1760s, but has also been identified in the Carolinas, with some arguing that anti-Scots prejudices facilitated internal solidarities, especially in the south.[6]

From the evidence of other overseas book-trade correspondence, many friendships were cemented by gifts or special services. In a studied gesture, Murray sent
Miller "a Morning Chronicle for his entertainment."[7] Henry Knox, the bookseller
of Boston, sent his book supplier Longman three pairs of ducks, a present that was
reportedly received with delight in Paternoster Row, even though "all but two of
the Drakes Dyed in the passage."[8] By contrast, the Charleston Library Society's
committee and correspondent seemed uninterested in flattering and encouraging
the London booksellers by sending them gifts. Beyond the odd word of praise and
expression of satisfaction, there is no example of spontaneous generosity on the part
of the Library Society. Given the stern language and strictures of the letters, the
bookseller, often the party who initiated the sending of presents, apparently saw no
reason to garnish the formal relationship. Of the few efforts at more general discourse was the promise to Nicoll in 1773 to send over the prefatory advertisement
to the society's rules so that "you will become better acquainted with us." Even this,
however, was not in fact sent until a year later and was little more than an attempt
to refine Nicoll's appreciation of the books members sought (letters 29, 31). The
only other sign of greater familiarity was McCall's comment to Nicoll about the
death of the former secretary and correspondent Colcock in 1783 (letter 33),
although again the depth of the bookseller's interest in this is not known.

For the Charleston Library Society the want of this more social intercourse was
not unimportant. The book trade was a particularly sensitive business. The whole
process of ordering books, of establishing the much wanted collection of great and
improving literature, was one in which the relations between trading partners were
delicate and finely balanced. Trust and judgment were expected on both sides. All
private and institutional customers in eighteenth-century America had no choice
but to allow their far-distant British bookseller a certain latitude in decision making if he was to be an effective agent. Indeed, the selection of a bookseller often
turned on his reputation as a well-informed and responsible operator in the world
of literature. He was to be not just a manufacturer and trader but a gentleman of
certain discernment and authority. Even more crucially, the "respectable bookseller"
elected at every anniversary meeting of the Library Society was expected to be a
good judge. This was no small matter. Information about books available—when,
where, for how much, and under what conditions—was often imperfect, especially
in the early years of the century. Even in the days of the periodical reviews, known
facts often amounted to little more than a vague ascription to a bookshop. London
newspaper advertisements, placed by publishing booksellers, were more helpful,
but received late and irregularly. It was, nevertheless, not perhaps with the greatest
tact that in writing to one of the longer-serving booksellers the Library Society's
correspondent referred to the society's being "*necessarily obliged* to leave the choice
of the best Editions to your Judgment" (letter 27). Throughout the correspondence

are examples of book orders comprising no more than a very brief and often inaccurate short title. Some of these remain unidentified in the notes to the letters collected below; among titles now identified but offering a challenge to the bookseller are John Heylyn, *An Interpretation of the New Testament,* published in two volumes in London in 1761, but ordered by the Library Society six years later as "Heylen's Lectures."[9]

Rumors about imminent publications were also to be investigated. As noted, the Library Society appears to have written on the basis of information that anticipated the issue of a new edition or compilation, and in a manner reminiscent of other colonial book collectors. In 1792 Edward Lloyd of Maryland requested from his book agent various books "if Published" and "if Translated into English" and left the general instruction, "If there are any New Publications within twelve Months past of real Merit either Travels, Voyages, Political or good Novels send them by the first Opportunity."[10] Lloyd's language of instruction is the same as that of the Charleston Library Society—not only the phrase (among others) "by the first Opportunity" but the reliance on the bookseller or merchant to be its eyes and ears in literary London. From the Library Society's list of May 1767 (appended to letter 17) the order for "The Mirrour" might have suggested Henry Dell's popular *The Mirrour: A Comedy in Three Acts* of 1756 and reissued in 1761, rather than the intended *Mirrour of Justices* "an old law book" (letter 24). The 1768 publication date in surviving editions, however, suggests (even if the imprint is a bookseller's postdating) that notice of its appearance reached a member of the society with remarkable haste. In another example, the library committee later asked Nicoll to assist in upgrading four elderly volumes of what seems to have been Whatley's edited *General Collection of Treatys, Declarations of War, Manifestos, and Other Publick Papers,* published in four volumes between 1710 and 1732, but "printed under rules somewhat differing & at different times." The bookseller was asked to find and send over "any other more perfect & compleat collection . . . but if not, send us any volumes that may have been printed to compleat this Sett" (letter 27). It seems that this was not possible.

Committee letters to the booksellers also disguised occasions when library members disagreed with each other about the books and other materials they needed. The gravest incident was a dispute in the 1760s about the importance of promoting the classics in Charleston. The earliest Library Society collection, as we can now see from the surviving 1750 *Catalogue* (see appendix 3), already included editions of Cicero, Cornelius Nepos, Herodotus, Horace, Justin, Livy, Ovid, Sallust, Tacitus, and Virgil. At the general meeting of June 1764 Christopher Gadsden proposed the establishment of a committee charged with preparing a list of the best editions of classics down to the fourth century to be sent for from London. The suggestion was approved, together with an allocation of £70 of the annual book-buying budget of £100.[11] At the next meeting, however, the librarian, William Carwithen, objected that few of the classics in the library were read, while the £30 residue from the purchase was far too little to cover the pamphlets and books already on order. Gadsden's resolution was duly rescinded, and the proposal was rejected by the autumn general meeting. In protest, Gadsden resigned from the society. Next year debate continued at the meetings of April and October, but a compromise was reached whereby the regular order was modified to include the classics. Gadsden rejoined the society, and, it might be argued, was entitled to claim victory. In February 1766 the secretary, William Mason, wrote to James Fletcher, the new bookseller, enclosing a "List of Classick's" to the value of £70 and followed this with a further list for £30's worth in May 1767.

There was, inevitably, an eclecticism in the Library Society's book ordering, reflecting the particular wants of members at any given time and almost certainly reflecting the particular clout of the more important members at the open meetings. The Gadsden debate about the classics also raises issues beyond the extent to which members were informed about new editions or the simple idea of cultural "lag." When writing to Fletcher in early 1766 the secretary reminded the bookseller that he must keep "strictly to the Editions particularly specified in the List" and that "many of them are only to be had at Second hand and some of them very scarce." The expertise of particular committees, secretaries, and correspondents was a key component in advising—and correcting—the bookseller. The other formative and often constraining feature was the book ordering process itself.

One of the most sensitive issues concerned the freedom allowed the bookseller to send over books and print not specifically ordered by the Library Society. Occasionally the committee was happy to be advised on a new and important publication or to receive an unsolicited shipment funded from the society's outstanding funds in London. When in 1774 the Charleston Library Society received "a Box of Books sent without Order" from its bookseller, Nicoll, the secretary's verdict was that "the Society did not disapprove of them & will not I dare say in future of your acting with discretion in the same manner where it is likely a book in esteem may not be had by the time we sho[d] take in ordering it" (letter 31). Such a reaction was a rarity, however, with booksellers receiving unsympathetic treatment, especially when involved in long-drawn-out transactions over subscriptions to publication by parts or series. Over the years instructions varied about the one or two copies of periodicals and journals sent with each vessel, the yearly or half-yearly volumes to be sent bound, or those sent to be bound locally.

All this was compounded by the complications of restarting from where past booksellers had left off or of attempts (probably because of lending casualties) to fill in gaps in back numbers. Catching-up was also required after the 1778 fire and the interruptions of the revolutionary period. The isolation and interruptions in supplies caused by the war led to a request to Nicoll in May 1783 for "late Pamphlets and Fugitive Pieces, that you imagine will be acceptable" as well as "the different Magazines & Fugitive Pieces as they come out, from time to time, by every Opportunity" (letter 33). The failings that led to Nicoll's dismissal only two years later clearly included the late receipt of periodicals and of-the-minute publications. Before that, however, an all too brief comment from the secretary points to controversy over what the Library Society regarded as Nicoll's timid response to a command to continue selecting pamphlets "as your own best Judgment shall direct." Nicoll, it seems, was falsely warned to steer clear of politically sensitive tracts following British acceptance of American independence at the Peace of Paris. The committee was appalled by what it saw as a questioning of the Library Society's belief in liberality and free discussion. Apparently anxious to dispel any sense that the library might be Loyalist, the secretary, McCall, succinctly noted that it was precisely because of the robustness of its attachment to the new government that a full range of opinions might now be read (letter 37).

Behind all this was the rapid expansion of the London print industry, increasing publication rates and widening choice. Quite apart from the fluctuations in the antiquarian market, books might be bought in different formats, in different bound or unbound states, and at different prices. Just as perplexing for the customer and the supplier was the increased speed as well as the output of printed controversies. Literary debates were the more furious as response time was cut and more contributors and presses entered a fray. During the second half of the eighteenth century an extraordinary variety of disputants exploited the new range of literary audiences and the new potential of print. Political agitation over American grievances and domestic reform vied with high-society scandals and the minutiae of religious controversy in the advertising puffs for new titles. Against this, colonial dependency on London booksellers brought ever greater complication. The more suspicious of customers believed that the necessary freedom allowed to their booksellers—to buy at a slightly higher price or in a different condition, for example—could lead to exploitation. It was for that reason that the Charleston library committees (like their counterparts in New York) put such effort into the writing of "general instructions" for their agents or booksellers in London.

In the case of the Charleston library, however, these instructions were particularly elaborate, not to say pedantic. The correspondent was charged with the composition of each letter, which was then discussed and approved by committee. The specifics (if not always the tone), they realized, had to be right. It seemed all the more frustrating when after such care, instructions were apparently misunderstood or ignored. Having sacked Fletcher as bookseller for "not attending to the spirit of the above General Instructions," the correspondent warned his successor, Nicoll, that small, sewed collections of plays and pamphlets "are not to be sent but by order of the Society" (letter 21). When, as noted, Nicoll was given more freedom after the war to send across his own selection of publications he was nevertheless soon dismissed, largely because of his perceived failure to adhere to the sacrosanct "Directions." He was especially censured because he had dared to send the library some of the "plainest and most ordinary editions," just, indeed, as his predecessor, Fletcher, had seen fit to send over "paltry" editions, which the society had duly returned (letters 23, 37, 39).

A recurrent suspicion by Charleston library members was that a devious bookseller might take advantage of them. In writing to Nicoll in 1769 the correspondent explained that the society would not trust him to send unsolicited material any larger than "Plays & Pamphlets" and up to "a Shilling or two" in price because of the previous behavior of Fletcher, sending books such as a "History of England" that was charged at two guineas—"certainly a Sum too large for the Society to be often surpris'd into" (letter 23). In the original letter of appointment, indeed, Fletcher had been told to confine himself "strictly to the Editions particularly specified" (letter 15). Stockdale hastened to emphasize that he would never wish to be "imprudent in my Selection" or send over unwanted goods, and that the society should auction off unapproved books at whatever loss to himself (letter 53). It was a brave act and a commercial risk to second-guess the society about an unsolicited publication or an addition and embellishment that they might appreciate. Successful actions here are rare. As already noted, Nicoll got away with sending books unordered in 1774, and late in 1793 no adverse reaction greeted a carefully worded letter from Bird, Savage, and Bird that they had "gone to the expence of the handsomest frames for the [Boydell] Prints." Given past history it was nonetheless rash of the merchants to write that "we have no doubt of the Society's approbation" for what they claimed as the added effect allowed by greater margins and larger frames, each of which had cost an "additional few shillings" (letter 62).

As a result of their experiences, many of the elected booksellers to the society must have felt that they had to be mind readers as well as miracle workers, and they knew that they had to take the consequences if things went wrong. Those serving the Charleston Library Society must certainly have wondered whether the trade was worth it when they received letters countermanding orders for books and materials not only already bought but shipped out several weeks before. The society also demanded quality. In May 1784 (letter 35) Nicoll was assured that copies in quarto were always preferred to octavo, where available, and "to send the very best Editions, in respect to Editor, Type, Paper and Binding." The same letter reminded Nicoll to leave out the "W" in renamed "Charleston" in lettering on the books, but also to expect a visit from Alexander Garden, then in London, to inspect his selection and work. The society also demanded value for money, allowing Wilson, for example, up to a year (but only up to year) to buy journals of the House of

Commons "as cheap as possible" (letter 25). The one bookseller who declined to serve the society, Charles Dilly, was told in his letter of appointment that he had been elected bookseller because members had been "of Opinion that Mr. William Nicoll of St. Paul's Church Yard their late Bookseller, had not served them with that Punctuality which the Spirit of their Society required, and which their Punctuality in Payment gave them a Right to expect" (letter 38). Quite apart from his concern over transatlantic credit, Dilly's refusal to act might well also have been based on shared memories of service to the society within the close-knit London trade. Four years later Wells was anxiously writing from London to request clarification of some of the titles in the society's order, lest he make a mistake (letter 41).

From other correspondence of the period it is clear that many London booksellers found it hard to satisfy demanding overseas customers. Murray apologized to Miller for his failure to locate all the foreign articles requested from London sellers—"at a future Period I may order what is wanting with some others [booksellers] from the Continent"—and he asked Miller to repeat orders for those he could not send "because they may be easier got at one time than another."[12] Longman's assistant Christopher Brown sent elaborate explanations and letters ahead to Knox in Boston, indicating why certain ships were missed or why others were chosen because of uncertainties about departure times, routes, or the weather. Similar comments, sent out as enquiries or demands by the library committee, pepper the Charleston letters. In the absence of other documents from the period, one of the letters received in reply from London offers an important and unique testimony. John Stockdale, summarily dismissed in 1792, fired off a letter of justification. Laboriously he explained that although many of the requests were "trifling in price," they were also the most elusive and "only to be got by accident as they came into the trade from private persons." As a result, he continued, "my Clerks and myself have traversed the streets of London from Bookseller to Bookseller I firmly believe an hundred times over at least. . . . I have executed my instructions to the best of my Judgment and this is no trifling task, as for instance it frequently happens that a scarce book is sold by one Bookseller at £14.14 and by another at £12.12d" (letter 53).

Stockdale's response was echoed by a similar cri de coeur from John Murray. Murray was never to be contacted directly by the Library Society, but he made various attempts to establish long-term custom from Charleston's elite. The three months taken to dispatch orders to Dr. Gates in Charleston had, insisted Murray, been not only on account of their small value, but because of failings in the original descriptions supplied by Gates. As he wrote to his customer, "I have done my best to execute your orders. But I still wish you to be more particular, being sensible of the difficulty of hitting anothers taste in books."[13] Stockdale, however, went far further and provides a graphic account of the methods used to search for books and of the intrinsic difficulty of ordering such a wide selection of publications, old, new, cheap, expensive, single- and multivolumed, through the agency of one dealer (letter 53).

In these quarrelsome exchanges specifications about bindings were a particular source of conflict. Instructions sent by the Charleston Library Society allude to a fast-changing but still poorly understood craft serving the book trade of the period. At the beginning of the century the great majority of books were sold unbound, ready for buyers to select their own London or local binders and styles of binding. Increasingly, bookseller-publishers offered binding services—although most depended on the out-house labors of humble binders, such as those living and working in the cramped alleyways off Paternoster Row. From the 1740s, trade bindings, or prepared stock in simple covers, became more easily available. Notices in the periodical reviews, for example, usually gave prices for a book "sewed" or "in boards." Most exported books were bound, if only to answer concerns about damage during transit. Thin "sheep, rolled" leather coverings were most commonly listed in the surviving overseas invoices of the period. The great majority of books imported by Knox of Boston in the 1770s were certainly so bound. Of the leather bindings, reddish-brown sheepskin was in fact a very popular material in England in the seventeenth and eighteenth centuries for account books and for school and cheap books.[14] Available in different tannings, sheepskin was nevertheless unsuitable for long-term preservation. What sheepskin did do was to provide protection until it could be discarded for local rebinding. Although this was deemed acceptable for some later periodicals to be rebound at Charleston, for almost all its ordered books the Library Society demanded quality London-executed morocco and calf leather binding, together with the labeling as decreed in the general instructions. To the exasperation of the library committee many of the books sent by Fletcher in 1769 arrived in boards and had to be sent off for rebinding (letter 22). The society's bookseller, in addition to searching for the books, was expected to send them out to a trusted London binder able to satisfy the exact requirements. Binding and lettering were demanded even for the additional small pamphlets that a bookseller was allowed to send without request (letter 23). The identity of the binder, as is the case in almost all surviving book order records of the period, is unknown, but many small binding firms were close by the booksellers in Paternoster Row and the Churchyard.

Binding orders for serial publications and periodicals added to the booksellers' difficulties, especially as the Library Society kept changing policy. Missing sets were to be sent bound according to a demand of 1760 (letter 6), but early in 1771 the correspondent insisted "that the Magazines & Reviews are not for the future to be sent out bound either ½ yearly or yearly, but instead thereof you are to furnish the Society with all necessary Prefaces, Frontispieces, tables of Contents, indexes &c in

order for their being bound up here, as we have been hitherto at a double expence"
(letter 26). Concern over the binding certainly remained a feature of the correspondence into the nineteenth century. In 1802, at the beginning of their service,
Lackington, Allen were quick to assure the society that the binding they offered "we
think will be found both neat & durable," enclosing charges by rivals for comparison (letter 86). A complaint by the Library Society about carelessness in the binding brought an anxious exchange in 1804–1805 (letters 100, 101), and central
to the firm's final plea for forgiveness was the need to secure an acceptable binder
(letter 113).

A further general but also growing difficulty was the contradiction between
Charlestonians' interest in the very latest and most fashionable literature and the
self-evident requirement to receive up-to-the-minute publications in good time.
"Latest print" and, most particularly, periodical publications and novels boosted
demand for imports, but also increased the pressure upon booksellers and agents
on both sides of the Atlantic. From the early 1750s interest in periodicals soared,
and some of the most insistent parts of the correspondence concerned orders for
periodical publications. By July 1760 (letter 6) the standard instruction from the
Charleston Library Society was for two copies of each *London, Gentleman's,* and
Universal magazine. These, together with the two periodical reviews, the *Monthly*
and *Critical,* seem to have been the leading exported monthlies. The *London* and
the *Gentlemen's* rank also, for example, among the six most popular titles imported
by Condy in New England.[15] These same publications, however, became a great
trial to colonial and London suppliers, with their information about the apparently
ready availability of London books, their attempts at comprehensive reviewing, and
above all, their telltale monthly masthead. The latter was indelible evidence of the
efficiency—or inefficiency—of transit. As in Philadelphia, where David Hall lost
customers because of breaks in the dispatch of the monthlies,[16] the Charleston
library rebuked its booksellers for their failure in magazine supply.

The record with the periodicals was not good from the beginning. Anxiety and
very often exasperation about delayed or lost periodicals are recurrent throughout
the span of the correspondence. In August 1758 the correspondent complained
that no periodicals had been sent for more than eighteen months, and that in any
case, the Library Society was also waiting for bound sets of the reviews for all of
1754 to 1757 (letter 1). In July 1760 the bookseller was again urged to send out
periodicals "as often as Opportunity offers," with a further calf-bound set at the end
of each year (letter 6). Two years later, the correspondent wrote to the new bookseller, Wilson, advising that "the Society are greatly disappointed in not having the
Magazines by every Vessel from London to this place" (letter 10). In the next communication from Charleston he was again reminded that the magazines were being
sent at only about six monthly intervals, something that was "of great disappointment

to the members" (letter 11). Change of bookseller made things worse, with the whole of 1764 left out in the periodical ordering as a result (letter 18). In 1766 Dodsley was told that he was no longer to be called bookseller because he had sent periodicals in a "packet & conveyance much too tedious to answer their expectations" (letter 16). Twenty years later Nicoll was sternly rebuked when the members' September periodicals arrived only in January "after a tedious Passage of 13 Weeks" (letter 36).

The reviews and magazines were among the most prized possessions of the Charleston library. Although each monthly part of a serial publication cost a fraction of one of the grand folios ordered by the society, each was of major value in reestablishing the connection between the members and the literary and intellectual heart of the empire. The periodical reviews brought the practical guidance to new publications and opinions about them, but they also affirmed a notion of imperial and international community. In addition to such periodical frontispieces as that to the *Universal Magazine,* noted already, the regular title-page engraving of the even more popular *London Magazine* displayed Mercury flying over a Thames busy with the freight of empire. It was also clear that the publishers of periodicals were not forgetful of their colonial audience. In 1769 the Charleston bookseller Nicholas Langford proclaimed of the *London Magazine* that "this periodical Production, from its Commencement in the Year 1731, hath ever been held in the greatest Estimation; and prefered, in the Opinion of the Judicious, to all the brother Publications of the Kind."[17] In advertisements for the first volume of a new series of the *Monthly Review* in 1790 its editor Ralph Griffiths announced, for the benefit of "Merchants, Captains of Indiamen, and of other Ships, and all Persons who send Books to their Friends abroad, that every Volume of his new Series consists of the Numbers for four Months, with an Appendix; and that complete Volumes will always be kept in readiness, as they come out, to supply immediate demands."[18]

What at least temporarily calmed the Library Society in its demands for periodicals was first, the appointment in the 1790s of the general merchants Bird, Savage, and Bird and then the apparently reassuring expertise of Lackington, Allen, and Co. The firm of Bird, Savage, and Bird offered the society, in the line of its general commerce, book and periodical collecting services, which included contacting and assembling book orders from the individual bookseller-publishers, and then handling the packing and shipping arrangements. After the firm's demise and the society's return to engaging a bookseller proper, Lackington, Allen offered the assurance of a vast stockroom, regular catalogues, and shelves boasting an extraordinary literary range. The firm might have been notorious in England for its motto "The Cheapest Bookstore in the World," but from the opening of correspondence in September 1801 and in service to the Library Society for the next eight years,

Lackington, Allen was viewed as one that had developed a successful new specialism in the London book export market. Apart from some disasters—the chief of which ultimately revived all the old claims of bookselling incompetence—the outgoing and incoming letters, orders, and accounts reveal a certain stability and at least new attempts at regularity in supply.

Perhaps the greatest contrast between the later London agents and the earlier booksellers appears in the Charleston commentary on invoices and billing procedures. A recurrent complaint from the Library Society correspondent concerned failure on the part of the bookseller to itemize accounts or to send due notice by letter or cocket of the contents of a particular shipment. The absence of adequate paperwork led to delays and misunderstandings in Charleston about the arrival of the parcels of pamphlets and periodicals and of the larger trunks of the book orders. Writing to Rivington in 1759 the correspondent complained that of the few consignments received none had been accompanied by "any Letter or account from you" (letter 5). Fletcher was reminded that invoices should be sent by separate letter and not in the actual trunk or book parcel. The secretary had only just found one such bill "by the meerest Chance" hidden in one of the books (letter 18). In 1763 Wilson was told to give the price not only of each book but also of its binding and lettering, in the manner, claimed the society, of all previous booksellers (letter 12). The request was seemingly ignored.

Subsequent correspondence repeatedly alludes to errors in accounting. In 1770 Nicoll was reprimanded for a catalogue of confusions and mischarging; at the end of the next year he was told that full paperwork from him was now urgent, not only for the completion of the society's records but so that they "may see in what manner you have rectified the mistakes I pointed out to you sometime" (letters 25, 27). Finally, in 1772, Nicoll is told that the accounts he has at last sent across are meaningless and that "we differ in amounts greatly" (letter 28). In fact, the society was itself guilty of poor record keeping on several occasions. The earliest surviving letters (1, 2) allude to controversy over an outstanding bill claimed by William Strahan, in which the widow of a former treasurer and the vice president Gabriel Manigault were called in to assist with the collective memory.[19] Even more embarrassingly, early in 1770 the society was obliged to send Nicoll—of whose accounts Colcock declared, "I can make nothing"—some additional funds to settle a newly discovered five-year-old debt to its former bookseller Wilson (letters 24, 28).

Such problems were exacerbated by the frequent change of booksellers. Outstanding credit was often left with those just dismissed, but the exact amount was not always clear given the billing failings. In the letter appointing Fletcher, the new bookseller was ordered to remonstrate with the discarded James Dodsley over his failure to supply proper invoices. These were now needed for the Library Society's accounts. Although records of these are lost, they were apparently "all regularly entered." Fletcher was also instructed to ensure that Dodsley did not overcharge in his retrospective billing (letters 15, 16, 17). The impression is not only that Dodsley was unconcerned, but that Fletcher made little haste in retrieving the account. Fletcher, indeed, seems to have effected nothing at all and later reported the situation as impossible (letter 18). It was left to Nicoll, Fletcher's successor as Library Society bookseller, to get satisfaction from Dodsley (letters 21, 23). Support from other quarters suggests Dodsley's imprecision and general laxity. Against the 1769–1770 entry for Dodsley in John Murray's accounts ledger, Murray has written "tho' irregularly stated I am of opinion is settled."[20] An obvious inference is that booksellers, having been awarded advance credit, were in no hurry to surrender it, especially those dismissed by customers several thousand miles distant. Booksellers faced constant cash flow crises, leading many to failure or to seek refuge in a declaration of bankruptcy.[21] In a business regime in which investment in copy ownership, paper, printing, and labor was balanced against sales that were normally made without secure guarantee of return, the sudden arrival of advance monies from afar was a blessing to be enjoyed for as long as possible. It was not, however, only the suppliers of print who had to confront financial embarrassments.

SIGILLVM SOCIETATIS DE PROMOVENDO EVANGELIO IN PARTIBVS TRANSMARINIS

TRANSIENS ADIVVA NOS

The Gift of the Society for propagating the Gospell in Foreign parts 1704

1. 1704 bookplate of the Society for the Propagation of the Gospel in Foreign Parts.
Reproduced by permission of the American Antiquarian Society, Worcester, Mass.

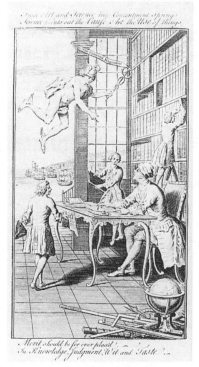

2. Library membership certificate of Charles Cotesworth Pinckney, 1769. Reproduced by permission of the Charleston Library Society, Charleston, S.C.

3. Frontispiece to the first volume of the *Universal Magazine* (1747). Reproduced by permission of the Syndics of Cambridge University Library.

4. The Charleston Courthouse, designed in 1792, from a photograph taken for Arthur Mazyck, *Charleston in 1883*.

OVERLEAF:

5. Map of the sites of the London booksellers, book agents, instrument makers, and merchant-brokers to the Charleston Library Society, 1758–1811 (with inset and enlarged section).

Booksellers and Agents

B1   **John Almon**, 178 Piccadilly

B2   **Bird, Savage, & Bird**, 12 Bury Court, S. Mary Axe

B3   **Charles Dilly**, 27 The Poultry

B4   **Robert and James Dodsley**, 59 Pall Mall

B5   **Thomas Durham & David Wilson**, Strand

B6   **James Fletcher**, St. Paul's Churchyard and Lovell's Court, Paternoster Row

B7   **Lackington, Allen, & Co.**, Finsbury Square

B8   **William Nicoll**, 51 St. Paul's Churchyard

B9   **John and James Rivington**, 62 St. Paul's Churchyard

B10 **John Stockdale**, 181 Piccadilly

B11 **William Strahan**, Little New Street, Fleet Street

B12 **Robert Wells** (from 1787), Salisbury Court, Fleet Street

Merchants

M1   **Sir George Colebrooke**, 9 New Broad Street

M2   **Greenwood & Higginson**, 25 Budge Row

M3   **Hanbury & Co.**, 33 & 34 Great Tower Street

M4   **Alexander Nesbitt**, 8 Bishopsgate Street Within

M5a **Sarah Nickelson & Co.**, Mansel Street, Goodman's Fields *and subsequently*

M5b Chequer Yard, Bush Lane

M6a **John Nutt**, 33 New Broad Street *and subsequently*

M6b 33 Old Bethlem

M7   **Richard Oswald & Co.**, 17 Philpott Lane

M8a **Richard Shubrick**, Barge Yard, Bucklersbury *and subsequently*

M8b 19 St. Peter's Hill

M9   **John Thomlinson**, Barge Yard, Bucklersbury

Instrument Makers

I1   **George Adams**, 60 Fleet Street

I2   **Peter Dolland**, 58 St. Paul's Churchyard

I3   **Benjamin Martin**, 171 Fleet Street

I4   **Jesse Ramsden**, 199 Piccadilly

Other

RE   **Royal Exchange**

CC   **Carolina Coffee House** and **Pennsylvania Coffee House**, 25 Birchin Lane

VC   **Virginia Coffee House**, 2 Newman's Court, Cornhill

6. Portrait of William Strahan (1715–1785) by Sir Joshua Reynolds, c. 1780. Reproduced by permission of the Syndics of Cambridge University Library.

7. Portrait of James Rivington (1724–1802) from a New York engraving by A. H. Petchie. Reproduced by permission of the Syndics of Cambridge University Library.

8. "John Stockdale, the Bookselling Blacksmith," c. 1781. Reproduced from a cartoon engraving in the possession of the author.

9. Exterior view of Lackington's Temple of the Muses, Finsbury Square, c. 1829. Reproduced from a Wallis engraving from a drawing by Thomas Shepherd in the possession of the author.

10. Interior view of Lackington, Allen, and Co., 1801. Reproduced by permission of the Lewis Walpole Library, Yale University.

diſtinct from that in which the young Gentlemen are to be.

PHILIP HAWKINS, & Comp.

Have juſt imported, in the MERMAID, *Capt.* SAMUEL BALL:

A FRESH Aſſortment of Iriſh Linens, a few Pieces of flowered Book Muſlins, Men and Womens Silk and Thread Hoſe: Which, with their large Aſſortment of Linen Drapery, and Hard Ware in general, will be ſold cheap, at their Store in Tradd-Street, lately poſſeſſed by JOHN EDWARDS, & Co.----Alſo, a large Quantity of beſt blue and white Watchet Plains, of an extraordinary Width and Quality, Briſtol and London Duffils.

For L O N D O N,

To ſail in a few Days:

The Ship M E R M A I D,

SAMUEL BALL, ſen. Maſter.

She has two-thirds of her Cargo already engaged.

FOR Freight of the Remainder, or for Paſſage (having ſuperior Accommodations to any Ship in the Trade) apply to ſaid Maſter on Board, or to ISAAC MOTTE, & Co.

A CONSIGNMENT of GOODS,

Lately imported, in the Ship NANNY, DAVID PERRY *Maſter, from* LIVERPOOLE, *conſiſting of*

11. Advertising woodcut of the ship *Mermaid, South Carolina Gazette,* 14 Sept. 1769.
Reproduced by permission of the Charleston Library Society, Charleston, S.C.

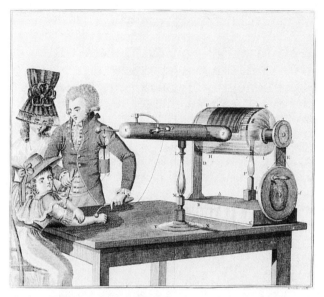

12. Demonstration of electrical experiments, frontispiece to George Adams, *An Essay on Electricity*, 4th ed. (London, 1792). Reproduced by permission of the Syndics of Cambridge University Library.

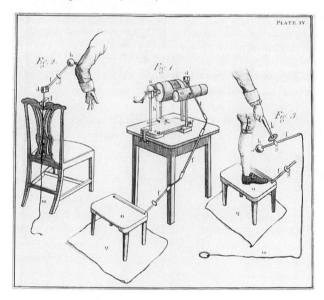

13. Detail of electrical experiments, plate 4 in Edward Nairne, *The Description and Use of Nairne's Patent Electrical Machine*, 8th ed. (London, 1796). Reproduced by permission of the Syndics of Cambridge University Library.

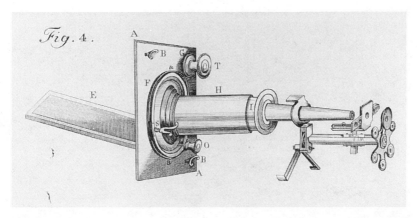

14. The solar microscope, fig. 4 in George Adams, *Micrographia Illustrata; or, the Knowledge of the Microscope Explain'd* (London, 1746). Reproduced by permission of the Whipple Museum of the History of Science, Cambridge.

15. Portrait of Jesse Ramsden (1735–1800), date unknown. Reproduced by permission of the Syndics of Cambridge University Library.

16. *The Merry Wives of Windsor*. From John Boydell, *A Collection of Prints, from Pictures Painted for the Purpose of Illustrating the Dramatic Works of Shakespeare, by the Artists of Great-Britain* (London: John and Josiah Boydell, 1803), volume 1, plate 9. Courtesy of the Department of Rare Books and Special Collections, Thomas Cooper Library, University of South Carolina.

Chapter Eight

FINANCING THE ORDERS

ALTHOUGH, AS WILL BE SHOWN below, the letters of the Charleston Library Society record mainly regular and substantial payments made to the London booksellers, the size and costs of the incoming consignments of books and pamphlets are, until the later letters, more indistinct. What stands out is the varying quantity of arriving publications, as well as the very high value of the biggest shipments. An early reported invoice of over £123 for a consignment in 1759 was itself substantial, but the controversial and long-awaited Stockdale trunks of 1792 were worth an extraordinary £436. This was by far the largest and most valuable of the known book cargoes sent to the society, greater even than the combined value of two large shipments of August 1809 (see table 6).

In attempting to best serve its members with their regular contributions to the library fund, the Library Society committee faced two financial problems. The first difficulty concerned the costs of the incidentals in overseas ordering—the expenses of freight, duty, official shipping charges and insurance, and the charges of interest incurred if, as was likely, communications and payment were delayed. The second, and on many occasions, the more difficult problem, concerned the securing of the actual means to make payment efficient and effective on the other side of the Atlantic.

The loss of the society's accounts makes it impossible to quantify full transaction costs (apart from early occasional insurance and captain's-bag references) until certain details are given in letters from Bird, Savage, and Bird and then more fully from Lackington, Allen (notably, letters 63, 67, 79, 86, 106, 107, 111, 115, 119). Most colonial booksellers and general merchants dealing in books had already found the import trade to be unpredictable and difficult. High transaction expenses prevented long-term investment. In the trade between the booksellers Matthew Carey of Philadelphia and Patrick Byrne of Dublin, for example, insurance after 1800 amounted to 8.5 percent of the wholesale cost, with duty at 13.5 percent and freight at 2 percent. In this case, then, the total import charge of 24 percent was close to the 25 percent discount offered to the bookseller.[1] Very few of the accounts within the Charleston Library Society correspondence offer details of freight and related shipping costs. In 1802 the society was charged, from a total bill of £208.3s.3d., a freight charge of £2.1s.10d. (or 1 percent) and £2.2s. (1 percent) for two packing cases and their shipping expenses (letter 86). In 1809 the society was charged, from a total bill of £292.6s.6d., a freight and primage bill of £1.15s.3d. (0.6 percent) and combined entry, cocket, shipping charges, and bills of lading of £1.2s.9d. (0.4 percent). The full bill also incurred a 2.5 percent commission from Goldingham (letter 115).

Usually, both smaller trader and individual customer were disadvantaged by economies of scale, with transport charges proportionately heavier the smaller the cargo. In his orders with John Murray, ranging from £14 to £56, Miller of Williamsburg spent about 2 percent of his total remittance on freight charges. For its freight the New York Society Library was charged the equivalent of 1 percent of their £70 order by John Ward at midcentury. The much larger shipments sent by Longman to Henry Knox gained from advantages of scale, and the Boston bookseller was charged carriage at only about half of 1 percent for orders valued at about £100. Large orders of some £400 invited a total freight charge of about a third of 1 percent including the expense of additional trunks. In consequence, as other importing problems or alternatives increased, smaller booksellers and individual customers were the more likely to count the cost of transport. In the case of the Charleston Library Society the full freight and shipping expenses of the 1802 consignment (1.8 percent) and that of 1809 (1 percent)—if representative of all their cargoes—suggest charges in line with the New York Society Library and somewhat better than those charged to smaller individual customers like those of Murray.

In any event, the increasing wealth of the Charleston Library Society, notably including the surplus funds let out at interest, made it well placed to absorb the additional costs of its London buying. But this did not make the library committee any less interested in cost cutting or suspicious of that attempted by a bookseller or agent. Examples of the society's accusations against its London suppliers have already been given (and more can be found in the letters below), but secretary-correspondents remained vigilant against the smallest irregularity. In 1769, in one of the rare comments on shipping costs, Nicoll was commanded not to pay two shillings for leaving pamphlets and letters via Captain Samuel Ball's bag. The secretary was indignant that "this is a new charge to the Society" and one quite uncalled for when the society was already paying the postage on small parcels when received, like letters, at Charleston (letter 23). Insurance costs, to be detailed below, were more problematic, but the biggest advantage, as a relatively modest customer when compared to major commercial importers like Knox, was the society's ability to maintain sufficient advance credit in London to spare it from heavy interest charges. The comparison here with other colonial libraries and book importers is a telling one.

Many colonial customers were unable to bear the interest charges caused by delay and transaction difficulties. For those dealing in books on both sides of the

Atlantic, the sheer distance and time involved created particular problems with credit terms. Short-term credit was frequently used by colonists for the purchase of British goods from Britain, and English merchants usually included a twelve-month interest charge in the price of the goods shipped. The credit charge was reimbursed (partially or completely) if payment was made before the twelve months elapsed. For the bookseller advancing credit, however, enormous and long-running complications could ensue at the distance of 6,000 miles and four to six months between each return correspondence. Longman allowed Knox twelve months' credit on what were often very large orders. One of the most exacting booksellers in the American trade, Adrian Watkins, who held the Bible patent in Scotland, allowed only two months' credit. As a result, Hall in Philadelphia had to pay in full before any part of the shipment arrived.

Many others placing orders from the colonies faced the same difficulty. The Atlantic made credit relations between these provincial customers and booksellers and the London wholesalers very different from those between the English provinces and London, where customers might expect and traders might be resigned to a year's credit (and sometimes more). After some years Watkins did extend Hall's credit to six months and even allowed a little discount.[2] Few financial records survive for the other library societies of the period, but when, in 1757, the New York Society Library's balance to Moses Franks of London of £28.10s. had been outstanding for three years the secretary discharged the debt by a total payment of £52 which included an extraordinary interest charge of 82 percent.[3]

By comparison, the Charleston Library Society never came close to suffering such heavy penalties. For an American customer the society's record was better than most, although not as exceptional as it might itself have believed. Pride in the achievement is understandable, however, given the customary reliance by the Carolina planters on purchase by credit and their consequent accumulation of a debt often equal to the value of one year's export. In its favor, the society was a wealthy eager purchaser never (apart from a few small oversights) in debt for long and often advancing substantial monies to London. Balances were regularly topped up in preparation for future orders, and the cast list of drawers and brokers was impressive. Behind the Charleston Library Society's advances was also a solid reserve, amounting, as already seen, to bonds and cash of over £9,000 in April 1767, £10,600 by July 1768, and £15,500 by July 1772.[4] In 1792 the library president assured Bird, Savage, and Bird that the dividends of no less than sixteen shares in the Bank of the United States were to be spent on book purchases, trusting that this would make it "worth the while of some eminent Bookseller to serve us Punctually and well" (letter 51).

Perceptions of the Library Society's liquidity and credit-worthiness seem to have varied among its London agents. At one extreme, Dilly would have none of this problematic institution, whereas Stockdale, bruised and rejected, nevertheless made the extraordinary plea (the order to him, after all, had been a valuable one) that in future the secretary should "order freely whatever Books you want . . . without any regard to the Amount or the payment, trusting that the remittances will be made as often as it is convenient to the Society" (letter 53). In a century when influential and demanding bibliophiles made nonpayment into an art form, booksellers certainly met with far worse customers than the Library Society. Robert Harley might have been one of the greatest book collectors of the age with enviable patronage to dispense, but his bookseller-agent Nathaniel Noel found him slow in settling bills. At one point in the 1720s Noel was owed some £3,000. The Earl of Sunderland, creator of the other great private library of the period, left the world owing his bookseller more than £500.[5]

Sudden death was less common among library societies. It was, however, the peculiarities of the colonial, transatlantic trade and supply of books that gave added concern to London booksellers. Against the generally sound payment record of the Charleston Library Society, it is worth reemphasizing that distance and time delays did ensure that many London booksellers suffered setbacks from the American trade. A good record in retrospect is very different from the sort of calculations that London booksellers might have had to make at any one particular time, especially given the short-term and relatively irregular relationships maintained by the Library Society. As creditors to American retailers, London wholesale booksellers were greatly disadvantaged by distance. Thomas Hancock considered that two years' credit was usual for colonial merchants and their customers, but twelve months seems to have been the norm between British book wholesalers and colonial clients. David Hall considered six months' credit too short as he could not sell all his imported cargo within that time,[6] but the difficulty for London suppliers in offering a full year of credit was that any discount rate, as expected by the colonial customer, then made the whole commerce seem unviable. Most colonial booksellers expected a 10 percent discount offered on bound publications, basing it, however, on the profit wholesalers made in provincial England. As a result, Strahan suggested that a wholesaler shipping out bound books might be paying in cash 85 percent of their value to their original bookseller-publishers. The wholesaler's profit margin might then be too low reasonably to support a year's credit with discount to the colonial customer.[7]

This question of discounts was a crucial one in the transatlantic book trade, and here the Library Society, even as a small, if rich, institutional customer, retained high expectations. The society's wealth, together with its mostly prompt payment and dispatch of new funds, underpinned a continuing fastidiousness. In 1767 Fletcher was told to remonstrate with Dodsley precisely because the members were "expecting from the punctuality of their payments to have been supplied on the most advantageous terms of the Trade" (letter 17). The great variable in book commerce remained the level of discount offered to retailers by the London wholesaler, with colonial booksellers demanding terms equivalent to those offered to English provincial booksellers. It might be thought that for the Library Society such discounts would have been trivial issues when compared to the apparent security of a direct London service and the promise of a swift delivery of new literature, periodicals, and newspapers. Most of the committee members were trading men, however. The "advantageous terms" expected by the society in return for its punctuality in settling bills implied good discounts, and possibly wholesale prices, and the decision to appoint James Rivington in the 1750s further suggests a merchant-like interest in discount offers. The challenge of Rivington in the late 1750s, paralleling English assaults on the London oligopoly, had certainly raised the stakes in the transatlantic book trade. What for Strahan were the "low, dirty, and unwarrantable Methods"[8] of Rivington were very attractive to many colonial clients. Rivington offered 16 percent discount and a year's credit to American customers in the late 1750s. William Hunter, the bookseller of Williamsburg, swapped Samuel Birt for James Rivington in 1755, enticed by notions of higher profits, but Hunter, after a visit to England in 1758, concluded that the business was fraudulent—at least according to the already biased Strahan.[9] It does seem that the quality of Rivington's imports was low and that many of his consignments contained curious books. His bankruptcy in January 1760, before he crossed the Atlantic, declared debts of £30,000. In addition to Rivington's eventual defeat by the fixed arrangements of the established London book trade, his already erratic career reached collapse because of the small profit margins of transatlantic business.

All this also provides background to the apparent inertness of some of the booksellers when faced by the Library Society's demands. The pricing constraints of the London trade often broke relationships between London booksellers and their American clients. The evidence from Murray's surviving correspondence and business records is that his colonial trade was hardly worth it. He always retained hopes that the trade would build up. Overseas orders did accumulate, but very slowly, and what appears to have been a normal credit agreement for payment within six months of the invoice dispatch, was honored by some but not every customer.[10] The Salem library found its local bookseller, Condy of Boston, very demanding that "urging [urgent] necessity gives you the trouble of this. I have had a Bill Excha' drawn upon me at Scotland for 50£ Sterling which is to be paid the 29th Currant, I must there fore request the Library Company to pay their Acc.ᵗ without which I see no way of paying the Bill in Season."[11] Longman gave Knox exactly the same terms as he gave an English provincial bookseller, but with the clear expectation that Knox would raise his prices above Longman's London retail prices.[12] Although Knox was providing an assured supply and able to offer unit-cost reductions on transport and the like, he was in effect held hostage to an agreed marginal rate of profit. At one point Longman suspected Knox of reneging on the agreement, a move, he argued, that "must be destructive to us both."[13] Both James Fletcher and James Dodsley, the latter managing a very considerable business, give every indication of deliberate inaction towards the Library Society. As Stephen Botein concluded, "the conventional pricing arrangements of the London booktrade presented only minimal incentive for expansion of transatlantic business."[14]

For London booksellers from Strahan and Nicoll to Stockdale and Lackington, long credit and fine margins of discount and pricing agreements might also result in irrecoverable nonpayment. English client-booksellers and many notable individual and institutional customers were notorious for holding long credit and being unresponsive to demands. American clients not only held credit at 3,000 miles distance, but their attempts to pay were often unsuccessful and in some cases less than serious. In 1748 William Strahan had been forced to sue James Read—the man who had first suggested the American market to him—when after three years no payment had been received for a large consignment. Strahan eventually abandoned the attempt to recover this debt when even a power of attorney proved ineffectual.[15] Three decades later, nothing had improved. When Strahan was still owed over £360 three years after the death of David Hall in 1772, he found it impossible to extract payment, even though he was assured by Franklin that the Hall family business was thriving.[16] Other silences resulted from business failure or the sudden closure of a colonial shop. In May 1774 Knox received a curt reprimand from the firm of Wright and Gill about his bill outstanding for some two years: "It was presuming on your Promised Remittances which induced us to ship your Last Orders, and it really hurts us, to be under the disagreeable Necessity of Thus Writing You. Your Correspondence will be a Real Pleasure to us, provided you were Careful to our Time of Credit, Twelve not to exceed fourteen Months would content us."[17] Henry—then general and minister—Knox still owed Longman £1,300 in 1789, fifteen years after Knox had left bookselling. It was not to be until 1805 that Longman's executrix, his widow, finally received full settlement of $4,461.[18] Longman was also the sufferer when Mein's bookshop closed because of his Loyalism in 1769. Longman was owed some £1,680, and in 1771 the Superior Court of Judicature at Boston assessed damages to be paid to Longman and Wright and Gill at £2,193, with power of attorney given to John Hancock with the right to seize Mein's books for nonpayment.[19] Nor was distinction a guarantee of reliability. Murray had to write to the president of the College of William and Mary to explain that he was failing to get the president's payments honored.[20]

Although the Charleston Library Society was not to prove a risk on this scale, there were many moments of crisis, and the society did fall into debt from time to time. Table 6 provides a basic chronology of the dispatch of monies to London as recorded by the letters, offset by references, also in the letters, to outstanding debts to the booksellers. No full invoices or accounts survive, so dating is approximate only and based on the date of the letters as written or received.

From the 1790s interest payments became a regular expense, but in the early years the committee tried hard to escape the charging of interest by its bookseller by sending advance credit. A reported debt to Rivington of over £65 in early 1759 increased to over £78 by the end of the year. Although news of the failure of his business is probably not unimportant here, payment was dispatched only in March 1761, some sixteen months after the original invoice (for £123.2s.6d.).[21] In September 1769 when the new bookseller Nicoll was sent funds largely to discharge a debt with Fletcher, Secretary Colcock hastened to explain that this was a most unusual circumstance, this particular debt being entirely a result of "that Gent.s complying so late with the Orders" (letter 22). Four months later, the embarrassing five-year accumulated debt with Wilson was directed to be paid by Nicoll with interest to be paid at the same rate chargeable by himself. This was obviously an agreed charge, although not specified (letter 24). Later that year a further debt to Nicoll was implied (letter 25) and after resumption of trade with the bookseller in 1784 a debt of more than £12 was rapidly established. Payment of the latter appears to have included interest of more than 5 percent, although by its settlement other orders might have been taken into account (letter 34). Bird, Savage, and Bird charged interest at 5 percent per annum and interest was levied in 1795 and 1797. In each case the period of indebtedness was taken into account, the actual charge amounting to 4½ percent of the outstanding debt (letters 67, 79). Also by then, the society seemed to be working to about a six months' lag between a demand made in the annual balance from Bird, Savage, and Bird and its payment (letters 79, 80, 82, 83). In Goldingham's 1810 account the number of days upon which interest was charged (33) was specified, again at an annual rate of 5 percent, the charge here amounting to just under half a percent of the total bill (letter 119). This was unlikely to cause enormous difficulty for the treasurer at any anniversary meeting.

By far the greater problem for the Library Society, obvious in the early years but recurrent in times of international tensions, was the actual making of payment and credit transfer. Like all other customers of London commercial suppliers, the Charleston Library Society faced particular difficulties here. For all parties concerned in the transatlantic book trade a significant transaction cost resulted from the complexities of securing credit and settling bills. Colonial money, both as a medium of exchange and as a standard of value, was represented by three separate tokens of transaction: paper currency (where colonial pounds were discounted against sterling[22]), bills of exchange, and promissory notes. Before the foundation of the Bank of England in 1694 and a protecting act of 1709, specie was a more

TABLE 6 *Monies Sent to London and Debts Recorded by the Charleston Library Society, 1759–1811*

DATE	CREDIT SENT TO LONDON	BOOKSELLER	RECORDED DEBT	BOOKSELLER
1759			£44.13s.1d.	Strahan
			£3.5s.2d.	
Feb. 1759	£100	Rivington		
	(£92.11s.)			
(Nov. 1759 invoice £123.2s.6d. Rivington)				
Dec. 1759			£78.9s.10d.	Rivington
Mar. 1761			£15.2s.10d.	Durham and Wilson
Mar. 1761	£150	Rivington		
		Durham and Wilson		
Oct. 1763	£100	Wilson		
Feb. 1765	£100	Dodsley		
Feb. 1766	£50	Fletcher		
Jul. 1769	£100	Nicoll		
Sept. 1769			£83.10s.8½d.	Fletcher
Jan. 1770	£50			
Jan. 1770[1]			£7.15s.11d.	Wilson
Oct. 1770	£57.10s.	Wilson	debt implied	Wilson
Dec. 1771	£70	Wilson		
Nov. 1773	£100	Wilson		
Feb. 1784			£12.10s.10d.	Wilson
Feb. 1784	£13.13s.4d.	Wilson		
Jan. 1785	£150	Nicoll		
Aug. 1788[2]	£80	Wells		
Nov. 1791	£150	Stockdale		
Jan. 1792	£150	Stockdale		
Jan. 1792	$2,092.93 as deferred stock, exchanged			
Aug. 1792	£324.1s.8d.	Bird, Savage, and Bird		
(Aug. 1792 invoice £435.17s.2d. Stockdale)				
Sept. 1792			unspecified debt	Bird, Savage, and Bird
Mar. 1793	£140	Bird, Savage, and Bird		
Apr. 1793	£100	Bird, Savage, and Bird		
(Dec. 1793 combined invoices minus Stockdale above, £299.1s.)				
Jan. 1794			£178.6s.10d.	Bird, Savage, and Bird
Dec. 1794	£120 but refused			
	and returned, Apr. 1795			
Aug. 1795	£100	Bird, Savage, and Bird		
Mar. 1795	£60	Bird, Savage, and Bird		
(Feb. 1796 invoice £89.18s.4d. Bird, Savage, and Bird)				
Aug. 1796	£150	Bird, Savage, and Bird		
(Oct. 1796 invoice £138.4s.8d. Bird, Savage, and Bird)				
(Oct. 1796 invoice £21.15s.9d. Bird, Savage, and Bird)				
(Oct. 1797 invoice £21.15s.8d. Bird, Savage, and Bird)				
Dec. 1797			£82.17s.2d.	Bird, Savage, and Bird
June 1798	£84	Bird, Savage, and Bird		

Date				
(Sept. 1798 invoice £41.12s.8d. Bird, Savage, and Bird)				
(Mar. 1796 invoice £59.14s. Bird, Savage, and Bird)				
Mar. 1799			£68.14s.5d.	Bird, Savage, and Bird
Oct. 1799	*£70*	Bird, Savage, and Bird		
Dec. 1800			£25.3s.5d.	Bird, Savage, and Bird
Sept. 1801	*£230*	Lackington, Allen	(cashed 3 Jan. 1802)	
Sept. 1801	*£26*	Bird, Savage, and Bird		
(Jan. 1802 invoices £392.3s.1d				
	£208.3s.3d)			
			£21.16s.9d.	Lackington, Allen
June 1802	*£200*	Lackington, Allen	(cashed 6 Sept. 1802)	
Feb. 1803			£170.6s.4d.	Lackington, Allen
Mar. 1803	*£150*	Lackington, Allen		
Apr. 1803	*£170*	Lackington, Allen		
(July 1803 invoice £178.8s.4d.)				
July 1803			£28.14s.8d.	Lackington, Allen
Mar. 1804	*£450*	Lackington, Allen		
(Aug. 1804 invoices £166.15s.10d.				
	£215.7s.1d. Lackington, Allen)[3]			
			(CLS now in credit £5.10s.)	
Dec. 1804	*£200*	Lackington, Allen		
(Apr. 1805 invoice £170.15s.11d. Lackington, Allen)				
			(CLS now in credit £29.19s.10d)	
(July 1805 invoice £18.14s.6d. Lackington, Allen)				
Dec. 1805	*£100*	Lackington, Allen		
(Feb. 1806 invoice £140.10s.11d. Lackington, Allen)				
Jan. 1807	*£100*	Lackington, Allen		
Apr. 1807			£186.13s.	Lackington, Allen
Aug. 1807	monies from underwriters £156.12s.5d.			
			£32.11s.1d.	Lackington, Allen
Nov. 1807	*£220*	Lackington, Allen		
June 1809	£101.18s.4d.	Lackington, Allen		
	cash via Goldingham			
(Aug. 1809 invoice £310.3s.5d. Lackington, Allen)				
(Aug. 1809 invoice £130.13s.3d Goldingham)				
Feb. 1810	*£400*	Goldingham		
		(for Rivington)		
(Jul. 1810 invoice £366.18s.8d. Rivington)				
Jan. 1811	*£110*	Goldingham		
Total	£4,869.14s.4d.			

Notes: Based on the correspondence; and apart from summary in letter 111, not on invoices or full balance sheets, none other of which survive.

£ represents pounds sterling (not colonial currency)

Italics represent gross amount by bill of transfer, prior to transaction cost deductions

1 Discovered then to be due since Jan. 1765.

2 Date of receipt in London; dispatch not recorded.

3 Excluding expenses, freight, insurance, etc.

reliable currency of credit, but the continuously adverse balance of payments in the colonies before about 1720 constantly drew specie back to Europe. Public bills of credit were issued first in Massachusetts in 1690 and then in South Carolina in 1703. By 1715 all colonies save Virginia, Maryland, and Pennsylvania had established a paper currency in the form of bills of credit.[23] Use of cash within the colonies was often impossible and by the late seventeenth century very little was sent by sea. In South Carolina large cash transfers were certainly out of the question. Here, as elsewhere along the Atlantic seaboard, the hunt for money was often serious, with the "dollar"—that is the Spanish or Austrian taler—frequently replacing the sterling pound when scarce.[24] More to the point, transatlantic conveyance of coin entailed high insurance and freight costs and, above all, the risk of complete loss. Agreements to barter or exchange like goods were possible, and general merchants importing books sometimes did so as part of a colonial cargo sale in London. This was relatively rare, however, involving both expensive negotiations with sales agents and acute problems of timing. Moreover, while such arrangements might suit certain planters or rich merchants, colonial importing booksellers and general customers were unlikely to have anything to sell in London to raise monies to secure their book order.

As a result, by far the most common way of securing payment to a distant supplier was by the protracted method of bills of exchange. In many instances it was the only method available. In the letters sent by the Charleston Library Society to its London booksellers anxieties and reassurances expressed about bills of exchange are second only to the details of the orders. Most of these bills were simple checks drawn on deposits kept by English and colonial merchants and agents. As an order to pay the specified amount at a future date, the bill was also effectively a loan involving what might be seen as an interest rate according to the maturity date of the bill. With the widening use of such customized notes and of bills of exchange, the availability of cash in hand increasingly depended on calling upon existing credits and on the anticipation of future resources.[25] In the words of one contemporary Boston authority, bills of exchange, like wives, were necessary evils.[26] The bills, bought in Charleston in Carolina currency, were in sterling value, the colonial rate of exchange fluctuating between 7 to 1 and 8 to 1, although during the second third of the century the terms, or "par," of exchange apparently remained relatively constant at £700 South Carolina to £100 sterling.[27] As many of the Library Society letters testify (and also the committee minutes) purchase of such bills was difficult at certain times. Once acquired, however, the bills offered a certain security of credit and a currency exchange.

Four parties were usually involved: a payer (buyer of the bill), drawer (seller of the bill), drawee, and payee.[28] In the first of the surviving letters from the Charleston Library Society its then correspondent, Robert Brisbane, attempted in

August 1758 to settle with its then bookseller, James Rivington. Brisbane, as payer, bought a bill from W. and J. Brisbane, merchants, drawn on their credit in London. The terms of exchange having been agreed between Robert Brisbane and W. and J. Brisbane, the latter became the drawers. Their bill was drawn on their drawees in London, J. Deneslone and J. Stevenson, who then sent the bill in the agreed sterling amount to the payee, Rivington, asking him to honor it. Any surplus remained in credit to the Library Society. As payee, Rivington agreed to honor the bill after whatever period "of sight" was stated in the bill. This "usuance" was usually set at sixty or ninety days. Rivington was then able either to cash the bill after that date or to endorse it to be passed on to another party to his own credit. Other merchants—and the various banks evolving later in the century—might also accept the note for cash at a discounted rate. Commission charges, which together with the discount, might come to between 5 and 9 percent of the total, were additionally liable, but generally the acceptance of bills of exchange became easier during the century—at least until new difficulties caused by the creation of the Republic. Published manuals, such as Hill's *Young Secretary,* helped establish common practice,[29] and a rough and ready standardization is evident from the surviving day books and ledgers of those engaged in book trades. The invoices, including risk, account of, and errors-excepted formulas, exactly match those of a century later.[30] One other feature of this early example from the Charleston correspondence was commonly repeated. As was essential for the drawer, the firm of W. and J. Brisbane maintained a regular trade with London, but in this matter also, they were related to the payer, Robert Brisbane (on behalf of the Library Society), and at least one of the drawees was also related to another member of the Library Society. In most cases, such connections provided important additional security.

Transaction costs on these bills were high. Of the £100 bill sent to Rivington in 1759, for example, 8.4 percent was lost in exchange and expenses. The period of "sight" also varied considerably—from twenty days on that sent in November 1773 to ninety days on many others, such as those of 1785 and 1791 (letters 30, 36, 50). This period of specified delay before the presentation and honoring of the bill was possible was determined by the circumstances of the enabling drawer (rather than the payer or buyer) of the bill. On at least one occasion the Library Society thought it necessary to apologize for the excessive sight-length (60 days) of the bill sent across (letter 27). Bills of longer sight usually cost less to buy, given that the drawers had effective use of the money for the period. By far the greatest difficulty, however, was in securing a bill at all, even at a high purchase (or "discounting") cost. In September Secretary Remington advised Wilson that the Library Society treasurer had been unable to buy a bill "they now being very Scarce" and warned that payment might be several months away. In fact a bill was secured in October (letter 12). The bill of £50 sent to Nicoll in January 1770 was "all I could procure" according to the then secretary, Colcock (letter 24). In November 1773 Colcock wrote that he had "found means at last to obtain a sett of Bills" (letter 30).

As an effective international currency, the availability (and discounting rates) of bills also varied markedly according to their size. Payment for a modest order of books might therefore be more problematic than for a costlier cargo. In the mid-1730s Thomas Dale, a member of the Library Society by 1750, apologized to his book supplier and correspondent Dr. Birch that "Bills of Exchange are so scarce & high, that people will not sell a small one."[31] In addition, at least in the earlier years, the difficulty in buying bills was also related not only to their poor availability in Charleston but to the inelasticity of Library Society funds. On two occasions, including when sending the relatively small bill to Nicoll in 1770, the correspondent admitted that the society was having to call in loans and interest on bonds to finance its bill purchase (letters 30, 40).

In trying to avoid these problems the society was able to draw upon some very influential and prosperous trading connections. Known and trusted associations were crucial for such operations—the first purchases for the Library Company of Philadelphia in 1732 depended upon a £45 bill of exchange sent to the Philadelphia lawyer Thomas Hopkinson then in London—but Charleston guarantors were somewhat grander. When, in October 1763, Secretary Remington was finally able to send David Wilson the £100 sterling bill of exchange, it was drawn by Gabriel Manigault, still perhaps the richest man in the colony, on Mrs. Sarah Nickleson and Co. for £100 sterling, payable to Wilson "or Order at thirty days sight" (letter 12).

The Nickleson (or Nickelson and sometimes Nicholson) firm headed a powerful and well-connected group of merchants and brokers all located in the commercial heart of London, close by the river wharves and the twin financial pillars of the Bank of England and the Exchange. Sarah Nickleson and Co. was based first in Mansell St., Goodman's Fields, London, and then, until 1768, in Bush Lane, Cannon Street. She was widow and successor to John Nickleson, a Charleston merchant who moved to London in the 1740s. He partnered his wife's brothers, Richard and Thomas Shubrick, involved in the 1740s in slave consignments.[32] Thomas Shubrick remained in Charleston, with Richard in Bucklersbury, London, becoming a London "Carolina merchant" inferior in wealth only to James Crokatt and John Beswicke.[33] Crokatt was also used as a bill guarantor by the Library Society (letter 1), as were major London-Carolina firms such as Thomlinson, Hanbury, Colebrooke, and Nesbitt, leading West India merchants and money contractors for the British forces in North America in 1761 (letter 7); Richard Oswald, wealthy merchant and a future peace commissioner in Paris (letter 14); and Greenwood and Higginson, the largest Carolina merchants on the eve of the Revolution (letter 36). Oswald traded from Philpott Lane, which ran towards the Thames, and Shubrick traded first at Barge Yard, Bucklersbury (from at least the early 1760s), and then from about 1780 at St. Peter's Hill, located near the river and Paul's Wharf, directly south of St. Paul's Cathedral (these and the following locations are all shown in plate 5). Sir George Colebrooke's premises were located in the prime location of New Broad St., a thoroughfare connecting Threadneedle St. with Throgmorton St., close by both the Royal Exchange and the Bank of England. From at least 1780 Hanbury and Gosling traded from Great Tower Street, at premises across the street from the buildings belonging to Hanbury and Lloyd (with, apparently, many warehouses adjacent) and close to one of the busiest wharves on the river. Arnold, Albert, and Alexander Nesbitt traded in Bishopsgate Within from before 1770, at one of the largest properties in the area. The Thomlinson Bucklersbury premises, expanded from midcentury, appear to have been particularly impressive, while the Nickleson firm owned many adjoining properties and warehouses concentrated around Chequer Yard, midway between Dowgate Hill and Bush Lane, close to the Thames wharves immediately west of London bridge.

Crokatt, his son-in-law John Nutt (see plate 5 for location), and the Beswicke-Greenwood-Higginson and Nickleson-Shubrick partnerships, headed the rising merchant class of the Carolinas. The Carolina Walk in the Royal Exchange served as a focal business point and a political rendezvous,[34] but the merchants also met regularly in London in the Carolina Coffee House in Birchin Lane (see plate 5). The Carolina or Caroline Coffee House, had been at 49 Birchin Lane since at least 1749, and was certainly in existence earlier.[35] It became a favored lodging, a resort, for example, of Gabriel Manigault when in London, and also of the many standard-bearers of prominent Charleston families entered in the nearby Inns of Court.[36] Above all, however, the coffeehouse continued as an effective center for trading and financial association when, as in insurance, "practice rather than formal organization remained the most important unifying force."[37] Many of these guarantors for the Charleston Library Society's bills were also shipowners. Both Nickleson and Crokatt are mentioned regularly in the Charleston shipping returns for the mid-1760s.[38] Their ships feature regularly in the correspondence. Sarah Nickleson, with Isaac King, for example, owned the ship *Charles-Town,* captained by John Barnes, when it transported a book consignment for the Library Society in 1762 (letters 10, 11).

After the Revolution various disputes, affecting the liabilities due these London firms, added to the turbulent trading conditions of the 1790s. In particular, in 1791 William Higginson, then surviving partner of Greenwood and Higginson, faced William Greenwood, surviving partner of Leger and Greenwood, in the new American federal courts, suing for a portion of nearly £300,000 claimed to be due to the firm from the citizens of the United States, and, in particular, for claims that interest was payable on debts existing during the war years as well as on those since

1783. After a succession of divided courts, a jury decided for Higginson in October 1793, although disallowing interest liability during the war years and all but the simple interest of five percent on dues outstanding since 1783. The partnership had last been used as a bill broker for the Charleston Library Society in 1785, and the absence of Higginson in the later records of the library might well reflect the resulting tensions of the lawsuits. These even threatened to turn moderates like the Rutledges and the Pinckneys against the British, until the pro-French enthusiasm of local radicals persuaded them to reconsider.[39]

Bills were also occasionally drawn on merchants outside London, such as that drawn on John Forrest of Edinburgh in 1771, presumably because this was the best then available (letter 27).[40] In 1804 Library Society bills drew on the security of Liverpool merchants Thomas and William Earle and Co. (letter 100). They were probably used because of the troubled money markets, but the decision might also reflect new mercantile contacts made by the Library Society. Earle and Co. had acted as the regular brokers of bills of exchange to library president Charles Cotesworth Pinckney for his foreign purchases in the early nineteenth century.[41] The shift in the slave trade from Bristol to Liverpool by the end of the eighteenth century must also have played its part. Bills sent in 1807 were drawn on William Lee (or Lees), a flour dealer of Liverpool, and on Harrison and Latham at Liverpool, payable in London (letters 105, 108). In the final transactions of 1810 Liverpool brokers were used again (letters 117, 118). The Library Society resorted to non-London and indeed non-British drawers in the troubled 1790s, notably Kirk and Lukens in London with Alstorphius and Van Hemert in Amsterdam, 1794–1796 (letters 66, 74), but the same bill-drawing crisis of the period also introduced Bird, Savage, and Bird to the society, the firm offering certain security on the drawing of bills in addition to completing the book orders (letter 44). At times, however, the society found international fissures unbreachable. Dilly declined service specifically because he was reported as "fearful to give Credit to the Society without good Security" (letter 63), and the first bill drawn on Alstorphius and Van Hemert was returned (letter 68).

Changing mechanisms for identifying and buying from bill providers was part of the wider question of the raising and organization of credit. In broad terms, there was again an improvement for overseas customers, with the cost of credit effectively reduced over the century. A general reduction in interest rates lowered the price of colonial imports, and to the extent that credit was used in trade to other areas, it cut the total differential as well. The reduced cost of credit and insurance also affected discounts on bills of exchange. Like the acceptance of bills of exchange, credit management depended on trust. Here, established connections told once more, even though merchants and individuals with capital to spare also publicly advertised as moneylenders. Payment was not an exact science, and very often, when bills of exchange or directions to ensure payment were sent with lists of books, secondary requests were also included in the event, in the words of Samuel Sewall, that "the Money doe more than hold out."[42] This was usually wishful thinking. Bird, Savage, and Bird, for example, thought it politic to settle Stockdale's bill even though existing funds from the Library Society were not sufficient (letter 52).

Further institutional development assisted at some levels, and general merchant firms also intervened to boost credit lines. Merchants like Bird, Savage, and Bird served as professional collectors in London and new and large bookselling firms like Lackington, Allen, and Co. developed an export and clearinghouse expertise. The four-party bill of exchange remained in staple use but with the complication that final receivers, like Bird, Savage, and Bird, were themselves ordering from other booksellers. It has to be noted that, as with the great majority of general, medium-sized merchant firms of the end of the eighteenth century, no London business papers of Bird, Savage, and Bird appear to have survived. Without them, further comparisons of their exact business practices and the credit terms offered are impossible. Nevertheless, such firms claimed to undercut the more old-fashioned types of wholesalers who were described as disenchanted and no longer efficient in the transatlantic trade. As Bird, Savage, and Bird took care to explain to their American customers in 1792: "we beg leave to remark that by the mode of a direct supply from the Bookseller the Book costs much more than if the order had passed thro our hands, Our Commissions as Merchants would have been far short of the difference between the Wholesale and exporting Price at which we should have bought them, and the retail price at which they are now charged" (letter 52). The firm was also acting as joint broker of bills and executor of Library Society orders. In 1791 Charles Goodwin, as a visiting agent for the society in London, explained that because he could not find either Wells or Nichols he was having serious difficulties in refunding Adams for his work in the long-running telescope saga, and had to pay out of his own pocket (letter 48). Bird, Savage, and Bird tried to ensure that such problems did not return, and Lackington, Allen seemed able to offer similar simplifications, with at least two of the society's bills drawn on the merchant John Price, himself a tenant of Lackington, Allen in Finsbury Square (letters 87, 92).

The role of such firms at the end of the eighteenth century should still not be overplayed. The immediate postwar boom proved highly unstable and plagued by failures in confidence. In 1784 the London *Morning Chronicle* advised that "the American markets are so overstocked, that our goods will scarcely be received there; and few of those who do receive them have the ability or honesty to pay for them. This has so hurt the American credit, and damped the spirit of our tradesmen, that although the names of so many ships are up at the different coffee-houses for the ports of North America, scarcely any but the most daring adventurers choose to trust them with a freight."[43] This was highly opinionated and" did not apply consistently to all American destinations, but there could be no doubting the difficulty in sustaining credit relations in the 1780s, as the correspondence of the Library Society, eager to reestablish its London book buying, amply demonstrates.

The financial problems of the 1790s wrought fresh complications in currency exchange and a fall in dollar credit-worthiness. In 1792 even the Charleston Library Society had to reassure Bird, Savage, and Bird, in a letter from its eminent president, Charles Cotesworth Pinckney, of the value of a certificate for 2,093 dollars of deferred stock (letter 45). A sorry correspondence ensued, with more reassurances from the society and a dismissive note from the agents explaining that "American stocks are just now very dull and deferred will not fetch above 7s. a price we are not disposed to take for this parcel" (letter 49). Eventually the stocks were sold but Stockdale, the bookseller for whom the funds were intended, had waited more than eight months for the completion of the transfer (letter 50). Certainly he had been warned that the society expected him to acquiesce in waiting two or three months if Bird, Savage, and Bird thought that delay would ensure a better rate of exchange on the stocks. In fact, quite apart from the fact that Stockdale had been given no option in the matter, the wait had been much longer. It was hardly an incentive for him to speed up on his infamous book-collecting exercises.

Nor did matters improve. In 1795 the Library Society suffered the indignity of receiving back its Dutch draft for £120 "sterling payable in London, which the communication between this Country and the United Provinces being cut off prevents the Acceptors making provision for in this country" (letter 68). What success the society did have in the transfer of funds in these years was indeed testimony to their ingenuity and perseverance. Knox's long-drawn-out attempts to settle with Longman and Wright and Gill were frustrated by similar wartime disruptions. Independence and continuing war in Europe appears only to have made refusals of credit notes more common. Bills of transfer had gained wider acceptance, but formal restitution had improved only slightly. "Protesting" the bill involved engaging a public notary to present the bill formally to the addressee, and then, if it was again refused, for a declaration of evidence to be made in court, with the protest—and consequent costs—returned to the drawer. In colonial South Carolina bills returned as protested were subject to a 15 percent damages penalty together with interest payment due from the date of protest.[44] Attempts to protest bills as well as other legal resorts remained common practice by the end of the century. Notorial charges on the protested bill from the Library Society were not crippling perhaps, and the bill was also successfully sent over again and accepted in London in late 1795 (letters 68, 70, 72), but institutional development had brought with it more incidental and transaction expense.

No bookseller dealing with the Charleston Library Society needed to fear obstinate or deliberate nonpayment; but loss at sea by natural disaster or by the intervention of privateers and financial exchange problems during international hostilities did create major difficulties. An enduring difficulty for the Library Society concerned the cost of protection against loss, even though insurance rates, always markedly fluctuating, generally improved over the period. As a precaution against loss, multiple copies of orders and payment papers were sent and insurance policies were taken out in London on the shipments of books sent over. Double or triple copies of outgoing orders and bills of exchange were the standard resort of colonial customers from at least the early eighteenth century.[45] Primarily a security consideration, firsts, seconds, and thirds of exchange were also sent on different ships to ensure the swiftest possible delivery (given the variable times of passage). Most of the letters reproduced in this volume provide details of copies sent out on different ships, usually with dates and sometimes with additional remarks. Any one, but only one, of the copies of bills of exchange could be used. Copying of the letters reinforced the importance of the master record of the copybook.

For return cargoes, the other precaution available was insurance, although this added, of course, to the costs of freight. During the eighteenth century the effective charge on transatlantic insurance had been lowered by between 10 and 20 percent, with coverage increasing to within 1 or 2 percent of the loss. It became common for ships to be insured at one port and their cargoes at another, while the underwriting itself remained the province of the merchants. Lloyd's List, established in 1734, and Lloyd's Register, founded by a group of merchant-underwriters in 1764–1766, confirmed also the European preeminence of London in marine insurance.[46] From the 1720s, rates on most crossings fell to a peacetime levy of 2 percent. This was a consequence of changes to business organization, economies of scale in inventorying, and later, the development of credit institutions. An apparent decline in piracy also contributed to more attractive terms.[47] With the decline in risks, crew sizes were also reduced, further cutting carriage costs. The Library Society, having already taken out a timely insurance on the entire collection in Charleston in 1773 (letters 29, 31), was nevertheless constantly concerned about the cost. The secretary had indeed complained about the 1½ percent charged on the London-brokered policy on the building (letter 31). From early 1762 the bookseller was instructed not to insure book cargoes of less than £50 in value.

Generally, the Library Society might have expected about a 2 percent insuring cost. The insurance taken out on packages sent by John Murray to his customer Robert Miller in Williamsburg in the 1770s averaged at just over 2 percent on each shipment. In the same decade the insurance bill for the much larger book cargoes sent by Thomas Longman to Henry Knox in Boston, also claimed 2 percent of total charges.[48] Nevertheless, insurance rates remained unpredictable and the outbreak of hostilities brought sudden hikes in charges. During the war years, 1757–1758, the books sent to the New York Society Library by its bookseller John

Ward were covered by an insurance which amounted to 16 percent of the total invoice.[49] During the American war British insurance rose again by 23 percent. For one of the small orders sent in 1772 Murray was forced to charge Miller 4 percent for the insurance, but in mid-1774 Nicoll was only able to insure the order for the Charleston Library Society at 11½ percent, much to the dismay of the committee.[50] Insurance rates were also volatile during the 1790s. The high value consignment from Stockdale in 1792 was insured at about 2 percent of the total charge (letter 52). Bird, Savage, and Bird arranged a similar insurance costing 2 percent to the Library Society in 1796, but a year earlier the charge had been 5 percent, and two years before that library members were warned of the possibility of extortionate premiums owing to "10 large Algerine Xebeques" prowling the Straits of Gibraltar (letter 62). The returns on claimed insurance also varied greatly, but it was rare for the bookseller or customer to recoup all losses. Judging by the complaints of others, Jeremy Condy, bookseller of Salem, was relatively fortunate in 1762 to receive £97.10s from his insurance on £100 of books carried in the *Lucretia,* Captain Green, "who was taken."[51]

On the basis of insurance claims, foreign hostilities were far more threatening than the weather. Between 1760 and 1762 Condy made at least three claims on his insurers, one of nearly £16 for imperfect and unordered books that he was returning to London booksellers but lost when Captain Dashwood was taken by the French (including, he notes, twelve copies of *Tristram Shandy*), another of nearly £100 when his entire order was lost by the capture of Captain Green's *Lucretia,* and another when a large order valued at more than £137 lost when the French captured the *Elizabeth Bradford* and took her to Martinique.[52] Other hazards to be covered included more domestic interference. In his account book in 1764 Condy recorded "ye Loss upon a Case remitted by Gideon Smith who was cast away at Mounts Bay, Cornwall, and who was pleased to plunder the Case he had saved. The Affair was settled by Wright & Gill of London, to whom it was committed by the persons to whom the case was consigned."[53] At the beginning of their service, Bird, Savage, and Bird assured the Library Society that in the event of any loss they would immediately dispatch a replacement order (letter 52). Certainly, as will be seen, the Charleston Library Society's great encounter with London insurers was to be over loss by the action of enemies at sea, but there was also the more humdrum but ever present question of the efficiency of the transport itself, and this certainly entailed issues of both weather and shipping practice.

Chapter Nine

GETTING THE BOOKS ACROSS

CHARLESTON'S EXISTENCE DEPENDED ON THE SEA. Ships were the lifeboats of the whole community, they were the conduits for produce, supplies, and economic survival, and the arrival and departure of the ships were the most visible embodiment of this support system. The entry to port, in particular, was the great event. A successive fleet of great ships, brigantines, and packet ships brought supplies and the season's stock. They brought the craved contact with European civilization as well as the continuing supply of slaves to work the plantations.

The London booksellers, not, after all, far from the wharves themselves, and trading in a city dominated by the Thames, could not have failed to appreciate this dependency on the ship. They must also have understood the symbolism of waterborne ceremonial—the Stationers' Company maintained its own barge on the river—just as most London traders could also be credited with a general familiarity with the more functional rites of seaborne trading. These ancillary skills certainly included the best procedures for packing, the completion of invoices, and of information needed for cockets and bills of lading, and arrangements for the payment of customs duties and other port-side costs—and yet it was in all of these that the merchants Bird, Savage, and Bird boldly suggested they were more expert than most booksellers.

To the Charleston Library Society members, indeed, it did not always seem that London booksellers fully appreciated their reliance on the Atlantic system or their understanding of the way in which their own ships and captains operated. In Carolina the provision of information was increasingly accomplished. Transatlantic passages were charted by print. The readers of Charleston newspapers were fed news of the progress and the last sightings of ships on routes destined for Charleston or for the return to Britain. News of ships clearing out from London or elsewhere provided reassurance for customers certain of the ship used to transport their completed order. This came by forwarded letter or by other ships arriving in port, with their observations often published in the *Gazette* or other later town newspapers. Many ships and sea captains were local,[1] and familiar ships regularly transported the letters, packages, and trunks of the Library Society. These were used less perhaps as favored vehicles, than because they were the most reliable and efficient carriers and ones most obviously tied in to information networks centered on

Carolina merchants, agents, and the colonial coffeehouse in London. Most of the letters sent by the society to its bookseller were written only a day or so before the sailing of the ship that carried them to Britain. Knowledge of when the ship was about to clear out was essential (see plate 11 for a typical *Gazette* advertisement of a ship much used by the Library Society).

This advantage could not always be repeated in London, however, despite the meticulous instructions to the bookseller about likely arrangements for the return of a particular ship. Here, the problems of transit added greatly to the growing tensions of the late-eighteenth-century overseas book trade. Expecting more and more, colonial customers' patience was stretched to breaking point. For many customers, including the Library Society, the optimum arrangement was for direct passage between Charleston and London and for the London order to be collected and dispatched by the return of the outgoing ship. Direct conveyance was the norm, and the letters suggest very few examples of indirect transport. One such, among the earlier correspondence, was the second copy of the appointment letter to Fletcher, apparently sent via Philadelphia (letter 15). Almost all the letters and orders were sent to and from London. An exception was the large order apparently sent to Nicoll in September 1772, put on board a ship bound for Falmouth, and in the 1790s at least one ship carrying a Library Society order and instructions for bill transfers sailed for Liverpool (letter 71). Later, Lackington, Allen was advised that a Charleston-bound ship from Liverpool was acceptable, although the firm's failure to consider that option, given overland transport costs as well as difficulties in obtaining accurate maritime information, should not, perhaps, have come as a surprise. The only attempt to use a Liverpool vessel to send books to Charleston came at the very end of this period, in the 1810 negotiations with the London merchant Nathaniel Goldingham, when indirect transport via New York or Philadelphia was also considered. Even then, the consignments were eventually shipped from London, one under convoy (letters 117, 118).

All London booksellers and agents were certainly instructed to wait for available Charleston-bound vessels. Demands for a "turn-round" passage further illustrated the urgency attending much of the ordering and the perceived isolation of the Library Society. Members pointed out that such orders-out, books-back by the same ship were possible, if not achieved as frequently as they wished. As early as 1700 Sewall sent out his request by a Capt. Mason from Boston and received his books by the same ship. Elsewhere on the Atlantic seaboard there is evidence to suggest that such turnarounds did increase during the century. Ships sending out orders from Henry Knox of Boston in the 1770s seem regularly to have returned with the books and stationery on board.[2]

For most London booksellers, however, such instructions were impossible. As the Stockdale letter to the Library Society insisted, many orders were complex and took weeks to gather, and packing and invoicing were often lengthy. When Murray received Gates's very modest order in April 1791, he took three months to send off the books.[3] It is evident from the correspondence that whereas customers and booksellers ordering from Boston or Charleston usually knew the captain well and also wrote only a day or so before the ship cleared port, many London booksellers were caught out by changes to the ship's timetable. Information on a ship's likely clearing-out date was often far from perfect (and likely to be changed at very short notice by weather or loading conditions). Nevertheless, the Library Society demanded that its London booksellers adhere to this arrangement whenever they could. Secretary-correspondents were often extremely displeased if the books-on-return target was not met. Just as irritating to the society, its committee might also be overwhelmed by the bunched arrival of a backlog of messages from London. As William Mason began a letter to bookseller Fletcher in May 1767 "Your several Letters of the 10th April, 20th May, 1st June, 7th July, 15th Octo[r], & 8th December 1766, I have received" (letter 17).

The emphasis on the turnaround ship was an attempt by the American customer to curb the booksellers' apparent dilatoriness in London, especially given the history of difficulties there for colonial agents and others involved in book purchase and shipment.[4] For similar reasons, as Robert Harlan has observed, colonial book buyers preferred infrequent and large orders to more frequent and smaller ones. Small packages and cases were assumed to be the more likely to disappear.[5] A related consideration was the uncertainty over the type of vessel engaged for the return journey, particularly if the specified Charleston-known ship was not used. Apart from the intervention of privateers or extremes of weather, variation in the lengths of books' transatlantic passage reflected the nature of the main cargo. Although large orders were heavy, valuable, and often cumbersome, books never commanded urgency on account of the volume transported. Books were not of high priority to ships' masters who might prefer to load up with other goods. As a result, books might be shipped in very different types of trading vessel. According to their freight, ships followed different routes, with different stop-off destinations, ranging from those on the Caribbean sugar route to those carrying tobacco from the Chesapeake. Most cargoes that included books were general, however, and usually contained a wide variety of merchandise. John Mein's 1770 import record lists the London cargo on the schooner *Yarmouth* which entered the port of Boston 1 March 1770. One box of "printed books" was typically packed alongside vast quantities of haberdashery, linen and cloths, fishing lines, iron, and wine. At Charleston, since at least the 1730s, dozens of importers like Peter Horry and Andrew Cowan, had brought in books, prints, and stationery included in general and varied supplies, which very soon after entering port were advertised in long newspaper lists like some cornucopia of domestic goods.[6]

The reality of the transatlantic passage was therefore often far from the ideal espoused by the Library Society. Even news of shipments might be slow and uncertain. Confirmation, for example, of the arrival in England of two ships carrying book orders and payments, both leaving in July 1760, did not reach Charleston until December of that year (letter 6). In January 1765 the Library Society had not heard, even apparently by the London newspapers, that its new choice of bookseller had in fact been dead for four months. Nor was advance news of the continuing progress of a transatlantic vessel always so advanced, even if it did alert customers to an imminent arrival. News that the ship *Two Friends,* carrying the society's latest order, had passed Deal on 14 April reached Charleston on 6 June 1807, but the ship itself arrived in Charleston only four days later.[7] The view from England was little better. In December 1773 Murray had still not heard whether the books he sent Miller on 1 July had safely arrived.[8] Nevertheless, when things did go well there was much to boast about, particularly if a service from and to Charleston seemed superior to that of another North American port. A Charleston newspaper proudly proclaimed the arrival of the ship *Cleopatra* in September 1803 after a sixty-day passage from London: "Our files of papers sent by the Cleopatra, are to 21st July, not so late by one day as those received at New York."[9] The Library Society, whose latest order of books was also carried by the ship, was also delighted (letters 94, 95). Only seventy-eight days had passed between the date of the invoice upon the dispatch of the books from Lackington, Allen's store and the arrival of the books in Charleston. The total length of time between dispatch of the order for the books and their arrival back at the port was 201 days (or some six-and-a-half months).

Such a time, however, was most unusual. The successful completion of an order from start to finish in just over six months was in fact a record among all the known journeys. Table 7 compares shipment times, from the dispatch of an order to the return of the books to the Library Society, for all those consignments where the dates of the complete passage—or significant parts of it—can be identified. The length of each transaction is reconstructed by using a combination of the Library Society letters, committee minutes, and newspaper maritime reports. Together, in whole or part, they locate the order date, shipping details, dates of loading and sailing, invoice dates, return passages, and the arrival of the books in the library. In all, twenty-eight passages can be reconstructed from piecing together a range of evidence. Greater completeness proved impossible. Newspaper runs (with almost no surviving official port records) often prevent identification of a ship's departure or arrival at Charleston. No full log of a Bird, Savage, and Bird order and shipment could be reconstructed, for example, although a projection from the three incomplete parts given in the table does suggest that the firm was indeed among the most efficient of those employed.[10] The orders to David Wilson in 1761–1762 were lost at sea and although it seems fair to include such losses within the total time calculated from dispatch of original order to the eventual arrival of the books, the exact dates for the receipt of orders by Wilson cannot be reconstructed (for suggestions see note 1 to table 7). Similarly, the 1792–1793 arrival in Charleston of Stockdale's infamous cargo on board the *Julius Pringle* is one of several key events that cannot be dated because no newspapers survive for the months concerned.

More broadly, other cautions need emphasis, even though the dates on letters, the notes about the ships used and the dates sent, and the shipping intelligence carefully recorded in the Charleston newspapers all seem to offer great precision. A few letter dates (noted in table 7) seem slightly in error, and in at least two instances the date given in the newspaper for the arrival of a ship in Charleston does not accord with the very few surviving official records of the port authorities (PRO, CO 5 series). Variation, however, is a matter of days only and nowhere exceeds a difference of more than a week. Another weakness is that although frequent mention in the letters of the transporting ship allows identification of the date of its arrival in port, only in rare cases do letters provide the date at which the books and magazines arrived at the library. This particular time lag (whatever it was) seems a minor point, but not—as will be discussed below—to the Library Society.

Even with these qualifications, table 7 offers a material survey of the times taken to cross the Atlantic and to complete the orders of the Charleston Library Society. The length of time between the sending out of the order and the receipt of the books ranged dramatically, and sometimes the wait was extreme. From the twenty-eight passages that can be reconstructed from beginning to end, the average length of wait during this period was 370 days or just over a year between writing the request and shelving the book. This, however, offers only the most general guide, when four orders took more than two years to arrive, and another two took more than eighteenth months. There is some evidence of improvement over the period, with the average time for the completion of the ten orders after 1800 standing at 345 days, or an impressive 241 days (or eight months) if the one catastrophic captured shipment in that period is excluded. Against this, the much hoped for swift passages appear to have been in decline. Of the three full passages completed in under 200 days, four were made before 1784 and only one after 1800. Charleston was by far the busiest mainland American transatlantic port after 1740, but it seems that the range of variability increased over the period, with both the shortest and the longest times of delivery recorded after 1800. What the table underlines is that even the shortest waiting period for the delivery of books remained at something like a full year—a period during which many members might themselves have made a crossing to London, and a period sufficient both to dull the enthusiasm for fashionable publications and to explain the vigorous language of complaint in the letters to the booksellers.

TABLE 7 *Charleston Library Society Book Orders and Shipments: Identifiable Transatlantic Passages, 1758–1810*

CLS ORDER DATE	DATE OF SAILING	BOOKSELLER	LONDON INVOICE DATE	DAYS SINCE ORDER	VALUE/SIZE	CHARLESTON ARRIVAL DATE	DAYS RETURN SEA PASSAGE	DAYS RETURN SINCE INVOICE	DAYS (TOTAL)
10 Aug. 1758	24 Aug. 1758	Rivington	30 Jan. 1757		reviews books/pamphlets £123.2s.6d.	early Nov. 59		–	c.450
24 Feb. 1759		Rivington	2 July 1757						
14 Aug. 1761	5 Sept. 1761	Wilson	–		c.£150	c.27 Feb. 1762		86	197
(27 Feb.1762 Wilson[1])			Dec. 1761			13 July 1762(p)		74	333
			30 Apr.1762	259		14/16 Aug. 1762(p)		80	367
			26 May 1762						
12 Oct. 1762	12 Oct.[1] or before	Wilson	17 Mar. 1763	158	£2.13s. £100	28 May 1763(p)		72	228
12 Feb. 1765	c.23 Mar. 1765 loading 2 Mar. 1765	Dodsley	–			15 Aug. 1763(p) "received answer" with books (?)			
5 Feb.1766	–	Fletcher	3 May 1766	90	£70	5 Feb. 1766			358
27 May 1767	3 June 1767 [2]	Fletcher				11 Oct. 1767		526	613
"	"	"			globes & scientific instruments	c.5 July 1769 part of consignment only; remainder arrives as below 16 Aug. 1769			c.769
					includes part remaining Fletcher	7 Mar. 1769(p) arrive CLS 9 Mar. 1769			620
9 Mar. 1769	–	Nicoll	9 June 1769	92		16 Aug. 1769(p)		78	170
24 July 1769	28 July 1769 regular order	Nicoll	21 Aug. 1769	165	pamphlets 3s.6d.	19 Dec. 1769(p?)		120	285
		Nicoll	8 Nov. 1769	107		before 25 Jan. 1770		78?	185?
			25 Sept. 1769			12 Dec. 1769(p)		94	
20 Oct. 1770	25 Oct. 1770	Nicoll	–	158	£57.10s. books & mirror	12 Sept. 1771(p)			327
6. Dec. 1771	–	Nicoll	4 June 1772			c. Sept. 1772(CLS)			c.290
3 July 1783	15 Aug. 1783	Nicoll	23 Oct. 1783	112	pamphlets & magazines £1.2s.6d.	30 Dec. 1783(p)		68	180

CLS ORDER DATE	DATE OF SAILING	BOOKSELLER	LONDON INVOICE DATE	DAYS SINCE ORDER	VALUE/SIZE	CHARLESTON ARRIVAL DATE	DAYS RETURN SEA PASSAGE	DAYS RETURN SINCE INVOICE	DAYS (TOTAL)
17 Feb. 1784	19 Feb. 1784	Nicoll	24 Aug. 1784	188	pamphlets	7 Dec. 1784(p)		105	293
1 May 1784	–	Nicoll	18 Sept. 1784	140	trunk & case	7 Dec. 1784(p)		80	220
2 Nov. 1791	21 Nov. 1791	Stockdale	14 Sept. 1792	316	£443.2s.7d.	c. late 1792			
17 Apr. 1793	–	BSB	7 Sept. 1793	143	books & instruments £121.10s.10d.	(?) late Dec. 1793			
17 Apr. 1793			13 Nov. 1793 (letter received 8 July 1793)	208	£126.7s.9d.				
1 Nov. 1794	5 Nov. 1794	BSB	8 Apr. 1795	188	£89.9s.1d.	(not sent by 25 Dec. 1795)			
25 Aug. 1795	–	BSB	19 Feb. 1796	188	£89.18s.4d.				
–	–	BSB	8 Dec. 1796	–	£21.15s.9d.	8 Feb. 1797(p)		62	–
7 Sept. 1801		LACo	9 Feb. 1802	155	£203.11s.11d.	8 Apr. 1802(p)		60	215
12 June 1802		LACo	20 Nov. 1802	161	£392.3s.1d. 4 trunks	29 Apr. 1803(p)		160 via New York	321
4 Mar. 1803		LACo	5 July 1803	124	–	21 Sept. 1803(p)		78	202
6 Mar. 1804		LACo	18 July 1804	134	£382.2s.11d.	17 Oct. 1804(p)		91	225
10 Dec. 1804		LACo	2 Apr. 1805	113	£170.15s.11d.	13 Oct. 1807(p)		888 pirate capture	1035
10 Dec. 1804		LACo	6 July 1805	207		21 Sept. 1805(p)	50(Dns.?)	77	284
24 Dec. 1805		LACo	20 June 1806	178 [3]	£235.4s.	1 Sept. 1806(p)	51	73	251
12 Jan. 1807	19 Jan. 1807	LACo	20 Apr. 1807	98	£281.8s.6d.	10 June 1807(p)	45(Dns.)	51	150 [4]
14 Nov. 1807		LACo	15 Aug. 1809	636		17 Nov. 1809	sent under convoy	97	733
3 Feb. 1810		LACo	16 July 1810	163 (33 days, between invoice and London sailing)	£329.3s.5d.	27 Oct. 1810+	70	103	266

1. Possible error in the copybook here or a postdated letter.
2. Second copy of order as sent.
3. Included newspapers to 5 July 1806.
4. Example of a "turn-round" passage, using the same ship outbound and inbound.

Key
BSB — Bird, Savage, and Bird
CLS — arrival of shipment at the Library
Dns. — at the Downs, in the English Channel
LACo — Lackington, Allen, and Co.
p — arrival of ship at port
Rivington — James Rivington

The quickest execution of an order, that sent out to Lackington, Allen in January 1807 with books received at the library door only 150 days (or five months) later, is remarkable in several respects. The fast return passage was compounded by what appears to have been both the invoicing of the books on the very day of the ship's clearing out from port in London, and by the arrival of the books in the library room on the very day that the ship entered at Charleston. Indeed, the paperwork and letters appear to reduce by a further day the proud boast in the local newspaper that the ship had returned after a 52-day passage. Even more clearly, it justifies the point constantly made by the Library Society about the ideal of the turnaround. The same ship, the *Two Friends,* under Captain Livingston, conveyed both order and books. Lackington, Allen managed to collect, pack, and send the required books to port some 98 days after the ship left Charleston. This is the shortest of the recorded completions of large book orders taken to that stage of the overall process. Although, as in every case given in table 7, we do not know when the outgoing ship entered at London and therefore do not know what sort of collecting period the booksellers had at their disposal, even a (generously estimated) 68-day outward passage allowed four weeks for the booksellers to process the order. This might not appear unreasonable and perhaps offers a critical gauge by which to compare some of the more extravagant time spans between the dispatch of an order from Charleston and the invoicing of the books from London. It also highlights Fletcher's achievement of 90 days for the first order he received from the Library Society in 1766 and that of 92 days achieved by Nicoll in the first half of 1769. Neither bookseller, incidentally, ever repeated such a quick book-collecting and invoicing completion time in subsequent dealings with the Library Society, and Nicoll's swift initial response was almost certainly because he was taking over much of the work already completed by Fletcher.

Among the shorter passages were those for the regular orders of pamphlets and periodicals, even though, as seen, the Library Society constantly complained that they were not sent with sufficient regularity. Because no order was needed to trigger these shipments (with the Library Society topping up its credit with occasional £100 sterling bills of exchange), most do not figure in table 7. One is given to gauge the length of transit from invoicing to delivery. The pamphlets sent by Nicoll in September 1769 took 94 days to reach Charleston, a slightly greater than average time for these orders. Some of the smaller parcels sent over by direct request, however, arrived remarkably swiftly. In 1783 it took just 180 days for an order worth just over £1 to be requested, bought, and received back in Charleston. Six months was still a frustrating wait for a topical publication, but this is one of the faster of the recorded conveyances.

Table 7 suggests that many letters with orders were written close to the date of a sailing, although there are also intriguing instances of severe delay between the completion of the letters and the clearing out of the ship. The ill-fated ship bearing the order for Wilson in August in 1761 did not leave for three weeks, with an equally ill-fated copy not leaving for a further five weeks after that. It was five weeks before the order written for Nicoll in July 1783 left harbor. The order sent to Stockdale was written (and presumably placed on board) on 2 November 1791, but the ship did not finally clear until 21 November. Once loaded and cleared out, a ship's passage to Britain met further obstacles in the shallows of the bar off the coast. Here, newspapers recorded many wind-bound delays offshore, including that carrying the order written to Dodsley on 12 February 1765. In addition to the continued loading of the ship, not completed until at least 2 March, the ship did not cross the bar until about 23 March. Countering this, successive recorded dates on the return leg can point to opportunities to shorten the communication time from port to port. Further confirmation is offered of overland dispatch of letters and small parcels to join a ship already cleared from London. The Charleston newspapers reported that the *Two Friends,* responsible for the Library Society's record run from order to completion in 1807, had "passed Deal 14th April."[11] Yet the invoice is dated 20 April and was therefore almost certainly in the bag of mail passed to the ship by small boat after the ship had passed the Channel. Similarly, the ship carrying the Lackington, Allen shipment to the library, invoiced 20 June 1806, also carried newspapers with dates up to 5 July.[12]

For comparison, table 8 records a range of book order and consignment passages from and to other colonial ports before the revolution. Delivery times for the Longman-Knox shipments to Boston appear more predictable than those from and to Charleston, ranging from 132 to 176 days (excluding the final shipment delayed because of the port difficulties of 1774). The average completion time for these Longman-Knox transactions is 155 days or just over 22 weeks from the dispatch of the order to the receipt of the books. This compares to the shortest listed Charleston completion of 21 weeks, and an average completion there (from a much greater range of times) of just under 53 weeks. Of 14 shipments to Carey in Philadelphia from Byrne in Dublin, 1793–1795, the average time of travel was about two months, with some shipments arriving in New York if they could not be sent directly to Philadelphia.[13] The average passage of news-bearing ships from London to New York, 1711–1739, has been calculated as 9.2 weeks, and that of similar ships to Philadelphia as 9.8 weeks.[14] The average of the four return journeys with books for Miller in Williamsburg as given in table 8 is 11.3 weeks. Return passages could, allegedly, be as short as 32 days, although the shortest recorded in table 8 are 51 days (Charleston) and 52 days (Boston). Against this a 65-day return to Charleston seems to have been the expected norm. The ship *Montezuma,* for example, sailed from Gravesend 8 March 1802, and arrived at Charleston after 64 days.[15] Nevertheless, it is obvious that different routes were followed by different general

TABLE 8 *Comparative Passages of Transatlantic Book Orders and Shipments, 1728–1774*

ORDER DATE	CUSTOMER	BOOKSELLER	PORT	INVOICE DATE	VALUE/SIZE	ARRIVAL DATE	DAYS (RETURN PASSAGE)	DAYS (TOTAL)	MISC.
1728 Oct. 7	James Logan, Philadelphia	Wm. Reading (agent), London	London	1729 Jan. 5	10 titles	1729 May 12	127	217	
1753 Dec. 8	David Hall, Philadelphia	Adrian Watkins, Edinburgh	Glasgow	1754 Sept. 2	3,275 books	1754 Dec. 18 (circa)	107	375	maximum arrival time to Philadelphia
1771 Nov. 21	Henry Knox, Boston	Thomas Longman, London	London	1772 Feb. 10	£678.12s.11d.	1772 Apr. 9	58	139	
1772 July 10	Henry Knox, Boston	Thomas Longman, London	London	1772 Sept. 16	£87.5s.3d.	1772 Nov. 19	68	132	
1771 Dec. 10	Henry Knox, Boston	Thomas Longman, London	London	1772 Mar. 6	£11.2s.8d.	1772 May 14	69	155	
1771 Jan. 20	Henry Knox, Boston	Thomas Longman, London	London	1772 Apr. 10	£157.8s.5d.	1772 June 11	52	142	
1772 May 9	Henry Knox, Boston	Thomas Longman, London	London	1772 Jul. 18	£249.3s.8d.	1772 Sept. 24	68	138	
1772 Nov. 2	Henry Knox, Boston	Thomas Longman, London	London	1773 Feb. 15	£318.16s.6d.	1773 Apr. 16	60	165	
1773 Feb. 24	Henry Knox, Boston	Thomas Longman, London	London	1773 May 19	£142.15s. 4 trunks	1773 Aug. 19	92	176	
1773 May 5	Henry Knox, Boston	Thomas Longman, London	London	1773 Aug. 10	£114.16 2 trunks; 1 case	1773 Oct. 28	79	176	
1773 Nov. 18	Henry Knox, Boston	Thomas Longman, London	London	1774 Mar. 10	£678.12s.11d. 8 trunks (incl. later orders)	1774 May 11	62	174	
1774 Mar. 30	Henry Knox, Boston	Thomas Longman, London	London	1774 July 29	£238.8s	1774 Oct. 13	76+	197+	additional time for shipment to Boston

ORDER DATE	CUSTOMER	BOOKSELLER	PORT	INVOICE DATE	VALUE/SIZE	ARRIVAL DATE	DAYS (RETURN PASSAGE)	DAYS (TOTAL)	MISC.
1773?	Robert Miller, merchant, Williamsburg	John Murray, London	London	1773 July 1	£2.3s.3d.	1773 Sept. 28	90		
1773?	Robert Miller, merchant, Williamsburg	John Murray, London	London	1773 May 24	£1.9s.	1773 Jul. 22	61		
1773?	Robert Miller, merchant, Williamsburg	John Murray, London	London	1773 Nov. 27	£56.12s.6d.	1774 Feb. 24	89		
1774?	Robert Miller, merchant, Williamsburg	John Murray, London	London	1774 July 7	£11.15s.	1774 Sept. 22	77		
1754 May 29	New York Society Library	John Ward, London	London			1754 Oct. 14		138	
1757 June 3	New York Society Library	John Ward, London	London	1757 Sept. 27	£70	1758 Mar. 27	181	297	
1761?	New York Society Library	William Johnston, London	London	1761 Apr. 13	£100.7s. (57 items)	1761 Aug. 27	136		
1762 Mar. 9	New York Society Library	John Ward, London	London	1763 Dec. 14	£39.12s.	1764 Sept. 3 1764 Sept. 20	264 281	560	
1760 Aug. 1	Salem Social Library	J. Richardson via J. Condy (agent), London	London	1760 Dec. 19	£172.7s.7d. (300 books)	1761 Mar. 13 1761 May 20	84 152	225 293	1st date Boston; 2d, Salem
1765?	William Stevenson, for John Robertson	?	Leith	1765 June 7	£75 valued (10 cwt); 6 trunks, 1 chest	1765 Aug. 29	83		

cargoes, with seasonal variation in addition. The combination of these factors makes analysis difficult. The cargoes for Miller, for example, could take half as long again to arrive despite being sent at about the same time of the year. Only three complete out-and-return passages can be reconstructed from the records of the New York Society Library and newspaper listings, but the average of the marked range (138 days in 1754; 560 days in 1763–1764) is 337 or 47.4 weeks. If this average is representative, then the New York library was far better served than its Charleston equivalent, and certainly, the order and delivery of 1754 was nearly two weeks faster than any such shipment for Charleston.

As the records used to compile these tables also make clear, the total length of delivery time included more than days at sea. Obviously, collecting and packing times in London varied greatly according to the nature of the order and the book-sellers employed, but a further concern was the speed with which a ship was loaded or unloaded. Because books were hardly the priority goods for any shipping merchant or ship's master, loading and unloading times (and the positioning of the trunks of books in the hold) were unpredictable. In some instances, consignments were unloaded and distributed with extraordinary speed. One example of the same-day delivery of books for the Charleston Library Society has already been mentioned, but among other examples, the September 1784 magazines sent by Nicoll arrived in port on 21 January 1785 and were with the library three days later (letter 36). More usually, however, unloading and collection by customers was slower. The New York Society Library (kept in rooms within sight of the harbor) received its latest order of books on 12 September 1764 from a ship, HMS *Cornelia,* that had docked at least nine days earlier.[16] In 1803 the *Cleopatra* entered Charleston port on 21 September, but confirmation of the books' arrival in the next letter (written in January) refers to their delivery in October so it must be assumed that unloading of the books took at least a week (letter 95).

Official procedure at both the clearing and the entry port was laborious and bureaucratic. To gain permission to unload, all ships' masters had first to submit their papers to the custom house for examination by both the collector of customs and the naval officer in charge. Chief among these papers were the ship's cockets, certifying that goods had been duly entered and duties paid and sealed by officials at the last port of call. The number, type, and sometimes volume and weight of cargo were then recorded, as well as the ship's registry and details of ownership. A tide waiter and surveyor searched the ship and listed all cargo on board, and then a land waiter recorded all items as they left the ship. The full entering process took about three days.[17] For loading new cargo and for permission to leave, the whole procedure was repeated in reverse. The length of time spent in port while a ship reloaded had implications for the time that books might be stored aboard before the ship was deemed, from a commercial viewpoint, full enough to sail. Some ships followed prearranged schedules, with full cargoes awaiting them (and additional goods such as trunks of books taken on if there was room). Others, however, advertised as being ready to carry general goods and then waited to load for a particular destination (which could sometimes also be open to negotiation). Masters of ships had to balance the commercial need to load vessels as fully as possible against the costs and wages payable for time spent crewed but not sailing. Some vessels and particularly those in colonial ownership aimed therefore at fast turnaround times.

An essential issue, therefore, concerned the quality of the shipping information available to London booksellers and agents. This appears to have caught out the less prepared London booksellers. As table 7 shows, Lackington, Allen ranged very greatly in the time taken to complete an order (even though we do not know the variation in the length of passage of each outgoing ship to London), and the firm was eventually to lose the contract to supply the Charleston Library Society because of the booksellers' failure to identify quickly departing ships. Sudden rerouting was another problem. It seems to have been very difficult for booksellers to ascertain shipping information, the veiled explanation offered by Lackington, Allen. In 1792 Murray excused himself to Dr. Gates: "Capt. Hale it now appears sails for Philadelphia and not for Charlestown, but never mentioned to me this alteration of his plan—on the contrary kept me in suspense till the last moment."[18] Such mishaps pointed again to the importance of good information and good contacts to ease the swift transmission of orders. In the colonies the marketing and shipping of goods were often undertaken by one merchant, and one who often owned his own vessel. While familiarity between colonial customer or bookseller and the local ship's captain (like William Coombes in the 1760s) assisted the speedy and safe dispatch of orders and bills of exchange, insistence on London booksellers' using the same or other colonial ships by return often proved a handicap.

Despite these difficulties, a general improvement in ships' turnarounds is reported over the century.[19] Particularly striking was the development of greater coordination of information about ships leaving and the more exact collection arrangements, both managed through interested traders and through the colonial coffeehouses in London. Sympathetic London booksellers, notably the Dillys and later Almon and Stockdale, offered their shops as mailing addresses for itinerant Americans in London.[20] More generally, the Pennsylvania Coffee House, the Virginia Coffee House, and the Carolina Coffee House were essential clearinghouses for news and contact points for captains of ships, booksellers, customers' agents, and even colonial customers when in London. The first instructions sent by the Library Society to Lackington, Allen reinforced the importance of using the Carolina Coffee House in Birchin Lane (letter 84). Many other Charleston book customers were served at some point by the Carolina Coffee House, while Murray had left his boxes for Miller at the Virginia Coffee House.[21] Merchants' houses offered similar services. From the 1790s Charleston orders and remittances sent to London were often left in the "bag at Mr Tunnos," the Loyalist Carolina merchant of Old Jewry who also acted as financial intermediary for bill transfers (letters 45, 70, 72, 80, and others). Later, Tunno and Loughnan of New Court, Swithins Lane, London, were regularly used by the Library Society as brokers for Lackington, Allen; the mail collection was almost certainly continued.

One particular instruction by the Library Society also explains the more efficient delivery of magazines, periodicals, and smaller publications in later years. From the earliest surviving letters secretaries complained of bundles left idling in Charleston because of poor paperwork. Rivington had been admonished by the report that pamphlets, magazines, and reviews have "generally put up in Packages to Other Houses here which have lain sometime unopened & by this means the Societys Intention of having them as early as possible has been utterly defeated" (letter 5). The solution was not only better labeling but the insistence that small parcels be carried in the captain's cabin rather than in the hold. The eagerly anticipated (and so often delayed) periodicals must be last on, first off. The order was a crucial part of the general instructions as conveyed to Wilson and Durham in 1760, repeated to Dodsley in 1764 and Nicoll in 1769 (letters 6, 13, 21), but strangely omitted from the commands to Dilly in 1786 (letter 38): "You will please likewise remember to give a particular Charge to the Master of the Vessell you Ship by to put the Society's Packages in the Cabbin, or in some place where they may be had immediately on the Arrival of the Vessell, as very often they are put in the hold & the Magazines &c are old before they come to hand."

Alarm was even expressed that an incoming ship might leave port or return to London with a package, letter, or invoice still on board. The letters sent by Thomas Dale to Dr. Birch include a remarkable report about a near miss with his own books sent from London. Notice of the box sent by Birch, together with a letter, was only given to Dale (by means that are not clear) two days before the ship left Charleston again. He rescued the books from the hold, but the captain denied all knowledge of an accompanying letter. The ship then departed "but the Wind being contrary, was obliged to anchor in Rebellion Road. . . . Our Post-master was out in his Boat, and happening to call on Board, the Capt. told him he had found a letter for me in one of his men's chests, a likely Story!"[22] Such reports reemphasized to library members the importance of good relations with the captain of a ship.

The one other concern of the society, and one shared by almost every American receiver of books, was the arrangements for packing. The letters from Charleston— just like the invoices of Longman and the correspondence between Hall and Strahan—noted anxieties about proper matting and crating. As cargoes increased during the eighteenth century, packing arrangements do seem to have improved, even though exact details are now difficult to recover. Procedures were clearly various, but the importance of the issue should not be underestimated. It was an old and vexed question. Complaints about damaged books, poor packing, or incorrect labeling pepper early accounts of transatlantic book traffic, including the Boston arrival in 1675 of hundreds of ruined Dutch Bibles pulverized by an unexpected detour via Barbados.[23] In response to such horrors, customers penned instructions and assurances about best practice. In 1729 William Byrd II sent instructions from Virginia to a Mr. Spencer in London to have his books sent over and be packed in bookcases with the shelves taken out "as you woud pack them in a chest, remembering to put brown paper next to the wood and between every book, otherwise the binding will bruise and fret to pieces . . . [and] fill up with shaveings, to keep the books tight."[24] For the Charleston Library Society consignments, safe packing in trunks, and for the smaller packages, the safety of the Captain's cabin, were regularly recommended by the secretary-correspondent. Stockdale put great emphasis upon the "utmost care" with which he had carried out the packing (letter 53), and David Ramsay reassured Bird, Savage and Bird of the "good condition" in which books had arrived (letter 77). Even in instructions to their last recorded London agent, Goldingham, in 1810, the Library Society ordered that he should be certain not to load the books on a ship "either wholly loaded with salt or having any quantity on board, as in that case I am told the books will run the risk of being materially injured" (letter 117).

There was of course, however, a more constant, final anxiety. Whatever the precautions and whatever the complaints about long delays caused by lengthy port processes, contrary winds, or adverse conditions in the hold, the ultimate disaster was always a threat on the transatlantic crossing. In this context the Library Society seems to have been fortunate, with few losses of letters and bills, and almost no losses of actual consignments from London. The cargoes of many other American customers were completely lost as a result either of enemy action or of severe storms (sometimes aided by the ailing condition of old or unsteady ships). Little could be done about the weather although the striking seasonality of imports reflects caution as well as practicality. Among bibliophiles, Governor Winthrop had been an early loser, learning in 1637 that "the Boxe of Boocks . . . with the passengers mooche Stuffe and goods, are all perished by the waye."[25] A century later we are offered the enduring image of a wet solitary page of Matthew Poole's magnificent four-volume folio *Synopsis criticorum* presented to James Logan in Pennsylvania. It was the only remnant salvaged from his order of London books that had crossed the winter Atlantic but then went down with the ship in Philadelphia harbor.[26] In Charleston Alexander Garden lost a large and important consignment of botanical specimens he was sending to London in 1757 when Samuel Ball's ship *Friendship* was captured by the French. Garden was also involved in correspondence resulting from a more sensitive loss to the literary community when a copy of an essay by

Cadwallader Colden sent to London for printing was also seized and apparently destroyed by the enemy.[27]

Although bad weather was a permanent threat, there were also few times when the seas were free of hostile ships. From the Dutch wars of 1666–1667 and 1672–1678 to the War of 1812, warfare repeatedly intervened in the rhythm of transatlantic book trade. In fact, disruption was caused far less by formal military engagement (although convoys did sometimes pass through hostile waters) than by the activities of privateers. Under letters of marque governments granted captors' rights to private citizens in time of war, but letters were often also issued for individual redress in peacetime.[28] French privateers were a particular threat off the Carolinas, but nowhere was entirely safe from them. During the War of Independence and again 1812–1815, American privateers also harried British shipping. Privateers often went beyond their commissions, with little accountability to home governments. In consequence, ships were usually armed. In the few surviving official shipping records of the period, the number of guns are recorded alongside crew size, tonnage, and other shipping details. Many American newspaper advertisements for ships ready to take cargoes to Britain also boasted of the weaponry aboard. Almost all the ships carrying orders to London and books back to Charleston were armed, and heavily so in times of war. Typically, in 1759 the ship *Elizabeth* was advertised in Charleston as sailing for Bristol "mounting 16 carriage guns, with men answerable."[29]

In times of serious conflict and offshore marauding, colonial shipping sought the protection of convoys under naval command. The earliest surviving Charleston Library Society letters were written during the Seven Years War (1756–1763), and naval vessels, often at the head of large transatlantic convoys of merchant marine, were favorite vehicles for the dispatch of book orders, payment, or return cargoes. As usual, it helped if there was friendship or kinship between trader, merchant, ship's master, or even convoy leader. In the summer of 1758 the society entrusted their orders for Rivington to Penhallow Cummings, RN, commander of the 60-vessel convoy then setting out across the Atlantic (letter 5). The Library Society's action was not exceptional, of course. When Jeremy Condy eventually sent off the order of books for the new Salem Social Library in November 1760, he shipped the first parcel aboard an eight-gun frigate, the majority on a ten-gun snow, and a letter to inform his customers of this on another ten-gun ship.[30] In July 1762 Condy also used a ship of the Royal Navy to import his London books.[31]

The threat of interception was a very real one, and Charleston was more exposed than Boston. Henry Laurens, who had just lost a brig to privateers, wrote that "the Islands Swarm with their Privateers," and the local newspaper had declared that the arrival of royal naval ships "affords us great Consolation."[32] In April 1760, HMS *Blandford,* which headed the 60-ship convoy out of Charleston in August 1758, was certainly involved in serious military action.[33] Despite this, Charleston found itself again exposed in late 1760 with four ships reported as taken by privateers within a month.[34] William Coombes, a Charleston sea captain used to convey Library Society letters, was himself captured in late 1760 and taken to Port-au-Prince.[35] In March 1761 a naval man-of-war escorted seventeen Charleston ships across the Atlantic, but as a "Petition of Several Merchants of Charlestown" of May 1761 reported, only two of them actually reached Britain. Among the shipments that got through were a consignment from Alexander Garden for Linnaeus containing tortoises, lizards, an alligator, and fourteen varieties of snake.[36] Another petition of the next month protested: "Your Petitioners being greatly interested in the protection and safe Arrival of the said Fleet, their Cargoes being very Valuable, are humbly to represent the insufficiency of the said Convoy for so great a number of Vessells, at a time when the British Channel swarms with French Privateers."[37]

As a result of the petition, further ships of the Royal Navy were sent, and one, HMS *Success,* conveyed one of the copies of the Charleston library's remittance to bookseller Wilson in 1763 (letter 12). In fact, however, copies of remittances to Wilson in 1761 had been carried on the 24-gun HMS *Dolphin,* one of the ships surviving the earlier, disastrous convoy (letter 7).[38] In the following communication in August 1761 a somewhat nervous library secretary referred to the *Dolphin* "which we hope has arrived safe" (letter 8). The society had to wait until October to learn in the newspaper of the *Dolphin*'s arrival in England "with some (if not all) of the vessells that sail'd from thence [Charleston] under her convoy 21st of June."[39] The next letter, as many others were to do, stressed the importance of repeated orders and copies of bills of transfers "lest they shou'd have miscarried." It was again, just as well. Two of the three copies were indeed lost, each carried by a ship captured. One of the taken ships was eventually recaptured and escorted to Plymouth; the other "entirely lost."[40] The Library Society could not escape these transatlantic confiscations—as it was to find to its particular cost early in the next century.

Chapter Ten

LITERARY PRIORITIES

IT IS IMPOSSIBLE TO BE CERTAIN about members' demands for new books at the Charleston Library Society general meetings. The accounts in the journals are necessarily formalistic, although the variation in the numbers of suggested titles is notable. The relative paucity of minuted proposals, the absence (save on one or two significant occasions) of recorded controversy, and the disparity between suggestions in the journal and the much larger number of titles actually listed in the orders sent to the booksellers, suggests that most library members were content to leave matters to the committee.[1] That said, the frequency with which very general or inaccurate titles were dispatched as orders (some confusing or confounding the London bookseller) does suggest a readiness to respond to propositions from the floor—and leave to others the matching of the suggestion to the actual title.

To this extent the Charleston Library Society conforms to what has been characterized by students of librarianship as an "autodidactic" purchasing policy. The choice of books originated with the members themselves, within the bounds of their accumulated purchasing fund. By its design, and by what we can tell of its practice, the Library Society did not build its collection under the instructions of administrators or donors, as did many colonial and British college and ecclesiastical libraries.[2] The Library Society committee was nevertheless an apparently powerful manager of the purchases, and requesting new books in Charleston was a cumbersome and more public performance than at the Library Company of Philadelphia. The Library Company became famous for its tin suggestion box of about 1750, painted with a lion's head and with a slot in the middle where "Gentlemen are requested To deposit in the Lion's Mouth the Titles of such Books As they may wish to have Imported." The Charleston Library Society offered no such anonymity or despite its lengthy procedural rules, much obvious consistency in practice.

What books actually arrived for the library from London is not simple to determine. With the exception of a manuscript volume covering 1798–1804 (and itself apparently incomplete) no Library Society accessions records survive until 1847. In the absence of these, the society catalogues provide basic stock records, by format and title, for 1750, 1770, 1772, 1806 and 1811. As noted, the 1750 *Catalogue* contained 365 short author entries; the 1770 *Catalogue*, 784 titles; and that of 1772,

989 titles. The Library Society journal also records some of the titles proposed at meetings (titles that had to be confirmed by one further meeting before being ordered), but those so approved and listed are few in comparison to the numbers eventually sent for. Additional comments in the journal are rare and are extensive only when controversy occurred. It is here that the letters to the London booksellers greatly amplify the record. Appended to many are lists of books ordered, supplemented in the text by continuing commentary and complaint about particular titles ordered, received, sent by error, or now countermanded by a further Library Society meeting. The bookseller is rarely congratulated.

The design of the catalogues of the period also offers certain clues about library objectives and its perception and usage by its members. Many library catalogues in Britain were "classical," or divided (or subdivided under format divisions) into subject arrangements. The choice of class headings, as with many circulating library catalogues of the period, gives an immediate insight into the way in which the librarian and the committee perceived the arrangement and rearrangement of knowledge on the shelves. Among colonial learned libraries, the Yale College Library catalogues of 1743 and 1755 and the Philadelphia Loganian Library catalogue of 1760 listed holdings under specified subject headings. The scheme was that of at least the first (and several other early) recorded colonial bookseller catalogues. The later Baltimore Library Company printed "a classical catalogue, alphabetically digested," without any format distinctions. The Savannah Library Society catalogue provided, under a primary alphabetical arrangement, fourteen separate headings, ranging from biography, history, and travels and voyages to law and political science, and "Ethic's," logic, and metaphysics.

This arrangement was also to be adopted by the Charleston library for its 1806 *Catalogue*,[3] but its earlier catalogues were structured only by primary format divisions, each (with the exception of the first, basic, 1750 *Catalogue*) comprising an alphabetical arrangement by author's name. The format-first design was that of many colonial booksellers' and auctioneers' catalogues, including Benjamin Franklin and David Hall in Philadelphia and more pertinently, the newspaper book advertisements of Robert Wells, Charleston library member and printer of its 1770 and 1772 catalogues.[4] The same format-led system was adopted by the 1723 and 1725 Harvard College Library catalogues (printed in Latin), the earliest surviving 1741 and 1757 catalogues of the Library Company of Philadelphia, the 1754 catalogue of the Union Library Company of Philadelphia, the 1754 catalogue of the New York Society Library, the 1758 catalogue of the Library Company of Burlington, New Jersey, and the 1760 catalogue of the College of New-Jersey (Princeton).[5] Such arrangements were practical finding aids, but of no assistance in giving us an indication of the perceived definition and relative importance of the different categories of literature held.

In the absence of most of the acquisition records for the Charleston library, the society's letter book offers a particular history of the books and pamphlets ordered and the means by which members sought to acquire different types of literature. The letters chronicle the orders, their dispatch, and concerns about particular titles received or requested, as well as anxieties over filling particular gaps on the shelves. In effect, the letters provide an index to the most eagerly awaited literature and prints. In 1770 there was even a debate about whether to postpone making a new catalogue until the bookseller sent over volumes wanted to complete sets. The result was an agreement not to print the *Catalogue* until the defects were remedied.[6] A couple of seasons later, in 1774, one letter conveyed a vast order for books. These were books lost in the catastrophic fire of 1778 and never to be listed in a printed catalogue (letter 31). In 1783, following both the fire and the halt to book ordering because of the war, Grimké's book collection, as offered the library at cost price, became the basis for the new holdings of the society. A year later, in 1784, a very extensive catalogue of orders was sent to London to extend the restocking. Further titles were discussed in the correspondence to new agents in the 1790s, and then, with much more vigor (if without at least surviving order lists) in letters to Lackington, Allen, and Co. to 1809.

The fullest existing account of the literary tastes of the Carolinas is given in Richard Beale Davis's magisterial interpretation of the culture and intellectual life of the colonial south. Davis emphasizes that religious and theological titles, headed relentlessly by the Bible and the Book of Common Prayer, comprised the largest single category of books in the southern colonies. Hooker and Tillotson were prominent imports, but the range of religious works was very wide and included numerous popular and collected sermons. Davis's second category is educational and occupational reading, ranging from elderly courtesy books and traditional texts on husbandry, to the medical textbooks required by physicians and navigational aids and charts for merchants and seafarers. Davis's final categories straddle "recreational reading," liberally including heraldry, genealogy, and novels; what he called the "functional artistic," including titles concerned with building, architecture, gardens, music, and rhetoric; and finally a very broad category of historical, political, and philosophical books.

From all of this Davis concludes that "there was no cultural lag in the South in the matter of reading current political philosophy and employing it in argument, as there was no cultural lag in other artistic and intellectual areas."[7] Such a wide-ranging survey is not only generalized (and inevitably based, as he makes clear, on a limited selection of southern inventories), but Davis is bullish in his insistence upon southern modishness and unexceptionalism. Evidence of the book-ordering policy of the Library Society, together with the commentary of the letters, offers certain reassessment of these claims.

The only existing supplement to Davis is Walter Edgar's pioneering survey of the libraries and book collections of colonial South Carolina based on the patchy survival of personal inventories. Some 2,800 different titles are listed in the 709 of the 2,200 surviving inventories that specify titles, with many of these titles listed only once. The inventories provide a sense of the variety of books arriving in Carolina. The most common title was the *Spectator* found in 27 collections, but also marked is the popularity of religious navigators like Matthew Poole's *Annotations upon the Holy Bible* and William Burkitt's *Explanatory Notes and Practical Observations on the New Testament*. A scattering of polemics include Nicholas Vincent's *The Morning Exercise Against Popery* and the anonymous *Frauds of Romish Monks,* all outweighed by expensive sets of John Tillotson's *Sermons* and popular titles by Isaac Watts, the latter especially common in the collections of Scots and Presbyterians.[8]

This balance between religious and secular works is probably the most significant issue in the characterization of South Carolina book collecting in the early eighteenth century. The original Bray and SPG Charleston library seems to have been unusually mixed, with some 83 nonreligious works among the 225 titles. Of these, the largest category comprised the 42 histories, voyages, and travels, followed by 15 works of physiology, anatomy, surgery, and medicine, 6 mathematics, 6 grammars, and 2 volumes of poetry.[9] The early inventories of private book collections seem to support this impression of diverse, not to say eclectic, tastes, probably in reflection of the different British immigrant groups. In the decade of the founding of the Charleston Library Society this latitude became the focus of bitter discussion. In the summer of 1740 George Whitefield fueled debates in the colony by condemning Tillotson and recommending a reading list that ranged from Bishop Hall to Allen's *Alarm* and Watts's *Hymns*. An immediate consequence of Whitefield's intervention seems to have been a public book burning and the destruction of a £40 library.[10] When James Walcot published an account of his Carolina adventures in the very year the library began, he advocated the intercession of "some prelate of sound learning" to act as "an Inspector of all Books upon Divine or religious Subjects." Walcot desired that no one was to be "star'd in the Face from every Bookseller's Shelves . . . by Hobbs, Tindal, Colins, Shaftesbury, Wolston, and the rest of that pernicious Herd."[11] The literary temperature-raising by Walcot and others almost certainly contributed to that early concern of library members to avoid "polemical divinity."

It has to be said at once that sources for the earliest years of acquisitions by the Library Society are not rich in detail. The sole surviving copy of the 1750 *Catalogue* provides the basic listing of the foundation collection, but then we have no more than a glimpse of what was ordered in the next eight years as members built up their new library. The first extant letter to a London bookseller was sent in 1758; earlier orders must have existed and the early collection was quite possibly also included a few donations from members. A newspaper notice following the anniversary meeting of 1754 announced the intention, extraordinarily, to spend £300 forthwith on new books.[12] In the absence of other notices it can only be assumed that the standard £100 was spent annually in the early years.

If length of borrowing is some guide to the popularity of the holdings, then we should take particular interest in the notice of overdue and missing books inserted in the *Gazette* for the first three months of 1756, just before the surviving letters to the booksellers begin. The advertisement listed some forty-nine titles of books (together with "a great number of pamphlets" overdue).[13] Among these were volumes by Bolingbroke and Locke, together with Demosthenes, Caesar, and Longinus. Some titles were, by inference from the *ESTC*, recent editions that were the first appearance in English of standard works. These included a recent translation of Jean Domat's *Civil Law in its Natural Order*. Perhaps the most popular of the listed volumes was William Wollaston's *Religion of Nature Delineated* of 1722, reprinted more than a dozen times before 1750. Among the belles lettres are an obscure novel, *The History of Cornelia*,[14] two volumes of the *Rambler*, the *Tales of an Old Tub*, and a report of the scandalous trial of Miss Blandy (the "lost" volumes are asterisked in the entries recreating the Library Society's foundation collection, appendix 3, below).

The Library Society letters to London, surviving from 1758 and with surviving book lists from 1761 (letter 8), reveal a remarkably broad selection of titles. As demonstrated below, both the letters and their appended book lists include dozens of titles, most of which have been identified (the original order often contains general or inaccurate titles and authors). The most detailed surviving lists and orders are those from 1769 to 1774, with a scattering of further orders from the late 1780s through the 1790s and 1800s. The earlier orders have been combined with a rearranged and researched version of the 1750 *Catalogue* to provide the reconstructed foundation collection of the Library Society given in appendix 3.

The earliest book arrivals uphold, in a practical if predictable manner, the aspirations of the Library Society's founding declaration. Foremost among the desirables were volumes of history, law, and natural science. In 1750 the library already boasted, among various such books, John Taylor, *Elements of the Civil Law* (Cambridge, 1755), De Blossiers Tovey, *Anglia Judaica: or the History and Antiquities of the Jews in England* (Oxford, 1738), and Montesquieu, *Persian Letters* (originally London, 1722, and about which a later complaint appears in letter 24 that an additional copy had been carelessly sent across instead of further writings by Montesquieu). Similar orders to extend and update these standards continued in the 1770s (not included in appendix 3 but traceable through the letters below and the 1770 and subsequent *Catalogues*). In 1771, for example, the library requested, among many popular learned works, various writings on Roman history, Jean

Jacques Burlamaqui, *Principles of Natural Law*, Beccaria, *On Crimes And Punishments*, and Joseph Priestley, *History and Present State of Electricity*. The *Encyclopédie* was sent for in 1773. In 1774 an order was placed for the works of Voltaire in English.

In the absence of particular accounts of library usage, the evidence of the book orders becomes more important, particularly where distinctions can be made within categories. The law books that were suggested by members are a particular instance of this. In confirming colonial enthusiasm for legal texts, Edwin Wolf cited Edmund Burke's 1775 statement that he had "been told by an eminent Bookseller, that in no branch of his business, after tracts of popular devotion, were so many books as those on law exported to the Plantations."[15] What the Charleston Library Society orders suggest, however, is an important distinction between practical working texts for lawyers and those who might require precise guidance or training and more general works that provided a polite education in British legal history and tradition.

Of these two types of legal literature, many practical manuals were ignored by the early Library Society, although they were common in certain private libraries, while the second, loftier but also pertinent category of publications, was the more familiar in library orders. The distinction between general legal literature and more practical conveyancing manuals, formularies for justices of the peace, and the like, are highlighted by comparisons with the holdings of other colonial eighteenth-century libraries.[16] Textbooks like the *Compleat Arbitrator* or the *Clerk's Manual*, listed in the inventories of many domestic North American collections, were not ordered by the Charleston Library Society. Although (as will be discussed in chapter 11) this was to change by the early nineteenth century, the colonial Library Society shelved few law dictionaries or how-to manuals for attorneys and clerks apart from Sir Geoffrey Gilbert's *Law of Evidence* (1756) and Thomas Simpson's *Annuities and Reversions* (1742). Other suggestions for reference volumes for the library included Emmerich de Vattel's *Droit de Gens* in French and English, *Journals* of the House of Lords, *Statutes at Large*, the *State Trials*, and *Biographia Britannica*. Interest in acquiring the much reprinted *Justice of the Peace, and Parish Officer* by Richard Burn, was presumably a simple administrative one. Burn was by far the most widely used magistrates' reference book in the eighteenth century, providing guidance for justices of the peace on the execution of their judicial duties.[17] An extremely battered and well-thumbed copy of Burn, with its London cover-lettering, survives in the library today.

In Carolina domestic libraries many such books were very common, notably Burn but also Michael Dalton's *Country Justice* (all but one of its owners from the surviving inventories were justices of the peace), Joseph Shaw's *Practical Justice of the Peace*, and William Nelson's *Office and Authority of the Justice of the Peace*. A very different but no less authoritative law text, Charles Malloy's *De Jure maritimo e navali,* was listed in the library of Joseph Wragg, along with Nelson's *Justice* and Kilburne's similar work in a library of 116 titles valued at just over £150.[18] Of these reference works, only Malloy was held by the Library Society in its first decades, and this had arrived by 1750.

Domestic collections, by contrast, could not hope to emulate the range of more general political, legal, and philosophical literature, although, exceptionally, at least seven of the inventories studied by Edgar did include Montesquieu's *Spirit of the Laws.*[19] The Library Society gained by bequest, of course, the outstanding library, replete with further legal and political texts, of John Mackenzie whose *Gazette* obituary praised him as "that jealous, disinterested and unshaken Patriot—that true Friend to *America* and the *English Constitution.*"[20] It was exactly the more general and philosophical legal works that were central to the Library Society collection, as confirmed by the orders sent to bookseller Fletcher in 1767 (letter 17). The library requested a cluster of fundamental legal texts, and it did so in the midst of colonial conflict over the Townshend duties and other complaints against Parliament. Bracton, the great classical Latin treatise on English laws and customs from the thirteenth century, represented a foundation work, a standard for the shelves.[21] *De laudibus legum Angliæ* written in about 1468 by Sir John Fortescue, chief justice of the King's Bench under Henry VI, attempted to explain the advantages of English law, contrasting this with Roman law and offering comments on the benefits of limited monarchy compared to despotic government. Published in parallel Latin and English texts from 1616 by followed editions in 1660 and 1672, a new translation, Latin text was issued in 1737.[22] This seems to have been the edition sent to the library. Providing the same mixture of essential heritage and contemporary relevance, *The Mirrour of Justices* (1768), written, it is thought, in 1289, claimed to have examined all branches of law from the time of King Arthur, offering in one renowned section criticism of the abuses of common law.

Also making up the Charleston library's reading-list on Englishmen's rights was a 1672 edition of William Hakewill's *Modus tenendi parliamentum; or, The Old Manner of Holding Parliaments in England* (first published in 1659). Notably present, given the arguments in this context about the intellectual preconditions for revolution, were a three-volume 1751 folio edition of *The Works of John Locke,* and a 1764 octavo edition of *Two Treatises of Government.* As noted in the 1756 list of overdue books, Locke's *Essays on Human Understanding* was also an early (if soon lost) acquisition of the library.[23] Both Harrington and Locke were listed by the New York Society Library in 1754. In modern (and much debated) historiography, James Harrington's *Oceana* (in the Charleston library in an edition of 1747) is even more associated with revived interest in constitutional rights and custom. In Charleston this culminated in the Christopher Gadsden furore, with appeals to broad constitutional rights. It led directly, five years after the Gadsden victory and the departure of Governor Boone, to the South Carolina Commons, without the sanction of either the council or the governor, sending £1,500 sterling to "support the Bill of Rights" and assist John Wilkes in London. An immediate result was the open conflict with the governor with no tax bill passed after 1769 and no legislation of any kind after 1772.[24]

Corresponding divisions among Charleston library members could not but affect the society. William Wragg, for example, a founder of the library, was a member of the South Carolina Commons, but then after 1769 a member of the council, appointed from England, financially dependent on the Crown, and fiercely opposing Gadsden. In 1769, 37 members of the Commons adopted the Virginia resolutions condemning as "oppressive and illegal" and "arbitrary and cruel" Westminster proposals to revive a statute of the previous century allowing the transportation of colonists to England for trial. In what one historian of these years has called a South Carolina "intense legislative devotion to principle," the empire was tested.[25] Loyalism extended to cultural ties, but the same ties also supported library orders for further reading on political rights and contested notions of freedom. No less than 43 of the 48 members of the Carolina Commons were to be members of the Revolutionary Congress, under its first president, Col. Charles Pinckney, and when in July 1774, 104 men of Charleston elected delegates to the Constitutional Convention in Philadelphia, an exuberant Peter Timothy wrote in his *South Carolina Gazette* that "such an example of pure democracy . . . has rarely been seen since the days of the Ancient city republics."[26]

The interest of members in the politics and ideological writings of the English Civil War, its antecedents and aftermath, gives certain support to notions of a mid-eighteenth-century colonial "Commonwealth" discourse, more specific than Lockean tribunes of enlightenment or liberalism, and revivified by a broader exposition of a "civic humanism."[27] Milton, Harrington, and Sidney were on the shelves of the Charleston Library Society, but so were dozens of tracts on legal precedents and the accumulated common law that supports certain scepticism about the Commonwealthmen paradigm.[28] In fact, of course, seventeenth-century British history and legal disputation are not easily divisible—well might George Rogers write of the South Carolina representative in the First Congress and distinguished judge Aedanus Burke, "he was a Carolinian imbued with the history of the English Civil War, looking for his heroes not among the trimmers of 1688 but among the regicides of 1649."[29] Burke was admitted to the Library Society in 1778 and was an active member in the 1780s.

In addition, the full and diverse holdings of the Charleston library also qualify any suggestion that American reprintings reflect a more representative measure of colonial intellectual discourse. The library held the 1715 Edinburgh edition of the works of George Buchanan but none of the other writings, either in their original or in their American editions, all suggested as being more influential than writers of the alleged Commonwealth idiom.[30] Rather, it might suggest that in any analysis of eighteenth-century colonial discussion of legal and religious liberties, greater account is needed of precise methods of literary access and of reading environments. Colonial publishing and reprinting, even where attempted—and this must not be overestimated for most of the eighteenth century—were of very little interest to the gentlemen of the Charleston Library Society. Many private collections did include some of the American publications at the center of the current historical debate about colonial political discussion. For most gentlemen, however, the London book consignments were not simply the foundation of the library's intellectual activity, but the only assured access to serious literature aside from newspapers, small cheap volumes, and the occasional second-hand volume from a local store.

A further consideration is the use of the library as an adjunct reading room for members of the colonial assembly. A statehouse library had been established when the colonial Statehouse was completed in 1756, and this collection was available exclusively to members of the Governor's Council and the Commons House of Assembly. Two volumes of Camden's *Britannia* and 20 volumes of the printed journals of the House of Commons were purchased from Benjamin Smith, Charleston merchant and former apprentice to James Crokatt, for just under £50 in 1756. Nine years later Smith was paid over £248 for all the printed volumes of the House of Commons, a huge outlay, yet one intended to support a lower house taking the lead in the 1760s in the championing of precedent and constitutional rights.[33] Twenty years later, near to the denouement of this opposition, the assembly appointed a committee to examine its library when uncrated after the British occupation. The committee listed a small but valuable library of working books, including both a 28-volume set and a broken set of the House of Commons *Journals*, 42 volumes of the journals of their own house, Trott's South-Carolina *Laws,* and 6 volumes of the *Statutes at Large.*[32] This library, then, duplicated many of the resources of the Library Society, but the assembly library was small and inadequate for anyone seeking broader historical legal and political reading. After 1790, and the move of the assembly to Columbia, the Library Society provided the only such collected resource in Charleston.

This is, of course, not to exclude the possibility that many of these texts were scattered between gentlemen's houses in the lowcountry. Among the most popular law books in leading colonial domestic libraries were Beccaria, Fortescue, Coke, and de Vattel.[33] In addition to these, the Lloyds' library in Maryland also held the Charleston-demanded Burlamaqui and Grotius. Certain of the surviving inventories also suggest that for a few gentlemen, their own private libraries supplemented the Library Society's legal holdings. At his death in 1765, Charleston lawyer James Grindlay's 187 law books (from a collection of 312 titles) notably included Coke's *Institutes* and Spelman's *Larger Treatise Concerning Tithes* (1647). Two legal publications in particular were favored by both domestic and institutional collections, Thomas Wood's *Institutes of the Laws of England* and Sir William Blackstone's *Commentaries*. Wood's *Institutes*, first published in 1720 and in the colonies especially, a precursor to Blackstone, certainly appears in the Library Society's 1770 *Catalogue* (in a 1730 edition). Wood was also in the first London order of the Library Company of Philadelphia of 1732, listed in the 1754 catalogue of the New York Society Library, and a regular feature of Nicholas Langford's "just imported" advertisements in Charleston.[34]

Given its other holdings, the Charleston Library Society order for Sir William Blackstone's *Commentaries,* the general history of English law, is hardly surprising. Each of the four volumes published between 1765 and 1769 addressed a different legal category and also stimulated wide-ranging debate. During publication, Blackstone, first Oxford Vinerian professor of law, became embroiled in the controversy over the exclusion of Wilkes from the Commons. The *Commentaries* was the only major law book to be reprinted in America before the Revolution, although the replacement volumes ordered by the library after the 1778 fire were also from London.[35] What is notable, however, is the speed with which the library asked its bookseller for the first volume in 1767 and to "continue his Vinerian Lectures as they come out." Blackstone also heads the list of law books in almost all known inventories of eighteenth-century private and institutional colonial libraries, where comparison further suggests the shared sense of the importance to the Library Society of a foundation collection of general legal literature as well as related philosophical treatises, notably including Grotius, *The Rights of War and Peace* (1738), and Pufendorf, *The Law of Nature and Nations* (1749 edition).

Such volumes were of evidently different intention and design to volumes of legal reports, held by the Charleston library as reference sources. These included the reports of King's Bench from William and Mary to Anne by William Salkeld, and the more ancient reports of King's Bench under Elizabeth and James compiled by Sir Henry Yelverton. Among other practical works of reference were Sir Matthew Hale's and William Hawkins's volumes of *Pleas of the Crown* (1736 and 1739), Sir Michael Foster's "Crown Law" (1762),[36] and the seven folio volumes of John Thurloe's *State Papers* (1742).

These holdings were obvious complements to the Commons *Journals* and the like, consulted by the politically active and concerned, but what we can reconstruct about the membership of the Charleston library is highly suggestive. While only one of the 129 members listed in the published advertisement of April 1750 was a member of a London Inn of Court (James Wright, late governor of Georgia), at least 15 of the sons of these early members went on to be admitted to one. Most were to inherit a share in the library where they joined other prominent South Carolina lawyers and Library Society members, including John Julius Pringle, Thomas Pinckney, Charles Cotesworth Pinckney, John Grimké, Henry Izard, Hext McCall, and Thomas Bee. The brothers Charles Cotesworth and Thomas Pinckney both attended Westminster School, then Oxford, and then the Middle Temple. Henry Laurens had served an apprenticeship at a London merchant house, and his son John entered Middle Temple where he read Blackstone. Peter Manigault and John Rutledge were also at the Inns of Court, and between 1764 and 1769 the only Anglo-Americans at Cambridge (where Grimké had studied) were Carolinians.[37] It was this generation that largely accounted for there being more members of the Middle Temple from South Carolina than from any other colony in the eighteenth century. They and their fathers, so many of whom were members of the Library Society, sought a select but weighty reading list of general legal literature. It offered a basic grounding in English law as a branch of civilized knowledge but also one with an increasing topicality. This small but deep reservoir of writing on legal customs and general philosophy was to sustain political debates about the rights of Englishmen and other questions of constitutional precedence and procedure that filled the newspapers and parliamentary reports.

What an examination of the Charleston Library Society's law books also illustrates most pointedly is the elision of antiquity and modernity, of precedent, tradition, and innovation in intellectual discussion. Obviously, without extensive evidence of members' responses, our understanding of the use of these volumes has to be speculative, but it is striking that while keen interest was taken in new publications in literature and science (and indeed, of course, in news itself), enthusiasm remained for relatively antique books, many not perceived as old or redundant. Notions of a circulating body of knowledge derived from a compound of texts and writers, ancient and modern, and these, in particular circumstances, displaced concerns about acquiring the latest and best-reviewed print.

Many of the works ordered because of historical or legal interest were themselves elderly or rare. Prominent among the antiquarian titles were the works of Robert Cotton dating from the mid-seventeenth century, an early printing of Henry de Bracton [Bratton], *De legibus et consuetudinibus Angliæ*, possibly the first London edition of 1569, the *Fleta seu commentarius Juris Anglicani sic nuncupatus, sub Edwardo Rege primo* (which arrived in its second edition of 1685), and Sir Henry Spelman's *Glossarium archaiologicum* of 1664 (which came in its third edition of 1687). Sometimes it seems that the bookseller was asked to find these books without any understanding that this might be a more difficult task for him than the purchase and dispatch of recently published titles. For example, the letter sent to the society's then bookseller James Fletcher, in June 1767 (letter 17), and containing an order for several of antique titles, including Bratton, Spelman, and the *Fleta,* calmly instructed Fletcher, "You have inclosed a small order (which you'll send out by the first Opportunity)." By contrast, some works of law and history were ordered, it seems, on the basis of news of imminent publication. *The Mirrour of Justices,* a text dating from the late thirteenth century, was published in duodecimo in 1768. If, as seems the case, this was the first printed edition,[38] then knowledge of its preparation had reached Charleston early—just as did news of fashionable histories early the next century (letter 98).

The mixture in the Library Society's orders of variously aged legal and intellectual histories and treatises adds, however, to the impression that for certain coveted titles, an imprint date was of little consequence. This is an important counterpoint to members' concern about "latest" publications from London, a concern so evident in library orders and correspondence over the full period. Such eagerness to have new, talked-about literature (as distinct from embarrassment about orders for fashionable belles lettres) remains an outstanding feature of the library's wants list, but it clearly co-existed with another, entirely different sense of literary currency, that of a corpus of publications contributing to a debate and intellectual canon irrespective of their age of publication.

From what we can tell of other collections of the period, the Charleston library's pursuit of a back-list of legal reference material was impressive. The society's much-vaunted Bracton is not recorded in the imported holdings of the twenty-two contemporary American libraries (including those of John Adams, Ralph Assheton, James Logan, John Jay, and Thomas Jefferson) examined in the fullest survey to date.[39] It seems that both wealth and determination were necessary to enhance the collection. The great Virginian bibliophile William Byrd is one of few colonial collectors who could match the Library Society in specialist legal stock. He owned a 1640 edition of Bracton and a *Fleta,* although it is not known whether this was the 1647 or 1685 edition.[40]

By comparison to the correspondence and orders for legal and political titles, the many works of history bought by the Charleston Library Society are in the main standard and predictable. Popular history was represented by George Lyttelton's *History of King Henry the Second* of 1767, abbé Millot's *History of England,* Thomas Leland's *History of Ireland,* and Nathaniel Hooke's *Roman History.* Among many other requests for history were those for the seasoned *Universal History,* but the gentlemen members also shared the passion of many of their British compatriots for guides to antiquarianism such as John Guillim's vintage *Display of Heraldry,* ordered in 1774, and later, in 1792, Francis Grose's *Antiquities.* In the collection already assembled by 1750 the new edition of Inigo Jones's seventeenth-century *Antiquity of Stone-Heng* (1725) was accompanied by three of William Stukeley's treatises, *Palæographia; or, Discourses on Monuments of Antiquity that relate to Ancient History*

(1736), *Stonehenge* (1740), and *Itinerarium curiosum* (1724). Also stocked by 1750 were John Arbuthnot's *Tables of Ancient Coins* (1727), and, more exotically, Samuel Dale's *History and Antiquities of Harwich and Dovercourt* (1730).[41] The last might well be explained by the fact that Samuel Dale, physician and botanist of Braintree, Essex, was the uncle of Dr. Thomas Dale, library founder—even though Dale had actually arrived in Charleston to escape family censure.[42] The Harleian catalogue of manuscripts was listed in the 1770 *Catalogue*. The numerous studies of ancient history sought by the library included *Antique Paintings of Herculaneum* and Cameron's *Baths of the Romans*.

The greatest contrast to Davis's assessment of southern literary tastes is provided by the relatively small number of religious books bought by the Library Society. Perhaps the uninterest of the members in this class of literature supports the claims of those, then and now, who emphasize the materialism of early Charleston society. Far more suggestive, however, is the command sent as part of the general instructions to the bookseller to at all times avoid "polemical Divinity," a stipulation that would seem to result from the diversity and attempted tolerance of the different communities in Charleston. As noted, the library had been founded in years when various clerics and religious zealots had launched impassioned criticism of literature entering Carolina.[43] Accepted precepts of literary sociability and political sensitivity appear to have informed the active membership by at least the 1760s.

Whatever the cause, sermons, other religious writings, and scriptural scholarship seem to have been relatively neglected in the early orders sent to London. Among exceptions were two Anglican handbooks, Edmund Gibson's *Codex juris ecclesiastici Anglicani,* and a 1750 *Appeal to Common Reason and Candour for Reviewing the Liturgy.* Louis Ellies Du Pin's *Compendious History of the Church* (1713), in a four-volume second edition of 1715–1716, was listed in 1770, together with Patrick Cockburn's *Enquiry into the Truth and Certainty of the Mosaic Deluge* (1750), Bishop Butler's *Analogy of Religion* (1740), and John Balguy's *Moral and Theological Tracts* (1734). Bernard Picart's *Religious Ceremonies and Customs of the Several Nations of the Known World,* originally published in 1731, and reissued in seven volumes, 1733–1739, was sent for in 1774, but his writings more resemble early anthropology than divinity. John Brown's *Dictionary of the Holy Bible* (1769) seems to have been the intended request in a letter of 1771, and late in the century (1792) the *Scripture-Dictionary* published by James Chalmers some twenty years before was also ordered. It was, perhaps, something of a give-away about the state of the theological shelves of the library. Different Bibles were held, including various donations and from the 1750 Library Society *Catalogue,* a large folio Bible "with maps and cuts." More striking in the 1770 *Catalogue,* was John Eliot's pioneering Algonquin translation of the Bible printed in Cambridge, Massachusetts, in 1685 (following a first edition of 1663). Unrecorded in the orders to London, it was almost certainly received from Boston. A curiosity, but also of linguistic interest rather than a volume with any practical use in the Carolinas,[44] Eliot's Algonquin Bible was also held by Byrd (along with another of Eliot's translations from the Algonquin).[45] Listed under "T" in the 1770 *Catalogue* was a 1739 "The Holy Bible."

The apparent religious somnolence was to change by the turn of the century, as will be discussed in a later chapter, but in the first Library Society collection (the one that predated the 1778 fire), the theological and ecclesiastical history holdings remained modest. Perhaps the only outstanding group of sectarian publications acquired by the library in its first decades were several books relating to Quaker lives and thought. Even these were hardly unusual titles, comprising George Fox's *Journals*, Robert Barclay's *Apology for the True Christian Divinity*, William Penn's *No Cross, No Crown*, William Sewel's *History of the Quakers*, and Joseph Besse's *The Sufferings of the Quakers*. Most, moreover, had been donated by the Society of Friends, and politely, if not effusively, received.[46]

As Kevin Hayes has written in a study of William Byrd II and his library at Westover, Virginia, most literate Americans of the period believed that most books should be useful.[47] Members of the Charleston Library Society ordered almost as many key practical works as they did popular academic writings. Works of technical reference featured strongly. Timothy Cunningham's *Laws of Bills of Exchange, Promissory Notes, Bank-Notes, and Insurances* (London, 1760) was sought, together with standard commercial law dictionaries such as William Guthrie's *Commercial Grammar* within a year of its publication in 1770 (letter 27). Allied holdings comprised the general commercial histories and commentaries that were popular in merchants' libraries in Britain. Many were ordered by the Library Society almost as soon as they were published, including Adam Anderson's *Historical and Chronological Deductions of the Origin of Commerce* of 1764. Closely related to these were legal and philosophical writings of particular interest to the merchant and professional members of the society. Adam Ferguson's *History of Civil Society*, second edition (London and Edinburgh, 1768), was ordered in 1769, and among the reference works, a compilation begun by Samuel Whatley and first titled *A General Collection of Treatys, Declarations of War, Manifestos, and Other Publick Papers*. This complex series opened in 1710 and continued in multiple volumes to at least 1732. Judging at least by the convoluted and insistent orders, the volumes were deemed of particular importance to the members.

In ordering other practical publications, Charleston library members followed interests in both agrarian science and domestic horticulture and cultivation. Theirs was the frontier commercial and agrarian world pictured by Henry Laurens, opponent of the classics in the library and champion of innovation. Here was the progressive optimism of an Eliza Lucas Pinckney or a James Crokatt, promoting the growing of indigo, and a climate in which the advocacy of improvement—both agricultural and mental (at least for the elite)—found no dissent. Changes in agriculture in the region can even chronicle the way in which white colonists of the lower south "redefined themselves as a modern people."[48] The Library Society selection rests well with what Joyce Chaplin offers as one of her most surprising findings, that lowcountry planters were more likely to keep bees than mules.[49] Between 1780 and 1810 nearly a fifth of all inland estates in the lower south gathered honey from their own hives. Nearly a third of all estates kept poultry. More than 80 percent of inventoried estates kept horses, and about 75 percent had cattle.[50] The improving works ordered by the Charleston Library Society in 1774 included du Monceau's *Elements of Agriculture* and Thomas Wildman's *Treatise on the Management of Bees.* These joined existing horticultural and apiarian volumes on the library's shelves, including Richard Bradley's *A General Treatise of Husbandry* (1721/22), John Gedde's *On the Management of Bees* (1721), John Laurence's *A New System of Agriculture: Being a Complete Body of Husbandry and Gardening in all the Parts* (1726), and Jethro Tull's *The Horse-Hoing Husbandry* (1731, bought in a 1742 edition).

Although books offering basic domestic advice were rare, an exception concerned volumes serving the kitchen garden and orchard. These extensions of the agricultural improvement manuals and treatises included Batty Langley's finely illustrated folio *Pomona: or, The Fruit-Garden Illustrated* (1728/29) and Philip Miller's *The Gardener's Dictionary* first published in 1731, bought in a 1752 edition. Miller (1691–1771) was employed as Chelsea gardener to the Society of Apothecaries after aid from Sir Hans Sloane (d. 1753). In addition to these, the library also invested in various treatises on simple manufacturing and extractive processes. A 1748 edition of William Brownrigg's *Art of Making Common Salt* was listed in the first, 1750 *Catalogue.*

Of the building guides offered, most were suitable for general architectural and design references rather than practical instruction.[51] What has been called a "West Indian" look to Charleston was developed by the building of "single" houses, gable-end to the street to maximize the use of the plot, but both single and double houses were also closely modeled on English styles, constructed from published builders' manuals. The country seats built on the main roads running north and south of Charleston, with show houses and formal and informal gardens, were clearly influenced by published design.[52] Of the building and architectural volumes bought by the Library Society, James Paine's *Elevations* offered certain inspiration for *beau monde* house building, while an earlier but less easily identifiable request was probably for William Jones's *Gentlemens and Builders Companion Containing Variety of Usefull Designs for Doors, Gateways, Peers,* published in London in 1739. William Pain's *The Builder's Companion, or Workman's General Assistant,* bought in the second edition of 1765, was a folio volume with many plates that could be used as a design manual. In 1774 the library committee ordered Sir William Chambers, *A Dissertation on Oriental Gardening*, published in London two years previously and the latest in a succession of guides to fashionable styles in the presentation of the country estate. It is perhaps worth noting the absence of any work by the Halfpenny brothers who very successfully exploited the market for manuals depicting fashionable garden design and architectural features (and one of whose volumes did appear in the New York Society Library foundation holdings in 1754).[53]

Somewhere between the practical and the fashionable were works on etiquette and civilized living. Although most were regarded as perfectly proper and serious publications in London, they were exactly the sort of titles mocked by visitors appalled by Charleston's nouveau-riche ostentation. Thomas Sheridan's *Course of Lectures on Elocution* of 1762 was ordered in 1771, while much energy was expended in ensuring that the Library Society was supplied with a guide to the art of dancing by Giovani Gallini (two attempts were made over three years before the exact title was located). Other publications that might be regarded as topical, fashionable belles lettres, were not as popular or at least deemed worthy for the Library Society in its first decades. The novels and fictional miscellanies imported by Wells from his earliest years—"entertaining books" as he described them[54]—were to be part of the library in large numbers only after the Revolution. More controversial and problematic in the first phase of the Library Society's development were orders concerning science and the classics.

Chapter Eleven

LEARNED AND SCIENTIFIC COMMUNITY

THE SENSE OF NEW SCIENTIFIC COMMUNITY created by prestigious British and European foundations spread far. Although colonial participants were in one sense situated at the extremities, their original contributions brought acknowledged credit, and the American correspondents and experimentalists should not simply be regarded as cultural debtors. Harvard, Yale, and other colleges were notable contributors by the end of the century, but even earlier, library societies and associated gentlemen's associations championed scientific discussion and experiment. Most conspicuous was the Library Company of Philadelphia, with Franklin as its guiding spirit. The library proudly displayed its air pump, sent over by John Penn in 1739. Housed in a specially commissioned glass-fronted cabinet, the pump graced a library boasting "a compleat Electrical Apparatus" by 1747. Like the American Philosophical Society of the same city, the Library Company gave increasing space to a museum cabinet with geological specimens, fossils, antique coins, parts of Egyptian mummies, and other curiosities.[1]

The gentlemen of Charleston envisaged a similar route for their learned society, but without guiding patrons like the Penns or learned promoters and performers like Franklin, the road was not easy. The correspondence and other records of the Charleston Library Society give much attention to the ordering of publications on science, medicine, botany, and natural history, but also to the purchase and care of scientific and mathematical instruments bought for the library for the use of members. This history adds to our understanding of the broader context of intellectual endeavor in the colonial south. The Carolinas were certainly not without their scholar enthusiasts, even if the southern colonies could not boast the illuminati of Philadelphia, New York, Boston, and the northern colleges (many of whose reputations now look suspiciously inflated by a politicized historiography).

Early leaders in Charleston included John Lining, second Library Society president, noted by Alexander Garden as being "vastly fond" of the subject of electricity.[2] Lining's "statical experiments" were published in the *Transactions of the Royal Society* of 1742–1743, and his studies of the Indian pink contributed notably to the advance of drug therapy. Both Lining and Lionel Chalmers attempted to establish connections between climate and local disease, and Lining wrote what has been called the first American account of the yellow fever.[3] Alexander Garden, country member of the library, gained international repute for his descriptive study of local plants, his correspondence and dispatch of specimens to Europe, and his botanical and zoological writings.

The fascination with the botany and wildlife of the colony promoted broader interest in natural history and proved an effective bridge to scientific experiment and discussion. The natural environment of Charleston and the lowcountry estates offered would-be savants an extraordinary opportunity to engage in an international exchange of information. For once, this meant that library members were far more than just supplicants for learning from the mother country and from past civilization. Early inspiration for the Carolina specimen collectors was provided by the visits and publications of John Lawson (d. 1711) and Mark Catesby (d. 1749), the latter staying three years and hosted, among others, at Bull's father's house at the Ashley Plantation.[4] Of particular assistance to Catesby was Dr. Thomas Cooper (d. 1734), father of the first president of the Library Society.[5] Among recipients of his specimens in England was Samuel Dale, fellow Essex man and author of the admired *Pharmacologia* (London, 1693). Dale was also originator of the *History and Antiquities of Harwich and Dovercourt* held by the Library Society and member of the Temple Coffee House Botany Club active in London from the 1690s. This club attracted numerous colonial members and visitors, including Edmund Bohun from Charleston. Son of the chief justice of South Carolina, Bohun briefly returned to Charleston in about 1700 and enthused a group of specimen collectors who then corresponded with the Royal Society and members of the scientific community in London.[6] Their interests attracted enterprising traders; the modest list of imported books advertised by Edward Wigg in 1732 included Bradley's *Botanical Dictionary* and a "Dictionaricum Botanical."[7]

In the next generation, physicians like Lining and John Moultrie became fascinated by botanical study. In London, Philip Miller, editor of the *Gardener's Dictionary,* read Lining's articles on the anthelmintic virtues of the Indian Pink in the Edinburgh *Essays and Observations,* and embarked on correspondence soon involving Garden. Garden's own contacts stretched very widely, including correspondence with John Ellis of the Royal Society and, most gratifyingly, Linnaeus. After insistent pressure by Ellis, Linnaeus eventually named the gardenia after the Charlestonian.[8] Garden was elected to the Royal Society and was also the first American corresponding member of the Royal Society for the Encouragement of Arts, Manufactures, and Commerce, founded in 1754. On his return to London in 1782, Garden took up his fellowship of the Royal Society, soon became a member of its council, and involved himself actively in its affairs.

In fact, Garden and many other Carolina naturalists often met with hostility and supercilious treatment abroad and in letters.[9] In his 1809 *History of South*

Carolina Ramsay recalled a common disdain for exotic provincials within London scientific circles and believed that most outsiders considered the colony as little more "than that it produced rice and indigo, and contained a large proportion of slaves, and a handful of free men, and that most of the latter were strangers to vigorous health—all self-indulgent, and none accustomed to active exertions either of mind or body."[10] If such puncturing of scientific ambitions was widespread in the colonial period, it must have tempered North American pride in the exploration of new flora and fauna and made some members of the Library Society even more defensive and alert to potential criticism.

Nonetheless, members of the London societies did offer certain encouragement to other groups in Carolina, while local commercial enthusiasm for cultivation and improvement dovetailed with international botanical interests. The Royal Society of Arts sent currant and vine cuttings to Christopher Gadsden and Henry Middleton in 1760, two years after Robert Pringle had submitted an application for support. In 1770 Governor William Bull demanded that the colony agent lobby the society on behalf of Christopher Sherb, who was attempting, in straitened circumstances, to plant vines and make wine.[11] Recipients of premiums and awards from the Royal Society of Arts had to demonstrate worth, understanding, and commitment, and a positive indication of this was the acquisition of relevant literature. In 1755 an issue of the *Gentleman's Magazine* featured an indigo machine and other illustrations produced by the colony's own writers, but much of the ongoing practical experiment with rice, indigo, and then cotton, was beyond established literature. The Winyah Indico Society was founded in 1757 to disseminate information about the cultivation of indigo. Very soon after the war, an even more ambitious association, the South Carolina Agricultural Society, was established in 1785. Founder members included Ralph Izard and Charles Cotesworth Pinckney, both presidents of the Library Society.

Whether, then, by positive encouragement or by the provocation of being thought second-rate and unworthy, the Charleston Library Society determinedly pursued its natural history and scientific interests. As already described, a museum was projected, and the results of the library committee appointed (at Bull's instigation) in 1773 to collect materials towards "a Natural History of this Province," were subsumed within the museum of the Literary and Philosophical Society in 1815.[12] In addition, and it would seem, more successfully, the library built up an extensive and lavish collection of botanical and related natural history, horticultural, and agricultural books. The collection established by 1750 already included one particular rarity. The two volumes listed by the library as "Natural History of Jamaica" were Sir Hans Sloane's *A Voyage to the Islands Madera, Barbados, Niewas* (1707 and 1725). Sloane, who had returned from Jamaica in 1689 and married a Jamaican widow in 1695, kept up an international scientific correspondence as president of the Royal College of Physicians from 1719 to 1735. Garden, to whom a copy had also been dispatched, regarded the work as eclipsed by Patrick Browne's new *Natural History of Jamaica* sent over by the author in 1757. This, in Garden's opinion was vastly superior to the version by "that Most pompous, confused, & illiterate Botanist Sir Hans Sloane."[13]

Both Catesby's *Natural History of Carolina* and John Lawson's *Travels* were ordered by the Library Society in 1770 (letter 24). What might be considered tardiness in acquiring these two works quite possibly points to their earlier arrival in a few eminent private libraries. It was not until 1769 that Catesby was proposed by Miles Brewton and, as noted, ordered in 1770, but neither the Catesby nor the Lawson volumes had arrived in time to be listed in the 1772 *Catalogue*.[14] Both do appear in the 1811 *Catalogue,* where Catesby's *Carolina,* with its magnificent and costly plates, is asterisked as "not to be taken out of the library." Catesby, much reprinted and much pirated in German, Latin, Dutch, and French became a standard work of reference, and a source for Linnaeus. Although replaced as a plant encyclopedia by Linnaeus's own compendium and then by Thomas Walter's *Flora Caroliniana* (1788), Catesby's discussion of Carolina fauna, and especially the ornithology, endured beyond the century.[15]

The horticultural and garden publications further informed the study of natural history. Peter Collinson, book agent for the Library Company of Philadelphia, served in his own right as a widely respected patron of naturalists and experimental philosophers, including Catesby. Elected to the Royal Society in 1728, Collinson maintained a huge correspondence and created his own magnificent specimen gardens at Peckham and then at Mill Hill. Garden fanciers gathering around Collinson and his colleagues in London included Garden, Thomas Dale, Henry Laurens, William Bull, and John Gregg of Charleston, all members of the library. Laurens's four-acre East Bay garden was laid out by a gardener brought over from England, and it attracted the interest of many like-minded gentlemen of the town. A formal association was even proposed by John Ellis, Fellow of the Royal Society (FRS) and member of the Linnean Society of London. A 1758 letter from Ellis to Garden suggested that he "form a Society of about 20 sensible men of consequence."[16]

In its enthusiasm for natural history the Charleston Library Society claimed particular affinities with leading European libraries and gentlemen's institutions, while the proximity of very real wilderness and unclassified exotica made the investigations all the more practical and pertinent. Botanical works included some of the grandest and most expensive editions ordered, notably the rare works of Charles Plumier, and James Lee's *Botany* in 1773. Plumier's *Filicetum Americanum, seu filicum, polypodiorum adiantorum etc,* had been published in folio in Paris in 1703 with a sumptuous 222 engraved plates and two years later was issued *Traité des fougères de l'Amerique*. As the library members found, however, these folios could not obtained separately from his other publications of 1693 (*Description de plantes de l'Amerique*), 1703 (*Nova plantarum americanarum genera*), or the folio *Plantarum Americanarum fasciculus primus/decimus* of 1755–1760. As might be expected, interested members also regarded the publications of Carl von Linné as essential reading. In 1771 the Library Society supplemented Lee's 1760 *Introduction to Botany*, "Extracted from the Works of Dr Linnæus," by "Linnais" proper, requesting his *Genera animalium* [*Systema naturæ*], published that year in Edinburgh and published in London two years later as the *Institutes of Entomology*.

The exploration of natural history as a way of understanding the world validated many of the avowed principles of the Library Society. Garden and his colleagues valued study of the natural world as an ethical and almost religious exercise, one, it has been claimed, with very particular political underpinnings. Intellectual boundaries dissolved when those who were Loyalists as well as scholars, investigated systems that they viewed as predicated on social stability and patronage.[17] To whatever extent this study reflected or strengthened political values, the emphasis upon reassurance is obvious. Intellectual satisfaction from the volumes themselves, together with the study they stimulated, echoed satisfaction in the establishment of a working collection of modern learning. Confirmation of the importance of scientific discovery was matched by apparent confirmation of the imperial and international standing of the Library Society.

During the 1770s in particular, a determined succession of books on geology, botany, zoology, ornithology, and the like, provided core reference literature within the society collection. In December 1771, for example, the library committee ordered Axel Cronstedt's 1770 *Mineralogy*, and John Swammerdam's study of insects of 1758; three years later the committee asked for both Rutty's and Sutherland's books on mineral waters, George Edwards's *A Natural History of Birds*, and Thomas Pennant's *British Zoology* and *Synopsis of Quadrupeds*. Many are magnificent productions. Edwards's *Birds*, published in London in four volumes between 1743 and 1751, with its exquisite drawings based on specimens sent to England, received the Copley Medal from the Royal Society in 1750.[18]

The environmental impetus behind Carolinians' exploration of natural history also encouraged interest in medicine. Of the thirty physicians known to have practiced in South Carolina before 1770, twenty-three were members of the Library Society.[19] These included John Moultrie, first president of the Charleston Faculty of Physic and a popular obstetrician; Lionel Chalmers, productive medical essayist; Thomas Dale, the botanist, Leiden graduate, and anti-innoculist; and, most notably, John Lining, whose belief in the relationship between the local climate and ill health and mortality led him to undertake regular meteorological recordings and experiments.[20] All three Drs. Caw were members of the society. Alexander Baron, a

Scot who arrived in 1769, and correspondent of Benjamin Rush of Philadelphia, was admitted to the Library Society in 1770, twenty years before becoming president of the St. Andrew's Society. It was an office he held for 28 years until his death in 1819. Among other Library Society physicians, the republican Dr. David Oliphant was imprisoned by the British during the occupation. At its end, his colleague, the Loyalist physician and library member Samuel Carne returned to London. Carne, who was described in the 1782 directory as "merchant," imported drugs and medicines from the 1750s, and between 1770 and 1775 took into partnership Elisha Poinsett (also a member of the library from 1777). As noted, Carne also imported many books on physick, anatomy, and surgery.[21] The association was a common one. Many booksellers in Britain dealt in medicine and drugs, most of which, including notable quack potions were extravagantly promoted in the newspapers. Of other library members, Dr. William Bull, was the first native-born American to receive the MD abroad. He was followed by John Moultrie's son, also called John, who graduated from Edinburgh.

Developments after the Revolution centered around the Medical Society of South Carolina founded in 1789. It seems never to have acquired a permanent home, but its library, begun in 1792, used first a room in a tavern and then a part of the house of Dr. Peter Fayssoux. The arrangement seems not to have been satisfactory, and finally, in September 1806, the medical society asked Davidson, librarian of the Library Society, to take charge of its books in return for $50 a year "as a compensation for his trouble."[22]

The medical society volumes supplemented a Library Society collection of medical books already extensive by the end of the century. Most had been bought to replace those lost in the 1778 fire, but the selection was notable given the strength of the holdings even by 1770. These included a 1752 edition of Lorenz Heister, *A Compendium of Anatomy*, first published in 1721; Thomas Glass, *Twelve Commentaries on Fevers* (1752); and John Ball, *A Treatise of Fevers* (London, 1758). Among the volumes advertised as overdue from members in 1756 were John Mitchell's *Treatise of Artificial Magnets* and William Clark's *Medical Dissertation Concerning the Effects of the Passions on Human Bodies* (although only a discreet short title is given in the advertisement).[23] Chalmers's many essays included a 1753 study of tetanus published in London ten years later in John Fothergill's *Medical Observations and Inquiries*. Chalmers published his *Essay on Fevers* in Charleston in 1767 and in London in 1768, but his major work, begun in 1750, *An Account of the Weather and Diseases of South Carolina*, was not finally published in London until 1776.

It has been suggested that compared to interest in natural history, medicine, and applied science, colonials were little interested in "chemistry, some aspects of physics (especially in studies of heat and light), and higher mathematics and the mathematical sciences generally."[24] An admitted exception is the familiarity of some Americans with Boerhaave's *Elementa chemie* and, oddly perhaps, Hales's *Vegetable Staticks*. Certainly, the Charleston Library Society held both volumes by 1750.[25] The society's acquisitions were also more extensive, however. Also in the 1750 collection were Hales's *Philosophical Experiments* (1739), and both his *Account of Some Experiments and Observations on Tar-water* (second edition, 1747), and *A Description of Ventilators* (1743), together with John Desaguliers's *Course of Experimental Philosophy* (1745) and Willem Gravesande's *Mathematical Elements of Natural Philosophy, Confirm'd by Experiments* (1720, bought in an edition of 1747). Later additions, bought soon after their publication, included Pierre Joseph Macquer's *Elements of the Theory and Practice of Chymistry* (1758), and *The Principles of Action in Matter* by Cadwallader Colden (1751).[26]

Books were not all, however. Correspondence continued in this enlarging community of scholars, recorders, and experimenters. Unusually for the perspective from eighteenth-century Charleston, it was a cultural resource that reached northwards in the American continent as well as across the Atlantic (with various letters and exchanges with New England and New York in particular). London remained the hub, however. Among many, Garden corresponded with Hales, adroitly naming a new tree after him (the Halesia) to secure good and enduring relations.[27] William Bull had studied at Leiden under Boerhaave who was also a dedicatee of Thomas Dale's Leiden dissertation.[28] A further bond was established when Cadwallader Colden's son David sought the advice of Dr. Garden on publication of an essay about electricity by his late father.[29] One or more scientific communities were constructed through this overlapping network of personal contacts and epistolary friendships and criticisms, supported by the availability and circulation of texts.

If projects were to be advanced and learning disseminated, however, solitary reading and study had to be accompanied by more public and communal activity. Like-minded individuals met to read papers or more usually and informally to share observations and ideas. Practical demonstrations and experiments became increasingly important in what developed as an often regular (and sometimes published) form of scholarly sociability.[30] The Library Society's books on electricity and physics and studies of cosmology, geology, zoology, and botany provided the reference and discussion texts to support an avid interest in scientific experiment. Evidence for such meetings held at the Library Society is slight, and few can have been suggested in the early years not least because library rooms were little more than book lodgings before use of the Manigault and then the Courthouse rooms. Members did meet in each others' houses, however, notably to conduct the experiments in electricity, such as those directed by Lining and then Johnson. The frontispiece engraving accompanying the 1792 edition of George Adams's *Essay on Electricity* depicts one such demonstration of medicinal electricity (plate 12). The dress and especially the hats of the figures shown in these opening illustrations to Adams's *Essay* were updated with each edition to preserve the modishness of the endeavor. Other plates in Adams and the works of rivals explained more technical applications to assist in public and private experiment (plate 13).

The inventories of private libraries often reflect the textual support for the explanation and use of scientific instruments to further the study of electricity and astronomy as well as of plants and animals. Many Charleston Library Society members must have owned such instruments, most notably Lining but also Garden, who in 1757 had been an early recipient of a microscope for viewing water animals. This equipment has been designed by John Cuff of London at the request of Garden's correspondent John Ellis, London merchant and FRS.[31] In addition to his library of 230 books, Chalmers owned electrical apparatus valued at £500. Individuals must have hesitated, however, to purchase the largest, most expensive instruments, especially if, for all the supporting promotional literature, they had not been tested for the tasks in hand. How much more sensible to pool resources and attempt a collective ownership of new apparatus.

In the view of many members a respectable learned society and library needed to possess its own collection of mathematical, optical, and other scientific instruments. As the committee's letters relate in increasingly pathetic detail, this became a principal aim of several members of the library. As the "Advertisement" or "Historical Introduction" to the 1762 *Rules* recorded, the original proposers of the Library Society "were soon joined by many lovers and encouragers of science."[32] It seems to have been hoped that in demonstrating the "advantages arising to mankind from learning" members might embrace a production of knowledge not simply derived from textual study.

Like the Library Co. of Philadelphia, the Charleston Library Society took its cue from the widely disseminated model of the Royal Society and foundation literature such as the *Philosophical Transactions*. The establishment of national scientific academies in Europe and burgeoning associations like the botanical study groups provided further inspiration. The Library Society owned Thomas Birch's *History of the Royal Society* (1756–1757), John Hill's *Review of the Works of the Royal Society* (London, 1751), and a fourth edition of Thomas Sprat's *History of the Royal Society* (London, 1734). Many of the mid-eighteenth-century academies or associations were modest gatherings of fellow enthusiasts, in which, to quote one of their historians, "well-written books or well-designed instruments often enjoyed comparable success as commodities."[33] James Lackington, founder of the firm of Lackington, Allen, and Co., recalled in his *Memoirs* meeting friends two or three times a week "for the purpose of improvement in science . . . with globes, telescopes, microscopes, electrical machines, air pumps, air guns, a good bottle of wine, and other philosophical instruments."[34]

The practical ambition was at least in place from the earliest days of the Library Society. As noted, the eleventh article of the 1750 printed rules stipulated that "when this society has at interest as much money as will purchase instruments for a course of experimental philosophy to the value of 8 or 900 l. Sterling, and likewise a fund, which, at interest, will annually produce 300 l. Sterling, the 8 or 900 l. Sterling shall be immediately applied towards the purchase of those instruments." The further annual fund of £300 was to be dedicated to the salary of "a professor of mathematicks and of natural and experimental philosophy, and to his successors for ever." This last, like the college it was supposed to herald, remained a pipe dream, at least until the external largesse of the final decades of the century.[35] In 1767 the Library Society did at least sponsor an exhibition of the electrical experiments of William Johnson, six years before the library's natural history committee was inaugurated.[36] Although Ann Manigault did not mention any reading in her journal, she did record a visit "to see experiments in Electricity" in May 1765, almost certainly those of William Johnson,[37] as advertised at Backhouse's tavern in April, although possibly at a more private venue. She makes no mention of accompanying her husband or other family member.[38]

Three general categories of scientific instruments were usually distinguished at this time: "mathematical," comprising technical measuring or drawing instruments used in navigation, astronomy, surveying, and other applications of practical mathematics; "optical," comprising telescopes, microscopes, and improvements to mathematical instruments such as telescopic sights in measuring devices; and "natural philosophical," comprising air pumps, electricity machines, and other apparatus designed less for passive observation of nature than for interventionist experiment. Members of the Library Society seemed most desirous for mathematical and optical instruments. Anxious always to order quality, the cost of larger philosophical instruments was probably prohibitive and requests for these were to be postponed until the college fund accumulated. Nor was the use of the smaller gadgets to be decried. "Mathematical instruments," advised the *Catalogue* of George Adams, maker of globes, surveying instruments, microscopes, compasses, barometers, quadrants, and the like, "are the means by which those noble sciences, geometry, philosophy, astronomy and opticks, are rendered useful in all the necessary occurences of human life."

The first attempt to acquire apparatus for the Charleston Library Society was extremely protracted. The general meeting in July 1759 (a few months after Halley's comet's appearance) recorded discussion of the "want of a pair of Globes in the Library" and the resolution "that a pair Suitable for a Library be sent for together with a Case of Mathematical Instruments."[39] Whether the mathematical instruments were then sent for is unclear, but the globes were not ordered for another eight years. All dealings over the globes were with the booksellers, and no manufacturer is mentioned in the correspondence or committee minutes. The most famous globe maker of the period, however, was George Adams the elder. Operating from Tycho Brahe's Head in Fleet Street, he was mathematical instrument maker to the king and to the Office of Ordnance until his death in 1772.[40] He was the named supplier of other apparatus to the Charleston library. His great and hugely popular treatise on globes was to appear in 1766, and a pair of his globes made for George III are today kept for display by the British Library. These, as was normal, comprise a terrestrial globe (or "terraqueous" in Adams's language) and a celestial globe, together designed to ensure "the attainment of astronomical and geographical knowledge."[41] As Adams opened his primer: "The connection of astronomy and geography is so evident, and both in conjunction are so necessary to a learned education that no man will be thought to have deserved ill of the republic of letters who has applied his endeavours to throw any new light upon such useful sciences."[42] All customers of globes and other apparatus needed to be cautious, however. Demand was rampant, the workshops were soon overstretched, and the blatant puffing by Adams and other instrument makers only put greater and often intolerable strain upon assurances of quality and service. Despite what we see today as the beauty and intricate tooling of the surviving examples, there are good reasons to believe the many contemporary complaints about faulty workmanship and overinflated claims.[43]

The first comment on instruments in the Library Society correspondence did not bode well. Writing to the bookseller David Wilson in September 1763, the secretary John Remington complained that the "Microscope Camera & Magic Lanthorn" recently received "no way answers the purpose of the Society: to be short, they have order'd 'em to be sold here on their own Account" (letter 12). Instead, Remington ordered "a new universal single Microscope together with the improved solar or Camera Obsura [*sic*] Apparatus, made & sold by George Adams. . . . The whole of which is particularly described in Adams' Micrographia Illustrata plates 1.2.3 & 4 the Instrument to be of brass."[44] Adams's *Micrographia Illustrata; or, the Knowledge of the Microscope Explain'd* was first published in 1746. Even when read today the enthusiasm of *Micrographia Illustrata* is infectious and makes very clear the interest in acquiring instruments.

Adams's volume, of course, was a clever promotional ploy and as has been pointed out, a reworking of existing guides to instruments, notably Henry Baker's *The Microscope Made Easy*, also on the shelves of the library.[45] Published by Robert Dodsley in 1742, Baker's book was the first to describe in detail the solar microscope, first demonstrated in London in 1740 by Lieberkühn. Baker was a correspondent of Alexander Garden and, with him, a critic of the work of Catesby's study of nature in the colonies.[46] In Adams's version of the guide, the camera obscura was to be attached to a solar microscope using light reflected from a mirror fixed outside the room in which it was used. For this, an aperture had to be cut into the outside wall to accommodate the telescopic tube. The room was to be darkened. As Adams enthused, "there are many conveniences in this, which no other Microscope has, for as it shows Objects larger than any other Way, there is reason to hope that further Discoveries will be made by it. Besides this particular Property it hath, that Numbers of People may view an Object at the same Time . . . and more probably find out the Truth, that when they are obliged to look one after another. Besides the weakest Eyes may use it without the least straining or Fatigue . . . an Object may be outlined exactly, and thereby a drawing of whatever is curious be easily obtained."[47]

In fact, despite the apparent clarity of Remington's instruction, the reference to the illustrations was almost certainly unhelpful. Figure 1 showed a single micro- scope with the additions illustrated in figure 2. Figure 3, however, featured a dou- ble microscope. Figure 4 (see plate 14) showed "this most surprising contrivance" of the camera obscura working with a single microscope. Adams introduced crucial variations between the different editions of his book. Significantly, although *Micro- graphia Illustrata* is listed in the 1770 *Catalogue* (as 4to no. 2), the request for a copy from London in 1763 seems to have been a re-order, following the listing of "Adams's designs" in the 1756 advertisement of lost books (see appendix 3 below). If, as seems very possible, either the bookseller or Adams's workshop did not appre- ciate that the Library Society's directions were based on engraved illustrative figures in a locally borrowed first edition rather than the latest (and far more popular) edi- tion of *Micrographia Illustrata,* further delay can be explained. The subsequent (and more widely circulated) editions bore different engraved figures.[48] At least specifi- cation of the illustrations confirms the particular importance attached by the Library Society to prints and figures (something, as will be discussed below, to cause further difficulties for later booksellers). In the 1811 *Catalogue,* "Adams's Micro- graphia Illustrata" is followed by a separate entry for a volume of plates or figures; forty years earlier the society had ordered a "Concave Glass Mirrour (to be b^{t} of Brass) for view^{g} prints of the best sort & largest dimensions (Mind a Common diagonal show glass is not meant)" (letter 27).[49]

Eighteen months after writing to Wilson about the proposed microscope, the Library Society's secretary had to repeat the order to its then bookseller James Dod- sley, adding that he should include "any late Improvements that may have been made upon the same," and that the instrument should be of brass and bought of Peter Dollond, "the Society being Informed that he is one of the best Optical Instrument makers in London." John Dollond (1706–1761), father of Peter (1730–1820), was renowned for the invention in 1758 of the achromatic telescope and lenses producing images devoid of color, revolutionizing the construction of optical instruments.[50] Rather as in their instructions for books, however, the

Charleston Library Society was not fully in command of its information—Dollond was misspelled Dollard, and they could supply no first name or address. As it happens, Dollond was soon to arrive in St. Paul's Churchyard (1766), where any bookseller of worth would know him. The order also attests to a shared community of instrument makers, supplying and supporting each other, not unlike the community of London booksellers providing parts for the whole consignment.

In May 1767 a further request was sent to James Fletcher, the next bookseller, for "An Astronomical Quadrant, Tellescope Sights Micrometer & the Usual Apparatus, 1 Fahrenheits Thermometer, 1 Reaumurs d.°; 1 Barometer, 1 Hygrometer, 1 p^r Globes of the best Sort 24 Inches Diameter at least and a Case of Mathematical Instruments Suitable for a Library" (letter 17). However, when Fletcher wrote for further specifications for the vaguely described "Astronomical Quadrant," the library committee informed him that the last meeting had voted to rescind the order, and a month later Fletcher was informed that "the members were much surprised at your delay in sending out the Instruments" (letter 19). The globes, barometer, two thermometers, and a case of mathematical instruments finally arrived in Charleston in March 1769 (letter 20). In October 1770 the secretary penned a follow-up request to the bookseller to have him commission protective leather covers. The thermometer had first been ordered in June 1767 (letter 17), but now, three years later, at least one was found to be "imperfect" and the new bookseller William Nicoll was asked to return it to the supplier Benjamin Martin "and get it exchanged." Martin, who began his instrument business in 1755, had been a traveling lecturer, and his *Catalogue* of 1757, listing 137 instruments, was aimed at the popular market. The Library Society's *Catalogue* of 1770 lists two of Martin's popularizing works, *A New and Compendious System of Optics* (1740) and the three-volume second edition of his *Philosophia Britannica: or a New and Comprehensive System of the Newtonian Philosophy* (1759). The cheapness of his products did not prevent some illustrious commissions, including an order from Harvard for a telescope and other equipment.[51] It also suggests that the Charleston Library Society was not the only institution anxious about the quality of its purchases, yet tempted by price-sensitive offers from tradesmen like Martin, Rivington, and Lackington, Allen, all regarded as upstart outsiders by their peers. Unfortunately, the return of the thermometer to Martin was another feature typical of his business. Martin, like Rivington, also suffered bankruptcy.[52]

Far more adventurously, members of the Charleston library embarked upon a further, abortive, attempt to procure an orrery or planetarium to enable calculations and demonstrations of planetary and stellar positions. A specially called extra general meeting of December 1773 debated whether "to engage an ingenious Artist one Mr Writtenhouse of Philadelphia who is a native of Pennsylvania to make an Orrery for this Society (he having made one and nearly finished another in which he seems greatly to have improv'd that Instrument)."[53] Members were anxious to secure the services of David Rittenhouse of Pennsylvania, who had been based in Philadelphia since 1770.

At forty-two, Rittenhouse's reputation was based on his mathematical work and astronomical observations, but most recently on his construction of working cosmological models. Seventeenth-century examples such as those built by Christian Huygens and by Steven Thrasi in Leiden in 1700 served as the prototypes for English orreries designed by John Rowley in the early eighteenth century and the more commercial clockwork machines sold by George Adams, Benjamin Martin, and others. In America, Rittenhouse began his innovative orrery design in early 1767. John Witherspoon, president of the College of New Jersey (later Princeton), bought Rittenhouse's first orrery for £300 (when still unfinished and at a time when Martin's most expensive model in London was priced at £150).[54] The Rittenhouse orrery comprised three faces, the largest being four feet square with ivory planets revolving on a vertical plane about a brass sun. Pointers determined the position of a planet within any day of the 2,500 years either side of 1767. Further calculations could be made of a planet's heliocentric or geocentric position by placing a small telescope, respectively, on the sun or the particular planet studied. The other faces demonstrated Jupiter and Saturn with moons and rings, and solar, lunar, and planetary representations to chart eclipses and the moon's phases.

The fame of the Rittenhouse orrery was spread by the first volume of the *Transactions* of the American Philosophical Society of 1771. The sale of the orrery to New Jersey College had also been controversial, given the original patronage of William Smith, provost of the College and Academy of Philadelphia, and a second orrery was rapidly completed for Smith in 1771.[55] It was reported to the Charleston Library Society that he was to leave for England, although the grounds for this are unclear. To prevent further delay, however, the special meeting unanimously agreed to empower the library committee to "procure for the Society the refusal of the next Orrery made by the said Mr Writtenhouse."[56] The excitement of the discussion is palpable still in the recorded minutes of this meeting and of the general meeting of April 1774, when the committee was further charged with investigating an exceptional orrery constructed for the Duke of Wurtenburg at his palace. Rittenhouse (now correctly spelled in the minutes) had replied and agreed to construct an orrery of 16 feet by 8 feet in height. This orrery was designed to be of the same proportions as that at the College of Philadelphia. It was to cost £350 pounds and was to take three years to complete. Rittenhouse included additional notice of his traveling expenses to Charleston for his visits during the construction.[57]

What happened next is not clear (and the official Library Society records are silent), but the failure of the Library Society to secure a Rittenhouse planetarium was not unique. A third orrery "for the use of the public" was ordered in 1771 by the Pennsylvania Assembly for £400. This also was never built.[58] The New Jersey College orrery had taken four years to build. From April 1775 Rittenhouse was caught up in the revolutionary cause in Philadelphia, first as engineer for the Committee of Safety and then, from July 1776, a member of the Constitutional Convention of Pennsylvania and eventually state treasurer.[59] No mention of the Charleston invitation and correspondence is made in the published lives of Rittenhouse. The Charleston Library Society, again attempting to emulate scientific developments elsewhere, was again frustrated. At least one aspect of the failure was different. The endorsement of Rittenhouse proclaimed an American advance in civilization, of instrument building more complete than anything available in Europe, and that in itself provides a significant contrast to the normal orientation of the early Charleston Library Society.

In contrast to the abortive Rittenhouse negotiations, most of the costs of the instruments ordered by the Library Society are not recorded in the library records. The equipment that did arrive could not have been cheap. The globes—each "of 28 Inches (the largest Size) in a Mahogany Stand with eagle claw feet"—were obviously top of the range. Even the Adams globes made for George III and now in the British Museum are not that large. The largest globes described by Adams in his promotional treatise were of eighteen inches diameter only, and these were advertised in his 1771 catalogue as nine guineas each. The globes ordered from Adams by the Royal Military Academy in 1767 cost eleven guineas the pair, and accompanying green covers (presumably like those ordered as an afterthought by the Library Society) were priced at fourteen shillings.[60] Globes of twenty-eight inches are said to have cost £35 or more.[61] The concave and convex mirrors advertised in the same catalogue ranged in price from 7s.6d to £26, the latter presumably closer to the cost of the order for one of "the best sort & largest dimensions," although the similar "zograscopes"[62] were priced at between eighteen shillings and three guineas. Later catalogues by Adams list opaque solar microscopes as costing from between sixteen and twenty-one guineas (or between a fifth and a sixth of the original annual book-buying budget of the Library Society).[63] In at least one case a member (and later president), Thomas Bee, first sent and then sold the society a hydrostatic balance, "which belonged to a gentleman about to leave the States," although the cost of the transaction is again unrecorded.[64]

The library committee also resolved to demand the biggest and best in order to facilitate shared use of the instruments and to display the results. Adams's propagandist treatises gave great emphasis both to the role of scientific discovery in this new enlightened age and to its social and communal context. The microscope enabled discovery of "the various and surprising contrivances, in the exact and uniform proportion of the minute parts of the creation; either in animals, insects, fossils, or vegetables," but the improved solar microscope (as ordered by the library) "from the very great extent of its magnifying power, and the convenience of viewing any object by many persons at one and the same time, gives more satisfaction and greater pleasure than any other microscope to the generality of observers." In particular, "you may make an exact drawing of every microscopic object that you chuse to convey to posterity, or to oblige your friends with your own remarks thereon."[65]

Despite the expense and problems over the exact orders and repairs, the Library Society pressed on with its collection of instruments and eventually considered the purchase of a telescope. Halley's comet, predicted in 1682, was seen over Charleston in April 1759, and must have boosted astronomical enthusiasms.[66] Yet action, presumably for financial reasons, was slow. The telescope was first proposed as "sights" in an order list of May 1767 (letter 17). Nearly three years later Nicoll was asked for an estimate "of such a one as you would recommend." Further discussion took place at the 1770 April and July meetings, and according to a letter then sent to Nicoll in October, the subsequent meeting "agreed to drop all thoughts of one for the present the Library room [in the Manigault Kinloch Court building] being at this time fixed where such a Instrument would be useless." In fact, although at this meeting it was "Ordered that the Secretary do write to the Bookseller countermanding the former order for a Tellescope,"[67] the bookseller had already conveniently misunderstood the order and held back from this expensive purchase without specific orders (letters 24, 25). Four years later, the former president of the Library Society, Gabriel Manigault, offered the library the telescope of his deceased son Peter to be "sold at first cost" and this was bought by the society.[68]

One of the instruments to escape the 1778 fire, the Manigault telescope was sent over to England for repair in 1784 (letter 34), beginning the most aggravating saga in the troubled history of the library's instrument collection. At exactly the same time, Gabriel Manigault was receiving letters from John Farquharson describing the current feats of the camera obscura (and especially one new model "on a new construction that folds up to the size of an Octavo volume"), air pumps, and electrical apparatus, all of which "might be purchased in Company and would be pleasing to the Ladies."[69]

In November 1789, five years after the Library Society–Manigault telescope arrived back in London, Robert Wells, then resident there, confessed to failure in his attempt to return the instrument to Charleston. Having asked Nicoll about it, Wells tracked it down to the repairers, Nairne and Blunt, who told him that they had lost it.[70] Nicoll then remembered that he had actually sent it to Jesse Ramsden, "who after many applications found it, but in the same state it was when he received it." The Wells reply is marked as received in January 1790 (letter 41). Such incompetence and the failure to have the telescope repaired after all this time must have caused great consternation in Charleston, but perhaps as great a vexation to

Library Society members was the realization that they were unable to command appropriate service in London. This was especially so given the celebrity of Ramsden of St. James's, Haymarket (1735–1800), Fellow of the Royal Society from 1786 and at the height of his success, employing some sixty workmen (plate 15).[71]

Matters, however, grew worse. By July 1791, and still without news of the Library Society's telescope, the secretary and correspondent William Blamyer was forced to write to Charles Goodwin, a merchant formerly of Charleston and now a resident of London. Blamyer asked Goodwin to call on Ramsden, to enquire whether the telescope was yet repaired and also to request "that a proper stand should be made for it & also an Accurate Micrometer." Goodwin was further asked to take the society's microscope, now also broken, to George Adams the younger. Adams operated as major repairer also,[72] and the society further requested that Adams should repair its telescope if Ramsden continued to be unforthcoming. This was not to be (or at least not yet). A letter of December 1791 relayed a still sorrier tale—that the society's telescope had in fact been repaired "2 or 3 years ago" but still languished in Ramsden's shop. Because Ramsden had not received any instructions about adding a micrometer further delay was to be anticipated. At least Adams set about repairing the microscope, although problems in paying all those involved caused further frustration for the library committee. In January 1792 the society had to send out another letter "on the Subject of our Telescope and Microscope in order to Know whether they are repaired, and if so, what the repairs amount to." Just over a year later, Goodwin reported that having called yet again on Ramsden he had found the earlier news of the telescope's repair to be completely false and had discovered the instrument to be in "nearly the same State it was when sent to him eighteen years ago." Goodwin therefore took the telescope to Adams. Finally, in July 1793 the society paid Adams for his work, taking receipt of their telescope nearly two decades after they had last used it (letter 63).

With commendable optimism, the president of the Library Society, when writing in 1792 to its new British agents Bird, Savage, and Bird, insisted that the members still intended to acquire further "philosophical instruments." In fact, however, the history of the purchase, maintenance, and effective detention of their most important instruments in London had been a chastening one. In some respects it was not unlike the tortuous acquisition of such instruments by other American colleges and learned societies, but the long-running predicament over the repairs was remarkable.[73] It is now clear, in fact, that the workshop of Ramsden, brother-in-law of Peter Dollond and feted in his own time, had a history of delays and imperfect service. According to one admirer "no person can be more reasonable, more attentive to business or more indifferent for pleasures or for riches than Mr Ramsden,"[74] but this is a verdict belied by the surviving evidence of his overstretched business. There is now available much testimony from distinguished customers—notably the agitated letters of the Duke of Saxe Gotha in the 1780s—about Ramsden's ability to fob off enquirers by showing a piece of another as proof of progress in his repairs.[75] The experience of the Charleston Library Society adds further evidence of this. Wells had believed an apparently false representation from Ramsden himself that, as original manufacturer of the telescope, only he could repair it (letter 41). It also confirms the close associations between the London makers and repairers of scientific instruments, all of whom made parts and sent instruments on.[76] The shops of some, like Adams and Martin, and Ramsden and Dollond, were not far apart (see plate 5), and both were also avid copiers of the products of other workshops. The shops, however, were in some respects no more than facades for the broader business. Some, like Ramsden, with workshops behind, barred all but the most privileged visitors from entry to the manufactory—Wells must have stayed in the shop to await the verdict on the society's telescope—and almost all makers relied on subcontracting and a brigade of outworkers, specialists in repair.[77] All the letters and those calling on the workshops do write of direct contact with Ramsden and the other makers: something rather rare perhaps, given the frequent absence from the shop of the head of these firms, notably the much-in-demand Ramsden.[78]

For all the disasters, the history of the Library Society's instruments provides a prehistory to accounts of the scientific experiment and discussion at the associated College of Charleston where the earliest records in this respect relate to 1805.[79] For those interested in scientific pursuit, the book collection also remained the greatest asset. Even if library members were unable to advance their own experiments or to follow the instructions of Adams in his volumes and experience visually all the wonders of creation he described, they could read about new discoveries and examine prints and drawings. Among the earliest orders to London were requests for Edmund Stone's translation of Nicolas Bion's *The Construction and Principal Uses of Mathematical Instruments* (1723), Robert Hooke's *Micrographia* (1665, in a 1667 reissue), Roger Long's *Astronomy* (1742), and a 1748 fourth edition of John Keill's *An Introduction to the True Astronomy* (1721). All of these were listed in the first 1750 *Catalogue,* and purchased anew (if in different editions) after the 1778 fire. Such books supported the broader endeavors of members, often far away from the library and even Charleston. They were part of a small community but one where all those interested knew each other.

The library served as the most distinguished resource in this net of intercommunications and mutual acquaintance. The collection both responded to and encouraged versatility, with no rigid demarcation between areas of investigation. All areas of natural philosophy, or the study of natural phenomena and their explanation, drew connections with each other. In a broader sense, at least by the early nineteenth century, however dominant the Charleston Library Society remained, the town's scholarly community was not focused on one institution.[80] The library had always been supplemented by other endeavors, ranging from the independent but widely disseminated activities of Lining and Garden to the numerous small associations designed to promote, from whatever motives, study of the natural world. Nevertheless, the newly founded college of Charleston was slow to acquire standing as well as resources. As George Rogers puts it, "neither the College of Charleston nor the South Carolina College took the role of an Oxford or a Cambridge to give special polish to the local society."[81] One illustration of the Library Society's achievement was that by the end of this period lectures followed the society's anniversary meetings. In 1803 Isaac Griggs, anniversary lecturer, even published his somewhat self-satisfied address on metaphysics in which he pointed out that "the man, who grasps at general knowledge, and tolerably well comprehends nearly the whole circle of arts and sciences, never passes for a man of genius, but is called a man of learning."[82] For many, however, this scholastic addition to the anniversary meeting was designed to mark the Library Society's seriousness in pursuit of its original objectives in distinction from more worrying trends in recent collecting and membership policy.

Chapter Twelve

FICTION, PRINTS, AND CHANGING ATTRACTIONS

In the early nineteenth century the literary tastes of the Charleston library members changed. Figures 2 and 3 compare by subject the holdings listed in the 1770 and 1811 *Catalogues*. Figure 2, based on the 1770 *Catalogue,* which offered no subject classification, adopts categories used in Edgar's survey of inventoried libraries in South Carolina.[1] In 1770, biography and history (19 percent) and religion and philosophy (13 percent) together comprised nearly a third of all titles held. The other substantial holdings of classics, law and politics, medicine and science, literature, and practical works were relatively evenly stocked, each with between 11 percent and 9 percent of all titles. Figure 3 is constructed from the subject categories used in the 1811 Library Society *Catalogue,* but combines various of the related classifications in order to provide the closest possible comparison with figure 2 (novels, plays/poetry, and foreign literature, for example, comprise the combined category "literature"). No obvious "practical literature" classification was made in the 1811 *Catalogue,* but this can probably be compared with at least some of the titles listed in 1811 under "miscellanies."

The earlier and later holdings of imaginative literature by the Library Society provide the surest and most obvious contrasts. "Literature" amounted to 10 percent of the total by title in 1770 but 23 percent in 1811, confirming the new enthusiasm of library members in the early nineteenth century for novels and romances. By comparison, the stock of classical literature diminished slightly over these forty years, law and politics remained roughly constant, but the proportion of travel writing doubled (from 4 to 9 percent). Biography and history declined slightly as a proportion of the total Library Society collection. The other important change between 1770 and 1811 concerns holdings in religion and philosophy. Despite the reticence about volumes of divinity in the early years and despite the dramatic increase in titles bought to restock the collection or to reflect new religious pressures in the opening decade of the nineteenth century, the 1811 proportion of religious holdings (7 percent of the total collection) is significantly lower than the 13 percent of 1770. Even allowing for the idiosyncrasies of subject boundaries, this represents a marked proportionate decline, although it is important not to neglect the broader context of an accumulating collection. Here, the extraordinary increase

FIGURE 2 *Titles Listed in the Charleston Library Society* Catalogue *of 1770, by Subject*

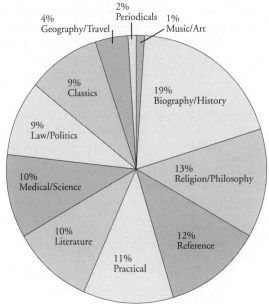

FIGURE 3 *Titles Listed in the Charleston Library Society* Catalogue *of 1811, by Subject*

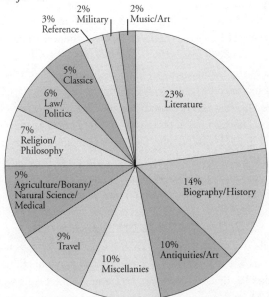

in belles lettres and novels in the library—from a very low base—dramatically distorts the appearance of change in other categories.

Collecting policy can also be glimpsed in new ways. For its 1806 *Catalogue* the Charleston library introduced subject divisions, even though this was at the expense of imprint dates and places of publication, a feature of both the 1770 and 1772 catalogues, In response to the increased size of library collections, subject divisions gained primacy. The Baltimore Library Company's first catalogue, printed in 1798, was similarly a "classical catalogue, alphabetically digested," with format size listed but not paramount. The new catalogue arrangement in Charleston quite probably reflected changes to the physical layout of the library room. According to the report of schoolmaster Kellogg, visiting in 1817, the library when installed in five or six divided "apartments" in the upper storey of the Statehouse, was indeed arranged according to subject.[2] Unfortunately, Kellogg does not describe shelving arrangements within each area, nor is it known whether a marked-up catalogue kept in the library assisted book location. Many of the subject divisions were relatively specific and compact, and presumably could be easily found.

The two Library Society catalogues of 1806 and of 1811 provide the fullest available profile of the expansion in the library holdings in the early nineteenth century. In total, seventeen original categories made up the society's collection in the 1806 and 1811 catalogues, together with a small "books omitted" section. Table 9 presents a comparison of these holdings, offering a more focused analysis of collecting trends during the great surge in book buying by the Library Society in the early nineteenth century.

Several notable changes over the five years are clear from table 9. Total holdings, by volume, increased by an extraordinary 40 percent between 1806 and 1811, but certain subjects expanded by an even greater amount. The small military category nearly doubled in size (an increase of 98 percent) and the smaller category of trade and commerce increased by 59 percent. Among the larger holdings, the number of church and theological volumes also nearly doubled (an increase of 95 percent); poetry and plays increased by 64 percent, books in French, Spanish and Italian by 58 percent, and novels by 49 percent. Subjects expanding at a slower rate than the norm included the prominent category of biography and history, which increased by a relatively modest 29 percent over the five years. Travel literature increased by 25 percent. Even more modestly, law and politics, and Greek and Latin found little new demand, increasing by only 9 percent and 8 percent, respectively.

An accent on modernity was especially apparent in law and politics. The rebuilding of the collection after the 1778 library fire put less emphasis on the ancient legal texts whose possession was regarded as so essential fifty years before. Fortescue, Hakewill, Bracton, Spelman, and even Locke were not replaced. The absence of Locke in the early-nineteenth-century library is particularly striking,

TABLE 9 *The 1806 and 1811* Catalogues: *Division of Charleston Library Society Holdings by Subject and Size*

1806 *Catalogue* in roman; 1811 *Catalogue* in italics

CATEGORY	FOLIO		QUARTO		OCTAVO & SMALLER		TOTAL	
	TITLES	VOLS.	TITLES	VOLS.	TITLES	VOLS.	TITLES	VOLS.
Antiquities, arts, &c.	51	90	58	87	66	133	175	310
	60	*105*	*68*	*107*	*80*	*166*	*308*	*378*
Biography & history	22	49	81	153	186	609	289	811
	22	*49*	*114*	*216*	*281*	*779*	*417*	*1044*
Agriculture, botany, &	12	15	30	49	80	237	122	301
natural history	*13*	*15**	*35*	*57*	*103*	*280*	*151*	*352*
Natural & moral philosophy	–	–	14	26	35	70	49	96
	–	*–*	*16*	*28*	*42*	*73**	*58*	*101*
Ecclesiastical history & theology	7	13	12	31	77	159	96	203
	10	*19*	*27*	*51*	*114*	*325*	*151*	*395*
Voyages & travels	8	9	77	117	129	237	214	363
	8	*9*	*96*	*148*	*177*	*298*	*281*	*455*
Trade & commerce	2	2	6	11	11	16	19	29
	2	*2*	*8*	*16*	*19*	*28*	*29*	*46*
Mathematics & mechanics	2	2	13	14	20	39	35	55
	3	*3*	*17*	*19*	*35*	*64*	*55*	*86*
Military	–	–	8	11	29	33	37	44
	–	*–*	*11*	*15*	*60*	*72*	*71*	*87*
Law & politics	20	63	21	40	104	217	145	320
	20	*70*	*25*	*43*	*133*	*236*	*178*	*349*
Medicine & chemistry	2	2	10	14	58	103	70	119
	2	*2*	*13*	*19*	*84*	*161*	*99*	*182*
Greek & Latin	11	13	25	48	115	193	151	254
	11	*13*	*30*	*56*	*117*	*206*	*158*	*275*
Grammars & dictionaries	10	53	20	42	31	53	61	148
	10	*53*	*26*	*45*	*37*	*84*	*73*	*182*
Poetry & plays	3	3	32	34	113	259	148	296
	3	*3*	*38*	*40*	*162*	*442*	*203*	*485*
Novels & romance	–	–	1	2	250	750	251	752
	–	*–*	*–*	*–*	*383*	*1118*	*383*	*1118*
French, Spanish, & Italian	10	46	29	99	55	154	94	299
	10	*46*	*31*	*102*	*60*	*325*	*101*	*473*
Miscellaneous	1	1	30	119	177	546	208	666
	1	*1*	*37*	*158*	*260*	*913*	*298*	*1072*
"Books omitted"	2	2	8	14	10	16		
	1	*1*	*4*	*11*	*5*	*12*		
Total	(1806)		2174		5082			
	(1811)		*3019*		*7092*			

* Apparent errors, but some are probably attributable to lost volumes.

especially when compared to the ranks of those that *were* replaced. New copies arrived of Blackstone (another whose absence would have been remarkable), and these were accompanied by replacement editions of Sidney, Pufendorf, Grotius, Harrington, Beccaria, and Foster.

Even more notable as an addition to modern political controversialism was the *Letters of Junius,* with its famous savaging of George III and the ministries of Grafton and North, and its laments over the repeal of the Stamp Act. Together with Blackstone's *Commentaries,* the *Letters of Junius* were used extensively by local essayists in Charleston. *Junius* in particular was demanded for its fame and literary value (including the question of its mysterious authorship). Indeed, the order for *Junius,* coming in 1807, caused some confusion in London and might even point to a degree of American information about forthcoming English publication unnoticed before. When the Library Society's committee specifically requested Woodfall's edition of *Junius,* the booksellers Lackington, Allen replied that it "had not come out." George Woodfall's famous edition, which incorporated for the first time an alleged correspondence between his father, Henry Sampson Woodfall, and *Junius* was not published until 1812. Woodfall the elder had died in 1805 and preparation of what became known as "Woodfall's edition" was public news some years before 1812. If the Charleston Library Society knew of its progress in 1807, then the broader history of this work is extended. The alternative explanation is that the library committee sought the original first collected edition. As the modern bibliographer of *Junius* points out, the term "Woodfall's edition" belongs more properly to the edition of 1772 published by Henry Sampson Woodfall, even though that label is not now used in this way.[3] The letters had first appeared in the *Public Advertiser* from 1769, but the "authorized editions" had been those of Woodfall the elder a year later. After many subsequent reissues a new two-volume edition by Robert Heron had appeared in 1802, and the library committee of 1807 might have referred to Woodfall to ensure that they received the 1772 rather than the 1802 edition. If this was the case, then it was Lackington, Allen who were the more informed about George Woodfall's intentions.

Another feature of these new accessions, visible across many categories, is the remarkably large number of publications relating to affairs in Bengal and the Indian subcontinent. By 1806 these volumes included Alexander Beatson's *View of the War with Tippo Sultan,* Thomas Maurice's *Modern History of Hindostan,* Robert Orme's *History of Military Transactions in Hindostan,* James Salmond's *Review of the War in Mysore,* a volume titled *Indian Antiquities,* and Sir William Jones's *Asiatic Researches, Dissertation on Asia,* and *Life of Nadir Shah* (listed as "Nader Shaw" in both the 1806 and 1811 *Catalogues*). Several other treatises explored the languages and philosophies of the subcontinent and southeast Asia. Among the novels and lighter works, the Indian and oriental influence was just as prominent and included, by

1806 also, Jonathan Scott's 1799 translation of the *Bahar Danush,* a collection of tales that were primarily satires on women.[4]

The most conspicuous of these acquisitions, however, were surveys and manuals of Indian law and commercial regulation. including *Ayeen Akbery or Institutes of the Emperor Akber, Gentoo Code of Laws,* William Jones's *Institute of Hindoo Laws,* the earl of Lauderdale on the government of India, Charles Maclean on India, Charles Boughton on landed property in Bengal, and numerous others. All attest to the sharp increase in commercial traffic to the Far East and trading and property interests in India. The digests and legal histories could provide a well-stocked armory for applications and appeals to both the consular and the Bengal courts for the determination of jurisdictions in commercial disputes and negotiations. The directories also stretched to more familiar inquests in maritime affairs, and Charleston Library Society members purchased other current legal manuals such as Martens's *Compendium of the Law of Nations on Privateers, Captures and Re-Captures.*

By contrast with the voracious purchase of practical and educational Eastern texts, enthusiasm for the classics was apparently drying up. The 1806 Library Society *Catalogue* listed 152 classics titles (255 volumes), but in the 1811 *Catalogue* this had only increased to 158 titles (278 volumes). The eagerness of an earlier generation to read classical authors appears to have waned, but there are also qualifications to this perception. First, the quality of the basic collection of classics should not be ignored, and second, the provision of new titles included numerous distinguished and rare volumes.

When subject divisions were introduced in the 1806 and 1811 *Catalogues* the sections headed "Greek and Latin Authors and Translations" included all texts in Latin and Greek, modern works as well as the classics. The collection was an impressive one, ranging from the restocking of classical authors after the 1778 fire that destroyed the original list of classics so hotly debated in the 1770s, to neo-Latin texts of the sixteenth, seventeenth, and eighteenth centuries. As Edgar shows, the classics held in most inventoried libraries in South Carolina were English translations, and of these the most popular were Caesar's *Commentaries,* Cicero's *Offices* and *Orations,* Seneca's *Morals,* and works by Ovid, Horace, Terence, and Homer, all variously in translation by Ruddiman, Chapman, Clarke, and above all, Pope.[5]

The classical texts eventually ordered by the Charleston Library Society after the Gadsden debate contributed largely to the 132 Greek and Latin titles of the 1772 *Catalogue.* The list confirms that this collection was a very fine one, certainly in the context of South Carolina private library holdings, and one based on a sound selection of classical texts established within two years of the Library Society's foundation.[6] The Library Society's continued collection included English translations of Cornelius Nepos, Caesar, Cicero, Livy, Justin, and Petronius, as well as Latin editions of Tacitus and Tertullian (the latter in a 1624 Paris edition). An order for the English Petronius followed a request for a Latin edition in 1761 (letter 8). This Burman edition of Petronius, with notes also in Latin, was certainly a scholarly addition to the library shelves, but it also offered convenient sanction of lewd material. The poems of Catullus were similarly held in both Latin and English. Many of the volumes were valuable acquisitions, notably the Stephanus Latin thesaurus, although the 1572 Greek thesaurus, set to cost the Library Society £25 in 1807 (letter 106), was deemed too expensive. Other items were rare or esoteric, suggesting the interests of particular members, including Polyaenus's *Strategems of War.* Horace in the Dacier edition was ordered in December 1771 (letter 27).

Aside from scientific and legal manuals and treatises written in Latin, the Charleston library also held a strong selection of modern classics ranging from Erasmus's *Colloquies* to the *Stradæ prolusiones.* Notable among other neo-Latin compositions were mid-eighteenth-century verses by Etonians (*Musæ Etonenses*), while Melchior de Polignac's *Anti-Lucretius* (ordered by 1811) was most definitely an example of the suspect "polemical divinity," albeit in the cause of Christianity against paganism. Creech's elderly translation of Lucretius's *De rerum natura* had been available in the library by 1806. Interest in Greek texts extended to Gilbert Wakefield's *Dio Chrysostom* and, intriguingly, a copy of Charles Boyle's controversial 1695 edition of *Phalaridis epistolae,* an attack on Richard Bentley's (by then vindicated) dismissal of the text.[7] This was despite, or perhaps because of, the notable absence of Bentley editions in the classics section of the society library—and in contrast to the acquisition of several works by his late-seventeenth-century foe, Charles Boyle.

Many of the reordered classics might also suggest a collection intended to support basic instruction in Latin and the classical authors. In addition to standard editions of Horace, the Library Society purchased various of the Delphin or Dauphin editions of the classics, and a notably large number of volumes of the lighter authors including Lucian and Petronius. Another indication that the collection assisted guided studies in Latin was the acquisition of the *Gradus ad Parnassum,* widely used for verse composition. In further testimony to continued interest in reading and writing in Latin, Thomas Mills, library member and rector of St. Andrews, undertook the unusual and laborious task of composing a *Compendium of Latin Grammar.* It was the first classical work published in South Carolina, printed and sold by Timothy and Mason in Charleston in 1795, followed by a much shorter *Compendium of Latin Syntax* later in the year.[8] By these standards, the society's librarian required certain assistance; the catalogues he was charged with compiling contain various muddles in the Greek and Latin authors section, including confusion between the elder and younger Pliny, and numerous spelling errors (although some were corrected in the 1811 version).

The near doubling of religious holdings between 1806 and 1811 attests to the increase in church activity and theological controversy in Charleston in the early years of the nineteenth century, even though the volumes of divinity, sermons, church history, and the like remained a modest proportion of the Library Society's collection. As the Episcopalians reorganized nationally in the early Republic (and adopted their founding constitution and canons in Philadelphia in 1789), the South Carolina constitution of 1778 disestablished the Anglican Church. The same constitution sanctioned the chartered incorporation of each Protestant congregation in the state. Carolinian Episcopalians largely avoided national connections and the selection of a bishop until 1795 when even the appointment of Robert Smith (Library Society member since 1763) seemed to be designed to avoid an imposition from outside. Relative calm followed his death in 1801, but it was short-lived. From 1803 attempts to energize the Episcopal Church in South Carolina led to the creation of a new church constitution at the annual convention in Charleston in February 1806. Uncertainty about the relationship to the national Episcopal Church continued, however, with sustained argument about the character of an episcopacy and the authority of recent canons passed since 1790. Dispute continued until at least 1812, when Bishop Smith's successor was also finally appointed.[9] During the same years the Presbyterian Church increased its influence. A new presbytery was incorporated at Charleston in 1790, to be followed by renewed evangelical activity that exacerbated tensions about institutional life within the Reformed tradition.[10] In 1810 the evangelizing Bible Society of Charleston was established by Charles Cotesworth Pinckney.[11]

In response to new sectarianism and new debate about authority within the churches, the Library Society avidly purchased religious texts between 1806 and 1811. It represented, in great measure, a catching-up strategy. Members now requested works of controversy and influence not formerly held by a library anxious to avoid denominational strife. This helps to explain the ordering of Thomas Secker's mid-eighteenth-century *Sermons* after 1806, as well as the much more recent *Sermons* of Paley. Of new editions of classics bought after 1806, and remarkable for their earlier absence, were John Foxe's *Book of Martyrs* (1563), and Bishop Gilbert Burnet's *Exposition of the XXXIX Articles* (1699), which was still not in the library in 1806 but bought before 1811 (although his *History of his Own Times* had been stocked by 1806). Striking proof of the ending of the ban on provocative works was also provided by the purchase after 1806 of the controversial 1749 *Free and Candid Disquisitions Relating to the Church of England* by John Jones, famously arguing for a new translation of the Bible and for a new liturgy.

Even more telling was the acquisition, under the banner of "ecclesiastical history," of both the great standards of deism and many of the most famous mid-eighteenth-century attacks upon it. Thus the anti-deist works of Charles Leslie were bought after 1806, together with the opposing volumes of Richard Simon's late-seventeenth-century *Critical History of the Old Testament,* a work used by many deists to attack the faith. With its seminal biblical criticism and the controversies it generated, the Simon represented a very significant (if belated) acquisition for the library. Other prominent additions after 1806 included the anti-deist tracts of John Leland on the divine authority of the Old and New Testament and the anti-deist *Scholar Arm'd.* For backup references to the anti-deist writings but also, perhaps, as a know-thy-enemy tactic, the Library Society bought a new copy of *Religion of Nature Delineated* by the great deist William Wollaston. Discussion of deism was revived for several reasons, notably as a consequence of the influence of Paine and the writings of radicals of the 1790s, but also as part of the told-you-so polemics that blamed the origins of both materialism and demagoguery on the deist beliefs of earlier generations. In addition, many linked deist writings with continued intellectual enquiry into Eastern religion, philosophy, and literature, as well as continued scientific interests, all sustained by the other new orders from the library committee. A critique of deism was offered, for example, by the natural philosopher and reader to Queen Charlotte, Jean André Deluc, whose *Recherches sur les modifications de l'atmosphère,* had been presented to the library thirty years before.[12]

A more straightforward series of purchases built up a stock of contemporary religious writings, several corresponding to the particular needs of members. The arrival of Thomas Belsham's *New Testament* and Francis Blackburne's *Confessional* probably signaled unitarian sympathies among some of the Library Society members, while evangelical zeal might have prompted the recommendation of the *Hutchinsonian Devotions* by William Andrews, as well as Joseph and Isaac Milner's more recent, evangelical *History of the Church of Christ,* both bought after 1806. Another order, of Bishop Benjamin Hoadly's mid-eighteenth-century works on the separation of church and state, made sometime between 1806 and 1811, probably reflected local concerns in the continuing debates in the American Episcopal Church. There also seems to have been an increased anxiety about the influence of the Catholic Church, with the arrival of various antipapal tracts as well as Francis Atterbury's *Sermons* and *Works,* both bought after 1806, despite their antiquity. Another post-1806 addition to the library, Bishop John Douglas's mid-eighteenth-century *Criterion: or, Miracles Examined with a View to Expose the Pretensions of Pagans and Papists,* attacked Hume as well as Hutchinson and came with some notable High Church volumes including John Henry Hobart's *Apology for the Apostolic Order* and many works by Thomas Hartwell Horne, another belligerent adversary of deism.

Other religious purchases can be explained in terms of working resources, also, of course, suggesting new ecclesiastical and evangelical activity. To standard works of divinity such as Mordecai's *Apology,* were added models of biblical exegesis and scholarly exemplars, such as Benjamin Blayney's 1784 translation, *Jeremiah and the Lamentations* (bought by 1806), and William Newcome's works on the nature of biblical translation and revision. Other church manuals included practical volumes on how to compose sermons, most notably Claude and Charles Simeon's *Helps to Composition or 600 Skeletons of Sermons* and George Pretyman's *Christian's Theology,* designed for students. The presence of works by Bishop Beilby Porteus further demonstrated an awareness of up-to-the-minute theology and practical religious exposition in the early nineteenth century. Missionary advice, some related to activity in India, was offered by several volumes, including *Oriental Customs* by the Congregationalist George Burder, one of the founders of the Religious Tract Society and of the British and Foreign Bible Society and founder and secretary of the London Missionary Society.

The demand for history and travels long represented the furthest extent of belles lettres interest. William Robertson's *Charles V,* perhaps the most famous historical work of the period aside from Gibbon's *Decline and Fall* (which also appears in the Library Society's 1784 manuscript "Catalogue of Books"), was ordered in the same year as its publication, 1769. The most anxiously awaited "travels," which included Indian and Asian as well as British and European, appear to have been American. It might now seem remarkable that almost all the Americana, so eagerly sought by library members, was printed and published in London, but a recent bibliography lists 3,212 pre-1760 British publications dealing with some aspect of North America.[13] In 1769 an order was placed for Thomas Hutchinson's *History of Massachusetts-Bay,* and in 1772 members requested Capt. Philip Pittman's *Present State of the European Settlements on the Mississippi.* The library also ordered *Travels into North America* by Peter Kalm, published in Warrington in 1772. Two years later the bookseller was asked to send across John Huddlestone Wynne's four-year old *General History of the British Empire in America,* as well as what was probably an early version of Hutchins's *Topographical Description of Virginia, Pennsylvania, Maryland, and North Carolina . . . Containing P. Kennedy's Journal up the Illinois River* (today, the only known edition of this was published in London in 1778). A later order for new geographies also illustrates the continuing difficulties faced by the bookseller. In 1807 the correspondent wrote for "Clarke's Maritime Discoveries," although it is not entirely clear whether the library wanted William Clark's *Travels in the Interior Parts of America* (London, 1805) or his *Journal of the Voyages of a Corps of Discovery* (London, 1807). Meanwhile, Clark's other *Discoveries Made in Exploring the Missouri River and Washita* had in fact been published in Washington in 1806.

Many rare and obscure works also featured among the lists, although it seems that members often did not realize that they were so recondite. Probably ordered on the recommendation of contacts in London or directly from the periodical reviews (including, perhaps, somewhat aged back numbers), many titles proved difficult or impossible to find. Individual back numbers of the *Botanical Magazine* ordered in 1807, for example, could not be found by the bookseller, although possibly this might have been his ploy to get an expensive collected volume bought instead. Some of the more inscrutable publications might well have been ghosts—recommendations that were in fact misremembered titles or taken from booksellers' newspaper puffs and never in fact published in the advertised form. The problem was probably exacerbated by the length of time that newspapers took to arrive and the transfer of advertisements between different advertising or reviewing publications, some of which carried very general titles for books and pamphlets. In any event, such requests continued to cause great difficulty for the booksellers.

Many of the rarer items were great folios with lavish illustration, and as Lambert's visit in 1810 confirmed, the Charleston Library Society not only collected but also made great efforts to display engraved and colored prints. Much of our knowledge of this (and of the importance attached to the prints) results from the complaints made by the Library Society to its bookseller—notably those over the illustrations to Holcroft's *Travels* (discussed below[14]) and the return of a fascicule of Smith's *Icones pictæ plantarum rariorum* sent over uncolored (letter 69). In addition to collections of scientific and botanical illustrations, library orders suggest other occasional print interests, such as the order of September 1772 (letter 27) for "Curious remains of Antiquity collected by the Society of Antiquarians in London," apparently a reference to published series of engravings. The supplement to the 1806 *Catalogue* listed "Twelve heads, from Michael Angelo" as new folio volumes. The enthusiasm of library members for the prints mirrored a general increasing interest in the domestic ownership of prints in Charleston during the second half of the eighteenth century. Some 26 prints were included in the 1769 inventory of Francis Stuart in a library valued at over £300, while the library of the Scots merchant and planter George Seaman of Charleston included 118 prints and pictures in a library of 53 titles valued at just over £100.[15]

The main objects of the Library Society's later print enthusiasm were the productions of Alderman John Boydell. Boydell, lord mayor of London in 1790, established his reputation by a series of landscape engravings and of prints of some of the most important paintings in England. Trading from 1772 with his nephew and later partner Josiah, Boydell was also sponsor of the public decorations of history paintings and portraiture at the Guildhall, Mansion House, Stationers' Hall, and other prominent sites. Known as the "Commercial Maecenas," he was by far the richest merchant printseller of his age. His business turned on his early import trade and then on his success in exporting his prints abroad.[16] In the early eighteenth century the great majority of prints in England were imported from the Continent, but by 1785—and very largely as a result of the industry of

Boydell—exports of engravings were valued at over £200,000 compared to £100 worth of imports.[17]

Boydell's most famous undertaking was his Shakespeare editions and prints, and he established his Shakespeare Gallery in Pall Mall to exhibit paintings of scenes from the plays, each commissioned by a leading artist (see plate 16). In 1786 Boydell issued a prospectus to publish the plays of Shakespeare in eight illustrated volumes (a further volume was declared in 1789), together with a two-volume prints edition, "the text to be regulated and the literary part of the undertaking conducted by George Steevens." With the assistance of Isaac Reed, Steevens prepared a new edition that depended significantly on his earlier work with Edmund Malone. When the Pall Mall gallery opened in 1789 it was an overnight sensation. The gallery then exhibited 34 pictures. More were added each year until, immediately prior to its dispersal in 1805, the total had reached 167 prints and paintings.[18] In his preface to his catalogue of 1789 Boydell announced his intention to "establish an English School of Historical Painting." The great Boydell edition of prints from the gallery was published in 1802–1803, but over the previous dozen years other subscription numbers—"a collection of capital prints"—had been available at three guineas per number, each of four to five main prints, and each extended by several small prints, available at an extra two guineas.[19] Artists included Wright of Derby and Fuseli. The whole amounted to a very prestigious and expensive undertaking. It was not until 1808 that final devastating reviews savaged the founder's reputation and the overextension of the Shakespeare Gallery prints almost ruined the Boydells.[20]

In fact, by the early 1790s, many influential voices scorned Boydell's proposals for arrangements of pictures in the halls of assemblies and other institutions. Boydell was caricatured as tainted by commercialism and populist bad taste.[21] This appears to have been a criticism not shared by a legion of print customers, and one that the gentlemen of the Library Society were either oblivious to or steadfastly ignored. The Boydell Shakespeare prints were apparently seen as a quality and appropriate embellishment for the library walls. As described, indeed, by the 1810 Lambert visit, the Charleston library seemed determined to maintain its claim as a major literary and learned institution. Boydell prints and other paintings might be less prestigious additions than scientific instruments, but they were supremely à la mode and typical of the adornments of similar libraries in cosmopolitan Britain. Following listings of its book stock, a comparable British printed library catalogue of 1795 provided separate headings for philosophical instruments, maps and charts, prints and engravings, busts, paintings, miniatures, small paintings unframed, and curiosities in the museum.[22]

The subscription price of the eighteen numbers originally envisaged by Boydell (with at least four prints per number) was 36 guineas (with the nine-volume text edition a further 54 guineas). The response to Boydell's subscription proposal was extraordinary, even though eyebrows were raised about the applicants. "Before the scheme was well-formed, or the proposals entirely printed off, near six hundred persons eagerly set down their names," reported Malone, but continued that "on looking over the list, there were not above twenty names among them that anybody knew."[23] This was nonsense. The list, placed in the Shakespeare Gallery for subscribers, survives today.[24] It comprises more than eighty vellum pages, the signatories headed by the king, queen, and Prince of Wales. The list of 1,384 names (from eight different countries) includes Warren Hastings, Josiah Wedgwood, Charles James Fox—as well as Charles Cotesworth Pinckney for the Charleston Library Society. Each subscriber was requested to make a down payment of three guineas for each number, with the remaining two guineas to be paid on receipt.

The Charleston Library Society was the first American subscriber to the Boydell Shakespeare series. Robert Wells, writing from London in late 1789, acknowledged the Charleston library's first request for the Boydell Shakespeare series (letter 41), but unfortunately, the signatures in the gallery book are undated. The order of signing is clearly chronological, however, and the entry "Charles Cotesworth Pinckney—President of the Charleston Library Society" is the 352d signature in the handsome green bound volume. It is only the second institutional subscription (after Emmanuel College Library, Cambridge, eight pages earlier), but more remarkably, it is only one of two signatures not made in the book itself but carefully cut from what seems to be a letter and pasted in.[25] The signature seems to be Pinckney's own and certainly does not match that of the secretary in the copybook of letters of the Library Society.

It is not clear why Pinckney's signature was cut out and stuck to the volume in this way. Other foreign individuals and societies often used trusted agents to sign on their behalf. One Arnold Kellogg signed *for* the duchess of Brunswick, as did an agent of a commercial firm at Danzig and a representative of a resident of Bengal. The next library to sign up after the Charleston Library Society, the Bristol Library Society (421st entry), is simply entered in the book under the library's name, although confusingly a Thomas Eagles later signs on behalf of the same institution (594th entry). Still later, the principal signs for the University of Edinburgh Library; Chetham's Library at Manchester is entered without a signature; and the bursar signs for the only other library listed among the subscribers, King's College Library, Cambridge. The next American subscriber after the Charleston Library Society—John Barker Church of New York, commissary general in Washington's Army, brother-in-law to Alexander Hamilton, and 310th in the order of names—signed in person.

One reason for the care with which Pinckney's name is attached to the book might be that subscribers were asked to sign accurately to assist in the engraving of their names on a celebratory silver medal. This was struck by Boulton at the Soho mint, on completion of the Shakespeare series, and eventually issued in March 1805. But the tone of the Library Society president's instructions might also have been such that his agents, almost certainly Bird, Savage, and Bird, thought it best to insist on the insertion of the original letter. Bird, Savage, and Bird referred to "Messrs Boydell's not having quite finished the Frames" in their letter to Pinckney of 11 October 1793, but also alluded to their earlier letter and what seems to have been the original order date from Charleston of 12 April 1793 (letters 61, 59). Whatever the cause of the enigmatic paste-in to the Boydell subscribers' book, the prominence of the Charleston Library Society is very evident. The only other American subscribers besides Church of New York were the great bibliophile Edward Lloyd of Wye, Maryland (549th), and Robert Burton of Richmond, Virginia (590th).

It took four years from the issue of the original prospectus before Boydell actually published his Shakespeare prints. The gallery had opened meanwhile in 1789, and Boydell deemed it necessary to offer reassurance about the production of the new series in the preface to the 1789 exhibition catalogue. The text edition appeared in parts from January 1791, with the first numbers of the print edition issued later that year. Publication of the prints of the Shakespeare paintings, following many new engraving commissions from a total of forty-six printmakers, proved particularly problematic. Work was much delayed and plans changed frequently during the course of publication from 1791 to 1803. Of the 189 prints taken from the paintings, only 16 were duplicated in the nine-volume text edition *Shakspeare.*

In response to the first Boydell order, Wells, in London, pointed out that the Charleston Library Society had not specified which series of prints it wanted and he sent the committee two copies of the Boydell *Catalogue* (letter 41). Four years later, in October 1793, Bird, Savage, and Bird advised the society of delay by Boydell's firm in the supply of frames for the prints (letter 61), but a June 1794 invoice for the fifth series included a ten-guinea charge for "5 Handsome Gold Frames with German Glass" (letter 65). The next letter sent from Charleston in November 1794 reported that the society was "exceedingly pleased, particularly as these Prints appear to be of more early impressions than those formerly sent." By return, the London agents expressed pleasure in serving and added that they would inform the Boydells about the Library Society's appreciation of the quality of these engravings (letter 67). The sixth and seventh series arrived in 1795, and at least two further series before the twelfth and thirteenth in 1799.

At the same time, the prints, as the Library Society letters reveal, became one of the most problematic items for transit.[26] Those supplying the library in the 1790s paid particular attention to sending further advice on aftercare: "We have sent frames for the Prints already gone, & we directed Messrs Boydell to put directions and a pattern in one of the frames, how the Prints were to be fix'd in by pins, there being a risk of spoiling them in pasting without being very conversant in the Method" (letter 62). Framed prints were often pasted on canvas stretchers, but this was not an easy procedure and it risked staining or injuring expensive prints. The Boydell firm seems therefore to have offered an alternative method of fixing the prints in the frames with pins at the side or by pinning them to a backboard.[27] Issue of the text edition of the *Dramatic Works* was finally completed in 1803, and the *Collection of Prints* in 1805 (although its title page was dated 1803). Many subscribers canceled as the series continued and the quality definitely diminished, attracting much adverse criticism. The Charleston Library Society, however, has left no record of adding its voice to those complaining about the later series. John Boydell, meanwhile, was forced to take out large bank loans to maintain publication. He finally accepted bankruptcy in November 1803 and a lottery of the Shakespeare gallery to recoup his losses in January 1805 (although he died a month before the drawing).[28]

In his account of his visit to the Charleston Society Library in 1817, Ebenezer Kellogg made special mention of the Boydell prints, following his meditation upon the library's dust-laden plaster cast of the Apollo Belvedere: "Here is also the whole Shakespeare Gallery; an immense number of elegant prints from scenes drawn by the poet, scattered through all the apartments [of the library's Courthouse rooms]. Most of them are in too faint a light."[29]

The popularity of the Boydell prints was relatively short-lived, however. As early as 1820 a general meeting of the Library Society discussed a proposal to sell the prints, but the authorization given to the book committee to dispose of them was found to be invalid as the general meeting had become inquorate at the time of the debate. Five years later a motion to present the Shakespeare prints to the Academy of Fine Arts was also postponed, but finally, in March 1836, a general meeting agreed to a proposal (from Rev. Gibbes) to transfer as many of the prints as possible to the new library building, but also remove other prints from the large gilt frames which were then to be sold. The Library Society's remaining Shakespeare prints were in fact sold in January 1842, following a decision of the August 1841 general meeting.[30]

Over these years, however, the greatest single change in the library's collecting policy was in its accession of novels and imaginative literature. Little fiction had been ordered in the early years. Exceptions, already part of the foundation collection by 1750, included Sarah Scott's *History of Cornelia* and Marie-Antoinette Fagnan's *Kanor.* These had both been published that year and had therefore quite possibly been sent over unsolicited by the bookseller as examples of current light reading. Less surprising inclusions in the 1750 *Catalogue* were Henry Fielding's *Joseph Andrews* and *Tom Jones,* but again, both were then very topical, having been published in 1749 and 1750, respectively, and the *Catalogue* contains no Richardson, Haywood, or other popular novelists of the 1740s. Gay's *Fables* and *Poems* were at least present. Later, Charles Johnstone's *Chrysal or the Adventures of a Guinea* and Hawkesworth's *Adventurer* were ordered in 1771, both of which were not only popular and favorably reviewed in Britain, but appealed to the serious male reader. Johnstone's novel also included some American episodes, although if that had been the basis for the choice, one might also expect the Charleston library to have ordered Defoe's *Moll Flanders* or Charlotte Lennox's *Harriet Stuart*. The 1770 *Catalogue* lists some additions since 1750, including Fielding's *Amelia*, Sterne's *Tristram Shandy*, Smollett's *Roderick Random* and *Ferdinand Count Fathom*, Dodsley's *Collection of Poems*, and Gay's *Beggar's Opera*. Shakespeare's *Works*, surprisingly absent from the 1750 *Catalogue*, were later ordered only in a duodecimo edition in the pre-1778 collection. By contrast, the 1750 holdings did include the works of Chaucer, and of Spenser (and later Spenser's *Faerie Queene* separately), and a 1738 two-volume edition of Milton's prose works (and, separately, his *Paradise Lost* and *Paradise Regained*).

By the final decade of the eighteenth century, however, and accompanied by shamefaced apologies from the Library Society's president and committee, orders for the classics (both ancient and modern) and the philosophical and natural science texts began to be diluted by requests for current belles lettres and other works of entertainment. As the president conceded of one 1793 order to Bird, Savage, and Bird, "the bulk of the Catalogue [the society's requirements] inumerates Books of much lighter reading than our last, but in a Society such as ours, we are obliged to consult all tastes and to have many books of mere amusement as well as books of instruction and science" (letter 57). When in September 1801 Charles Cotesworth Pinckney opened the library's business correspondence with Lackington, Allen, and Co., he again confessed to the change, "apprizing you that as our Society is numerous & of course variant in the taste, that we trust you will adapt your selection to suit as well those who are fond of serious & erudite subjects as those who love to amuse themselves with light & trivial reading" (letter 84).

The Charleston Library Society's experience was far from unique. If, as it seemed to some, the founding motto, *et artes trans mare currunt*, had now been reinterpreted or forgotten, the amnesia of the Charleston library was repeated in other, similar institutions in America. In the same year of 1801 the secretary of the New York Society Library declared to his British agent that "the Taste of several of the Members of the Library is so much turned to the reading of novels that it will be absolutely necessary to have a supply of this kind of Books."[31] In Baltimore the Library Company's founding committee decreed that acquisitions were to "consist chiefly of books in general demand" and "of general utility."[32] The largest class in the 1809 Baltimore catalogue was theology followed by history, then politics, and only then fiction. Even so, the library directors decreed that "they were not unmindful of employing a competent share of [the funds] for gratifying the taste of genius and providing for the entertainment of those readers who seek amusement and instruction in works of a lighter and less durable kind."[33] From its foundation in 1809, the Savannah Library Society also bought large quantities of fiction, and novels comprised the main category in its first printed catalogue of 1838—16 percent of the total (20 percent including novels and belles lettres), compared to just 3 percent theology.[34]

The few surviving borrowing records of the period also suggest an advancing demand for fiction. In the remaining early register for the Baltimore Library Company (covering the years 1800–1803), the popularity of fiction is clear. In 1800 the borrowing of modern novels far exceeded that of any other literature in the library. In that year almost exactly a quarter of all books borrowed (24.9 percent) were novels. Biography, the next most popular category, comprised 16.4 percent of all borrowings, followed by literature and criticism (15.8 percent), voyages and travel (14.8 percent), and history (13.7 percent). An 1822 borrowing register from the Savannah library charts the great popularity of the novels of Frances Burney, Henry Brooke's *Fool of Quality*, and much other seasoned fiction besides. All these registers offer an important cautionary record to compare with the stock lists of the society libraries. Of course, the breadth of the holdings was important to a few members, many of whom might have consulted in the room as well as borrowed, and the compass of the holdings was important also to the stature and esteem of the library. However, in terms of popular borrowing tallies (which we can only assume echoed reading experiences) fiction and belles letters were well out in front.

The earliest extant borrowing records of the Charleston Library Society, dating from 1811, amply demonstrate this uptake in fiction lending, although many practical manuals and volumes of accessible scholarship continued to be taken out. In July 1811, for example, Nathaniel Russell borrowed Robertson's ever popular *History of Charles V,* and in August he took out Goldsmith's *History of England.* In November W. P. Young, member but also local bookseller, borrowed Sully's *Memoirs.* In the same month, Dr. David Ramsay signed for various historical works, but Thomas Lowndes borrowed a succession of novels. As already noted,[35] certain borrowing appears to have been on behalf of other family members, especially for a wife or daughter, but there is no way of determining this from borrowing registers. In July and August 1811, for example, Gabriel Manigault borrowed Murphy's *Tacitus,* General Pinckney borrowed the *Memoirs of Richelieu,* and James Kennedy and William Johnson took out several novels including *Celestina* and volumes by Madame de Genlis, but are we right to assume a greater likelihood that Kennedy and Johnson borrowed the books for others?[36]

The "novels and romances" pages of the 1806 and 1811 Charleston *Catalogues*, differed from all other sections in being ordered alphabetically by title, irrespective of any given author (although most volumes were in fact listed, as they were mostly published, anonymously). These early-nineteenth-century holdings included various American novels, notably Walter Kennedy's *An American Tale* and *Rosa or American Genius and Education,* as well as the unambiguously titled *Wieland: An American Novel, Laura: An American Novel, Lawyer: An American Novel,* and *Margaretta: An American Novel,* the last printed in Charleston in 1807.

Editions of plays also featured strongly in the restocking of the Charleston library after 1800. Popular plays on the shelves by 1806 included those in Kotzebue's *Works* (as well as his *Life*), and Kotzebue's *False Shame or the American Orphan in Germany,* which had been produced at Charleston and printed there in 1800. The Library Society did not list copies of local dramas in its stock lists, but the 1806 *Catalogue* did give a general entry to fifty-two volumes of "plays by different authors," which might well have included copies of local pieces such as James Workman's 1804 *Liberty in Louisiana* or William Ioor's 1805 *Independence; or Which Do You Like Best, the Peer or the Farmer . . . Performed at the Theatre, Charleston, with Unbounded Applause.* Nor do we know whether the library's large play collection included a copy of the local reprinting of James Cobb's *The Siege of Belgrade* or of the 1800 Charleston-printed *Preservation; or, The Hovel of the Rocks . . . performed in London and at Massachusetts with the most flattering success by the director of the Charleston theatre, John Williamson.* A possible indication that local celebrity pieces might not have been customarily bought by the Library Society is the further absence of *Alfred,* a 1799 college commencement poem by William Soranzo, a Carolinian student at Yale.

Before about 1810 the production of both American fiction and American reprints of British novels and plays remained relatively modest, however, and from the London perspective, the new demands of the Charleston Library Society and its like suited Lackington, Allen's shelves and connections very well. For many London booksellers and Charleston novel readers, new market trends had been observable for a generation or more, with local Charleston circulating libraries, supplied by imported books, satisfying much of the demand for the lending of fiction. Broadening tastes were also associated with new readers. When George Wood established his circulating library in Charleston in 1763 he specifically included women in his invitation to read, as did Samuel Gifford, appealing to both ladies and gentlemen in his 1772 advertisements for his new library.

In its early decades, masculine interests were paramount to the Library Society. By the standards of the time, the society built up (and then after the fire, reassembled) a fine stock of reference works, practical manuals, and other publications that might be expected to provide the recommended reading material for an educated gentleman. It is harder to gauge the success of the Charleston library as a working resource, but the improving and utilitarian texts imported by members were mostly addressed to male occupations and concerns. The library offered a supportive reference collection for the colonial assembly, before the capital was moved to Beaufort and then permanently to Columbia. The enduring Charleston location of most lowcountry elite residences then ensured that the society's collection continued to serve as an accessible resource for members of the male political establishment. Other practical texts for gentlemen readers included the lately acquired guides to sermon writing and classical language composition.

The paltry selection of novels and lighter belles lettres before about 1790 included almost no volume addressed specifically to women. One exception, the seventeenth-century manual of essays *The Accomplish'd Woman* by Jacques du Boscq, translated into English in 1753, carried a translator's preface addressed to women readers.[37] This emphasized that the work was "all calculated, it seems, for the entertainment and instruction of the fair sex in virtue and good morals."[38] Another rare title from the foundation collection implying a specifically female readership was George Berkeley's *The Ladies Library.* Published in 1714, much of the text was plagiarized from Jeremy Taylor. Volume one discusses employment, wit and delicacy, recreation, dress, chastity, modesty, meekness, charity, envy, detractions, censure and reproof, ignorance, and pride. Volume two describes the duties of women as daughters, wives, mothers, widows, and mistresses.[39] Benjamin Franklin advised his daughter Sally to read *The Ladies Library* "over and over again."[40] Popular works like Dr. Fordyce's *Sermons to Young Women, The Gentleman and Lady Instructed,* and *The Ladies Diary* were not bought by the Library Society.

All this makes the contrast with the acquisitions of the early years of the nineteenth century all the more remarkable. Doubtless, as already noted, some women had always read Charleston Library Society volumes, when borrowed by male members of their household, but now the library appeared to undergo a certain feminization that invited or at least sanctioned female participation (if still indirectly). The change supports other indicators of women's increased influence in both the social and intellectual life of South Carolina from the final third of the eighteenth century. Even Charleston societies proscribing female membership, such as the St. Cecilia Society, simply could not exclude women from their public events. In March 1773, for example, 250 women were recorded as present at the St. Cecilia Society concert.[41] In similar vein, local printing initiatives for volumes for women commenced as early as Peter Timothy's issue of Henry Heywood's *Two Catechisms* in 1749, dedicated to four wives and mothers to instruct their children.[42] Nevertheless, few books written solely for women were generally available until the end of the century. In the inventories of Carolina libraries surveyed by Edgar very few women's titles appear. Hannah Glasse's *Art of Cookery* and Eliza Smith's

Compleat Housewife were rare exceptions.[43] It was only by the beginning of the new century that the wives and daughters of the propertied began to acquire substantial collections of modern literature for themselves. Emma Philadelphia Middleton, for example, daughter-in-law of the Charleston library president Ralph Izard, owned at least twenty-five books of her own (as confirmed by book plates in the Izard library), and these included popular novels by Bage, Burney, Brooke, and Edgeworth, travel books, and two magazines, the *Lady's Magazine* and *The Literary Magazine and British Review*.[44]

The choice of novels by the Charleston Library Society might indeed indicate a certain despairing and indiscriminate ordering policy. Hundreds of novels did arrive from London in the early nineteenth century, but many were clearly the detritus of London bookshops. Of the seven titles cited by Kevin Hayes as the most favored by women readers of the period, the Charleston library stocked only one, the novel *Almoran and Hamet*.[45] Requests for miscellany titles like Fénelon's *Education of Daughters* and Gisborne's *Duties of the Female Sex,* both appearing in the 1806 *Catalogue,* might well have been initiated by gentlemen members themselves. If the dilution of scholarly literature did amount to a feminization of the Library Society or, as perceived by its president and committee, a pandering to lower tastes, it was on a privileged basis. Evidence of certain broader developments for women's education in Charleston ranges from modest early schools like that established by Widow Varnod in the 1730s through to the academy of Mrs. Duncan, "gentlewoman from England," who claimed in 1770 to have kept "one of the genteelest Boarding-Schools about London." Mrs. Duncan offered instruction in "English Languages grammatically—Geography—History—and many interesting Amusements to improve the Mind."[46] Membership of the Library Society remained with elite families, however, and most of the women obtaining access, via marriage or paternity, to the society's collection were unlikely to have been taught by a Mrs. Duncan.

Chapter Thirteen

PIRATES, REPRINTS, AND THE FINAL LETTERS

THE CHANGING LITERARY TASTES OF CHARLESTON and its Library Society, so marked in the opening decade of the nineteenth century, responded to and prompted far-reaching changes in the book trades, both overseas and domestic. From the late 1780s booksellers in Charleston managed a new volume of trade that expanded notably from the mid-1790s. In 1803 Ebenezer Thomas, nephew of Isaiah and a major bookseller in Charleston, imported more than 50,000 volumes in a single shipment, "by far the largest [book] importation ever made into the United States."[1] The Scottish trade in particular appears to have flourished. The merchants James and Edward Penman developed the contacts left by Cowan and others. Charles Elliot, the Edinburgh bookseller who had been exporting to America since 1777, gave Edward Penman (also deputy collector of the customs at Greenock), the task of organizing book shipments to Carolina, including many quality publications. Surviving records from as early as 1784 and 1785 mention the export of new medical books and novels.[2]

As the book trade escalated so did the problems of shipment. The overseas traffic in books, maintained by the desirability and, in most cases, by the necessity of continued importation from London, had to confront the possibility of loss in addition to the existing aggravations of lengthy and convoluted transactions. The Charleston Library Society complained insistently about the loss of copies of bills and orders, but the ultimate disaster, of course, was the destruction of book consignments in transit. In relative terms, the Library Society was fortunate in suffering very few sinkings or seizures on the high seas in its first fifty years. Captain Corrie "was lost" carrying pamphlets and small publications in 1761 (letter 10), and in early 1799, the *Pacific*, carrying two of the latest numbers of Boydell's Shakespeare prints for the library, was captured by privateers just off the Carolina coast. This order was not recovered although it was replaced without too great a delay (letters 81, 82).

With the recurrence of the Napoleonic wars and their encouragement of privateering, the perils of English Channel crossings and transatlantic passages were exacerbated rather than reduced. In April 1800 the directors of the Baltimore Library Company learned that the latest consignment of books from London had been lost, apparently by capture. The directors collected £250 on insurance.[3] Seven years later another ship bearing library company purchases was lost, "cast away early in the winter" according to the directors' report. Again, remedy was sought from the insurance, but the loss also caused the directors to express renewed interest in ordering, where possible, from American reprint publishers.[4]

The Charleston Library Society was to suffer similar trials. Early in the century, one particular disaster revived all the old problems encountered in the pursuit of learning from London. Already, between 1803 and 1805 successive letters from the society had issued minor warnings about Lackington, Allen's conduct. In 1804 these included both the familiar (and unfulfilled) request for a turnaround conveyance and a countermanding of orders. The last was a particularly spectacular example, the society writing three months after the original order to inform Lackington, Allen that "the French books" were no longer required. Not unreasonably, Lackington, Allen sent the books anyway, having already bought them in Paris and having had them bound in London (letters 96, 98).

A year later, however, broader hostilities brought genuine crisis. On 2 June 1805 the Library Society's large winter consignment of books from Lackington, Allen was forty-two days out from Gravesend and virtually within sight of Charleston when its journey was arrested. The *Charleston Gazette* reported five days later, "It is with sincere regret we inform our readers that on Wednesday evening last, the regular trading ship Two Friends, capt M'Neil, from London, was captured when within a few miles of our bar, by the French privateer which has been cruising in the offing since Saturday last."

The privateer *Emerance* from Guadalope sailed under French letters of marque during the second year of renewed war between Britain and France. She carried seven guns and a total crew of ninety-seven. According to the Charleston newspapers the *Two Friends* was seized because she had no certificate from the American Consul declaring her or her cargo to be American property. Captain McNeil, the cook and two boys were detained aboard, but the five gentlemen passengers from London and the remainder of the crew were allowed to take the pilot boat to Charleston. On landing they reported that the intention of the privateers was to sail the *Two Friends* to Guadaloupe or Cuba.[5]

It was a catastrophe. The *Charleston Courier* of 7 June estimated that the full cargo was worth between £80,000 and £100,000 and observed that its plunder "has produced a sensation in this city of a stronger kind than any that has been felt for several years. . . . The cargo of the Two Friends was composed of a considerable part of the Spring and Summer supply of Goods for this State – none other being expected till the Fall." As a further report exclaimed, "by the daring and piratical proceeding of a small picaroon, is our port completely blockaded, and our citizens wantonly robbed of their property!"[6]

The literary loss was especially severe. The cargo of the *Two Friends* included thirteen trunks of books from Lackington, Allen, containing the Library Society's books (worth a little over £170), but also a special order to supply a library and some scientific instruments to the South Carolina College, founded at Columbia in late 1801. The college order, credited to Judge William Johnson,[7] was valued at over £970. Lost also were 2,000 letters in the ship's bags "all of which were detained by the Frenchman."[8] The newspapers, with knowing political bias, proclaimed disgrace: "What must the nations of the world think of a country whose commerce extends all over the globe, insulted in all its ports by paltry privateers. . . . It is said by some that America could not in many years build a navy able to cope with that of England – True; but it might build enough to make the country respected, in its harbours, to repress those paltry aggressions, which are disgraceful to us in proportion to their smallness."[9]

Moreover, although redress was unexpectedly at hand, the assistance was not American. First, the *Emerance,* together with two of her prize vessels, was captured by a British frigate early in July.[10] Then, the British brigantine *Hunter* recaptured the *Two Friends* off Barracoa, and escorted her, with McNeil restored to command, to Jamaica.[11] The *Two Friends* arrived at Kingston on 9 July, news reaching Charleston three weeks later. Documents certifying the ship and cargo as American property were then immediately sent to Jamaica. There, the Admiralty Court had ordered the *Two Friends* and her cargo to be sold in order to ascertain their value before salvage compensation was paid to the British recaptor. As part of this it was publicly reported that "Captain McNeil, having been deprived of all his papers, it became requisite, in order to get at the invoices, to open the greater part of the letters. This was to the navy agents a very disagreeable duty, but absolutely indispensable; and you may assure the parties that every scrupulous delicacy was observed, that was possible in such a case – not a single letter of them was read: the invoices were taken out of such as contained any, and the letters were instantly sealed again. One letter only is retained, that being written on the back of an invoice, could not be separated from it. The invoice appears to be from *Lackington* to judge Johnson, of articles for the South Carolina College."[12] McNeil bought back the *Two Friends* in the Jamaica sale, and the ship and the books for the Library Society and the college finally arrived at Charleston under British naval convoy on 13 October.[13]

By this time the capture of the *Two Friends* had become a political cause célèbre up and down the East Coast. At least since 1793 the Library Society had warned its suppliers of the absolute necessity for cargoes to be shipped in an "American Bottom" (letter 57). Only then might a shipment be protected from French privateering during wartime. In response, Bird, Savage, and Bird had taken care in their letters to preface "American" to all references to the American vessels used. Even earlier, in the years leading up to the Revolution, the secretary had written anxiously to the bookseller to ensure that all trunks and packages were carefully labeled so as not to run foul of nonimportation resolutions (letter 24). A later quarterly meeting agreed that all such packets would also be opened only in the presence of the librarian.[14] The question of neutrality led in 1806 to the publication in Charleston of long closely argued pieces first published in the *Courier* on the subject of neutral rights, also reissued at London the same year under the title "American arguments for British rights."[15]

Many observers were ready to question the exact ownership of the *Two Friends* and to explain the pained outrage over its seizure as Federalist troublemaking. If, the argument went, Charlestonians had risked their cargoes on what were in reality British-owned ships then they had to take the consequences. This was certainly the contention of the New York *Farmer's Register,* reprinted also in the *Baltimore Evening Post.* The writer denounced the "virulence" of the *Charleston Courier,* asserting that the *Two Friends* was London owned, and concluding that "sailing under the American flag is a mere cover to save risks."[16] The Federalists (led by the president of the Library Society) were accused of seeking vengeance against Jefferson (Pinckney had commanded only fourteen electoral votes in 1804). All this was refuted during the summer in the Charleston newspapers, notably by William Boyd and William Muir. Both were merchants of Charleston and former part-owners of the ship who confirmed their American citizenship (at least since 1793) and the sale of the ship to Captain McNeil in 1799. The charge that a London-based brother of Boyd was now one of the partners in the ship was denied. McNeil, it was said, had paid $18,000 for the ship and thereafter addressed his vessel to the house of Hopkins, Grey, and Glover, not Boyd. A declaration of American registration was also produced from the Charleston custom house.[17]

Lackington, Allen was therefore unlikely to have remained ignorant for long about the fate of the *Two Friends,*[18] but it was only with the new winter order conveyed by the redoubtable Captain McNeil himself in late December 1805 that the Library Society informed its booksellers of the events of the summer. The immediate concern was clear. As the librarian and acting secretary John Davidson explained it, the society's consignment "was retaken & carried into Jamaica where it was exposed to public Sale & bought in . . . [by Captain McNeil] for the Society, as will appear from a certified copy of his Acc.ᵗ" (letter 103). To reclaim the costs of buying back the books, the Library Society demanded full compensation from the £150 of their order that was insured from the underwriters engaged by Lackington, Allen. The South Carolina College pursued a similar claim for £950 (letter 107).

The episode reaffirmed the importance of insurance. In Pinckney's opening letter of 1801, the Charleston Library Society excused Lackington, Allen from the task of securing insurers, but Davidson quickly reversed this and demanded the inclusion of insurance from the next order onwards (letter 87). It had, indeed, been only during the last year that the society had successfully claimed a £44 recovery from insurance on the capture and loss of the Boydell prints carried on the ship *Pacific* in 1799–1800 (letters 81, 82). In line with all the early Lackington, Allen invoices, the combined charge for insurance and duty paid on the confiscated cargo of 1805 was 3 percent. Insurance, however, had been taken out for only £150 of the total consignment value of £170.15s.11d. After the debacle, in December 1805, Davidson instructed Lackington, Allen "that in future Insurance may be made in full so as to cover the premium & all charges" (letter 103).

More aggravating than the uninsured portion was the time that it took to settle with the underwriters. In June 1806, six months after the Library Society's instructions reached London, Lackington, Allen reported that the underwriters had not yet paid out but that at least "we are now in expectation of the produce of the Sale being remitted from Jamaica" (letter 104). The thirteen trunks of the combined Library Society and South Carolina College order were sold for a little over £1,058 Jamaican, but from this the brokers, Tunno,[19] deducted one third of the remittance, or just over £354 Jamaican to cover "landing charges, public sale expences, Brokers, Agents & Registers Commissions, Salvage – 12½ p^{r}Cent to Recaptors, Proctors Accounts, Premium on Bills 10 p^{r}Cent." The total returned was £703.12s.10d. Jamaican or £502.12s. sterling. A year later, payment had still not been received from the underwriters, who, according to Lackington, Allen, "made many objections principally as to the sale & re-purchase at Jamaica which we have had to combat – these we believe are now done away with & the delay is occasion'd by their refusal to allow the heavy commissions & charges which the agents have put on them" (letter 106).

The settlement was finally made in August 1807, but by 14 November, when a new order was sent, the Library Society remained ignorant of its details (letters 107, 108). These were not pleasing. "We regret to find," wrote Lackington, Allen, "that a loss tho small will fall on your Acc.^{t} arising partly from the Policy not covering the whole amount of Invoice & partly from a refusal on the part of the Underwriters to admit the enormous charges on acc.^{t} of Sale in Jamaica, as well as home expences. We have had great difficulty in bringing the matter to an issue; & after advising with our sollicitor, we thought it more to your interest to refer the affair to an arbitrator than adopt legal measures" (letter 107). The total claim against the insurers amounted to the £1,100 of the entire loss of £1,149.5s.5d. for the combined Library Society and South Carolina College books, excepting the total of £502.12s. returned from the Jamaican sales. This last was reduced (and the insurance claim increased therefore) by a total claim against charges in London of £45.13s.10d. which included a proportion of the charge of sending pilot boats to Havana and Jamaica in search of the *Two Friends* and with documents to prove the neutrality of the cargo (£8.12s.4d.), small brokers' and postage charges

(£11.18s.10d.), and Tunno's 5 percent commission (£25.2s.8d.). It was this last commission that the underwriters would not accept.

Resentments hardened when another familiar grievance surfaced. Engraved and colored plates continued to be highly esteemed by the Library Society members and many expensively illustrated botanical, natural history, topographical, and travel volumes were the pride of the collection. The seized *Two Friends* carried a keenly awaited copy of Thomas Holcroft's *Travels.*[20] When the consignment eventually reached Charleston, Davidson wrote to confirm that all "arrived in good Order, but I must inform you that the Plates which should have accompanied Holcroft's Travels were omitted to be sent" (letter 103). In response, Lackington, Allen argued that "the volume of Plates to Holcroft was assuredly packed, & we imagine, if you have not yet found it, that it must have been taken out & not replaced, either by the Captors or Recaptors." The riposte did not go down well. Then some two years since the Holcroft was originally ordered, Davidson insisted that "some mistake must have taken place with regard to the Plates for Holcroft, as the Packages had never been opened 'till deliver'd here when I took out the contents with my own hands" (letter 105). In April 1807 the London booksellers surrendered: "As to the plates of Holcroft we cannot account for them being missing: we will however endeavour to procure another set" (letter 106).

In Charleston incompetence and obstinacy now seemed to accompany interminable delays for the latest publications from London. Library Society frustration turned to real anger, however, when not only their books and journals but also acknowledgments of payments and orders failed to arrive. Between August 1807 and March 1809 the librarian heard nothing from Lackington, Allen, and no advance notice therefore of whether any of the society's books were carried by the vessels that did arrive at Charleston—or that were reported as lost or captured.

It might be argued that the Charleston Library Society was once again assuming that it could ignore worldly realities. Britain and France were still at war, and American vessels were especially disrupted by the Berlin Decree and the retaliatory orders-in-council of 1806. A year later, one attack too many led to the American nonimportation act against Britain and then the embargo act suspending all commerce with the rest of the world. In March 1809, after the election in which the Library Society's president benefited greatly from an anti-Jeffersonian and Federalist resurgence, Congress replaced the "dambargo" with a nonintercourse act— which still prohibited trade with Britain and France. There was, perhaps, unhelpful ambiguity in the last closing courtesy from Lackington, Allen assuring Davidson "that no change of circumstances affecting the amity of our countries (which would be deeply lamented here) will affect our situation with you" (letter 107).

By November 1808 the librarian's patience had expired. Davidson wrote to Finsbury Square, noting that a year had passed since his last letter, order and bill of exchange for more than £200, and that "the Society feels much hurt & disappointed in neither having received the books, nor even an acknowledgement of the receipt of the Bills." This was the more so given that one ship had just arrived from London—without the books—and another was anticipated. Davidson seems almost resigned to that ship's also failing to deliver, but added that a new order for the booksellers was ready to send once the expected shipment arrived (letter 109).

In the following March Lackington, Allen expressed surprise that their earlier receipt had not yet reached Charleston. They insisted that the books had been collected and packed although "the only vessel our broker has apprised us of for Charleston direct . . . suddenly changed her destination, in consequence we imagine of the uncertain state of American Affairs. Since that time no vessel has sailed either from London or Liverpool for your port" (letter 110). By then, however, the new president of the Library Society, Henry William DeSaussure,[21] had written to John Hopton, a leading London Carolina merchant and member of the society,[22] noting that "considerable sums of money" had been sent to Lackington, Allen for some years, and that the firm "have had an Order for Books for nearly a Year & a half, which they have not complied with." During the past eighteenth months, continued DeSaussure, the booksellers had been in receipt of "a Bill of Exchange for £220 on Mess[rs] Harrison, the payment of which they have never acknowledged, tho' we have learnt collaterally that the Money has been paid them – Having behaved thus improperly, the Society have resolved to change their Correspondent."[23] Hopton was asked to reclaim the outstanding balance from Lackington, Allen and "to retain the same in your hands until the commercial intercourse between Great Britain & America, now unhappily interrupted, shall be restored; & upon that event to cause a shipment to be made by some eminent bookseller on whom reliance can be placed. . . . We should be glad to establish a regular correspondence with some really respectable & exact Bookseller whom you could recommend to us & beg that you would make such recommendation." DeSaussure had no objection to Lackington, Allen's completing the Society's last order, but he was clear that it would be their last: "We know that this is a bad course in the unsettled state of affairs between the two countries, but it is better than bringing a suit for the recovery of it" (letter 111).

Two months later, in May 1809, the Library Society turned to an American bookseller supplier not just for American publications and reprints (which appear to have been bought in small numbers in Charleston from the 1790s), but for imported London books. Until then, the society had appeared resolute in depending almost entirely on London booksellers, even though New York, Boston, and Philadelphia wholesalers were now the main and often cheaper suppliers of London-imported books to American customers and increasingly of American publications and reprints. The Charleston library's policy was shared by the Baltimore

Library Company in its early days. When founder members placed their first orders for books in 1796, some 700 titles were ordered from American booksellers, but more than 1,300 titles were ordered from London.[24] Similarly, in Charleston, the Medical Society, established in 1789, sent a £50 bill to London in 1792 to purchase their books.[25]

In despair about the apparent inefficiencies of Lackington, Allen, John Davidson wrote to William W. Woodward of Philadelphia who had been importing books from London as well as dealing in American imprints.[26] Davidson ordered $302 worth of books. In response, Woodward commended his new shipment of books from London—testimony to the poorly enforced nonintercourse act— offering to search through his new stock for any books that he was unable to supply to date, but warning that "if any should have been imported they will be extravagantly dear."[27] The librarian was horrified by the new charges, replying that "as the Books from London come so high you will please to stop sending any more of that description."[28]

Notwithstanding evasions like Woodward's consignment, the nonimportation, embargo and nonintercourse acts effected critical changes in the book trade. The American printing and publishing industry had grown rapidly since 1790s, but cultural and even economic determinants continued to sustain an elite custom with the booksellers in Britain and, to a lesser extent, in Europe. When forced to examine possible American book supply, many librarians and bibliophiles were surprised by what they found. The directors of the Baltimore Library Company, for example, reported in 1813 that the "talents and industry of our own Country afforded facilities greater than was generally foreseen. . . . Many [American reprints] are no wise inferior in typographical excellency, quality of paper, correctness of execution" to the best English editions.[29]

In Charleston's case the sheer volume of the 1806–1811 stock increase might suggest (in the absence of full domestic purchase records) that American books had been bought for some years before the 1809 crisis, but in fact the Lackington, Allen shipments from London remained massive. London invoices totaled £949.4s.7d. for consignments arriving in the years between the printing of the catalogues (see table 6). If the 2,010 volumes added to the Library Society's 1811 *Catalogue* since 1806 were supplied by Lackington, Allen this represents an average expenditure of 9s.5d. per volume. Although variation in costs per volume was obviously great, an average of 9s.5d., including binding and transaction costs is perfectly commensurate (and indeed, verges on the generous) with average volume prices. The average cost per title (from the 845 titles added to the collection 1806–1811) of 17s.8d. seems almost extravagant. It compares to a modern calculation of an average retail price of 14s.4d. per title for the years 1824–1827 (that is, more than a decade later) and to Charles Knight's contemporary estimate in 1828 of 16s.[30]

These calculations suggest that much before 1810 (at least) domestic supply records are absent because they were never written. The Library Society's 1811 *Catalogue* confirms this, listing only a handful of identifiable American editions. The *Supplementary Catalogue of Books,* published by the society in 1816 and recording volumes purchased since 1811, lists general titles only. It is not always clear whether certain of these are American reprints or British originals.[31] Some titles are unproblematically American and include Jefferys's folio *American Atlas,* Arrowsmith's and Bradley's maps, Jedidiah Morse's *Gazetteer* and *The American Universal Geography,* printed in Boston, but also advertised in the imprint as sold by William Price Young in Charleston in 1793. In addition, the library bought the *American Philosophical Transactions,* the American edition of Biddle's *Carpenter's Assistant,* and three biographies of Washington by Marshall, Corry, and Weems. Even more outstanding were Ramsay's local *History of South Carolina* and *American Revolution of South Carolina,* Stith's *History of Virginia,* and Smith's *History of New-York.* The various American agricultural, botanical, and natural history publications included the *Transactions of the New York Society for the Promotion of Agriculture* and Wilson's *Ornithology,* bought together with medical texts such as those on pestilential fevers by Rush and Chisolm. Prominent among the legal works, ordered for reference necessity and respectability, were the *Journals, Public Acts,* Adams's *Defence of the* [American] *Constitutions,* and *The American Citizen's Sure Guide.* The library also bought the American edition of the *Encyclopaedia Britannica* which had been extensively revised for an American audience and published by Thomas Dobson in Philadelphia in the mid-1790s. It was catalogued as "The American Encyclopaedia" and stacked with the *Supplement to the Encyclopaedia Britannica.*[32] Much admired and used though many of these American volumes were, their number must not be overestimated. In total, American publications amounted to about fifty titles from the 3,019 listed in the 1811 *Catalogue.*

This also means that there were significant omissions of American publications from the 1811 *Catalogue.*[33] Despite the handful of American novels, the only Charles Brockden Brown work was *Wieland* (1798), and not his more celebrated *Arthur Mervyn* (1799). Other fiction casualties included *Charlotte Temple* and *Modern Chivalry.* Missing from expected reference works were Belknap's *American Biography,* Graydon's *Abridgment of the Laws of the United States,* and Hazard's *Historical Collections.* The *Monthly Magazine and American Review* was bought, but not, apparently, the *Columbian Magazine* or Barlow's *Columbiad.* Perhaps understandably, but still, in the American context, pointedly, none of Thomas Paine's works were on the library shelves. Many of the standard American books of the period have a northern register so that their absence in Charleston is perhaps not as remarkable as we might suppose, especially given the library's purchase of equivalents to Warren's *History of the . . . Revolution,* and Hannah Adams's histories, all missing from the shelves.

The only extant purchasing records for the American editions taken by the Charleston Library Society are haphazard and incomplete. What evidence there is resides in the scrawls of a small waste book, later labeled "Accessions 1798–1805."[34] It lists fourteen books, including Thomas Holcroft's *Hugh Trevor* (1794 and continued in 1797) from Bailey in 1798, four from Aertsen and Co., eight from Young in about 1798, a further five from D. Smith in 1799, two volumes of the *American Encyclopedia* from Freneau and Paine, and a total of thirty-one titles from Bailey and Waller, all apparently bought between 1799 and 1802. Other long lists of books seem to be proposals rather than definite orders, and still others seem to be those sent for binding locally at Bailey's shop.

The listed local book dealers and importers were now well established and well connected. Bailey and Waller, merchants and booksellers of Elliot Street, Charleston, printed a thirty-three page *New Catalogue of Books, of the latest publications, newest editions, & in elegant bindings, just imported from Europe* in about 1796, listing 875 author entries under subjects and including many novels.[35] William Aertsen, cashier of the State Bank and senior grand warden of the Grand Lodge of Masons from 1787, was a member of the Library Society from at least 1788.[36] William Price Young (1760–1820), library member, and printer of the 1806 and 1811 *Catalogues*, arrived in Charleston in 1788 and began printing in 1791. He worked in Columbia 1794–1799, but was offering a sixteen-page catalogue of books at Franklin's Head, Broad Street, Charleston in 1793, and another Charleston catalogue of imports from London in 1796. Sometime thereafter Young served as a silent partner in the firm of his brother-in-law, Thomas Campbell Cox.[37]

The history of the Library Society's early-nineteenth-century acquisitions should also be considered in relation to local literary developments. These made the preponderant London stock of the library increasingly explicit. At the same time, local readers in search of serious or rare literature were offered more choice with the foundation of the other Charleston and Carolina public and scholarly libraries. They included the library of the South Carolina College, whose books had also been detained by the privateers. The college published its first catalogue in 1807, although it survives only in an imperfect copy, listing 1,105 titles (but with most of the duodecimos missing).[38]

Increased if intermittent publishing activity in Charleston itself further extended the availability of books. Figure 1 has already demonstrated the overall trends, with no sustained advance in the number of titles published locally before 1811 (certainly considering the spurts of activity in the mid-1770s and mid-1790s), and with an average of about fifteen titles per annum issued in the first decade of the new century. To recap, in the colonial period almost the only locally printed books were laws and proclamations (with Peter Timothy acting as printer to the General Assembly), sermons (such as those by Rev. Alexander Garden and

Josiah Smith), and almanacs. Early rarities included *The Chapman's Companion* of 1748, some notable tracts on the cultivation of indigo, and a few early medical and disputatious works, notably James Kirkpatrick's *Full and Clear Reply to Doct. Thomas Dale.* In 1761 Robert Wells printed the *Practical Justice of the Peace* by the chief justice of South Carolina, William Simpson. Charleston reprints included an edition of Beccaria's *Essay on Crimes and Punishments* issued by David Bruce in 1777.

Twice during the revolutionary period more than twenty-five different publications were issued in a year by Charleston printers, including in 1776 a reprinting of the Philadelphia edition of Paine's *Common Sense* (not apparently stocked by the library), as well as a reprinting of the London-produced *Observations on the Nature of Civil Liberty* by Richard Price. Publishing activity in Charleston in the early national period was unprecedented but erratic (see figure 1). Prominent among the new publications were natural histories, travel books, medical tracts, and grammars, including Henry Osborne's *English Grammar* (1785), John Drayton's *Letters Written during a Tour through the Northern and Eastern States of America* (1794), his *View of South-Carolina* (1802), and David Ramsay's *Dissertation on the Means of Preserving Health* (1790). Ramsay's *Observations on the Impolicy of Recommencing the Importation of Slaves* (1791) was much shorter but far more contentious. Throughout these years local printers also worked to provide copies of new state laws and ordinances, House resolutions, and the regulations, reports, and special publications of local churches and societies. The latter included many new special-interest associations such as the South-Carolina Society for Promoting and Improving Agriculture, whose rules were printed in 1798. Charleston printing in the late 1790s was also notable for the sort of literature that supported both increased sectarianism and the growing concern about insurrectionist tendencies. By the late 1790s, hostility to the French replaced earlier Francophilia, resulting in particular concern about inflammatory printed materials. In 1804 the Carolinian authorities made great efforts to suppress reprints of the Declaration of Independence of the French colony of Sainte Domingue.[39]

Clearly, the alterations in the literary market did not always converge with the acquisitions of the Charleston Library Society, still bound by London connections and priorities, and complemented now by the servicing of different demands by different libraries and booksellers. What has been described in an earlier chapter as a part feminization of the library also seems to have resulted in an increased circulation of the collection. In 1808 David Ramsay reported that Secretary Davidson believed "that the number of books lent out for reading has increased astonishingly in the period of eleven years, during which he has been charged with the care of the society's books."[40] Ramsay further observed that after the 1778 fire, the library was "deficient in ancient Literature" and that "since the establishment of peace the attention of the society has been principally directed to the most valuable modern authors."[41] Local anti-insurrectionist material was certainly among these. The Library Society bought a copy of the 1802 Charleston-printed translation by Dubroca of Herbemont's *Vie de Toussaint Louverture,* the former governor of Sainte Domingue, and it also stocked various accounts of slave revolts including John Stedman's *Narrative of a Expedition Against the Revolted Negros of Surinam* (1796), as well as Thomas Clarkson's classic essay, *The History of the Rise, Progress, and Accomplishment of the Abolition of the African Slave-Trade by the British Parliament* (1808).

Locally printed novels as well as more substantial volumes seem, however, to have been excluded from the new acquisitions of the library. This was quite possibly because of their ready availability either by purchase from the booksellers or by loan from local circulating libraries. The importing and publishing Charleston bookseller Ebenezer Thomas was a partner in the Boston printing of Susanna Rowson's *Reuben and Rachel* of 1798. This edition does not appear in either the 1806 or 1811 Library Society *Catalogues.* Thomas also shared in the Boston reprinting of Lewis's *The Monk.* The novel is listed in the 1806 *Catalogue,* but it was almost certainly the London edition. Among more earnest publications, William Best's *Dissertation upon Oratory* printed in Charleston in 1800, seems not to have been stocked by the library, nor by 1811, does Carter's 1806 Charleston-printed *Physiological Essay on the Yellow Fever.* An edition of John Ash's *Grammatical Institutes* printed by Young in 1795 and reprinted in 1798 was also not held by the library. Even more oddly, John Shecut's *Flora Carolinaeensis* printed in Charleston in 1806 remained unlisted by the 1811 *Catalogue.*

The importation of books from London therefore remained the focal policy of the Charleston Library. Following the urgent request from the library president DeSaussure to John Hopton to find a London successor to Lackington, Allen, Hopton replied first to his Charleston brother-in-law, Nathaniel Russell (1738–1820), by whom the president had introduced the library's suit. Russell offered authoritative credentials. A native of Rhode Island, he had arrived in South Carolina in 1765 as a northern commercial agent, amassing a vast fortune by the 1790s.[42] Two weeks later Hopton wrote directly to the president and vice president of the Library Society, recommending that its affairs be entrusted to the general commercial firm of Nathaniel Goldingham, merchant of 59 Old Broad Street.[43] Goldingham was to receive orders and credit and would then ship the books "in due time," as well as deal with custom house procedures and duties, insure the cargoes, and send on both invoice and bill of lading. "All this part of the mercantile business," asserted Hopton, "is quite foreign to a Bookseller: from this cause arose the disappointment which the Society have just now experienced." Goldingham was to charge a commission of £8.10s for his services, but Hopton, calling it "trifling," presumed that this "can't be any object, & in return for which their business will be faithfully & punctually executed" (letter 112). Because of Goldingham, the society was assured, "disappointment won't again occur – the books will be sent by the very first conveyance, but when, is not fixed; the amount of the first cost will exceed your balance about £100 which he will advance, besides the duty, freight &c – hence the whole will go on equal terms & prevent any more, already too long, delay" (letter 114).

After eight troubled years of service, a bookseller was for the second time rejected for a general mercantile firm. Hopton further reported on a visit he made to Lackington, Allen: "I hinted that Interest should be allow'd on the Balance they held, to which they object, in my opinion without reason." The firm had also "protested their innocence about the ship that had been sailing for Charleston a month before – an ignorance which I can readily believe as they are mere booksellers" (letter 112). In the same month, Lackington, Allen managed to send another letter defending their conduct. They insisted that although they would now obey Hopton's instructions to deliver the books for shipment to Goldingham, "it cannot expedite the business since it is a ship only that is wanting & that we shall ourselves make every search for, since we trust it must be evident to every person that the delay is as detrimental to our interest as to your convenience" (letter 113). The booksellers were more than aware that they were in danger of losing a rich if curmudgeonly customer. Many customers, indeed, might be more troublesome.[44] In late August the firm reported that Goldingham had duly shipped the books to the Library Society and that they "therefore anxiously solicit a return of your good opinion which from this unpleasant affair we shall undertake unusual care to preserve" (letter 115).

It was not to be. Lackington, Allen's correspondence with the Library Society ceased, ending also this rare chronicle of long-distance ordering. When, in June, Hopton had replied directly to the president and the vice president of the Charleston Library Society, he suggested that "if you continue resolved to change your correspondent, I recommend to your attention Mess[rs] F. C. & J. Rivington, who as well as their Father & Grandfather, were Booksellers on the same site, St Paul's Church Yard, for about a Century, & are undoubtedly as respectable as any in that trade." He added that the Rivingtons' prices were slightly higher than those of some booksellers, but that they were quality suppliers (letter 114). The irony, of course, was that both their grandfather and great uncle, until declared incompetent, had already been one of the elected respectable booksellers of the Library Society. How long the Rivingtons stayed the course this time is not known.

What is clear is that the war of 1812 ensured that the interruption to the Library Society's London book supply continued. In the society's new journal opened in 1815 it was noted at the quarterly meeting of 15 March that for the previous three years there had been "no opportunity of purchasing Books." The result was that the $4,240 otherwise to be spent on books had been invested in stock, and that now the society was resolved to spend $5,000 on ordering new books.[45] Importation from London was still regarded as a necessity for many books, however, despite the additional cost of purchasing in sterling. Other major American libraries, notably the Library Company of Philadelphia, also persisted with direct London suppliers, but the Library Company's committee, like that of the New York Society Library, conducted its affairs through established agents and trading relationships.[46] What happened in Charleston is not clear. Although the secretary of the Charleston Library Society carefully minuted continuing expenditure on books, no bookseller's name (and certainly no formal election of a bookseller to the society) was mentioned.

Chapter Fourteen

EPILOGUE

THE EPIGRAPH FROM HORACE that prefaces this book[1] was adapted by the colonist George Mason when writing in 1766 to the Committee of Merchants in London: "In crossing the Atlantic Ocean, we have only changed our climate, not our minds: our natures and dispositions remain unaltered."[2] The Charleston Library Society was founded to prove that the civilization of Britain and Europe was transportable and sustainable. To its members the Library Society answered both the needs of colonial social ambition and a quest for connections. The library offered tangible affiliation to a European and to an intellectual community.

Great hopes were raised by the foundation of library societies, despite supercilious reportage in London. A front-page essay on the state of Rhode Island in the *London Chronicle* in 1775 declared that "Arts and sciences are almost unknown; except to some few individuals; and there are no public seminaries of learning; nor do the Rhode Islanders in general seem to regret the want of them. The institution of a Library Society, which has lately taken place, may possibly in time produce a change in these matters."[3] A quarter of a century later, the *General Evening Post* looked forward to a global devotion to improvement, noting that "the Philo-historic Society in Pennsylvania have opened a communication with similar Societies in the other provinces of the Western World, for the diffusion of Useful Knowledge. Medals are given for the best Orations, and the choicest Collections of Books have been purchased in different languages. Philo-harmonic Assemblies are also forming, and the Fine Arts and Belles Lettres are making the greatest progress on the other side of the Atlantic."[4]

In writing the history of the Charleston Library Society, crude and instrumentalist explanations must be avoided. Perceived communities were not necessarily envisaged as mapped exactly one upon the other, and they were represented in different ways to different people. From John Cooper, first library president, merchant, and distiller, to Pinckney, DeSaussure, and the grander, later presidents, the Library Society supported the aspirations of upwardly mobile men of property, but its members were also independently minded. They boasted different (if subtle) ethnic and religious affiliations and demonstrated marked political differences that led some to be expelled from Charleston for Loyalism and others to be deprived for supporting the Patriot cause.

In the design of the Library Society, the familiar wrestled with the unfamiliar. The grounding ideals of all its founders were those of English gentry society, but expressed from a particular sense of isolation. Self-representation as an outstation of civilization in the wilderness gave the institution an acute sense of purpose, however fancifully expressed. The library was, after all, in the words of its own manifesto, established to save Charlestonians' descendants from sinking into "the gross ignorance of naked indians." Bulwark civility demanded unity wherever possible, and the Charleston elite, for whom the library became a cultural and political focus, seems genuinely to have attempted to bridge differing or even opposing interests. In a setting that now seems bizarrely brutal and morally contradictory, the leading gentlemen of the colony sought pragmatic, rational values, founded, wherever possible, on a dispassionate regard for legitimate claims of interest. The resulting exclusivity of the Library Society derived from an enlightenment mission proclaimed in a fluid but highly polarized and defensive society.

In many ways, the situation of Charleston pushed to the limits the transatlantic connections to cosmopolitan community. Until at least the early national period, Charleston remained remarkably isolated. The Carolinas boasted no system of roads like those in the middle and northern colonies and postal services were poor. Ships sailing to northern communities were slow and journeys problematic. A letter sent to New York or Philadelphia via the West Indies or England might be faster than one sent on a northbound coastal ship. Charleston remained a real English province, whose natural orbit was the Caribbean and whose connections with London were savored as stronger and far more consequential than those with the cities of the American north. Charleston's transatlantic links were tested by the Revolution, but also survived it. In the early national period political geographical reorientation was not matched by cultural reorientation.

This is by no means, however, to discount change in either the perception or practice of transatlantic community over this period, and particular aspects of this change are emphasized by the history of the Library Society, its membership, and its acquisitions. The development of the library depended upon links between the technicalities of communications and financial transactions, the different literary and scientific interests, and the members' own particular conceptualization of an international republic of letters. A few would-be savants, like Alexander Garden, pursued a transatlantic intellectual sociability in which the mere fact of knowing another scholar provided an indication of status in a community.[5] John Ellis of the Royal Society urged Garden to resubmit his name to Linnaeus to ensure that a plant was named after him.[6] Towards the end of his life, when Peter Collinson recalled a list of contacts in the colonies, they were headed by those in Carolina.[7] In Charleston itself, men of literary and scientific eminence were further distinguished by their apparent rarity. Charlestonians alluded to this themselves as did far more censorious visitors. Thomas Dale noted in his letters to Dr. Birch that one of the most pleasing aspects of life in Charleston was that he was looked upon as a learned man. He had been appointed judge of the Supreme Court and a justice of the peace and had been asked to write a prologue for a new play.[8] In Charleston one might perform with distinction because of isolation as much as in spite of it.

As all the earlier chapters have attempted to demonstrate, the success of the Charleston Library Society has to be gauged carefully. An early historian of the library earnestly exaggerated the plebeian profile of the founding members, writing that "a more democratic group can scarcely be found than those seventeen men held together by the bond of the reading habit."[9] In this, and in other, later accounts, the Charleston Library Society has been contextualized within the familiar notion of a democratic America born from book-learned self-help and the rights of free expression. But such portrayals are clearly circumscribed in several respects. The assertion of privilege and status by the library founders was elementary, and the Library Society's elitism appears to have been increasingly savored by the later membership. The library's character, at least in theory, was to be determined by the particularity of its literary and philosophical inheritance. And women, lest we forget, featured very little in its early history. It has been noted that one of the most liberal South Carolinians of the late eighteenth century (and a prominent member of the society), David Ramsay, maintained great respect for the intellectual abilities of his wife and yet also praised her for her dutiful "submissiveness."[10] What might be called the "feminization" of the library in the early nineteenth century did reflect, it seems, pressure from women readers of the library's books and periodicals, but their demands were represented only indirectly, through the requests made by the exclusively male membership. Very probably, the new orders for novels and the like also reflected a broadened, more relaxed attitude by many of the gentlemen members themselves towards the sorts of books the library might properly stock.

Contrary also to extravagant accounts of the development of the library, many of its endeavors were thwarted or delayed. The society suffered recurrent periods of low attendance in the 1760s and again in the 1790s. Early attempts to organize a college, a medical society, and a society for scientific agriculture all failed. Gadsden's move to bolster the library's stock of the ancient classics resulted in an embarrassing and negative debate, even if most of his proposed volumes arrived at the library in due course. The pursuit of public science became almost farcical when the library committee attempted to wrestle back the telescope from the hands of its repairer in London where it had lain—as they were later to learn—completely neglected for decades. The proposed Rittenhouse orrery was never built. The attempt at a natural history cabinet resulted in a disorderly hoard of curios that was soon superseded by the specialist collections of others.

Failures hurt. When the library was founded, and again through the revolutionary period and the establishment of the new state, many of the propertied and the professionals of Carolina publicly rehearsed their commitment to better themselves and to ensure the intellectual advancement of succeeding generations. In January 1756 Alexander Garden wrote that "books to me of all things must be the most valuable, as they more immediately tend to my improvement, which I value above all the riches in the world besides."[11] In June 1776 Henry Laurens wrote from Geneva to Gabriel Manigault (shortly to resume the presidency of the library): "I don't think it too much to repeat it, Americans are particularly call'd upon now to improve themselves, you will upon Reflection be convinced of this, and will I hope in consequence act a part which will do you Honour."[12]

Failures also brought redemption. The fire of 1778, no fault of the library itself, of course, resulted in new donations and, after the war, a fresh energy in rebuilding the library's collection. The growing wealth of the society, sustained by the astute if high-risk money-lending policy of its committee, underwrote the extensive book ordering from London, however prickly and tortured the relationship with the supplying booksellers. The genuine difficulties of transatlantic transport and communication encouraged new resourcefulness from both London suppliers and library secretaries and presidents.

The new fiction and miscellanies apart, the overall impression from the titles ordered over these sixty years is of a determined but somewhat clumsy attempt to emulate the learned societies of Britain and Europe. The anxieties and frustrations of the book ordering process led to the appearance of bluster and, occasionally, not a little ignorance. The mercantile and planter wealth that was essential to support this library in South Carolina must also have suggested a certain arrogance in some quarters in London. Yet the cause was a noble one—and one attended by many difficulties. The isolation that lent the enterprise both its vigor and urgency was a very real challenge that had to be overcome by methods not confronted by similar institutions in Europe.

Indeed, one measure of the success of Charleston library members in creating a worthy literary and scientific collection was the relative speed with which they acquired new and important books. The early record, at least, is patchy, with obvious enthusiasms at certain times, but with notable lethargy or myopia at other times. Partly, this might be explained by the changing composition of the library committee and its failure to meet for long periods when quorate attendance proved impossible. One constant concern was to hasten the arrival of the monthly periodical reviews and magazines. A source of up-to-date information in their own right, the periodicals also served as dictionaries to both the latest publications in Britain and to how the critical world received them. With books also, orders such as those for Anderson's *Trade and Commerce* (1764) and Robertson's *Charles V* (1769), dispatched in the same year as the books were published, might well suggest that there was no "Southern cultural lag," as Davis proposes and Hayes seconds.[13] It would, nevertheless, have been hard to ignore what were among the most famous books of their day.

In other respects, the Charleston library was not always at ease in its attempts to secure fashionable literature, or at the very least, the ordering processes proved complex and frustrating. Two examples from an order of early 1804 make the point. Members had obviously heard of William Roscoe's forthcoming book on Pope Leo X, but in fact it had not yet been published and Lackington, Allen, and Co. admitted defeat in the book search. They also informed the society that "Radcliffe's Julia" was unpublished when it must have been clear to them that the society was muddled or at least asking for a very arcane text. What was apparently meant was a 1798 translation into French of Ann Radcliffe's popular 1790 *A Sicilian Romance* whose title, in the hands of Moylin Fleury, was rendered *Julia; ou, les souterrains du château de Mazzini.* Where did a member of the library come by that title, and why did he want it?

It is now difficult to gauge how the resulting collection harmonized with domestic libraries and with the later commercial lending libraries of Charleston and South Carolina. Both private and circulating libraries increased markedly in number and range in the final third of the eighteenth century. Booksellers seem to have extended their modest lending services, although evidence is slight and business methods might not have been the most efficient. On the failure of Carne and Wilson's bookshop in 1763, a *Gazette* advertisement listed various volumes including Rabelais, Horace, Smellie's *Midwifery,* Russell on glandular diseases, and odd volumes of Shakespeare and *The Craftsman,* all "being lent to persons whose names I have forgot, they are requested to return them, as are all those who have any other books belonging to Samuel Carne."[14] In the same year, George Wood commenced his circulating library, announcing that "great care will be taken to add thereto all new books as soon as possible.[15]

Of domestic libraries at the plantations and in the town houses of Charleston, the impression is of small but carefully chosen collections. William Middleton of Crowfield Plantation owned more than 300 books in the mid-eighteenth century.[16] The surviving library of Ralph Izard (d. 1804) and his son Henry (d. 1826) extends to 394 titles and 867 volumes, but how complete it is remains unclear (and the collection was also augmented by descendants). The Izard volumes replicated many of those in the Library Society, notably the historical works that made up more than a fifth of the collection. One of the best surviving domestic libraries is that of Charles Pinckney, deposited in the special collections of the Thomas Cooper Library at the University of South Carolina in Columbia. Notably, it includes the 1811 *Catalogue* of the Library Society (the current edition; Pinckney died in 1824, well before the 1826 edition), as well as that Demosthenes lent to Eliza Pinckney. Also among the Pinckney volumes were various classical authors not kept in the Charleston library, the speeches of Isaeus, and Winckelmann's *Reflections on the Painting and Sculpture of the Greeks*. Many early Carolina libraries were professional, working ones, such as that of Dr. William Pillans (d. 1769) comprising 119 titles, two thirds of which were medical and scientific works, as well as many very small collections formed by artisans, ship carpenters, silversmiths, and modest shopkeepers (among others).[17] If Edgar is right in insisting that "the libraries of these artisans and mechanics belie the usual idea that outside a select group the remainder of Carolina society was ignorant,"[18] then this lower-order bookishness must have exacerbated tensions between those included and those excluded from the Library Society.

A large proportion of books in Carolina domestic collections catered to neither practical nor professional interests, but were bought for simple entertainment and general education. This suggests that domestic libraries might have worked well in concert with the literary supplies offered by the early Library Society. Two-thirds of all titles listed in the 1770 *Catalogue* were not listed in the surviving (if sometimes scant) inventories of private libraries. Conversely, under a tenth of the titles listed in the 1770 *Catalogue* appear in the inventories.[19] The society managed to acquire a formidable range of large, expensive, and rare books, and the notable absences of the early years, most obviously religious works and lighter *belles lettres,* could be left to the individual (and less public) desires of the gentleman's own purse. The library's acquisition of standard histories, legal treatises, travels, memoirs, scientific tracts, and general reference works was of particular importance for those members, most conspicuous perhaps in the founding years, who were not among the wealthiest families in the colony.

We do, in fact, have some glimpse of the private libraries of certain early library members. As discussed in chapter three, many founders of the Library Society, including John Lining, James Michie, and Daniel Crawford, left large and important book collections at their death. William Bull also acquired a substantial book collection and loaned John Clayton's *Flora Virginica* to Alexander Garden.[20] We know that books by Charles Alston, the king's botanist, Linnaeus, and Robert Whytt were all owned by Lining by 1752, the year in which he lent them to Garden.[21] Alston was not on the Library Society's shelves, but Whytt (*Essay on the Vital and Other Involuntary Motions of Animals,* 1751) was. Garden himself built up a specialist collection slowly and with some difficulty. He constructed his own library building in the shape of a miniature temple beneath a large magnolia tree on his plantation, but his collection was shipped out when he left Charleston, his land confiscated, in December 1782.

The continuing assemblage of private libraries, as well as the advance of bulk book importation by Charleston booksellers and general merchants, exacerbated the perceived failures of the Library Society's London book suppliers. Frustration worked both ways. Much of the transatlantic trade seemed increasingly exasperating for the colonial customer, but also less and less worth the attention of many London booksellers. Certain American clients proved especially troubling both for London wholesalers and for importing American merchants. Exacting customers demanded single copies, odd periodicals, books out of print, special bindings, or even particular methods of conveyance. The result, when it often seemed hardly to the advantage of the London bookseller to export and ever more problematic for the customer to take receipt, was that both the supply and the demand for imported books became more specialist. After the conflict with Britain and the financial difficulties of the 1790s, elite customers like the Charleston Library Society and specialist merchants like Bird, Savage, and Bird and then Lackington, Allen resumed the transatlantic trade where others gave up.

Apparent in different ways on both sides of the Atlantic was a commercial escalation of the book trades that involved the creation of larger firms and more regularized practices. General merchants like Bird, Savage, and Bird served as professional collectors in London and the large firm of Lackington, Allen developed an export and clearinghouse expertise. The four-party bill of exchange remained in staple use, but with the complication that final receivers, like Bird, Savage, and Bird, were themselves ordering from other booksellers. Such firms claimed to undercut the more old-fashioned type of wholesalers who were described as disenchanted and no longer efficient in the transatlantic trade. As Bird, Savage, and Bird took care to explain to their American customers: "we beg leave to remark that by the mode of a direct supply from the Bookseller the Book costs much more than if the order had passed thro our hands, Our Commissions as Merchants would have been far short of the difference between the Wholesale and exporting Price at which we should have bought them, and the retail price at which they are now charged."[22]

This contributed, by the end of the century, to greater distinctions between traders and a more tiered structure of bookselling, wholesale and retail. In London, as in other major European cities, large bookselling firms now offered a range of services formerly conducted at different sites and by different personnel. The advent of steam-powered presses, revolutionizing printing and publishing output in the second decade of the new century, reinforced the new hierarchy. In North America, even before the war, a few very large importers, like Leverett and Cox of Boston, had come to dominate their regional market. These main importers then supplied a second level of booksellers, often by coastal trade. The result was a far greater concentration of importing firms, now increasingly distinct from local publishers, in New York, Philadelphia, and Boston. Even in Charleston, where local book publishing advanced very slowly, indirect overseas supply began to dilute the direct commercial transatlantic book trade by the early nineteenth century. In 1797 the London bookseller Henry Lemoine observed that now "in North Carolina they do not import from Europe but purchase, at an unreasonable high price, of the Northern booksellers."[23] During the 1790s the Charleston Library Society made reluctant recourse to a Philadelphia book merchant to obtain a few London books and again for several dozen more volumes (presumably from existing imported stock) during international trade disruptions in 1809–1810 and 1813.

Before local American supply finally came of age, the demands and expectations of colonial customers remained fixed to the east. In the absence of local publications and reprints there was no alternative to imported books, but even when the American presses were more active, the social valuation of imported literature remained strong. Comparisons were also made up and down the eastern seaboard. The speed of news from London and Europe had always been important and competitive. A Charleston newspaper boasted in September 1803 that "our files of papers sent by the Cleopatra, are to 21st July, not so late by one day as those received at New York" (letter 93). The fashionable customer was also the customer who most expected to be able to order new things from London.

By 1812 a social dimension to the London book export trade still contributed to the evaluation of the costs and attractiveness of the product. In North America demand for British and European books had never been uniform, but now it was increasingly driven by particular groups and interests. As with the book boom in England, increased demand had derived as much from those already active in the market and from institutions such as the new proprietary and circulating libraries, as from the increase in the total number of book buyers. In America, this was paralleled in the profile of the relative decline of book imports, but certain outstanding features remained as the more general demand for overseas print began to dissolve (also precipitated by trade embargoes and war). At the turn of the nineteenth century demand in the book import trade appeared narrower, both socially and geographically.

By the end of the century it was clear that the first general cause of the weakening of the book import trade (detectable since the early 1770s) was a structural one. Foremost were the payment, credit-extension, and delivery problems caused by distance and time. Although, as detailed above, new services and expertise were all advanced during the century, information, transport, and associated transaction costs always threatened to make transatlantic trade unviable—and certainly did so once the handicapped domestic American printing industry reached an effective stage of development. Distance ensured lapses of time that aggravated the trials of credit, money transfers and interest. Long-term planning was made difficult by all the transatlantic obstacles.

Underpinning these commercial initiatives on both sides of the Atlantic was the particular nature of colonial demand and the endurance of the relationship with Britain. Despite the many difficulties involved, the British colonial book trade expanded because of the strength of cultural and social imperatives. Eighteenth-century book imports can be explained as lifelines to identity. In essence, books were the physical, readable manifestations of a past and a present European culture, and it was literary fashion—and fashion of largely a secular kind—that played a prominent part in growing demand. In Charleston the wealthy clearly valued the link to London and Britain and were especially anxious to gain access to the latest reading. Independence brought no less and in certain areas even greater clamor for things European. The economic, political, and social advance of the planters, increasingly distancing themselves from the merchants of the town, further exaggerated the social dimension of imperial and European connections.

To some extent Loyalism derived from the trading history of individual library members. Many of those seeking compensation from the Loyalists' Commission in the late 1780s had been prominent in the Charleston Library Society. The situation was common to other Charleston societies, with their overlapping memberships. The St. Andrew's Society, a Loyalist stronghold that ceased to meet between 1775 and 1780, reemerged during the British occupation with James Brisbane, on the police board, as its secretary.[24] Colonial publishers of British best-sellers and book merchants like Robert Wells were also obviously predisposed to Loyalism because of business connections—and back in London Carolina Loyalism lived on. In 1801, Wells's daughter Helena, author of two novels, applied for financial relief to the Royal Literary Fund where she was described as "the daughter of a Royalist from South Carolina."[25]

Carolina had always been closer to Britain than all the other colonies save the West Indies. French sympathies in the 1790s were short-lived, especially after the arrival of Genet in Charleston. Apparent British economic and social stability in the first decade of the nineteenth century gained new respect and envy. With those pictures of King George and Queen Charlotte still displayed in the library rooms in the Charleston Courthouse in the early nineteenth century, the Library Society seems to have sponsored a resurgent Anglophilia that carried particular messages about order, civility, and social standing. By jointly configuring empire and civilization, the society assisted a very particular cultural domination by an elite group. Part of this repositioning involved the subsumption or even suppression of separate former ethnic and sectarian identities within the broader print diaspora of civilized and learned knowledge from Europe. Although we must not overlook the new evangelicalism and religious debates of the early national period, these provoked fresh energies within the Library Society that did not necessarily undermine but rather enhanced London and European connections. The revitalization was obviously effective in the boost to London book ordering in the first decade of the new century and, judging by the later records, in swelling attendance at the general meetings and dinners.

The Library Society, indeed, was established to empower—and not just by the acquisition of textual knowledge, but by the pursuit of particular formal and informal social practices. The texts resided and were used in a specific cultural and political context. Reading and dining, private discussion and public parade, were consorting activities. The development of the Library Society underscores the importance of a literary sociability in which books and bookish interests provided the catalyst for social and political exchange. Many historians have looked *in* texts to understand a local culture; how much more can be gained by study of the broader social history of texts in order to appreciate wider cultural practices.[26]

The library operated at several levels, as a repository of learning and instruction, but also as a social passport and a conduit for polite society. There was both overlap and tension. Quincy's account of his 1773 visit to Charleston quoted at the beginning of this book has featured in many verdicts about the vulgarity of the town. Although it is an account much contradicted by earlier chapters of this study, it does offer further clues about the origins and character of the prejudice. Quincy suggested that "there is an affectation too prevalent in South Carolina of superiority over the Northern colonies, especially over poor North Carolina." Even in North Carolina, he thought, "arts and sciences are certainly better understood, more relished, more attended to." This seems startling and unlikely to be true in terms of books and access to literature, but it does reveal something about the cultural conduct of the society centered on Charleston. As Quincy continued, in South Carolina's northern neighbor "there is real hospitality, less of what is called politeness and good-breeding and less inhumanity."[27]

Together, therefore, the attractions of both sociability and participation in an imagined community explain much about the involvement of members in the library. Both convictions laid certain claims to intellectual commitment. Michael Warner cast the colonial experience of reading as "normally impersonal" whereby the reader subsumed within the reading experience an appreciation of what was imagined to be the rest of the audience for the book. He or she read and in reading assumed links with numberless others also reading the text, extending the notion of a participatory culture.[28] The further possibility here is that readers imagined contrary or more advanced or simpler (or in other ways, different) readings experienced by others. Library members' concerns about free-ranging reading underpinned their attempts to impose ideological and political controls. These included both the early filter against "polemical divinity" and the later restocking of religious controversy, a catching-up exercise designed to understand and contain particular convictions.

Library members' construction of a wider intellectual consortium also contributed to a progressive distancing of refinement from commodification in eighteenth-century Charleston. From the late 1740s it is possible to detect new interest in the plantation as a source of pleasure and status as well as of commercial endeavor.[29] In similar fashion, men of property regarded books as vehicles of enlightenment and instruction, but also, in consequence, as instruments of social and cultural assertiveness. The library was inescapably bound to the intricacies of elite social and political consolidation, where planter claims to public leadership were founded not only on wealth but on education, fashion, and etiquette— precisely the sort of badges and rituals of gentility nurtured by a literary society. At all times aware of their vulnerable position, members of a privileged and wealthy elite employed the Charleston Library Society to reinforce political and cultural unity.

The social and political engagement of the Library Society, while not overt in terms of ideological stances and interventions (both specifically denounced by its constitution), was therefore by no means passive. In this respect, its history offers certain caution to those who have sought to qualify Habermasian emphasis upon communities of conscience. Various concepts of sociability have been proposed in refinement of or in contrast to the idea of stringently politicized communities. A sociability commonly based on taverns, salons, coffeehouses, and the like has been considered in its wider, discursive, effects as unbounded or at least only informally contained. Questions of access and of the construction of class identities are apparently downgraded in such arenas. The development of the Charleston Library Society suggests a more socially instrumental institution, formally organized, and in the context of neighboring and overlapping associations, a European print-supplying and would-be academic organization that encouraged hierarchical division and the establishment of community boundaries as much as any democratizing sociability.

This was, in effect, the most far-reaching contribution of the Charleston Library Society during its first sixty years. When attempting to rehouse the library in the 1760s, Gabriel Manigault described the society as a "private community."[30] His terminology conceptualized exactly the existence of a separate but unified group acting within a broader local society. This was, moreover, an association that did significant cultural work, mostly by cultivating a sense of literary and social belonging. The abstraction of a community that reached back and forth across the Atlantic, fueled and supplied by texts and ships, was designed to counter the fear of loss by the extension and consolidation of an intellectual heritage. The library supplied the texts to foster political argument and mobilization, but also ensured a sociability that survived political divisions among members during and after the revolt against England. It encouraged interest in modern science and ancient scholarship, yet assisted in the transference of notions of civil society and sensibility to the support of slave owning as part of customary social relations. Above all, it constructed and sustained a particular vision of civilized identity that outlasted local political transformation and the conspicuously changing economic relationships with London, Great Britain, and the northern American states.

PART TWO

THE LETTER BOOK

THE CHARLESTON LIBRARY SOCIETY's "Copy Book of Letters" details the literature bought by the Library Society, the booksellers contacted by the society, and the mechanics of ordering the books and getting them across the ocean. In addition, the letter book offers commentary on its own construction. Letter books have in recent years provided detailed firsthand evidence of eighteenth-century commerce conducted by a range of entrepreneurs from tobacco merchants to London booksellers.[1] Crucial questions about the function of the copybooks and their exact compilation are not always easy to answer, however. The Library Society's letter book offers some new suggestions. In the first place, the letter book confirms that the Library Society needed to retain (and preserve) an accurate master copy not only as a simple record but also because secretary-correspondents were required to send out several copies of the same letter. Sometimes further copies were also demanded. In establishing the master record, the copying from the original letters appears to have been good but not always meticulous. Despite considerable variation between secretaries, the hand is usually clear, although marginal comments on the ships used to convey the letters are prone to error and correction.

More revealing is what the letters suggest about the role of the original writing and copying. It is clear that the letter book was used as a record to be consulted by the Library Society committee and members to ensure continuity and to check past ordering. The record was especially vital to reestablish correspondence following the Revolution. In June 1783 John McCall, Jr., wrote to William Nicoll after the gap caused by the war and enclosed a letter that he "found in the Society's Letter Book," originally written by the former correspondent John Colcock, lately deceased (as he informs Nicoll), and repeating the society's order (letter 33 below). There is, however, also evidence that the copybook was used for composing the original draft, with corrections made to it. The alterations obviously prompt questions about authenticity in the event (not uncommon in these letters) of a dispute about the orders sent out to the secretary. Sometimes a change was made in order to record revised shipping arrangements. Against one letter the name of the supposed carrying ship, the *Briton*, was crossed out. The ship had left Charleston some two weeks earlier. A further explanation for the corrections (and oddities of spelling in book titles even by the standards of the day) is that some letters were dictated into the copybook. At the end of letter 46, for example, the ship named after Henry Laurens is misspelled as "Laurence." This is unlikely to be a textual transcription error over one of the most easily recognized family names in Carolina. Newspaper and other contemporary sources offer verification of many of the references—notably the ships and captains—and false details are very few (the apparent mistake about conveyance by Capt. Curling, letter 24, for example).

Occasionally, the letter book suffers from a few lapses and unexplained absent letters. The accuracy of transcription seems to be good, although obviously we have no true measure of this. All financial accounts add up, with one exception (a difference between letter 101 and 106 where, somewhat crucially, £170.15s.11d. is later repeated as £175.11d.). If the Library Society correspondent or secretary did obey such orders as that from the committee in November 1759 to "write to Mr Strahan to desire him to send a discharge or Acquittal of his Demands on the Society,"[2] the resulting letter was not copied into the letter book. The response from Robert Wells in 1789 also points to an unrecorded letter of 1788 explaining the dispatch of monies and the proposed role of an intermediary (letter 41). In addition to the failure to record early incoming letters, it is at least possible that later letters from London booksellers and agents were not entered into the copybook if they were of no relevance to current business. The sudden and disastrous ending to some of the appointments might have elicited further justification and pleas from abandoned booksellers. The abruptness of the Stockdale exchange is a case in point. It is, however, even more likely that a conscientious secretary-correspondent would record all contributions with some bearing on past and present orders.

In chronicling the progress of the Charleston Library Society, the letter book provides unrivaled detail—and a much needed supplement to the other surviving Library Society records of the period. The later part of the committee minute book, for example, is little more than a list of the names of members appointed to the committee, with no records of decisions of meetings, and this record ends completely in 1791. The journal records the proceedings of the anniversary and quarterly meetings from 1759 to 1780, and then again 1783–1790. Also copied into the letter book were various of the society's early book orders, although the earliest and more modest requests, which were written out, according to the letters, on the other side of the original letter, were not thought worthy of entry in the copybook.

All but one of the 120 letters are numbered in the order that they appear in the letter book with a note against those that were copied into the letter book out of sequential date order. The other letter (numbered here as 17a) is a draft letter that appears to have been sent, but was recorded in the committee minute book rather than in the journal.

Original spellings and punctuation have been retained, not least because of the ambiguity they sometimes involve. I have followed the practice of citing a calendar year as beginning from January and of giving the last of the two publication dates in one issue of a newspaper. Thus "February 16–23 1745/6" is given as "February 23 1746." The symbol "❡" has been transcribed as "pr" (i.e., "per").

CHARLES TOWN LIBRARY SOCIETY LETTER BOOK, 1758–1811

"Copy Book of Letters"

[1]
Chas Town August 10th 1758
M^r· Jam.^{s} Rivington[1]

Sir,

    Have yours of Jan^{ry} 30th & July 2^d [1757] with the Books and Pamphlets, On the other Side you have an order for Books which ship p^r first Opportunity, with two Magazines of Each Sort two monthly Reviews,[2] and any pamphlets or papers of Character useful or entertaining. you are not to send any News papers, Votes of Parliam^{nt}, Lloyds Lists or Bills of Entrys.[3] make Insurance as in our Last (the Society not to Suffer in Case of a Loss & to replace ye Order if taken) If any Book sent for is Scarce and not to be had but at an extravagant price, much trouble & charge, you are not to send it. We have had no Reviews since Jan^{ry} 1757, be sure to send two Copys of evry month since and have added to the order the Volumes of the Reviews for the years 1754.5.6. & 1757 to compleat our Set, bound & titled as formerly directed and continue to send the Volume for the year bound up. There was an order drawn on Mr. Crokatt[4] July 19th 1756 and advices to pay to Mr. Wm Strachan[5] out of the Societys Money in his hands £44..13..1 Ster.[6] and now £3..5..2 to d.^{o} [ditto] the Rem.^{r} to be paid to you, inclosed in Copy of advice to him. Also W. & J. Brisbane's Bill on J. Deneslone & J. Stevenson[7] for One Hundred pounds Str when paid pass to the Credit of the Societys Acco. and send a State thereof. Please take notice of the returned premium on last Invoice. Your Complim.^{ts} were made to the Society & they are satisfyd of your Honour & diligence in their Affairs, your hints on the pamphlets are approved, you are desired to continue them.[8]

    y.$^{&c}$ Ro Br [Robert Brisbane][9]

[2]
To Jam.ˢ Crokatt Esqʳ

Sir

I have the Orders of the Society to advise the paym.ᵗ of £3..5..2d due from them to Wᵐ Strachan, the Ballance of their money remaining in your Hands, please pay to Mr. Jam.ˢ Rivington on the Societys Accᵒ. Accept of their Compliments

Augᵗ 10ᵗʰ 1758 y&c R Br [Robert Brisbane]

[3]
Mr. Jam.ˢ Rivington
Febry 24ᵗʰ 1759

Sir Our Last was Augᵗ 10ᵗʰ cover'd W. J. Brisbanes Bill for £100 Ster. Also an order on Jam.ˢ Crokatt Esqʳ for Ballᶜᵉ in his hands of the Societys Money, Also an Order for Books, which hope are with you and Bill & Order honoured with paym.ᵗ. Since have none of yours but had some pamphlets & 2 Magazines, on the other side is an Order for Books which send pʳ first opportunity with such papers and pamphlets as are of Character, always taking Care to make Insurance as formerly directed

y&c R Br [Robert Brisbane]

[4]
South Carolina Charles Town 6ᵗʰ August 1759
James Crokat Esqʳ

Sir,

I am directed by the Charles Town Library Society to acknowledge the receipt of your Esteemed favour of 28ᵗʰ March last, to their Correspondent, inclosing William Strachan & James Rivington's Receipts for the Ballance of the Societys Money in your hands, paid over to them, agreable to the Orders given you for that Purpose. – The President & members of the Society have in their former Letters done themselves the pleasure to testify their Esteem & Gratitude for the Polite favours this Society has received from you, and on this Occasion have commanded me to repeat them.¹⁰

By Order of the Society¹¹

Jⁿᵒ Butler Secʳʸ¹²

[5]
South Carolina Chas.Town 6th August 1759
Mr. James Rivington

Sir

In Consequence of an Order made at a General Meeting of the Charles Town Library Society on the 5th July last, I am to inform you that their late Correspondent Mr. Robert Brisbane then laid before the Society a Copy of his Letter to you of 10th August 1758 p^r the Blan[d]ford Man of Warr,[13] inclosing you a list of Books to be sent Over for the Societys Account, as also a Bill of Exchange for One Hundred pounds Sterling, The receipt of which you have not as yet thought proper to acknowledge, nor have you duly answered any of the Correspondents Letters since that date, in some of which a Second List of Books was sent you, Tho' they must have got safe to your Hands.[14]

The Society some time since received a Letter from James Crokatt Esqr in which was Inclosed your receipt for £92..11.. say Ninety Two pounds Eleven shillings Sterling paid you by him on the Societys account,[15] tho' you are silent about it.[16] I am also directed to inform you that very few Pamphelets, Magazines or Reviews have for many months past appeared from you, Notwithstanding the Positive instructions of this Society lodged in your hands to send them out regularly & what few have been sent, come unaccompanied with any Letter or account from you & generally put up in Packages to Other Houses here which have lain sometime unopened & by this means the Societys Intention of having them as early as possible has been utterly defeated.[17]

The Society is quite at a Loss to judge of your Reasons for neglecting their Orders & paying no Regard to their repeated Letters, They cant but look upon themselves as entitled to the same punctuality which every Private person in Tra[de] expects from his Correspondent & as matters now appear to them, they think themselves much slighted. As the Society presumes the Books so long agoe sent for will either be shipped or ready to ship before this Letter reaches you, they hope you [have] Strictly followed their Correspondents Directions about them, Particularly Of omitting any Book which on account of its Scarcity should bear a very advanced Price with you, and about such Books to wait the farther orders of the Society. What the Society now desires from you is that you will immediately on receipt of this Letter furnish them with an exact State of your account from the Commencem^t of their dealings with you that they may be able to form a true Judgement of them which your long silence & delay in sending Over any accounts has put out of their Power, And as they have & intend to observe the greatest punctuality in paying off every account against them they expect for the future some Regard may be paid to their Letters, as they cannot think of continuing as [*sic*] Correspondence under the same Disadvantages which their Dependance on you has subjected them to for more than Twelve Months past

By order of the Society[18]

Jon°· Butler Sec[ry]

PS
What Letters or Packages &c you may for the future send Over, please direct to the Secretary of the Charles Town Library Society.

[At the committee meeting of 7 Nov. 1759 "a Letter lately received from Mr. Rivington was read as also an Invoice of Books Amo.[t] £123..2..6 Strg with s[ai]d Rivington's Acco.[t] by which the Ballance appears due to him £65..14..10 Strg. It was observed, that in the last Acco.[t] the Pamphlets & Magazines were charged in the Lump, Order'd that the Secretary desire Mr. Rivington for the future to send the Cost of each pamphlet &c."[19] No record of such a letter to Rivington survives, nor is there a copy of a letter to accompany the order of the Committee, 10 Dec. 1759, "that the Correspondent purchase a Bill to remitt to the Assignees of Mess[rs] Rivington and Fletcher for the Ballance of their Account being £78..9..10 St[rg]."[20] At the anniversary meeting of 9 Jan. 1760 "Mr. James Rivington's letter was read, & the apology he made for the Neglect of the Society's orders, was admitted."[21]]

[6]
[to] Mess[rs] Durham & Wilson of London[22]
Chas.Town S° Carolina
17th July 1760

Gentlemen,

I'm order'd by the Charles Town Library Society to inform you that on the 2[d] Instant being a general meeting of the said Society, they were of Opinion, from the recommendation of some of their own Members & your established Character, that you were Gentlemen properly qualified to Serve them as Booksellers & you were accordingly elected.[23]

You'l please therefore take Notice that you are to forward as often as Opportunity offers, two Copys of the London, Gentleman & Universal Magazines for each Month[24] with the like Number of Reviews beginning with February last, also the Universal Review & Smollets British Magazine from 1st Jan[ry], with all pamphlets,

Plays, Tragedys &c, published since that time, either useful or entertaining, & at the end of the year a Sett of each Magazines & Reviews bound up in Calf & Letter'd on the outside of the Cover next the Titlepage Charles Town Library Society, & on the back under the Title C T.L.S, This you are to Observe as a Standing Order & as the Society will be very punctual in their payments, they expect you'l be at some pains to find out Conveyances for this place, to forward their orders as quick as possible, You will please likewise remember to give a particular Charge to the Master of the Vessell you Ship by to put the Society's Packages in the Cabbin, or in some place where they may be had immediately on the Arrival of the Vessell, as very often they are put in the hold & the Magazines &c are old before they come to hand. Next meeting of the Society I believe they will send you an order for some Books &c, mean time please call on Mr. John Rivington[25] & pay him 45/8 sterling for some Pamphlets &c he sent since his Brother failed, for which take his Receipt in full & Charge the Same in the Societys Account.

by order of the Society

Wm Michie Sec^ry[26]

P.S. I forgot to mention that we want [*missing*] Magazines & Reviews for 1759 bound, [*missing*] to Complete our Setts, Please send Ainsworths [*missing*][27] the best Latin Dictionary Extant, Letterd as Described above.

[*note in margin*] p^r Capt Muir   p^r [Capt] Smith[28]

[Meanwhile, at the committee meeting of 4 Feb. 1761, it was agreed to recommend at the next general meeting "to appoint certain Members, to purchase such usefull Books, for the Society as may happen to be sold at Auction in this Province" and it is also "Agreed, that the Vols of the Critical Reviews be compleated to wit, the first six Volumes, & the 18th and 19th Vol^s of the Monthly review be sent for."[29] Some local purchase is therefore to be attempted but there is no more mention of this until Baskerville's Bible is bought in town of Messrs. Jones and Fisher, Merchants, 1 May 1765.[30]]

[7]

[To] Mr. David Wilson[31] Chas Town S^o. Carolina 19th March 1761

Sir I have the Orders of the Charles Town Library Society[32] to send you the Inclosed Bill of Exchange for One Hundred & fifty Pounds Sterling drawn on Messrs. Thomlinson Hanbury Colebrooke & Nesbitt, by Ch^a W^d Apthorp[33] in Order to discharge the undermentioned accounts when you are in Cash Viz^t

To the Assignees of the Creditors of
James Rivington   £78..12..10
To Mr. Potts, Comp^r. at ye Gener^l Post Office &
acquaint him the Society have no further Occasion
for the papers formerly sent by him   9.. 3.. –
To Messrs. Wilson & Durham p^r Acco^t   15.. 2..10
                              total £102..18.. 8

And the remainder is directed by the Society to rest in your hands till our further Orders

I am S^r your &c Jno Remington Sec^ry[34]

[*note in margin* "Copy Bill Sent"]

Exch^ge for £150   N° 5304 New York 19th DeceM^r. 1760 At Thirty days Sight of this first p^r Exchange (second third and fourth unpay'd) Pay unto Mr. Edward Martyn[35] or Order One hundred & fifty Pounds Sterling value received, and Charge it, without further advice, to account of

To Messrs Thomlinson Hanbury Colebrooke	Gentlemen
& Nesbitt Merchants in London (Endors'd)	Your humble
Pay the Contents to Mr. David Wilson or	Servant
Order	Cha Wd Apthorp

Value rec^d of the Charles Town Library Society Edward Martyn [?New York]

[*note in margin*] This Bill paid 7th Nov 1761

1st p^r The Pitt Herriot, Cowes[36]
2^d p^r The Bristol Packet, Marshall, Bristol[37]
3^d p^r His Majesty Ship Dolphin Capt Marlowe[38]

[8]
Chas Town 14^h Augt 1761
Mr. David Wilson

Sir

The Inclosed List of Books* you will please to send out for the Charles Town Library Society by the first Opportunity letterd as before directed, the Magazines &c as for February with a few Pamphlets came to hand the 30^t May last without Letter or Bill of Parcels being the last parcel rec^d. Our last to you was 19^t March 1761 by the Pitt Herriot, the Bristol Packet, Marshal, & his Majesty's Ship Dolphin inclosing Bills of Exch^e for One hundred & fifty Pounds Strg wch hope are safe arrived & Paid.

I am S^r yr &c Jno Remington

p^r Bance Island Cap$^{t.}$ Stephens[39]
p^r Prince Edwd Capt. White[40]
* vide Journal for Quarterly meeting July 1761

[Journal, fol. 24, quarterly meeting, 1 July 1761: Petronius Arbiter Burmans Edit Leyden[41]

the 6 first Vol^s of the Critical Review

the 18th & 19th Vol^s of the monthly Review

Trublets Essays Literary & Moral;[42] Biographia Britannica in 6 Vol^s to the present times;[43]

An Enquiry into the Beauties of Painting by Daniel Webb 3/6 St^{rg}.[44] A Supplement to the English Universal History designed as an Improvem^t & Illustrations of that Work translated from the Original of Dr Baumgarten 2 Vol^s 10^s.[45] Parliamentary History from 1756 to 1760 2 Vol^s

A General Index to all the Articles in the first 20 Vol^s of the Monthly Review to June 1759[46]]

[9]
Mr. David Wilson[47]
Chas Town 27th Feb^{ry} 1762

Sir

Your Letter of the 10th Novr last with Magazines Reviews &c p^r Capt Mitchell & the Packett by Mr. Murray came safe to hand.

My last was 14^h Augt inclosing an Order for a few Books for the Society, the first by the Bance Island, Stephens & Copy by the Prince Edward, White, lest they shou'd have miscarried I now repeat the Order.[48]

[*note in margin*] this l^{tr} is acknowledg'd to be rec^d the 27th April 1762.

As some Pamphlets &c have been taken, and a Parcel came to hand without Letter It would be agreeable to send a general Account D^r & C^r of the Society now with you, that it may be Entred in their Books & from thence their Accounts will be regulated.

I am directed to desire you not to make Insurance on the Society's Account, unless the Value of the Books sent, Amount to Fifty Pounds Sterling or upwards,[49]

I am y^r &c

Jno Remington Sec^{ry}

[10]

Sir,

I was favour'd wth yours of the 30^t April & 26 May past with the receipt of two boxes & one paper parcel by Cheesman & Barnes[50] [*also written but crossed through:* There is wanting in the box first Ship'd the Article Chargd in the Acco^t 1 Univ Mag 1761 w^h Supp 2 Vol £0..10..0 all the rest are] very right & in good Order. The Articles Ship'd by Corrie that were taken[51] shou'd be replaced, & if Trublets Essays are not come out, they need not be sent as they are in the Library already.[52]

The Society are greatly disappointed in not having the Magazines by every Vessel from London to this place wh^ch is hop'd will not be neglected for the future You will please to send out the paper called the Monthly Chronicle from the beginning & Continue it by all Opportunity's with the Mag^s &c.

At the next meeting of the Society your Letters & Acco^t will be laid before them wch no doubt will meet with their Approbation after wch meeting I shall have in Charge a pretty large Order for Books & shall acquaint you fully with the Society's Sentim^ts[53]

I am Y^r &c

J^no Remington Scry

Mr. David Wilson
24^h August 1762
Original p^r Royal Charlotte Woolf[54]

["Copy" *crossed out*] returnd & Sent p^r Barnes[55]

[11]
Chas Town 12^h October 1762

Sir

My Last was the 24^h August past acknowledging the receipt of yours of the 30^h April & 26 May with receipt of two boxes & one paper parcel by Cheesman & Barnes all very right & in good Order –

You have now Inclosed an Order for Books &c wch you will please to send out p^r the first Opportunity for the Charles Town Library Society, directed to me or the Secretary for the time being.[56] two sets of the Monthly Chronicle with the Magazines are expected by every Vessel that comes from London to this port,[57] the latter are not sent hardly once in six months which is a great disappointment to the Members. it's requested you'l send them for the future by every vessel bound here.[58]

The Articles you ship'd by Corrie who was taken shou'd be sent out again, & whenever any vessel is taken by which you have sent any thing for the Society, the like sho^d be forwarded by another, As to Insurance you will refer to my Letter of the 27th February last i:e Only to Insure on the Society's Acco^t when the Value Ship'd is fifty pounds Sterling Value or upwards.

I am y^r &c

Jn Remington Sec^ry

Mr. David Wilson
Orig^ls p^r the Chas Town ^cBarnes[59]
Copy p^r the Eliz^a Mallard[60]

[There is now an interval of nearly a year in the recorded correspondence, a reflection of the desultory state of the society with a committee appointed to consider the "poor spirit" of the membership (AM, 11 Jan. 1763, J, fol. 34).]

[12]
Mr. David Wilson
Chas Town 7th 7^ber [Sept] 1763

S^r

I was favour'd with yours of 17^h March inclosing Bill lading & Inv^o p^r Capt Coombes[61] from whom rec^d a trunk Case & paper parcel in the latter was wanting, <u>Cocoa tree letter,</u>[62] all the rest with your Acco^t Curr^t were right.

The second Mention of <u>Modern part of the Universal history</u> in the Order, was superfluous & it happens right, you did not send them, there is no parcel at present wants replacing. As to the Microscope Camera & Magic Lanthorn, am sorry to acquaint you no way answers the purpose of the Society: to be short, they have order'd 'em to be sold here on their own Account & I have orders to desire you to send over a Microscope as follows.

A new universal single Microscope together with the improved solar or Camera Obsura [*sic*] Apparatus, made & sold by George Adams at Tycho Brahes Head in Fleet Street London,[63] The whole of which is particularly described in Adams' Micrographia Illustrata plates 1.2.3 & 4[64] the Instrument to be of brass.[65]

To your N.B. I am directed to observe, that if you [*word missing*] a charge of the Books, binding & lettering, each seperate, the Society cou'd better judge of the prices, as former Booksellers in their Accounts with the Society have so stated them.

Your Letter with Inv⁰ pʳ Capᵗ Ball⁶⁶ & paper parcel Amoᵗ £2..13.. is safe arrived & right; I should have acknowledged the receipt of your several parcels before, had I not expected to have the Opportunity of sending a bill for the payment of your Account, which the Society had Order'd; but the Treasurer has not been able to get one, they now being very Scarce – & very probable cannot be had before Novemʳ· or Decemʳ·

I am yʳ &c J R

Mr. David Wilson

13ᵗʰ Octʳ 1763

Sir

The above is Copy of my last, this serves to inclose first Bill of Exᵃ drawn by Gabˡ Manigault Esqʳ on Mrs. Sarah Nickleson & Co⁶⁷ for one hundred Pounds Sterling payable to yourself or Order at thirty days sight, when paid place to the Credit of the CTLS.⁶⁸

I am yʳ &c J R

1ˢᵗ pʳ the Adventure, Heidlam⁶⁹
2ᵈ per His Majʸˢ Ship Success⁷⁰

[During this interval in correspondence, there appears to have been a further reflection upon the possibility of using local booksellers. At the anniversary meeting of 10 Jan. 1764, "Also agreed, That any Books hereafter to be sent for, if they can be bought here at near the Sterling Cost, or not exceeding ten Pʳ Cent Advance, on the first Cost, shall be purchased here," J, fol. 38.]

[13]
Charles Town S⁰ Carolina, 8ᵗʰ October, 1764
Mr. Robert Dodsley⁷¹

Sir,

I am ordered by the Charlestown Library Society, to which I have lately been appointed Secretary, to inform you that at the Anniversary meeting of the said Society, held the 10ᵗʰ day of January Last,⁷² they were of Opinion from the Recommendation of some of their own Members and your Established Character, that you was a Person properly Qualified to serve them as their Bookseller, and you was accordingly elected as such. The former Secretary's having neglected to comply with the directions given him by the Society on this head, is the reason of your not having been sooner made acquainted with this your Election.

If you think proper to serve the Society in this Capacity, you will please to Observe, that you are to forward as often as an Opportunity offers, two Copies of the London, Gentleman's and Universal Magazines for each Month; with the Like Number of Monthly and Critical Reviews, beginning with April Last: Also Smolletts Brittish Magazine, with all Pamphlets, Plays, Tragedy's &c, published since that time, which are either usefull or entertaining; and at the end of the Year a Sett of each of the Magazines and Reviews, bound up in Calf and Letter'd on the out side of the Cover next the Title Page, Charles Town Library Society, and on the back under the Title C.T.L.S. This you are to Observe as a Standing Order, and as the Society will be very punctual in their payments, they expect you'l be at some pains to find out Conveyances for this place, to forward their Orders as Quick as possible; You will Likewise please to remember to give particular Charge to the Master of the Vessell you Ship by, to put the Societys Packages in the Cabbin, or in some place where they may be had immediately on the Arrival of the Vessell, as very often they are put in the hold, and the Magazines &c are old before they come to hand.

I have Orders also to desire you'll please to send out at the same time the following Books Letter'd as before directed Viz^t

The Continuation of Biographia Britanica, In Folio, from the fifth Volume Exclusive

The Annual Register from the beginning & to be continued occasionally (Excepting 1761 & 1762, which we have)[73]

The Continuation of the Modern Universal History In Folio, from the Twelfth Volume Exclusive[74]

The Continuation of Smolets history of England from the Treaty of Aix La Chapelle in Quarto, if to be had, if not in Octavo[75]

The Continuation of Blackwell's Court of Augustus from the Second Volume Exclusive[76]

The Philosophical Transactions abridged from the Year 1745 to 1750 both Inclusive[77]

Taylor on the Civil Law[78]

Anglia Judaica by Dr Tovey of Oxford[79]

Anderson's Historical & Chronological Deduction of Trade and Commerce, from the Earliest Account of Time.[80]

At the next Meeting of the Society I believe they will send you a Larger Order accompanied with a Bill.[81]

I am Sir,

Your most Obed^t Hum: Servt

W. Mason[82]

To

Mr. Robert Dodsley

in Pall Mall London

P^r the Africa Capt Moth[83]

[14]

Mr. James Dodsley[84]

Charles Town S^o Carolina February 12th 1765[85]

Sir,

I am Ordered by the Charleston Library Society to acquaint you that having heard the news of y^r brothers death sometime before the Anniversary meeting of the said Society which was held the 8th of January Last, the members then met were of Opinion from the recommendation of some of their Members that you was a Person properly Qualified to succeed y^r Brother as their Bookseller, and you was accordingly elected as such.[86]

. . .

[The letter then follows, word for word, the formula of letter 13 above to Robert Dodsley: "If you think proper to serve the Society in this Capacity . . . the following Books Letter'd as before directed Vizt." The same list given in letter 13 is then repeated, but also with the following additions, as approved at the anniversary meeting of 8 Jan. 1765, J, fol. 50.]

Musaeum Rusticum et Commerciali[87]

Chavalier Ramsays Principals of Natural and Revelead [sic] Religion[88]

The Builders Companion[89]

Parlimentary [sic] Debates, by Anchitel Grey Esqr[90]

[and then added, following part of order in letter 12 above to Wilson] A New Universal Single Microscope together with the Improved Solar or Camera Obscura Apparatus &c. The whole of which is particularly described in Adams's Micrographia Ilustrata plates 1.2.3 & 4 (with any late Improvements that may have been made upon the same;) The Instrument to be of Brass – For this Instrument you are desired to apply to Mr. Dolland the Society being Informed that he is one of the best Optical Instrument makers in London.[91]

Inclosed is a Bill for £100 Sterling drawn on Richard Oswald Esqr[92] by Jno Lewis Gervais & J F Rossel,[93] made payable to you with which you'll please to credit the Society.

I am
Sir

Your most Obed[t] Hub[le] Ser:[t] W Ms. Sec[ry][94]

To
Mr. James Dodsley
In Pall Mall
London 1st P[r] The Prince of Wales. Cap[t] Rod Wilson[95]
2nd The Success Cap[t] Jos: Cookson

[*note added*] Cookson sailed 20th April 1765 & arrived at Bristol the 13th June[96]

[N]B Rece[d] an Answer to y[e] above L[tr] 5th Feb[ry] 1766.[97]

[Following the writing of this letter, the quarterly meetings of 3 Apr. 1765 and 2 Oct. 1765 are preoccupied with the heated debate over a list of "Classicks" to be sent for and its appropriate expense. At the October meeting it is resolved to postpone the discussion over a letter to Mr. Dodsley (who has, in any event, not yet responded to the 12 Feb. letter) until the next anniversary meeting, J, fols. 54, 61]

[15]
Charles Town, South Carolina, 5th February 1766
Mr. James Fletcher[98]

Sir,

I am Ordered by the Charles Town Library Society, to which I am Secretary, to acquaint you that the Members thereof being of opinion that Mr. James Dodsley of Pall Mall their late Bookseller had not served them with that punctuality which the Spirit of their Society required & which their punctuality in payment gave them a right to expect, did at their Anniversary meeting held the 14th January last upon the recommendation of several of their members unanimously elect you as a person properly Qualified to be their Bookseller in the room of the said James Dodsley.[99]

[There then follows the long detailed formula outlining the "General Instructions" adopted in letters 13 and 14 above, "If you think proper to. . . ."]

As the above General Orders together with a List of Books &c were transmitted to Mr. Dodsley upon his being elected Bookseller some of which he has sent out you will please to call upon him & inform yourself how far he has gone & begin by sending out such as he has Omitted, with the Magazines, Reviews &c where he left off as also the Magazines & Reviews bound up for 1764 & 1765, if not already forwarded by him together with Douglas's Peerage of Scotland[100] and the Continuation of Tristram Shandy from the 6th Volume Exclusive.[101]

I have also Orders to transmit you the Inclosed List of Classick's and to desire that you will send them out to the Amount of Seventy pounds Sterling's worth of them as soon as they can conveniently be purchased, and also thirty pounds Sterlings worth more of them in the course of the present Year, to which amount the Society intend annually to send you Orders untill the whole shall be compleated: In complying with this part of the Society's directions it is expected that you will confine yourself strictly to the Editions particularly specified in the List and as many of them are only to be had at Second hand and some of them very scarce it is hoped that you will be at some pains in Collecting them in the best condition and on the most reasonable terms possible. You will please to deliver the inclosed to Mr. Dodsley from whom get his Account against the Society which you will take the trouble to settle with him taking his Receipt; and as from the Money sent him there must be a Ballance in his hands due to the Society you will receive the same & pass it to their Credit, together with the Inclosed Bill for £50 drawn on Denys Rolle Esqr made payable to yourself[102]

> I am
> Sir
> Your most Obed^t humb: Ser^t

> W: Ms. Sec^ry

To Mr. James Fletcher
In St. Pauls Church-Yard
1st p^r: –
2nd p^r: Chas Town Packet[103]

[16]
Chas: Town, S^o Carolina 5th Febru^ry 1766
Mr. James Dodsley

Sir

I am Ordered by the Charlestown Library Society to acquaint you that the members thereof, from the backwardness which you seemed to show in serving them and from their never having heard from you since yours of the 10th of January 1765 rece^d by the packet & conveyance much too tedious to answer their Expectations and also imagining that from your situation in Business some person in the City wou'd be much more proper for them to Corrispond with; they did at their Anniversary on the 14th January Last & before the receipt of yours of the 21st of August Last, chuse Mr. James Fletcher their Bookseller in your room, who will deliver you this and settle with you on the Societys Account, to whom you will please to pay any Ballance of theirs that may be in your hands. You will also please to inform Mr. Fletcher how far you have gone in complying with the Orders which have been sent you to enable him to take them up where you have left Off.

I am, Yours &c

W M Sec^{ry}

To Mr. James Dodsley
in Pall Mall
London

[17]
South Carolina, Charles Town 27th May 1767

Sir,

Your several Letters of the 10th April, 20th May, 1st June, 7th July, 15th Octo^r, & 8th December 1766, I have received,[104] and must Observe to you in answer to y^{rs} of the 20th May, wherein you acquaint me of having settled with Mr. Dodsley on the Society's behalf, that he has not transmitted as full an Acco^t as expected having in his of the 24th of April 1766 (rece^d with yours) only sent the particulars of the last Articles shipped by him, and at the foot charges the Amo^t of a former Order of which I received no Bill; now as the Society's Accounts of Books &c received are all regularly entered it wou'd be very agreeable to have a full and particular Acco^t Deb^{tr} & C^{dr} of Mr. Dodsley from the first of his Acting as Bookseller to the Society, that their Accompts may be continued & regulated therefrom. I must likewise observe here, that proper regard was not paid by him to the Orders of the Society, he having in his Shippings, sent several Copies of Different pamphlets, which were only an Additional Expence, and that many of his Charges are looked upon as high, the Society expecting from the punctuality of their payments to have been supplied on the most advantageous terms of the Trade; which you may represent to him.

In answer to that part of yours wherein you desire to know whether any subject is excluded, I am desired to acquaint you that in the General Directions given in my first no Subject is excluded, which is either usefull or entertaining, at all times avoiding polemical Divinity in every shape, unless, particularly Ordered.[105]

With Mr. Dodsley's you'll please forward, pr next Opportunity, your own Account against the Society, that I may have it also entered and in future whenever you Ship anything on the Society's Acco.t let a Bill accompany the Letter which you'll take care not to inclose in the Pacage [*sic*] as the last had liked to have been Lost for want of his precaution.

You have inclosed a small order (which you'll send out by the first Opportunity) and may expect with my next a further One for the Classic's; The Society having upon my laying yr last (of the 8th of December) before them given in Charge to the Committee to prepare a list to be laid before the Society at the next Quarterly Meeting for their approbation.

I am Sir
Your Obt huml Servt

W: M: Secry & Correspt.

1st pr –
2d sent 3d June 1767 pr the –[106]
Mr. James Fletcher St. Pauls CYd London[107]

[*appended*]

List of Books &c referred to in the annexed Letter of the 27th May 1767

Bracton,[108] Fleta,[109] Sr Henry Spelman's Glossary,[110] Giovani upon Dancing,[111] History of Ireland by Warner,[112] The Laws of Several provinces of America,[113] The Mirrour,[114] Fortescue de Laudibus Legum Anglia,[115] Blackstones Analysis 4to continue his Vinerian Lectures as they come out,[116] Shenstones Works London Edition,[117] Robert Dodsley's Collection of poems,[118] Continuation of Swift's Works London Edition small 8vo[119] – Francis's Demosthenes,[120] The Court Calendar to be sent Annually,[121] Chas Churchill's Works,[122] The Newest and Best Gazetteer,[123] Bishop Gibson's Codex,[124] Edmondson's peerage,[125] State Trials from ye 6th Volume Exclusive,[126] Young Gents & Lady's Magazine by Martin,[127] Lowth's Grammar,[128] Kilpatrick's Translation of Tissot,[129] Heylen's Lectures in two parts[130] – An Astronomical Quadrant, Tellescope Sights Micrometer & the Usual Apparatus, 1 Fahrenheits Thermometer, 1 Reaumurs d.o; 1 Barometer, 1 Hygrometer, 1 pr Globes of the best Sort 24 Inches Diameter at least and a Case of Mathematical Instruments Suitable for a Library.[131]

[Despite the many letters received, the minutes of the quarterly meeting of 1 July 1767 record "a Motion made that the Committee be directed to meet on Fryday next, and that they do then prepare and send such a Letter to the Bookseller, for his late Extraordinary neglect in complying with the Orders of the Society, as they shall think requisite on the Occasion," J, fol. 83. The committee meeting is held Friday, 3 July 1767, recording "in Obedience to the Orders of the Society at the Last Quarterly Meeting proceeded to take under Consideration the Letter Ordered to be wrote the Bookseller, when it was recommended to each member [*seven committee members attended*] to consider of a proper draught, by Tomorrow 5ºClock to which time the Committee adjourned" (C, fol. 42). At the Saturday, 4 July, meeting "Mr. Wells[132] produced a draught of a Letter to be sent the Bookseller, which being read Debated and amended was agreed to and is as follows. Viz.t" (C, fol. 42)].

[17a]
Charles Town Sº Carolina 4 July 1767

Sir,

The Charlestown Library Society at a General Meeting on the 1st Inst: His Excellency Lord Charles Greville Montagu[133] President of the Society in the Chair, were pleased to express their great dissatisfaction with your Conduct as their Bookseller, it then appeared that 'though numbers of Vessells have arrived here from London, some of which left that place so late as the end of April that no Magazine's, Reviews or pamphlets, or even a single Line had been received from you since December nor had any of the Orders for Books sent you been complied with.

The Members of the Standing Committee appointed by the Society were directed to acquaint you with the Society's Sentiments of your Conduct. You cannot, Sir, expect that any private person much less a Society will put up with such remissness and you have certainly laid your friends who recommended you under great difficulties to find excuses for your Neglect.

The Society expect that their Orders will be punctually complied with and Desire that you will immediately on receipt of this Letter send out their Account and an Answer to such Letters as you have not hitherto taken Notice of.

We are Sir,
Your most hum.b Serv.ts

George Saxby, Miles Brewton, Robt Wells, Robert Smith,[134] James Simpson

Ordered that a fair Copy of the above Letter be transcribed and sent by the very first Opportunity that Offers [C, fols. 42–43]

[This letter was not transcribed into the letter book possibly because, uniquely, it was so fully copied here in the minutes, but it was sent for at the committee meeting of 2 Dec. 1767: "A Letter from the Bookseller in answer to the one wrote him by the Committee was presented (by the Correspondent) & being read It is ordered that the same be laid before the Society at their next General Meeting" (C, fol. 46).]

[18]
Chas Town, So. Carolina, March 31st 1768
Mr. James Fletcher

[*note in margin*] – pr the Mary Capt Gordon April 15th 1768[135]

(Copy) pr the Nancy Capt Jordan 25th May[136]

Sir,

The Members of the Charlestown Library Society having at their last Anniversary meeting done me the Honor to elect me Secretary to the same;[137] I was directed to Inform you that altho' they had great reason to disapprove and were highly Offended at your remissness in Several Particulars (especially in sending out the Classics unlettered contrary to the full and clear Instructions given you by their late Secretary) they had at the intervention of your Friends Re-elected you the Societys Bookseller; & that it is expected you wou'd be more attentive to & diligent in the Execution of the future Orders of the Society.[138]

Since the last Letter wrote you by Mr. Mason, several of yours have been received & are all now before me. – The first of the 24th May last relating to the Classics you have the Secretary's sentiments upon above – Yours of the 30th August mentions your not being able to get a Particular accot from Mr. Dodsley, for which I am very Sorry, as it will be impossible to Settle his accot properly in the Society's Books without – I must beg therefore you'd still endeavour to obtain one from him – Your General Accot recd at the same time, has been examined – & is very right – I Observe that you request further Instructions with regard to the Astronomical Quadrant; The Committee before whom your Letter was Laid, recommended to the Society at their last meeting to Countermand the Order Sent for that instrument which I believe wou'd have been done, but through the hurry of Other business, no order was made, You'll be pleased therefore to wait for the further Instructions of the Society.

By the Portland Captn Higgins[139] the late Secretary recd yours of the 3rd Septr last inclosing a Bill of some Pamphlets, which however did not arrive for above a Month after.

Your last of the 30th September inclosed a Bill of some Magazines & Pamphlets which were regularly received – I must observe to you that several Prcells of books have been nearly lost for want of advice by Letter, particularly one of the 3rd May last, which was not received till Octo^r following by the America Captn Rainier,[140] and altho' you sent a Duplicate of yours of 24th May by the same Vessell, you gave no Advice of those Books. Your Letters too in General I am sorry to Inform you seldom come to hand in Less than 4 or 5 Month after the date of them.

Mr. Mason in his last to you, I observe directs that the Bills P^{r}cells should be inclosed in a Letter and not as had been done before in the Package, yet two or three Bills have been received in this manner Since you have had that direction, One of the Packages came to my hands since my Election & it was by the meerest Chance I discovered the Bill between the Leaves of one of the pamphlets You'll be pleased therefore to write however short by every Vessell in which you may send any Packages for the future; as by this means the Society will be always acquainted with the Arrival of any such package; or with the loss of it in case of any & will be also enabled to give you proper Credits.

I have no further Orders from the Society at present, therefore will conclude with requesting that you will Compleat if not already done the Orders sent you so long ago as May last.

I am Sir
Y^r very Hble Servt

J^{no} Colcock Sec^{ry}[141]

[*added*] April 7th 1768[142]

Since writing the above there has been a meeting of the Society when the recommendation of the Committee for Countermanding the Order for an Astronomical Quadrant being taken under Consideration, I was Ordered to direct you not to send one out.[143] The Magazines & Reviews, which you'll observe in the first letter wrote you, you are directed to send out at the end of every Year Bound; by the Change of Booksellers were Omitted for the Year 1764 Be pleased therefore to send them & Observe the Universal Magazine & Monthly & Critical Reviews are to be in two Volumes each, but the Gentlemans London & British Magazines in one Volume each.[144]

I am Sir
as before Y^{rs} &c

J^{no} Colcock S.

[19]
Mr. James Fletcher
Charles town May 25th 1768

Sir

Above is Copy of what I did myself the pleasure of writing you by Capt: Gordon, since which I have received yours of 8th February last, accompanying some Pamphlets and Magazines and inclosing a Bill of them, which all came safe to hand – The members were much surprised at your delay in sending out the Instruments, which you say are done, altho' you have not received further Intructions, relating to the Astronomical Quadrant, and more especially at your not mentioning a Syllable about the books ordered by the late Secretary at the same time as the Quadrant and other Instruments

I am Sir
Y^r very hble Ser^t

Jno Colcock Sec^{ry}

[*note at top in margin*]

p^r the Nancy
Capt. Jordan[145]

[20]
Mr. James Fletcher March 9th 1769

Sir

The Society taking greatly amiss your neglect of their Orders sent you so long ago as May 1767[146] thought proper at their Anniversary meeting in January last to appoint Mr. William Nicoll to succeed you in the Office of their Bookseller.[147]

I have just received by Capt. Laslie[148] the Globes Barometer & 2 Thermometers[149] with a Case of Mathematical Instruments being part of the above Order and also a Lre of Advice & Bill Lading of them – and by Capt. Coombes I rec^d a Duplicate of the same Lre but no Bill of Pcells in either nor even in the Packages.

You will be pleased to give in your Acco. to Mr. Nicoll and as by the Receipt of these last Articles the Society will be in Debt to you, a Bill will be remitted him for your Satisfaction.

The exact Acco.^t I have kept will save you a great deal of trouble in draw^g out yours, it will not be necessary to give the particulars of any Pcell antecedent to the

Articles now received – but of them & also of all Pcells sent afterwards and before this reaches you you will be pleased to give the particulars least they should not come to hand.

I am Sir y^r Hble Ser^t

J. C.

[*note at top in margin*]

P^r the Ship St. Helena[150]
Goes as those for Bristol
Copy – p^r the Dolphin Simblett[151]

[21]
Mr. William Nicholl[152]
March 9th 1769

Sir,

The Incorporated C: T: L: S: finding their late Bookseller Mr. James Fletcher extremely remiss in the Execution of their Orders did at their Anniversary meeting held the 10th January last unanimously elect you their Bookseller upon the recommendation of several of their Members.

Shou'd it be agreable to you to serve the Society in this Capacity . . . [There follows the explanation of "General Instructions" as in letters 13 and 14, with the qualification (cf. letter 17 above) that the bookseller when selecting "Pamphlets, Plays, Tragedy's &c" should be "of Character which are either useful or entertaining always avoiding Polemical Divinity unless particularly Ordered." The paragraph then concludes:] The late Bookseller not attending to the spirit of the above General instructions, supplied the Society not only with all the unsaleable hawk of his Shop, but with many books about the size of Plays & Pamphlets & which being Sewed in Boards too were often doubly unfit to have places in our Library – books therefore of that size you will take Notice are not to be sent but by order of the Society.

By every Vessell in which you may ship be pleased to write a letter of advice of the same inclosing a Bill of Parcells & with every subsequent bill a Copy of the preceding that in case of a loss the Society may be early inform'd of it and the Secretary give you proper Credits.

As the Society will be always very punctual in their payments they expect to be supplied upon the most reasonable terms as also that you will be dilligent in searching for & careful in complying with their Orders by the earliest opportunities. The late Pacquets which were sometimes made use of by Mr. Fletcher were very improper conveyances as this was the last Port of many they went to; but the new Pacquets & also the Vessells in this Trade of whose sailing you can always be inform'd at the Carolina Coffee-house[153] I recommend to you. You will also be pleased to give particular Charge to the Captn to put the Society's Packages containing occasional & Periodical publications in the Cabbin or some other place where they may be conveniently had immediately upon their Arrival.

Inclosed you have a Letter for Mr. Fletcher & his Account with the Society as far as it can be made out on this side the Water, which is given to enable you to check his Accompts, which you'll be pleased to settle with him & as there will be a Ballance due him I shall in my next transmit you a Bill for payment thereof: By his Accompt you will perceive how far he is gone in complying with the above mentioned Gen^r as well as the particular Orders of the Society (of which you have a Copy at foot given him so long ago as May 1767, now near two Years* past) and you will therefore take them up where you find he has left off.

Mr. Fletcher by order of the Society settled with his Predecessor Mr. James Dodsley but neglected to obtain a regular acco^t from him & notwithstanding the repeated directions given him has not as yet obtained one. I must beg you'd take this further trouble upon you & get if possible a particular acco^t of 2 parcels of Pamphlets sent by that Gentleman those being all that are wanting to settle his Acc^{ts}: one Shipt in July 65 & called 33 Pamphlets without particularizing the Name or price of any & the other in March 66 in the same manner. This if you can obtain of him you'll be pleased to transmit together with Mr. Fletchers Acc^{ts} & the remaining part of the Order not complied with by him, as soon as possible directed to

Sir

y^r very hble Ser^t

Jno Colcock Secretary

* for this Order Vide 3 pages ante[154]

The following are now Ord^d for the first time

Ld Lytteltons Hist: of Henry 2:^{d},[155] Hutchinsons Hist: of Massachusett's Bay,[156] Mosheims Ecclesiastical History,[157] Hookes Roman Hist:,[158] Salmons Abridgmt of State Trials[159] – Montesquieu's Letters[160] – Vattell's Droit DeGens in French & also a Copy in Eng^{sh} as translated[161] – Cays Edits of Statutes at large from 1758 30th Geo: 2^d [162] – Rougheads Edit. of Statutes at large[163] – The Philadelphia Farmers Letters[164] –

[22]
Mr. William Nicoll
Charles town July 24th 1769

Sir

I wrote you some Months ago informing you of your being elected Bookseller to the Charles town Library Society & altho' Capt. Arthur by whom I sent the Original has since returned here,[165] I have not had the pleasure of hearing from you – by which I fear that Letter miscarried; but am in daily hopes of doing so as I am now informed of Capt. Simbletts arrival by whom I sent a Duplicate of the same Letter.

I now enclose you the 1st of a Sett of Bills of Exch^a for £100 St^g the most part of which will be sunk in the Discharge of Mr. Fletchers Acct. – It is not usual for the Society to be so largely indebted to their Bookseller, their being so now is entirely owing to that Gent.^s complying so late with the Orders of the Society.[166]

I must beg you'd not pay his Demand without a particular Acco. of such Parcells as I have not already acknowledged the rec^p of by the Acco. Curr.^s inclosed.

At foot you have a New Order which with the former & the remaining part of that sent Mr. Fletcher not complied with by him you'll be pleased to Ship by the first opportunity. I am Sir

Yr hble Ser^t J. C.

[*note at top in margin*]

P^r the Polly Rainier saild[167]
copy p^r the Beaufain Curling[168]

[*listed at end*]

Tertullian; Opera,[169] Perry's State of Russia,[170] Ferguson's Hist. of Civil Society[171] – S^{ir} James Stewart on Government[172] – X [*sic*] Stewart Mathem.^s Works[173] – Robertson's Hist. of Emp. Chas. 5[174] Priestley's Eng^l Grammer[175] – Rhimers Federa,[176] Dr Middleton's Works 5 Vols 8vo.[177]

[23]
Mr. William Nicoll
Charles town 28th September 1769

Sir

Yours of the 9th June by Capt Ball I have rec^d together with the Pamphlets sent with it and also your other Letter of the 18th July with the Pamphlets then sent.[178]

I shall in the first place answer your remarks on the Instructions sent you The reason for that confin'd one of Plays & Pamphlets is as I before inform'd you owing to Mr. Fletchers sending books of no little Value without the express directions of the Society in particular among the last books sent us by that Gent. is Grainger's [*sic*] Hist: of England in Boards Price 2 Guineas:[179] This is certainly a Sum too large for the Society to be often surpris'd into; But the intention of the Society (before whom I have not had an opp^y of laying your L[ett]^{rs} & shall not till 4:th Oct. next one of their Gen.^r Meetings) was not I believe to restrain any Political or other publication of Character whose price might exceed the gen.^l one by a Shilling or two – Sho^d you be inclin'd at any time to send any such & which may be worthy of a binding I apprehend you might easily get it bound before it is sent out as the expence is greater on this side the Water than with you in that case you'll observe it must be letter'd also.

I am sorry Mr. Fletcher wou'd not be more particular in informing you what pamphlets he had sent out as by that means we have more than one Copy of the State of the Nation & the observations on it – indeed that Gent. himself sent us two Copies of the first, which without any other is suff.^t instance of his inattention to the business of the Society.

The publications on American affairs will not be disagreeable I believe unless some of them may be tho.^t to be the Eccho of others; of that you can easily be a Judge & I dare say you will not send any such merely because they relate to us whether well wrote or not.

I am obliged to you for the trouble you have taken with Mr. Dodsley.

In answer to what you say of Ld Lyttletons Hist:[180] you will on all cases send out the best Edition Extant of the Books Ord^d by the Society; the paltry Editions sent us by your Predecessor was one great cause of Complaint against him. Edmondson's Peerage a Book of Cost had nearly been retd to him for that Reason.[181]

You have omitted send^g 2 copies of the London Magazine with the others for May & June they need not be sent for those Months you have or may omit as they will have been read before they can arrive here by all the Gent. of the Society but as soon as this reaches you be pleased to let them be sent for the last Months together with the others.

I observe you pay 2s p^r Balls Bag this is a new charge to the Society & need not be paid by you I apprehend for such small parcells as I pay postage for them here as L[ette]rs.

Mr. Fletcher has sent us 2 or 3 Acc.ts Curr^s & one by the Packet for wch I pd 2s Stg post^{ge} & desires he be speedily paid his Acco. which I have examined & found right bal^{ce} due him £83.10.8½ which I suppose you will have paid him ere this comes to your hands. I shall lay your L[ette]rs before the Society on Wednesday next when I shall have their future Orders to transmit. In the meantime

I am yr very hble Sec^t

J: C: Sec^y

P.S.
Some Gent. having an inclination to propose sending for the Journals of the H: of Comm^s I must beg you'd inform me what they may be purchased for.

[*note at top*]

p^r the Mermaid
Capt Ball[182]

[24]
January 25th 1770

Sir,

I wrote you sometime since p^r the Mermaid Capt Ball, since which I have laid a Copy of the same before the Society who approved of the answer I gave you in explanation of the General Instructions, The last which was the Anniversary meeting the 9th Instant was the first Opportunity I have had of laying your Letters before the Society and I was desired to inform you that the Members were much Pleased at the Inclination you express to serve them and the Attention you promise to pay to their Orders. Your several Letters and Bills of 21st August 9th & 25th Septr and 8th Novr have been duly received. The Books mentioned in That of the 21st Augt were not received till 19th Decem^r after Capt. Gun[183] who brought them was again sail'd for England which was owing to a Neglect of Sending the Bill of Lading. The Books not sent for the several reasons given by you will be remarked upon at foot. The Pamphlets mentioned in Bill of 9th Septr being an Ode to Shakespeare &c said to be ship'd by Markell[184] I applied for frequently but never received and instead of them I received 2 Parcells of Magazines and Dr Musgrave's Reply[185] – Your last of 8th November by Curling[186] gave me Advice of a Trunk of Books which were duly received in good Order. Mr. Fletcher's Account as Settled by you

is very right The Book mentioned in this Bill not sent is also remarked upon at foot
– Inclosed you have 1ˢᵗ of Sett Bills Exchᵃ for £50 only being all I could procure to
be sent you at Present, the Society having lately Let a Sum to Interest – Mr. David
Wilson formerly a Bookseller to our Society has lately made a Demand for a Ballance due him. It was thought his Acco.t had been long ago settled but upon examination it was found that the sum of £7.15.11 was due him since the 16ᵗʰ Janʳʸ
1765 The Society have therefore Ordered that the said Ballance be paid him with
Interest from the above date at the Rate with you which you will be pleased to do[187]
I observe by your letter you mistook the Order sent you for a Tellescope &c and
thought we had one – the Order was meant to stand thus. A Tellescope – with
proper Sights a Micrometer and the Usual Apparatus fitting for a Place in our
Library but those as well as the Laws of the Provinces the Society have since
thought proper to Countermand and you will wait further Orders Concerning
them,[188] with regard to the Tellescope &c be pleased to inform me in your next
what wou'd be the Cost and Size of such a one as you would recommend and also
what woud be the Cost of Hills Eden[189] neatly bound and Collᵈ Be pleased to add
to your General Instructions the Court Calendar which you are to send out Annually. I am sorry you sent the Farmers Letters[190] sewed we cou'd have got them here
in the same manner in a former letter I requested that when any new publication
worthy of a Binding was Ordered you woud get it bound before you sent it. Be
pleased to direct any Trunk or Box you may send me in future For the Charles
Town Library Society and to my care at Large this is more particularly Necessary
at this time as the Committee of yᵉ Inhabitants are calling on me to know what it
is I import Contrary to the Resolutions of the People. At foot you have some new
Orders you will Comply with as soon as possible

> I am Sir
> yʳ very Hble Sevᵗ
>
> J: C: Secretary

Books Ordered from Mr. Fletcher & yourself & not yet received to be sent now[191]
– A Treatise on Dancing by Giovanni Andraea Gallini (Mistitled before)[192] History
of Ireland by Warner (not of England)[193] The Mirrour of Justices – an old Law
Book[194] Continuation of Swifts Works, We have 13. Volˢ 12ᵐᵒ London Edition
1749 State Tryals from 6ᵗʰ Vol. exclusive[195] (This you forgot) Magazines and
Reviews bound & letterᵈ for 1764 Omitted by a Change of Booksellers, & Mon-
tesquieus Letters– (you sent us Montagu's Persian Letters instead of them.)[196] Stew-
arts Mathematical tracts in 8ᵛᵒ London Cost 7/6–[197]

Books now first Ordered, Catesby's Natural History of Carolina Collᵈ.[198] Lawson's
Account of his Travels through Sᵒ Carolina in 1711.[199]

[*note at top*]

p^r Nancy Jordan[200]
p^r the Minerva Arnott[201]

[25]
Chas Town October 20th 1770

Sir,

I am directed by the Society to request you would send the above Books by the first Opp^y [Montesquieus Letters on the Roman Republick / St. Evremond's works; The Frederician Codes / British Magazine Bound for the year 1764 & any other year after 1766 for which they may be had[202]], & also take the trouble of informing Mr. Fletcher that the Copy of Edmondson's Peerage sent us by him wants the 2nd Sheet of the Geneaological table of Harley Lord Oxford's family to Compleat it.[203] if he will not, you will be pleased to provide us with it.

You are requested also to purchase as cheap as possible a Copy of the Journals of the House of Commons;[204] in order for your better doing So, you will take such time to procure them as you please not exceeding 12 months.

Fletcher also sent us a p^r Globes of 28 Inches (the largest Size) in a Mahogany Stand with eagle claw feet but neglected to send proper covers for them, the Society beg the favour of you Sir to get a p^r of Covers fit for them made & transmitted as soon as possible.[205]

The Society at their last Meeting took under Consideration the Acc^t of the Expences of a Tellescope sent us by you & it was agreed to drop all thoughts of one for the present the Library room being at this time fixed where such a Instrument would be useless.[206]

Inclosed you have 1st: 2nd of a Sett of Bills of Exchange for £57.10s.[207] which will not only Settle the Ball^e of your Acco.^t but also put you pretty well in Cash for the Books now Ord^d.

Your Acco^t Curr^t to 13th April Last I have rec^d & Ex^d you have C^r for a few pamphlets rec^d by Maitland, Shipd by you 25th September 1769[208] amot^g to 3/6 which you do not charge us with, on the other hand you charge us with Sundries p^r Markall 6/8 which as I before informed you were never received & also 9/1½ for sundries p^r Gun for which also you are not Credited & which were never received, the acct. is otherwise very right.

I am
Sir
Y^r very Hble Sev^t

Jn: Colcock Sec^ry

P.S.

Since writing the above I have recollected that I rec^d a parcell of Pamphlets p^r Duncan being a Narrative of complaint against Melville &c without Letter or Bill.

[*note at top*]

p^r the Swallow Packett
Capt Wauchop[209]
sail'd 21st October 1770
Copy p^r the Charm^g Sally
Capt Rainier saild the [*space left; never filled in*] Novr 1770[210]

[26]
Mr. William Nicoll
10th January 1771

Sir,

You are desired by the Society to send out the Books mentioned at foot as soon as possible, and also to take notice that the Magazines & Reviews are not for the future to be sent out bound either ½ yearly or yearly, but instead thereof you are to furnish the Society with all necessary Prefaces, Frontispieces, tables of Contents, indexes &c in order for their being bound up here, as we have been hitherto at a double expence,[211]

I am Sir yr very hble Ser^t J: C.

The Septuagint[212] – Cottons Abridgm^t of the records of the Tower[213] – Beccaria's Essay on Crimes & Punishments[214] – Chambauds French Dict.[215] Delpino's Spanish d^o [216] – Barretti's Italian d^o[217] – Baron Bielfeld's Elements of universal erudition[218] –

[QM, 2 Oct. 1771: "The Concave Mirrour proposed and agreed to at the last Meeting was also agreed to at this. Ordered that the Secretary does direct the Bookseller to send one of the best sort and largest Dimensions" (J, fol. 136). If the direction was sent, no copy now survives.]

[27]

Mr. William Nicoll Chas Town Decr 6th 1771

Sir,

I have now the pleasure of transmitting you the first of a Sett of Bills of Exchange drawn by Mess$^{rs.}$ John Simpson & Co[219] on Mr. John Forrest Junr Merchn^t in Edinburgh[220] for £70 St.^{g} which I am extremely sorry we cou'd not obtain at a shorter sight than 60 days.

At foot you have a list of Books which you will send out by the earliest opp.^{y} some of them may give you some trouble in procuring as the Society has been necessarily obliged to leave the choice of the best Editions to your Judgment.

The Trunks p^r Ball[221] were duly rec^d agreable to the Bill of P^{r}cells – Be pleased to send me by the next opp.^{y} after receipt of this a full Acco.^{t} Current that I may see in what manner you have rectified the mistakes I pointed out to you sometime ago & carry the ball^{ce} if found right to a new Acco.^{t}.

There are several works as St. Evremont & others which being out of print & from other Causes you have not sent when ord^d, these you will always have an eye to when those causes are removed.[222]

It is with concern the Society whilst it commends y^r dilligent execution of its orders is obliged to condemn any part of your Conduct; but I am orderd to inform you that you are thought not sufficiently careful in your choice of the Pamphlets you send many which are the dry jejune performances of writers of mean parts & little Genius; & not only so, but by not keeping (as it wou'd seem) the titles of them you sometimes send us Duplicates; of the former kind may be instanced most of the several pamphlets you sent us on the intrigue of the D: of C: (with LHG)[223] & many others & of the latter Clementine, Falklands Islands &c[224] – A more strict Attention to these particulars in future will make your Conduct altogether agreable to every member of the Society, which cannot give greater pleasure to you than, Sir,

yr very hble Sert

J^{no} Colcock Secr^y & Corresp^t.

Books &c to be sent

Brown's[?] Scripture Chronological tables fol,[225] Priestly on Electricity[226] Burns Justice fols.[227] Congreves plays 3 Vols[228] Burlamaquis Nat^l & polit^l law 2 vols.[229] Adventurer by Hawkesworth 4 Vol^s[230] Swammerdam's Hist of Insects fol[231] Linnais [*sic*] Systema Natura last Edit.[232] Harris's Hermes 8°[233] Cronstedt's mineralogy 8vo[234] Sheridan on Elocution last Edit.[235] Cunningham's Law of Bills of Exch^g 8vo dittos Law Dictionary fol[236] Sidneys discourses on Governmen^t fol^s[237] Beattie's Essay on truth[238] Baburye's book of rates last Edit.[239] Guthrie's Geographl Grammar 8vo[240] Chrysal or the Adventures of a Guinea 2 Vols[241] Horace by Dacier[242] A collection of the Laws of Trade particularly those respecting America[243] The Marquis Beccaria's Lectures & in general all the works of this Author & of Baron Bielfeld which have been translated into English,[244] except those you have already sent us which are the Essay on Crimes & Punishments of the former & the Elements of Education of the latter.[245] A Collection of all the treaties of Commerce, Friendship and Alliance between Great Britain & foreign powers. We have an old collection of 4 Vols 8vo which was printed under rules somewhat differing & at different times the first in 1710 the 2d in 1713 & the 2 last in 1732 if therefore there is any other more perfect & compleat collection you will send it out, but if not, send us any volumes that may have been printed to compleat this Sett.[246] A Concave Glass Mirrour (to be bt of Brass) for views prints of the best sort & largest dimensions (Mind a Common diagonal show glass is not meant) were initialy at a loss with regard to the Value of the mirrour, but it is supposed it will not cost above or at most not much above £15 Sg.

[*note at top*]

pr Wilson[247]

[28]

[*no date and no addressee*]

[*note in margin*] Pr Liberty Lesslie sail'd Sept 1772[248]

Books to be sent for the C:T:L:S:
Instructions for a Code of Laws for the Empire of Russia[249]
Curious remains of Antiquity collected by the Society of Antiquarians of London[250]
Lelands Antiquities,[251] Sr Chas Whitworth's Edition of Dr Davenants Works[252]
Martin's Hogarth Moralized[253] – Knox's Campaigns in America 2 Vols 4to[254]
Prints Draughts & prospects of the Mississippi River by Pittman, when published –[255]
Caves Lives of the Apostles[256] – best Edit, 3d & 4th Vols. of Ld.Lytteltons Life of Henry 2d –[257]
Lee's Botany 4to[258] Dr Priestly's Geograpl & Chronoll tablets with the 2 pamphlets of explanation[259]

Sir,

Above you have a list of Books which you are to send by the first conveyance for the Society[260] – Yours of the 4th June I have just reced together with the Books & Mirrour then sent – The Acc.t Currt you then sent, I can make nothing of, as there are not those Charges which agree with your Bills of parcells in date & amount – I sho.d be glad you'd send a General Acc.o Curr.t from the beginning – I am extremely sure that I have regularly credited you for every parcel of books I have rec^d but we differ in amounts greatly.

I am Sir y^r very hble Se^v J: C: Sec^ry

[29]
Mr. William Nicoll August 8th 1773

Sir,

Having been a long while silent I seize this opp^y of informing you that I shall in a day or two enclose you a large order of the Society – A Bill for £100 St^g is Ord^d to be sent you but a Bill is not to be purchased even for a Prem^m. The Treasurer of the Society informs me he is endeavouring to collect as many Guineas, if he succeeds, I shall transmit them by Capt. Dove who will sail in the course of the next week.[261]

You are desired to insure £1000 St.^g value on the Books of the Society which are kept in a large Room in a Brick building situated in Union Street on the corner of a side alley a lane leading into that Street – The underpart of this building is divided into two stores which are sometimes lett to persons who keep liquors in them but not selling by retail. As they are not used as dwellings there is no fire kept but by our Librarian in his office house in Winter. The Society are of opinion that, as the risque is small considering the circumstances above mentioned, also considering the great activity of our people in cases of fire, our being well supplied with fire bags, the number of our members (to whom the books are more valuable than the prices of them) &c, you may get this sum insured for one p^rCent – You will however get it insured as low as possible – Sho.^d you be at a loss to transact this business you will probably get information from some of the Carolina Factors who insure for their Correspondents here for one P^rC^s Prem^m. You are particularly requested to be very careful to have the names of indisputable men to the policy, a Copy of which you will please transmit.[262]

Mr. Wells promised some time ago to write & let you know that the Drawing of the Paintings of the Herculaneum[263] are proposed & likely to be agreed to be sent for that you might have time to lay your hands on a Copy – You are desired to send them out –

I am desired to inform you that the Society take greatly amiss to your neglecting some of their orders long ago sent Viz.^t the 5th Vol. of Edmondsons Peerage wantg to compleat our Sett.[264] – The Vols want^g to compleat our sett of Cays Edition of the Statutes at Large & of the State Trials.[265] On this Acc^t I think it will not be improper to send you Copies of our Catalogues by which you will see several other works of which we have incompleat setts – As these or at least our appendix has been finished since your appointment you will from them & your Acc^ts since, be fully acquainted with all the Books the Society is possessed of I propose sending them to you by the first person going to England with whom I may be acquainted & who will take the trouble of delivering them himself & shall also send you a Copy of our Rules from which & the Advertisement prefixed to them you will become better acquainted with us – You will observe that several volumes have been lost of some history, romances & other paltry books which found their way into our library in the infancy of the Society, if you can easily & cheaply lay your hands on the missing volumes you may send them out

I am, Sir Y^r very Hble Servt J: C: Sec^ry

[30]
Mr. Wm Nicoll
November 10th 1773

Sir,

Our Treasurer having found means at last to obtain a sett of Bills of Exch^ge I now inclose you the first of the same drawn by Mr. J: Scold on Greenwood and Higginson[266] for £100 Stg at 20 days sight which you will be pleased to receive & carry to the Credit of the Society.

I am, Sir

Yr very hble Servt J: C.

[At the quarterly meeting of 6 Apr. 1774 it was "Order'd that in future all Packages Pacquets or other things sent over to the Society be directly carried to the Library & be there open'd in the presence of the Librarian & that no Packet or Package be on any account whatever open'd at any other place" (J, fol. 160).]

[31]
Mr. Wm Nicoll
Charles town S. Carolina Aug 10th 1774

Sir,

You now have at foot a long list of Books which have been ord^d to be sent for a great while past & at many meetings of the Society, but which I neglected send^g as I found some of the Books proposed were in the Library but had miss'd the eyes of the proposer by being placed in our Catalogues under improper letters while others were twice proposed for various other reasons – Having now corrected the list let me beg you will be as expeditious as possible in sending them out.[267] In my last Order I made mention of the Drawing of the Antique paintings of the Herculaneum & also of the 5th Vol. of Edmondsons Peerage & others want.^g to compleat diff.^t setts of our Books,[268] The Statutes at large & the State trials in particular,[269] which I have never rec^d nor have you made mention of in your letters – As I now send you by Co M^r. Shirley[270] the Copies of our Rules, Catalogues & Appendix long since promised you will be at once acquainted with all the Books we are possessed of & be enabled to see what works we have incompleat setts of & which you will be pleased to compleat as soon as possible.

You are desired to subscribe in the name of the Society for a Copy of the Encyclopedia 25 Vol^s Fol^o at the Booksellers who advertise that work in London if the Subscription is not already closed & the work published – if it is – to purchase a Copy if possible –[271]

Since my last I have duly rec^d yours inclosing Bills of Pamphlets & also the Magazines & Reviews – I have also the Copy of Policy of insurance made on our Books which is approved of by the Society tho' they are sorry you cou'd not get it done at less than 1½ p^rCt –

By Capt. Urquhart[272] I rec^d a Box of Books sent without Order The Society did not disapprove of them & will not I dare say in future of your acting with discretion in the same manner where it is likely a book in esteem may not be had by the time we sho^d take in ordering it

I hope to hear from you soon & am
Sir Y^r very hble Ser^t

J. C.

[in small writing in two columns]

[first column]

Picarts religious Ceremonies – 6 Vol^s Fol^s English[273] M. Vitruvius Pollio transl^d from Lat. by M^r. Newton[274] – 4th vol: Hooks rom: Hist[275] – Inigo Jones's designs[276] – Rollins Methods[277] – Philosophical transactions from 1762, to be cont. as they come out[278] Voltaire's works compleat in English[279] – Principles & power of Harmony[280] Medical Observat^s & inquiries by a Society of Physicians in London[281] – Bougainvilles voyage[282] – Annual register from 1767[283] Introduct. to ye Theory of Human mind[284] – Pennants tour in Scotland[285] British Zoology[286] – Synopsis of Quadrupeds[287] – Burneys Hist. of Musick[288] Boyce's Cathedral musick[289] – Wynns Genl Hist. of Brit: Emp:^re in America[290] Dalrymples Memoirs[291] – DuHamel on Agriculture[292] & Chambers on d^o.[293] Mr. De Guys sentimental Journey thro' Greece

transl^d into English[294]
All the Vol^s of M^r. Bufons Nat. Hist. plates coloured[295]
Dr Peter Kalms tour thr' N^o. America[296] –
Hist. of Ramsehatka, lately travel^d from Russia[297]
Th[?] Hutchins's acct of the Country of the Illinois[298]

[*second column*]

A genteel collect. of the most eleg.^t publick & private buildings to be bound in
Boards with leather Back[299] Ruthy and Sutherland on Waters w:^th one or 2 others
the most appr^d authors on y: Subject[300] Geo: Edwards's Nat. Hist: compleat with
plates col'd[301] Cameron's baths of the Romans illustrated & explained Fol^o[302] Collections of curious discoveries written by em.^t Antiquarians 2 vols. 8vo[303] McBrides
introduct. to the Theory & practice of Physick[304] Mylne's translat. of Linnaeus's
institutes of Botany[305] Wildman's treatise on Bees[306] – Guillims Heraldrye[307] A Voyage from Eng^d to India also a Journey from persia to England by a unusual rout by
Edwar^d Ives[308] India tracts by Mr. Holwell & friends[309] – Lelands Hist: of Ireland[310]
Best Edit. Fol.^o of Antient part of Universal History[311] –Dr Kennicott's Bible[312] –
Price on Annuities[313] – Greys Memoria Technica[314] Lowes Mnemonics delineated.[315]
The largest, latest & best map of the City of London[316] Journals of the House of
Lords. Drury's illustrat^s of Nat. History[317] Icon Basilicon.[318] Voltaires essay on Genl
Hist: & manners & spirit of state 2 vols 12°[319] Milots – all his works ord^d above.[320]

[In the journal, books are still being proposed and sent for in 1775 (J, fols. 166–69)
but no correspondence is recorded. There is mention of a letter received from the
bookseller at the quarterly meeting of 5 July 1775 (J, fol. 169). During 1777 books
from local auctions and by gift are noted at meetings (J, fols. 177–78).]

[Fearful of destruction of the books, the quarterly meeting had debated moving
them (QM, 4 Oct. 1775), and boxes are prepared for the move (9 Oct. 1775, J,
fols.170, 171), but in 1778 the collection was destroyed by a disastrous fire. The
doleful entry in the journal says it all: "The Librarian reported that on the fifteenth
day of January last the Library Room together with the Books instruments Charter Box and its contents &c the property of the Society and also the Books late of
Mr. McKenzie were all consumed by Fire except the Books & instruments mentioned in the List delivered by him" (1 Apr. 1778, J, fol. 185). In mid 1783 Mr.
Justice Grimké offered to let the society have his London-purchased books at cost
price, to replace those lost in the 1778 fire, and this was agreed by the anniversary
meeting of 1784 (1 Oct. 1783, J, fol. 199; 13 Jan. 1784, J, fol. 201).]

[32]
Mr. William Nicholl
Charles Town January 12th 1780

Sir,

Your letter in March last found it's way to my hands after a long delay, and I had the pleasure of presenting it for the first time to the Society at the Anniversary Meeting thereof held Yesterday.[321]

Circumstances of a private nature inducing me to change my Residence from Charles Town to a distant part of the Country, the Society chose John McCall Junr Esq their Secretary in my stead,[322] by whom this will be enclosed you – From this Gentleman you will learn how agreably your proposal was received, and be informed of the Orders of the Society thereupon.

I return your thanks for the polite manner in which you have been pleased to express your sorrow, for the long interruption of our Correspondence & can assure you it is not more regretted by you, than by

Sir,
Your very humble Servt

John Colcock

[There is a break between the anniversary meeting of 4 Jan. 1780 and that of 5. Feb. 1783: "The Chasm in the Journal was occasioned by the State being invaded in the beginning of the year 1780 by the British, to whom the Garrison of Charles Town surrendered on the 12th of May following – the Capitol remained in their possession until the 14th of December 1782, during which time a meeting of the Society was not held, until the 5th of February 1783" (note by McCall, J, fol. 193). The anniversary meeting for 1784 is advertised as normal in the supplement to *SCG,* 23 Dec. 1783.]

[33]
So. Carolina Charles Town July 3d 1783
Mr. William Nicholl

[*note in margin*]

trav'd by Mr. Julius Smith
Charles Town packt Capt Hill[323]

Sir,

The Members of the Charles Town Library Society having at their Anniversary in January 1780, done me the Honor to elect me their Secretary and Correspondent, I was then directed to inform you thereof, and also to acquaint you the Society had received your Letter dated in March 1779, and did accept and note their thanks for your kind offer to "supply them with Pamphlets & Fugitive Pieces, as usual, and to wait for payment until a Peace" – the Delay in not applying to you before this, was occasioned by the unsettled State of this Country, being from that period, until last December, the seat of War; during which time, there has been no Meetings of the Society, until the 5th of last February. I am now directed[324] to desire you will send for the Society, under direction to me, Annual Register from January 1770 to January 1783 each Year bound seperate, and Letter'd as usual. The different Magazines from January 1780, to the last publication. Some late Pamphlets and Fugitive Pieces, that you imagine will be acceptable; and also that you will continue to send the different Magazines & Fugitive Pieces as they come out, from time to time, by every Opportunity.

Enclosed is a Letter (I found in the Society's Letter Book) from our mutual friend John Colcock Esqr – I am sorry to inform you, that he died last summer at Jacksonburgh in this State, after a few days Illness.

You will please transmit your account, with the above Order as soon as possible.

I am Sir Your most Obedt Serv.

John McCall Junr. [325]

[34]
Mr. William Nicoll
Charleston February 17th 1784

Sir,

Your favour of the 23d October last pr the Peggy, Scott[326] I received as also the parcel of Magazines and Pamphlets amounting to £1..2..6 I have laid your account before the Society balance in your favour £12..10..10 which is approved of, and ordered to be paid[327] – since the receipt of the above, I have delivered into the Library, sundry packets more of Magazines and pamphlets, but by what vessel they came by, I am ignorant of, as I had no advice of them – Enclosed you have a Bill of Lading of a Box ship't by the Britannia, Ball,[328] containing a Telescope, out of repair – I am directed by the Society to send it you, and to request the favour, you will have it put in complete Order, and sent back by the First opportunity – The Committee are preparing an Order for Books &c which hope to transmit you soon

– I forgot to mention that the books are now to be marked on the outside of the cover next to the Title page "Charleston Library Society," and on the back underneath the Title the initial Letters CLS – this alteration being made, since the Town has been Incorporated, now called the City of Charleston.

I am, Sir
your most Obed^t Servt

John McCall Junr Secretary.

[35]
Mr. William Nicholl
Charleston May 1st 1784

Sir,

I wrote you last by the Britannia, Ball,[329] and enclosed you a Bill of Lading of a Box, containing a Telescope, which belongs to the Charleston Library Society, requesting you would have it put in good repair – Since which have been favoured with yours, and One sett of the November & Magazines [*sic*] – Enclosed you have a Catalogue of Books, which is to be sent out for the Society – the Committee requested me, to inform you, that Doctor Garden (one of our Members, now in London)[330] will be desired to call on you, and will be authorized to Inspect the choice of Books; but if you should not hear from the Doctor, within a month after the receipt of this, you will be pleased in that case, to exercise your own Judgement and Discretion, under the following Directions.

1st to pay particular attention, to send the very best Editions, in respect to Editor, Type, Paper and Binding.

2dly Provided the Editions are equal in point of Merit, to transfer as many as possible, from the other heads to Quarto, that is, to send as many in the Quarto size as possible.

I beg leave to remind you leaving out the W in the Lettering of the Books, that is, they are now to be lettered with the Initials CLS, under the outside Title, and Charleston Library Society, on the outside, next the Title page.

I shall write you again soon, when I hope to enclose you a Bill.
Interim

I am Sir
Your most obed^t humble Servt

John McCall Junr Secretary

[There follows an extensive "Catalogue of Books for the Charleston Library Society" marked with "+" and "v" as a stocktaking exercise. Listed are 15 titles in 2°, 54 4ᵗᵒs, and 90 "8°,12° & Infra," with a further 19 titles on a separate loose paper, including Gibbon, *Decline and Fall,* and Adams, *On Vision.*]

[36]
Charleston Sᵒ Carolina January the 24ᵗʰ 1785
Mr. William Nicholl[331]

Sir,

Pʳ the Hunter, Jay,[332] I have only Time to acknowledge the Receipt of your Favours of the 24ᵗʰ August pʳ Hill and of the 18ᵗʰ September pʳ Ball enclosing me Invoice and Bill of Lading pʳ Ball[333] of a Trunk and Case of Books for the Charleston Library Society, which I have received in good Order and find them right except Meyer Observations Politick 3s[334] left out the Package – would be obliged you will send Book for Priestly; chart of Biography.[335]

I herewith enclose you a Bill of Exchange at 90 Days sight drawn by John Dawson and N. Russell[336] on Messʳˢ Greenwood and Higginson Merchants in London[337] payable to yourself or order for £150 Sterling which when paid please pass to the Cʳ. of the Library Society.

The Eleanor Henderson[338] by whom I recᵈ September Magazines (the noble Peasant[339] charged in the Bill left out) arrived last Week after a tedious Passage of 13 Weeks.

The Lightening, Briton and Sally[340] is just arrived, the Letters by them are not delivered out as yet – I am Sir

Your most obedᵗ humble Servᵗ

John MᶜCall Secretary

[37]
Charleston Sᵒ Carolina August the 6ᵗʰ 1785
Mr. William Nicholl

Sir,

Your Favour of the 30ᵗʰ May last I received this Day, also three Packets, with March April and May Magazines. With respect to new Pamphlets you'l please proceed in your former Tract making such a Selection as your own best Judgment shall direct. The Person who undertook to give you Advice upon the Subject must have entertained a poor Opinion of our Liberality of Sentiment, as well as our

Confidence, and decided attachment to our present Form of Government, to have conceived, that we feared a free Discussion of that, or any other Subject – I am sorry to inform you that the Committee were far from being pleased with the Books you sent last, as they expressly ordered the best and most elegant Editions of each Author, whereas those sent are in General the plainest and most Ordinary. I am directed to inform you that if you wish to continue in your present Connection with the Society, it will be necessary to be more attentive to Directions – By next Opportunity I shall be able to answer your Letter more fully, as in the mean Time I am to lay it before the Committee, the Bill for 150 Pounds I observe is duly honoured and placed to the Credit of the Society – You will please go on in compleating the Order and also have a Stand for the Mirror made, so as not to be in too an expensive a Style.

I am Sir
Your most obed.ᵗ Serv.ᵗ

John MᶜCall Secretary

[38]
Sᵒ Carolina Charleston January 14ᵗʰ 1786
Mr. Charles Dilly

Sir,

I am directed by the Charleston Library Society (to which I am Secretary) to acquaint you that the Members thereof being of Opinion that Mr. William Nicholl of St. Paul's Church Yard their late Bookseller, had not served them with that Punctuality which the Spirit of their Society required, and which their Punctuality in Payment gave them a Right to expect, did at their Anniversary Meeting held the 10ᵗʰ Instant, elect you as a Person properly Qualified to be their Bookseller (in the room of the said Mr. William Nichol) upon the recommendation of Reverend Mr. Robert Smith Rector of St. Philip's Charleston, one of the Members of the Society.[341]

If you think proper to serve the Society in this Capacity . . . [the "General Instructions" follow—lettering, binding etc.—but without mention of placement of packages in the cabin].

The enclosed List of Books,[342] is what Mʳ· Nicholl has been difficient in not sending out to the Society, from orders he had transmitted to him in May 1784 – you will please call upon him, and inform yourself, if he has sent any part of them since – what he is [*sic*] omitted, the Society requests you will send out under direction to me as their Secretary with Invoice of the Cost & Bill of Lading thereof –

and also inquire of him when he sent the last Magazines, Reviews &c in order that you may begin, by sending them out where he left off –

The enclosed Letter you will please Seal and forward to Mr. Nicholl; and receive from him the Telescope sent to have repaired, which if he has compleated, send by first Conveyance, if not done, beg you will give the necessary Orders respecting it.

You have also inclosed a Copy of our Rules for your Government.

I shall write you again soon; Interim

I am Sir
Your most obed^t humble Servt

John McCall Secretary

[39]
S^o Carolina Charleston Jan^ry 14th 1786
Mr. William Nicoll

Sir,

I am ordered by the Charleston Library Socicty, to acquaint you, that the Members thereof, from the backwardness you seem to shew in serving them, did at their Anniversary Meeting the 10th Instant, elect Mr. Charles Dilly, their Bookseller in your stead.

Mr. Dilly will hand you this, to whom deliver your Account with the Society, that the Balance may be transmitted you immediately, you will also be pleased to inform him the Time you sent the last Magazines Review &c and if you have shipped any more of the Books continued in the Order of 1784 – if the Telescope is finished and shipped, otherwise to give Orders for him to receive it.

I am Sir,
Your most Obed: Sevt

John McCall Secretary

[40]
Sº Carolina Charleston 14th April 1787
Mr. Robert Wells,

Dear Sir,

At a Quarterly Meeting of the Charleston Library Society, held the 4th Instant; our President the Hon. Thomas Bee Esqr mentioned, that some time ago he had received a Letter from you,[343] kindly offering to serve the Society as their Bookseller, in case of a Vacancy – the last Anniversary (Mr. Bee being absent & the Society not then Knowing of your being in that way of business) chose Mr. Charles Dilly in the room of Mr. William Nicoll who on my application to him, answered in a manner as being fearful to give Credit to the Society without good Security &c, the society having thought proper to dismiss Mr. Dilly and to elect another person in his stead on casting up Ballots it appeared that you were unanimously elected as their Bookseller.[344]

[The "General Instructions" follow, noting that "Charleston Library Society (in words of full length)" be lettered on the titlepage.]

You will please ask Mr. Charles Dilly for the order I sent him which you are directed by the Society to compleat and send out as soon as possible & add thereto Machivals Works[345] – Knoxs Essays moral & Literary[346] – Treatise on Road-making by John Scott printed 1778[347] – also inquire of him if the Telescope is mended and ready to be sent – We have taken in the Library Gillies's History of Greece 2 Vols Quarto,[348] which you sent Mr. Bee, who has spared it to the Society – you will please debit the Society therefore you also please command the Magazines Reviews &c from July 1786 those of June 1786 being the last we have received from England –

Joshua Ward Esqr our Treasurer informs me, he is now calling in the Interest and the Bonds due the Society which money is intended to purchase a Bill to remit you. I refer you for particulars to Mr. Bee who intends writing you on this Subject by this Conveyance – Interim

I am with my best respects to Mrs. Wells & family
Dear Sir,
Your most obedient humb Servt

John McCall

Charleston Sº Carolina 14th April 1787
Robert Wells Esq.
John McCall[349]

[41]
Rec'd the 26 Jan^ry 1790
London November 7th 1789

Sir,

It was not till a few weeks since that I received your letter of August 1st written by direction of the Charleston Library Society, A delay occasioned by its not being put into the Bag with the other Letters. I have also received a list of Books, many of which are out of Print but all of them that are to be had shall be made ready and forwarded with expedition. I am truly sorry that I have not been able to send the Telescope. Mr. Nicholl informed me that it was with Narne & Blunt[350] ready to be delivered on the repairs being paid for, of which I informed the Society – I call'd repeatedly on N&B and was always put off, till at last they assured me that after the most diligent search they could find no such thing – A considerable time afterwards Mr. Nicolls recollected that he was mistaken & now believed it was sent to Mr. Ramsden,[351] who after many applications found it, but in the same state it was when he received it. R. said the reason he had done nothing to it was because he could not learn whether a new stand was to be provided none having been sent with it to him. I went again to N. who said that he had written to the Society but had received no answer about the Stand. Judging from this that none was wanted I directed Mr. Ramsden to proceed in the other repairs with all possible expedition which he promised to do, but as he has a great deal too much to do I have not been yet able to get it out of his Hands, though I assured him his Bill should be paid on demand, this is many Months ago and though his House is near two Miles from mine I have gone myself and sent my Clerk time almost innumerable but without effect, tho' every time he repeated his promise of having it ready immediately – I should have taken it out of his Hands but as he was the Original maker no other person could properly repair it – I was in daily expectation of Receiving the List of Books with which I am now favoured, as I found it impossible to proceed on the List which I received from M^r. Dilly which prevented me from writing to the Society till I should receive the new list, and as it differs not a little from the former I apprehend the Society's intentions will be more fully answered than if I had done otherwise. I also postponed acknowledging the receipt of the Bill £80 – on Racquet & Co of Rotterdam which was paid and is at the Credit of the Charleston Library Society with me August 21st 1788, Eighty Pounds. – Mr. John Ward did not pay me any Money, as I presume he has informed the Society.[352] I saw him a few weeks before he embarked but as he said nothing to me on the Subject I did not think it necessary to mention it to him – In the List of Books now received are the following which I must request you to describe more fully to prevent any mistake in procuring & sending them – Modern History – Belles Letters – Sallust[353] – I am also directed to Subscribe for the Society to Boydells Shakspeare but the Society have not mention'd which I have therefore enclosed two Copies of the proposals for their goverment [*sic*] & shall wait for their further commands.[354] – Permit me to request you to present my best compliments to the Hon^bl Mr. Bee & inform him I shall write to him by the Olive Branch which will sail in a few days[355] – I shall be glad to learn how the Magazines &c come to hand as I omit no opportunity of sending them as soon as they are published*

[*written sideways by copyist in left margin*] *I am sorry the Britan [*sic*][356] had gone down the River, before those for October were published – With my gratefull acknowledgements to all the Members of the Charleston Library Society – I am Sir

y^r very Ob^t H^bl Servt

Rob Wells

To Philip Prioleau Esqr[357] or the Secretary for the time being of the Charleston Library Society, South Carolina

[42]

Charleston South Carolina July 29th 1791

Sir,

The Charleston Library Society have in the hands of M^r. Ramsden a celebrated Optician in London,[358] a Telescope which was sent to him in order to be repaired, the Society are desirous to have it put in Complete repair, and that a proper stand should be made for it & also an Accurate Micrometer. This Instrument was placed in Mr. Ramsdens hands by a Mr. Nicholl our former Bookseller and Mr. Wells writes us word that he has frequently requested Mr. Ramsden to expedite the repair. We beg the favor of you Sir to call on M^r. Ramsden on your arrival in London and desire him to complete the Telescope with the stand and Micrometer without delay, on its being finished Mr. Wells who has money of ours in his hands will (we Presume pay for it) but should he not as we are about remitting Monies to England, we will inform you when Mr. Ramsden may be paid; and as soon as he is paid we will request the favor of you to forward the Instruments to us here. We will also be obliged to you to take charge of Our Microscope for us and put it in the Hands of M^r. Adams the Optician[359] to get it repaired, and if you find that M^r. Ramsden will not proceed immediately to repair our Telescope we request the favor of you to take it out of his hands and place it also in the hands of M^r· Adams to be repaired and to have the additions expressed above.[360]

> I am Sir with respect
> y^r Ob^t H^{bl} Servt
>
> W Blamyer Sec^{ry} & Corresp^t [361]

To
Charles Goodwin Esqr [362]

[43]
Charleston S° Carolina 2^d Novr 1791

Dear Sir,

With this you will receive a bill for One hundred and fifty pounds and a Catalogue of Books for the Charleston Library Society. This has been framed by a Committee and is forwarded to you as the Bookseller of the Society in order that you may send them out the Books contained therein with all convenient speed. It is not supposed that One hundred and fifty pounds will pay for the whole of the Books, but it is left to your discretion to send out as many as One hundred and fifty pounds will pay for, or the whole, or any number you please. The Society have lately subscribed for fifteen shares in the Bank of the United States which will absorb near fifteen hundred pounds of their Capitals but produce them about One hundred and fifty pounds of an Annual Income. They have also a thousand pounds in good Bonds which are in a time of recovery. It is the intention of the society to lay out as much of their money when recovered as will make a complete Library. If you think proper to send the whole of the Books in the Catalogue, I can assure you the Society will esteem it as a favor, and that it is their intention to remit as fast as they receive money untill you are wholly paid. In the mean time they begin with One hundred and fifty Pounds which is all they can at present spare consistent with making up this subscription to the Bank: the Society has been incorporated since the year One thousand seven hundred and forty nine and consists upwards of One hundred of the most respectable Gentlemen in this State it would be absurd in me a Private member to guarantee their future payments. I therefore only state facts and leave it to yourself to determine whether you will send out the whole of the Books, or only a part. The Society wishes for the first and your compliance will cement the connection which already subsists between you and them. I beg it may be remembered that I do not make myself Responsible for any Credit you may give the Society, but at the same time give it as my opinion that if you send out the whole of the Books in the Catalogue you will not only oblige them but yourself. Please address your letters out to M^r. Wm Blamyer the Librarian of the Charleston Library Society, and believe me to be with respect & Esteem the unknown.

yr most Ob.^t & very H^bl Servt

David Ramsay[363]

Copy
M^r. John Stockdale Bookseller
Piccadilly
London[364]
By the Olive Branch[365]

[There follows a letter from Charles Pinckney to General Charles Cotesworth Pinckney about the library building, 12 Jan. 1792. A further copy is sent 14 Jan. 1792.[366]]

[44]
M^r. Stockdale
S. Carolina
Charleston, 14th Jan^ry 1792

Sir,

Inclosed I transmit to you by the Britannia Captn Kerr[367] a copy of a letter written to you by Doctor Ramsay dated the 2^d of November 1791 in which he sent you a Catalogue of Books to be sent out for the Charleston Library Society and the first bill of exchange drawn by James Theus on Messrs Bird, Savage & Bird Merchants in London[368] – dated the 3^d of November 1791 for £150. and payable Ninety days after sight to William Blamyer who endorsed it to you. Herewith I now send you the second bill of the same tenor and date together with a Copy of the Catalogue sent by Doct. Ramsay. Also acquaint you the Society have sent Public securities of the United States to Ms^rs Bird Savage & Bird to be disposed of by them in order to pay the ballance which your Account may Amount to. Should those Gentlemen apprehend a Probabillity of disposing of the above to a better advantage in the space of two or three months hope you will acquiesce therein
Charleston, 14th Jan^ry 1792

I am Sir
y^r most Ob^t Servt

Wm Blamyer Sec^ry & Lib.

[45]
Charleston Jan^ry 14 1792

Gentlemen –

The Charleston Library Society has desired me as their President, to remit to you the inclosed Certificate for two thousand and ninety two Dollars and Ninety three Cents of deferred Stock, to sell to the best advantage in order to pay the ballance of their account to their Bookseller M^r. Stockdale, which they request you will do when in cash. – A Bill of One hundred and fifty Pounds sterling has already been remitted to him. Should any depression of the American Stock have taken place on Account of the defeat of General St. Clair,[369] you are to be so obliging as not to sell, till they have got up again. The Stocks here are not in the least affected by it; but I am told that in your Market a similar event may affect ours. The defeat of the few troops engaged was total, but there is no doubt but the Troops now preparing to march against the Indians, will be in sufficient power to obtain ample reparation.

I remain very respectfully
Gentlemen
y^r most Ob^t Servt

(signed) Charles Cotesworth Pinckney[370]

Messrs Bird Savage & Bird[371]
Merchants in London
by the Britannia
NB. Letter put in the bag at Mr. Tunno's[372]

[46]
Charleston Feb^ry 5th 1792

Gentlemen –

On the 14th of last Month at the desire of the Charleston Library Society I inclos'd you in a letter (which I put into the bag of the Britannia) a Certificate for two thousand and ninety two Dollars & Ninety three Cents of deferred Stock made out in the name of Bird Savage and Bird and requested that you would sell it to the best advantage for the Society, in order to pay the ballance of their Account to their Bookseller M^r. Stockdale, and also some repairs done to the Philosophical Instruments, which M^r. Goodwin of this town but now in England[373] had undertaken to get done for the Society. The Society will be much obliged to you for your attention to this business. A Bill for One hundred and fifty Pounds Sterling has already been transmitted to Mr. Stockdale and after the payment of his and M^r. Goodwin's Accounts, & your own Commissions the Society by you will return the residue in your hands till you hear further from them. We have kept a Notarial Copy of the Certificate, and M^r. Neufville's Books[374] will shew the transfer to you, that in case of miscarriage of the letter inclosing the certificate, no loss will accrue, as no persons have a right to transfer or sell that Certificate but yourselves.

I remain very respectfully
y^r most Ob^t Servt

C. C. Pinckney

Messrs Bird Savage & Bird
Merchants in London
by the ["Britannia" *crossed out*] Laurence [*sic*][375]

[47]

["Omitted" *(i.e., out of order) written in margin*]

Dr Sir

The Library Society has requested me to write to you on the Subject of our Telescope and Microscope in order to Know whether they are repaired, and if so, what the repairs amount to, that we may direct this expence you have been at or may be at relative to them, to be paid to you. We send funds by this Opportunity to Messrs Bird Savage and Bird sufficient to pay for the Books we have ordered and to pay for those repairs; and to have we hope a ballance in hands. We shall esteem your attendance to this business as a particular favor, as we wish to have those instruments here as soon as possible.

I remain with great respect
y^r most Ob^t H^ble Servt

C. C. Pinckney

Charleston ["Library Society" *crossed through*]
Jan^ry 17th 1792
To Charles Goodwin Esqr
p^r the Britannia (Copy)

[48]
London 14ᵗʰ Decʳ 1791

Sir,

In compliance with the wishes of the Charleston Library Society, expressed in your letter of the 29ᵗʰ of July I waited on Mr. Ramsden the Optician, from whom I learned that the Telescope belonging to the Society had been done 2 or 3 years ago & was then lying his Shop waiting their orders, but as he had never before received Instructions to add a Micrometer I found it would not be possible to send it by the Hanbury,[376] as from him I learnt it would take sometime to have that addition made. I therefore told [him] to finish it agreeable to the orders by me, & he says I shall have it to send by the first Vessel after Christmas – The Microscope has been repaired by Mr. Adams and I have now intrusted it to the particular care of Captⁿ McNeil who I make no doubt will deliver it safe. I cannot find either Mr. Wells or Mr. Nichols in order to obtain the money to pay these Gentlemen, I shall therefore do it myself and will thank you to write to your Agent here to pay it either to me or Messrs Goodwin & Co, No 25, Park Street, Southwark. Before my departure from London, which will not be till later next year, if the Society can point out any other way wherein I can serve them, I shall be happy in doing it.

I remain Sir, with Respect
yʳ most Obᵗ Servᵗ

Charles Goodwin

Mʳ· William Blamyer
Secʳʸ & Correspondᵗ of the Libʳʸ Socʸ
Charleston   (Copy)

[49]
Charleston – Genˡ C. Cotesworth Pinckney
London 14 April 1792

Sir,

We have before us your esteemed favors of the 14 Janʳʸ and 5ᵗʰ February inclosing a Certificate for two thousand and Ninety two dollars Ninety three Cents of deferred Debt the property of the Charleston Library Society and we shall attend to your direction as well in the payment of Mʳ· Stockdale and Mʳ· Goodwin's Accounts as in not forcing the sales – American Stocks are just now very dull and deferred will not fetch above 7s. a price we are not disposed to take for this parcel. We have the honor to be with great respect, Sir

y^r most Ob^t Serv^{ts}

Bird Savage & Bird

Copy–
Original p^r Capt. Marston[377]
Hon^b Genl C. Cotesworth Pinckney, Charleston
by Britannia[378]
Captn Kerr

[50]
Charleston, South Carolina July 18th 1792

Sir,

By the Britannia Captain Kerr on the 14th of last January I inclosed you a bill of exchange dated the 3^d November 1791 for One hundred and fifty Pounds Sterling and payable Ninety days after sight; drawn by James Theus on Messrs Bird Savage and Bird in my favor, and indorsed by me to you, in order to be applied towards the payment of some Books I requested you to send out for the Charleston Library Society agreeably to a Catalogue transmitted you at the same time I also informed you that the Society had forwarded Public Securities of the United States to Messrs Bird Savage and Bird in order fully to discharge what your Account might amount to. The Britannia has returned to this Port, and several other Vessells have come from England since she arrived there and I have received no intimation from you whether you mean to comply with the order sent you or not, and not even an acknowledgment of my letter and the bills, altho- I sent duplicates of both; the Society therefore apprehend that it will not suit you to send them, and therefore they have desired me, if the order for Books has not been complied with before you receive this letter, that you will pay the amount of the above bill of Exchange (if you have received the same) to Messrs Bird Savage and Bird who are Authorized to make you any reasonable allowance for any trouble you may have been at in this business — I am Sir

Your Ob^t H^{ble} Servt

Wm Blamyer Secretary

To M^r· John Stockdale
Bookseller in Piccadilly
By the Britannia[379]
Duplicate by the Westberry[380]
dated 14 August 1792 & a
Catalogue

[51]

Gentlemen

I inclose you a letter from the Secretary of the Charleston Library Society to M^r· Stockdale, you will find by it that he has not complied with our Order for Books, and that the Society think themselves not well treated by his inattention I am authorized by the Society as their President to beg the favor of you if M^r· Stockdale has not complied with our Order (a Copy of which is herewith sent) to receive from him One hundred and fifty pounds the Amount of the bill of exchange sent him drawn by M^r· James Theus on you, after allowing him any reasonable expence he may have been at, and put our Order into the hands of some Bookseller of Reputation and punctuallity, who will without delay procure and forward to us the Books mentioned. We are obliged to you for your Attention to our Interest with regard to the Certificates, the receipt of which you acknowledge in your favour of the 14th of last April And I am desired by the Society to assure you that all the expences and Commissions that may arise about their business, they will with Pleasure discharge The Society have Sixteen Shares in the Bank of the United States, and they have directed the whole of the dividends to be regularly applied to the Purchase of Books and Philosophical Instruments, so that I should think it would be worth the while of some eminent Bookseller to serve us Punctually and well. I have the honor to be

Gentlemen
Your most Ob^t H^ble Servt

Charles Cotesworth Pinckney

Charleston July 17th 1792
Messrs Bird Savage & Bird
Merchants in London
By the Britannia (Copy)
Duplicate sent by the Westberry
dated 14 August 1792[381]

[There follow two letters from Sarah Butler of Philadelphia to Pinckney, 18 Aug. and 28 Oct. 1792.]

[52]
London 18th Augt 1792

Sir,

We inclose you sales for two Certificates rec^d^ p^r^ St. John Laird Nett proceeds £914..16..3 at your Credit 29 July & also for 1 Certificate p^r^ Britannia Kerr Nett proceeds £324..1..8 to the Credit of the Library Society, we have written Mr. Stockdale that we are ready to pay his Acc^t^ against the Society and the ballance we shall hold subject to your future orders

Copy
London 22d Septr 1792

Sir,

Refering you to the above copy of our last, we have to remark that we were fortunate in our sales of American Stock, the Markett for which, owing to the quantity here for Sale is since become very dull, 3 pr Cts being offered at 63 deferr'd at 67 & 6 pr Cts at 104. We are since favor'd with yours of the 17 of July inclosing a letter from the Secretary of the Charleston Library Society to Mr. Stockdale with an Order in case he had not complied with their order for Books, for us to withdraw it and put it into the hands of some other Bookseller. On presenting this letter to Mr. Stockdale, we found that notwithstanding his extreme negligence in delaying so long the execution of the Order, he had provided most of the scarce books, and on his promise to get the whole ready immediately, we thought it best to let him do it, as it would have taken any other Bookseller much time to have collected the Scarce Editions. We have the Satisfaction to inform you that the whole Order is now shiped in 6 Boxes on board the Julius Pringle Capt Callahan[382] and we inclose your bill of lading, bill of parcels & Invoice amounting to £435..17..2 which we have covered by Insurance of £596 at 2prCent & Policy 7s £12..5..5. To the Debt of the Society £4. We thought it most proper to make this Insurance the expence which is not to be confused with the inconvenience and disappointment of the Society would Suffer in case of a Loss, and we shall be pleased if our Conduct meets with their approbation. If a loss should take place in the European Seas we shall immediately issue an order for the same Books.

Tho- the Cash of the Society in Our hands was not sufficient, concluding that Mr. Stockdales neglect would deprive of their future Orders, we determine to pay him in full as pr his inclosed Receipt, having advanced the balance which you will remit us when convenient to the Society we beg leave to remark that by the mode of a direct supply from the Bookseller, the Books cost much more than if the order had pased thro our hands, Our Commissions as Merchants would have been far short of the difference between the Wholesale and exporting Price at which we should have bought them, and the retail price at which they are now charged. In addition to the 5 Cases Books Captn Callahan has especial charge of a Small Case containing a Pocket Compass, directed to Mr. William Blamyer which we suppose is for the use of the Society. We request you to present our respects to the Members of the Society, and assure them that feeling ourselves highly honored by their confidences we shall pay very particular attention that their orders are executed in the best manner. We have the Honor to be with great regard

Dr Sir,
Yr most devoted hble Servts

Bird Savage & Bird

Honble
Govr Charles Cotesworth Pinckney

[53]

[Letter from John Stockdale]

14th September 1792
Piccadilly, London

Sir,

I received your favour of the 17th July by the Hands of Mr. Savage which distressed me very much as the whole or nearly so of your Order was compleated, which I shewed to Mr. Savage. I was in hopes of collecting them in a much shorter time and sending the whole together, had I acted as I first intended and sent out such Books as I had in readiness in my own Shop I should have given greater satisfaction to you and myself. Many of the Articles tho' trifling in price were the most difficult to procure and were only to be got by accident as they came into the trade from private persons, for this reason my Clerks and myself have traversed the streets of London from Bookseller to Bookseller I firmly believe an hundred times over at least, which is no trifling trouble considering that there are near two hundred which cannot be gone thro' in less than two days they lying at so great a distance from each other. There are still a few Articles wanting that I shall endeavour to pick up but shall send nothing untill I receive your further orders which you may be assured shall be executed with the greatest punctuality and sent by return of the ship or at least such articles as can be procured. I have executed my instructions to the best of my Judgment and this is no trifling task, as for instance it frequently happens that a scarce book is sold by one Bookseller at £14..14 and by another at £12..12. A number of instances I could give in this order (did it not take up too much time) in lesser Articles, but as I have probably added Articles that you may not approve being too dear, or not wanted; should this be the case I beg that you will be so obliging as to order them sold by Public Auction, and whatever loss should there be any attending the sale I will chearfully pay it as I would much rather put up with any reasonable loss than that the Gentlemen should think I wished to land them with Books that they did not want, or that I had been imprudent in my Selection, in short I beg you to understand that it is my wish that there may be no ground left for any complaint against me with respect to the present Order. The following Articles if the[y] are not approved must not be sold for one shilling less than they are charged in the bill as they are all as good as Gold in the London Markets, and the first Article is seldom to be met with in such excellent condition. I have three Orders for the same Book now altho I send it to your Library

Gentlemans Magazine 71 Volumes[383]	£31..10
Bucks Antiquities 3 Vol.[384]	21
Chalmers Dictionary 5 Vol.[385]	13..13
Camdens Britannia 3 Vol.[386]	11..11
Groses Antiquities 10 Vol.[387]	22..11..6
Latham's Synopsis 7 Vol.[388]	12

Wherever you find any of the Articles charged above the prices marked in the Catalogue, you may safely conclu[d]e that they are very scarce and out of print, notwithstanding some of them are lately published, as for instance many of Pennants works, Irelands' tour in Holland and some of Gilpins works, his forest scenery[389] I picked up by mere chance the day that the order was compleated, on the other hand where ever I could purchase the Books under the Price I have charged you accordingly allowing myself a reasonable profit. I have packed up the whole of the Books myself with the utmost care and I trust you will receive them in good condition, they are shiped [*sic*] on board the Julius Pringle, Callahan by Mess[rs] Bird, Savage & Bird who will transmit you a Copy of my bill. They have promised to pay me the Amount tomorrow, including the £150 – which I received from you by the Britannia. I beg my very sincere thanks may be given to the Gentlemen of the Society, and that they will still continue to send their future Orders which shall be executed with the utmost care and attention, and I do solemnly assure you that had the Order been for as many thousands as it is hundreds I should have executed it with the utmost pleasure from the confidence I have in so respectable a Society. I do not say this because you have remitted the Cash, had I not received one shilling my language would have been the same with the first parcel of Books which would have been sent at this time had I not received your last letter. Notwithstanding this Cash is as pleasant and as acceptable to me as to other Persons. I mention this that you Order freely whatever Books you want for the Society, without any regard to the Amount or the payment, trusting that the remittances will be made as often as it is convenient to the Society. I have two capital works that will be ready for Publication before I can hear from you, the first is by Captn Hunter of the Navy, <u>Historical proceedings in & about New South Wales</u> it will consist of near 600 pages in quarto closely printed,[390] the other is the history of the West India Islands by Bryan Edwards Esqr late of Jamaica but now in England, it will make two large Volumes in quarto[391] – the Life of Doctor Franklin is not yet published nor is it certain when it will be as it is not yet gone to press.[392]

I am Sir, with all due respect to you

& the Gentlemen of the Society
y^r much obliged & very humble Servt
(signed) John Stockdale

Piccadilly London
14th Sept. 1792

[54]

[*no date*]

Gentlemen,

The Books you were so obliging as to send to the Library Society arrived safe. The Society return you their best thanks for the polite advance of the ballance of M^r. Stockdale's Bill, & they have given directions to the President to collect as much money without delay as will reimburse you. Their general Annual meeting will be this Month when they will form a Plan for their future supply of Books, and I imagine the Mode suggested by you will be adopted[393] – I remain with great respect

your most Ob^t humble Servt

(signed) C. C. Pinckney

Messrs Bird Savage & Bird

[55]
London 29ᵗʰ January 1793

Dear Sir,

I should have answered your Letter sooner on the subject of the Telescope, belonging to the Library Society, but I waited until Ramsden had compleated it, which he promised me week after week should be done, finding that there was no prospect of that being the case, I determined to take it from him several Months ago, and fortunately at last I effected it yesterday. It is nearly in the same State it was when sent to him eighteen years ago. I have lodged it with Mr. Adams with the necessary directions, who has promised I shall have it in a Month or six weeks, and I know that I can rely on his punctuallity. When done I shall send it by the first Vessel that may offer, unless that should be within a short space of my return, when I shall delay it in order to take charge of it myself. I should have been glad if the Secretary had acknowledged the Receipt of the Microscope. Believe me Dear Sir

yʳ most Obᵗ Servᵗ

(signed) Chaˢ Goodwin

C.C. Pinckney Esq
Charleston
Sᵒ Carolina

[56]
Charleston March 2ᵈ 1793

Gentlemen,

At the desire of the Charleston Library Society I now remit you with their best thanks for the advance made by you on their Account £140 in a bill drawn by Messʳˢ Legare Theus & Prioleau[394] on you for that sum in favor of their Treasurer Mʳ· Beekman,[395] and endorsed by him to you – the Society is collecting money and they will soon trouble you with an Order for Books and a remittance to pay for them. I have the honor to be with respect –

Your most Obᵗ Servᵗ

(signed) C C Pinckney

Messʳˢ Bird Savage & Bird
by the Carolina Planter[396]
& the Major Pinckney[397]

[57]
Charleston April 17th 1793

Gentlemen,

   By the Carolina Planter and the Major Pinckney at the desire of the Charleston Library Society, I remitted you a bill of Exchange for One hundred and fifty Pounds in a bill drawn by Messrs Legare Theus and Prioleau and indorsed by him – I now inclose you a bill of Exchange on Account of the Society for One hundred Pounds, and in next July the Society will remitt you fifty Pounds more. I enclose also the within order for Books and Mathematical Instruments, which as soon as you are in Cash on the Society's Account they will be obliged to you to procure for them of such Bookseller as you think proper. The Bulk of the Catalogue inumerates Books of much lighter reading than our last, but in a Society such as ours, we are obliged to consult all tastes and to have many books of mere amusement as well as books of instruction and science. I remain with much respect,

   yr humble Servt

   C. C Pinckney

Messrs Bird Savage & Bird
by the Federalist³⁹⁸

N.B. you will please send our Books &c in an American Bottom and have them insured – the Society request you will subscribe for them to Kerr's Animal Kingdom or Zoological System of the celebrated Dr Charles Linnæus, and also Smellie's Natural history of Birds translated from Buffon.

[58]
London July 8th 1793

Sir

   We duly have been favored with your much esteemed Letters of the 2d March and 17th April, inclosing Legare Theus & Prioleaus drafts on us for £142 and for £100..–..– on Acct of the Charleston Library Society, which have been accepted and will be at the Credit of their Accot. Your last favor inclosed an Order for Sundry Books for the use of the Society, which we shall pay particular attention, adverting to the direction of their being insured and shipped on an American Bottom. –
   We have this day paid George Adams the Optician, for Telescope for the use of the Society, ordered by Mr. Goodwin, who shewed us his directions to apply

to us for payment of the same. We debit the Society's Acco^t £38.9.6.– for this payment.

> We remain with much respect
> Sir your most Obed^t Servt

> Bird Savage & Bird

Honble
Charles Cotesworth Pinckney Esqr
Charleston S^o Carolina
Pr Caroline Hilton[399]

[59]
Charleston, General Charles Cotesworth Pinckney
London Septr 7th 1793

Sir,

We have attended to the Postscript in Copy of your favor of the 17th of April last, desiring that we should subscribe for the Charleston Library to Kerr's Animal Kingdom or Zoological System of the celebrated Sir Charles Linnëus, and also Smellies's natural history of Birds, with which we shall punctually comply. We have now the pleasure to inclose you bill of Parcels, bill of lading & Invoice of sundry Books shipt by your Order, and for account of the Charleston Library Society on the American Vessel Fame, Captn Blair[400] amounting to £121.10^s.11^d at the debit of the said Library Society. The Mathematical Instruments will be forwarded by the next Ship.

> We are with great respect & Esteem
> Sir
> your most Ob^t Serv^{ts}

> (signed) Bird Savage & Bird

[60]
Charleston,
Honble Genl C. Cotesworth Pinckney
London 20 Novr 1793

Sir,

In your letter of 12th Inst: per Lively,[401] & Copy per this Vessel, we were not able to fill up the blanks left for the Premium of insurance of the things ship'd for the Charleston Library Society. On the first alarm about the Algerines, the Premium ask'd was 10 Guineas p^{r}C^t – but by waiting to the last moments, we have succeeded in effecting it at 7.$^{g.s}$ p^{r}C^t. –

The Invoice Amounted	£120. 7. 9
Insured on £140 at 7$^{g.s}$ p^r.C^t & policy 7/–_	10.12.10
In all	£131. –. 7

to the debit of the Society.

We are with esteem & regard –
Sir
y^r most Ob^t Serv^{ts}

Bird Savage & Bird

[61]

[*note in margin:* "Omitted to be copied"; *applies also to letter 62 below*]

Honble Genl Charles Cotesworth Pinckney
Charleston
Triplicate
London October 11th 1793

Sir,

We hope the Articles mentioned in our last of which the above is a copy will be safe arrived, and that they will prove to the satisfaction of the Library Society. –

Messrs Boydell's not having quite finished the Frames of your Shakespeare Prints; we shall send them by the next opportunity, with the other things ordered. –

Dr Sir
your most Obed^t Serv^{ts}

[Bird Savage & Bird]

Original p^r Sally & Polly – Rich[402]
Duplicate p^r Ruby – Atkins[403]

London 30th October 1793

Sir, (Duplicate)

The above is a Copy of ours of 11th last: by the Sally & Polly. The remainder of the order for the Library Society & the Air Pump will be shipped by the American

Brig Lively, to sail in about ten days, and which we believe will be the first conveyance to hand.

We are very respectfully, Sir

your most Obed^t Serv^ts [Bird Savage & Bird]

Original p^r Ruby Atkins

[62]
London Nov^r: 13 1793

Sir,

We have now the pleasure to inclose you Invoice bill of lading & bills of Parcels of some mathematical instruments, Books and Prints of Boydells Shakespeare for the Charleston Library Society amounting to £126. 7. 9
on which we have insured £[*figures lacking*] at p^rC^t & policy   7/–
In all   £[*figures lacking*]
to the debit of the Society. We shall be obliged to give a high premium owing to accounts of 10 large Algerine Xebeques[404] 30 to 36 Guns having come out of the Streights of Gibraltar to cruize against your Ships, of which one is said to have been taken. The Portuguese used to keep them in the Streights, but have lately made a truce with them. We have gone to the expence of the handsomest frames for the Prints, as they admitted of the whole Print with its margin which has a favorable effect, and they are otherwise so much in richness surpassing the value of a few shillings difference in each frame that we have no doubt of the Society's approbation. We have sent frames for the Prints already gone, & we directed Messrs Boydell to put directions and a pattern in one of the frames, how the Prints were to be fix'd in by pins, there being a risk of spoiling them in pasting without being very conversant in the Method.[405] We hope the binding &c of the Books will be satisfactory, and with the offer of our services to the Society we are with much regard and esteem

Sir
your most Obed^t Serv^ts

(signed) Bird Savage & Bird

[63]
Charleston General Charles Cotesworth Pinckney
London January 25th 1794

Sir,

    This being the season of the year at which we close our Accounts, we beg, through you to convey to the Members of the South Carolina Library Society, their Account Current with us, ballance due to us on the 31st December last, One hundred and seventy eight pounds, six shillings and ten pence, carried to the debit of the new Account under that date. We trust on examination it will be found free from error, and request the ballance due to us may be acknowledged.

    We pray the favor of your presenting our respectful compliments to the Gentlemen of the Society & believe us to be with great respect

> Sir
> your most Obed^t Serv^{ts}
>
> (signed) Bird Savage & Bird

To the Honb^{le}
Genl Chas Cotesworth Pinckney
Charleston
S^o Carolina
p^r Major Pinckney
Captⁿ Grice[406]

Deb^r Charleston Library Society their Account Currrent
Cred^r

[*left column*]

1792

Septr 29	To Sundries by the Julius Pringle	£443. 2. 7

1793

July 8	Paid Adams	38. 9. 6
Septr 7	Sundries by the Fame	121.10.10
Novr 16	Sundries by the Lively	137. –. 7
Decr 31	Postages 14/2 Stamps 3/	17. 2
	Commission on £278.9.6 Receipts and	
	Payments 2½ prCt	1. 7.10
		£742. 8. 6
Decr 31	Ballance due this day brought from	
	Old Account	178. 6. 8

[*right column*]

1792

Augt 18th   Net proceeds of D^rs 2092.93 deferred
             by the Britannia   £324. 1. 8

1793

July 20   Remittance from C C Pinckney Esqr   140.

Octor 6   ditto   ditto   100.

Decr 31   Balance due this day carried to the
            debit of New Account   <u>178. 6.10</u>
                                            <u>£742. 8. 6</u>

Errors Excepted
London 31 Decr 1793

   (signed) Bird Savage & Bird

[64]
London Augt 21 1794

Dear Sir,

   We duly received your favor of the 28th March last, covering a remittance for £100 – on account of the Library Society, which being paid as to their credit. We are much pleased that out attention to their orders meets with their approbation. We have on board this Vessel shiped a Case directed to you and included in another bill of Lading we send you, containing the fifth Number of Boydells Shakespeare,[407] amounting as per Invoice with insurance to £18.18^s.8^d Ster^g to the debit of the Society

   We are with great regard
   your most Obed^t Serv^ts

   (signed) Bird Savage & Bird

Genl C. Cotesworth Pinckney
Charleston
So Carolina
p^r Mary
C^t McNeil

[65]
London June 6th 1794
Messrs Bird Savage & Bird
To Messr Boydell's
Dr

Subscription to Shakespeare N.º 5 for the Charleston Library Society	£5.	7.
5 Handsome Gold Frames with German Glass to dº	10.10	
Case " "		5
	£16.	2

[66]
Charleston Novr 1st 1794

Gentlemen,

We duly received your favour of the 21st of August and the fifth number of Boy-dells Shakespeare, with the Large Pictures in gilt frames, with the whole of which we are exceedingly pleased, particularly as these Prints appear to be of more early impressions than those formerly sent. The small Prints to this number have not come.[408] We now inclose you a Bill for One hundred & twenty pounds sterling, drawn by Kirk and Lukens in your favour, and payable in London, and Messrs Alstorphius & Van Hemert merchants in Amsterdam, which when paid will throw a ballance in our favour, in your hands; we also intend to remit in February fifty Pounds more, when Bills will become more reasonable, than they are at present. We also inclose an Order for some Books, which the Society will be obliged to you to expedite as soon as possible. With every acknowledgement for your attention to the Society. I remain

your most Obet hble Servt

Charles C. Pinckney

Messrs Bird, Savage & Bird (sign'd)
London
pr the Federalist[409]
& Minerva[410]

[67]
London 24th Decr 1794

Dear Sir,

We are happy to find that the fifth number of Boydell's Shakespeare gave so much satisfaction to your Library Society by the early impression of the prints of which we shall not fail to inform Messrs Boydell's and claim an equal attention, in future; We shall learn why the small prints of this number were not sent at the same time and have the omission remedied. We have forwarded your Bill for £120 Sterling on Messrs Alstorphius and Van Hemert for acceptance and unless you hear to the contrary, you may conclude that it is honor'd. We shall pay attention to have your first order for Books expedited as soon as possible. As we close our Accounts at this season of the year, we inclose that of the Society, by which it appears that if the above bill is paid, they will be creditors for balance in £13.11^s. ^d order date of 5th April 1795 with great respect to the Society we are

Dear Sir,
y^r most Obed^t Serv^ts

(signed) Bird Savage & Bird

P.S. The Bill on Alstorphius & Co. was accepted 2^d January 1795 and becomes due 5th April 1795.
The Honorable General C. Cotesworth Pinckney
Charleston
So. Carolina
p^r Romulus
Captn Wallace[411]

Charleston Library Society their Acc^t Curr^t with Bird Savage & Bird, Interest to 5th April at 5p^r C^t p^r Annum

[*left column*]

Deb.^t
1793
Oct. 31st   £178.. 6..10   Debtors for balance of old Account
                                     due this day 15..5 £11.. 5.. 5
1794
Augt 19   18..18.. 8   Prints by the Mary
1795
April 5   7..18.. 7   Interest as p^r Contra
                 2..11   Postage 2/7 Stamps 4^d

1.. 2..		Commission on £220 Receipts at ½ p^{r}C^t
13..11..		Creditor for balance to new Acco.^{t} under this date
220.. ..		

[*right column*]

C^r
1794
Augt 4th £100.. ..   1 Rem⁻ from C. C Pinckney Esqr on Simpson & Co 1.. 8.. 1 £8.. 6..10

1795
April 5th 120   1 Rem⁻ from ditto on Alstorphius & Co

Balance of Interest Carried to the Debit

7..18.. 7

£220   £11.. 5.. 5

1795
April 5th £ 13..11   Creditors for Balance of old Accot under this date

Errors Excepted
London 31 December 1794

(signed) Bird Savage & Bird

[**68**]
Charleston, Charles Cotesworth Pinckney Esqr
London April 7th 1795

Sir,

We have already written you by this conveyance on the business of the Charleston Library Society, and are sorry now to address you by inclosing under protest for non payment Kirk & Lukins draft on Alstorphius & Van Hemert for £120. Sterling payable in London, which the communication between this Country and the United Provinces being cut off prevents the Acceptors making provision for in this Country. We debit you (say the Society) 5/6 for Notarial Charges on the same, and remain with great respect,

Sir

y^r most Ob^t Serv^{ts}

(signed) Bird Savage & Bird

To the Honble
Genl Charles Cotesworth Pinckney
Charleston
South Carolina
p^r Trial
Vicary[412]

[There follow two letters, both Aug. 12 1795, containing an exchange between Pinckney and Ramsay about teeth and bones to be placed in the new museum.]

[69]
London 2d April 1795

Dear Sir,

Inclosed are bills of Parcels, bill of lading and Invoice of two Cases directed to you n° 142 Containing Books from Ogilvie & Speare,[413] and the Sixth and Seventh Numbers of the Shakespeare Prints from Boydells[414] Amounting to £89.9^s.1^d to the debit of the Charleston Library Society including £4.4^s for the insurance of 100 at four Guineas p^{r}C^t – Commission £4.9.5. and Policy 7s.

After the Cases were packed we received a parcel of Books from Adams, being his Lectures[415] contained in the invoice, and packed in a Case RI N°4. sent by this Vessel to M^r R Izard[416] from whom you can procure them; Messrs Boydells suppose that the small Prints to the fifth Number of Shakespeare were put into the Book, which is their usual way of Sending them.[417] We refer you to the remarks at the foot of Ogilvie and Speares bill about some Articles not sent, and desiring the return of the third Fascicules of Smiths Plantarum Icones[418] to be exchanged for a coloured one – We shall be happy to attend to the future orders of the Society and am with great regard

Dr Sir,

y^r most Ob^t Serv^{ts}

(signed) Bird Savage & Bird

[70]
Charleston Augt 25th 1795

Gentlemen,

I inclose you in Account of the Charleston Library Society the Second of a Bill of Exchange for One hundred Pounds Sterling drawn by John Price & Co[419] in your favor, on Thos Mullet Esqr London.[420] Also I return the Protested Bill & Protest of Kirk & Lukens for £180 Sterling, also the second of Exchange of the same Bill, they having entered into an obligation to us that the same shall be paid immediately to you, with Interest from the time it became due, & by this Opportunity the Brig Seven Sisters Farqhar, Master, they send a Cargo addressed to Mr. John Tunno[421] who is to take it up. I inclose you also a list of Books for the Society which they will be obliged to you to send them as soon as possible – I remain with great respect –

y^r most Obed^t h^{ble} Servt

(signed) C C Pinckney

Messrs Bird Savage & Bird
by Brig. Seven Sisters
Farqhar Mast.
duplicate 4th Sept.
triplicate 9 Sept.[422]

[71]
Charleston March 1st 1796

Gentlemen,

The Charleston Library Society are in daily expectation of receiving the Books they wrote for in August last, in addition thereto, they request you would procure and forward to them the Books mentioned in the inclosed list. At their desire, I now transmit you a Bill of exchange for Sixty Pounds Sterling, drawn on you by John Price & Co in favor of Mr Samuel Bakman, and indorsed by him to you, –

I remain with great Respect
Gent^n – y^r most Ob^t Servt

(signed) – Chas Cotesworth Pinckney

Messrs Bird Savage & Bird
London
By the Roebuck, Wilson, via Liverpool[423]
(Duplicate) by the Washington[424]

[72]
Extract of a Letter from Messrs Bird Savage & Bird to Charles Cotesworth Pinckney, dated London 23^d Decr 1795–

Sir,

We now have to acknowledge the receipt of your much extended favor of the 25th Aug^t, 4th Septr and 9th Oct^r – The Bill for One Hundred Pounds on Thomas Mullet & Co drawn by John Price & Co has been paid as has Kirk and Luken's with charges by John Tunno,[425] both these are at the Credit of the Library Society – The Books you have ordered for yourself as well as those for the South Carolina Library Society will be sent by an early opportunity – we are with regard

Dear Sir
y^r most Ob^t Serv^ts –

(signed) Bird Savage & Bird

[73]
London 19 Feby 1796

Sir,

Inclosed you have the triplicate of Ours of the 28th Ult.^o on the Subject of our own business, which we recommend to your particular attention. – We now inclose you bill of lading, bills of Parcels and Invoice of Sundries for Account of the Charleston Library Society

amounting to	£89..18^s.. 4^d
insured in cover'd Sum of	
£95.23 guineas p^rC^t duty 2/6	2.. 2..4
	£92.. 8

which we pass to the Society's debit in addition to £8.8.1 due to us on the 31 Decr last for the balance of their account to that time, agreeable to the inclosed statement which if found right you will please to acknowledge – Since Adams's death, his Widow has declined making several of the Articles in the Mathematical way, & we in consequence procured the Gunners Compasses from Dolland.[426] In the bill of lading we have included a Case P N° 5, sent to us by some Person unKnown, for the freight & Shipping charges of which we debit M^r· Pinckney £1.4.6 – We are with great regard

Sir

y^r Ob^t Serv^ts

(Copy) Bird Savage & Bird
by the Powhatan
Capt Shaw

[74]
Charleston Augt 17th 1796

Gentlemen,

I now inclose you on account of the Charleston Library Society, a Bill for One hundred and fifty Pounds Sterling, drawn by Kirk & Lukens at Ninety days sight on Alstorphius & Van Hemert, in Amsterdam, payable in London, in favour of Samuel Bakman, and indorsed by him to you. Our last order for Books we expect shortly to receive – I remain with great Respect –

Your most Ob^t Serv^{ts}

(signed) Charles Cotesworth Pinckney

Messrs Bird Savage & Bird
Original by the Ruby

[75]
(Copy)
London 5th October 1796

Sir,

Inclosed we send you Invoice bill of lading & bills of parcells for sundry Goods shiped on Account of the Charleston Library Society on board the Winyaw Captn Richards amounting to £138.4.8 to the debit of the Society. We beg to refer you to Ogilvey & Spear's bill for observations relative to sundry Books which were ordered. We are

very respectfully
Sir
y^r most Ob^t Servt^s

Bird Savage & Bird

rec^d by the S^o Carolina
the 21 Nov 1796[427]
& the Original by the Winyaw

[76]

Doctor David Ramsay London 8th Decr 1796

Dear Sir,

By direction of Genl Pinckney we address you as vice President of the Charleston Library Society & inclose you invoice, bill of lading and bill of parcells of a Case of Books directed to you and Ship'd on board the Federalist Capt Pratt[428] amounting to £21.15.9 – to the debit of the Society. By the next opportunity we shall send you an account of the balance due to us by the Society, to whom it will always give us pleasure to render our best services. –

we are respectfully
Dear Sir
Y^r most Ob^t Serv^{ts}

(signed) Bird Savage & Bird

by the Pacific
Captⁿ Kennedy[429]

[77]

Charleston April 2^d 1797

Gentlemen

Your favor dated London 30th December 1796 addressed to me as vice President of the Charleston Library Society, by the direction of Genl Pinckney, I received by the Pacific, Captⁿ Kennedy, as also the invoice, bill of lading and bill of parcels, the Books you mentioned therein, were also received by the Federalist Captn Pratt in good condition and agreeably to the list sent you, (except the two) which you noted could not be got. Viz –

Repton's Sketches & tints with coloured plates &c[430] Le Grande's Tour thro⁻ Auvergne.[431] The Society are very much obliged by your past attention to their orders for Books, as also your polite offer to continue to oblige them

I am Gent^m
respectfully
y^r Ob^t Servt

(signed) David Ramsay

Messrs Bird Savage

[78]
Dr David Ramsay
London 26th April 1797

Sir

We have the pleasure to inclose you bill of Lading, bill of parcels and Invoice of a Case of Prints, shipt to your address by the Two Brothers, Captn Rust for Acco^t of the Charleston Library Society Amounting to £21.15^s.8^d– for which we debit the Society's Acco^t and hoping the Case may arrive safe we are with great esteem.

Sir
y^r most Obed^t Serv^ts

(signed) Bird Savage & Bird

[79]
Charleston Doct^r David Ramsay
Vice President of the Charleston
Library Society
London 9th Decr 1797
Orig.^l p^r S^o Carolina
Copy

Sir,

We had the pleasure on the 26th April last to send you the invoice of a Case of Prints for the Society amounting to £21.15.8 which we trust came safe to hand.

We now inclose you the Acct of the Society made up to the 31st inst^t when the balance due to us will be £82.17.2– British Sterling & we request your attention to our recovering a remittance from the Society

We are with great regard

Dear Sir
y^r most obed^t Serv^ts

(signed) Bird, Savage & Bird

Deb^r The Charleston Library Society their Account Curr.^t with Bird Savage & Bird, with Int.^t to 31. Decr 1797 @5p^rC^t p^rAnn. C^r

[*left column:* Deb^r]

1797

Feb^{ry} 6	Debtors for balance of old Account	
	under this date	£55 13 2
Jan^{ry} 1	Publications to 31st Decr 1796	
	Reviews & Magazines	2 14
April 14	Shipment by the Two Brothers	21 15 8
Decr 31	Interest on £55..13..2 from 6th	
Feb^{ry} to 31st	Decr 10 m^{ths} 25 Days	2 10 3
	2..14..– from 1st	
	Jan^{ry} to do 12 mth.	2 9
	Postages	1 4
1797		
Decr 31	Debtors this day for balance carried	
	to new Account	£82 17 2

[*right column:* Cr (*blank*)]

Errors excepted
London 9th Decr 1797

(Signed) Bird Savage & Bird

[80]

Gentlemen

At a Meeting of the Committee of Purchases at the Charleston Library Room the 26th April last it was ordered that the Treasurer purchase a bill to be transmitted to you for £82.17.2 being the Amount of your Acct against the Society to 31st Decr 1797.

Conformably thereto I now transmit to you the first of Exchange drawn by Messrs Kirk & Lukens on Mr John Tunno at 90 Days for Eighty four Pounds Sterling in your favor. I am very respectfully

Your most obedient
humble Servant

Joseph Peace

Treasurer of the Charleston Library Society[432]
Charleston
23^d June 1798

To
Messrs Bird, Savage & Bird
By the Pacific, Captn Kennedy[433]
Duplicate 28th July 1798
By the Julius Pringle[434]

[81]
Charleston Joseph Peace Esqr London 29th Septr 1798
Original p^r Pacific, Kennedy
Copy

Sir,

We inclose Invoice, bill of lading & bills of parcels for one case containing two Numbers of Shakespear sent by the Pacific, Captn Kennedy,[435] for the Amount we debit the Library Society in the Amount of £41..12..8– and are truly

Sir
your most obed.^t Serv^ts

(signed) Bird Savage & Bird

[82]
Charleston M^r. Jos. Peace Esqr   London March 15th 1799

Sir,

The Pacific which we shipt the 12th & 13th Numbers of Boydells Shakespear having been captur'd, we have shipped them & the 14th since published on board the Recovery, Captn Butler, for which we inclose bill of lading & Invoice amounting to £59..14.. to debit of the Charleston Library Society – We also inclose Acc.^t Curr.^t by which you will see that after having credited then for loss recover'd on the Pacific, particulars of which at foot & having debited them £5..16..7–for Interest, Commission & Postage, we have carried the balance. To debit of n/a under date of 12th April next in Sixty eight Pounds, fourteen shillings & fivepence.

We are truly
Sir
your most obed^t Serv^ts

(signed) Bird Savage & Bird

1799

March 12th Amount recovered of the Underwriters		£44.. –..
Off Brok[r], settling ½ p[r]C[t]	4..5	
Commission 2p[r]C[t]	17..7	1.. 2
		42..18..

[83]

Gentlemen

I acknowledge the receipt of you Letter of the 15th of March last, covering Bill of lading of one Case of Boydell's Shakespeare p[r] the Ship Recovery, Capt[n] Butler; and your Acc[ts] Curr[t] striking a bal[ce] against the Charleston Library Society of £68..14..5.

Enclosed is the first of Exchange drawn by M[r.] James Hamilton on Mess[rs] H. Bethune & C[o] of London[436] for £70..0..0– which you will please to place to the credit of the Society in due time.

I am respectfully

your obed[t] hbl Serv[t]

Joseph Peace

Treas[r] Ch.ton Liby Soc[y]
Charleston
12th Oct[r] 1799

To Mess[rs] Bird, Savage & Bird
By the West Indian
Capt[n] Chisolm
Duplicate Nov[r] 28th
By the Maria, Capt[n] Inglis

[This final letter to Bird, Savage, and Bird is followed in the letter book by a misplaced copy of a letter about a book purchase from Benjamin Leefe, CLS librarian 1813–1815, to the bookseller, John Vaughan of Philadelphia, 28 Oct. 1813. The letter book then continues with copies of the correspondence below.]

[84]

Charleston S°. Carolina Sept[r] 7th 1801

Gentlemen,

The Charleston Library Society being desirous to increase their collection with the Books enumerated in the inclosed List, & being informed of your Attention & punctuality in the supply of your Customers, and of the reasonable rates at which you dispose of your Books, they have determin'd to purchase of you while they shall be satisfied with your mode of dealing, such Books as they shall want.[437] For this purpose they inclose you the first (second, third) of a Bill of Exchange for £230 Sterling drawn by Mess[rs] Edwin Gairdner & C°[438] at Sixty Days sight in your favour on Mess[rs] Simpson & Davison Merchants in London,[439] and you will please to apply the same as far as it will extend towards the purchase of the Books enumerated in the inclosed List, and have such Books carefully packed up in strong cases and shipped to us in one of the first American Vessels bound for this port, apprizing us of the shipment by two or three other opportunities that we may make insurance here – We must leave it to your judgment to select such part of the inclosed list as can be purchased with the bill of Exchange now forwarded, apprizing you that as our Society is numerous & of course variant in the taste, that we trust you will adapt your selection to suit as well those who are fond of serious & erudite subjects as those who love to amuse themselves with light & trivial reading. — You will please to furnish us without delay with the probable cost of such part of the list as cannot be immediately complied with, on account of the money remitted not being sufficient to complete the purchase, that another bill may be transmitted to you for the amount – We wish you to furnish us with triplicates of every letter you favour us with to guard against miscarriage, to supply us regularly with your catalogues; and to apprize us of every new publication of considerable merit & importance which may appear in the various branches of Literature – All books sent us must be bound & lettered – you will be able to learn at the Caroline Coffee House in Birchin Lane Cornhill[440] what vessells are ready to sail for this port; & you will be careful to forward our books to this port & to no other.

Be so good as to direct your Letters & Packages to the Charleston Library Society to the care of Mr. John Davidson, Librarian & Treasurer, Charleston, South Carolina,[441] and this Gentleman will in future correspond with you, and his Letters you will consider as coming from the Society – As the present President of the Society it is part of my duty to open this Correspondence, and I flatter myself that you will reap emolument & the Society benefit from the intercourse. I have the honour to be with great respect

Gentlemen
your most obed.ᵗ hum: Servant

Cha.ˢ Cotesworth Pinckney

Messʳˢ Lackington, Allen & Cº.

[85]
Charleston 9ᵗʰ Septʳ 1801

Gentlemen

Mʳ· Joseph Peace[442] having in the beginning of last year declined serving as Treasurer to the Charleston Library Society I was then appointed to that Office & received from him your Letter of the 4ᵗʰ of April last inclosing your Accᵗ Current to 31ˢᵗ Decʳ 1800 – from which it appears that the Society was then indebted to you in the Sum of £25..3..5.

By direction of the Committee I now transmit to you the first of Exchange for £26 Sterling drawn by Messʳˢ Edwin Gairdner & Cº at sixty days sight in your favour on Messʳˢ Simpson & Davison Merchants in London

I am very respectfully

Gentlemen
Your most Obedᵗ humᵇˡᵉ Servant

John Davidson Treasʳ C L, S

Messʳˢ Bird, Savage & Bird

[86]
London 15ᵗʰ Febʳʸ 1802

Sir,

We were duly honored with Mr. Pinckneys esteemed favour of Sept.ʳ 7ᵗʰ & having lost no time in the completion of the Order inform you of its Shipment on board the Ranger, Capt.ⁿ Lovell, Feb.ʳʸ 6.[443] well packed in Two Cases, Freight paid, but no Insurance made with us.– We flatter ourselves that the execution of this Order will meet the approbation of the Society as we have been very diligent in collecting the several Articles, many of which being out of print & scarce could only be procured with difficulty – The Omissions are principally Novels & such as we trust are least anxiously wished; many of these however are now reprinting & will be sent with your next Order – The binding we think will be found both neat &

durable – To our prices we have annexed those generally charged by the trade & from the comparison anticipate your favorable opinion – We are the more led to expect this from your having expressed a conviction that the funds sent would be found insufficient for the discharge of the Order which they certainly would had we made the usual charges – We have inclosed our new Catalogue, which with the Reviews will be found an adequate guide to the further selections – The most celebrated works now in the press are a new & fine edition of Milton,[444] with notes by Mr. Todd – Lord Bacon's Works[445] – a new Cyclopedia – a Collection of periodical Papers about 40 Vols to be called the British Classics[446] – a translation of the Works of Linnëus by Dr Truron[447] – Travels in Russia, by Pallas[448] – a new Farmers Dictionary in 2 Vols, 4to Swifts' Works with some posthumous pieces, 19 Vols – Charnock's Marine Dictionary[449] – a new Copy of Dryden and a new Shakspere with Notes in 20 large Volumes.

The late very heavy duties on Paper have not only advanced the prices of all works, but have deprived the public of many new & important publications; but as we are in daily expectation of a repeal of those grievous taxes, the present year will present a greater variety & at more reasonable rates than the last – We have only to add our best thanks for the confidence you have placed in us which it shall be our study to merit on all occasions – We remain Sir

Yours &c

Lackington, Allen & Co.

Mr. John Davidson

Amount of Books pr List	£203.. 11..11
3 Postages	7.. 6
Freight	2.. 1..10
2 Cases & Shipping Expences	2.. 2.. –
	208.. 3.. 3
Balance Carried to Cr.	21..16.. 9
	£230.. –.. –

[87]
Charleston 12th June 1802

Gentlemen,

I have to acknowledge the receipt of yours of the 15th Feb.ry and also of the Two cases by the Ranger, Capt.n Lovell who had arriv'd here about ten days before your Letter,[450] which appears to have come round by the way of New York. I would therefore submit to you the propriety of accompanying every shipment with a few lines by the same Vessel –

I have the pleasure to inform you that the execution of the order has given satisfaction to the Society who have directed me to send you the inclosed Catalogue accompanied with this First of Exchange on Mr. John Price Merchant in London[451] for £200 – which with the Balance in your hands they hope will be nearly sufficient to cover the Order. In any case it will give them satisfaction to have an acknowledgement of the receipt of the Bill; & if from your calculation there appears a probability of any deficiency in the Money sent, another remittance shall be immediately made, as it is their wish to have you always fully provided. They also request that you would be pleased in future to have insurance made on any packages for the Society & have the Amount charged with the other expences. A speedy execution of this Order will much oblige them.

Gentlemen,
your very hum: Serv.[t]

John Davidson

Mess[rs] Lackington, Allen & C[o].

[88]
London Sept[r] 26th 1802

Sir

We have to return the Charleston Library Society our most sincere thanks in acknowledging the receipt of their Bill for £200 on our tenant Mr. Price,[452] & we beg further to assure them that the most particular attention shall be given to this & their future commands. The only difficulty occurring in this Order is in the Article Philosophical Transactions – We have searched every Library in London & have also sent to Oxford & Cambridge without being able to meet with a Copy made up by the Abridgement. We have therefore ventured on sending an entire set, the finest we are confident that ever was seen: the price is £120 – which is very reasonable, considering the scarcity & value of the Article – we have every reason to hope that the difference in charge will be amply compensated by the utility of the work & its ornament to your Library.–[453]

The present Order (as nearly as we can now judge) will exceed the remittance & balance in hand by about £100 – such further sum as you may think proper to send shall be passed to the Credit of the Account without delaying the Order, which we hope to ship in a fortnight from this date. – Many works of credit have been recently published, of which we shall take the liberty to send De Non's

Travels in Egypt,[454] Barthelemies in Italy,[455] Dean Paley on Theology & the Bishop of Londons Lectures,[456] all of which are to you indispensable – We shall send a Register of new publications which is published monthly:[457] from this you will no doubt select many others. – We request Sir you will accept our best thanks for the clearness & accuracy in which the Orders are conveyed – very few mistakes we trust have yet occurred: if any, they must wholly be attributed to us.

We remain, Sir
your very humble Serv.[ts]

Lackington, Allen & C[o].

Mr. John Davidson

[89]
London Nov[r] 20th 1802

Sir

We had the honor to address you Sept[r] 26th in acknowledging the receipt of the Library Society's Order, the Shipment of which you are now apprized of by the inclosed Bill of lading, duplicates of which will be sent in course – Every attention having been paid to the execution of the Order, we trust it will meet with your approbation – In the Article Philosophical Transactions we beg to refer you to our former Letter – we continued our search for the Copy you ordered 'till the last day of shipping, but without effect, nor did we find another entire copy in any booksellers hands, so that we are led to hope it will prove acceptable to the Library. The Articles omitted are few, being only such as could not be found on the most diligent search – The Balance is in our favor – we rely on your punctuality for a remittance – I remain

your very humble Serv.[ts]

Lackington, Allen & Co.

Mr. John Davidson

[90]
London Feb[ry] 18th 1803

Mr. Davidson

We take this opportunity of forwarding 3[d] duplicate of goods sent in 4 Trunks, by the Brothers, Rising, in Nov.[r] last[458] – We have taken every care in completing the Order & trust it will give satisfaction. The balance is stated as above & we request to be favor'd with your remittance–

We remain, Sir
your obliged humble Serv.ts

Lackington, Allen & C°.

Amount of Books & Charges	£392.. 3.. 1
Sundries Janᵗʸ 28ᵗʰ 1802	£208.. 3.. 3
	600.. 6. .4
Cash Janᵗʸ 3ᵈ £230 – –	
Septʳ 6ʰ 200 – –	
	430.. –.. –
Balance due to L, A & C°	£170.. 6.. 4

[91]
Charleston 30ᵗʰ April 1803

Gentlemen,

Yours of 20ᵗʰ Nov.ʳ last came to hand by the Ship Brothers which had been obliged to put into New York, from whence she arrived here the evening before last[459] – The Books are not yet landed but I hope will be found in good order & I have no doubt will prove satisfactory to the Society – On the 4ᵗʰ of March I wrote You per the Polly[460] & on the 19ᵗʰ sent a duplicate per the Ruby[461] inclosing another Order with the 2ᵈ & 3ᵈ of Exchange on Mr. John Price[462] for £150. I now send you the 1ˢᵗ of Exchange on Messrs Tunno & Loughnan[463] for £170 –. Should you find it difficult to procure any of the Books in the last Order I am directed to request that you would send on the rest without delay, reserving the others for a future opportunity – I am

Gentlemen
Your very hum: serv.ᵗ

John Davidson

Messʳˢ Lackington, Allen & C°.

[92] [*recorded out of order*]
Charleston 4th March 1803

Gentlemen

Your last of the 26th Sept. was not received here till the 20th Dec^r – Since that time the Society has been in daily expectation of the Books, which however have not yet arrived – Inclosed you will receive a fresh Catalogue to be sent on as soon as possible, with this 1st of Exchange on Mr. John Price for £150 – which on the arrival of the last Order shall be speedily followed by another remittance to the full supposed value of the whole –

I beg leave to refer to your own accuracy & knowledge of business the compliment you have been so polite as to pay me. –

I remain
Gentlemen
your very hum: Servt

John Davidson

Messrs Lackington, Allen & Co.

[93]
Charleston 17th May 1803

Gentlemen

On the 30th of last Month I took the opportunity of addressing you p^r the Maria, Captⁿ Chisolm,[464] & on the 7th Instant p^r the Isabella, Captⁿ Green,[465] inclosing the 1st & 2^d of Exchange on Messrs Tunno & Loughnan for £170[466] – I now send you the 3d & have the pleasure to inform you that the Books have come safe to hand.

I am

Gentlemen
your very hum: Servt

John Davidson

Messrs Lackington, Allen & Co.

[94]
Mr. John Davidson
London July 5th 1803

Sir,

We have to acknowledge the receipt of your two kind favors covering remittances which are duly credited for in the following statement of your account, for which please accept our best thanks.

We here advise you of the shipment of your Order on board the Cleopatra, Davenport,[467] insurance on which you will perceive we have effected at a very low rate. It is with satisfaction we state that but few omissions will be found in the Order, the chief Articles being Sir Joseph Banks's Catalogue, which could not be procured even by a personal application to Sir Joseph[468] who is a good friend of ours & we are certain would have accommodated us if a spare copy had remained in his possession. Campbell's Vitruvius also cannot be got with the supplement – We have one by us without it, in 3 Vol.s folio if that will answer –

We have every reason to hope a continuance of your favors & remain

your obliged humble Serv.ts

Lackington, Allen & Co.

Amount of Books & charges	£178.. 8.. 4	
1802 – Novr 20th Sundries	392.. 3.. 1	
Janry 28th Do	208.. 3.. 3	
	778..14.. 8	
Contra Cr.		
1802 Janry By Bill	£230	
Sepr Do	200	
1803 April Do	170	
June Do	150	
	750.. –..	
Balce in favor of L, A, & Co.	£ 28..14.. 8	

[corrected in original from £228..14.. 8]

[95]
Charleston 31st Janry 1804

Gentlemen

I have to acknowledge the receipt of yours of the 5th July, with the Books in good order by the Cleopatra in Octr[469] – The Society appears to be indebted to you for a Balance of £28..14..8 – which shall be remitted to you soon with a sum to cover a large Order now making out a part of which I have now sent by the Two Friends, Captn McNeill[470] & the rest with the Bills shall be forwarded by the first Opportunity.

I am

Gentlemen
your very humble Servt

John Davidson

Messrs Lackington Allen & Co.

[96]
Charleston 6th March 1804

Gentlemen,

On the 31st Jan^ry I wrote you by Captn McNeill with such part of the Order as could then be made out. I now inclose you a compleat copy with the 1st of Exchange on Messrs Mackmurdo, Hicks [*sic*] and C^o[471] for £450– which it is expected will be more than sufficient to cover the Order & discharge the former balance. The French books I am directed to countermand & to request that you would if possible have the rest ready to be sent by the return of Captn Mackneill.[472]

I am
Gentlemen
Your very humble Servt

John Davidson

Messrs Lackington, Allen & Co.

[97]
Charleston 16th July 1804

Gentlemen

On the return of Captn McNeill to this Port[473] the Society was much disappointed in not receiving a part at least of the Order transmitted by him. Since that time I have sent on Triplicates under date of 6th & 24th March & 28th April, inclosing fuller Copies of the Order with the 2^d & 3^d of Exchange on Messrs Mackmurdo, Hicks & Co for £450 – drawn in your favor by Messrs Ogier & McKinney. Of the receipt of these the Society also expected to have been informed & beg that this may always be done in future by the first opportunity of which you will also be pleased to avail yourselves for sending on the books – I am

Gentlemen
your very hum: Servt

John Davidson

[98]
London July 20th 1804

Sir

We wrote by this Month's Packet advising of the shipment of the Articles agreeable to the Invoice on board the George Washington Enoch Parrott[474] in six matted Trunks; the freight of which £3..17..7 is paid here – Annexed is a Copy of our Letter of July 18th –

We received your favours in due course, but the return of Captn McNeill was so sudden[475] that tho' the Order was put in hand immediately we were not in time for him: ever since which the books have lain pack'd waiting a vessel for Charleston direct. This we have at length procured, & we hope you will receive them in safety – They are insured, but as we have not yet the Brokers Account we are unable to state the balance, which however will be done by next Packet – The French books we are sorry to say were procured many of them purposely from Paris & bound, before we recieved your Counter Orders – As they were books far from being of general demand their [*sic*] would have been a very considerable loss on their re-sale & therefore we have thought it advisable to send them which we have done agreeably to our Letter to that effect of April 28th. – There will be found to be very few omissions in the present order & those are chiefly of modern books, which are temporally [*sic*] out of print – To Charnock's Marine Architecture there is no Supplement,[476] neither are there any more papers on Naval Architecture – Roscoes Leo[477] & Radcliffe's Julia[478] are not yet published & Plumiers Ferns cannot be procured without his other works[479] – The newspapers & Debates shall be sent in parcels by Trading vessels: this we conclude is what you desire, in preference to their conveyance by the New York Packet. Should any preferable mode present itself you will have the goodness to inform us – Would you not chuse all the periodical works which you subscribe to & the new Plays sent in the same manner?

We are Sir
your humble Serv.^ts

Lackington, Allen, & Co.

Mr. John Davidson

[99]
London Aug^st 28th 1804

Sir,

We beg leave to refer you to our former Letters for particulars of the Execution of your two last Orders & here hand you a general Statement of Account. We shall continue forwarding the Papers in the mode you will herewith them [*sic*] – The periodical publications could also be added if you thought fit.

We remain, Sir
your very humble Serv.^ts

Lackington, Allen & Co

Mr. John Davidson

Amount of books	£166..15..10
Sundries May 1st	215.. 7.. 1
Balance as before stated	28..14.. 8
Paid for Trunks	5.. 4.. –
Custom House Duties, & Shipping, Bills of lading &c	15..19.. –
Paid Freight	3..17.. 7
Paid Insurance	9.. 1.. –
	444..19.. 2
Balance carried to new Acc^t	5.. –..10
	£450.. –.. –

[100]
Charleston 10th Decr 1804

Gentlemen,

By the George Washington, Captn Parrot your Invoice with the books came safely to hand, & shortly after your duplicate with the statement. These are the only communications received from you since the original Order sent by Captn McNeill & I am now directed by the Society to request that you will in future immediately acknowledge the receipt of any Bills that may be forwarded[480] – In examining the books I was sorry to find that in several of them, by the carelessness of the binder, some of the leaves were left loose & in a few instances pieces torn out, both of which will I hope in future be guarded against – You will now receive inclosed a new Order with the 1st of Exchange on Messrs Tunno & Loughnan for £200 –

Should any difficulty arise respecting the Bills in London, you will please to forward the inclosed to Mess.rs Tho.s & Will.m Earle & Co481 Liverpool, by whom they will be duly honored. The books mark'd with a cross in the list are some which had been formerly sent for but not transmitted.

I am
Gentlemen
your very hum: serv.t

John Davidson

Mess.rs Lackington, Allen & Co.

[101]
London April 2d 1805

Sir

We beg to refer you to a duplicate of this with a bill of lading inclosed which we have sent by Capt.n McNeill,482 & a further duplicate by Packet – You will have to regret but few Omissions in this Order & the complaint against the binding we trust is <u>fully</u> obviated. We beg to return you our best thanks for this additional proof of your kindness & by increased attention shall hope a long continuance of your correspondence, Sir, we remain,

your obliged Servants

Lackington, Allen & Co.

The recent advances on paper, printing & binding shall stimulate us still farther to keep down our charges – a circumstance of the greatest importance to large purchasers –

Mr. John Davidson

Amount of books		£170..15..11483
Balance of last Acc.t as stated	£5..10..	
By Bill of Exchange	200.. ..	
	205..10..	
Balance in favor of the Library		34.. 4..10
Do bro.t forward	34.. 4..10	
		205.. –..10
Paid Insurance & Duty on £150	4.. 5..	
	£29..19..10 due to the Society	

[102]
London July 6th 1805

Sir

We send you by the St. Andrew, Captⁿ John Pratt[484] a box of Books as p^r annexed Statement, for the purpose of making a package which might include the papers – Leo 10th which is just published we doubt not you will be glad to receive – it is purchased in England with great avidity. The Non Military Journal is very scarce; the copy sent came in a Library while we were packing the box & we thought it advisable to send it even tho' unbound[485] – We trust you have received the former in safety & we rely on its having given satisfaction & being favoured with a continuance of your favours. We are, Sir

your obliged

Lackington, Allen & Co.

Mr. John Davidson
Am.^t of books £18..14..6

[103]
Charleston 24th Decr 1805

Gentlemen,

I take this opportunity by Captⁿ McNeill[486] to inform you that we recieved by him our last Order which after being captur'd off the Bar by a French Privateer was retaken & carried into Jamaica where it was exposed to public Sale & bought in by him for the Society, as will appear from a certified copy of his Acc.^t herewith inclosed. You will therefore be entitled to receive from the underwriters the sum of £150 being the amount insured, & I am instructed by the Society to request that in future Insurance may be made in full so as to cover the premium & all charges. The books by Captⁿ McNeill, as also the Package by the St. Andrew, Captⁿ Pratt arrived in good Order, but I must inform you that the Plates which should have accompanied Holcroft's Travels[487] were omitted to be sent. – You will now receive a fresh Order which we hope may be got in readiness by the return of the Vessel. There is also inclosed the 1st of Exchange for £100 drawn in your favor by Messrs Shoolbred & Williams,[488] out of which you will please to pay to Messrs Bird & Savage £20– to cover a Balance due from the Society.[489] After the receipt of this you will please discontinue the London Papers – I am

Gentlemen

your very hum: Serv.ᵗ

John Davidson

Messʳˢ Lackington, Allen & Cᵒ.

[104]

London 20ᵗʰ June 1806

Sir,

We were duly favoured with your remittances & Order: the latter has been executed some Months waiting a Vessel & is now shipped on board the Wanderer, which we hope will make a more fortunate voyage than the Vessel we last freighted – There are few omissions in this Order & they are principally of the works relative to America. – the Nᵒ. from our Catalogue was sold, & Thomsons Chemistry[490] – The Rules for French Infantry[491] & some other modern publications are in the press for new editions. – We have not yet recovered from the underwriters on the Two Friends, tho' we are now in expectation of the produce of the Sale being remitted from Jamaica – when we have received it the amount shall be placed to your Credit – We paid Messʳˢ Bird & Cᵒ on your account £20 – The volume of Plates to Holcroft was assuredly packed, & we imagine, if you have not yet found it, that it must have been taken out & not replaced, either by the Captors or Recaptors.

Sir

we remain

your Obed.ᵗ Servants

Lackington, Allen & Co.

Mr. John Davidson

Amount of Books & Charges £140..10..11

[105]

Charleston 12ᵗʰ Janʳʸ 1807

Gentlemen,

Our last Order was duly received by the Wanderer[492] & I now inclose you a fresh one[493] in which are inserted the omissions in the last. It is particularly requested that you would immediately compleat it & send it if possible by the return of the Two Friends – You will also receive inclosed the 1ˢᵗ of Exchange for £100 – drawn in your favor by Mr. John Haslet,⁴⁹⁴ accompanied by a Letter of Advice to Mr. William Lees⁴⁹⁵ at Liverpool.

I am sorry to mention that some mistake must have taken place with regard to the Plates for Holcroft, as the Packages had never been opened 'till deliver'd here when I took out the contents with my own hands.

I am
Gentlemen
your hum: Servt

John Davidson

Mss^rs Lackington, Allen & C°.

[106]
London April 20th 1807

Sir,

Annexed we hand you our Acc.^t – These sundries are shipped on board the Two Friends⁴⁹⁶ & we hope will be more fortunate than those formerly sent by that Vessel – We are sorry to say that we have not yet been able to credit your acc.^t by payment from the underwriters, who have made many objections principally as to the sale & re-purchase at Jamaica which we have had to combat – these we believe are now done away with & the delay is occasion'd by their refusal to allow the heavy commissions & charges which the agents have put on them. We shall do our best endeavour to have the Acc.^t settled as speedily & advantageously for your interest as possible – You will find but few omissions in the execution of this Order – Holcroft's Recorder⁴⁹⁷ being of no repute is discontinued – we thought you would not wish the few N.^s that were publish'd –

Many N.^s of the Botanical Magazine being out of print, we could only meet with a copy splendidly bound⁴⁹⁸ – Woodfall's Junius⁴⁹⁹ is not out, nor is the 2^d volume of Clarkes Maritime Discoveries⁵⁰⁰ – Stevens's Greek Thesaurus is exceedingly scarce – the only copy we can find they demand £25 for – We would not purchase without consulting you⁵⁰¹ – As to the plates of Holcroft we cannot account for them being missing: we will however endeavour to procure another set. We remain, Sir

your obliged Serv.^ts

Lackington, Allen & C°.

Amount of books & charges		£235.. 4.. –
Acc.ᵗ		
1805		
April 2ᵈ	Sundries	175.. –..11⁵⁰²
July 6ᵗʰ	D.º	20..18.. –
1806		
	Paid Bird & Savage	20.. –.. –
Febʳʸ 20ᵗʰ	Sundries per Wanderer	140..10..11
		£591..13..10

Contra	
Balance of Old Acc.ᵗ	5.. –..10
1805 Bill of Exchange	200.. –.. –
1806 D.º	100.. –.. –
1807 D.º	100.. –.. –
	405.. –..10
Balance in favor of L. A & Cº	186..13.. –
	£591..13..10

Balance	186..13.. –

Mr. John Davidson

[107]
London Augˢᵗ 5ᵗʰ 1807

Sir

    We herewith hand you a statement of a settlement we have this day made with the Underwriters on the unfortunate shipment on the Two Friends – We regret to find that a loss tho small will fall on your Acc.ᵗ arising partly from the Policy not covering the whole amount of Invoice & partly from a refusal on the part of the Underwriters to admit the enormous charges on acc.ᵗ of Sale in Jamaica, as well as home expences. We have had great difficulty in bringing the matter to an issue; & after advising with our sollicitor, we thought it more to your interest to refer the affair to an arbitrator than adopt legal measures. This was accepted & the deduction of 5 prCent excepted, the Acc.ᵗ as rendered by Mr. Tunno is admitted & the loss is paid & placed to your credit. – We have annexed our current Account, for the balance of which we shall rely on your usual punctuality in next remittance.

    We beg to assure you that no change of circumstances affecting the amity of our countries (which would be deeply lamented here) will affect our situation with you, being desirous of acting with the most perfect honor in all our transactions. – We remain, Sir

your obedient Serv.ts

Lackington, Allen & Co

P.S. – The Amount of Sales on two Invoices you will perceive has been rendered to us in one, supposing the Articles to sell at an average rate it can be of no disadvantage to you or the other party, Mr. Johnson of the South Carolina College,[503] but should you think otherwise, on application to him he will we are certain do what is just.

Mr. John Davidson

Charleston Library Society In Acc.t with Lackington, Allen & Co.
London Augst 5th 1807

Dr

1805
April 20th Sundries as prAcct render'd pr Two Friends

			£175.. –..11
July 6th	D.o	D.o	20..18.. –

1806
April 3d Acceptance in favor Bird, Savage & Bird

20.. –.. –

Febry 20th Sundries as prAcct render'd per Wanderer

140..10..11

1807
April 4th D.o D.o per Two Friends

235.. 4.. –

Augst 5th Paid Brokerage & expences attending recovery
of Insurance from Underwriters 2..10.. 6

£594.. 4.. 4

Cr

1805	Balance as pr Acct Rendered	5.. –..10
April	By Bill	200.. –.. –
1806		
Febry 13th	D.o	100.. –.. –
1807		
Febry 27th	D.o	100.. –.. –

Augst 5th Rec^d of Underwriters of £150
@ 58.. 1..2 p^rCent Tunno & Co.

proceeds of cargo	87.. 1.. 9
on £175 @ 39..14..8 prCt	69..10.. 8
* ———	
97..15..10 p^rC^t	

* This deficit is occasioned by a commission charge in Mr. Tunno's Acc.t which the Underwriters would not allow

Balance in favor of L. A & Co to new Credit	32..11.. 1
	£594.. 4.. 4
Balance brought forward	32..11.. 1

Statement of the Proceeds of sundry Goods shipped by Messrs Lackington Allen & Co pr Two Friends, McNeill bound for Charleston, but captur'd & recaptur'd on her voyage & sent to Jamaica, where Ship & Cargo were sold by Order of the Judge of the Admiralty Court in that Island to ascertain the amount due for Salvage

Jamaica currency	
13 Trunks of books	1058.. 1..11

Copy of Tunnos Acct [*written in left margin*]
Charges in Jamaica
To proportion of landing charges, public
sale expences, Brokers, Agents & Registers
Commissions, Salvage – 12½ prCent to
Recaptors, Proctors Accounts, Premium on
Bills 10 prCent, making together as pr

Jamaica Sales 33..10 prCent	354.. 9.. 1
Jamaica currency	703..12..10
Or Sterling 140 prCent	502..12.. –

Charges in London
To your proportion of a Pilot Boat at
Charleston which was sent to the Havanna
& Jamaica in search of the Two Friends at
the time she was captured, with documents
to prove the neutrality of the cargo

£ 8..12.. 4

To your proportion of Shaw & Le Blanc &
Hopkins Gray and Glovers Accounts   9.. 8.. 7
Packet, Postages Stamps & petty

charges	2..10.. 3	
* Commission 5 prCent	25.. 2.. 8	
		45..13..10
		456..18.. 2

Underwriters Acc.t [*written in left margin*]
* Deduct Commission as above which the Underwriters
would not admit   25.. 2.. 8

                                                           482.. –..10

C.L.S.	175.. –..11
S.C.C.	974.. 4.. 6

1149.. 5.. 5 – if 1149..5..5 gives 482..–..10 the loss pr Hund^d is 58..1..2 Insurance only being made on £150 – C,L,S – & £950 – S,C,C –. Recd of Tunno £456..18..2 which is 39..4..8 prCent as credited

[108]
Charleston 14th Novr 1807

Gentlemen,

By the Ship Two Friends our last Order was duly received & I now inclose you a new one[504] in which are inserted the Omissions of the former – you will also receive the 1st of Exchange for £220 drawn in your favour by Mr. T. Hindley[505] on Messrs R & A Harrison & Latham Liverpool,[506] payable in London – Out of this you will please to pay Messrs Bird & Savage £7..18..9 being a Balance due to them by the Society –

From the high price of Stevens's Greek Thesaurus it has been thought proper to postpone the purchase for the present[507] – I hope before this time you have been able to settle with the Underwriters & have only to intreat that the Order may be forwarded by the very first opportunity – I am

Gentlemen
Your very humble Servt

John Davidson

Messrs Lackington, Allen & Co.

[109]
Charleston 26th Novr 1808

Gentlemen,

It is now fully Twelve Months since I wrote you by the Ship Caledonia, Henderson,[508] inclosing an Order for Books & the 1st of Exchange for £220 – Soon afterwards I forwarded a duplicate with the 2d of Exchange. – The Society feels much hurt & disappointed in neither having received the books, nor even an acknowledgement of the receipt of the Bills. – The Montezuma arrived here lately from London[509] & another vessel is said to be daily expected, an opportunity of which it is hoped you have not neglected to avail yourselves.

A new Order has been in readiness for some time but will not be forwarded till the receipt of the former. I am

Gentlemen
your very humble Serv.t

John Davidson

Messrs Lackington, Allen, & Co.

[110]
London March 1st 1809

Sir,

We learn with surprise that our last acknowledging the receipt of your Order covering a remittance of £220 has not reached your hands. We wrote to thank you for that favor & to say that the Order should be put in hand immediately & forwarded by the first opportunity – It was prepared accordingly & the only vessel our broker has apprised us of for Charleston direct is the Diana, Captn Tibbits, by which we were prepared to send when she suddenly changed her destination, in consequence we imagine of the uncertain state of American Affairs. Since that time no vessel has sailed either from London or Liverpool for your port. Be assured, Sir we are as desirous of sending the Order as you can be of receiving it, & we hope a very short time will elapse before we shall be enabled to announce a vessel which shall have received them. In the meantime your further Orders shall meet every attention. We remain, Sir

your obed.t Serv.ts

Lackington, Allen, & Co.

Mr. John Davidson, Charleston

[111]
Charleston March 31st 1809

Sir,

The Library Society of this City have been for some years past in the habit of Corresponding with Messrs Lackington, Allen & Co remitting them considerable sums of money & receiving in return Books, Maps &c conformable to Order. By the enclosed Account it will appear that they are indebted to the Society to the amount of £179..10..2. They have had an Order for Books for nearly a Year & a half, which they have not complied with, a Catalogue of which we enclose. The last remittance made to them was in Novr 1807, by a Bill of Exchange for £220 on Messrs Harrison, the payment of which they have never acknowledged, tho' we have learnt collaterally that the Money has been paid them – Having behaved thus improperly, the Society have resolved to change their Correspondent. We will therefore be obliged to you to demand the payment of the balance in the hands of Lackington, Allen & Co due to the Library Society, & to retain the same in your hands until the commercial intercourse between Great Britain & America, now unhappily interrupted, shall be restored; & upon that event to cause a shipment to be made by some eminent bookseller on whom reliance can be placed, of such Books of the enclosed Catalogue as can be obtained, to the amount of the sum received by you. We should be glad to establish a regular correspondence with some really respectable & exact Bookseller whom you could recommend to us & beg that you would make such recommendation – Our demand for Books would be to the amount of about £200 pr annum.

Should Messrs Lackington, Allen & Co make any difficulty in paying you the Money, we should have no objection to their compleating the Order & delivering you the Books properly packed for shipment, to be forwarded as soon as commercial intercourse is renewed – We know that this is a bad course in the unsettled state of affairs between the two countries, but it is better than bringing a suit for the recovery of it – We should not trouble you with this small agency but upon a conviction that you continue to respect many members of our Society who remember you with esteem – Should it not be convenient for you to perform it, be pleased to place the business in the hands of some respectable person on whom you can rely – I am &c

H. W. DeSaussure[510]

John Hopton Esqr[511]

Messrs Lackington, Allen & Co.

D.ʳ

1801		
Sepᵗ 7ᵗʰ	To Gardner & C.ᵒˢ Bill[512]	230.. –.. –
	To Balᶜᵉ brought down	21..16.. 9
1802		
June 12ᵗʰ	To Bill on John Price of London	200
	To Balᶜᵉ carried to you C.ʳ	170.. 6.. 4
		392.. 3.. 1
1803		
april 30	To Bill on John Price	150
	To Dᵒ on Tunno & Loughnan	170
	To Balᶜᵉ carried to your C.ʳ	28..14.. 8
		348..14.. 8
1804		
March 6ᵗʰ	To Bill on Mackmurdo & Hicks	450.. –.. –
	To Balᶜᵉ brought down	5.. –..10
Dec 10ᵗʰ	To Bill on Tunno & Loughnan	200
		205.. –..10
	To Balᶜᵉ due the Society	29..19..11
1805	To Bill	100
1807	To Bill	100
	To Balᶜᵉ in favor of L. A & Co	186..13.. –
		416..12..11
	To Monies recᵈ from Underwriters	87.. 1.. 9
	D.ᵒ	69..10.. 8
	To Balᶜᵉ due to L. A & Co	32..11.. 1
		189.. 3.. 6
Nov 14th	To Bill on Messʳˢ Harrison	220.. –.. –

C.ʳ

1802		
Febʳʸ 15ᵗʰ	By Books	208.. 3.. 3
	By Balᶜᵉ	21..16.. 9
		230.. –.. –
1803		
Febʳʸ 18ᵗʰ	By Books	392.. 3.. 1
	By Balance brought down	170.. 6.. 4
1803		
July 5ᵗʰ	By Books	178.. 8.. 4
		348..14.. 8

	By Balance brought down	28..14.. 8
1804		
Augt 28th	By Books & Charges	416.. 4.. 6
	By Bal^{ces} due the Society	5.. –..10
		450.. –.. –
1805		
April 2d	By Books	170..15..11
	Insurance & Duty 4.. 5..	
	By Bal^{ce} due the Society	29..19..11
		205.. –..10
July	By Books	18..14.. 6
1807	Charges	2.. 3.. 6
April	By Books	235.. 4.. –
	By Bird & Savage	20.. –.. –
	By Books	140..10..11
		416..12..11
	By Bal^{ce}	186..13.. –
	By Cash p^d Brok^{ge} on recov'g	
	Insurance	2..10.. 6
		189.. 3.. 6
	By Bal^{ce}	32..11.. 1
	By Bird & Savage	7..18.. 9
	By Bal^{ce} due the Society	179..10.. 2
		220.. –.. –

[112]
Extract of a Letter from J^{no} Hopton Esqr to Nathl Russell Esqr[513]
London 10th June 1809

Dear Sir

   I shall put the business of your Library Society into Goldinghams hands[514] &
recommend that in future their Order for books & remittances to pay for them be
sent to him, so that he may take care to have them shipped in due time, d^o the Custom House business, pay the duty, make the Insurance & forward the Invoice &
Bill of Lading – All this part of the mercantile business is quite foreign to a Bookseller: from this cause arose the disappointment which the Society have just now
experienced – to them, his trifling commission of £8 or £10 pr Ann: can't be any
object, & in return for which their business will be faithfully & punctually executed. I have seen Lackington, Allen & Co and they acknowledge the balance they

hold belonging to the Society, & the books ordered will be or are ready to be shipped by the first opportunity. They know nothing of the Montezuma that sailed from hence to Charleston about a Twelve Month ago, at least they say so & which I can readily believe as they are mere booksellers. Pray communicate all this or as much as you may think proper to the President & Vice President of the Society.

Dear Sir
your friend & hum: serv.^{t}

John Hopton

Nathl Russell Esqr

[113]
London June 9th 1809

Sir,

We beg to refer you to our last dated March 1st which we trust has allayed your displeasure relative to our supposed neglect in the execution of your order. We have since had a communication with a Mr. Hopton & have assured that Gentleman, as we have also declared to you that the delay is by no means imputable to neglect on our part, the books having actually been purchased by us on the immediate receipt of the order & put into the binders hands, direction at the same time having been given to our Brokers Messrs Hopkins & C^{o515} to give us timely notice of the first vesel destined for your port – After a tedious delay we accordingly had notice of the Diana's being put up & in consequence gave immediate direction for the package of books which was scarcely issued when her destination was suddenly changed & no other vessel has since replaced her, nor to our knowledge was previously put up. – We have Mr. Hopton's Instructions to deliver the books for shipment to Mr. Goldingham – we can have no objection to that arrangement if it is your request, tho' it cannot expedite the business since it is a ship only that is wanting & that we shall ourselves make every search for, since we trust it must be evident to every person that the delay is as detrimental to our interest as to your convenience. – That our acknowledgment of the receipt of your Order & Remittance should have failed to reach your hands is a circumstance as extraordinary as it is to be lamented – That we wrote we give you our honor's – a copy of the letter in our regular letterbook Mr. Hopton shall see when he next calls – We certainly did not send duplicates of that letter, because as we were in immediate hope of handing you an invoice of the books, the necessity of such acknowledgment would we hoped have been superseded. – In the expectation of our being honor'd with a continuance of your confidence which we shall study more than ever to preserve

We remain Sir
your Obed.ᵗ Servants

Lackington, Allen & Cᵒ.

Mr. John Davidson

[This is followed by copies of four letters exchanged between Davidson and Wood-ward of Philadelphia, 8 May, 24 May, 20 June, 2 Aug. 1809.]

[114]
London 24ᵗʰ June 1809

Sirs,

I am debtor for your favor of 31ˢᵗ March last; both original & copy have reached me, with them several inclosures – the introduction by Mʳ· Russell would under any circumstances have commanded my attention; independent of which I cant have the least objection to do any thing within my reach to serve the Charleston Library Society.

I lost no time in calling on Lackington Allen & Co who at once acknowledged the Balance in their hands to agree with the statement of your Secretary, & shew'd by their books that the Bill of Exchange & Order for Books did not get to their hands until the last day of the Year 1807 – the receipt they acknowledged by a vessel then on the point of sailing for Charleston, & they immediately began to collect the books order'd, intending to embrace the first opportunity of shipping, since which they never heard of any; on this point they have certainly been negligent. – I hinted that Interest should be allow'd on the Balance they held, to which they object, in my opinion without reason – give me leave to refer to you what I have written to our friend Mr. Russell, & as I told him, having entirely declined business,⁵¹⁶ I shall place yours under the care of a person on whom I can depend, Mr. Nathˡ Goldingham, Merchant, of this city – the little commission he will charge, can't be any object to the Society & disappointment won't again occur – the books will be sent by the very first conveyance, but when, is not fixed; the amount of the first cost will exceed your balance about £100 which he will advance, besides the duty, freight &c – hence the whole will go on equal terms & prevent any more, already too long, delay – if you continue resolved to change your correspondent, I recommend to your attention Messʳˢ F. C. & J. Rivington, who as well as their Father & Grandfather, were Book-sellers on the same site, St. Pauls Church Yard, for about a Century, & are undoubt-edly as respectable as any in that trade – I have mentioned your Society to them & am instructed to say, they are ready to receive & execute your Orders on the very best terms circumstances will admit, which I dare say they will faithfully do – their books may perhaps be somewhat dearer than you have been accustomed to, but, if so, I am satisfied the quality will be proportionably better.

I am very respectfully
Sirs
your most Obed^t hum: Servt

John Hopton

Henry Willm DeSaussure
& Thos Roper^{517} Esquires
President & Vice President
of the Library Society Charleston

[115]
London Augst 30th 1809

Sir

We trust you will believe our sincerity when we assure you that the delay which has arisen in forwarding these books has been as much regretted by us as it could possibly have been by your Society – indeed no circumstance in the whole course of our trades has given us greater vexation. To the neglect of our broker in omitting to apprise us of the sailing of the Montezuma the whole is to be imputed, our reliance on him having been such as precluded us from making any enquiries ourselves. – You may readily conceive that for the future we shall place no such confidence in any one, & therefore anxiously solicit a return of your good opinion which from this unpleasant affair we shall undertake unusual care to preserve.

Mr. Hopton surprised us greatly by reading a paragraph in your letter stating that no acknowledgement of the Order & remittance had reached your hands – We instantly referred to our Letter Book & clear'd ourselves from the imputation of such neglect by reading to him a copy of our letter of acknowledgement which was dated Jan^{ry} 20th 1808, & which we forwarded for your address thro' our Post Office in London – that it failed to reach you is matter of great surprise as well as regret, but that we sent it is an absolute certainty – We have as you will perceive forwarded the periodicals in continuation up to this period, which will no doubt meet your approbation – the articles not sent are not numerous & are such as could not be met with on a second search, which we have made now, in addition to that we did when the Order was collected which was in Feb^{ry} 1808.

Mr. Goldingham having shipped the Books will no doubt have handed you bills of lading & made Insurance – With sincere thanks for the liberality we have always experienced from you, not doubting that the same will be extended to our further intercourse We remain Sir

your Obed.ᵗ Serv.ᵗˢ

Lackington, Allen & Cº.

John Davidson Esqʳ
Library Society
Charleston
General Account

Balance of former Acc.ᵗ in favʳ of L. A & C.º	£32..11.. 1
Paid Messʳˢ Bird & Savage as pʳ Recᵗ.	7..18.. 9
Sundries pʳ Hamilton Moore	281.. 8.. 6
	£321..18.. 4

Contra	
By Bill	220.. – .. –
Cash pʳ Mr. Goldingham	101..18.. 4
	£321..18.. 4

Invoice of sundry Books shipp'd by Nathˡ Goldingham on board the Hamilton Moore, John le Bosquet Master[518] for Charleston So. Carolina on accᵗ. & risque of the Charleston Library Society & consign'd to John Davidson, Esqʳ Secretary

---

C.L.S. Nº: 1 @ 4 Four Packages

[*in margin:* N.1@4]

To Lackington Allen & Co. for Books pʳ Bill 15ᵗʰ Augˢᵗ 09 Nº 1

	£281.. 8.. 6

Charges are Vizᵗ

Entry, Cocket & sundry shipping charges	£ –..18.. 9	
Convoy Duty on £200 @ 4 pʳCent	8.. –.. –	
Freight & primage £1..15..3		
Bills lading 4s	1..19.. 3	
		10..18
		£292.. 6.. 6
Commission on £292..6..6 @ 2½ pʳCent		7.. 8.. 2
		£299..14.. 8

Prem. Insurance on £310 @ 2½

G^s P^rCent & Policy 15s   £ 8..17.. 9

Commission effecting d.° ½ p^rCent   1..11.. –

                                                    10.. 8.. 9

London 12th August 1809   310.. 3.. 5

Interest on £130..13.. 3 to commence from this date

Errors excepted

N. Goldingham

[116]

London 9th Septr 1809

Sir,

   Mr. John Hopton having placed in my hands a Letter under date of 31st March last, from the President & Vice President of the Charleston Library Society – I have in consequence taken the necessary steps to have their wishes carried into effect – referring to what that Gentleman has already written on the subject I have the pleasure to forward the enclosed Bill of Lading & Invoice of the Books shipped on the Hamilton Moore John Le Bosquet Master for Charleston[519] amounting to £310..3..5 Messrs Lackington, Allen & Co. having nearly finish'd the Order previous to the receipt of the above mention'd Letter it was thought advisable to suffer them to complete it & I have paid them the Balance of their Account £101..18..4 – this sum with Insurance & Charges amounting together to One Hundred and thirty Pounds thirteen Shillings & three Pence I have carried to the Debit of the Charleston Library Society & I beg you will assure them that any Commission they may transmit me in future shall be particularly attended to. I was rather fortunate in effecting the Insurance as the Prems have had a rapid rise from 2½ G^s which you perceive I paid to 4 & 5 G^s p^rCent the present rate on the said Ship & I remain

   Sir
   your most Obedient Servt

   N. Goldingham

John Davidson Esqr

[Two brief letters follow between Woodward of Philadelphia and Davidson, Jan. 4 and 31, 1810.]

[117]
Charleston 3 Feb^ry 1810

Sir,

Yours of the 9th Septr last with the books was duly receiv'd by the Hamilton Moore & I have to return you the thanks of the Society for your attention on the occasion – I have herewith sent you another Order which on the recommendation of M^r. Hopton you will please to procure from Messrs Rivington – Inclos'd you will also receive the 1st of Exchange for £400 drawn in your favor by Messrs Hindley & Gregorie[520] on M^r. John Garnett Liverpool, payable in London, from which you will deduct the amount due on your former advance – Should the remainder be insufficient to fulfill the Order, on intimation from you of the probable deficiency another remittance shall be immediately made – As it is a great object with the Society to have the books as soon as possible, it is submitted to you whether if the opportunity should occur from London to this port, it might not be proper to send them by the way of Liverpool either to New York or Philadelphia – If to the former to the care of M^r. Arch^d Gracie Merch^t or to Philadelphia to John Vaughan Esqr either of whom will directly forward them here. If the latter mode of conveyance should be preferr'd, it will be necessary to guard against their being shipp'd in any vessel either wholly loaded with salt or having any quantity on board, as in that case I am told the books will run the risk of being materially injured. I need not recommend to you to have full insurance made as usual, & am, with respect

Sir
your very hum: Servt

John Davidson

Mr. Nath Goldingham
1st p^r Hindley & Gregorie
2 12th April

[118]
London 11 April 1810

Sir,

I have the pleasure to acknowledge the receipt of your Letter of 3^d Feb.^ry enclosing Hindley & Gregory's Bill on Js Garnett of Liverpool for £400– which has been accepted, & when paid, shall be passed to the credit of the Charleston Library Society –

The Order for Books which accompanied the Bill shall have every attention from me, & should there not be any vessel about sailing from this Port for America, when the Books are ready, I will endeavour to procure freight from Liverpool, either direct to Charleston, or in failure of this to New York or Philadelphia – I have some Idea that Hamilton Moore will sail about the time, but this is at present uncertain. I shall not however allow any good opportunity to escape & the Society may rely upon having the Books as early as practicable. – I have the Honor to be

Sir
your most Obedient Servant–

N. Goldingham

J. Davidson

[119]
London 11 Augst 1810

Sir

I have the pleasure to enclose Invoice, Bill of Lading 7 Account Current with the Charleston Library Society, Balance in my favor £104..2..4 (say One Hundred & four Pounds, Two Shillings & four Pence) which I trust you will find correct – The Books have been shipped on board the Neutrality, Captn Asa Miller[521] in four Packages marked CLS N.º 124. –

Some of the Books have not been sent – the reasons you will find in the Memorandum from Messrs Rivington & Co accompanying, which I trust the Society will find satisfactory. – Waiting the further commands of the Society I remain

Sir
your most Obed^t Servant

N. Goldingham

Dr Charleston Library Society in Account Current with N. Goldingham C^r

[*left column:* D^r]

1809
Augst 12th To Balance of Amount of
Invoice this date   £130 13 3
1810
July   To Int^t on d^o 33 days @5PCent   6 – 7
           To Amount Invoice p^r Neutrality

As Miller Master for Charleston	366 18 8	
To Cash paid Postage & Stamps		
to this date	6	
	£505 18 6	

[*right column:* C^r]

1810

June 10th	By Bill on J. Garnett of Liverpool	
	due this Day	£400
July 16th	By Int^t 33 Days on d^o @5PCent	1 16 2
	By Balance carried to debit	
	new Account Current this	
	date barring Interest	104 2 4
		£505 18 6

London 16 July 1810
Errors Excepted
N. Goldingham

Invoice of Sundry Books shipped by Nathl Goldingham on board the Neutrality, A. Miller, Master for Charleston S^o Carolina on Account & risque of the Charleston Library Society & consigned to John Davidson Esqr Secretary – viz –

CLS N° 124 Four Trunks of Books

N° 124 To J C & J Rivington for Books p^r Bill			
dated 6th July		£329 3 5	
Charges are Viz –			
To Cash paid Entry, Cocket & sundry			
shipping charges	£ 2..10.. 2		
D.^{o} Duty on £300 – 14 p^{r}Cent	12		
D.^{o} Freight & Primage £1.17.. Bills			
Lading 4s–	2.. 1		
		16 11 2	
		£345 14 7	
Commission on £345.14.7 @ 2½ p^{r}Cent		8 12 10	
Prem^m Insurance on £370 @ 2½ G^s p^{r}Cent &		£354 7 5	
Policy 20s	10..14.. 3		
Commission effecting d^o ½ p^{r}Cent	1..17.. –	12 11 3	
		£366 18 8	

London 16th July 1810
Errors Excepted
N. Goldingham

[120]

Charleston 23^d Jan^ry 1811

Sir

I have the pleasure to inform you that the Books by the Neutrality arriv'd safe & in excellent Order. The Committee have since been employ'd in making a proper selection for another Order, but not having yet compleated it, have directed me in the mean time to send you a remittance for the purpose of covering your kind advance. – I have therefore inclos'd the 1st of Exchange for £110 – drawn in your favor on Messrs Hindley & Gregorie – I am, with respect

Sir

your very hum: Servt

M^r. Nathl Goldingham
John Davidson
p^r Ship Isabella, Captn McNeill[522]

[The letters end without explanation. The remainder of the large copy ledger is blank.]

Appendix 1

Members of the Charleston Library Society before 1779

An alphabetical list of the founders is followed by an alphabetical list of those advertised in the 23 April 1750 *South Carolina Gazette,* supplemented by the CLS journal records of attendance and elections to 1779. The transfer and mode of acquisition of shares is also recorded with the (often vague) phrasing taken from the journal. The trades of members as advertised in the *Gazette** are given in parentheses, although such descriptions are often too limiting for men engaged in various forms of commerce; occupational listings and titles given in square brackets are taken from the 1782 Charleston *Directory.*

The 1748 founders

Baron, Alexander (schoolmaster)
Brailsford, Morton (dry goods merchant)
Brailsford, Samuel (dry goods merchant); share transferred after death to Bee
Brisbane, Robert (merchant, medical supplier)
Burrows, William (lawyer)
Cooper, John (merchant, distiller); Prioleau buys share Oct. 1766
Douxsaint, Paul (dry goods merchant)
Grindlay, James (lawyer)
Logan, William (merchant)
Macaulay (or McCauley), Alexander (peruke maker); his share given by his widow
    to William Scott
Mackie (or McKie), Dr. Patrick (physician, medical supplier)
Middleton, Thomas (planter, merchant)
Neufville, John (dry goods merchant)
Sacheverell, Thomas, Esq. (planter); Hewitt takes over share Jan. 1765
Sinclair, John (librarian) (food, dry goods merchant)
Stevenson, Charles (madeira, dry goods merchant)
Timothy, Peter (printer; silkworm seeds, stationery wares)
Wragg, Joseph (dry goods merchant)
Wragg, Samuel (dry goods merchant)

*From the 1750 advertisement and also as given, from *SCG* advertisements, in Calhoun et al., "Geographic Spread of Charleston's Mercantile Community," pp. 197–203.

*Additional members by 1750, and later members known
to have been admitted before 1779*

Unless specified, those listed appeared in the *SCG* advertisement of 23 April 1750 as members before 21 April. The first attendance date after 1759 is given for members not listed in the 1750 advertisement. Subsequent admission dates are given when recorded in the surviving journal after 1759. Where the manner of share acquisition is not specified in these later admissions, the new member was purchasing a new share.

This list excludes Lyttelton and Montague, governors of the colony, elected as presidents of the Library Society in 1759 and 1767, respectively.

Addison, Benjamin

Ancram (or Ancrum), William, admitted Oct. 1770 [merchant]

Atkins, Charles, admitted Jan. 1773 [merchant]

Atkinson, Joseph, admitted Jan. 1778 [merchant]

Austin, George, member before Jan. 1761 (and probably before 1759)

Baddeley, John, admitted Jan. 1777

Bampfield, William, Apr. 1772

Baron, Alexander (not the founder member; arrived Charleston 1769), admitted
    Oct. 1770 "in room of" Burn [physician]

Bassnett, John

Baxter, Rev. John

Bee, Thomas, admitted Jan. 1771, having taken the share of late Samuel Brailsford

Bellinger, George, Esq.

Berenger de Beaufain, Hector, Hon. Gent.; leaves share to Rhind (already a member) who presents it to Chiffelle

Beresford, Richard

Blake, Daniel, member before July 1760 (and probably before 1759)

Blake, Joseph, Hon. Gent.

Bond, Jacob

Bonneau, Josiah, admitted July 1772

Bonner, William

Boone, William, Esq.

Bostock, Capt. Peter

Bremar, John, admitted July 1772

Brewton, Miles, admitted July 1759; share inherited by Charles Pinckney, Jr. (after
    Mrs. Pinckney and Mrs. Motte waived their right)

Broughton, Nathaniel, member before Jan. 1759

Browne, Francis (medicines/dry goods merchant)

Bull, William, Hon.

Bull, William, admitted Oct 1773

Bullman, Rev. John, admitted Jan. 1773

Bulloch, James, Esq.

Burke, Aedanus, admitted July 1778

Burn, John, admitted Apr. 1765 having been assigned share by William Murray; share transferred to Baron

Butler, John

Campbell, Dougal

Cape, Brian, admitted Oct. 1770 [merchant]

Carne, Dr. Samuel (dry goods merchant); sells share to Shirley [merchant]

Carson, James

Carss, William, admitted Oct. 1772 [merchant]

Carter, Dr. George, admitted Jan. 1778 [physician]

Carwithen (or Carwithin), William, member before Jan. 1759

Cattell, William, admitted Aug. 1771

Caw, Dr. David (parish doctor of St. Phillip's); share bequeathed to son Thomas

Caw, Dr. Lewis; share sold at public "outcry" (auction), bought by Philip, July 1774

Caw, Dr. Thomas, admitted Apr. 1772, inheriting share of father, David

Chalmers, Dr. Lionel

Chisholme, Alexander (orange trees, seeds, vinegar) [factor]

Chiffelle, Philotheos, admitted Jan. 1768; takes over share from Berenger de Beaufain

Cleland, John (merchant-planter), Hon. Gent.

Cochran, Dr. John

Colcock, John, admitted as minor Apr. 1763, inheriting share of uncle, Job Milner, on paying arrears; Campbell offers surety [attorney-at-law]

Corbett, Thomas, Esq.

Cosslett, Charles, member before Jan. 1773 (assistant justice)

Crawford, Bellamy, bequeathed share of Daniel Crawford and admitted (after payment of arrears) Apr. 1763

Crawford, Daniel, Esq.; bequeaths share to Bellamy Crawford

Crokatt, John (hemp seed merchant)

DaCosta, Isaac, member before Oct. 1761 (and probably before 1759)

Dale, Dr. Thomas

Dart, Benjamin (dry goods merchant)

Dart, John, admitted July 1773; name struck off July 1778

Davidson, James

Deas, David, Esq. (dry goods merchant)

Deas, John, member before Oct. 1762 (and probably before 1759); after his death share bought by Alexander Inglis

Dewar, Robert, admitted Jan. 1778

Downes, William, admitted Jan. 1778

Doyley, Daniel, admitted July 1762, having acquired (and possibly bought) stock of Seymour

Drayton, John, assigned share by brother William, Oct. 1767

Drayton, William Henry, admitted Jan. 1766

Drayton, William, admitted Apr. 1761; resigns share to brother John

Dunbar, Simon

Dupont, Gideon, admitted Oct. 1772 [merchant]

Durand, Rev. Levi (dry goods merchant)

Edwards, John, admitted Oct. 1770

Elliott, Barnard, member by Oct. 1777

Evance, Bransill (dry goods merchant)

Evance, Thomas, member before Jan. 1759

Fardo, George John, admitted July 1777

Fayssoux, Dr. Peter, admitted Oct. 1770

Fenwicke, Edward, Esq., member before Jan 1775 (and possibly before 1759, remaining a nonattending country member); resigns share to son Edward

Fenwicke, Edward, admitted Jan. 1775, with share transferred from father, Edward

Fleming, William, Esq.

Foissine, Elias, Esq.

Fyfe (or Fyffe), Dr. Charles [physician to the refugees]

Gadsden, Christopher (dry goods merchant)

Garden, Dr. Alexander, country member before May 1784 (and probably before 1759; not listed in journal but referred to as a member living in London, in letter 35)

Gibbes, William

Gibbes, William Hasell, admitted Apr. 1778

Gibbs, John Walter, admitted Jan. 1778

Glen, William [merchant]

Gordon, Thomas Knox, Hon., admitted Aug. 1771

Graeme, David

Grimball, Thomas, admitted July 1766, having bought share of late William Scott

Grimké, John Faucheraud, Esq., admitted Oct. 1778

Guerard, John, member before Apr. 1759

Hall, Daniel, admitted Jan. 1778

Hall, George Abbott, admitted July 1772

Halliday, Robert Dalway, admitted Jan. 1774

Harcourt Henderson, William

Harleston, John. Jr., admitted Oct. 1777

Harvey, Maurice

Hatton, Capt. Joseph

Hawkins, Philip, admitted Oct. 1770

Hayne, Isaac, admitted Oct. 1769

Hayward, Thomas, admitted Feb. 1771

Henderson, William, member before Jan. 1759; resigned share to Robert Smith

Heron, Alexander, Lt. Col.

Hewat (or Hewitt), Rev. Alexander, admitted Jan. 1765, share from Sacheverell; share bought by Moncrief

Holmes, Isaac, Esq.

Hopton, William, member before Jan. 1759 [Esquire]

Horry, Thomas, admitted July 1772

Hort, William, admitted Oct. 1770

Huger, Benjamin, Esq., admitted Oct. 1772

Hume, John, admitted July 1759; transferred share to Alexander Wright

Hummel, John, member before Jan. 1760 (and probably before 1759)

Hurst, Samuel (dry goods merchant)

Hutson, Richard, member before Oct. 1775

Inglis, Alexander, admitted Jan. 1777, after buying share of Dr. Deas, deceased [merchant]

Inglis, George

Inglis, Thomas, admitted Oct. 1773 [merchant]

Irving, Dr. James (dry goods merchant)

Jamieson, James, admitted Oct. 1772

Johnston, Andrew

Johnston, Charles, admitted Apr. 1771, with share from Andrew Robertson who had left the province

Johnston, James, Esq., admitted July 1773; resigns share in favor of Robert Johnston

Johnston, Robert, admitted July 1777, having taken over share of James Johnston

Keenan, Henry (foodstuffs)

Keene, Dr. James, admitted Oct. 1777

Keith, Rev. Alexander (St. George Parish)

Ladson, Robert, admitted Apr. 1774

Laurens, Henry (dry goods merchant)

Laurens, James, member before Apr. 1762 (and probably before 1759)

Legare, Benjamin, admitted Jan. 1778, having bought share of Lightwood

Leger, Peter, admitted Jan. 1777

Lenox, James

Lightwood, John, admitted July 1773; share sold to Legare

Lining Thomas

Lining, Dr. John, (library president, 1750) (spirits and cordial waters merchant)

Livie, Alexander; share bequeathed to son Robert

Livie, Robert, admitted Jan. 1773 on inheritance of share from father Alexander

Livingston, Abraham, admitted Apr. 1778

Logan, George

Logan, John, admitted Apr. 1772

Logan, William, member before Apr. 1762 (and probably before 1759)

Loocock, Aaron, admitted Jan. 1777

Lynch, Dr. Thomas, admitted Oct. 1777

Lynch, Thomas, Esq.

Manigault, Gabriel, Esqr. (planter, sugar, oil merchant)

Marr, Andrew, admitted Apr. 1772

Marshal, George

Martson, Richard (dry goods merchant)

Mason, William, admitted June 1764

Mathewes, Anthony, Esq.

Mathews Cos[s]lett, Charles, admitted July 1772

Matthews, John, admitted July 1772

Mayrant, John, Esq.

Mazyck, Isaac, admitted Apr. 1775 [Esquire]

Mazyck, William, admitted Jan. 1771, buying new share, having been refused admission earlier at the same meeting when proposed in letter from Mrs. Carwithen to take her late husband's share

McQueen, John

Michie, James, Esq.

Michie, William, member before Jan. 1759

Middleton, Arthur, admitted Jan. 1765

Middleton, Henry, Esqr. (dry goods merchant)

Middleton, William, Hon. Gent.

Milligen, Dr. George (drugs)

Milner, Job, member before Jan. 1759; share inherited by nephew Colcock

Moncrief, Robert, admitted July 1777, having bought share of Hewat

Montaigut, David

Moreau, Rev. Charles Frederick, admitted Oct. 1778

Morrison, Rev. Philip, member before July 1760 (and probably before 1759); assigned share to Rowand when left province

Motte, Jacob, Jr., admitted Sept. 1770, having been left his late father's share

Motte, Jacob, Esq.; share bequeathed to son Jacob

Moultrie, Alexander, admitted July 1772

Moultrie, Dr. John, Jr.

Murray, George (misc. goods merchant)

Murray, Dr. John, member before Jan. 1759

Murray, John, member before Jan. 1759 (the two John Murrays are different members)

Murray, William, probably member before 1759 and certainly a member before Apr. 1765 when, on leaving province, assigned share to Burn

Neilson, James, admitted Jan. 1778

Neufville, Edward, member before Jan. 1759 [merchant]; "disposed" share to Rhind

Nisbett, William, admitted Oct. 1774

Oliphant (or Olyphant), Dr. David (dry goods merchant, salt, medicines; medical partner of Lining)

Ouldfield, John

Owen, John, admitted Oct 1777

Palmer, John

Panting, Rev. Thomas (first entered as John, in error), admitted Oct 1769; share transferred to Webb via Rev. Cooper

Parnham, John (dry goods merchant)

Parsons, James, member before Jan. 1759

Perry, Benjamin

Petrie, Alexander, member before Jan. 1759; share inherited by son Edmund

Petrie, Edmund, admitted Oct. 1773 on inheriting share from father, Alexander

Phepoe, Thomas, Esq., admitted Jan. 1773 [attorney-at-law]

Philip, Robert, admitted July 1774, after buying share of Lewis Caw at auction [Esquire]

Philp, Robert, member before Jan. 1759

Pickering, Joseph (Philadelphia goods merchant)

Pike, Thomas, admitted Jan. 1771

Pinckney, Charles, Hon. Gent. (d. 1758)

Pinckney, Charles Cotesworth (b. 1746), admitted Oct. 1769

Pinckney, Charles, Jr. (b. 1757), admitted Apr. 1778, share inherited from his uncle, Miles Brewton

Pinckney, Charles, Col. (b. 1731), admitted Oct. 1770

Pinckney, Roger, Esq., admitted July 1772

Pinckney, Thomas, admitted Oct. 1777 in room of father, Charles (d. 1758)

Pinckney, William, Esq. (d. 1766)

Poinsett, Elisha, admitted Jan. 1777 [physician]

Porcher, Isaac, admitted Oct. 1774

Powell, George Gabriel

Powell, Robert William, admitted Oct. 1773

Powell, Thomas, admitted Feb. 1771

Price, Rice (vinegar, wine, dry goods merchant); bequeaths share to Samuel Price

Price, Samuel, admitted Oct. 1770, bequeathed share of Rice Price

Prioleau, Philip, admitted Jan. 1778

Prioleau, Samuel, admitted Oct. 1766, having bought share from Cooper

Pryce, Charles

Radcliffe, Thomas, Jr., admitted Jan. 1778

Ramsay, David, admitted Apr. 1776

Rantowle, Alexander, member before Jan. 1760 (and probably before 1759)

Raven, John (foodstuffs, beer)

Read, Jacob, admitted Jan. 1777

Reid, Patrick (misc. goods, dry goods merchant)

Remington, John (secretary, 1750)

Rhind, David, admitted Jan. 1765, having taken over (bought?) share of Edward Neufville

Richardson, Capt. William, admitted July 1770; resigned share to John Smyth

Robertson, Andrew, member before Jan. 1759; on leaving province, share transferred to Charles Johnston

Robinson, A., member before June 1764 (and probably before 1759)

Rose, Alexander, admitted July 1769

Rowand, Robert, admitted July 1763, having been assigned share of Morrison [merchant]

Rudhall, William, admitted July 1777

Rutledge, Andrew, Hon. Gent.

Rutledge, Dr. John

Savage, Edward, Hon., admitted Apr. 1772 [judge, Court of the Vice-Admiralty]

Saxby, George, member before Jan. 1760 (and probably before 1759)

Schwabb, Rev. Christopher, admitted Apr. 1772

Scott, John "Merchant" (Philadelphia flour, soap, dry goods merchant)

Scott, William (dry goods merchant); share bought by Grimball

Scott, William, admitted Jan. 1763, with share transferred from McCauley via his widow

Seaman, George

Seymour, John, member before Apr. 1759; disposed of stock to Doyley

Sharp, James (steward, 1750)

Shirley, Thomas, admitted Apr. 1766, having bought share from Carne

Shubrick, Thomas, admitted Jan. 1776 after transfer of share from father, Thomas
Shubrick, Thomas; transfers share to son Thomas
Simons, Maurice, admitted Oct. 1777
Simpson, James, admitted June 1764
Smith, Benjamin, Esq.; share bequeathed to son, Thomas
Smith, Job, member before Apr. 1763, when share bequeathed to (minor) Colcock (Job Smith probably member before 1759)
Smith, Rev. Dr. Robert, admitted Apr. 1763, assigned share by Henderson
Smith, Roger, admitted Jan. 1765, having been given share of Peter Taylor [merchant]
Smith, Thomas (vice president 1750)
Smith, Thomas, admitted Jan. 1771, bequeathed share by father Benjamin
Smith, Thomas, of Broad St., admitted Jan. 1771
Smyth, John, admitted July 1777, share transferred from Richardson
Stewart, Alexander, Esq.
Stoutenburgh, Luke, Esq.
Stoutenburgh, William, admitted Apr. 1767
Taylor, Alexander
Taylor, Peter, member before Jan. 1765, when share assigned to Roger Smith (Peter Taylor probably a member before 1759)
Taylor, Ralph (rum, sugar, dry goods merchant)
Tidyman, Philip, admitted Oct. 1770
Trail, James, admitted July 1772
Trapier, Paul, admitted July 1770
Wakefield, James, admitted Oct. 1777
Walton, Peter, admitted Jan. 1771
Ward, John, Esq.
Ward, Joseph
Ward, Joshua, admitted Jan. 1771 [attorney-at-law]
Waties, William, Esq.
Webb, Benjamin, admitted Apr. 1771 "in room of" Panting, whose share he purchased from "Rev. Mr. Cooper" (unclear whether Cooper had been member)
Wedderburn, James, Esq.
Wells, Robert, member before Jan. 1759
Wragg, John (dry goods merchant) [Esquire]
Wray, Charles, Esq.
Wright, Alexander, admitted Oct. 1773, on transference of share from Hume [Esquire]
Wright, James, Esq.

Honorary Members

Crokatt, Charles(?), admitted Oct. 1765
Fothergill, Dr. John, admitted Oct. 1765

Appendix 2

Chronological List (By Date of Admission, 1759–1779) of New Members Purchasing New Shares

Brewton, Miles, July 1759
Hume, John, July 1759
Drayton, William, Apr. 1761
Mason, William, June 1764
Simpson, James, June 1764
Middleton, Arthur, Jan. 1765
Drayton, William Henry, Jan. 1766
Stoutenburgh, William, Apr. 1767 (like Middleton, proposed by father, and so, like his brothers, also in the Society, representing an independent household; see above, p. 69)
Rose, Alexander, July 1769
Hayne, Isaac, Oct. 1769
Panting, Rev. John, Oct.1769
Pinckney, Charles Cotesworth, Oct. 1769
Richardson, Capt. William, July 1770
Trapier, Paul, July 1770
Ancram, William, Oct. 1770
Cape, Brian, Oct. 1770
Edwards, John, Oct. 1770
Fayssoux, Dr. Peter, Oct. 1770
Hawkins, Philip, Oct. 1770
Hort, William, Oct. 1770
Pinckney, Charles, Oct. 1770
Tidyman, Philip, Oct. 1770
Cattell, Mr., Aug. 1771
Gordon, Hon. Thomas Knox, Aug. 1771
Mazyck, William, Jan. 1771, buying new share, having been refused admission earlier at the same meeting when proposed in letter from Mrs. Carwithen to take her late husband's share
Pike, Thomas, Jan. 1771
Smith, Thomas, of Broad St., Jan. 1771

Walton, Peter, Jan. 1771
Ward, Joshua, Jan. 1771
Heyward, Thomas, Feb. 1771
Powell, Thomas, Feb. 1771
Bampfield, William, Apr. 1772
Logan, John, Apr. 1772
Marr, Andrew, Apr. 1772
Savage, Hon. Edward, Apr. 1772
Schwabb, Rev. Christopher, Apr. 1772
Bonneau, Josiah, July 1772
Bremar, John, July 1772
Hall, George Abbott, July 1772
Horry, Thomas, July 1772
Mathews Coslett (or Cosslett), Charles, July 1772
Matthews, John, July 1772
Moultrie, Alexander, July 1772
Pinckney, Roger, Esq., July 1772
Trail, James, July 1772
Carss, William, Oct. 1772
Dupont, Gideon, Oct. 1772
Huger, Benjamin, Esq., Oct. 1772
Jamieson, James, Oct. 1772
Atkins, Charles, Jan. 1773
Bullman, Rev. John, Jan. 1773
Phepoe, Thomas, Esq., Jan. 1773
Dart, John, July 1773
Johnston, James, Esq., July 1773; resigned share in favor of Robert Johnston
Lightwood, John, July 1773; share sold to Legare
Bull, William, Oct.1773
Inglis, Thomas, Oct. 1773
Powell, Robert William, Oct. 1773
Halliday, Robert Dalway, Jan. 1774
Ladson, Robert, Apr. 1774
Philip, Robert, bought share of Dr. Caw, sold at public "outcry" (auction),
    July 1774
Nisbett, William, Oct. 1774
Porcher, Isaac, Oct. 1774
Mazyck, Isaac, Apr. 1775
Ramsay, David, Apr. 1776
Baddeley, John, Jan. 1777

Leger, Peter, Jan. 1777
Loocock, Aaron, Jan. 1777
Poinsett, Elisha, Jan. 1777
Read, Jacob, Jan. 1777
Fardo, George John, July 1777
Rudhall, William, July 1777
Harleston, John, Jr., Oct. 1777
Keene, Dr. James, Oct. 1777
Lynch, Dr. Thomas, Oct. 1777
Owen, John, Oct. 1777
Simons, Maurice, Oct. 1777
Wakefield, James, Oct. 1777
Atkinson, Joseph, Jan. 1778
Carter, Dr. George, Jan. 1778
Dewar, Robert, Jan. 1778
Downes, William, Jan. 1778
Gibbs, John Walter, Jan. 1778
Hall, Daniel, Jan. 1778
Neilson, James, Jan. 1778
Prioleau, Philip, Jan. 1778
Radcliffe, Thomas, Jr., Jan. 1778
Gibbes, William Hasell, Apr. 1778
Livingston, Abraham, Apr. 1778
Burke, Aedanus, July 1778
Grimké, John Faucheraud, Esq., Oct. 1778
Moreau, Rev. Charles Frederick, Oct. 1778

Appendix 3

Reconstruction of the Foundation Collection of the Charleston Library Society during Its First Twenty Years, 1748–c.1769*

Unless specified, titles are taken from the sole surviving 1750 *Catalogue of the Charleston Library Society* printed by William Strahan in London and now held at the Library of Congress. Given the slightness of the original listing, many of these titles and an even larger number of the authors have had to be reconstructed entirely (together with edition date and place of publication).

Additional titles ordered by or given to the Library Society before the printing of the 1770 *Catalogue* are also indicated, with references given to the annotated letters to and from the booksellers above.

Books are listed in alphabetical order by author, preceded by anonymous works (the original 1750 *Catalogue* was designed as a format classification, although Strahan badly misordered the titles).

The abbreviation (p) indicates a title listed as a pamphlet in the 1750 catalogue. Place of publication is London unless otherwise specified.

An asterisk at the end of the entry indicates a volume listed as missing in the public advertisements of early 1756 (*SCG*, 6 Jan. 1756 and at least ten further issues to 8 Apr. 1756).

Two asterisks indicates that the volume, listed as missing in 1756, arrived after compilation of the 1750 CLS *Catalogue*. Nine titles listed in the 1756 *SCG* advertisements are unidentified, and the advertisement also noted, as lost, "a great number of pamphlets."

Acta Germanica or, the Literary Memoirs of Germany &c. . . . by a Society of Gentlemen, 1743, 1 vol., 4to.
The Annual Register, ordered Oct. 1764; see letter 13.
Bible, large folio, with maps and cuts.
Bible in a new translation, presented by Dr. John Fothergill at a special meeting set up to receive it, July 1765 (J, fol. 59).
Biographia Britannica, ordered Aug. 1761; see letter 8; and *Continuation*, ordered Oct. 1764; see letter 13.

*Completed with the generous assistance of Patricia Aske, Corpus Christi College, Cambridge, and Nigel Hall.

The British Magazine, ordered Oct. 1764; see letter 13.

Canons of Criticism (p).

Catalogus Plantarum By a Society of Gardners, 1730, 2o.

A Collection of Friends Sufferings, 2 vols, presented by the Society of Friends, Apr. 1768 (J, fol. 89).

Common Sense, 1738, 2 vols., 12mo.

The Compleat Florist, colored, 1747, 8vo.

A Compleat History of the Piratical States of Barbary . . . by a Gentleman who Resided There . . . , 1750, 8vo.

Complete System of Geography, 1744–1747, 3 vols., 2o.

Conversations Moral and Entertaining, between an English Gentleman and a Knight of Malta, 1740, 12mo.

The Contrast (p).

Court and City Register, ordered May 1767; see letter 17.

The Craftsman, 14 vols., 12mo.

The Critical Review; 1st vols. ordered Aug. 1761 (and subsequent vols. thereafter); see letters 8, 13, 18, etc.

Declaration of Universal Laws **

Determinations of the Honourable House of Commons, Proceedings 1747, published 1753, 3d ed., 12mo.

Epistle to the Admirers of the Bishop of London's Letter, 1750, 72 p., 8vo.

Essay on Modern Gallantry [1750?], 50 or 51 p., 8vo.

The Gentleman's Magazine, commenced publication 1731; ordered July 1760; see letter 6.

German Spy [*Gentleman on his Travels Thro' Germany*], 1740, 2d ed., 8vo.

Historie des Martyrs, Geneva, 1619, 2o, presented by Samuel Prioleau, July 1767 (J, fol. 83).

Independent Whig, 4 vols., 12mo.

An Introduction to the History of the Kingdoms and States of Asia, 1705, 8vo.

Life of Augustus Caesar, 1748, 2 vols., 12mo.

The London Magazine: or Gentleman's Monthly Intelligencer, began 1732; ordered July 1760; see letter 6.

The Magazine of Magazines vol. 1 (Jan.–June 1751), Limerick, 8vo (p).

Marriage of Venus, 1750, 8vo.

Memoirs of the Life of Robert Devereux, Earl of Essex, 1753, 8vo**.

Mirrour of Justices, ordered May 1767; see letter 17.

Miss Blandy's Trial ** (this could be one of several accounts).

Modern Universal History, ordered Oct. 1764; see letter 13.

The Monthly Review 1748, 1749, 4 vols., 8vo; first vols. ordered from at least Aug. 1758 (and subsequent vols. thereafter); see letters 1, 8, 11, etc.

[*Monthly Review*] *Compleat Catalogue . . . for Ten Years Past . . .* [of the *Monthly Review*], ordered Aug. 1761; see letter 8 and n. 278.

Museum rusticum et commerciale; ordered Feb. 1765; see letter 14.

The Nominal Husband, or Distress'd Innocence, 1750, 12mo (p).

Parliamentary History, ordered Aug. 1761; see letter 8.

A Philosophic Ode on the Sun and Universe, 1750, 26 p., 4to.

Philosophical Transactions, ordered Oct. 1764; see letter 13 [1st vol.* indicating CLS holding before 1756].

Polygraphic Dictionary, 2 vols., 8vo.

Preceptor: Containing a General Course of Education, 1748, 2 vols., 8vo.

Prodigal Son Returned, 1750, 16 p., 8vo.

Prospa alpini historiae naturalis Egypti, Ludg. Bat., 1735, 2 vols., 4to.

*Review of British Liberty***

The Spectator, 1749, 8 vols., 12mo.

State-Trials, ordered May 1767; see letter 17.

[*The Tatler*] *The Lucubrations of Isaac Bickerstaff, Esq.,* 1728, 4 vols., 12mo.

Trial of the Seven Bishops in 1688, 1716, 8vo.

An Universal History, From the Earliest Account of Time, 1747– , 20 vols., 8vo.

The Universal Magazine, from first vol. of 1747; ordered July 1760; see letter 6.

Wealth of Great Britain in the Ocean, 1749, 71[1]p., 8vo.

[Académie Royale de Chirurgie], *Memoirs of the Royal Academy of Surgery at Paris,* 1750, 8vo.

Acherley, Roger, *The Britannick Constitution,* 1741, 2o.

Adams, George, *Micrographia illustrata,* 1747, 4to; and also ordered Sept. 1763; see letter 12 ["Adams's designs"*].

———, *On the Microscope,* 1747, 4to.

Addison, Joseph, *Anacreon,* 12mo.

———, *The Evidences of the Christian Religion,* 1742, 12mo.

———, *The Freeholder,* 1744, 12mo.

———, *The Guardian,* 1745, 2 vols., 12mo.

———, *Petronius Arbiter,* 1736, 12mo.

———, *Works,* 1746, 5 vols., 12mo.

Ainsworth, *Thesaurus linguae latinae compendiarius,* ordered July 1760; see letter 6.

Akenside, Mark, *The Pleasures of Imagination. A Poem,* 1744, 8vo.

Albini, *Explicato tabularum Eustachii,* 2o.

Albinus, Bernhard Siegfried, *Anatomical Tables,* 1749, 2o.

Ali, Sharaf al-Din, Yazdi, *The History of Timur-Bec, Known by the Name of Tamerlain the Great,* trans. Petits de la Croix, 1723, 8vo.*

Anderson, Adam, *An Historical and Chronological Deduction of the Origin of Commerce,* ordered Oct. 1764; see letter 13.

Anderson, James, *Royal Genealogies, or the Geneaological Tables,* 1732, 2o.

Anson, George, *A Voyage Round the World,* 1749, 4to.

Arbuthnot, John, *Tables of Antient Coins,* 1727, 4to.

Arrian, *Arrian's History of Alexander's Expedition . . . By Mr Rooke,* 1729, 2 vols., 8vo.

Atkyns, Robert, *Parliamentary and Political Tracts,* 1741, 8vo.*

————, *Parliamentary Tracts,* 1734, 8vo.

Bacon, Nathaniel, *An Historical and Political Discourse on the Laws and Government of England,* 1739, 4th ed., 2o.

Bacon, Francis, *Works,* 1740, 4 vols., 2o.

Baker, Henry, *The Microscope Made Easy,* 2d ed., 1743, 8vo.

Bancks, John, *A Short Critical Review of the Political Life of Oliver Cromwell,* 3d ed., 1747, 12mo.

Banier, M. l'abbe (Antoine), *The Mythology and Fables of the Ancients,* 1739–1740, 4 vols., 8vo.

Barclay, Robert, *An Apology for the True Christian Divinity,* 1765, 8vo, presented by the Society of Friends, Apr. 1768 (J, fol. 89)

Barrow, John, *Navigatio Britannico,* 1750, 4to.

Baumgarten, Siegmund Jakob, *Supplement to the English Universal History,* ordered Aug. 1761; see letter 8.

Baxter, Andrew, *Appendix to the First Part of Enquiry into the Nature of the Human Soul,* 1745, 8vo.

————, *Enquiry into the Nature of the Human Soul,* 1745, 2vols., 8vo.

————, *Matho, or, the cosmotheoria puerilis,* 1745, 2d ed., 2 vols., 8vo.*

[Bayle, Pierre], *The Dictionary Historical and Critical,* 1734–1741, 10 vols., 2o.

Bion, Nicolas, *The Construction and Principal Uses of Mathematical Instruments by Stone,* 1723, 2o.

Birch, Thomas, *An Historical View of the Negotiations,* 1749, 8vo.

Blackstone, William, *Commentaries on the Laws of England,* ordered May 1767; see letter 17.

[Blackwell, Thomas], *An Enquiry into the Life and Writings of Homer, with the Proofs,* 3d ed., 1757, 8vo.

————, *Letters Concerning Mythology,* 1748, 8vo.

————, [and John Mills], *Memoirs of the Court of Augustus Continued and Completed from the Original Papers of the late Thomas Blackwell,* ordered Oct. 1764; see letter 13.

Bland, Humphrey (entered as Blood), *A Treatise of Military Discipline,* 2d ed., 1727, 8vo.

[Bodley, Thomas], *Reliquiae Bodleianae,* 1703, 8vo [1770 *Catalogue: The Remains of Thomas Bodley*].

Boerhaave, Herman, *A New Method of Chemistry by Shaw,* 1721 [or 1741?], 2 vols., 4to.

Bolingbroke, Viscount (Henry St. John), *A Dissertation upon Parties in Several Letters to Caleb D'Anvers, Esq.,* 8vo.

————, *Reflections Concerning Innate Moral Principles,* 1752, 8vo.**

Bolton, Robert, *On the Employment of Time,* 1750, 8vo.

[Bond, John], *An Essay on the Incubus, or Night-Mare,* 1753, 8vo.**

Bonneval, Claude Alexandré, comte de, *Memoirs of the Bashaw Count Bonneval,* 1750, 8vo.

Bott, Thomas, *An Answer to the Reverend Mr. Warburton's Divine Legation,* 1743, 8vo.

[Bourn, Samuel], *A Vindication of the Principles and Practice of Protestant Dissenters,* 1748, 12mo.**

Boyle, Robert, *Works,* 1744, 5 vols., 2o.

Bracton, Henricus de, *De legibus et consuetudinibus Angliae,* ordered May 1767; see letter 17.

Bradley, Richard, *A General Treatise of Husbandry and Gardening,* 1721, 4to.

Bréquigny, M. de (Louis-Georges-Oudard Feudrix), *The History of the Revolutions of Genoa,* 1751, 3 vols., 12mo.

Brightland, John, *A Grammar of the English Tongue,* 1746, 12mo.

Brownrigg, William, *The Art of Making Common Salt,* 1748, 8vo.

Buchanan, George, *Opera omnia,* Edinburgh, 1715, 2 vols., 2o.

[Bulwer, John], *Anthropometamorphosis, Man Transform'd, or, the Artificial Changeling,* 1650, 4to.

Bunyan, John, *The Pilgrim's Progress,* 1741, 8vo.

[Burgh, James], *An Hymn to the Creator of the World,* 1750, 2 p, 8vo.

Burnet, Gilbert, *History of His Own Time,* 1724, 2 vols., 2o.

Burnet, Thomas, *A Treatise Concerning the States of Departed Souls,* 2d ed., 1739, 8vo.

————, *The Sacred Theory of the Earth,* 1726, 2 vols., 8vo.

Burrish, Onslow, *Batavia Illustrata,* 1728, 2 vols., 8vo.

Buschings, Anton Friedrich, *A New System of Geography,* 1762, 6 vols., presented by William Bull, July 1765 (J, fol. 60).

[Burton, John?], *Narrative of the Young Chevalier,* [1749?], (p).

Butler, Joseph, *The Analogy of Religion, Natural and Revealed,* 1740, 8vo.

[Butler, Samuel], *Hudibras,* 1750, 12mo.

[Cæsar, Julius], *C. Jullii commentaria de bello gallico,* 1755, 8vo.**

Caille, Nicolas Louis de la, *The Elements of Astronomy,* trans. John Robertson, 1750, 8vo.

Campbell, Archibald, *An Enquiry into the Original of Moral Virtue*, 1734, 8vo.

Cary, John, *A Discourse on Trade*, 2d ed., 1745, 8vo.

Cato's Letters, 1748, 4 vols., 12mo.

Cay, John, *Statutes at Large*, ordered Mar. 1769; see letter 21.

Chambers, Ephraim, *Cyclopædia, or, an Universal Dictionary of Arts and Sciences*, 1750, 2 vols., 2o.

Chandler, Edward, *A Vindication of the Defence of Christianity from the Prophecies*, 1728, 3 vols., 8vo.

Chandler [Richard?], *Debates of the House of Lords and Commons*, 22 vols., 8vo.

Chaucer, Geoffrey, *Works*, 1721, 2o.

Child, Josiah, *A New Discourse of Trade*, 1669, 12mo.

Churchill, Charles, *Poems*, ordered May 1767; see letter 17.

Cicero, Marcus Tullius, *The Morals of Cicero*, trans. William Guthrie, 1744, 8vo.

————, *The Orations of Cicero*, trans. William Guthrie, 3 vols., 8vo. (1st ed., 1743).

————, *Tully's Three Books of Offices*, trans. Thomas Cockman, 6th ed., 1739, 12mo.

Clarendon, Edward Hyde, *The History of Rebellion and the Civil Wars*, Oxford, 1732, 2o.

Clarke, John, *An Essay upon the Education of Youth in Grammar Schools*, 3d ed., 1740, 12mo.

————, *An Essay upon Study*, 2d ed., 1737, 12mo.

Cleghorn, George, *Observations on the Epidemical Diseases in Minorca*, 1751, 8vo.

[Coade, G. George?], *Letter on the 30th January*, 12mo (1st ed., 1747).*

Cockburn, Patrick, *An Enquiry into the Truth and Certainty of the Mosaic Deluge*, 1750, 8vo.

[La Combe de Urigny de], *Travels through Denmark etc. in the Year 1702*, 1707, 8vo.

[Committee Appointed for Relieving the Poor Germans], *The Proceedings of the Committee appointed for relieving the poor Germans who were brought to London and there left destitute in the month of August 1764*, presented by William Bull, Nov. 1765 , 1765, 2o (J, fol. 61).

[Commynes, Philippe de], *Memoirs of Philip de Commines*, 2d ed., 1723, 2 vols, 8vo.

Condamine, Charles-Marie de la, *A Succinct Abridgment of a Voyage Made Within the Inland Parts of South-America*, 1747, 8vo.

Congreve, William, *Works*, 5th ed., 1730, 3 vols., 12mo.

Constable, John, *Reflections upon Accuracy of Style*, 1734, 8vo.

Cooper, John Gilbert, *The Life of Socrates*, [2d or 3d ed.], 1750, 8vo.

[Costard, George], *A Letter to Martin Folkes Concerning the Rise and Progress of Astronomy*, 1746, 8vo.

Cowley, Abraham, *Works,* 1721, 2 vols., 12mo.

[Cox, Thomas], *Magna Britannia & Hibernia, antiqua & nova,* 1720–1731, 6 vols., 4to.

Coxe, Daniel, *A Description of the English Province of Carolina,* 1741, 8vo.

Cramer, Johann Andreas, *Elements of the Art of Assaying Metals,* 1741, 8vo.

Crouch, Henry, *A Complete View of the British Customs,* 4th ed., 1745, 2 vols., 8vo.

Cumberland, Richard, *Origines gentium antiquissimæ,* 1727, 8vo.

———, *A Treatise of the Laws of Nature,* 1727, 4to.

Cunn, Samuel, *On Fractions,* 1724, 12mo.

Curtius Rufus, Quintius, *The History of the Wars of Alexander the Great,* trans. John Digby, corrected and revised by William Young, 1747, 12mo.

Davenant, Charles, *Essays,* 1701, 5 vols., 8vo.

———, *Discourses on the Publick Revenues, and on the Trade of England,* 1698, 2 vols., 8vo.

Decker, Sir Matthew, *An Essay on the Causes of the Decline of the Foreign Trade,* 2d ed., 1750, 12mo.

De Foe, Daniel, *A Plan of the English Commerce,* 3d ed., 1749, 8vo.

De Piles, Roger, *The Art of Painting,* 1744, 8vo.

Derham, William, *Astro-Theology,* 6th ed., 1731, 8vo.

———, *Physico-Theology,* 10th ed., 1742, 8vo.

Desaguliers, John Theophilus, *Course of Experimental Philosophy,* 2d ed., 1745, 2 vols., 4to.

Dickinson, John, *Letters from a Farmer in Pennsylvania,* ordered Mar. 1769; see letter 21.

[Dodd, William], *A New Book of the Dunciad,* 1750, 36 p., 4to.

Dodsley, Robert, *A Collection of Poems,* ordered May 1767; see letter 17.

[Dodwell, Henry], *Christianity not Founded on Argument,* 1746, 8vo.

Domat, Jean, *The Civil Law in Its Natural Order,* 2d ed., 1737, 2 vols., 2o.*

Douglas, Sir Robert, *The Peerage of Scotland,* ordered Feb. 1766; see letter 15.

Dufresnoy, Charles-Alphonse, *The Art of Painting,* with a preface by Dryden, 1716, 8vo.

Du Halde, Jean-Baptiste, *The General History of China,* 1741, 4 vols., 8vo.

Edmondson, Joseph, *Baronagium genealogicum,* ordered May 1767and arrived by Sept. 1769; see letters 17 and 23.

Ellis, William, *The Country Housewife's Family Companion,* 1750, 8vo.

———, *Husbandry,* 1744, 8 vols., 8vo.

———, *The London and Country Brewer,* 6th ed., 1750, 8vo.

———, *The Practical Farmer,* 4th ed., 1742, 8vo.

Emerson, William, *The Projection of the Sphere*, 1749, 8vo.

———, *The Elements of Trigonometry*, 1749, 8vo.

Erasmus, Desiderius, *All the Familiar Colloquies of Desiderius Erasmus*, trans. N. Bailey, 2d ed., 1733, 8vo.

[Estienne, Robert?], *Roberti Stephani thesaurus linguae latinae*, 1734–1735, 4 vols., 2o.

[Fagnan, Marie Antoinette], *Kanor, A Tale*, 1750, 12mo.*

Farquhar, George, *Works*, 1742, 2 vols., 12mo.

Ferguson, Adam, *An Essay on the History of Civil Society*, ordered July 1769; see letter 22.

Fielding, Henry, *The History of Joseph Andrews*, 1749, 2 vols., 12mo.

———, *Histoire de Tom Jones, with Examen*, 1750, 4 vols., 12mo.

———, *Miscellanies*, 1743, 3 vols., 8vo.

Florus, Lucius Annaeus, *Epitome of Roman History*, 2d ed., 1725, 12mo.

Floyer, John, *Sybilline Oracles*, 1713, 12mo.

Fontaine, Nicolas [entered under the name of the book's bookseller Richard Blome as "Bloom"], *"History of the Bible"* [*History of the Old Testament, History of the New Testament*], 1690 [reprint of 1688], 2o, presented by Alexander Rantowle, Jan. 1767 (J, fol 76).

Forbes, Duncan, *Reflections on the Sources of Incredulity*, [1750?] (p).

[Fordyce, David], *Dialogues Concerning Education*, 1757, 2 vols., 8vo.

Fortescue, John, *De laudibus legum Angliae*, ordered May 1767; see letter 17.

———, *The Difference Between an Absolute and Limited Monarchy*, 1714, 8vo.

[Fortescue, James], *Science: An Epistle*, Oxford, 1750, 4o (p).

Foster, James, *Sermons*, 1724, 4 vols., 8vo.

Fothergill, John, *Some Account of the Late Peter Collinson*, 1770, 8vo, "left by the author Dr Fothergill," Feb. 1771 (J, fol. 129).

Fox, George, *Journal*, 1765, 2o, presented by the Society of Friends, Apr. 1768 (J, fol. 89).

[Francis, Philip], *A Letter from the Cocoa-Tree*, ordered Sept.1763; see letter 12.

———, *Orations of Demosthenes*, ordered May 1767; see letter 17.

[Frederick II, King of Prussia], *Memoirs of the House of Brandenburg*, [1751?], 12mo.

Freind, Johannis, *Serenis simae Reginae Carolinae archiatri, opera omnia medica*, 1733, 2o.

Gale, Theophilus, *The Court of the Gentiles*, Oxford, 1669, 4 vols., 4to.

Gallini, Giovani-Andrea, *A Treatise on the Art of Dancing*, ordered May 1767; see letter 17.

Gay, John, *Fables*, 6th ed., 1746, 2 vols., 8vo.

————, *Poems on Several Occasions,* 1745, 2 vols., 12mo.

Geddie [Gedde], John, *The English Apiary: or, the Compleat Bee-master,* 1721, 12mo.

Gibson, Edmund, *Codex juris ecclesiastici Anglicani,* ordered May 1767; see letter 17.

[Gifford, Andrew], *A Dissertation on the Song of Solomon,* 1751, 8vo.**

Granger, James, *A Biographical History of England,* arrived by Sept. 1769; see letter 23.

Graunt, John, *Observations on the Bills of Mortality,* 5th ed., 1676, 12mo.*

Gravesande, Willem Jacob, *Mathematical Elements of Natural Philosophy,* trans. J. T. Desaguliers, 6th ed., 1747, 2 vols., 4to.

Greaves, John [published by Thomas Birch], *The Miscellaneous Works of Mr Greaves,* 1737, 2 vols., 8vo.

Greenwood, James, *An Essay Towards a Practical English Grammar,* 1740, 12mo.

Grotius, Hugo, *The Rights of War and Peace,* 1738, 2o.

Guicciardini, Francesco, "History of the Wars in Italy" (probably *Histoire des guerres d'Italia,* Londres [Paris], 1738), Venice, 1738, 2 vols., 2o, presented by Lyttleton, Apr. 1760 (J, fol. 17).

Gurdon, Thornagh, *The History of the High Court of Parliament,* 1731, 8vo.

Guthrie, William, [trans. of Cicero] *On the Character of an Orator,* 1745, 8vo.

Hakewill, William, *Modus tenendi Parliamentum: or, The Old Manner of Holding Parliaments in England,* 1671, 12mo.

Hale, Matthew, Sir, *The Original Institution, Power and Jurisdiction of Parliaments,* 1707, 8vo.

Hales, Stephen, *An Account of Some Experiments and Observations on Tar-Water,* 1747, 8vo.

————, *A Description of Ventilators,* 1743, 8vo.

————, *Philosophical Experiments,* 1739, 8vo.

————, *Statical Essays: Containing Vegetable Staticks,* 1738, 2 vols., 8vo.

[Halifax, George Savile, marquis of], *A Character of King Charles the Second,* 1750, 8vo.

Hall, Richard, *Acts, Passed in the Island of Barbados,* ordered May 1767; see letter 17.

Hare, Francis, Bishop, *Works,* 1746, 4 vols., 8vo.

Harrington, James, *The Oceana,* 3d ed., 1747, 2o.

Harris, John, *Lexicon technicum,* 1736, 3 vols., 2o. [1770 *Catalogue:* Third volume was a supplement published in 1744].

Hauksbee, Francis, *Physico-Mechanical Experiments on Various Subjects,* 2d ed., 1719, 8vo.

Hayes, Richard [entered as Heyer], *Negotiator's Magazine,* [1740?], 8vo.

Hénault, Charles-Jean François, *A New Chronological Abridgement of the History of France,* 1762, 2 vols., 8vo, presented by William Bull, Nov. 1765 (J, fol. 61).

Herbert, Edward [Baron Cherbury], *The Life and Reign of King Henry VIII,* 1672, 2o (1st ed., 1649).

Herodotus, *The History of Herodotus,* trans. Isaac Littlebury, 3d ed., 1737, 2 vols., 8vo.

Heylyn, John, *An Interpretation of the New Testament,* ordered May 1767; see letter 17.

[Hill, John], *A New Tale of an Old Tub,* 1752, 8vo.**

Hodges, Walter, *Elihu, or an Enquiry into the Principal Scope and Design of the Book of Job,* 1750, 4to.

Hodgson, James, *A System of the Mathematicks,* 1723, 2 vols., 4to.

Hooke, Nathaniel, *The Roman History,* ordered Mar. 1769; see letter 21.

Hooke, Sir Robert, *Micrographia,* 1667, 2o.

———— [entered as Hawke], *Philosophical Experiments,* 1726, 8vo.

————, *Posthumous Works,* 1705, 2o.

Horace, *The Odes, Epodes, and Carmen Seculare of Horace,* with notes by Rev. Philip Francis, 1742, 4 vols., 8vo.

————, *The Satires of Horace in Latin and English,* 1746, 2 vols., 8vo.

Hospital, marquis de l' [Guillaume François Antoine], *An Analytick Treatise of Conick Sections,* trans. E. Stone, 1723, 4to.

Hotman, François, *Franco-Gallia: or, An Account of the Ancient Free State of France,* 2d ed., 1721, 8vo.

Hume, David, *Philosophical Essays,* 12mo (1st ed., 1748).

[?Hume, Sophia], *An Essay upon Christian Education,* presented by Mrs. Sophia Hume, a Quaker preacher via the lt. gov., William Bull, Jan. 1768 (J, fols. 86–87).

Hutcheson, Francis, *An Essay on the Nature and Conduct of the Passions and Affections,* 3d ed., 1742, 8vo.

————, *An Inquiry into the Original of our Ideas of Beauty and Virtue,* 4th ed., 1738, 8vo.

Hutchinson, Thomas, *The History of the Colony of Massachusets-Bay,* ordered Mar. 1769; see letter 21.

James, Robert, *A Dissertation on Fevers and Inflammatory Distempers,* 1749, 8vo (p).

Johnson, Samuel, *An Account of the Life of Mr. Richard Savage,* 1748, 8vo.

————, *The Rambler,* Edinburgh, 2d ed., 1751, 4 vols., 12mo [2 vols.*].

Johnson, Thomas, *Quæstiones philosophiæ,* Cambridge, 1732, 8vo.

Jones, Inigo, *The Most Notable Antiquity of Great Britain, vulgarly called Stone-Heng,* 2d ed., 1725, 2o (1st ed., 1655).

[Jones, John], *An Appeal to Common Reason and Candor,* 1750, 8vo.

Jones, William, *The Gentlemens and Builders Companion* [?], ordered Feb. 1765; see letter 14.

Justin[us], Marcus Junianus [Trogus Pompeius], *M. J. Justiniex Trogi Pompeii historiis externis,* trans. N. Bailey,1732, 8vo.

———, *Justinus de historiis Philippicus* [probably 1721 ed.], presented by James Brisbane, Jan. 1765 (J, fol. 54).

Kaempfer, Engelbert, *The History of Japan,* trans. J. G. Scheuchzer, 1738, 2 vols., 2o.

Keill, John, *An Introduction to the True Astronomy,* 4th ed., 1748, 8vo.

———, *An Examination of Dr. Burnet's Theory of the Earth,* [Oxford?], 1734, 8vo.

Kennett, Basil, *Romæ antiquæ notitia: or, the antiquities of Rome,* 11th ed., 1746, 8vo.

[King, Charles], *The British Merchant,* 2d ed., 1744, 3 vols., 12mo.

King, William, *An Essay on the Origin of Evil,* Cambridge, 3d ed., 1739, 8vo.

Langley, Batty, *Pomona; or the Fruit Garden Illustrated,* 1729 [or 1728?], 2o.

———, *A Sure and Easy Method of Improving Estates,* 8vo (1st ed., 1728).

Laurence, John, A *New System of Agriculture,* 1726, 2o.

Leake, John, *Practical Observations on the Childbedfever,* [1772], 8vo, presented by the librarian (Samuel Price) in the name of the author, July 1773 (J, fol. 152).

Le Cat, Claude Nicolas, *A Physical Essay on the Senses,* 1750, 8vo.*

Le Clerc, Sébastien, *Practical Geometry,* 1742, 12mo.

Le Sage, Alain René, *The Adventures of Gil Blas de Santillane,* 4 vols., 12mo.

Lediard, Thomas, *The Naval History of England,* 1735, 2 vols., 2o.

Lee, Henry, *Anti-Scepticism: or, Notes upon Each Chapter of Mr. Lock's Essay Concerning Human Understanding,* 1702, 2o.

Leland, John, *The Divine Authority of the Old and New Testament Asserted,* 2d ed., 1739, 8vo.

Lhwyd, Edward, *Archaeologia Britannica,* Oxford, 1707, 2o.

Livy, *The Roman History by Titus Livius,* [trans. John Freinsheim?], 1744–1745, 6 vols., 8vo.

Locke, John, *Works,* 3 vols., 2o (1st ed., 1714); [*Essays on Human Understanding**].

Long, Roger, *Astronomy,* Cambridge, 1742, 2 vols., 4to.

Longinus, Dionysius Cassius, *The Works of Dionysius Longinus on the Sublime,* trans. Leonard Welsted, 1712, 8vo.**

Lowe, Solomon, *Arithmetic in Two Parts,* 1749, 12mo.

Lowth, Robert, *A Short Introduction to English Grammar,* ordered May 1767; see letter 17.

Lucas, Richard, *An Enquiry after Happiness,* 1749, 2 vols., 8vo.

[Lucas, William], *A Five Weeks Tour to Paris &c,* 1752, 42 p., 8o (1st ed., 1750).

Lyttelton, George, *The History of the Life of King Henry the Second,* ordered Mar. 1769; see letter 21.

Mabbut, George, *Sir Isaac Newton's Tables for Renewing and Purchasing Leases,* 1742, 12mo.

Madox, Thomas, *Firma burgi,* 1726, 2o.

Malynes, Gerard, *Consuetudo, vel, Lex mercatoria,* 1686, 2o.

[Manly, Captain, or Richard Manley], *A Summer Voyage to the Gulph of Venice,* 1750, 4to.

[Marana, Giovanni Paolo], *The Eight Volumes of Letters Writ by a Turkish Spy,* 24th ed., 1748, 8 vols., 12mo.

Martin, Benjamin, *Optics,* 1740, 8vo.

————, *The Young Gentleman and Lady's Philosophy,* ordered May 1767; see letter 17.

[Maupertuis], *The Figure of the Earth Determin'd,* 1738, 8vo.

[Mauvillon, Eleazer de], *The Life of Frederick-William I, Late King of Prussia,* 1750, 8vo.

[Michell, John], *A Treatise of Artifical Magnets,* Cambridge, 1751, 2 vols., 8vo.**

Middleton, Conyers, *Life of Cicero,* 4th ed., 1750, 3 vols., 8vo.

————, *Miscellaneous Tracts,* ordered July 1769; see letter 22.

————, *A Treatise on the Roman Senate,* 2d ed., 1748, 8vo.

Midon, Francis, *The History of the Rise and Fall of Masaniello,* 1729, 8vo.

Milton, John, *Paradise Lost,* 1741, 8vo.

————, *Paradise Regained,* 1727, 8vo.

————, *Works,* 1738, 2 vols., 2o.

Molesworth, Robert [entered as Snellgrove], *An Account of Denmark,* 1745, 8vo.

Molloy, Charles, *De jure maritimo et navali,* 8vo (1st ed., 1676?).

Montaigne, Michel de, *Essays,* 1743, 3 vols., 8vo.

[Montesquieu, baron de (Charles de Secondat)], *Persian Letters,* 12mo; in the 1750 *Catalogue,* but then lost and reordered Mar. 1769; see letter 21.

————, *Reflections on the Causes of the Grandeur and Reclension on the Romans,* 1734, 12mo.

————, *The Spirit of the Laws,* 1750, 2 vols., 8vo.

Mortimer, John, *Husbandry,* 5th ed., 1721, 2 vols., 8vo.

Mosheim, Johann Lorenz, *An Ecclesiastical History,* ordered Mar.1769; see letter 21.

Mottley, John, *The History of the Life of Peter I, Emperor of Russia,* 2d ed., 1740, 3 vols., 12 mo.

[Mozeen, Thomas], *Young Scarron,* 1752, 12mo.**

Muilman, Teresia Constantia [entered under Philips], *An Apology for the Life of Mrs T. C. Phillips,* 1750, 3 vols., 12mo.

Muller, John, *The Attack and Defence of Fortify'd Places,* 1747, 8vo.

————, *Elements of Mathematicks,* 1748, 2 vols., 8vo.

————, *A Treatise Containing the Elementary Part of Fortification,* 1746, 8vo.

Musschenbroek, Petrus van, *The Elements of Natural Philosophy,* trans. John Colson, 1744, 2 vols., 8vo.

Nepos, Cornelius, *The Lives of Illustrious Men,* trans. Finch and Creech, 12mo (1st ed., 1713).

[Osterwald, Jean Frédéric], *La Sainte Bible, qui contient le Vieux et le Nouveau Testament,* Amsterdam, 1724, presented by Samuel Prioleau, July 1767 (J, fol. 83).

————, "Réflexions sur la livre de la Genève," [assumed to be *Argumens et réflexions sur les livres et sur les chapitres de la Sainte Bible,* Neuchatel, 1720], presented by Samuel Prioleau, July 1767 (J, fol. 83).

————, "Système de la religion protestante," [untraced], presented by Samuel Prioleau, July 1767 (J, fol. 83).

Ovid, *Epistles, Latin and English,* 1746, 8vo.

————, *Metamorphosis, Latin and English,* 1748, 8vo.

Paris, Matthew, *Historia major,* 1686, 2o.

[Patrick, Simon], *Advice to a Friend,* 1673, 12mo.**

Pennington, Isaac, *Works,* 1761, 8vo, presented by the Society of Friends, Apr. 1768 (J, fol. 89).

Perry, John, *The State of Russia under the Present Czar,* ordered July 1769; see letter 22.

Persius, *The Satyrs of Persius,* trans. Thomas Sheridan, Dublin, 1728, 12mo.*

Petty, Sir William, *Several Essays in Political Arithmetick,* 1699, 8vo.

Petyt, William, *The Antient Right of the Commons of England Asserted,* 1680, 8vo.

Phaedrus, *Fables, Latin and English,* 1745, 8vo.

[Philomath, S. F. (pseud.)], *The Petticoat Pensioners,* c. 1749, 12mo.**

[Philips, George], *Lex Parliamentaria,* 3d ed., 1748, 8vo.

Pictet, Benedict, *La Théologie Chrétienne,* Amsterdam, 1702 [possibly 1721 ed.], 3 vols., presented by Samuel Prioleau, July 1767 (J, fol. 83).

Plato, *Works,* 4th ed., 1749, 2 vols., 12mo.

[Pliny], *Letters of Pliny the Consul,* trans. William Melmoth, 3d ed., 1748, 2 vols., 8vo.

Plot, Robert, *The Natural History of Oxford-shire,* Oxford, 1677, 2o.

————, *The Natural History of Stafford-shire,* Oxford, 1686, 2o.

Plutarch's Lives, Frankfurt?, 1620?, 8 vols., 8vo [1770 *Catalogue:* 2 vols.].

[Pöllnitz, Karl Ludwig, baron von], *La saxe gallante: or the Amorous Adventures and Intrigues of Frederic-Augustus II, late King of Poland,* c. 1750, 12mo.**

Pope, Alexander, *Works,* 9 vols., 8vo (1st ed., 1751).

Popple, Henry, *A Map of the British Empire in America,* 1733, 2o.

Postlethwayt, Malachy, *The Merchant's Public Counting-House,* [1750 or 1751], 4to.

Potter, John, Bishop, *Archæologia Græca: Or, the Antiquities of Greece,* 1740, 2 vols., 8vo.

Price, Francis, *The British Carpenter,* 1735, 4to.

Priestley, Joseph, *The Rudiments of English Grammar,* ordered July 1769; see letter 22.

Pufendorf, Samuel Freihass von, *An Introduction to the History of the Principal Kingdoms and States of Europe,* 1748, 2 vols., 8vo.

———, *Law of Nature and Nations,* 5th ed., 1749, 2o.

Rabelais, François, *Works,* 1750, 5 vols., 12mo.

Raleigh, Sir Walter, *The History of the World,* 2 vols., 2o.

———, *Works,* preface by Thomas Birch, 1751, 2 vols., 8vo.

Ramsay, Allan, *Poems,* [1751?], 2 vols., 12mo.

———, *Songs,* [1750?], 2 vols., 12mo.

Ramsay, Andrew Michael, *The Philosophical Principles of Natural and Revealed Religion,* ordered Feb. 1765; see letter 14.

[Ramsey, Chevalier (Andrew Michael)], *Travels of Cyrus,* 12mo (1st ed., 1736).

Rapin, René, *The Whole Critical Works,* trans. by Basil Kennet, 2 vols., 8vo (1st ed., 1706).

Rapin de Thoyras [Paul], *The History of England,* 5 vols., 2o.

Rawlinson [Richard?], *A New Method of Studying History,* 1728, 2 vols., 8vo (a trans. of Nicolas Lenglet du Fresnoy).

Ray, John, *On the Creation,* 11th ed., 1743, 8vo.

———, *Travels,* 2nd ed., 1738, 2 vols., 8vo.

Robertson, William, *The History of the Reign of the Emperor Charles V,* ordered July 1769; see letter 22.

Rohault, Jacques, *System of Natural Philosophy by Clarke,* 3d ed., 1735, 2 vols., 8vo.

Rollin, Charles, *The Antient History of the Egyptians . . . and Greeks,* Glasgow, 1759–1763, 10 vols., 12mo.

———, *The Method of Teaching and Studying the Belles Letters,* 2d ed., 1737, 4 vols., 8vo.

———, *The Roman History,* 1739–1750, 16 vols., 8vo.

Rowe, Nicholas, *Works,* 1747, 2 vols., 12mo.

[Royal Society of Great Britain], *The Philosophical Transactions and Collections,* abridged by John Lowthorp, 5th ed., 1749, 5 vols., 4to.

Ruffhead, Owen, *Statutes at Large,* ordered Mar. 1769; see letter 21.

Rymer, *Fœdera,* ordered July 1769; see letter 22.

Sallust, *Caius Crispus Sallustius the Historian,* preface and trans. by John Rowe, 1739, 12mo.

————, *Works,* [trans. Thomas Gordon?], 1744, 4to.

Salmon, Thomas, *An Impartial Examination of Bishop Burnet's History of His Own Times,* 1724, 2 vols., 8vo.

————, *New Abridgement and Critical Review of the State Trials,* ordered Mar. 1769; see letter 21.

[Scott, Sarah], *The History of Cornelia,* 1750, 12mo.*

Selden, John, *Fleta seu commentarius Juris Anglicani,* ordered May 1767; see letter 17.

————, *Titles of Honor,* 1672, 2o.

Sewell, William, *History,* 1735, 4to, presented by the Society of Friends, Apr. 1768 (J, fol. 89).

Shaftesbury, Earl of [Anthony Ashley Cooper], *Characteristicks of Men, Manners, Opinions, Times,* 1749, 3 vols., 8vo.

Shaw, Thomas, *Travels,* Oxford, 1738, 2o.

Shenstone, William, *Works,* ordered May 1767; see letter 17.

Sherwin's Mathematical Tables, revised by William Gardiner, 1742, 8vo.

Short, Thomas, *A General Chronological History of the Air etc,* 1749, 2 vols., 8vo.

————, *Discourses on Tea etc,* 1750, 8vo.

————, *New Observations on the Bills of Mortality,* 1750, 8vo.

Sidney, Algernon, *Discourses Concerning Government,* Edinburgh, 1750, 2 vols., 8vo.

Simpson, Thomas, *Doctrine of Annuities and Reversions,* 1742, 8vo.*

————, *The Doctrine and Application of Fluxions,* 1750, 2 vols., 8vo.

————, *Elements of Plane Geometry and Trigonometry,* 1747, 8vo.

————, *Essays on Speculative and Mixed Mathematicks,* 1740, 4to.

————, *A Treatise of Algebra,* 1745, 8vo.

Sloane, Sir Hans, *A Voyage to the Islands . . . with the Natural History of Jamaica,* 1707–1725, 2 vols., 2o.

Smart, Christopher, *The Horatian Canons of Friendship,* 1750, 4to (p).

Smith, John, *Memoirs of Wool,* 1747, 2 vols., 8vo.

Smith, Robert, *Harmonics, or the Philosophy of Musical Sounds,* Cambridge, 1749, 8vo.

Smollett, Tobias, *The Adventures of Roderick Random,* 3d ed., 1750, 2 vols., 12mo.

————, *Continuation of the Complete History of England,* ordered Oct. 1764; see letter 13.

Snelgrave, William, *A New Account of Some Parts of Guinea,* 1734, 8vo.

Spelman, Henry, *Glossarium archaiologicum,* ordered May 1767; see letter 17.

Spenser, Edmund, *Works,* preface by Hughes, 1750, 6 vols., 12mo.

Squire, Samuel, *An Enquiry into the Foundation of the English Constitution; or, an Historical Essay upon the Anglo-Saxon Government in Germany and England,* 1745, 8vo.

Stackhouse, Thomas, *A New History of the Bible,* 2d ed., 1742–1744, 2 vols., 2o.

Stanhope, George, *Epictetus His Morals,* 5th ed., 1741, 8vo.

Stanley, Thomas, *The History of Philosophy: Containing the Lives of the Philosophers,* 4th ed., 1743, 4to.

Steele, Richard, *The Christian Hero,* 9th ed., 1741, 12mo.

———, *Lady's Library,* 1739, 3 vols., 12mo.

Sterne, Laurence, *Tristram Shandy,* continuation vols., ordered Feb. 1766; see letter 15.

Steuart, James, *An Inquiry into the Principles of Political Œconomy,* ordered July 1769; see letter 22.

Stewart, Matthew, *Tracts, Physical and Mathematical,* ordered July 1769; see letter 22.

Stukeley, William, *Itinerum curiosum,* 1724, 2o.

———, *Of the Spleen,* 1723, 2o.

———, *Palaegraphia sacra,* 1736, 4to.

———, *Stonehenge, A Temple Restor'd to the British Druids,* 1740, 2 vols., 2o.

Swift, Jonathan, *Works,* ordered May 1767; see letter 17.

Switzer, Stephen, *The Practical Fruit-Gardener,* 1724, 8vo.

Sykes, Arthur Ashley, *An Examination of Mr. Warburton's Account of the Conduct of the Antient Legislators,* 1744, 8vo.

Tacitus, Cornelius, *Works* [trans. Thomas Gordon?], 1737, 4 vols., 8vo.

Taylor, Jeremy, *Ductor dubitantium,* 2o (1st ed., 1660).

Taylor, John, *Elements of the Civil Law,* ordered Oct. 1764; see letter 13.

Taylor, Silas, and Samuel Dale, *The History and Antiquities of Harwich and Dovercourt,* 1730, 4to.

[Tencin, Claudine Guérin de], *The Siege of Calais, an Historical Novel,* 1751, 2 vols., 8vo.**

[Tertulian], Q. Septimij, *Florentis Tertulliani Opera,* ordered July 1769; see letter 22.

Thomson, James, *Works,* 1744, 2 vols., 8vo.

Tillotson, John, *Sermons on Several Subjects and Occasions,* 1742, 12 vols., 8vo.

Tissot, Samuel Auguste David, *Advice to People in General,* ordered May 1767; see letter 17.

Titi Petronii arbitri satyricon, ordered Aug. 1761; see letter 8.

Tooke, Andrew, *The Pantheon,* 1750, 8vo (trans. of Françoise Antoine Pomey).

Tournefort, Joseph Pitton de, *A Voyage into the Levant,* 1741, 3 vols., 8vo.

Tovey, de Blossiers, *Anglia Judaica,* ordered Oct. 1764; see letter 13.

Trott, Nicholas, *The Laws of the Province of South-Carolina,* ordered May 1767; see letter 17.

Trublet, Abbé Nicholas-Charles-Joseph, *Essays upon Several Subjects of Literature and Morality,*** and a replacement ordered Aug. 1761; see letter 8.

Tull, Jethro, *The Horse-Hoing Husbandry,* 1742 [or 1733, 1736, 1740?], 2o.

Turnbull, George, *The Principles of Moral and Christian Philosophy,* 1740, 2 vols., 8vo.

Varenius, Bernhardus, *A Compleat System of General Geography,* 1736, 2 vols., 8vo.

Vattel, Emer de, *The Law of Nations,* ordered Mar. 1769; see letter 21.

Vertot, Abbé de, *The History of the Revolution in Rome,* 5th ed., 1740, 2 vols., 8vo.

———, *The History of the Revolution in Sweden,* 7th ed., 1743, 2 vols., 8vo.

Virgil, *The Works of Virgil Translated into English Prose . . . with the Latin Text and Order of Construction on the Same Page,* 2d ed., 1748, 2 vols., 8vo.

[Voltaire, François Marie Arouet de], *Micromegas; A Comic Romance,* 1753, 12mo.**

Waller, Edmund, *Works,* 1747 [or 1730, 1744?], 12mo.

Walsingham, Sir Francis, *Instructions pour les Ambassadeurs,* 4 vols., 12mo.

Warburton, William, *The Divine Legation of Moses Demonstrated,* 1742, 3 vols., 8vo.

Warner, Ferdinando, *The History of the Rebellion and Civil-War in Ireland,* ordered May 1767; see letter 17.

Watts, Isaac, *The Doctrine of the Passions Explained and Improved,* 1739, 12mo.

———, *The Improvement of the Mind,* 1743, 8vo.

———, *The Knowledge of the Heavens Made Easy; or, the First Principles of Astronomy,* 1745, 8vo.

———, *Logick: or, the Right Use of Reason in the Equiry after Truth,* 1745, 8vo.

———, *Philosophical Essays,* 1742, 8vo.

Webb, Daniel, *Inquiry into the Beauties of Painting,* ordered Aug. 1761; see letter 8.

[Whiston, James], *A Discourse of the Decay of Trade,* 1693, 2o.**

Whiston, William, *Chronological Tables,* Cambridge, 1702, 8vo (p).

———, *Josephus,* 1737, 2o.

———, *Memoirs of the Life and Writings of Mr. William Whiston,* 1749, 2 vols., 8vo.

———, *Sacred History,* 1745–1746, 6 vols., 8vo.

———, *Tracts,* London and Canterbury, 1707–1734, 29 vols., 8vo.

Whitlocke, Bulstrode, *Memorials of the English Affairs,* 1732, 2o.

Whytt, Robert, *An Essay on the Virtues of Lime-Water in the Cure of the Stone,* Edinburgh, 1752, 12mo.**

Wollaston, William, *The Religion of Nature Delineated,* 1750, 8vo.*

Wood, William, *A Survey of Trade,* 2d ed., 1719, 8vo.

Woodward, John, *An Attempt Towards a Natural History of Fossils,* 1728–1729, 2 vols., 8vo.

————, *An Essay Towards a Natural History of the Earth,* 3d ed., 1723, 8vo.

————, *Natural History of the Earth, Illustrated, Inlarged, and Defended,* 1726, 8vo.

————, *Naturalis historia telluris illustratæ aucta,* 1714, 8vo.

[Wren, Christopher], *Parentalia, or Memoirs of the Family of the Wrens,* 1750, 2o.

Young, Edward, *The Complaint, or, Night Thoughts,* 1767, 12mo.

————, *Poetical Works,* 1741, 2 vols., 8vo.

————, *A Vindication of Providence: or, a True Estimate of Human Life,* 1747, 8vo (p) .

Young, George. *A Treatise on Opium,* 1753, 8vo.**

NOTES

Notes to Chapter 1

1. From time to time early library records resurface. Among new material advertised for sale during the completion of this study were documents relating to the Philogrammatican Library subscription library, Joseph Rubinfine, *Catalogue* 133 (West Palm Beach, Fla., 1996), item 32.

2. *The Rules and By-Laws of the Charleston Library Society: Together with the Act of the General Assembly of South-Carolina for Incorporating the Society, Confirmed by His Majesty: and a Brief Historical Introduction* (Charlestown: Robert Wells, 1762), 5th rule, ratified 4 Apr. 1759 (hereafter, as with the published 26 Apr. 1748 and 23 Apr. 1750 *SCG* advertisement and then all the printed editions of the rules from 1750, cited as *Rules and By-Laws* followed by edition date). An earlier version was contained in rule 17 of the original rules advertised in the *South Carolina Gazette* (hereafter *SCG*), 26 Apr. 1750.

3. Library Company of Philadelphia (hereafter LCP) minute books, 1 (1731–1768), 2 (1768–1785), 3 (1785–1794), 4 (1794–1816), 5 (1816–1832); and box files of additional correspondence, invoices, and photocopies of letters held at the Historical Society of Pennsylvania.

4. Marcus A. McCorison, ed., *The 1764 Catalogue of the Redwood Library Company at Newport, Rhode Island* (New Haven and London: Yale University Press, 1965), pp. x, xvii. See also details in Jesse H. Shera, *Foundations of the Public Library in New England* (Chicago: Chicago University Press, 1949).

5. New York Society Library (hereafter NYSL) first minute book (1754–1772); second minute book (1773–1832); and cf. Austin Baxter Keep, *History of the New York Society Library* (New York: New York Society Library, 1908). I am extremely grateful for the assistance of Sharon Brown, assistant librarian, and Mark Piel, librarian, for allowing me access to these and other materials. A much fuller discussion of the NYSL and the other early American libraries will appear in a subsequent study.

6. As in letter 23, for example.

7. James E. Tierney, ed., *The Correspondence of Robert Dodsley, 1733–1764* (Cambridge: Cambridge University Press, 1988); William Zachs, *The First John Murray and the Late Eighteenth-Century London Book Trade* (Oxford: British Academy and Oxford University Press, 1998); William Zachs, "'An Illiterate Fellow of a Bookseller': John Murray and His Authors, 1768–1793," in Robin Myers and Michael Harris, eds., *A Genius for Letters: Booksellers and Bookselling from the 16th to the 20th Century* (Winchester and New Castle, Del.: Oak Knoll, 1996), pp. 123–43; L. H. Butterfield, "The American Interests of the Firm of E. & C. Dilly," *Papers of the Bibliographical Society of America* 45 (1951): 283–332. The Joseph Johnson letter book is now available at the New York Public Library (and in facsimile at the British Library). Stockdale's letters remain

in private hands: Eric Stockdale, "John Stockdale of Piccadilly: Publisher to John Adams and Thomas Jefferson," in Robin Myers and Michael Harris, eds., *Author/Publisher Relations during the Eighteenth and Nineteenth Centuries* (Oxford: Oxford Polytechnic Press, 1983), pp. 63–87.

8. Cited in John Tebbel, *A History of Book Publishing in the United States,* 3 vols. (New York and London: R. R. Bowker, 1972–1978), 1:1.

9. Scottish Record Office, E504/22/12, Customs Ledgers, Leith, 1765–1766, 27 Sept. 1766 (sent by the *Kinoul,* Alexander Alexander, master). I am grateful to Warren McDougall for locating this reference.

10. The only exceptions, towards the end of the century, were short novels, Robert B. Winans, "Bibliography and the Cultural Historian: Notes on the Eighteenth-Century Novel," in William L. Joyce et al., eds., *Printing and Society in Early America* (Worcester, Mass.: American Antiquarian Society, 1983), pp. 174–85 (pp. 178–81).

11. Hannah D. French, "Early American Bookbinding by Hand 1636–1820," in Hellmut Lehmann-Haupt, ed., *Bookbinding in America: Three Essays* (Portland, Maine: Southwold-Anthoensen, 1941), pp. 3–127; and William Spawn, "The Evolution of American Binding Styles in the Eighteenth Century," in John Dooley and James Tanis, eds., *Bookbinding in America 1680–1910* (Bryn Mawr, Penn.: Bryn Mawr College Library, 1983), pp. 29–36.

12. Stephen Botein, "The Anglo-American Book Trade before 1776: Personnel and Strategies," in Joyce et al., eds., *Printing and Society,* pp. 74–79.

13. See Elizabeth Carroll Reilly, "The Wages of Piety: The Boston Book Trade of Jeremy Condy," in Joyce et al., eds., *Printing and Society,* pp. 83–131. Condy's son, John Foster Condy, continued the business through the 1770s.

14. James A. Henretta, *The Evolution of American Society, 1700–1815: An Interdisciplinary Analysis* (Lexington, Mass.: D. C. Heath, 1973), pp. 41–42.

15. John Clive and Bernard Bailyn, "England's Cultural Provinces: Scotland and America," *William and Mary Quarterly,* 3d ser., 11 (1954): 200–13. See also Ralph Davis, *The Rise of the Atlantic Economies* (London: Weidenfeld and Nicolson, 1973), esp. pp. 304–8; and Carole Shammas, "Consumer Behavior in Colonial America," *Social Science History* 6 (1982): 67–86.

16. T. H. Breen, "'Baubles of Britain': The American and Consumer Revolutions of the Eighteenth Centuries," *Past and Present* 119 (1988): 87.

17. Samuel Eliot Morison, *The Maritime History of Massachusetts 1783–1860,* 4th ed. (Cambridge, Mass.: Riverside Press, 1961), p. 35, and see also pp. 25, 125–33. Although in vogue in recent studies these observations have a long pedigree, including, for example, Thomas J. Wertenbaker, *The Golden Age of Colonial Culture* (New York: New York University Press, 1949).

18. See Edwin Wolf II, *The Library of James Logan of Philadelphia 1674–1751* (Philadelphia: Library Company of Philadelphia, 1974).

19. See James Raven, "From Promotion to Proscription: Arrangements for Reading and Eighteenth-Century Libraries," in James Raven, Helen Small, and Naomi Tadmor, eds., *The Practice and Representation of Reading in England* (Cambridge: Cambridge University Press, 1996), pp. 175–201.

20. See Paul Kaufman, "The Community Library: A Chapter in English Social History," *Transactions of the American Philosophical Society,* n.s., vol. 57, pt. 7 (1967). As of December 1998 Robin Alston's "Library History Database" website (www.r-alston.dircon.co.uk/contents.htm) listed 3,071 libraries operating at some time between 1700 and 1799.

21. Joseph Breintnall, secretary of LCP, to Peter Collinson, 7 Nov. 1732, LCP minute book 1, fol. 13.

22. Various examples from the Winthrop papers and collection of the Massachusetts Historical Society (hereafter MHS), cited in Thomas Goddard Wright, *Literary Culture in Early New England 1620–1730* (New Haven: Yale University Press, 1920), pp. 25–61.

23. MHS, Henry Knox Papers, 1719–1825 (hereafter HKP), 5:237, Longman to Knox, 18 Jan. 1772.

24. John Murray Archives, Albemarle St., London, John Murray I letter books (hereafter JMLB) 4, Murray to Miller, 26 Mar. 1773 (relating to order for £6, John Murray I day book (hereafter JMDB), fol. 353, invoice, 10 Mar. 1773).

25. Wright, *Literary Culture in Early New England,* p. 113; letter to John Winthrop, 26 Dec. 1720, "The Mather Papers," *Collections of the Massachusetts Historical Society,* 4th ser., 8 (1868): 440.

26. Notably, M. Halsey Thomas, ed., *The Diary of Samuel Sewall 1674–1729,* 2 vols. (New York: Farrar, Straus and Giroux, 1973), 1:229, 19 July 1689; *The Letter-Book of Samuel Sewall, Collections of the Massachusetts Historical Society,* 6th ser., 1–2 (1886, 1888), 1:199, 25 Apr. 1698, sent by Capt. Thomas Carter (recipient unknown).

27. MHS, Usher letter book, with surviving invoices, 1679–1685 (total £567); Worthington Chauncey Ford, *The Boston Book Market 1679–1700* (Boston: Club of Odd Volumes, 1917), pp. 19–21; *Letter-Book of Samuel Sewall,* 1:271–72, Sewall to Ive, 13 June 1702.

28. Logan to J. [William] Reading, 12 July 1727, Logan letter book 3:81–83, Historical Society of Pennsylvania, cited in Edwin Wolf II, "James Logan's Correspondence with William Reading, Librarian of Sion College," in Hellmut Lehmann-Haupt, ed., *Homage to a Bookman: Essays on Manuscripts, Books and Printing* (Berlin: Mann Verlag, 1967), p. 210.

29. LCP minute book 1, fols. 45, 58 (reprimands to William Meadows, 12 Aug. 1734, 5 Nov. 1735); fol. 189 (Meadows dismissed, 9 July 1739); fol. 163 (first resignation of Collinson, 13 Aug. 1759).

30. NYSL first minute book, 1754–1772, fol. 29, 27 Mar. 1758.

31. Logan to John Whiston, 27 July 1748, copy, Historical Society of Pennsylvania, Logan Papers, letter book 5, 1748–1750, cited in Marie Elena Korey, "Three Early Philadelphia Book Collectors," *American Book Collector,* n.s., vol. 2, no. 6 (Nov.–Dec. 1981): 8.

32. Receipt to Cabot from George Pearch, London, 18 May 1771, Cabot Family Papers, box 2, folder 4, James Duncan and Stephen Phillips Libraries, Peabody Essex Museum (hereafter PEM), Salem, Mass.

33. L. B. Namier, *England in the Age of the American Revolution* (London: Macmillan, 1930), pp. 286–90.

34. Samuel Reade to Wait Winthrop, 12 Oct. 1708, "The Winthrop Papers: Part VI," *Collections of the Massachusetts Historical Society,* 6th ser., 5 (1892): 171.

35. I am indebted here and in the following remarks to Ian K. Steele, *The English Atlantic 1675–1740: An Exploration of Communication and Community* (New York and Oxford: Oxford University Press, 1986), see esp. pp. 7–9, 10; table 1.1, p. 59.

36. Various examples, including Hall's orders to Watkins (see table 4), are given in Warren McDougall, "Scottish Books for America in the Mid 18th Century," in Robin Myers and Michael Harris, eds., *Spreading the Word: The Distribution Networks of Print 1550–1850* (Winchester and Detroit: St. Paul's Bibliographies, 1990), pp. 21–46.

37. Steele, *English Atlantic,* pp. 15, 273, 275.

38. James F. Shepherd and Gary M. Walton, *Shipping, Maritime Trade, and the Economic Development of Colonial North America* (Cambridge: Cambridge University Press, 1972), p. 50.

39. George C. Rogers, Jr., *Charleston in the Age of the Pinckneys* (Norman: University of Oklahoma Press, 1969), p. 4.

40. Huguette Chaunu and Pierre Chaunu, "Économie Atlantique, Économie Mondiale (1504–1650): Problèmes de fait et de méthode," *Journal of World History* 1 (1953): 91–104. Translation in Peter Earle, ed., *Essays in European History, 1500–1800* (Oxford: Oxford University Press, 1974), pp. 113–26.

41. Ann Laura Stoler and Frederick Cooper, "Between Metropole and Colony: Rethinking a Research Agenda," in Cooper and Stoler, eds., *Tensions of Empire: Colonial Cultures in a Bourgeois World* (Berkeley, Los Angeles, and London: University of California Press, 1997), pp. 3–4.

42. Bernard Bailyn, "Atlantic History: The View from the Moon," and David Armitage, "An Overview," papers read at the International Seminar in the History of the Atlantic World, Harvard Universiy, Nov. 1998.

43. See, for example, Breen, "Baubles of Britain"; Timothy Breen, "An Age of Goods: The Anglicanization of Colonial America, 1690–1776," *Journal of British Studies* 25 (1986): 467–99; and Cary Carson, Ronald Hoffman and Peter J. Albert, eds., *Of Consuming Interests: The Style of Life in the Eighteenth Century* (Charlottesville and London: University Press of Virginia, 1994). Underlying theories are discussed in Robert Bocock, *Consumption* (London: Routledge, 1993); and Martyn J. Lee, *Consumer Culture Reborn: The Cultural Politics of Consumption* (London: Routledge, 1993).

44. See in particular Richard D. Brown, *Knowledge Is Power: The Diffusion of Information in Early America, 1700–1865* (New York: Oxford University Press, 1989), a study of the tidewater Virginian gentry and their consolidation of political power.

45. Most influentially, perhaps, aspects of Benedict Anderson's "print capitalism," *Imagined Communities: Reflections on the Origin and Spread of Nationalism* (London: Verso, 1983), pp. 42–48, but also in numerous studies by Roger Chartier, Robert Darnton, and David D. Hall.

46. Jurgen Habermas, *The Structural Transformation of the Public Sphere,* trans. T. Burger and F. Lawrence (Cambridge, Mass.: Polity, 1989); Craig Calhoun, ed., *Habermas and the Public Sphere* (Cambridge, Mass., and London: MIT Press, 1992).

47. Michael Warner, *Letters of the Republic: Publication and the Public Sphere in Eighteenth-Century America* (Cambridge, Mass.: Harvard University Press, 1990).

48. Christopher Looby, *Voicing America: Language, Literary Form, and the Origins of the United States* (Chicago and London: University of Chicago Press, 1996), p. 3.

49. Jay Fliegelman, *Declaring Independence: Jefferson, Natural Language, and the Culture of Performance* (Stanford: Stanford University Press, 1993).

50. See Michael Warner, "The Public Sphere and the Cultural Mediation of Print," in William S. Solomon and Robert W. McChesney, eds., *Ruthless Criticism: New Perspectives in U.S. Communications History* (Minneapolis: University of Minnesota Press, 1993).

51. Richard L. Bushman, "American High-Style and Vernacular Culture," in Jack P. Greene and J. R. Pole, eds., *Colonial British America: Essays in the New History of the Early Modern Era* (Baltimore and London: Johns Hopkins University Press, 1984), p. 358.

52. Dena Goodman, *The Republic of Letters: A Cultural History of the French Enlightenment* (Ithaca, N.Y., and London: Cornell University Press, 1994); Robert Darnton, *The Forbidden Best-Sellers of Pre-Revolutionary France* (New York and London: W. W. Norton, 1995).

53. David S. Shields, *Civil Tongues and Polite Letters in British America* (Chapel Hill and London: University of North Carolina Press, 1997).

54. Bushman, "American High-Style and Vernacular Culture," p. 368.

55. Notably, David Hancock, *Citizens of the World: London Merchants and the Integration of the British Atlantic Community, 1735–1785* (Cambridge: Cambridge University Press, 1995).

56. Mark D. Kaplanoff, "How Federalist Was South Carolina in 1787–88?" in David R. Chesnutt and Clyde N. Wilson, eds., *The Meaning of South Carolina History: Essays in Honor of George C. Rogers, Jr.* (Columbia: University of South Carolina Press, 1991), pp. 67–103.

57. Rebecca Starr, *A School for Politics: Commercial Lobbying and Political Culture in Early South Carolina* (Baltimore and London: Johns Hopkins University Press, 1998), p. 4.

58. As Rebecca Starr has described it, "this highly interactive, interconnected, cosmopolitan social world was a far cry from the solitary, independent, rural world of the Virginia tobacco grower," *School for Politics,* p. 19. Cf. the merged discourse of a radical country ideology and an analogous elite agrarian rhetoric derived from the tobacco culture of Virginia described in T. H. Breen, *Tobacco Culture: The Mentality of the Great Tidewater Planters on the Eve of the Revolution* (Princeton: Princeton University Press, 1985).

59. James Raven, "New Reading Histories, Print Culture, and the Identification of Change: The Case of Eighteenth-Century England," *Social History* 23 (1998): 268–87.

Notes to Chapter 2

1. Robert M. Weir, "'The Harmony We Were Famous For': An Interpretation of Pre-Revolutionary South Carolina Politics," *William and Mary Quarterly* 26 (1969): 473–501.

2. Clarence L. Ver Steeg, *Origins of a Southern Mosaic: Studies of Early Carolina and Georgia* (Athens: University of Georgia Press, 1975), pp. 120–32.

3. *Gentleman's Magazine* 25 (London, 1755): 344. For a survey of the Charleston economy see R. C. Nash, "South Carolina and the Atlantic Economy in the Late

Seventeenth and Eighteenth Centuries," *Economic History Review,* 2d ser., 45 (1992): 677–702.

4. James Percival Petit, *South Carolina and the Sea: Day by Day toward Five Centuries 1492–1976 AD,* 2 vols. (Charleston: Maritime and Ports Activities Committee of the States Ports Authority, 1976), 2:2.

5. Joyce E. Chaplin, *An Anxious Pursuit: Agricultural Innovation and Modernity in the Lower South, 1730–1815* (Chapel Hill and London: University of North Carolina Press, 1993), p. 59.

6. David Moltke-Hansen, "Protecting Interests, Maintaining Rights, Emulating Ancestors: US Constitution Bicentennial Reflections on the Problem of South Carolina, 1787–1860," *South Carolina Historical and Geneaological Magazine* (hereafter *SCHM*) 89 (1988): 160–82; Mark D. Kaplanoff, "Making the South Solid: Politics and the Structure of Society in South Carolina, 1790–1815," Ph.D. diss., Cambridge University, 1979; Rachel N. Klein, *Unification of a Slave State: The Rise of the Planter Class in the South Carolina Backcountry 1760–1808* (Chapel Hill: University of North Carolina Press, 1990).

7. M. Eugene Sirmans, *Colonial South Carolina: A Political History 1663–1763* (Chapel Hill: University of North Carolina Press, 1966), p. 233.

8. Evarts B. Greene and Virginia D. Harrington, *American Population before the Federal Census of 1790* (New York: Columbia University Press, 1932), pp. 174–76.

9. Cited in Carl Bridenbaugh, *Cities in Revolt: Urban Life in America, 1743–1776* (New York: Alfred A. Knopf, 1955), p. 333.

10. Dr. [George] Milligan [Milligen-Johnston], *A Short Description of the Province of South Carolina . . . In the Year 1763* (London, 1770). The British Library copy with marginal annotation is dated 1775; I am most grateful to Rebecca Starr for this information.

11. Greene and Harrington, *American Population,* tables from the census, pp. 177–79.

12. For details see Converse D. Clowse, *Measuring Charleston's Overseas Commerce, 1717–1767* (Washington, D.C.; University Press of America, 1981).

13. Peter H. Wood, *Black Majority: Negroes in Colonial South Carolina from 1670 through the Stono Rebellion* (New York: Alfred A. Knopf, 1974), pp. 80–90.

14. "The Diary of Samuel Sewall," *Collections Mass. Hist. Soc.,* 5th ser., vol. 6, pt. 2 (1879), pp. 11–12.

15. [Josiah Smith], *Mr. Smith's Sermon Occasioned by the late Terrible Fire in Charlestown, South-Carolina, November 18, 1740* ([Boston], 1741), pp. 16–17.

16. See Robert M. Weir, *Colonial South Carolina: A History* (Millwood, N.Y.: KTO Press, 1983), pp. 211–13, 218; and Weir, "The Harmony We Were Famous For."

17. Jerome J. Nadelhaft, *The Disorders of War: The Revolution in South Carolina* (Orona, Maine: Orona Press, 1981), pp. 2–3.

18. Petit, *South Carolina and the Sea,* 2:33.

19. George C. Rogers, Jr., *Evolution of a Federalist: William Loughton Smith of Charleston (1758–1812)* (Columbia: South Carolina University Press, 1962), p. 375.

20. Starr, *School for Politics,* p. 12.

21. See the conclusions of Starr, *School for Politics,* pp. 161–66.

22. Mark A. DeWolfe Howe, ed., "Journal of Josiah Quincy, Junior, 1773," *Proceedings of the Massachusetts Historical Society* 49 (1916): 454.

23. Rogers, *Evolution of a Federalist,* p. 9.

24. Cited in Nadelhaft, *Disorders of War,* p. 4.

25. Nadelhaft, *Disorders of War,* p. 5.

26. Kaplanoff, "Making the South Solid," pp. 20–26.

27. See in particular, Edward Pearson, "'Planters Full of Money': The Self-Fashioning of the Eighteenth-Century South Carolina Elite," in Jack P. Greene, Randy Sparks, and Rosemary Brana-Shute, eds., *Money, Trade and Power: The Evolution of Colonial South Carolina's Plantation Society* (Columbia: University of South Carolina Press, 2001), pp. 299–321. I am very grateful to Ted Pearson for advance copy of his work.

28. Cited in Kaplanoff, "Making the South Solid," p. 20.

29. See Weir, *Colonial South Carolina,* pp. 191–203.

30. Richard Beale Davis, *Intellectual Life in the Colonial South 1585–1763,* 3 vols. (Knoxville: University of Tennessee Press, 1978), 3:1119, 1294–97, 1396–98; Edgar Legaré Pennington, "The Reverend Thomas Morritt and the Free School," *SCHM* 32 (1931): 45.

31. "William Logan's Journal of a Journey to Georgia, 1745," *Pennsylvania Magazine of History and Biography* 36 (1912): 163–64.

32. Plowden C. J. Weston, ed., *Documents Connected with the History of South Carolina* (London, 1856), pp. 84–85.

33. Sirmans, *Colonial South Carolina,* pp. 232, 233.

34. David S. Shields, *Oracles of Empire: Poetry, Politics, and Commerce in British America, 1690–1750* (Chicago and London: University of Chicago Press, 1990), pp. 17–20.

35. Cited in Edwin Wolf II et al., *"At the Instance of Benjamin Franklin": A Brief History of the Library Company of Philadelphia,* 2d ed. (Philadelphia: Library Company of Philadelphia, 1995), p. 11.

36. See in particular Shields, *Oracles of Empire,* esp. pp. xiii–xxxii. Further research to understand the nature of early Charleston community, particularly given the archival possibilities, is much needed and Shields's study offers many suggestions.

37. Howe, ed., "Journal of Josiah Quincy," p. 455.

38. Cf., for example, Sirmans, *Colonial South Carolina,* pp. 231–32, with the revisionist tone of Weir, *Colonial South Carolina,* pp. 210–13, 219–20 (qualified by emphasis on Anglican inclusivist ambitions, pp. 221–23).

39. See, for example, Klein, *Unification of a Slave State,* chap. 9.

40. Sirmans, *Colonial South Carolina,* pp. 229, 232.

41. Weir, *Colonial South Carolina,* p. 261.

42. Michael O'Brien, preface to Michael O'Brien and David Moltke-Hansen, eds., *Intellectual Life in Antebellum Charleston* (Knoxville: University of Tennessee Press, 1986), p. ix, with reference to the work of Thomas Bender. Although focusing on the nineteenth century, see also David Moltke-Hansen, "The Expansion of Intellectual Life: A Prospectus," in O'Brien and Moltke-Hansen, eds., *Intellectual Life in Antebellum Charleston,* p. 23; and Davis, *Intellectual Life in the Colonial South 1585–1763,* esp.

2:491–626 on books, libraries, and printing; and the earlier Frederick P. Bowes, *The Culture of Early Charleston* (Chapel Hill: University of North Carolina Press, 1942).

43. Shields, *Civil Tongues and Polite Letters in British America.*

44. Jack P. Greene, *Imperatives, Behaviors, and Identities: Essays in Early American Cultural History* (Charlottesville and London: University Press of Virginia, 1992), p. 357.

45. John J. McCusker and Russell R. Menard, *The Economy of British America 1607–1789* (Chapel Hill and London: University of North Carolina Press, 1985), pp. 103, 136, 172, 218, 226–30.

46. Cynthia Z. Stiverson and Gregory A. Stiverson, "The Colonial Retail Book Trade: Availability and Affordability of Reading Material in Mid-Eighteenth-Century Virginia," in Joyce et al., eds., *Printing and Society,* pp. 140–41.

47. *SCG,* 12 Feb. 1750. Among Viart advertisements, *SCG,* 9 Mar. 1752.

48. Two Whitmarsh pieces survive from what must have been dozens of other examples. Both are ascribed to 1731. One further Whitmarsh survival is the more substantial *Full and Impartial View of Mr Bowman's Visitation Sermon* by Rev. Alexander Garden. I am most grateful for the assistance of Alan Degutis in working with the North American Imprints Program at the American Antiquarian Society. See also figure 1 below.

49. The pioneering study is Calhoun Winton, "The Colonial South Carolina Book Trade," *Proof: The Yearbook of American Bibliographical and Textual Studies* 2 (1972): 71–87.

50. Leonard W. Labaree et al., eds., *The Papers of Benjamin Franklin,* 31 vols. (New Haven: Yale University Press, 1959–1995), 1:205–8 (esp. n. 5).

51. A summary is offered by Davis, *Intellectual Life in the Colonial South,* 2:606–7; and Hennig Cohen, *The South Carolina Gazette 1732–1775* (Columbia: University of South Carolina Press, 1953), pp. 4–14.

52. See Douglas C. McMurtrie, "The First Decade of Printing in the Royal Province of South Carolina," *Library,* 4th ser., 13 (1933): 425–52. Cf. Richard Parker Morgan, *A Preliminary Bibliography of South Carolina, 1731–1800* (Clemson, S.C.: Clemson University, [1966?]); and Lawrence C. Wroth, *The Colonial Printer,* 2d ed., revised and enlarged (Charlottesville, Va.: Dominion Books, 1964 [1st ed., Portland: Southworth-Anthoensen Press, 1938]), pp. 43–47.

53. Rosalind Remer, *Printers and Men of Capital: Philadelphia Book Publishers in the New Republic* (Philadelphia: University of Pennsylvania Press, 1996).

54. Douglas C. McMurtrie, "A Bibliography of South Carolina Imprints, 1731–1740," *SCHM* 34 (1933): 132. This "choice collection" was regularly advertised through the 1740s (e.g., *SCG,* 1 Mar. 1740).

55. J. L. E. W. Shecut, *Shecut's Medical and Philosophical Essays. Containing: 1st Topographical, Historical and Other Sketches of the City of Charleston* (Charleston, 1819), pp. 54–55.

56. *SCG,* 5 Feb. (*Poor Richard's Almanacks*), 26 Mar. 1737.

57. Advertised, *SCG,* 27 Jan. 1759.

58. *SCG,* 26 June and 3 July 1749 (reprinting London advertisement of 31 Jan 1749);

59. *The Memoirs of Major Robert Rogers* (London, 1765), advertised, *SCG,* 27 Feb. 1762; notably for histories, *SCG,* 18 Nov. 1756; and Rivington, now in New York, for the

Complete Works of Charles Churchill, SCG, 13 Oct. 1766. Rivington's fuller career features in chap. 6 below.

60. *SCG,* 1 Sept. 1758; and *SCG,* supplement, 15 Feb. 1770.
61. *SCG,* 29 Dec. 1746; and still for sale, *SCG,* 19 Jan. 1747.
62. Various advertisements in the *SCG* (such as that for Wigg, 8 Apr. 1732, and for the Perroneaus, 26 June 1736), now recorded in John H. Wilson and Gary S. Wilson, *Early South Carolina Newspapers Database Reports: South Carolina Gazette 1732–* (Charleston: South Carolina Historical Society, 1995–). I am most grateful to John Wilson for his generous supply of references during his compilation of these invaluable guides.
63. *SCG,* 15 Apr. 1732, 16 Nov. 1738.
64. *SCG,* 21 Dec. 1738.
65. *SCG,* 26 Sept. 1748.
66. Cohen, *South Carolina Gazette,* pp. 130, 134, 138, 139.
67. Notable advertisements include *SCG,* 21 May 1754, 6 Mar. 1755.
68. *SCG,* 10, 17 Aug. 1752.
69. *SCG,* 11 Apr. 1761.
70. *SCG,* 5 Feb., 12 Feb. 1753.
71. *SCG,* 12 June 1753.
72. "Merchantable rice will be taken in all payments at market price," Cowan advertisement, *SCG,* 8 Jan. 1750.
73. *SCG,* 27 Mar., 29 May 1749; Scottish Record Office, E504/22/3; *SCG,* 8 Jan. 1750. I am greatly indebted to Warren McDougall for assistance in locating the Scottish Record Office items.
74. Scottish Record Office, E504/22/5 and 6, Leith, 19 Oct. 1752, 27 Aug. 1753, 18 Sept. 1754; *SCG,* 5 Feb. 1753 and repeated next issue; *SCG,* 2 Dec. 1754 and repeated next two issues.
75. See McDougall, "Scottish Books for America in the Mid 18th Century."
76. *SCG,* 24 June 1751.
77. *SCG,* 16 Jan. 1762, 14 Dec. 1769; but also many other examples.
78. When in London, prior to his bankruptcy in 1759, Rivington had served the CLS as its bookseller; see below, chap. 6.
79. *SCG,* 16 May 1761; 18, 25 June, 10 Sept. 1763.
80. *SCG,* 24 Dec. 1763.
81. Isaiah Thomas, *The History of Printing in America,* 2d ed., 2 vols. (Albany, N.Y., 1874), 2:240.
82. *SCG,* 2 Apr. 1763.
83. See R. C. Nash, "Trade and Business in Eighteenth-Century South Carolina: The Career of John Guerard, Merchant and Planter," *SCHM* 96 (1995): 16–19.
84. *SCG,* 29 June 1738.
85. Joseph Towne Wheeler, "Thomas Bray and the Maryland Parochial Libraries," *Maryland Historical Magazine* 34 (1939): 246–65; Charles T. Laugher, *Thomas Bray's Grand Design: Libraries of the Church of England in America, 1695–1785* (Chicago: American Library Association, 1973); H. P. Thompson, *Thomas Bray*

(London: SPCK, 1954); and James Raven, "Sent to the Wilderness: Mission Literature in Colonial America," in James Raven, ed., *Free Print and Non-Commercial Publishing since 1700* (Aldershot, Hants., and Burlington, Vt.: Ashgate, 2000), pp. 135–61.

86. Nicholas Trott, *The Laws of the Province of South-Carolina* (Charleston, 1736), pp. 77–81.

87. Edgar Legaré Pennington, "Beginnings of the Library in Charles Town, South Carolina," *Proceedings of the American Antiquarian Society,* n.s., 44 (1935): 159–87; Bowes, *Culture of Early Charleston,* p. 55.

88. Louis B. Wright, *The Cultural Life of the American Colonies, 1607–1763* (New York: Harper & Brothers, 1957), p. 147.

89. This was the key explanation of Alexander Hewat, *An Historical Account of the Rise and Progress of the Colonies of South Carolina and Georgia,* 2 vols. (London, 1779), 1:147.

90. Shecut, *Shecut's Medical and Philosophical Essays,* p. 40.

91. Lambeth Palace Library, SPG Papers, xvi, fols. 186–87, "Books with ye Societys Marke found by the Executors of the Late Reverd Mr Samll Thomas and left in the parish where he dyed," 2 Nov. 1707.

92. Lambeth Palace Library, SPG Papers, xvi, fols. 258–64, "Proposals for the Founding and Endowing of a School, in Charles Town in South Carolina," 6 Jan. 1709/10.

93. Pennington, "The Reverend Thomas Morritt and the Free School," p. 41.

94. The list is given by Walter Bellingrath Edgar, "The Libraries of Colonial South Carolina," Ph.D. diss., University of South Carolina, 1969; but see also Davis, *Intellectual Life in the Colonial South,* pp. 519, 569–77; and below, chaps. 10, 11, and 14. Edgar notes that of the total of 4,700 inventories recorded for 1736–1776, 2,051 mentioned books.

95. David D. Wallace, *The History of South Carolina,* 4 vols. (New York: American Historical Society, 1934), 1:96. For clerical libraries, see Bowes, *Culture of Early Charleston,* p. 57.

96. South Carolina Department. of Archives and History, Columbia, Recorded Instruments, Inventories of Estates, 1736–1776, Records of the Secretary of State, 73: 101–3.

97. Edgar, "Libraries of Colonial South Carolina," p. 20. For Mackenzie's collection see also below, chap. 5.

98. How books were purchased for the Izards' impressive library is, however, largely a matter of conjecture; Robert F. Neville and Katherine H. Bielsky, "The Izard Library," *SCHM* 91 (1990): 164–65. Further discussion of private libraries, in relation to the fuller history of the Library Society, is given below, chaps. 10, 11, and 14.

99. *SCG,* 8, 15 Dec. 1737. I am grateful to John Wilson for this reference.

100. *SCG,* 27 June 1748; Cohen, *South Carolina Gazette,* p. 133 (and cf. further advertisements, pp. 121–56); Winton, "Colonial South Carolina Book Trade," p. 75.

101. *SCG,* 22 March 1735. I am grateful to Ted Pearson for this reference.

102. Cited in Cohen, *South Carolina Gazette,* p. 124.

Notes to Chapter 3

1. The rules were then published in the *SCG,* 23 Apr. 1750, together with a list of members.

2. The basic details are given by Virginia Rugheimer and Guy A. Cardwell, Jr., "The Charleston Library Society," *South Atlantic Bulletin* 8, no. 2 (Oct. 1942): 4–5; but an earlier, fuller account is also given in the preface to the printed Library Society *Catalogue* of 1826.

3. The Samuel and Joseph Wragg listed were the sons of Joseph Wragg (d. 1751) the wealthy merchant, slave trader, and assemblyman, even though he is listed as a member of the library in his entry in Walter B. Edgar and N. Louise Bailey, eds., *The Commons House of Assembly 1692–1775*, vol. 2 of *Biographical Directory of the South Carolina House of Representatives* (Columbia: University of South Carolina Press, 1977), p. 728.

4. James L. Petigru, *Oration delivered before the Charleston Library Society at its First Centennial Anniversary June 13, 1848* (Charleston, 1848); and a full list with professions is reproduced in Anne King Gregorie, "The First Decade of the Charleston Library Society," *Proceedings of the South Carolina Historical Association* 5 (1935): 5–6. William Fleming, founder member and Scottish merchant of Georgetown, S.C., also in Philip M. Hamer, et al., eds. *The Papers of Henry Laurens* (hereafter *PHL*), 13 vols. (Columbia: University of South Carolina Press, 1968–), 1:54.

5. E. Haviland Hillman, "The Brisbanes," *SCHM* 14 (1913): 115–33.

6. *Rules and By-Laws,* 1762, p. 22.

7. CLS journal book, 1759–1780 and 1783–1790 (hereafter J), records membership elections, and various computations have been based upon this source, such as those by Richard Waterhouse, *A New World Gentry: The Making of a Merchant and Planter Class in South Carolina, 1670–1770* (New York and London: Garland, 1989), pp. 94–95, but, as is explained below, it is not clear that the record in this matter is comprehensive.

8. A clue about the disappearance of these pre-1758 records is provided by a minute of the AM of Jan. 1762 (J, fol. 29), when members resolved to ask John Butler, who even more significantly had been secretary for a year in 1759, "to endeavour to recover the Journals and Papers belonging to the Society." The general meetings, held each quarter, are more usually described as quarterly meetings after 1 Apr. 1761 (J, fol. 23); the abbreviation QM is therefore adopted below for all general meetings except for the first of the year, the anniversary (formerly "annual") meetings (AM).

9. Owing to the loss of the journal before 1758, it is not clear when Garden was first elected a country member (or indeed whether he was at first a full member and then asked to be translated into a country member at Goose Creek), but this must have been after 1750 (the date of the *Gazette* newspaper advertisement).

10. Jeanne A. Calhoun et al., "The Geographic Spread of Charleston's Mercantile Community, 1732–1767," *SCHM* 86 (1985): 186.

11. Arthur Mazyck, preface to the *Catalogue of the Charleston Library Society 1876,* reproduced in *SCHM* 23 (1922): 169; Edmund Berkeley and Dorothy Smith Berkeley, *Dr. Alexander Garden of Charles Town* (Chapel Hill: University of North Carolina Press, 1969), p. 72.

12. As given, from *SCG* advertisements, in Calhoun et al., "Geographic Spread of Charleston's Mercantile Community," pp. 197–203.

13. "Records Kept by Colonel Isaac Hayne," *SCHM* 10 (1909): 170; *PHL* 3:282; *Charleston Directory* 1790; *Supplement to the State Gazette,* 18 Nov. 1784.

14. *SCG,* 2, 9 Nov. 1767.

15. *SCG,* 29 Oct. 1764; 30 Apr. 1772.

16. For Wells's career see David Moltke-Hansen, "The Empire of Scotsman Robert Wells, Loyalist South Carolina Printer-Publisher," M.A. thesis, University of South Carolina, 1984; and Christopher Gould, "Robert Wells, Colonial Charleston Printer," *SCHM* 79 (1978): 23–49.

17. Thomas, *History of Printing in America,* 1:344.

18. For the full sentence, see below, p. 42. His 1762 edition had been correct.

19. Verso of a Wells publication, 1771, cited in Winton, "Colonial South Carolina Book Trade," p. 81.

20. Robert M. Weir, "The Role of the Newspaper Press in the Southern Colonies on the Eve of the Revolution: An Interpretation," in Bernard Bailyn and John Hench, eds., *The Press and the American Revolution* (Worcester, Mass.: American Antiquarian Society, 1980), p. 104.

21. "The Sale of Negroes belonging to Mr John Miles," printed 3 Feb. 1768, Charleston; American Antiquarian Society (hereafter AAS) Broadsides 1768, also no. 2964 in Roger P. Bristol, *Supplement to Charles Evans' American Bibliography* (Charlottesville, Va.: Bibliographical Society of America and Bibliographical Society of Virginia, 1970), hereafter cited as Bristol.

22. Library Company of Philadelphia, Articles of Association, Philadelphia, 1 July 1731, with illustration given in Wolf et al., *"At the Instance of Benjamin Franklin,"* pp. 5–6; Articles of the Subscription Roll of the New York Library, 1754 [2 April 1754] reprinted in *The New York Society Library: History, Charter and By-Laws* (New York: New York Society Library, 1985), p. 11.

23. *Rules and By-Laws,* 1762, pp. iii–iv.

24. Samuel Purchas, "A Discourse of the Diversity of Letters . . . ," in *Hakluytus Posthumus, or Purchas His Pilgrimes,* 20 vols. (Glasgow: James MacLehose and Sons, 1905), 1:486. Cf. Stephen Greenblatt, *Marvelous Possessions: The Wonder of the New World* (Oxford: Clarendon Press, 1991), pp. 10–11.

25. Cf. the notion of the "bible transaction" in Leslie Howsam, *Cheap Bibles: Nineteenth-Century Publishing and the British and Foreign Bible Society* (Cambridge: Cambridge University Press, 1991), pp. 2–3.

26. The bookplates are reproduced and discussed in more detail in James Raven, "The Representation of Philanthropy and Reading in the Eighteenth-Century Library," in *Libraries and Culture* 31, no. 2 (Spring 1996): 492–510.

27. *Rules and By-Laws,* 1762, p. iv.

28. Rev. Charles Woodmason, cit., Richard Hofstadter, *Anti-Intellectualism in American Life* (New York: Jonathan Cape, 1963), p. 75.

29. I am grateful to Catherine Sadler and Patricia Glass Bennett for allowing me to consult letters to the Library Society from David Heisser (the Citadel, Charleston) and Eric-Christopher (fine art designer), regarding the design of the seal.

30. Wolf, "At the Instance of Benjamin Franklin," p. 5.
31. Alexander Keith commonplace book, South Caroliniana Library, University of South Carolina, Columbia. Keith then copied remarks from Daniel Waterland's *Advice to a Young Student*, given in Edgar, "Libraries of Colonial South Carolina," pp. 176–79. Here, and below, I have modernized the spelling of Winyaw to "Winyah."
32. *Rules and By-Laws*, 1748 advertisement and 1750, rule 11; 1762, rule 24.
33. *SCG*, 23 Apr. 1750: CLS committee minute book, 1759–1780 and 1785–1791 (hereafter C), pp. 16–17; *SCG*, 21 Jan. 1772; Berkeley and Berkeley, *Dr. Alexander Garden*, pp. 241–43; J. H. Easterby, *A History of the College of Charleston Founded 1770* (Charleston: Scribner Press, 1935), pp. 13, 20.
34. Rogers, *Charleston in the Age of the Pinckneys*, pp. 22–23.
35. [Edmund Gibson], *Two Letters of the Lord Bishop of London* (London, 1727), pp. 12–13.
36. Ordered by the library in 1771 (see below, letter 27).
37. Notably, *London Magazine*, July 1746, pp. 325–26.
38. Including *Charleston, July 24th, 1769. To be sold, on Thursday the third day of August next: a cargo of ninety-four prime, healthy Negroes . . . by David and John Deas* (Charleston, 1769).
39. Cited in Harvey H. Jackson, "Hugh Bryan and the Evangelical Movement in Colonial South Carolina," *William and Mary Quarterly* 43 (1986): 610.
40. *SCG*, 22 Mar. 1734/5. The epithet "mulatto" came to be widely applied in Britain for returning Creoles with great fortunes, many accused of dissipated lifestyles. See Ivor Waters, *The Unfortunate Valentine Morris* (Chepstow, Monmouthshire: Chepstow Society, 1964); and James Raven, *Judging New Wealth: Popular Publishing and Responses to Commerce in England, 1750–1800* (Oxford: Oxford University Press, 1992).
41. See below, between letters 14 and 15; and Edgar C. Reinke, "A Classical Debate of the Charleston, South Carolina, Library Society," *Papers of the Bibliographical Society of America* 61 (1967): 83–99.
42. Laurens to John Rose, 28 Dec. 1771, *PHL* 8:141.
43. Examples discussed below are given further attention in Raven, "Representation of Philanthropy and Reading."
44. It remained the great model. Near the close of the century "Philonaus" proposed the setting up of the Baltimore Library Company (founded 1795) "similar to the Philadelphia Library Company," *Baltimore Daily Repository*, 29 Jan. 1793.
45. Alston, "Library History Database."
46. Examples are given in Raven, "From Promotion to Proscription."
47. *SCG*, 3 Mar. 1757 (sale of Rutledge library by Wells); Davis, *Intellectual Life in the Colonial South*, 2:570, 573–74, 576; Edgar, "Libraries of Colonial South Carolina," pp. 220–23.
48. P[ierce] Tempest, *Iconologia: Or, Moral Emblems, by Caesar Ripa* (London, 1709), p. [i]. This was the first English translation of this much reprinted (and redrawn) collection, published at Rome in 1593, and with figures, in 1603. The next English edition, by George Richardson, was printed in 1779.

49. Further discussed in Raven, "Representation of Philanthropy and Reading."
50. Cited in Steven C. Bullock, *Revolutionary Brotherhood: Freemasonry and the Transformation of the American Social Order, 1730–1840* (Chapel Hill and London: University of North Carolina, 1996), p. 68.
51. As claimed by Sirmans, *Colonial South Carolina*, p. 230. Later advertisements, such as that in the *City Gazette and Daily Advertiser*, 11 Feb. 1790, suggest the society's continuing health. Cf. J. H. Easterby, *History of the St. Andrew's Society of Charleston, 1729–1929* (Charleston: Walker, Evans and Cogswell, 1929).
52. *SCG,* 25 Oct. 1770. See also Ellen Heyward Jervey, "Items from a South Carolina Almanac," *SCHM* 32 (1931): 73–80. See also Arthur Mitchell, *The History of the Hibernian Society of Charleston, South Carolina, 1799–1981* (Charleston: Hibernian Society, [1985]); and George J. Gongaware, *The History of the German Friendly Society of Charleston, South Carolina, 1766–1916* (Richmond, Va.: Garett and Massie, 1935), p. 11.
53. Gongaware, *History of the German Friendly Society*, p. 11.
54. *SCG,* 5 Dec. 1754, 9 Jan. 1755; and brief note in Albert Gallatin Mackey, *The History of Freemasonry,* 7 vols. (New York: Masonic History Co., 1898–1906), 5:1230.
55. Joseph Ioor Waring, *A History of Medicine in South Carolina, 1670–1825* (Columbia: South Carolina Medical Association, 1964), p. 255.
56. *SCG,* 26 Mar. 1741; 3 Apr. 1742. The Charleston Lodge apparently dissolved between 1742 and 1752; see Bullock, *Revolutionary Brotherhood,* p. 76.
57. Easterby, *History of the St. Andrew's Society,* p. 20.
58. Waring, *A History of Medicine,* appendix.
59. Cynthia B. Wiggin, *Salem Athenaeum: A Short History* (Salem, Mass.: Forest River, 1971); Salem Athenaeum Records, PEM.
60. Robert D. Winans, *A Descriptive Checklist of Book Catalogues Separately Printed in America 1693–1800* (Worcester, Mass.: American Antiquarian Society, 1981), no. 65, held at the New York Public Library (hereafter NYPL), New York.
61. Shields, *Civil Tongues and Polite Letters,* p. xvi.
62. Erskine Clarke, *Our Southern Zion: A History of Calvinism in the South Carolina Low Country, 1690–1990* (Tuscaloosa: University of Alabama Press, 1996), p. 47.
63. See James C. Scott, *Domination and the Arts of Resistance: Hidden Transcripts* (New Haven and London: Yale University Press), esp. chap. 3, "The Public Transcript as Respectable Performance."
64. See Shields, *Civil Tongues and Polite Letters,* pp. xvii–xviii, with particular emphasis upon Shaftesbury's contemporary cultural analysis. Cf. Lawrence E. Klein, *Shaftesbury and the Culture of Politeness: Moral Discourse and Cultural Politics in Early Eighteenth-Century England* (Cambridge: Cambridge University Press, 1994).
65. See Bullock, *Revolutionary Brotherhood,* esp. pp. 26–29.

Notes to Chapter 4

1. QM, 4 Apr. 1759, J, fols. 3–9; QM, 3 Oct. 1759, J, fol. 13; AM, 27 Jan. 1761, J, fol. 21 (with copy, fols. 21–23); *Rules and By-Laws,* 1762. Individual rule clarifications

and revisions were approved July 1771, J, fol. 134; Oct. 1771, J, fol. 138; Jan. 1772, J, fols. 139–40; Oct. 1772, J, fol. 147; July 1777, J, fol. 180; with more major corrections to wording and updating, Oct. 1783, J, fols. 198–99.

2. QM, Oct. 1769, J, fols. 103–14, and printed as a preface (with the historical "Advertisement" of 1760) to the *Rules and By-Laws,* 1770 (known as the "Third Edition").

3. *Rules and By-Laws,* 1750, rules 2 and 3, after a rule declaring the title of the society; 1762, rules 1 and 2.

4. *Rules and By-Laws,* 1748 advertisement and 1750, rule 22; 1762, rule 33.

5. Virginia Rugheimer, "Charleston Library Society," *Southeastern Librarian* 5 (1955): 137.

6. *Rules and By-Laws,* 1762, rule 6; 1770, rule 8. In fact, in a revision to the rules approved at the QM, Apr. 1765, the summer hours were agreed to be from 4 to 7 PM (J, fol. 55), but this was changed to 6 PM in the 1769 revision (J, fol. 105) to be printed in 1770.

7. *Rules and By-Laws,* 1785, rule 8; manuscript annotation on AAS copy of 1785 *Rules and By-Laws* indicates the change; *Rules and By-Laws,* rule 7.

8. *Rules and By-Laws,* 1762, rule 6.

9. See Berkeley and Berkeley, *Dr. Alexander Garden,* pp. 235–37.

10. By-Laws, prefacing *Catalogue of the Books, &c Belonging to the Library Company of Baltimore* (1797).

11. QM, Apr. 1762, J, fol. 31.

12. QM, July 1775, J, fol. 169.

13. AM, Jan. 1768, J, fol. 87.

14. *Rules and By-Laws,* 1770, rule 13 (strengthening rule 11 of 1762).

15. *Rules and By-Laws,* 1762, rule 18; *Rules and By-Laws,* 1770, rule 20. See also below, chap. 5.

16. Including *SCG,* 6, 13, 22, 29 Jan.; 3, 19, 26 Feb.; 3, 18 Mar.; 1, 8 Apr. 1756 (for titles see asterisked entries in appendix 3 below); Gregorie, "First Decade of the Charleston Library Society," p. 9.

17. Milligen-Johnston, *Short Description of the Province of South Carolina,* p. 37.

18. AM, Jan. 1763, J, fol. 34.

19. AM, Jan 1763, J, fol. 34.

20. C, fols. 33–38; J, fol. 80; and see letters below, n. 86.

21. Committee meeting of the Charleston Library Society (hereafter CM), 6 June 1767, C, fol. 40.

22. The society was inquorate for ten successive meetings between that proposed for 7 Aug. 1765 and that proposed for 12 Mar. 1767, C, fols. 59–61.

23. Rule 7, cited in Joseph I. Waring, *Excerpts from the Minute Book of the Medical Society of South Carolina from 1789 to 1820,* 2 vols. (Charleston: Nelsons Southern Printing Company, 1959), 1:2.

24. CLS, MS 29, "Financial Records," receipt book, 1770–1789, entry for 1 July 1778.

25. Brown, *Knowledge Is Power,* p. 49.

26. Cf. Barbara G. Carson, *Ambitious Appetites: Dining, Behavior, and Patterns of Consumption in Federal Washington* (Washington, D.C.: American Institute of Architects Press, 1990).

27. *SCG,* 2 Jan. 1755.

28. AM, 8 Jan. 1765, J, fol. 50.

29. *SCG,* 28 Sept. 1767.

30. *CGDA,* 18 Jan. 1804; *City Gazette* (hereafter *CG*), 19 June 1805.

31. Cf. Donald G. Davis, Jr., and John Mark Tucker, *American Library History: A Comprehensive Guide to the Literature* (Santa Barbara, Calif., and Oxford: ABC-CLIO, 1989), p. 56.

32. C, fols. 39, 48, 70, 86.

33. CM, 6 Jan. 1768, C, fol. 49, schedule of outstanding bonds; CM, 13 Jan. 1772, C, fol. 86.

34. CM, 5 Jan. 1775, C, fol. 48.

35. CM, 16 June 1773, C, fol. 91; CM, 17 June 1792, C, fol. 87.

36. CM, 6 Nov. 1771, C, fols. 84–85.

37. CM, 6 May 1767, C, fol. 40.

38. QM, 7 July 1762, J, fol. 31.

39. CM, 5 Dec. 1764, C, fol. 29.

40. QM, 6 July, Oct. 5 1774, J, fols. 163, 164.

41. W. Robert Higgins, "The South Carolina Revolutionary Debt and Its Holders, 1776–1780," *SCHM* 72 (1971): 15–29.

42. AM, 13 Jan. 1784, J, fol. 200; QM, 2 July 1788, J, fol. 222.

43. QM, 7 July 1790, J, fol. 233.

44. *SCG,* 24 July 1749, 1 Jan. 1750, 22 Jan. 1752, 1 Jan. 1754, 2 Jan. 1755.

45. *SCG,* 22 Jan. 1756.

46. Cited in *Catalogue* of 1826, p. xi.

47. QM, 3 Oct. 1764, J, fols. 45–46.

48. Extra meeting, 19 Jan. 1764, J, fol. 40. Members required, they said, the insurance of an act of the governor, council, and assembly, and royal confirmation of the act.

49. Weir, *Colonial South Carolina,* pp. 292–93.

50. CM, 2 Oct. 1764, C, fol. 26, and confirmed at QM, 3 Oct. 1764, J, fol. 45; CM, 12 Dec. 1764, C, fol. 30.

51. CM, 7 Aug. 1771, C, fol. 83.

52. Howe, ed., "Journal of Josiah Quincy," p. 447.

53. More than 1,400 houses were also consumed in the conflagration. For details and descriptions see Richard Walsh, ed., *The Writings of Christopher Gadsden, 1746–1805* (Columbia: University of South Carolina Press, 1968), p. 125; Samuel G. Stoney, ed., "The Great Fire of 1778 Seen through Contemporary Letters," *SCHM* 64 (1963): 23–26.

54. AM, 4 Jan. 1780, J, fol. 191.

55. Report to the society, cited in preface, *Catalogue* of 1826, p. v (also p. xii). Society meetings were held in different houses, including that of Peter Lesesne in Feb. and July 1783, and William Thompson, Oct. 1783, Jan. 1784, and Edward McCrady (sometimes McCredy or McCredie), meetings, April 1784 to Oct. 1787, J, fols. 194–95, 197, 200, 203–17.

56. Extra meeting, 9 Apr. 1789, J, fol. 227.

57. Extra meeting, 9 Apr. 1789; QM, 1 July 1789; extra meeting, 29 July 1789; J, fols. 227–29.

58. In 1772 the governor had also moved the meeting of the assembly from Charleston to Beaufort.

59. Carl R. Lounsbury, *From Statehouse to Courthouse: An Architectural History of South Carolina's First State House and Charleston County Court House* (Columbia: University of South Carolina Press, 2001), p. 60, and see fig. 28.

60. Sidney Walter Martin, ed., "Ebenezer Kellogg's Visit to Charleston, 1817," *SCHM* 49 (1948): 12.

61. *Catalogue of the Books Belonging to the Savannah Library Society* (Savannah, 1839), rules 9 and 11 (from inaugural meeting Jan. 1809).

62. *New-York Mercury,* 21 Oct. 1754, cited in Keep, *History of the New York Society Library,* p. 157.

63. Duke University, Rare Book, Manuscript, and Special Collections Library, John Rutledge, Jr., Papers, "Journal 1788," fols. 6–7.

64. The full notice is reproduced in Albert E. Sanders and William D. Anderson, Jr., *Natural History Investigations in South Carolina from Colonial Times to the Present* (Columbia: University of South Carolina Press, 1999), p. 19.

65. W. G. Mazyck, "The Charleston Museum, Its Genesis and Development," *Year Book, City of Charleston, 1907,* pp. 13–36; Easterby, *History of the College of Charleston,* pp. 5, 110.

66. QM, July 1773, J, fol. 152.

67. QM, July 1773, J, fol. 153.

68. QM, Oct. 1773, J, fol. 154.

Notes to Chapter 5

1. Waterhouse, *New World Gentry,* p. 187; Jack P. Greene *The Quest for Power: The Lower Houses of Assembly in the Southern Royal Colonies, 1689–1763* (Chapel Hill: University of North Carolina Press, 1963), pp. 475–88.

2. Waterhouse, *New World Gentry,* pp. 94–95 (indicating that only 39 men were admitted to library membership between 1761 and 1770).

3. Shecut, *Shecut's Medical and Philosophical Essays,* p. 41. The first surviving indication of numbers attending a general meeting from the early nineteenth century is the 143 names of members recorded at the QM, 15 Mar. 1815, CLS journal, 1815–1841.

4. Stella H. Sutherland, *Population Distribution in Colonial America* (New York: AMS Press, 1966); and *Census for 1820* (Washington, D.C.: Gales and Seaton, 1820), p. [105].

5. *A Catalogue of the Books, &c Belonging to the Library Company of Baltimore to which are prefixed, the Bye-Laws of the Company and an Alphabetical List of the Members* (Baltimore, 1797), listing 207 members (but one given as deceased) and 20 members elect; Stuart C. Sherman, "The Library Company of Baltimore, 1795–1854," *Maryland Historical Magazine* 39 (1944): 6–24.

6. Sherman, "Library Company of Baltimore," p. 16.

7. Preface, *Catalogue of the Books Belonging to the Savannah Library Society: Instituted in the Year 1809 and Re-organized in the Year 1838* (Savannah: Thomas Purse, 1839).

8. "Josiah Smith's Diary, 1780–1781," *SCHM* 34 (1933): 78–83, 194–95, 196.

9. 1748 advertisement, rule 15; *Rules and By-Laws,* 1750, rule 15; *Rules and By-Laws,* 1760, rule 22; and *Rules and By-Laws,* 1770, rule 24.

10. I owe this point to Catherine Sadler, current librarian of the Library Society, who has traced the way in which a more formalized nineteenth-century restriction of one membership per household effectively excluded female membership.

11. QM, Apr. 1778, J, fol. 185.

12. Wolf et al., *"At the Instance of Benjamin Franklin,"* pp. 19–20. By 1800 there were 29 women shareholders. The first woman member of the New York Society Library was recorded in 1773. Kevin J. Hayes, *A Colonial Woman's Bookshelf* (Knoxville: University of Tennessee Press, 1996), p. 12.

13. Hayes, *Colonial Woman's Bookshelf,* p. 12.

14. Elise Pinckney, ed., *The Letterbook of Eliza Lucas Pinckney 1739–1762* (Chapel Hill: University of North Carolina Press, 1972; Columbia: University of South Carolina Press, 1997). See also Harriott Horry Ravenel, *Eliza Pinckney* (New York: Charles Scribner's Sons, 1896).

15. Memo of letter to her father, Jan. 1741/2, and letter to Mary Bartlett, [1742], Pinckney, ed., *Letterbook of Eliza Lucas Pinckney,* pp. 24, 35–37.

16. Letter to Mrs Boddicott, 2 May 1740, and to Elizabeth Lamb Pinckney [1741], Pinckney, ed., *Letterbook of Eliza Lucas Pinckney,* pp. 6–8, 19.

17. Letter to Mary Bartlett, [1742], Pinckney, ed., *Letterbook of Eliza Lucas Pinckney,* pp. 47–48.

18. Letter to Mary Bartlett, c. Mar.–Apr. 1742, Pinckney, ed., *Letterbook of Eliza Lucas Pinckney,* pp. 32–33.

19. Letter to Lady Carew, [1754], Pinckney, ed., *Letterbook of Eliza Lucas Pinckney,* pp. 82–83.

20. Charleston County Records, Probate Court, Inventories, 1748–1751, p. 230.

21. Weir, *Colonial South Carolina,* p. 252.

22. *SCHM* 9:86, 87, 91.

23. H. Roy Merrens, "A View of Coastal South Carolina in 1778: The Journal of Ebenezer Hazard," *SCHM* 73 (1972): 177–93.

24. Mary Stead Pinckney to Rebecca [Izard], 11 Jan. 1797, reproduced in Charles F. McCombs, ed., *Letter-Book of Mary Stead Pinckney, November 14th 1796 to August 29th 1797* (New York: Grolier Club, 1946). The account concerned was Raynal's *Histoire philosophique et politique des etablissements et du commerce des européen dans les deux Indes* (Amsterdam, 1770), bk. 5, chap. 13. The first English translation appeared in 1771.

25. CLS MSS 29, borrowing ledger, 1811–1814, entries for 26 July 1811.

26. *Rules and By-Laws,* 1762, rule 14, a refined version of original 1750, rule 6.

27. *Rules and By-Laws,* 1762, rule 22. Members were not allowed to leave shares to other members.

28. J, fol. 142. Dott died in 1775 (*SCHM* 17 [1916]: 90) and is listed as a merchant in the town. Mabel L. Webber, "Abstracts from the Records of the Court of Ordinary, 1764–1771," *SCHM* 31 (1930): 156. For the librarian contest see also below, p. 76.

29. *Rules and By-Laws,* 1762, rule 18; *Rules and By-Laws,* 1770, rule 20.

30. QM, Oct. 1777, J, fol. 182; QM, July 1778, J, fol. 186.

31. QM, Sept. 1770, J, fol. 121.

32. AM, Jan 1763, J, fol. 33.

33. AM, Jan. 1771, J, fol. 127.

34. AM, Jan 1778, J, fols. 183–84.

35. *Charleston Directory,* 1782; Henry A. M. Smith, "Charleston and Charleston Neck," *SCHM* 19 (1918): 3–76; Robert Bentham Simons, "Muster Roll of Capt. James Bentham, 1778–1780," *SCHM* 53 (1952): 167; Howe, ed., "Josiah Smith's Diary," p. 196.

36. J, fol. 15, with copy and Manigault's response, fols. 16–17. Cf. Public Record Office, Kew, London (hereafter PRO), CO 5/377, pt. 1, fol. 13, Lt. Gov. William Bull to the Board of Lords Commissioners for Trades and Plantations, 14 May 1760.

37. Kinloch Bull, Jr., *The Oligarchs in Colonial and Revolutionary Charleston: Lieutenant Governor William Bull II and His Family* (Columbia: University of South Carolina Press, 1991), p. 138.

38. Attending his first CM, 1 Aug. 1770, C, fol. 77.

39. See Mark D. Kaplanoff, "Charles Pinckney and the American Republican Tradition," in O'Brien and Moltke-Hansen, eds., *Intellectual Life in Antebellum Charleston,* pp. 85–122.

40. See Marvin R. Zahniser, *Charles Cotesworth Pinckney: Founding Father* (Chapel Hill: University of North Carolina Press, 1967).

41. See Neville and Bielsky, "The Izard Library," p. 160.

42. A native of Scotland, Davidson died in office in 1813; *SCG,* 1 July 1813.

43. Corrected from the list given, with errors, in the preface to the 1876 CLS *Catalogue.*

44. CLS MSS 29, CLS receipt books, 1758–1769, 1770–1789.

45. QM, Sept. 1770, J, fol. 121.

46. QM, Feb. 1771, J, fol. 129.

47. QM, Apr. 1772, J, fol. 142.

48. See above, chap. 4.

49. Cohen, *South Carolina Gazette,* p. 121.

50. *SCG,* 28 Oct. 1756

51. *SCG,* 24 and 31 Oct. 1761.

52. J, 21 Aug. 1771.

53. CM, 7 Aug. 1771, C, fol. 83.

54. Easterby, *History of the College of Charleston,* pp. 115, 358 n. 54.

55. Catalogue available under http://cofc.edu/MARION. The eventual return of the books to the college was reported in the *Charleston News and Courier,* 12 Mar. 1970.

56. Henry Adams, *History of the United States of America during the First Administration of Thomas Jefferson,* 9 vols. (London: G. P. Putnam's Sons, and New York: Charles Scribner's Sons, 1891–1892), 1:149.

57. Shecut, *Shecut's Medical and Philosophical Essays,* pp. 48–49.

58. Shecut, *Shecut's Medical and Philosophical Essays,* p. 47.

59. Pelatiah Webster, "Journal of a Visit to Charleston, 1765," in H. Roy Merrens, ed., *The Colonial South Carolina Scene: Contemporary Views 1697–1774* (Columbia: University of South Carolina Press, 1977), pp. 223, 224.

60. See below, letters 41, 61, 62, 64–67, 69, 81–83, 86. The Boydells always adopted the spelling "Shakspeare" for their gallery and prints.

61. A Mr. Gagne persuaded the medical society, also on the third floor of the Courthouse, to allow him to use their room next to the Library Society for an additional display of his own collection. This comprised mostly birds and was distinct from the library's own natural history and curiosity collection. Lounsbury, *From Statehouse to Courthouse,* pp. 60–63.

62. John Lambert, *Travels Through Lower Canada, and the United States of North America, in the Years 1806, 1807, and 1808,* 3 vols. (London: Richard Phillips, 1810), 2:363–65. I am grateful to Robert Leath for this reference.

63. Raymond A. Mohl, "'The Grand Fabric of Republicanism': A Scotsman Describes South Carolina 1810–1811," *SCHM* 71 (1970): 172. For other views see Alan M. Greenburg, "'A Splendid Establishment . . . Charmingly Arranged': 18th and 19th Century Observers of the Charleston Library Society," *South Carolina Librarian* 24, no. 2 (Fall 1980): 5–10.

64. Henry Lemoine, writing to the *Gentleman's Magazine,* 1797, reprinted in Henry Lemoine, *Present State of Printing and Bookselling in America [1796],* ed. Douglas C. McMurtrie (Chicago: private ed., 1929), p. 17.

65. Shecut, *Medical and Philosophical Essays,* pp. 54–55.

66. Mohl, "Grand Fabric of Republicanism," p. 172.

67. *Report of the Committee of the Charleston Library Society* (Charleston, 1853), p. 7.

68. Bridenbaugh, *Cities in Revolt;* Bowes, *Culture of Early Charleston;* Richard Waterhouse, *A New World Gentry,* p. 87.

69. Waterhouse, *New World Gentry,* p. 93.

70. Starr, *School for Politics,* p. 164.

71. Starr, *School for Politics,* esp. chap. 1; and private communication to the author.

72. Winans, *Descriptive Checklist of Book Catalogues,* no. 20, catalogue of the CLS, printed by W. Strahan for the society, 1750, held at the Library of Congress, Washington, DC.

73. The catalogue was drawn up by William Floud, to whom the CLS paid £73.10s for his troubles; CLS, "Financial Records," receipt book, 1770–1789, entry for 30 July 1770.

74. Only 185 volumes survived the fire.

75. *Catalogue of the Charleston Library Society,* 1806; *Catalogue of the Charleston Library Society,* 1826 (comment, p. vi).

76. *A Catalogue of the Books belonging to the Bristol-Library Society* (Bristol, 1790).

77. Shecut, *Shecut's Medical and Philosophical Essays,* p. 41.

78. Sherman, "Library Company of Maryland," pp. 18, 22.

79. See below, table 6.

80. CM, 3 Aug 1768, C, fol. 62.
81. Joseph Towne Wheeler, "Thomas Bray and the Maryland Parochial Libraries," *Maryland Historical Magazine* 34 (1939): 246–65; Charles T. Laugher, *Thomas Bray's Grand Design;* Anne Stokely Pratt, *Isaac Watts and his Gifts of Books to Yale College* (New Haven: Yale University Library, 1938); W. H. Bond, *Thomas Hollis of Lincoln's Inn: A Whig and his Books* (Cambridge: University Press, 1990).
82. Berkeley and Berkeley, *Dr. Alexander Garden,* pp. 124–25; Stephen Hales, *A Description of Ventilators* (London, 1743).
83. QM, Apr. 1760, J, fol. 17.
84. QM, Apr. 1768, J, fol. 89.
85. QM, July 1767, J, fols. 82, 83; QM, Oct. 1767, J, fol. 85. For the Prioleau donations, and their assumed provenance, see appendix 3 under Osterwald and Pictet.
86. Berkeley and Berkeley, *Dr. Alexander Garden,* p. 246.
87. Bernard Forest de Belidor, *Architecture hydraulique* (Paris, 1737).
88. As reported at AM, Jan. 1777, J, fol. 177; QM, Apr. 1777, J, fol. 178.
89. See below, chap. 6.
90. Gregorie, "First Decade of the Charleston Library Society," p. 7.

Notes to Chapter 6

1. AM, 10 Jan. 1764, J., fol. 38.
2. Moltke-Hansen, "Empire of Scotsman Robert Wells," pp. 1, 31.
3. See above, p. 82.
4. Zahinser, *Charles Cotesworth Pinckney,* p. 267.
5. *SCG,* 8 June 1771.
6. *SCG,* 13 Dec. 1783, 1st col.
7. Notably, Jacob Deveaux and sons at Graeme's wharf, advertising imported books, *CGDA,* 7 Mar. 1793.
8. *CGDA,* 6 May 1803; Marion R. Hemperley, "Federal Naturalization Oaths, Charleston, S.C. 1790–1860," *SCHM* 66 (1965): 183–92 (p. 185).
9. Salem Athenaeum Records, 1760–1889, MSS 56, series I, Social Library Records, box 1, vol 1, Treasurer's Book, 1761–1810, fols. 7, 11.
10. American Philosophical Society (hereafter APS), Philadelphia, Pa., Hall Papers and Hall letterbook (hereafter HP); see Robert D. Harlan, "William Strahan's American Book Trade, 1744–76," *Library Quarterly* 31 (1961): 235–44; and Harlan, "David Hall's Bookshop and Its British Sources of Supply," in David Kaser, ed., *Books in America's Past: Essays Honoring Rudolph H. Gjelsness* (Charlottesville, Va.: Bibliographical Society of the University of Virginia, 1966). For the Murray archive, see notes 9 and 25 above.
11. JMLB 10, fol. 38, Murray to James Scott, Charlestown, 29 May 1786.
12. Murray confirmed that he was happy to supply Smith. JMLB 11, fols. 57–58, Murray to Rev. Dr. Gates of Charlestown, 9 June 1792.
13. Winans, *Descriptive Checklist of Book Catalogues,* xviii, table 1; 4, no. 2.
14. Wolf, *Book Culture,* 38–39.

15. BL Add MSS 48800, fols. 113, 129, 145, 146, 149; and APS, HP.
16. Wroth, *William Parks,* p. 25.
17. Tracy W. McGregor Library, University of Virginia, Daybooks of William Hunter (1750–52) and Joseph Royle (1764–66); Stiverson and Stiverson, "Colonial Retail Book Trade," pp. 146–47, 154.
18. *Papers of Henry Laurens* 1:79–80; Manigault Papers, South Caroliniana Library, Corbett to Peter Manigault 30 May and 20 Oct. 1755, cit., Edgar, "Libraries of Colonial South Carolina," p. 52.
19. MHS, HKP 1:43, 99, 117, Longman to Knox; 1:131, Wright and Gill to Knox.
20. American Antiquarian Society, Condy Account Book, 1758–70 [hereafter CAB], fol. 57 [1761]; Botein, "Anglo-American Book Trade," p. 72.
21. Stockdale's American contacts are discussed in Stockdale, "John Stockdale of Piccadilly."
22. SPG "Proposalls," Lambeth Palace Library, Fulham Papers, xxxvi, fol. 192.
23. A few of the labels with their original lettering survive in the Library, including *Critical Review* volumes 9 and 10 for 1760 (AP.C86.1).
24. C. fol. 72.
25. Edwin Wolf II, *The Library of James Logan of Philadelphia 1674–1751* (Philadelphia, 1974); and in particular, Logan to John Whiston, 27 July 1748, copy, HSP, Logan Papers, letterbook 1748–50, fol. 5.
26. J. A. Cochrane, *Dr Johnson's Printer: The Life of William Strahan* (London: Routledge and Kegan Paul, 1964); Robert Dale Harlan, *William Strahan: Eighteenth-Century London Printer and Publisher* (Ann Arbor, Mich.: Ann Arbor Publications, 1960); O. M. Brack, Jr., "The Ledgers of William Strahan," in D. B. Smith, ed., *Editing Eighteenth-Century Texts* (Toronto: University of Toronto Press, 1968): 59–77.
27. In addition, extracts from a 1734–1747 ledger of Henry Woodfall [d. 1747], now lost, were published in the nineteenth century, and the later Henry Woodfall's accounts for 1765–1771 are also preserved; "Pope and Woodfall," and "Woodfall's Ledger, 1734–1747," *Notes and Queries* 11 (1855): 377–38, 418–20; 1765–71 Woodfall accounts, BL Add MSS 38,169.
28. William Strahan to David Hall, 1 Nov. 1753, APS, HP.
29. See above, pp. 54–55.
30. A family tree of the early Rivingtons is given in Ian Maxted, *The London Book Trades, 1775–1800: A Preliminary Checklist of Members* (Folkestone: Dawson, 1977), p. xxxv.
31. Septimus Rivington, *The Publishing Family of Rivington* (London: Rivingtons, 1919), p. 71.
32. John Nichols, *Literary Anecdotes of the Eighteenth Century,* 9 vols. (London, 1812–15, reptd. New York: Kraus, 1966), 3:400.
33. Thomas Rees and John Britton, *Reminiscences of Literary London from 1779 to 1853* (London, 1896), p. 32.
34. [Henry Dell], *The Booksellers: A Poem* (London, 1766), p. 19.
35. See Catherine Snell Crary, "The Tory and the Spy: The Double Life of James Rivington," *William and Mary Quarterly* 3rd ser. 16 (1959): 61–72.

36. Botein, "Anglo-American Book Trade," p. 68.

37. *SCG,* 14 October 1756.

38. See also below, p. 119.

39. James E. Tierney, ed., *The Correspondence of Robert Dodsley, 1733–1764* (Cambridge: Cambridge University Press, 1988), p. 24.

40. Harry M. Solomon, *The Rise of Robert Dodsley: Creating the New Age of Print* (Carbondale and Edwardsville: Southern Illinois University Press, 1996).

41. Nichols, *Literary Anecdotes,* 6:438; and E. Marston, *Sketches of Booksellers of Other Days* (London, 1901), pp. 85–86.

42. This is the most usual spelling. Some Library Society letters also spell his name as Nicholl; but elsewhere it appears as Nicol, Nichol, Nicholls, and variants.

43. *Royal South Carolina Gazette,* 11 July 1782, cit., George Smith McCowen Jr., *The British Occupation of Charleston, 1780–82* (Columbia: University of South Carolina Press, 1972), pp. 119–20.

44. CLS, "Financial Records," Receipt Books, 1770–1789, entry for 19 Oct. 1784, payment for £5.12s.6d.

45. Nichols, *Literary Anecdotes,* 3:191.

46. William Granger, *New Wonderful Museum and Entertaining Magazine,* 6:3135, cited in Belanger, "Bookseller's Directory," p. 48.

47. Further details on Edward and Charles are offered by L. H. Butterfield, "The American Interests of the Firm of E. & C. Dilly," *Papers of the Bibliographical Society of America* 45 (1951): 283–332.

48. Stockdale, "John Stockdale of Piccadilly."

49. George C. Rogers Jr., "The Charleston Tea Party: The Significance of December 3 1773," *SCHM* 75 (1974): 153–62 (p. 161).

50. South Caroliniana Library, Columbia, Manigault Family Papers, Bird, Savage and Bird to Gabriel Manigault, Feb., 23 Mar., 1785.

51. Rogers, *Evolution of a Federalist,* p. 99.

52. Rogers, *Evolution of a Federalist,* pp. 202–3, 273–75.

53. Maxted, *London Book Trades,* p. 165; Nichols, *Literary Anecdotes,* 3:649; 8:463; Catalogues, *ESTC* t030187, t113264, n030099, t090420.

54. Edwin Wolf II, "The Library of Edward Lloyd IV of Wye House," *Winterthur Portfolio* 5 (1969): 87–121. Thomas Eden and Co. traded at 2 New Court, Crutched Friars, and later at 9 Savage Gardens, Tower-hill, from at least 1783 until at least 1801 (but not by 1808), *A London Directory, or Alphabetical Arrangement* (London, 1801) and *Kent's Directory* (London, 1808).

55. Listed that year as at 15 John Street, Minories, in *A London Directory, or Alphabetical Arrangement* (London, 1797), p. 112.

56. Rogers, *Evolution of a Federalist,* pp. 274, 355 note 63.

57. Henry Curwen, *A History of Booksellers, The Old and the New* (London: Chatto and Windus, 1874), p. 75.

58. Charles Knight, *Shadows of the Old Booksellers* (London, 1865), pp. 282–99; George Paston [pseud.], *Little Memoirs of the Eighteenth Century* (London and New York,

1901), pp. 205–34; Richard G. Landon, "Small Profits Do Great Things: James Lack-ington and Eighteenth-Century Bookselling," *Studies in Eighteenth-Century Culture* 5 (1976): 387–99; and others listed in James Raven, "Selling One's Life: James Lacking-ton, Eighteenth-Century Booksellers, and the Design of Autobiography," in *Writers, Books, and Trade: An Eighteenth-Century English Miscellany for William B. Todd,* edited by O. M. Brack Jr. (New York: AMS Press, 1994): 1–23 (notes 33–35).

59. In 1827 the firm moved to 4 Pall Mall East; it variously changed partners and was finally Harding, Triphook and Lepard.

60. Knight, *Shadows of the Old Booksellers,* p. 283.

61. The British Library and Cambridge University Library hold annual catalogues, 1787–89, 1792–94, 1796–1811, 1814, and 1817–20.

62. *Second Part of Lackington's Catalogue for 1787: Consisting of About Thirty Thousand Vol-umes,* p. 1.

63. *Second Part of Lackington's Catalogue for 1787,* p. 1. Coastal ships cannot entirely account for this emphasis.

64. The phrase of Landon, "Small Profits Do Great Things," p. 387.

65. James Lackington, *Memoirs of the Forty-Five First Years of the Life of James Lackington* (London, 1791), dedicated to "sordid and malevolent booksellers"; and *The Confessions of J. Lackington, Late Bookseller, at the Temple of the Muses, in a Series of Letters to a Friend* (London, 1804).

Notes to Chapter 7

1. South Caroliniana Library, Manigault Family Papers, 5, fol. 18, Thomas Corbett to Peter Manigault, 30 May 1755.

2. Bernard Bailyn and Lotte Bailyn, *Massachusetts Shipping 1697–1714: A Statistical Study* (Cambridge, Mass.: Harvard University Press, 1959), pp. 56–57.

3. JMLB 3, Murray to Robert Miller of Williamsburg, 17 Aug. 1772.

4. JMLB 4, Murray to Robert Miller of Williamsburg, 5 Dec. 1773.

5. See below, CLS letters, n. 4.

6. Weir, "Role of the Newspaper Press in the Southern Colonies," pp. 123–24, 141.

7. JMLB 4, Murray to Robert Miller of Williamsburg, 24 May 1773.

8. MHS, HKP 5:237, Longman to Knox, 18 Jan. 1772. Convenient deaths, perhaps, on a long, poorly victualed voyage.

9. The quality of the original manuscript sent to Strahan must have accounted at least in part for the numerous blunders in the 1750 printed *Catalogue,* including, for example, Richard Hayes (*Negotiator's Magazine*) printed as Heyer; Humphrey Bland (*Treatise of Military Discipline*) printed as Blood; Robert Molesworth (*Account of Denmark*) printed as Snellgrove; and Sir Robert Hooke (*Philosophical Experiments*) printed as Hawke; see below, appendix 3.

10. Cited in Edwin Wolf II, "The Library of Edward Lloyd IV of Wye House," *Winterthur Portfolio* 5 (1969), p. 92.

11. CM, 3 July 1764, C, fols. 21–23; the dispute is further discussed in Reinke, "Classical Debate."

12. JMLB 4, Murray to Miller, 1 July 1773 (Murray often used Bennet and Hake of Rotterdam); JMLB 4, Murray to Miller, 5 Dec. 1773.

13. JMLB 11, Murray to Rev. Dr. T. Gates, Charlestown 4 July 1791.

14. Roy Stokes, ed., *Esdaile's Manual of Bibliography* (London: George Allen and Unwin, 1967), p. 159.

15. Elizabeth Carroll Reilly, "Common and Learned Readers: Shared and Separate Spheres in Mid-Eighteenth-Century New England," Ph.D. dissertation, Boston University, 1994, appendix A4.

16. Harlan, "David Hall's Bookshop," p. 240.

17. *SCG,* 28 Dec. 1769.

18. *St. James's Chronicle,* 6 July 1790. I am grateful to Antonia Forster for this reference.

19. Discussed by the committee, C, fols. 4, 10.

20. John Murray Archives, John Murray I Account Ledger, 1768–80 (hereafter JMAL), fol. 49.

21. A table of bankrupts in the London book trades, 1772–1805, is given in Ian Maxted, *London Book Trades, 1775–1800: A Preliminary Checklist of Members* (Folkestone, Kent: Dawson, 1977), p. xxxiii.

Notes to Chapter 8

1. Vincent Kinane, "'Literary Food' for the American Market: Patrick Byrne's Exports to Mathew Carey," *Proceedings of the American Antiquarian Society* 104 (1995), p. 320.

2. Harlan, "David Hall's Bookshop," p. 13.

3. NYSL Archives, NYSL first minutes book, fol. 25.

4. C, fols. 39, 48, 70, 86; see above, chap. 4.

5. Katherine Swift, "Bibliotheca Sunderlandiana: The Making of an Eighteenth-Century Library," in Robin Myers and Michael Harris, eds., *Bibliophily* (Cambridge and Alexandria, Va.: Chadwyck-Healey, 1986), pp. 69, 78, 79.

6. APS, HP, Hall to Strahan, 27 Sept. 1750, 7 Oct. 1755.

7. APS, HP, Strahan to Hall, 3 Mar. 1755.

8. APS, HP, Strahan to Hall, 11 July 1758; cited in Harlan, "David Hall's Bookshop," p. 241.

9. APS, HP, Strahan to Hall, 11 July 1758; J. A. Cochrane, *Dr Johnson's Printer: The Life of William Strahan* (London: Routledge and Kegan Paul, 1964), p. 84. Strahan had, after all, predicted this; Strahan to Hall, 3 Mar. 1755; cited in Cochrane, *Dr Johnson's Printer,* p. 81.

10. Of various examples, JMDB 4, fol. 409 (27 Nov. 1773); JMAL, fol. 170 (6 June 1774, 7 July 1774, 16 Feb. 1775), and invoice copy, JMDB 4, fols. 295–96.

11. Jeremiah Condy to William Browne, Esq., of Salem, Boston, 21 Apr. 1768, PEM, MS 56, series I, Social Library Records, box 2, folder 2, "Shareholders and Correspondence."

12. MHS, HKP 5:237, Longman to Knox, 18 Jan. 1772.

13. MHS, HKP 5:244, Longman to Knox, 21 July 1773.

14. Botein, "Anglo-American Book Trade," pp. 20, 27.

15. Robert D. Harlan, "William Strahan's American Book Trade, 1744–76," *Library Quarterly* 31 (1961): 238.

16. Harlan, "William Strahan's American Book Trade, 1744–76," pp. 243–44.

17. MHS, HKP 1:104, Wright and Gill to Knox, 24 Mar. 1774.

18. Extraordinary negotiations were involved for what was to be settlement of a 30–year debt; relevant letters include HKP 18:158; 20:26, 99; 23:158; 26:71, 144; 27:138; 28;166; 34:65, 173; 35:57.

19. MHS, Suffolk Court Files, no. 89428, and Records of Superior Court of Judicature, 30:210; see John E. Alden, "John Mein, Publisher: An Essay in Bibliographical Detection," *Papers of the Bibliographical Society of America* 36 (1942): 199–214.

20. JMLB 10, fol. 35, Murray to Rev. Mr. Maddison, president of the College of William and Mary, Virginia, 29 May 1786.

21. CM, 7 Nov., 10 Dec. 1759, C, fols. 10–12; letter 7.

22. That is, "a colonial exchange transaction consisted of paying some premium in colonial currency for the delivery of a certain sum in the metropolis or vice versa. Thus colonial rates of exchange were usually expressed as a percentage of colonial currency"; John J. McCusker, *Money and Exchange in Europe and America, 1600–1775: A Handbook* (Chapel Hill: University of North Carolina Press, 1978), p. 18.

23. Curtis P. Nettels, *The Money Supply of the American Colonies before 1720,* rept. ed. (Madison, Wisc.: Curtis Putnam, 1934; reprint, New York: Sentry Press, 1964), pp. 12, 168–70, 185.

24. For failure to solve the colonial monetary problem, see Leslie V. Brock, *The Currency of the American Colonies 1700–1764: A Study in Colonial Finance and Imperial Relations* (New York: Arno Press, 1975).

25. Nettels, *Money Supply of the American Colonies,* pp. 250–51.

26. William Douglass, *A Discourse Concerning the Currencies of the British Plantations in America* (Boston, 1740).

27. McCusker, *Money and Exchange in Europe and America,* p. 220.

28. See McCusker, *Money and Exchange in Europe and America,* p. 20.

29. In 1703 Thomas [John] Hill's popular *Young Secretary's Guide* was republished in Boston (it reached a 27th edition in London in 1764).

30. Francis G. Clarke, *The American Ship-Master's Guide and Commercial Assistant* (Boston: Allen, 1850).

31. British Library (hereafter BL), Add. MS 4304, Thomas Dale to Thomas Birch, 6 June 1736.

32. *PHL* 1:9 n. 6.

33. *PHL* 1:184 n. 7.

34. A plan of the Exchange, showing the Carolina walk in the southwest corner, was included in the *London Directory or Alphabetical Arrangement* (as surviving, for example, in a copy of the 1797 edition in the Bodleian Library, Oxford). See also Perry Gauci, "The City as Exchange: Merchant Culture 1660–1720," *Centre for Metropolitan History: Annual Report 1997–8* (London: University of London, Institute of Historical Research 1999), pp. 60–65.

35. Bryant Lillywhite, *London Coffee Houses: A Reference Book of Coffee Houses of the Seventeenth, Eighteenth and Nineteenth Centuries* (London, 1963), no. 223 (pp. 147–49). Occasional reference in Carolina letters home is also made to a "Carolina coffee house" in Chancery Lane, although Lillywhite is silent on this.
36. Rogers, *Evolution of a Federalist,* pp. 71, 81, 89–90.
37. A. H. John, "The London Assurance Company and the Marine Insurance Market of the Eighteenth Cetury," *Economica,* n.s., 25 (1958): 129. The form of marine insurances was not confirmed by statute until 1795.
38. PRO, CO 5/511, South Carolina Shipping Returns, "1746–65" (actually 1764–1767), manifests of cargoes, nos. 3, 13, 24. Manifest no. 13 lists 7 cargoes, largely indigo and rice in great bulk, all to Sarah Nicholson.
39. See Rogers, *Evolution of a Federalist,* pp. 250–53.
40. The Forrests seem to have been a long-established and highly reputable firm with a network that might also have influenced this purchase; see n. 220 to letter 27.
41. Duke University, Rare Book, Manuscript, and Special Collections Library, Charles Cotesworth Pinckney Papers, bills and receipts, 1788–1819.
42. *Letter-Book of Samuel Sewall,* 1:237–38, Sewall to John Love, 10 June 1700.
43. *Morning Chronicle and London Advertiser,* 12 Oct. 1784.
44. McCusker, *Money and Exchange in Europe and America,* p. 221.
45. Among many early examples, *Letter-Book of Samuel Sewall,* 1:300, Samuel Sewall to Sir William Ashhurst, 21 July 1704.
46. John, "London Assurance Company."
47. Gary M. Walton and James F. Shepherd, *The Economic Rise of Early America* (Cambridge: Cambridge University Press, 1979), pp. 89–90.
48. JMLB 3 and 4 (various entries) and JMDB, fol. 384 [July 1773]; MHS, HKP, vol. 48 (invoices from Thomas Longman).
49. NYSL Archives, NYSL first minute book, 1754–1772, fol. 29, 27 Mar. 1758 (order arrives); invoice copy (27 Sept. 1757), fol. 30.
50. Colcock to Nicoll, 10 Aug. 1774, letter 31 below.
51. AAS CAB, fol. 57, 29 Oct. 1762.
52. AAS CAB, fol. 57.
53. AAS CAB, fol. 108, April 1764. The distinguished stationery firm of Wright and Gill was also the main supplier of Henry Knox.

Notes to Chapter 9

1. The annotations to the letters below detail many of the syndicates owning the ships.
2. *Letter-Book of Samuel Sewall,* 1:248, Sewall to John Ive, 20 Dec. 1700.
3. JMLB 11, Murray to Rev. Dr. T. Gates, Charlestown, 4 July 1791.
4. As discussed above, chap. 1.
5. Harlan, "David Hall's Bookshop," p. 240.
6. See above, pp. 31–32.
7. *CGDA,* 6 and 10 June 1807.
8. JMLB 4, Murray to Miller, 5 Dec. 1773.

9. *CGDA,* 22 Sept. 1803.

10. Among the absences are failures to record the ship's name (and hence arrival time) against shipment of the order sent 1 Nov. 1794 and acknowledged with invoice 8 Apr. 1795 (letters 66, 69); but in most cases where reconstruction has not been possible the cause is the loss of newspapers and records of shipping of relevant weeks and months.

11. *CGDA,* 6 June 1807.

12. *CGDA,* 1 Sept. 1806.

13. Kinane, "Literary Food," p. 320.

14. Steele, *English Atlantic,* pp. 299, 301, tables 4.9, 4.13.

15. *CGDA,* 22 May and 24 Apr. 1802.

16. *New York Gazette,* 3 Sept. 1764.

17. A contemporary description of colonial entering is given in Barrow, *Trade and Empire,* p. 265, appendix B.

18. JMLB 1, fols. 57–58, Murray to Rev. Dr. Gates, Charlestown, 9 June 1792.

19. Shephard, *Shipping, Maritime Trade,* pp. 87–88. The increased efficiency of port-side procedure and inventory times was especially noted in the Chesapeake.

20. Butterfield, "American Interests of the Firm of E. and C. Dilly," 290; Stockdale, "John Stockdale of Piccadilly."

21. JMDB 4, fol. 384, record of invoice, 1 July 1773. For location, see plate 5 above.

22. BL, Add. MS 4304, Thomas Dale to Thomas Birch, 20 Oct. 1735.

23. MHS, Usher letter book, Usher to Ive, 2 July 1675; Ford, *Boston Book Market,* p. 8 n. 2. Contrary to orders, the Bibles were also bound in the Netherlands.

24. Byrd to Mr. Spencer, 28 May 1729, cited in Marion Tinling, ed., *The Correspondence of the Three William Byrds of Westover, Virginia 1684–1776,* 2 vols. (Charlottesville: University Press of Virginia, 1977), 1:400.

25. Robert Ryce to John Winthrop, 17 Jan. 1637, *Winthrop Papers,* 6 vols. (Boston: MHS, 1929–1992), 3:346.

26. Matthew Poole, *Synopsis criticorum aliorumque s. scripturae interpretum* (London 1669–1676); Logan to J. [William] Reading, 12 May 1729, Logan letterbook 3:232–35, HSP, cited in Wolf, "James Logan's Correspondence," p. 217.

27. Berkeley and Berkeley, *Dr. Alexander Garden,* pp. 91–92, 127.

28. British prize acts were passed in 1708 and 1739.

29. *SCG,* 27 Jan. 1759.

30. Essex Institute, Condy to Stephen Higginson, London, 5 Nov. 1760, and invoice, 19 Dec. 1760, reprinted in Harriet Silvester Tapley, *Salem Imprints 1768–1825: A History of the First Fifty Years of Printing in Salem, Massachusetts* (Salem, Mass.: Essex Institute, 1927), p. 229; AAS CAB, opposite fol. 57; PRO, CO 5/851, fols. 66, 66v, William Rhodes, *St. Christopher,* frigate, arrived at Boston, 18 Mar. 1761, 180 tons, 8 guns, 22 men; Richard Newton, *Hawk,* snow, 120 tons, 10 guns, 12 men, arrived at Boston, 13 Mar. 1761; William Vernon, ship *King of Prussia,* arrived at Boston, 12 Jan. 1761, 145 tons, 10 guns, 14 men.

31. AAS CAB, 3 July 1762, order in HMS *Launceston,* Edmund Afflich, commander.

32. Hamer, et al., eds. *Papers of Henry Laurens,* 2:448–49, Laurens to Thos Frankland, 11 Feb. 1757; *SCG,* 18–25 Aug. 1758.

33. *SCG,* 10–14 June 1760.
34. *SCG,* 1–8 Nov., 30 Dec. 1760.
35. *SCG,* 16 Dec. 1760.
36. Berkeley and Berkeley, *Dr. Alexander Garden,* pp. 163–64.
37. PRO, ADM 1/1608, petition to Governor Bull, 18 June 1761.
38. HMS *Dolphin,* Capt. Benjamin Marlowe, 24 guns; P. C. Coker, *Charleston's Maritime Heritage* (Charleston: Cokercraft, 1987), p. 296.
39. *SCG,* 10 Oct. 1761.
40. See below, letter 9 and n. 48.

Notes to Chapter 10

1. Of the very few records of individual book purchase requests is the attribution to Miles Brewton of the (successful) proposal to buy Catesby's *Natural History of Carolina* at the QM of July 1769, J, fol. 101.
2. Edwin Wolf II, *Book Culture of a Colonial American City: Philadelphia Books, Bookmen, and Booksellers* (Oxford: Clarendon Press, 1988), pp. 31–32.
3. See below, p. 186.
4. As, for example, in *SCG,* 24 Apr. 1755 and 1 July 1756.
5. For these and later examples, see Winans, *Descriptive Checklist of Book Catalogues.*
6. J, fol. 118, 4 Apr. 1770.
7. Davis, *Intellectual Life,* 2:595; and cf. Richard Beale Davis, *A Colonial Southern Bookshelf: Reading in the Eighteenth Century* (Athens: University of Georgia Press, 1979).
8. Edgar, "Libraries of Colonial South Carolina," with his classification scheme on p. 22.
9. Lambeth Palace Library, SPG Papers, x, fols. 247–48, "The Missionaries Library," 15 Mar. 1705; fol. 264, list of books for missionary library, n.d. (before 1710); Laugher, *Thomas Bray's Grand Design,* p. 38.
10. *SCG,* 30 Aug. 1740.
11. *The New Pilgrim's Progress: or, the Pious Indian Convert* (London, 1748), pp. 93–94, cited in Edgar, "Libraries of Colonial South Carolina," p. 29.
12. *SCG,* 15 Jan. 1754.
13. *SCG,* 6, 13, 22, 29 Jan., 3, 19, 26 Feb., 3, 18 Mar., 1, 8 Apr. 1756.
14. Attributed to Mrs. Scott and published in 1750; James Raven, *British Fiction 1750–1770: A Chronological Check-List of Prose Fiction Printed in Britain and Ireland* (Newark, London, and Toronto: Associated University Presses, 1987), entries 38 and 39.
15. Cited in Wolf, *Book Culture,* p. 131.
16. For this section I am most grateful for the advice of Kathryn Preyer.
17. Its use in the colonial context is discussed in Susan Lethwaite, "The Pre-Trial Examination in Upper Canada," in Greg T. Smith et al., eds., *Criminal Justice in the Old World and the New: Essays in Honour of J. M. Beattie* (Toronto: Centre for Criminology, University of Toronto, 1998), pp. 85–103.
18. Edgar, "Libraries of Colonial South Carolina," pp. 29, 104.
19. Edgar, "Libraries of Colonial South Carolina," p. 38.
20. *SCG,* 30 May 1771.

21. The text has also been the center of debate; see Samuel E. Thorne, trans. and ed., *Bracton on the Laws and Customs of England,* 5 vols. (Cambridge, Mass.: Belknap Press, 1968).

22. W. Harold Maxwell, comp., *A Bibliography of English Law to 1650,* vol. 1 (London: Sweet and Maxwell, 1925), sect. 1, no. 24.

23. For a comparative brief survey of the availability of Locke in Pennsylvania (with the conviction of its influence on the "thoughtful leaders of colonial America"), see Wolf, *Book Culture,* p. 115.

24. Discussed in Nadelhaft, *Disorders of War,* pp. 2–3.

25. Nadelhaft, *Disorders of War,* p. 2.

26. Cited in Nadelhaft, *Disorders of War,* p. 14.

27. Notably, Caroline Robbins, *The Eighteenth-Century Commonwealthman: Studies in the Transmission, Development, and Circumstance of English Liberal Thought from the Restoration of Charles II until the War with the Thirteen Colonies* (Cambridge, Mass.: Harvard University Press, 1959); J. G. A. Pocock, *The Machiavellian Moment: Florentine Political Thought and the Atlantic Republican Tradition* (Princeton, N.J.: Princeton University Press, 1975); J. G. A. Pocock, ed., *The Political Works of James Harrington* (Cambridge: Cambridge University Press, 1977).

28. J. C. D. Clark, *The Language of Liberty 1660–1832: Political Discourse and Social Dynamics in the Anglo-American World* (Cambridge: Cambridge University Press, 1994).

29. Rogers, *Evolution of a Federalist,* p. 167.

30. Clark, *Language of Liberty,* pp. 27–29, nn. 102–8.

31. Edgar, "Libraries of Colonial South Carolina," p. 83. See also Jack P. Greene, *The Quest for Power: The Lower Houses of Assembly in the Southern Royal Colonies 1689–1776* (Chapel Hill: University of North Carolina Press, 1963).

32. *Report to Journal of the House,* 6 Jan.–17 Mar. 1783, pp. 75–76; further detailed in Edgar, "Libraries of Colonial South Carolina," p. 84.

33. Herbert A. Johnson, *Imported Eighteenth-Century Law Treatises in American Libraries 1700–1799* (Knoxville: University of Tennessee Press, 1978).

34. Including *SCG,* 14 Dec. 1769. For Wood, see Johnson, *Imported Eighteenth-Century Law Treatises,* pp. 56–57.

35. The *Commentaries* were republished in Charleston in 1799 when Thomas joined the consortium producing the second American edition, printed at Boston.

36. Michael Foster, *A Report of Some Proceedings on the Commission of Oyer and Terminer and Gaol Delivery for the Trial of the Rebels in the Year 1746 . . . and of other Crown Cases* (London, 1762).

37. Rogers, *Evolution of a Federalist,* pp. 71, 89 (with further examples in n. 141), 113.

38. Maxwell, comp., *A Bibliography of English Law to 1650,* vol. 1, sect. 1 no. 17.

39. Johnson, *Imported Eighteenth-Century Law Treatises.*

40. Kevin J. Hayes, *The Library of William Byrd of Westover* (Madison: Madison House, 1997), nos. 421, 425. On the ownership of Bracton, Hayes corrects Johnson, *Imported Eighteenth-Century Law Treatises.*

41. The volume is also associated with Silas Taylor and William Holman of Halstead.

42. Christy, "Samuel Dale," p. 53.

43. See above, pp. 21, 27, 153.

44. "A marvel of patience and ingenuity than an attempt to meet a market," in the words of Wolf, *Book Culture,* p. 40.

45. Hayes, *Library of William Byrd,* nos. 1522, 2377.

46. See above, p. 82.

47. Hayes, *Library of William Byrd,* p. 73.

48. Chaplin, *An Anxious Pursuit,* p. 3.

49. Chaplin, *An Anxious Pursuit,* p. 252.

50. Chaplin, *An Anxious Pursuit,* pp. 335–36.

51. An exception was Francis Price's 1735 *British Carpenter; or, a Treatise on Carpentry,* but no similar volumes were stocked and must either have been regarded as beneath interest or were acquired privately.

52. Weir, *Colonial South Carolina,* pp. 244–46.

53. See James Raven, *Judging New Wealth: Popular Publishing and Responses to Commerce in England 1750–1800* (Oxford: Oxford University Press, 1992), pp. 206–9.

54. In, for example, his advertisement, *SCG,* 21 May 1754.

Notes to Chapter 11

1. Cf. Robert P. Multhauf, *Catalogue of Instruments and Models in the Possession of the American Philosophical Society* (Philadelphia: American Philosophical Society, 1961); Murphy D. Smith, *A Museum: The History of the Cabinet of Curiosities of the American Philosophical Society* (Philadelphia: American Philosophical Society, 1996). A excellent guide to surviving collections in North America is G. L'E. Turner and D. J. Bryden, eds., *A Classified Bibliography on the History of Scientific Instruments* (Oxford: International Union of the History and Philosophy of Science, Scientific Instrument Commission, 1997).

2. Berkeley and Berkeley, *Dr. Alexander Garden,* p. 35.

3. See Waring, *A History of Medicine,* pp. 254–60.

4. Raymond Phineas Stearns, *Science in the British Colonies of America* (Urbana, Chicago, and London: University of Illinois Press, 1970), pp. 296–326; John Lawson, *A New Voyage to Carolina* (London, 1709); Mark Catesby, *The Natural History of Carolina, Florida, and the Bahama Islands,* 2 vols. (London, 1731–1743).

5. See Waring, *A History of Medicine,* p. 200.

6. Stearns, *Science in the British Colonies of America,* pp. 295–96.

7. *SCG,* 8 Apr. 1732.

8. Berkeley and Berkeley, *Dr. Alexander Garden,* pp. 29–30, 161.

9. See for example, Berkeley and Berkeley, *Dr. Alexander Garden,* pp. 252–53.

10. David Ramsay, *History of South Carolina, from its First Settlement in 1670 to the Year 1808,* 2 vols. (Charleston, 1809), 2:512.

11. Chaplin, *An Anxious Pursuit,* pp. 138–39.

12. CLS journal, 1815–1841, QM, June 1815, with agreement to transfer the collection of natural curiosities to the Literary and Philosophical Society "together with the cases containing them." See also above, chap. 4.

13. Cited in Berkeley and Berkeley, *Dr. Alexander Garden,* p. 90.

14. QM, 5 July 1769, J, fol. 101.

15. Stearns, *Science in the British Colonies,* p. 323.

16. Stearns, *Science in the British Colonies,* pp. 515–16, 519; Linnean Society of London Archives, (draft) letter, 11 Sept. 1758.

17. Nina Reid, "Loyalism and the 'Philosophic Spirit' in the Scientific Correspondence of Dr. Alexander Garden," *SCHM* 92 (1991): 5–14.

18. Stearns, *Science in the British Colonies,* pp. 522–24.

19. Waring, *History of Medicine,* appendix; cf. appendix 1 below.

20. Waring, *History of Medicine* pp. 188–97.

21. Of many advertisements, *SCG,* 6 Mar. 1755; see also above, chap. 2.

22. Waring, *Excerpts from the Minute Book of the Medical Society,* 1:6–7, 9–10, 40–41.

23. *SCG,* 22 Jan. 1756.

24. Stearns, *Science in the British Colonies,* p. 524.

25. Herman Boerhaave, *A New Method of Chemistry,* 2 vols. (London, 1721); Stephen Hales, *Statical Essays,* 3d ed., 2 vols. (1738) (vol. 1 originally appeared as *Vegetable Statics* in 1727). The first printed catalogue of the New York Society Library (n.d., c. 1758) also listed "Hale's Vigitable Statics."

26. Colden was also author of the *History of the Five Nations of Canada,* 1747, held by the library in a 1755 3d ed.

27. Berkeley and Berkeley, *Dr. Alexander Garden,* p. 37. Garden exchanged letters with Hales until the latter's death in 1761.

28. Miller Christy, "Samuel Dale (1659?–1739), of Braintree, Botanist, and the Dale Family: Some Genealogy and Some Patriots," *Essex Naturalist* 19 (1918–1921): 53.

29. Berkeley and Berkeley, *Dr. Alexander Garden,* p. 127.

30. Of various surveys see in particular the collected studies in Alan Q. Morton, ed., *Science Lecturing in the Eighteenth Century: A Special Issue, British Journal for the History of Science* 28 (1995).

31. Berkeley and Berkeley, *Dr. Alexander Garden,* pp. 90, 128.

32. *Rules and By-Laws,* 1762, p. v.

33. Alice Nell Walters, "Tools of Enlightenment: The Material Culture of Science in 18th-Century England," Ph.D. diss., University of California–Berkeley, 1992, p. viii.

34. *Memoirs of the Forty-Five First Years of the Life of James Lackington,* new ed. (London, 1827), p. 236.

35. See below, chap. 13 n. 7

36. Easterby, *History of the College of Charleston,* p. 4.

37. William Johnson (1771–1834), judge of the S.C. Court of Common Pleas, 1798–1804, associate justice of the U.S. Supreme Court from 1804; see also Herbert A. Johnson, "The Constitutional Thought of William Johnson," *SCHM* 88 (1989): 132–45; and below, p. 206.

38. Mabel L. Webber, "Extracts from the Journal of Mrs. Ann Manigault 1754–1781," *SCHM* 20 (1919): 57–63, 128–41, 204–12, 254–59, entry for 14 May 1765; *SCG,* 13 Apr. 1765.

39. QM, 4 July 1759, J, fol. 12.

40. See John R. Milburn, *Adams of Fleet Street, Instrument Makers to King George: The History of a London Business, 1735–1830* (Aldershot, Hants.: Ashgate, 2000).

41. George Adams, *A Treatise Describing and Explaining the Construction and Use of Celestial and Terrestrial Globes* (London, 1766), p. vii.

42. Adams, *Treatise,* p. vii.

43. See, for example, Walters, "Tools of Enlightenment," pp. 132–34.

44. For surviving instruments of this type see Olivia Brown, comp., *The Whipple Museum of Science: Catalogue 7, Microscopes* (Cambridge: Whipple Museum, 1986), nos. 141–45; and G. L'E. Turner, *The Great Age of the Microscope: The Collection of the Royal Microscopical Society through 150 Years* (Bristol: Hilger, 1989), pp. 223–24.

45. As also listed on the shelves of the New York Society Library in 1754.

46. Berkeley and Berkeley, *Dr. Alexander Garden,* pp. 55–56.

47. George Adams, *Micrographia Illustrata; or, the Knowledge of the Microscope Explain'd* (London, 1746), p. 11.

48. The relevant illustration in the 1771 4th ed. is plate 11.

49. It is possible that what was in mind was a "zograscope," the term coined by Adams to market these glasses; see J. A. Chaldecott, "The Zograscope or Optical Diagonal Machine," *Annals of Science* 9 (1953): 315–22; and C. J. Kaldenbach, "Perspective Views," *Print Quarterly* 2 (1985): 86–104.

50. The Dollonds were also of Huguenot origin; see Tessa Murdoch, *The Quiet Conquest: The Huguenots 1685 to 1985* (London: Museum of London, 1985), p. 130.

51. Invoice details and a reprint of the catalogue are given in John R. Millburn, *Benjamin Martin: Author, Instrument-Maker, and "Country Showman"* (Leiden: Noordhoff International, 1976), pp. 214–15, 219–23.

52. Millburn, *Benjamin Martin;* Roy Porter et al., eds., *Science and Profit in 18th-Century London* (Cambridge: Whipple Museum, 1985), pp. 32–33.

53. CLS extra general meeting, Dec. 1773, J, fol. 156.

54. Brooke Hindle, *David Rittenhouse* (Princeton: Princeton University Press, 1964), pp. 72–73.

55. Edward Ford, *David Rittenhouse: Astronomer-Patriot, 1732–1796* (Philadelphia: University of Pennsylvania Press, 1946), p. 33.

56. CLS extra general meeting, Dec. 1773, J, fol. 156.

57. QM, Apr. 1774, J, fol. 160.

58. Ford, *David Rittenhouse,* p. 33.

59. Hindle, *David Rittenhouse,* chaps. 9, 10.

60. John R. Millburn, "The Office of Ordnance and the Instrument-Making Trade in the Mid-Eighteenth Century," *Annals of Science* 45 (1988): 261.

61. Walters, "Tools of Enlightenment," p. 171.

62. See above, n. 49.

63. Brown, comp., *Microscopes,* no. 143.

64. QM, Apr. 1778, J, fol. 184.

65. Adams, *Micrographia Illustrata,* 4th ed., pp. i, vi, xi.

66. Berkeley and Berkeley, *Dr. Alexander Garden,* p. 126.

67. QM, 3 Oct. 1770, J, fol. 123.

68. QM, 6 Apr. 1774, J, fol. 161.

69. South Caroliniana Library, Columbia, Manigault Family Papers, John Farquharson to Gabriel Manigault, 5 Apr. 1784.

70. Edward Nairne (1726–1806), trading opposite the Exchange in Cornhill from 1748, was partnered by Thomas Blunt (c.1740–1822); see plate 5.

71. Allan Chapman, "Scientific Instruments and Industrial Innovation: the Achievement of Jesse Ramsden," in R. G. W. Anderson et al., eds., *Making Instruments Count: Essays on Historical Scientific Instruments Presented to Gerard L'Estrange Turner* (Aldershot, Hants.: Variorum, 1993), pp. 418–30.

72. Millburn, "Office of Ordnance."

73. Cf. I. B. Cohen, *Some Early Tools of American Science* (Cambridge, Mass.: Harvard University Press, 1950); David Wheatland, *The Apparatus of Science at Harvard 1765–1800* (Cambridge, Mass.: Harvard University Press, 1968); S. A. Bedini, "Of 'Science and Liberty': The Scientific Instruments of King's College and Eighteenth Century Columbia College in New York," *Annals of Science* 50 (1993): 201–27.

74. Prof. Piazzi of Palermo, "Account of the Life and Labours of the late Mr Ramsden," *Philosophical Magazine* 16 (1803): 262.

75. See Anita McConnell, "From Craft Workshop to Big Business: The London Scientific Instrument Trade's Response to Increasing Demand, 1750–1820," *London Journal* 19 (1994): 36–53, esp. p. 50.

76. Cf. Piazzi, "Life and Labours of the Late Mr Ramsden," p. 254; Millburn, "Office of Ordnance."

77. McConnell, "From Craft Workshop to Big Business," pp. 38, 40–41.

78. McConnell, "From Craft Workshop to Big Business," p. 46.

79. Barbara Hughes, *Catalog of the Scientific Apparatus at the College of Charleston: 1800–1940* (Charleston: College of Charleston Library Associates, 1980), p. i.

80. Stearns, *Science in the British Colonies,* pp. 533–34; Ernest P. Earnest, *John and William Bartram, Botanists and Explorers* (Philadelphia: University of Pennsylvania Press, 1940), p. 68.

81. Rogers, *Evolution of a Federalist,* p. 491.

82. Isaac Griggs, *Discourse Delivered at the Anniversary Meeting of the Charleston Library Society* (Charleston, 1803), p. 17.

Notes to Chapter 12

1. Edgar, "Libraries of Colonial South Carolina," appendix 6.

2. Martin, ed., "Ebenezer's Kellogg's Visit," p. 12.

3. Francesco Cordasco, *Junius: A Bibliography of the Letters of Junius with a Checklist of Junian Scholarship and Related Studies* (Fairview, N.J., and London: Junius-Vaughn Press, 1986), p. 64. The Lloyds' Maryland library held the 1772 edition of *Junius.*

4. See James Raven and Antonia Forster, eds., *The English Novel 1770–1799: A Bibliographical Survey,* vol. 1 (Oxford: Oxford University Press, 2000), entry no. 1799: 51.

5. Edgar, "Libraries of Colonial South Carolina," p. 32.

6. See above, pp. 105–6, and below, appendix 3.

7. See the discussion in David Money, *The English Horace: Anthony Alsop and the Tradition of British Latin Verse* (London and Oxford: British Academy and Oxford University Press, 1999), chap. 4.

8. Charles Evans, *American Bibliography: A Chronological Dictionary of All Books, Pamphlets and Periodical Publications Printed in the United States,* 14 vols. (New York: Peter Smith, and Worcester, Mass.: American Antiquarian Society, 1941–59), entry no. 29084; Morgan, *Preliminary Bibliography of South Carolina.*

9. Rogers, *Evolution of a Federalist,* pp. 388–91.

10. Erskine Clarke, *Our Southern Zion,* pp. 112–13.

11. Zahniser, *Charles Cotesworth Pinckney,* p. 272.

12. See above, p. 82; for Deluc and deism see also Clarissa Campbell Orr, "Charlotte: Scientific Queen," in Campbell Orr, ed., *Queenship in Britain, 1660–1837: Royal Patronage, Court Culture and Dynastic Politics* (Manchester: Manchester University Press, 2001).

13. R. C. Simmons, *British Imprints Relating to North America, 1621–1760* (London: British Library, 1996).

14. See below, p. 209.

15. Edgar, "Libraries of Colonial South Carolina," pp. 118, 128–31.

16. See Timothy Clayton, *The English Print 1688–1802* (New Haven and London: Yale University Press, 1997), pp. 177, 196, 209–10, 236, 238.

17. Sven H. A. Bruntjen, *John Boydell, 1719–1804: A Study of Art Patronage and Publishing in Georgian London* (New York and London: Garland, 1985), pp. 38–39; Winifred H. Friedman, *Boydell's Shakespeare Gallery* (New York and London: Garland, 1976), p. 42.

18. Friedman, *Boydell's Shakespeare Gallery,* pp. 74, 83.

19. According to the original proposals in the *World,* 1 Jan. 1787.

20. Friedman, *Boydell's Shakespeare Gallery,* pp. 215–16.

21. See Marcia Pointon, *Hanging the Head: Portraiture and Social Formation in Eighteenth-Century England* (New Haven and London: Yale University Press, 1993), pp. 26–27, and plate 41.

22. *An Alphabetical Catalogue of all the Books in the Library belonging to the Bristol Education Society* (Bristol, 1795).

23. Edmund Malone to Lord Charlemont, 9 June 1787, cited in Evelyn Wingate Wenner, "George Steevens and the Boydell Shakespeare," Ph.D. diss., George Washington University, 1952, p. 114.

24. Boston Public Library, Rare Books Room, **G.164.2, "Boydell's Shakespeare Subscribers' Signatures" (1792).

25. The other paste-in, much later in the volume (641st entry), is from a James Mingay of Thetford, Norfolk.

26. Letters 41, 61, 62, 64–67, 69, 81–83, 86.

27. I am grateful to Timothy Clayton for this observation.

28. Bruntjen, *John Boydell*, pp. 113, 115, 117. Boydells eventually recouped £66,000.

29. Martin, ed., "Ebenezer Kellogg's Visit to Charleston, 1817," pp. 12–13.

30. CLS journal, 1815–1841, fols. 5, 6, 10, 11 (general meetings 15 Mar., 21 June 1820; 15 June 1825; 11 Mar. 1836; 27 Aug. 1841; 11 Jan., 31 Jan. 1842).

31. NYSL Archives, Keep Papers, J[ohn] Forbes, draft of a letter for the purchasing committee, to Rev. John M. Mason, Glasgow, 1 Oct. 1801. I am indebted to Sharon Brown, NYSL, for her assistance in locating this item.

32. Sherman, "Library Company of Baltimore," p. 9.

33. Directors' report, 26 Apr. 1802, cited in Sherman, "Library Company of Baltimore," p. 16.

34. *Catalogue* of the Savannah Library Society, 1838. I am grateful to Michael O'Brien for lending me a copy of this.

35. See above, pp. 71, 83.

36. CLS borrowing ledger, 1811–1814, July 1811.

37. Raven, *British Fiction*, entry 178.

38. Jacques du Boscq, *The Accomplish'd Woman*, 2 vols. (London, 1753), 1:[i–ii].

39. The library held a 5th edition of 1739, listed in the 1770 *Catalogue* as by Sir Richard Steele. More details of this publication and the *Ladies Calling* are given in Julia Cherry Spruill, *Women's Life and Work in the Southern Colonies* (Chapel Hill: University of North Carolina Press, 1938), pp. 208–31. See also Stephen Parks, "George Berkeley, Sir Richard Steele, and the Ladies Library," *Scriblerian* 8 (1980): 1–2.

40. Franklin to Deborah Franklin in Labaree et al., *Papers of Benjamin Franklin*, 3:383–84, cited in Hayes, *Colonial Woman's Bookshelf*, p. 65.

41. Cited in Spruill, *Women's Life and Work*, p. 101.

42. Noted in Hayes, *Colonial Woman's Bookshelf*, p. 28.

43. Edgar, "Libraries of Colonial South Carolina," p. 46.

44. Neville and Bielsky, "Izard Library," p. 162.

45. Hayes, *Colonial Woman's Bookshelf*, p. 12.

46. *SCG*, 17 June 1770.

Notes to Chapter 13

1. E. S. Thomas, *Reminiscences of the Last Sixty-Five Years, Commencing with the Battle of Lexington*, 2 vols. (Hartford, Conn: Case, Tiffany, and Burnham, 1840), 2:35, cited in Winton, "Colonial South Carolina Book Trade," p. 72.

2. Warren McDougall, "Charles Elliot's Book Adventures in America 1777–1790, and the Trouble with Thomas Dobson," unpublished paper, 1997. I am very grateful to Warren McDougall for these references.

3. Sherman, "Library Company of Baltimore," p. 12.

4. Directors' report, 27 Apr. 1807, cited in Sherman, "Library Company of Baltimore," p. 17.

5. *City Gazette* (hereafter *CG*) and *Charleston Courier* (hereafter *CC*), 7 June 1805.

6. *Poulson's American Daily Advertiser*, 18 June 1805.

7. William Johnson (see above, p. 174), graduate of Princeton, was an early trustee of the

college (later University of South Carolina), established by state act in 1801 with a capital of $50,000 and an annual grant of $6,000. See Daniel Walker Hollis, *South Carolina College,* vol. 1 of *University of South Carolina* (Columbia: University of South Carolina Press, 1951), pp. 22–26.

8. *CC,* 7 June 1805.
9. *CC,* 7 June 1805.
10. Report from Savannah, *CG,* 15 July 1805.
11. Report dated 20 July from Charleston, in *Poulson's,* 2 Aug. 1805.
12. Report from Kingston dated 18 July, in a report from Charleston, dated 1 Aug., reprinted in *Poulson's,* 16 Aug. 1805; and "Extract of a Letter from Kingston" (Jamaica) received at Charleston, 13 July 1805, in the *Political and Commercial Register,* 15 Aug. 1805.
13. *CG,* 30 July and 14 Oct. 1805.
14. QM, 6 Apr. 1774, J, fol. 160.
15. *The Numbers of the Phocion: Which were originally published in the Charleston Courier, in 1806, on the subject of neutral rights* (Charleston, 1806).
16. *CC,* 31 July 1805
17. *CC,* 1 Aug. 1805, and *CG,* 2 Aug. 1805. William Muir, merchant, resided at Store 1, Bull Street, Geyer's north wharf; Eleazer Elizer, *A Directory for 1803; Containing The Names of all the House-Keepers and Traders in the City of Charleston* (Charleston, 1803), p. 42.
18. The firm had not been informed by 6 July 1805 when writing to express the hope that the winter order had arrived "in safety & we rely on its having given satisfaction" (letter 102).
19. See above, p. 146, and below, p. 443n. 372.
20. The exact title was not specified but it was probably Holcroft's recent *Travels from Hamburg through Westphalia, Holland, and the Netherlands to Paris,* 2 vols. (London, 1804), rather than his earlier *Travels through Germany,* 2 vols. (London, 1796–1797).
21. H. W. DeSaussure (1763–1839), director of the Mint in Washington, D.C., in 1794, returned to Charleston 1795, was elected to the Chancery Bench in 1808, and served as president of the Library Society, 1807–1812.
22. John Hopton (1748–1831), son of William Hopton (1712–1786), partner with Robert William Powell (his brother-in-law) in one of the largest importing and slave-importing firms. In *Holden's Directory* of 1808 he is listed as merchant, 1 Angel Court, Throgmorton St., London. See also below, p. 451n. 511.
23. The term "Bookseller" is dropped.
24. Sherman, "Library Company of Baltimore," p. 10.
25. Waring, *Excerpts from the Minute Book of the Medical Society,* 1:9–10. A *Catalogue* of their books, appended to their *Laws and Resolutions* was printed in 1806.
26. William Wallace Woodward, printer, bookseller and stationer of Chestnut St. (1796–1801) and South Second St. (1802–1820), Philadelphia. See H. Glenn Brown and Maude O. Brown, *A Directory of the Book-Arts and Book Trade in Philadelphia to 1820, Including Printers and Engravers* (New York: New York Public Library, 1950).
27. CLS letterbook, Woodward to Davidson, 24 May 1809.
28. CLS letterbook, Davidson to Woodward, 20 June 1809.

29. Cited in Sherman, "Library Company of Baltimore," p. 18.

30. John Sutherland, "The Book Trade Crash of 1826," *Library,* 6th ser., 9 (1987): 151.

31. *Supplementary Catalogue of Books, Belonging to the Charleston Library Society; which have been purchased, or presented since January, 1811* (Charleston, 1816).

32. This seems a more likely candidate for the *Catalogue* title, "American Encyclopaedia," than the American edition of Abraham Rees's *The Cyclopaedia; or Universal Dictionary* published in parts in 41 vols. from 1805, but not completed until 1825.

33. I am much indebted to the advice of James Green in this section.

34. Included in CLS, MS 29.

35. Bristol B901; Winans, *Descriptive Checklist of Book Catalogues,* no. 2106. David Bailey died in 1799.

36. Biographical listings, *SCHM* 30:123; 32:78; attendance list, QM, 1 Oct. 1788, J, fol. 223; and AM, 13 Jan. 1789, J, fol. 224.

37. Winans, *Descriptive Checklist of Book Catalogues,* p. 149.

38. *Catalogue of Books belonging to the South-Carolina College Library* (Columbia, 1807), giving 62 folio titles, 312 quarto, 665 octavo, and (to letter J only) 66 duodecimo. No copy survives at the Library Society.

39. See Edward A. Pearson, *Designs against Charleston: The Denmark Vesey Conspiracy of 1822* (Chapel Hill: University of North Carolina Press, 2000), p. 104. I am grateful to Ted Pearson for advice on this section.

40. Ramsay, *History of South Carolina,* 2:380.

41. Ramsay, *History of South Carolina,* 2:379.

42. Together with that of Adam Tunno, Russell's was "the last great wealth to be gained by Charlestonians in the carrying trade"; Rogers, *Charleston in the Age of the Pinckneys,* p. 54.

43. *Kent's Directory* of 1808 and 1813 (but not in *Kent's Directory* of 1801 or the *Post Office Directory* of 1802).

44. Richard Heber, the book collector, was one such. He sent back a book to the firm as unwanted four years after receiving it, Arnold Hunt, "Bibliotheca Heberiana," in Robin Myers and Michael Harris, eds., *Antiquaries, Book Collectors and Circles of Learning* (Winchester and New Castle, Del.: St. Paul's Bibliographies and Oak Knoll Press, 1996), p. 106.

45. CLS journal, 1815–1841, 15 Mar. 1815.

46. LCP minute books, 2 (1768–1785), 3 (1785–1794), 4 (1794–1816), 5 (1816–1832), copies of correspondence with Joseph Woods and William Dillwyn, 1783–1812 (and with Samuel Woods from 1812 to at least 1824).

Notes to Chapter 14

1. *Caelum, non animum mutant qui trans mare currunt,* Epistles of Horace, 1.2.27.

2. Cited in Richard M. Gummere, *The American Colonial Mind and the Classical Tradition* (Cambridge, Mass.: Harvard University Press, 1963), p. 2.

3. *London Chronicle,* 12 Oct. 1775. I am grateful to Antonia Forster for drawing my attention to this essay.

4. *General Evening Post,* 22 May 1798.

5. Cf. Anne Goldgar, *Impolite Learning: Conduct and Community in the Republic of Letters 1680–1750* (New Haven and London: Yale University Press, 1995), p. 157.

6. Berkeley and Berkeley, *Dr. Alexander Garden,* pp. 112–13.

7. E. G. Swam, "Brothers of the Spade: Correspondence of Peter Collinson, of London, and of John Custis, of Williamsburg, Virginia, 1734–1746, " *Proceedings of the American Antiquarian Society* 58 (1948): 19–20.

8. BL, Add. MS 4304, Birch Papers.

9. Gregorie, "First Decade of the Charleston Library Society," p. 5.

10. Cited in Weir, "The Harmony We Were Famous For," p. 232.

11. Cited in Berkeley and Berkeley, *Dr. Alexander Garden,* p. 73.

12. South Caroliniana Library, Columbia, Manigault Family Papers, John Laurens to Gabriel Manigault, 16 June 1776.

13. Hayes, *Library of William Byrd,* p. 43 n. 120.

14. *SCG,* 12 Dec. 1763.

15. *SCG,* 2 Apr. 1763.

16. Langdon Cheves, "Middleton of South Carolina," *SCHM,* 1 (1900), p. 233n. 1.

17. Edgar, "Libraries of Colonial South Carolina," pp. 115, 144–48.

18. Edgar, "Libraries of Colonial South Carolina," p. 148.

19. See Edgar, "Libraries of Colonial South Carolina," pp. 48, 85.

20. Berkeley and Berkeley, *Dr. Alexander Garden,* p. 33.

21. Berkeley and Berkeley, *Dr. Alexander Garden,* p. 35.

22. Below, letter 52, Bird, Savage, and Bird to Gov. Charles Cotesworth Pinckney, 22 Sept. 1792.

23. Lemoine, *Present State of Printing and Bookselling,* p. 19.

24. McCowen, *British Occupation of Charleston,* pp. 123–24.

25. British Library, Royal Literary Fund MSS 3:103, letter to the committee, 21 May 1801.

26. Cf. the discussion in chaps. 5 and 6 of Rhys Isaac, *The Transformation of Virginia 1740–1790* (Chapel Hill: University of North Carolina Press, 1982).

27. Howe, ed., "Journal of Josiah Quincy," p. 462.

28. Warner, *Letters of the Republic,* p. xiii.

29. I am most grateful to Max Edelson for discussion about this point.

30. QM, 3 Oct. 1764, J, fols. 45–46.

Notes to Letter Book Introduction

1. Cf. for example, Jacob M. Price, *Joshua Johnson's Letterbook, 1771–1774: Letters from a Merchant in London to his Partners in Maryland* (London, 1979); and Zachs, *First John Murray.*

2. CM, 7 Nov. 1759, C, fol. 10.

Notes to the Letter Book

1. James Rivington (1724–1802), sixth son of Charles Rivington (1688–1742), bookseller of St. Paul's Churchyard. Until March 1756 James continued his father's business with his brother John (1720–1792). Thereafter, James went into partnership with

James Fletcher and together published the hugely profitable Smollett's *History of England.* By 1760, however, Rivington was bankrupt and left England for America. He opened a shop in Market Street, Philadelphia, but by December was trading from premises in Hanover Square, New York. During the next decade he expanded his business to Boston and Annapolis, and from 1773 began Rivington's *New-York Gazetteer.* Attacked for his Loyalism he returned to London in 1776 but after a year was back in New York as king's printer. His survival, albeit with mixed success, in the United States until his death, has been linked to allegations that he was a spy for Washington; see Crary, "Tory and the Spy." A portrait by Gilbert Stuart hangs in the New York Historical Society. See also Leroy Hewlett, "James Rivington, Loyalist Printer, Publisher and Bookseller of the American Revolution, 1724–1802: A Biographical-Bibliographical Study," Ph.D. diss, University of Michigan, 1958.

2. The *Monthly Review* and the *Critical Review* commenced publication in 1749 and 1752, respectively.

3. For the publication of these see John McCusker, "The Business Press in England before 1775," *Library,* 6th ser., 8 (1986): 205–31.

4. James Crokatt (or Crockatt), merchant of Cloke Lane, London, had been prominent in the foundation of the CLS, securing the 1754 charter and its ratification by Lords in Council, 24 June 1755. His "care & diligence" were applauded in the CLS printed rules ("Advertisement," *The Rules and By-Laws of the Charleston Library Society,* 3d ed. [Charleston, 1770], p. 5). The son of Charles Crokatt of Edinburgh, James was a merchant of standing in Charleston before leaving for England in 1737. He established himself as the foremost "Carolina merchant" in London where he was referred to as "a Scotch Jew Lately come from So. Carolina." He traded as James Crokatt & Co until 1763 and was the colony's agent in London from 1749 to 1756. He was prominent in the establishment of the Masons in the colony and was master of Solomon's Lodge in 1738; Bullock, *Revolutionary Brotherhood,* p. 80. His brother John (d 1740), sometime resident of Portugal, had been a merchant in Charleston, and a sister also lived there. Other siblings lived in Edinburgh. See *PHL,* 1:2 n. 7; Lothrop Withington, "South Carolina Gleanings in England," *SCHM* 6 (1905): 117–25 (pp. 121–22); Walter B. Edgar, ed., *The Letterbook of Robert Pringle,* 2 vols. (Columbia: University of South Carolina Press, 1972). He is not to be confused with Dr. James Crokatt, country member of the CLS (d. c.1765), whose books are noted in Davis, *Intellectual Life in the Colonial South,* 2: 574. For other aspects of his life, including his interest in and publications on indigo cultivation, see Rogers, *Evolution of a Federalist,* pp. 9–11, 14, 22, 31; and Starr, *School for Politics,* p. 22.

5. William Strahan (1715–1785), printer of Johnson's *Dictionary* and Gibbon's *Decline and Fall,* friend to Benjamin Franklin, and MP from 1774 to 1784; he was established at Wine Office Court, off Fleet Street, until 1748 when he moved to Little New Street. In 1753 this shop was rebuilt and extended on to the site of six houses pulled down by Strahan. In a letter to America, he proudly proclaimed it to be "the largest and best Printing-house in Britain"; Strahan to David Hall, 1 Nov. 1753, David Hall Collection, American Philosophical Society. Later, a second office—the King's Printing

Office—was opened in East Harding Street. Strahan's younger son, Andrew, succeeded to the business in 1785. Strahan's ledgers comprise only the third substantial surviving printing business record of this period, after Ackers and Bowyer, and the later Henry Woodfall accounts for 1765–1771. For an account of his career see Cochrane, *Dr Johnson's Printer;* Harlan, *William Strahan;* and Patricia Hernlund, "William Strahan's Ledgers: Standard Charges for Printing, 1738–1785," *Studies in Bibliography* 20 (1967): 89–111, and "William Strahan's Ledgers II: Charges for Papers, 1738–1785," *Studies in Bibliography* 22 (1969): 179–95. The Strahan-Hall correspondence is a key and much-used record of transatlantic book-trade dealings of the period; see Harlan, "David Hall's Bookshop and Its British Sources of Supply."

6. This did not reach him. See below, n. 10.

7. W. & J. Brisbane were part of the firm founded by William Brisbane of Glasgow (1670–1733) whose successor, Walter (b. 1706), was brother to Robert Brisbane (see below, n. 9). J. Stevenson was almost certainly a relative of Charles Stevenson (see below, n. 10); possibly he was the Capt. John Stevenson who lost property in a 1774 fire in Charleston; *South Carolina Gazette and Country Journal,* 22 Dec. 1774.

8. Letter sent by *Blandford,* Man of War, as noted below, letter 5.

9. Robert Brisbane (1707–1781), native of Glasgow and graduate of Glasgow University, arrived in Carolina in 1733. He joined the St. Andrew's Society in 1740 and in 1746 was secretary of the Right Worthy and Amicable Order UBIQUARIANS. In 1748 he was a founder member of the CLS, and elected correspondent at the anniversary meeting (hereafter AM), 9 Jan. 1759 (CLS journal [hereafter J], fol. 1). He is mentioned as "new appointed" (CLS committee meeting [hereafter CM], 4 Apr. 1759, C, fol. 1), having been appointed at the general (later, from 1761, regularly styled quarterly) meeting (hereafter QM) of that day (J, fol. 10). He retired from the committee at the QM of 3 Oct. 1759 (J, fol. 14). His will was proved 28 Dec. 1781; Caroline T. Moore, *Abstracts of the Wills of the State of South Carolina, 1740–1760* (Columbia, S.C., 1964), pp. 162, 329. Robert's brother, Dr. William Brisbane (1710–1771), who arrived in Carolina c. 1731–1733, was a surgeon and apothecary; E. Haviland Hillman, "The Brisbanes: First Part," *SCHM* 14 (1913): pp. 123–27. The brothers bought land in Granville County in June 1764, South Carolina Department of Archives and History, Columbia, S.C., Deeds DDD, 735–49. See also above, n. 7, and *PHL,* 2:73 n. 5.

10. The dispute was discussed 20 June 1759: "Mr Robert Brisbane laid before the Committee a Letter received by him from James Crokatt Esqr of London which served to inclose two Receipts Viz One of William Strahans [corrected from "James"] for £3..5..2 Sterling One of James Rivingtons for £92..11..– . . . The Committee taking said Letter into consideration observed that Mr Crokatt had not paid William Strahan the sum of £44..13..1 which was ordered by the Society formerly, as no Bill had appeared for that Purpose but had paid the Whole Balance of the Money's in his Hands to James Rivington as appears by the receipt inclosed in his Letters upon which It was resolved that said sum be immediately remitted William Strahan" (C, fols. 3, 4). For Crokatt see above, n. 4. At the same meeting a Mr. Charles Stevenson was ordered to attend the next committee meeting "with Mr Strachan's Account, that they [the committee] may

then finally adjust and settle the same" (C, fol. 4). Charles Stevenson (d. 1762), appointed to the CLS committee at the QM of 4 Apr. 1759 (J, fol. 13), was a Charleston merchant, importing as Charles Stevenson and Co.; "Records Kept by Colonel Isaac Hayne," *SCHM* 10 (1909): 161; *PHL*, 1:181, 182.

11. At the meeting of 1 Aug. 1759, "The Secretary was directed to write Letters to Mr Strahan & Mr Rivington agreeable to the directions given in the Minutes of the Society" (C, fol. 5).

12. John Butler, secretary since the AM of 9 Jan. 1759 (J, fol. 1).

13. HMS *Blandford,* 20 guns, Commander Penhallow Cummings, Esq., arrived at Charleston from Jamaica, Sunday, 7 Aug. (*SCG,* 11 Aug. 1758), and sailed, with the *Winchelsea* at the head of "our grand Fleet"—a convoy of nearly 60 vessels—going over the bar on 24 Aug. and following the embargo imposed until 6 Aug., after which 84 vessels set out in 2 weeks (*SCG,* 25 Aug. 1758).

14. QM, 4 July 1759: Committee informs the QM that they have gone through the accounts of Strahan and find that there is a balance due to him of £49.15s.7d. and "at the sametime laid before the Society all the Vouchers &c necessary to ascertain said Balance, which were examined & approved," and ordered that Strahan's account be paid to "his Attorney here, or provide a Bill of Exchange for that purpose to be remitted him as soon as possible" (J, fol. 11).

15. See above, n. 10.

16. Rivington, ruined by losses at Newmarket races in 1759, had fled to America, opening shop first in Philadelphia in 1760 and then a year later in New York; Isaiah Thomas, *History of Printing in America,* ed. Marcus McCorison (New York: Weathervane Books, 1970), p. 478 (1st ed., 1810). See also below, n. 23.

17. The QM of 4 July 1759 is followed by a committee meeting (J, fol. 12): "A Complaint being made by several of the Members that the Bookseller had not only neglected to furnish the Society with Pamphlets &c for some time past, but had also omitted to send over his accounts, or answer any of the Correspondents letters for many Months, some of which inclosed him payments on the Society's account." The QM has ordered the committee to order the secretary "to write the Bookseller, & Inform him that the Society Expects he will for the future give no cause for such a Complaint."

18. CM, 1 Aug. 1759, C, fol. 5.

19. C, fols. 10–11.

20. C, fols. 11–12.

21. J, fol. 15.

22. Thomas Durham and David Wilson, booksellers in partnership from 1753 at Plato's Head near Round Court, Strand. Durham ceased trading c. 1775, and Wilson died in July 1777; Nichols, *Literary Anecdotes,* 3:671.

23. QM, 2 July 1760, learned that a new bookseller was required "as the situation of Mr James Rivington's Affairs had put it out of his power to Serve the Society any longer in that Capacity," and "the Correspondent was desired to inform Messʳˢ Durham & Wilson that they were elected the Society's Booksellers & to desire them to forward Pamphlets Magazines &ᶜ by every Conveyance" (J, fol. 18).

24. The *Gentleman's Magazine* commenced publication 1731; the *London Magazine: or Gentleman's Monthly Intelligencer* began 1732 and was collected as an annual volume until 1782; the *Universal Magazine* began in 1747. The *London* was one of the most popular of the periodicals in America; Reilly, "Common and Learned Readers"; and James Raven, "The Importation of Books in the Eighteenth Century," in Hugh Amory and David D. Hall, eds., *The Colonial Book in the Atlantic World,* vol. 1 of *A History of the Book in America* (New York: Cambridge University Press, 2000), pp. 183–97. Cf. the local advertisement for the *London* by Nicholas Langford, bookseller on the bay, in the *SCG,* 28 Dec. 1769: "This periodical Production, from its commencement in the Year 1731, hath ever been held in the greatest Estimation; and prefeered [*sic*], in the Opinion of the Judicious, to all the brother Publications of the Kind."

25. John Rivington (1740–1792), bookseller and publisher in St. Paul's Churchyard, in partnership with his brother James until 1756. John was the son of Charles Rivington I and from 1760 was bookseller to the Society for Promoting Christian Knowledge. In 1775 he was master of the Stationers' Company.

26. John Butler had resigned as secretary (CM, 31 Oct. 1759, C, fol. 9), and he is dead by 12 Jan. 1762 (J, fol. 29). William Michie is elected secretary and correspondent at the AM of 8 Jan. 1760 (J, fol. 15), having been elected to the committee on 4 July 1759 (J, fol. 13).

27. This must be Robert Ainsworth, *Thesaurus linguæ Latinae compendiarius,* 2 vols. (London, 1736), *ESTC* t065492. An abridgment had been issued in 2 vols. in 1758, *ESTC* t089748.

28. These are the first of these indications of the copies and ships. The snow *Polly and Betsey,* William Muir, loading since the week beginning 28 June, sailed 26 July, and the ship *Elizabeth,* James Smith, was "windbound" 26 July, sailing some days thereafter. News that both ships had arrived safely at London reached Charleston in early December 1760; *SCG,* 5, 26 July, 16 Dec. 1760. The *Polly and Betsey,* cleared out 19 July; a snow of 130 tons, 6 guns, and a crew of 10; built in Sussex in 1752, registered at Charleston in Dec. 1759, and owned by William Ellis, John Hodsden, and Isaac Holmes of Charleston; bond was given on 3 Apr. 1760, and she arrived in London with a great cargo of about 600 lbs. of rice and over 2,000 lbs. of indigo (PRO, CO5/510, fol. 92). The *Elizabeth* was a ship of 160 tons, 2 guns, and a crew of 12, built in New England in 1753 and registered in London in Jan. 1758, cleared out on 26 July (PRO CO5/510, fol. 92).

29. C, fol. 15.

30. C, fol. 32.

31. Hereafter letters are addressed only to Wilson (the elected bookseller), and without address to Durham. See above, n. 22.

32. CM, 4 Feb. 1761, as agreed by last AM, to purchase a bill for £150 "payable to Mr. David Wilson Bookseller at Plato's Head in the Strand, & pay rest to his account to wait future Orders" (C, fols. 14–15). At the AM, 13 Jan. 1761, report was made of £15..2..10 sent to "Willson and Dunbarr" (*sic*) and "To the assignees of the Creditors

of James Rivington late Bookseller, to be remitted by the Correspondt £78..12..10 Stg" (J, fol. 20).

33. Thomlinson, Hanbury, Colebrooke, and Nesbitt were money contractors for the British forces in North America; Henry Laurens is relieved in Nov. 1764 to have secured his part in a bill of Apthorp drawn on Thomlinson, Hanbury, Colebrooke, and Nesbitt, so their security must have been sought after; Laurens to William Hodshon, 3 Nov 1764, *PHL*, 4:490. John Thomlinson (1731–1767) was a London merchant born in Antigua and was a government contractor; Jack M. Sosin, *Agents and Merchants: British Colonial Policy and the Origins of the American Revolution, 1763–1775* (Lincoln, Neb.: University of Nebraska Press, 1965), pp. 9–10; *PHL*, 1:184 n. 6. In 1763 Barlow Trecothick, Charles Apthorp, and John Thomlinson were West Indian merchants in Bucklersbury, London (with Thomlinson established at Barge Yard, Bucklersbury, since at least 1753; see plate 5 above). Thomlinson was MP for Steyning, 1761–1767. The 1763 *London Directory* lists Arnold, Albert, and Alexander Nesbitt as West India merchants of Bishopsgate within. Arnold, brother-in-law to Henry and Hester Thrale, was MP, 1753–1768, 1770–1779; Alexander Nesbitt, *History of the Family of Nisbet or Nesbitt in Scotland and Ireland* (Torquay, 1898), pp. 57–58; *PHL*, 2:381 n. 6. Sir George Colebrooke (1729–1809), son and eventually sole successor of a London banker, MP for Arundel, 1754–1774, and later chairman of the East India Company, 1769–1771, 1772–1773, was also a contractor until 1765 for victualing the forces in America. His firm was based at 9 New Broad St. (see plate 5, with sites of Hanbury, Nesbitt, and other firms also).

34. John Remington elected secretary and correspondent at AM, 13 Jan. 1761, J, fol. 19. He was notary public, having arrived in Charleston in 1748 with a commission from the Archbishop of Canterbury, successfully challenging his governor-appointed predecessor, John Rattray. A public quarrel continued in the *SCG*, 27, 30 Aug., 12, 20, 26 Sept., 3, 30 Oct., 1748; *PHL*, 1:9 n. 5. Remington died Sept. 1775; "Records Kept by Colonel Isaac Hayne," *SCHM*, 10 (1909): 222.

35. Edward Martyn, partner with Thomas Shirley (CLS committee in 1770) and importers of slave cargoes, 1763–1765. The partnership was dissolved in 1765. Martyn was a planter on the Waccamaw River at his death; *PHL*, 4:96, n. 4.

36. Ship *Pitt*, Master Benjamin Herriot, sailed for Cowes, 5 Apr.; *SCG*, 11 Apr. 1761.

37. Brigantine *Bristol-Packet*, Master John Marshal, sailed for Bristol, 23 Mar.; *SCG*, 28 Mar. 1761

38. HMS *Dolphin*, Capt. Benjamin Marlowe, 24 guns; Coker, *Charleston's Maritime Heritage*, p. 296; sailed "for England," 18 June; *SCG*, 20 June 1761. The *Dolphin's* arrival in England "with some (if not all) of the vessells that sail'd from thence [Charleston] under her convoy 21st of June" is announced in the *SCG*, 10 Oct. 1761.

39. Ship *Bance-Island*, Master John Stephens, sailed 1 Sept.; *SCG*, 5 Sept. 1761. See also below, n. 48.

40. *Prince Edward*, Master John White, sailed for London (after weeks windbound) 12 Oct. 1761; *SCG*, 17 Oct. 1761. See also below, n. 48.

41. There were many London editions available (e.g., 1707, *ESTC* t118803), but this request must be for *Titi Petronii arbitri satyricon,* with preface by C. Burman, 2 vols. ("Amsterlaedami, Lugduni Batavorum," 1743; Leiden colophon dated 1742). Amsterdam edition listed as 4to no. 76 in the 1770 *Catalogue,* p. 15.

42. First edition in English, M. [Nicolas C. J.] l'Abbé Trublet, *Essays upon Several Subjects of Literature and Morality* (London, 1744), *ESTC* t183354; listed as London 1745 edition, "Octavo et Infra" (hereafter 8^{vo-}) no. 457 in 1770 *Catalogue.*

43. *Biographia Britannica: or, The Lives of the Most Eminent Persons who have Flourished in Great Britain,* 7 vols. (London, 1747–1766; 7th vol. published 1766), *ESTC* t139261; 6 vols., listed as 2° no. 21 in 1770 *Catalogue.*

44. Daniel Webb, *An Inquiry into the Beauties of Painting* (London: R. and J. Dodsley, 1760), *ESTC* t131072; listed as 8^{vo-} no. 492 in 1770 *Catalogue.*

45. Siegmund Jakob Baumgarten, *A Supplement to the English Universal History,* 2 vols. (London, 1754–1758), *ESTC* n037461.

46. *A Compleat Catalogue of all Books and Pamphlets Published for Ten Years Past . . . The Whole Forming a General Index* (London: R. Griffiths, 1760), *ESTC* n029128.

47. The election of bookseller to the society is reaffirmed at the AM, 12 Jan. 1762 (J, fol. 29).

48. The orders did miscarry. The ship *Bance Island,* Master John Stephens, bound for London, was captured by a Bayonne privateer of 22 guns and 200 men, 23 Oct., "& vessel and cargo entirely lost the 28th, going into St Jean de Luz." The same report notes the capture by the French of the ship *Prince Edward,* Capt. John White, from Charleston for London, but also its rescue and the capture of the privateer by the frigate *Escorte* and its conveyance to Plymouth; *SCG,* 13 Feb. 1762.

49. At the AM of 12 Jan. 1762, "a letter from Mr Wilson Bookseller dated 10th Novr last was read, & Order'd, that the Correspondent write him, not to make Insurance on Books sent out to the Society, unless their Value Amount to Fifty Pounds Sterling or upwards" (J, fol. 29).

50. Brigantine *Hopewell,* Master Christopher Cheesman, arrived at Charleston from Bristol 13 July 1762; *SCG,* 17 July 1762. Arrival dated 14 July and as brig. of 100 tons, no guns, and crew of 6, with "British" 1749 registration and ownership in the name of Poole, carrying "Sundry British Goods"; PRO, CO5/510, fol. 109. Cheesman was a vessel-owner and his brother George a merchant in London; *PHL,* 4:230. Ship *Charles-Town,* Master John Barnes, arrived at Charleston from London 14 Aug.; *SCG,* 21 Aug. 1762. Arrival dated 16 Aug. and as a ship of 200 tons, 16 guns and a crew of 16, built New York in 1750, registered London in May 1762, and owned by Isaac King and Sarah Nicholson of London, with "Sundry British Goods"; PRO, CO5/510, fol. 110. Barnes leaves again for London early Oct.; see below, n. 55.

51. This appears to indicate the capture of Corrie's ship and cargo, although no reference survives in the *SCG.* The firm of Corrie and Scott advertises in the newspaper, including, for example, for goods imported by Capts. Cheesman and White; *SCG,* 30 Jan. 1762.

52. Ordered in July 1761, see letter 8 (above), but not listed in the 1770 or 1772 *Catalogues.*

53. At the QM of 7 July 1762, "the Lists of Books proposed by the last Committee were read for the first time" (J, fol. 31).

54. Ship *Royal Charlotte,* Master Ephraim Woolf, sailed for Cowes, 17 Sept. 1762 (*SCG,* 18 Sept. 1762), but returned to Charleston.

55. Ship *Charles-Town,* Master John Barnes, sailed for London, first week of October; *SCG,* 2 Oct. 1762. Officially cleared out on 9 Oct., with ship details as above, n. 50, but now with 12 guns and crew of 14, and large rice and indigo cargo, and bond given London on 4 May; PRO, CO5/510, fol. 102.

56. At the QM of 6 Oct. 1762, "the List of Books proposed at the last meeting, was again considered & debated & agreed to be sent for" (J, fol. 32).

57. The CM of 4 Aug. 1762 decided to send for the *Monthly Chronicle* (it is unclear if this was approved by a QM) (C, fol. 18).

58. An example of a demand which is not recorded in the C or J.

59. Sent out therefore with letter 10 (above). Barnes sailed as above, n. 55.

60. Ship *Elizabeth,* Master John Mallard, sailed for London, 19 Nov.; *SCG,* 20 Nov. 1762. Cleared out on 20 Nov., ship of 150 tons, 4 guns, 12 men, built Philadelphia in 1756, registered Dec. 1760, owned by Peter Mallard, London, with large cargo of rice, indigo, pitch, tar, and turps; PRO, CO5/510, fol. 103.

61. Ship *America,* Master William Coombes, arrived from London, 28 May; *SCG,* 28 May 1763. Arrival dated 30 May as ship of 170 tons, no guns and crew of 14, built New England in 1760, registered London in Sept. 1761, and owned by John Beswicke, William Greenwood, and William Higginson of London, with "Sundry British Goods"; PRO, CO5/510, fol. 120. Coombes was a Charleston sea captain; *SCG,* 16 Dec. 1760.

62. [Philip Francis], *A Letter from the Cocoa Tree, to the Country Gentlemen* (London, [1762]), *ESTC* t010157, a brief sixteen-page pamphlet, much reprinted, referring to the formation of an opposition party by the Duke of Cumberland.

63. George Adams, the elder, d. 1773, mathematical instrument maker to George III. His great work on globes was to appear in 1766, with a 30th edition by 1810.

64. George Adams, *Micrographia Illustrata; or, the Knowledge of the Microscope Explain'd* (London, 1746), *ESTC* t039334; "Adams on the Microscope," London, 1747, listed as 4to no. 2 in 1770 *Catalogue.* In the 1811 *Catalogue,* "Adams's Micrographia Illustrata" is followed by a separate entry for the plates (p. 35).

65. As agreed, in almost the same words, QM, 6 July 1763. The unwanted instrument was to be sold by Mr. Wells (see below, n. 132), and the treasurer is ordered to procure a bill for payment of the bookseller's account (J, fol. 36). Demands for telescopes and other instruments had been made earlier, including a proposal by Daniel Crawford that "an Astronomical Quadrant with Tellescop [*sic*] Sights, Micrometer & the usual Apparatus be sent for" (QM, 4 July 1759, J, fol. 12; QM, 3 Oct. 1759, J, fol. 13).

66. Ship *Friendship,* Master Samuel Ball, arrived from London, 15 Aug.; *SCG,* 20 Aug. 1763. Arrival dated 17 Aug. and as British-built in 1754, but with no crew or registration details, owned by Benjamin and Thomas Smith, George Inglis, Isaac Holmes, Henry Peronneau of South Carolina, and James and Charles Crokatt of London, with "Sundry British Goods"; PRO, CO5/510, fol. 122.

67. Sarah Nickleson (or Nickelson) & Co., of Mansell St., Goodman's Fields, London, and then no. 15 Bush Lane, Cannon Street, until 1768, *London Directory,* 1763, 1768; *PHL,* 1:9 n. 6 (see plate 5 above). She was widow and successor to John Nickleson, a Charleston merchant who moved to London in the 1740s. He partnered Richard and Thomas Shubrick, involved in the 1740s in slave consignments, who "now reside in England"; *SCG,* 26 Sept. 1754. Thomas Shubrick remained in Charleston, with Richard in Bucklersbury, London, becoming a London "Carolina merchant" second only in wealth to James Crokatt and John Beswicke; *PHL,* 1:184 n. 7. The Shubrick plantation figured in the 1781 conflict with the British army; Wallace, *History of South Carolina,* 2:283.

68. QM, 5 Oct. 1763: "It appearing that a Ballance of £87..18..8 is due from the Society to Mr Wilson Bookseller, Order'd that the Treasurer procure a good Bill of one hundred Pounds Sterg upon the best Terms he can, to be remitted to the said Mr Wilson" (J, fol. 37).

69. Ship *Adventure,* Master Thomas Headlam, sailed for London, 25 Oct.; *SCG,* 29 Oct. 1763. The ship had arrived at Charleston from Havana, 7 Aug.; *SCG,* 13 Aug. 1763.

70. HMS *Success,* Capt. John Botterell, 20 guns; Coker, *Charleston's Maritime Heritage,* p. 296 (sailing of the naval ships apparently unlisted in the *SCG*).

71. Robert Dodsley (1703–1764), bookseller, poet, and playwright, trading at Tully's Head, Pall Mall, from 1735. Friend of Johnson and Pope, "Doddy's" letters (with none to South Carolina) are collected in Tierney, ed., *Correspondence of Robert Dodsley.*

72. The delay in informing the bookseller of the appointment seems extraordinary, probably another indication of the problems besetting the society. Whatever the cause, it is only at the QM of 3 Oct. 1764 that it is "Ordered that the Secretary do Write to Mr Dodsley and Acquaint him that he is appointed Bookseller to the Society and as such constantly to send out the Magazines, Reviews and other Occasional papers &c by the first Opportunity" (J, fol. 45). The approved list of books is also recorded with the list of classics rejected. In addition, "it being reported that several Volumes of different Setts of Books in the Library was wanting to render them compleat – Ordered that the Librarian do furnish the Secretary with a List of such, and that the Secretary do Write to the Bookseller to send them out."

73. Printed by R. and J. Dodsley, it began publication in 1758. "Annual Register Compleat" listed as 8^{vo-} no. 15 in 1770 *Catalogue.* See also below, n. 283.

74. Began publication in 1762. Listed in 1770 *Catalogue* as 2° no. 104, 15 vols., 1759.

75. Tobias Smollett, *Continuation of the Complete History of England,* 5 vols. (London, 1763), *ESTC* t055305; listed as 8^{vo-} no. 424 in 1770 *Catalogue,* supplementing the 4 vols., 1757, listed as 4to no. 84. The appendix of the 1772 *Catalogue* lists a further set, 7 vols. 1758, as 8^{vo-} no. 157.

76. Thomas Blackwell, *Memoirs of the Court of Augustus,* 3 vols. (Edinburgh 1753), listed as 4to no. 9 in 1770 *Catalogue.* The first 2 volumes were published in Edinburgh in 1753 and 1755. The posthumous third volume by John Mills, *Memoirs of the Court of Augustus Continued and Completed from the Original Papers of the late Thomas Blackwell,* was published in London in 1763 (*ESTC* t142701).

77. Listed in 1770 *Catalogue* as 4to nos. 70–75, *Philosophical Transactions,* all "Ludg. Bat" (Leiden), abridged by Lowthorp to the end of 1700 (vols. 1–3), 1749; by Jones 1700–1720 (vols. 4–5), 1749; by Eames & Martyn, 1719–1733 (vols. 6–7), 1734; by Martyn 1732–1744 (vols. 8–9), 1747; by Martyn, 1743–1750 (vols. 10–11), 1756; and "vol. 47th to 42d" (from 1751 to 1762), n.d.

78. John Taylor, *Elements of the Civil Law,* first published in Cambridge, 1755, *ESTC* t134034. A London edition, n.d., appears as 4to no. 112 in the McKenzie bequest appended to the 1772 *Catalogue,* but not in the main entries of the 1770 or 1772 *Catalogues.*

79. De Blossiers Tovey, *Anglia Judaica: or the History and Antiquities of the Jews in England* (Oxford, 1738), *ESTC* t021895, listed in 1770 *Catalogue* as 4to no. 99. Both the Taylor and Tovey were proposed at the CM, 26 Sept. 1764 (C, fol. 25). Two other works then proposed do not appear in the final order until letter 14 (below). One proposed work, "To: Aug: Ernesti Apuscula Oratoria Orationes &c 1st vols. 8$^{vo–}$ Vaillant," was not apparently sent for.

80. Adam Anderson, *An Historical and Chronological Deduction of the Origin of Commerce,* 2 vols. (London, 1764), *ESTC* t079288. This edition is listed as 2° no. 8 in 1770 *Catalogue.*

81. "The Committee appointed to make out a List of the best Edition of the Classic's, deliver'd a Small Catalogue to be sent for, which was read, & proposed to be sent for; for the first time [i.e., discussed]" (QM, 4 Apr. 1764, J, fol. 40), marking the beginning of a bitter struggle over ordering the classics, chronicled by Reinke, "Classical Debate."

82. Remington resigned as secretary after a furious argument with the committee when ordered before it (CM, 6 June 1764, C, fols. 19, 20; QM, 11 June 1764, J, fol. 41). No secretary-correspondent is forthcoming at the extraordinary meeting of 11 June 1764, although Brisbane volunteers to fill the gap. William Mason is then admitted member and immediately elected secretary and correspondent (J, fol. 42). Mason was appointed clerk of the South Carolina Court of Common Pleas in Apr. 1766, was expelled from Charleston by the British in Apr. 1782, but returned as clerk two years later, and died May 1795; Mabel L. Webber, "Marriage and Death Notices from the City Gazette," *SCHM* 23 (1922): 26–33 (p. 32). Mason is listed as residing at the Academy, 19 Ellery-Street, in Elizer, *A Directory for 1803,* p. 37.

83. *Africa,* Hugh Moth, loading on 5 Nov., and sailed on 12 Nov. 1764; *SCG,* 5, 12, Nov. 1764.

84. James Dodsley (1724–1797), younger brother of Robert, and his partner since 1750, succeeding him at Tully's Head in 1764.

85. In fact not sent until March. At the CM of 6 Mar. 1765, "the Secretary laid Before the Committee the Letter Ordered by the Society at the Anniversary to be wrote to Mr Dodsley to acquaint him of his being Elected Bookseller to the Society, which was read and approved of. The Secretary then reported that he had delayed sending the said Letter on Acco^{t} of the Treasurer's not being able to procure the Bill Ordered to be sent therewith – On which The Chairman [Henry Laurens] made an Offer of a Bill

(provided the Treasurer cou'd not get One) payable at Sixty days Sight 3 p^{r}Cent Advancd." The CM accepts Laurens's offer without waiting "in order that it may be transmitted with the Letter to the Bookseller" (C, fol. 31). The sagging spirits of the society also continue, with repeated difficulties in being quorate, Nov. and Dec. 1764 postponements (C, fols. 28, 29).

86. AM, 8 Jan. 1765, J, fol. 52. Also ordering "that the Treasurer do purchase a Bill of £100 Sterling, and deliver the same to the Secretary to be by him transmitted with the said letter."

87. *Museum rusticum et commerciale: or Select Papers on Agriculture,* vols. 1–2 (London, 1764), vols. 3–5 (London, 1765), with a 6th vol. (London, 1766), *ESTC* t164213. A London 1764 edition, 5 vols., listed as 8^{vo-} no. 302 in 1770 *Catalogue.*

88. Andrew Michael, Chevalier Ramsay, *The Philosophical Principles of Natural and Revealed Religion,* 2 vols. (Glasgow, 1748–1749), *ESTC* t068477, with London reissue 1751. A Glasgow 1748 edition, 2 vols., listed as 4to no. 80 in 1770 *Catalogue.*

89. Probably William Jones (d. 1757) *The Gentlemens and Builders Companion Containing Variety of Usefull Designs for Doors, Gateways, Peers . . .* (London, 1739), 4to, *ESTC* t014933.

90. "Grey's debates in the House of Commons," 10 vols. (London, 1763), listed as 8^{vo-} no. 174 in 1770 *Catalogue.*

91. "Ordered . . . that the Secretary do write the Bookseller to apply to Mr Dollard [*sic*] for the same" (AM, 8 Jan. 1765, J, fol. 50). Peter Dollond, of Huguenot origin, had set up his optician's shop in Vine St., Spitalfields in 1750, and was joined by his father, John (d. 1761). John pioneered the development of achromatic lenses, the Dollonds revolutionizing the construction of optical instruments. Peter Dollond is first recorded in the land tax records as being at 59 St. Paul's Churchyard in 1767–1768. He was joined in partnership by his son John; see also below, n. 426.

92. Richard Oswald 1705–1784, an extremely wealthy merchant with various interests. He gave £50,000 bail to Henry Laurens in 1781 and was a peace commissioner in Paris in 1782 (*DNB*).

93. John Lewis Gervais (1741–1795) and James Theodore Rossel, arrived in Charleston from London, June 1764. Oswald, who had sent them out to establish a plantation for him in the Carolina backcountry, recommends them to Henry Laurens, Laurens to Oswald, 7 July 1764; *PHL,* 4:331–32 n. 3. Gervais and Rossel were of French Huguenot extraction and had originated from Hameln near Hanover. Rossel died in 1767; Gervais became a planter, merchant in Charleston, and trusted aide of Laurens.

94. Having been found in an emergency, Mason is reelected as secretary and correspondent (AM, 8 Jan. 1765, J, fol. 51).

95. Ship *Prince of Wales,* Capt. Roderick Wilson, sailed for London, loading on 2 Mar., cleared out and reported as windbound on 16 and 23 Mar., but had left by 23 Mar.; *SCG,* 10, 17, 24, 30 Mar. 1765.

96. *SCG,* 2 Mar., reports arrival of ship *Success,* Joseph Cookson, at Antigua, and *SCG,* 9 Mar., reports Cookson's arrival at Charleston on 8 Mar. Cookson loaded again 30 Mar. and cleared out for Bristol on 13 Apr., leaving 20 Apr.; *SCG,* 20 Apr. 1765.

97. See below, n. 99.

98. James Fletcher, Jr. (1731–1798), bookseller of St. Paul's Churchyard, and the Turl, Oxford, from 1756, son of James Fletcher, Sr., bookseller of Oxford, St. Paul's Churchyard, and at Westminster Hall. James Fletcher, Jr., was partner with James Rivington (as noted in committee minutes following letter 5, above) until the latter's bankruptcy in 1759, and in 1769 was taken into the business of his father.

99. "Mr Dodsley's letter [i.e., from the CLS] being taken under Consideration, It was Agreed, that as he had neglected to send out the Books wrote for or Answer the Letter sent him by the Correspondent, [Dodsley's reply arrives 5 Feb. according to note added to copy of letter 15 (above)] that a New Bookseller be chosen in his room; when Mr James Fletcher of St Pauls Church Yard bookseller, being recommended as a person proper to serve the Society in that Capacity . . . on being ballotted for was declared duly elected" (AM, 14 Jan. 1766, J, fol. 64).

100. Sir Robert Douglas, *Peerage of Scotland* (Edinburgh, 1764), 2º. Unlisted in the 1770, 1772, and 1811 *Catalogues*.

101. No works by Sterne are listed in the 1770 or 1772 *Catalogues*.

102. The treasurer was ordered to obtain a £50 bill to give to the secretary to accompany this letter (AM, 14 Jan. 1766, J, fol. 64).

103. Unidentified in the newspapers; the *Charles Town Packett,* Master Thomas Eastwick, brigantine, 60 tons, leaves for Philadelphia on 15 Feb. 1766 (and returns to Charleston on 3 Apr.); PRO, CO5/511, fols. 38, 104).

104. It was at the QM of 1 Oct. 1766 that "The Secretary reported he had received several Letters since the Last meeting, from Mr Fletcher and One from Mr Dodsley, which being read; It is Ordered that the Correspondent do prepare Answers to them and acquaint Mr Fletcher in answer to his of 20th May last that in the General directions given him he is not confined to any particular Subject" (J, fol. 73). See paragraph later in the letter incorporating the last instruction.

105. No reference to this qualification is given in J or C.

106. Nearest recorded sailing is the ship *Carolina Packet,* Master William White, bound for London, sailing on 3 June 1767; later London ships, 4 June and 15 June; *SCG,* 8, 15 June 1767.

107. Confirmed as bookseller to the society, AM, 13 Jan. 1767 (J, fol. 76).

108. The great mid-thirteenth-century legal treatise, first printed as Henricus de Bracton, *De legibus et consuetudinibus Angliæ* (London, 1569); listed as 2º no. 18 in 1770 *Catalogue* (the 1569 edition was in fact 4to but the only other pre-1767 edition, that of 1640, was 8vo).

109. *Fleta seu commentarius Juris Anglicani sic nuncupatus, sub Edwardo Rege primo,* 2d ed. (London, 1685), *STCii* 1291; listed as "Fleta Seldeni, seu comment [etc] 1685," 4to no. 31 in 1770 *Catalogue.* John Selden's *Ad Fletam Dissertatio* was appended to both the 1647 and 1685 editions of *Fleta.*

110. Sir Henry Spelman, *Glossarium archaiologicum,* 3d ed. (London, 1687), *STCii* 4926 (1st ed., 1664); listed as "Spelmanni glossarium archæologicum London 1687," 2º no. 135 in 1770 *Catalogue.*

111. Giovani-Andrea Gallini, *A Treatise on the Art of Dancing* (London, 1765), *ESTC* n013981 (1st ed., 1762); listed as 8^{vo-} no. 196 in 1770 *Catalogue*.

112. Ferdinando Warner, *History of the Rebellion and Civil-War in Ireland* (London, 1767), *ESTC* t061699 (1st ed. 1763); listed as 4to no. 106 in 1770 *Catalogue*.

113. [Chief Justice] Nicholas Trott, *The Laws of the Province of South-Carolina* (Charlestown, 1736); Richard Hall, *Acts, Passed in the Island of Barbados* (London, 1764), *ESTC* t019072; listed as 2° nos. 84 and 85.

114. *The Mirrour of Justices,* now known to date from c.1289, was published in duodecimo in 1768. It was later described as "an old law book" when the request was repeated (see below, n. 194). There seems to have been no earlier printed edition (W. Harold Maxwell, comp., *A Bibliography of English Law to 1650* [London: Sweet and Maxwell, 1925], vol. 1, sec. 1, no. 17); if this is the case then knowledge of its imminent publication had reached Charleston.

115. Sir John Fortescue, *De laudibus legum Angliæ* (London, 1737), *ESTC* t140177; listed as 2° no. 54 in 1770 *Catalogue*.

116. William Blackstone, *Commentaries on the Laws of England,* 4 vols. (Oxford, 1765–1769), *ESTC* t057753; listed as 4to no. 14 in 1770 *Catalogue*.

117. William Shenstone, *The Works in Verse and Prose,* 2d ed., 2 vols. (London, 1765), *ESTC* t092446; listed as "Shenstone's poetical works, 2 vols. London 1765," 8^{vo-} no. 441 in 1770 *Catalogue*.

118. *A Collection of Poems in Six Volumes: By Several Hands,* 6 vols. (London, Robert Dodsley, 1763), *ESTC* t131163; listed as 8^{vo-} no. 140 in 1770 *Catalogue*.

119. *The Works of Jonathan Swift,* 8 vols. (Dublin, 1747), *ESTC* n031104; listed as "Swift's (Dean) works [damaged] vols. London 1747," 8^{vo-} no. 444 in 1770 *Catalogue*.

120. [Philip] Francis, *Orations of Demosthenes,* 2 vols. (London, 1757–1758), *ESTC* t138464; listed as 4to no. 34 in 1770 *Catalogue*.

121. *Court and City Register,* published at least since 1742 (see *ESTC* t034299); listed as 8^{vo-} no. 108 in 1770 *Catalogue*.

122. Charles Churchill, *Poems,* 2 vols. (London, 1769), *ESTC* t173072; listed as 8^{vo-} no. 77 in 1770 *Catalogue*.

123. Not identifiable in 1770 *Catalogue*.

124. Edmund Gibson, *Codex juris ecclesiastici Anglicani* (Oxford, 1761); listed as 2° no. 61 in 1770 *Catalogue*.

125. *Baronagium genealogicum: or, The Pedigrees of the English Peers, Deduced from the Earliest Times . . . by Sir William Segar . . . and Continued to the Present Time, by Joseph Edmondson,* 6 vols. (London [1764]–1784) (first 5 vols. undated), *ESTC* t147241; listed as "4 vols. London 1764," 2° no. 51 in 1770 *Catalogue*. Edmondson's Peerage was first proposed, but not sent for, 2 July 1766, J, fol. 71. See also below, nn. 181, 203, 264.

126. *A Complete Collection of State-Trials,* 6 vols. (London, 1742), *ESTC* t148933; listed as 2° no. 155 in 1770 *Catalogue*.

127. Benjamin Martin, *The Young Gentleman and Lady's Philosophy,* 2 vols. (London, 1759–1763), *ESTC* t025359; but also Martin, *General Magazine of Arts and Sciences,* 14 vols. which incorporated the above in part 1. Neither is listed in 1770 *Catalogue*.

128. Robert Lowth, *A Short Introduction to English Grammar* (London, 1763), *ESTC* t143997; listed as 8^{vo-} no. 278 in 1770 *Catalogue.*

129. Samuel Auguste David Tissot, *Advice to People in General, with Regard to their Health,* 3d ed. (London, 1768), *ESTC* t076080; edition listed as 8^{vo-} no. 458 in 1770 *Catalogue.*

130. John Heylyn, *An Interpretation of the New Testament,* 2 vols. (London, 1761), *ESTC* t094864 (second part only); listed as 4to no. 47 in 1770 *Catalogue.*

131. The "List of Instruments" proposed at the last QM, was agreed to be sent for (AM, 13 Jan. 1767, J, fol. 76), and "List of Books sent for" at QM, 1 Apr. 1767 (J, fol. 81). Eight years before, "the Want of a pair of Globes in the Library being mentioned, it was proposed also that a pair Suitable for a Library be sent for together with a Case of Mathematical Instruments" (QM, 4 July 1759, J, fol. 12).

132. Robert Wells (b. Dumfries, 1728; d. 1794), printer and bookseller of Charleston. After his arrival in the town in 1752 Wells revolutionized the South Carolina book trade, first by acquiring a printing house (corner of Meeting and Tradd Streets) and then, in 1764, a newspaper of his own, the *South Carolina and American General Gazette.* In this he listed his wares from "the Great Stationery and Book-Store, on the Bay" in very large and bold advertisements for imported books. The entire collection, announced the verso of one of his publications in 1771, comprised "the LARGEST STOCK and greatest VARIETY of BOOKS to be met with in all America, consisting of many THOUSAND Volumes." He did not embark on a reprint trade until the eve of the Revolution, however, after which he left for London (below, n. 337). See Winton, "Colonial South Carolina Book Trade," and the extensive study by Moltke-Hansen, "Empire of Scotsman Robert Wells." A colorful vignette is given by Thomas, *History of Printing in America,* 2d ed., 1:344.

133. Lord Charles Greville Montagu, second son of the Duke of Manchester, governor of South Carolina, 1766–1773. At the Jan. AM of the CLS William Bull, lieutenant governor, resigned as president of the CLS to give the place of honor to Montagu. Manigault resigned as vice president at the same AM, but both Bull and Manigault returned to their positions three years later when Montagu was "unceremoniously dumped as head of the Society"; Bull, *Oligarchs in Colonial and Revolutionary Charleston,* p. 138.

134. See below, n. 340.

135. Ship *Mary,* James Gordon, sailed from Charleston for London on 17 Apr.; *SCG,* 18 Apr. 1768. The *Mary* had arrived at Charleston on 3 Mar.; *SCG,* 8 Mar. 1768. Gordon might have been related to the Charleston merchant John Gordon, extensively engaged in the East Florida trade from the 1760s; William S. Coker, "Entrepreneurs in the British and Spanish Floridas, 1775–1821," in Samuel Proctor, ed., *Eighteenth-Century Florida and the Caribbean* (Gainesville: University Presses of Florida, 1976), 15–39 (p. 17).

136. Sent with copy of letter 19 (below). The *Nancy,* Capt. George Jordan, having been windbound for some days, sailed for London on 26 May; *SCG,* 30 May 1768.

137. AM, 12 Jan. 1768, J, fol. 87.

138. At the QM of 7 Oct. 1767, note was made of the secretary's receipt of a letter from the bookseller together with the classics and "was moved that they be Lettered in the same manner as the rest of the Books belonging to the Society" and that because the bookseller had neglected to have them so lettered "that the expence arising from such his neglect be deducted out of his account against the Society" (J, fol. 85). This motion is however rejected at the AM of 12 Jan. 1768, "but it was Ordered that the Secretary do write him, that the Society were much Surprised at his Omission and that it was expected he would be more attentive to their Orders in future" (J, fol. 86). At a CM of 3 Feb. 1768, "it appearing by the said Minutes [of special meeting of 11 Jan. 1768] that Mr Campbell, Mr Wells and Mr Brisbane, were appointed to look over, inspect and compare the Classics sent out by the Booksellers, with the orders sent him for the same and Ord^d to report thereon; which Order does not appear to have compli'd with" (C, fol. 57) (there was a succession of inquorate CMs in 1768 [C, fols. 59–61]).

139. Snow *Portland,* George Higgins, arrived Charleston from London on 25 Oct. 1767; *SCG,* 26 Oct. 1767.

140. Ship *America,* John Rainier, arrived Charleston from London on 20 Sept.; *SCG,* 21 Sept. 1767.

141. John Colcock (1744–1782) was admitted to the practice of law in the Court of Common Pleas, Feb. 1767. He was not reappointed as JP in 1770, however, apparently because he had been a Son of Liberty; A. S. Salley, Jr., "Capt. John Colcock & Some of His Descendants," *SCHM* 3 (1902): 218–20; *PHL,* 5:212 n. 8. Colcock was admitted to the CLS in Apr. 1763 as a minor (see appendix 1), and recorded as "now of age" at the QM of 3 July 1765 (J, fol. 58). In Jan. 1769 he was appointed secretary of the CLS.

142. Mention is made of the full letter which the secretary puts before the QM of 6 Apr. 1768, explaining that it could not have been sent earlier as the committee has not met (J, fol. 89). This also accounts for the difference between the date of writing and that of the dispatch by the ship noted in the copybook.

143. "The Secretary laid before the Committee a Letter he had received from the Bookseller which being read was intimating that he was desirous of further Instructions about the Quadrant Ordered to be sent out, when the same being taken under Consideration, It is Agreed that it be recommended to the Society to Countermand the Orders sent therefor, as the Committee is of Opinion it is rather too expensive and wou'd if sent out, at present, be of little or no Service to the Society" (CM, 2 Dec. 1767, C, fol. 46), repeated when laid before a special meeting on 11 Jan. 1768 (C, fol. 56) and confirmed at the QM of 6 Apr. 1768 (J, fol. 90).

144. Ordered at QM, 6 Apr. 1768 (J, fol. 90), where a list of books, in addition to the periodical magazines, received from Fletcher was also recorded: "Peep behind the Curtain, Considerations on the Douglas Cause, Essence of ditto, Letters of Lady Jane, Harveys Pamphlet on Midwif^y."

145. Ship *Nancy,* George Jordan, sailed for London on 26 May; *SCG,* 30 May 1768. The same ship was used in Jan. 1770; see letter 24.

146. Letter 17 (above). At the QM of 5 Oct. 1768, "the Sec. reported that he had received several small parcells of Pamphlets from the Bookseller but none of the Books so long ago Ordered by the Society" (J, fol. 93).

147. AM, 10 Jan. 1769, J, fol. 94. There is no indication of discussion or process of election, merely Nicoll's listing as the bookseller.

148. Ship *Pitt*, John Lasley (*sic*), arrived Charleston from London on 16 Feb.; *SCG*, 7 Mar. 1769.

149. At the CM of 2 Aug. 1769, a motion was agreed for presentation at the next QM "that the Thermometer which is found imperfect sent over by our late bookseller be sent back to England & that our present bookseller Mr Nicoll be requested to return the same to Mr Martin & get it exchanged" (C, fol. 71). The thermometer was first proposed in letter 17 (above) to Fletcher in June 1767.

150. Ship *St. Helena*, Master George Arthurs, entered and loading for Bristol on 16 Feb. (*SCG*, 16 Feb. 1769), and sailed 5 Mar. (*SCG*, 9 Mar., 1769). The "St. Halena," 170 tons, owned by Francis Stuart of Beaufort and Nathaniel Wraxall and George Abbot Hall & Co., merchants of Bristol, registered in 1764; R. Nicholas Olsberg, "Ship Registers in the South Carolina Archives," *SCHM* 74 (1973): 262.

151. Ship *Dolphin*, Henry Simbletts, sailed for London, 5 Mar.; *SCG*, 6 Apr. 1769.

152. William Nicoll, bookseller of the Paper Mill and then no. 51 St. Paul's Churchyard, trading 1761–1775, a publisher of political pamphlets, many printed by Strahan.

153. Established at 49 Birchin Lane since at least 1749; see Lillywhite, *London Coffee Houses*, no. 223 (pp. 147–49), and above p. 127 and plate 5.

154. See above, letter 17.

155. George Lyttelton, *The History of the Life of King Henry the Second*, 4 vols. (London, 1767), *ESTC* t079258, but the issue of this and subsequent editions was complicated by a publication interval between the first and the final two volumes. See below, nn. 180 and 257.

156. Thomas Hutchinson, *The History of the Colony of Massachusets-Bay* (*sic*), 2d ed. (London, 1760 [1765]), *ESTC* 7121382.

157. Johann Lorenz Mosheim (trans. Archibald Maclaine), *An Ecclesiastical History, Antient and Modern, from the Birth of Christ*, 2 vols. (London, 1765), *ESTC* t136145, but also 2d ed., corrected, 5 vols. (London, 1768), *ESTC* t135753.

158. Nathaniel Hooke, *The Roman History, from the Building of Rome to the Ruin of the Commonwealth*, 4 vols. (London, 1738), *ESTC* t071736, but with an eleven-volume edition (London, 1767), *ESTC* t072962.

159. Thomas Salmon, *A New Abridgement and Critical Review of the State Trials* (London, 1737), published in parts, *ESTC* t174071.

160. Charles de Secondat, Baron de Montesquieu, *Persian Letters: Translated by Mr Ozell* (London, 1722), *ESTC* t090449; most recently 5th ed., 2 vols. (Dublin, 1767), *ESTC* t197467; and 4th ed., trans. Mr. Flloyd, 2 vols. (London, 1762), *ESTC* n020116. First proposed at QM, 5 Oct. 1768 (J, fol. 93). But this work was already listed in the 1750 *Catalogue* and is apparently ordered in error (and one blamed on the bookseller; see below, n. 196). Montesquieu's *Spirit of the Laws*, 2 vols. (London, 1750), *ESTC* t090872; listed as 8^{vo-} no. 314 in 1770 *Catalogue*.

161. Emer de Vattel, *The Law of Nations; or Principles of the Law of Nature*, 2 vols. (London, 1759–1760), *ESTC* t112820.

162. John Cay, *The Statutes at Large, from Magna Charta, to the 30th Year of King George the Second, inclusive*, had been published in 6 vols. in 1758 (*ESTC* t145898) and this is apparently a request for a continuation. The nearest available seems to have been Henry Boult Cay, *An Abridgement of the Public Statutes now in Force and in General Use from the Eleventh Year of King George II to the First Year of his Present Majesty King George III*, 1 vol. (1766), *ESTC* t145080.

163. Owen Ruffhead, *The Statutes at Large; from Magna Charta, to the end of the Last Parliament, 1761*, 8 vols. (London, 1763–1764), *ESTC* t134761; and a new edition also in 8 vols., 1768–1770, *ESTC* t134762.

164. John Dickinson, *Letters from a Farmer in Pennsylvania, to the Inhabitants of the British Colonies* (Philadelphia, 1768), *ESTC* w019245, and various subsequent American editions. John Almon published an edition in London, 1768, *ESTC* t062910.

165. *St. Helena*, George Arthur, arrived Charleston on 1 July 1769, and sailed again for Bristol on 17 July; *SCG*, 6, 20 July 1769.

166. Reported, QM, 5 July 1769, that "the late bookseller [Fletcher] had sent over some of the books long ago Ordered and among them Dodsley's Poems and Blackstones Law Tracts which the Society had already received in the present from Lord Hope." The duplicates are sold off and bought by two members (J, fol. 100). Also agreed to purchase the bill of £100 and reported that the books just received were "all unletter'd & some of them in boards which being taken into consideration it was Ordered that they be bound & letter'd by the next Meeting" (J, fols. 100–101).

167. Snow *Polly*, John Rainier, sailed for London on 28 July; *SCG*, 3 Aug. 1769.

168. Ship *Beaufain*, Daniel Curling, sailed for London on 30 July; *SCG*, 3 Aug. 1769. Curling was among the many masters to have been captured at one time by privateers (*SCG*, 14 Nov. 1761, reporting capture of Curling and the *Alexander*).

169. Q[uintus] *Septimij Florentis Tertulliani opera, argumentis, explicationibus, notis illustrata: Authore I.L. de La Cerda*, 2 vols. (Paris, 1624); listed as 4to in 1770 *Catalogue*, appendix, p. 4.

170. Capt. John Perry, *The State of Russia under the Present Czar* (London, 1716), *ESTC* t105640; listed as 8^{vo-} no. 357 in 1770 *Catalogue*.

171. Adam Ferguson, *An Essay on the History of Civil Society*, 2d ed. (London and Edinburgh, 1768), *ESTC* t134320 (1st ed., 1767); listed as 4to no. 35 in 1770 *Catalogue*.

172. Sir James Steuart, *An Inquiry into the Principles of Political Œconomy*, 2 vols. (London, 1767), *ESTC* t128831; listed as 4to no. 88 in 1770 *Catalogue*.

173. Matthew Stewart, *Tracts, Physical and Mathematical* (Edinburgh and London, 1761), *ESTC* t130107; listed as 8^{vo-} no. 425 in 1770 *Catalogue*.

174. William Robertson, *The History of the Reign of the Emperor Charles V*, 3 vols. (London and Edinburgh, 1769), *ESTC* t130107; listed as 4to no. 82 in 1770 *Catalogue*.

175. Joseph Priestley, *The Rudiments of English Grammar; Adapted to the Use of Schools*, new edition (London, 1768), *ESTC* t046907 (1st edition, London 1761); listed as 8^{vo-} no. 362 in 1770 *Catalogue*.

176. Thomas Rymer, *Foedera, conventiones, literæ, et cujuscunque generis acta publica, inter*

reges Angliæ, et alios, 20 vols. (London, 1704–1735), *ESTC* t148099; listed as "Lond. 1727," 2° no. 134 in 1770 *Catalogue.*

177. Conyers Middleton, *Miscellaneous Tracts by the Late Reverend and Learned Conyers Middleton* (London, 1752), *ESTC* n005222; listed as "Miscellaneous works, 5 vols. Lond. 1755," 8vo– no. 294 in 1770 *Catalogue.*

178. The *Mermaid,* Samuel Ball, arrives Charleston from London, 16 Aug. (*SCG,* 17 Aug. 1769); the 12 July letter must have been sent separately. For newspaper advertisement of the *Mermaid,* see above, plate 11.

179. Reported at the AM of 9 Jan. 1770 that Granger's *History of England* "received from our late bookseller in boards be bound" (J, fol. 117). This is James Granger, *A Biographical History of England, from Egbert the Great to the Revolution,* 2 vols. (London, 1769), *ESTC* t090309; listed as 4to no. 40 in 1770 *Catalogue.*

180. See above, n. 155, and below, n. 257.

181. *Baronagium genealogicum . . . by Sir William Segar . . . and continued . . . by Joseph Edmondson;* see above, n. 125.

182. The *Mermaid,* Samuel Ball, sailed for London on 2 Oct.; *SCG,* 5 Oct. 1769. The *Mermaid* had arrived in Charleston on 16 Aug. (see above, n. 178).

183. Ship *Heart of Oak,* Henry Gunn, arrived Charleston from London on 30 Oct., 1769, and sailed out on 28 Nov., but for Lisbon, not London; *SCG,* 2, 30 Nov. 1769.

184. Ship *Dolphin,* Thomas Mackrell, arrived Charleston from London, 21 Nov.; *SCG,* 23 Nov. 1769.

185. Samuel Musgrave, *Dr Musgrave's Reply to a Letter Published in the News Papers, by the Chevalier d'Eon* (London, 1769), *ESTC* n008940. Unlisted in the 1770 and 1772 *Catalogues.*

186. There seems to be some error here. Ship *London,* Alexander Curling, arrived Charleston from London, 22 Sept. (*SCG,* 28 Sept. 1769); it left again for London in January 770.

187. At an "Extra meeting" of the committee, 26 Nov. 1769, "Mr David Wilson formerly a Bookseller his Acco^t with the Society being Examined a Ball^ce of £7..15..11 St^g was found due to him which is recommended to be paid" (C, fol. 72). Recommendation repeated at the CM of 9 Jan. 1770 (C, fol. 73), and the AM of the same day ordered that Wilson be paid off "with interest" on the outstanding balance, and also ordered a bill for £50 to be sent to Mr. Nicholl (J, fol. 116).

188. AM, 9 Jan. 1770: The secretary was ordered to write to the bookseller "and countermand the Order for the Laws of Several Provinces in America" (J, fol. 117).

189. John Hill [as Thomas Hale, gardener], *Eden: or, A Compleat Body of Gardening,* issued in 60 nos., 1756–1757, *ESTC* t032413 (collected later in a 1773 ed.).

190. Probably John Dickinson's *Letters,* see above, n. 164.

191. AM, 9 Jan. 1770, books "now be sent for": Gallini "on dancing, mistitled formerly," Warner's *Ireland, Mirrour of Justices* (J, fol. 117).

192. Gallini, *Treatise on the Art of Dancing;* see above, n. 111.

193. Warner, *History of . . . Ireland;* see above, n. 112. Only the first volume was published.

194. *The Mirrour of Justices: Written Originally in the Old French, before the Conquest* (London, 1768), *ESTC* t114858; see also above, n. 114. Described as law book here (when

earlier it was in a list of legal texts) to avoid any confusion with Henry Dell, *The Mirrour: A Comedy in Three Acts* (London, 1756), *ESTC* t039414, with a 1761 ed. (*ESTC* n004567).

195. Presumably *A Collection of State-Trials, and Proceedings upon High-Treason,* vols. 7 and 8 (London, 1766), *ESTC* 148947, a continuation of 6 vols. published in 1730 (and originally published 1719).

196. See above, n. 160. The unwanted edition was possibly *The Persian Letters, Continued* (London, 1735), *ESTC* n011440.

197. Matthew Stewart, *Tracts, Physical and Mathematical* (Edinburgh, 1761), *ESTC* t130107.

198. Mark Catesby, *The Natural History of Carolina, Florida, and the Bahama Islands,* 2 vols. (London, 1731–1743), *ESTC* t147030, with various later editions; proposed by Miles Brewton at the QM of 5 July 1769 (J, fol. 101), and sent for at the QM of 4 Oct. 1769 (J, fol. 115). Neither Catesby nor Lawson, below, is listed in the 1772 *Catalogue,* but both appear in the 1811 *Catalogue,* pp. 34, 60, with Catesby's *Carolina* asterisked as "not to be taken out of the library."

199. John Lawson, *A New Voyage to Carolina* (London, 1709), *ESTC* t133233, but reissued in 1711 in *A New Collection of Voyages and Tales,* with later editions titled *The History of Carolina;* proposed by the president in absentia at the QM of 5 July 1769 (J, fol. 101), and sent for at the AM, 9 Jan. 1770 (J, fol. 117).

200. *Nancy,* Capt. George Gordon, sailed for Cowes (with George Rolle, MP, on board, it is noted) 31 Jan.; *SCG,* 1 Feb. 1770. The ship had arrived from London with distinguished passengers again listed; *SCG,* 4 Jan. 1770.

201. Ship *Minerva,* Thomas Arnott, sailed out, for Gosport, 5 Feb., after several weeks' windbound delay; *SCG,* 15 Feb. 1770. *Minerva* was 80 tons, owned by Edinburgh merchants and built at Massachusetts Bay in 1766, registered in 1770 (Leith master, Robert Alexander); Olsberg, "Ship Registers," p. 247.

202. Montesquieu, *Reflections on the Causes of the Grandeur and Declension of the Romans* (London, 1734), *ESTC* t139718; listed as 8^{vo-} no. 315 in 1770 *Catalogue;* Saint-Evremond, *The Posthumous Works of Mr. de St. Evremont,* 3 vols. (London, 1700, 1705, 1714), *ESTC* n036429 and n025833; *The Frederician Code; or, A Body of Law for the Dominions of the King of Prussia,* 2 vols. (Edinburgh and London, 1761), *ESTC* t114264. QM, 3 Oct. 1770, confirms order for "Montesquieux miscellaneous works on the Roman Republick, St Euvremonts works, The Frederician Code, & the Journals of the House of Commons" (J, fol. 123).

203. See above, nn. 125, 181.

204. Order confirmed at QM, 3 Oct. 1770, requesting the bookseller "to purchase this last book as cheap as possible and that the better to enable him to do, he may take any time for sending it out not exceeding twelve months," and with a bill of £50 ordered for the bookseller (J, fol. 123).

205. Globes acknowledged in letter 20 (above). QM, 3 Oct. 1770, "Ordered that the Secretary do write to the Bookseller to send a p^r Leather Covers proper for the Globes" (J, fol. 124).

206. The question of the telescope, first proposed ambiguously (as "sights") in the list appended to letter 17 (above), May 1767, and clarified in 1770 (letter 24), was referred

to the next meeting by QM, 4 Apr. 1770, and referred again at QM, 4 July 1770 (J, fols. 119, 120), and finally, at QM, 3 Oct. 1770, it was "Ordered that the Secretary do write to the Bookseller countermanding the former order for a Tellescope" (J, fol. 123). The saga continued when the former president Manigault offered the society the telescope of his deceased son, Peter, to be "sold at first cost" and it was bought by the society (QM, 6 Apr. 1774, J, fol. 161). The question was next raised in 1784 (letter 34), when a telescope—probably the Manigault one—was sent over for repair.

207. In fact, QM, 3 Oct 1770, ordered the treasurer to purchase a bill for £50 sterling to be sent to the bookseller (J, fol. 123).

208. Ship *Little Carpenter,* Master Richard Maitland, arrived Charleston from London, 12 Dec.; *SCG,* 14 Dec. 1769.

209. HM Packet Boat *Swallow* (also referred to as Snow *Swallow*), George Wauchop, sailed for Falmouth on 21 Oct.; *SCG,* 25 Oct. 1770. The *Swallow* was new, having arrived at Charleston in the new year: "a new Snow Packet-Boat commanded by Capt. George Wauchop, arrived here in seven weeks from Falmouth; reckoned as complete and handsome a Vessel as any in service. She sails again from hence, with the Mails for Great-Britain, on Monday next"; *SCG,* 4 Jan. 1770.

210. *Charming Sally,* Master Peter Rainier, sailed for London on 6 Nov.; *SCG,* 8 Nov. 1773. The *Charming Sally,* ship, 170 tons, Charleston, owned by John Neufville, merchant, built South Carolina in 1769, registered in 1770.

211. CM, 7 Nov. 1770, "agreed that it be recommended to the Society to countermand the former Order of the same for the Magazines & Reviews to be sent us annually bound & in place thereof to order Prefaces indexes, tables of Contents Frontispieces &c to be transmitted us, that we may have them bound here at less expence" (C, fols. 79–80).

212. The Greek translation of the Hebrew Scriptures commissioned from 70 scholars by Ptolemy Philadelphus for the library at Alexandria. The edition requested is uncertain. It might even be Henry Owen, *An Enquiry into the Present State of the Septuagint Version of the Old Testament* (London, 1769), *ESTC* t083580.

213. Sir Robert Cotton, *An Exact Abridgement of the Records of the Tower of London from the Reign of Edward the Second* (London, 1657), a version of his *Abstract of the Records of the Tower* (London, 1642).

214. Cesare Beccaria [Bonesana], *An Essay on Crimes and Punishments, Translated from the Italian; with a Commentary, attributed to Mons. de Voltaire, translated from the French* (London, 1767), *ESTC* t138985. A local edition was published in 1777: "Printed and sold by David Bruce, at his shop in Church-Street, Charlestown," *ESTC* w018691. See also below, n. 245.

215. Lewis Chambaud, *A Dictionary French and English* (London, 1761), *ESTC* t201661.

216. Hipólito San José Giral del Pino, *A Dictionary, Spanish and English, and English and Spanish* (London, 1763), *ESTC* t099944.

217. Giuseppe Marco Antonio Baretti, *A Dictionary of the English and Italian Languages* (London, 1760), *ESTC* n030800, but also a new edition in 1771 (*ESTC* t081920).

218. Jacob Friedrich von Bielfeld, *The Elements of Universal Erudition . . . Translated from the Last Edition Printed at Berlin by W. Hooper* (London, 1770), *ESTC* t128060.

219. John and Thomas Simpson, merchants of 32 Bay, Charleston, *Charleston Directory,* 1782.

220. John Forrest, son of John Forrest (d. 1778) and grandson of John Forrest (d. 1767), Edinburgh merchants and burgesses since at least 1752, commanded considerable wealth and property at Castle-Hill and Charles Street in Edinburgh by the time of his death in 1786; Scottish Record Office, Part. Reg. Seisins 305 (Dec. 1786–Jan. 1787), RS 27/305, fols. 18–26; Com. Edinburgh Testaments 127:2 (Sept. 1787–Dec. 1788), CC8/8/127/2; James Gilhooley, comp., *A Directory of Edinburgh in 1752* (Edinburgh: Edinburgh University Press, 1988); Charles B. Boog Watson, *Roll of Edinburgh Burgesses and Guild-Brethren 1761–1841* (Edinburgh: Scottish Record Society, 1933), p. 59.

221. The *Mermaid,* Samuel Ball, arrived Charleston from London on 8 Sept.; *SCG,* 12 Sept. 1771.

222. "St Euvrements works" ordered by QM, 3 Oct 1770 (J fol. 123). See above, n. 202.

223. Henry Frederick, Duke of Cumberland, and (Lady) Henrietta, wife of Richard Lord Grosvenor. Popular pamphlets included *The Genuine Copies of Letters* (London, 1770), *ESTC* n030585, with a 7th ed. within the year; *Free Thoughts on Seduction, Adultery and Divorce* (London, 1771), *ESTC* t117150; *The Whole Proceedings at Large* (London, 1770), *ESTC* n012530; *A Defence of His Royal Highness the Duke of Cumberland* (London, 1770), *ESTC* n028892.

224. *Papers Relative to the Late Negotiation with Spain* (London, 1771), *ESTC* t043596; [Samuel Johnson], *Thoughts on the Late Transactions Respecting Falkland's Islands* (London, 1771), *ESTC* t050220.

225. Probably John Brown, *A Dictionary of the Holy Bible, Containing an Historical Account of the Persons,* 2 vols. (Edinburgh, 1769), *ESTC* t144070, and adopting chronological tables in the title of later editions.

226. Probably Joseph Priestley, *The History and Present State of Electricity, with Original Experiments* (London, 1767), *ESTC* t036344.

227. Richard Burn, *The Justice of the Peace, and Parish Officer,* 2 vols. (London, 1755), *ESTC* t068627, with many subsequent editions.

228. The most recent of many editions was *The Works of Mr William Congreve,* 3 vols. (London, 1761), *ESTC* t026067.

229. Jean Jacques Burlamaqui, *The Principles of Natural Law* (London, 1748), *ESTC* t112806, with a second edition in 1763 (ESTC t107029) and Dublin edition in 1769 (*ESTC* n020839).

230. John Hawkesworth, *The Adventurer,* 2 vols. (London, 1753), and a new edition in 4 vols. London 1770 (*ESTC* t097916).

231. John Swammerdam, *The Book of Nature; or, The History of Insects* (London, 1758), *ESTC* t022987.

232. Carl von Linné, *Genera animalium* [*systema naturæ*] (Edinburgh, 1771), *ESTC* t009551; first London edition, *Institutes of Entomology,* 1773 (*ESTC* n016970).

233. James Harris, *Hermes or a Philosophical Inquiry Concerning Universal Grammar,* 3d ed. (London, 1771), *ESTC* t146749 (1st ed., 1751).

234. Axel Frederik Cronstedt, *An Essay Towards a System of Mineralogy* (London, 1770), *ESTC* t134557, and 2d ed., 1772 (*ESTC* t033443).

235. Thomas Sheridan, *A Course of Lectures on Elocution* (London, 1762), *ESTC* t090536. The "last edit." was technically the Dublin third edition, 1770 (*ESTC* t166913).

236. Timothy Cunningham, *The Law of Bills of Exchange, Promissory Notes, Bank-Notes, and Insurances* (London, 1760), *ESTC* t108507, with 1766 3d ed. (*ESTC* t140363); and *A New and Complete Law-Dictionary, or, General Abridgment of the Law,* 2 vols. published in 140 parts (London, 1764–1765), *ESTC* t140761, with 2d ed., 2 vols., 1771 (*ESTC* 140762).

237. Algernon Sidney, *Discourses Concerning Government* (London, 1704), with various later editions, most recently London, 1763 (*ESTC* t131336).

238. James Beattie, *An Essay on the Nature and Immutability of Truth* (Edinburgh and London, 1770), *ESTC* t138995, with 2d ed. in 1771 (*ESTC* t138977).

239. Not identified.

240. William Guthrie, *A New Geographical, Historical, and Commercial Grammar* (London, 1770), *ESTC* t149699.

241. Charles Johnstone, *Chrysal; or, The Adventures of a Guinea,* 2 vols. (London, 1760), *ESTC* t089195, with a two-volume 5th ed., 1766 (vols. 3 and 4 were published in 1765).

242. The M. Dacier and P. Sanadon editions were *Oeuvres d'Horace en latin et en françois,* 4 vols. in 4to and 10 vols. 12mo (Hamburg, 1733), *ESTC* t013699, t013700, or the more recent *The Odes, Epodes, & Carmen Seculare of Horace,* 2 vols. (London, 1741), *ESTC* t042038, and *The Satires, Epistles and Art of Poetry of Horace* (London, 1743), *ESTC* t047089.

243. Possibly a request for John Almon's publication, *A Collection of the Most Interesting Tracts, on the Subjects of Taxing the American Colonies, and Regulating their Trade,* 2 vols. (London 1766), *ESTC* n027849, with a four-volume edition in 1773 (*ESTC* t004123).

244. Cesare Beccaria, *A Discourse on Public Œconomy and Commerce* (London, 1769), *ESTC* n008843; Jacob Friedrich von Bielfeld, *Letters of Baron Bielfeld,* 2 vols. (London, 1768), *ESTC* t112978, with 2 further vols., 1770 (*ESTC* t112977).

245. Beccaria, *An Essay on Crimes and Punishments* (London, 1767), *ESTC* t138985, and later edition, listed as London, 1770, 8vo no. 518 in the 1772 *Catalogue,* appendix (see also above, n. 214); Bielfeld, *The Elements of Universal Education,* 3 vols. (London, 1770), *ESTC* t128060; listed as 8vo no. 520 in 1772 *Catalogue,* appendix, (see also above, n. 218).

246. Samuel Whatley (supposed editor), *A General Collection of Treatys, Declarations of War, Manifestos, and Other Publick Papers* (London, 1710), *ESTC* t096502; *A General Collection of Treaties, Manifesto's, Contracts of Marriage, Renunciations, and Other Publick Papers* (London, 1713), *ESTC* t096504; *A General Collection of Treatys of Peace and Commerce, Renunciations, and Other Publick Papers,* vol. 3 (London, 1732), *ESTC* t096506; *A General Collection of Treatys of Peace and Commerce, Manifestos, Declarations of War, and Other Publick Papers,* vol. 4 (London, 1732), *ESTC* t096507. Any later volumes, if published, are unidentified.

247. Ship *Portland*, James Wilson, "new loaded and may sail between this and our next [newspaper edition]"; *SCG*, 5 Dec. 1771. The following weeks' *SCG*, presumably with Wilson's exact sailing date and destination, are missing.

248. Ship *Liberty*, Capt. John Lasley, sailed for Falmouth on 11 Sept.; *SCG*, 17 Sept. 1772.

249. *A Description of the Manner in which the Commission, for Establishing a New Code of Laws, was Opened at Moscow, on Friday the Third Day of August, 1767* (London, 1769), *ESTC* t103581.

250. Probably a general reference to a series of prints published by the Society of Antiquarians (unless to John Strange, *An Account of Some Remains of Roman and Other Antiquities . . . of Brecknock* [London, 1769], *ESTC* t183308, but this appears too specialist).

251. *Joannis Lelandi antiquarii de rebus Britannicis collectanae*, 6 vols. (London, 1770), *ESTC* t136035.

252. *The Political and Commercial Works of that Celebrated Writer Charles D'avenant LLD . . . Collected and Revised by Sir Charles Whitworth*, 5 vols. (London, 1771), *ESTC* t081620.

253. *Hogarth Moralized: Being a Complete Edition of Hogarth's Works* (London, 1768), *ESTC* t010099, but without mention of Martin. It was published by John Trusler.

254. Capt. John Knox, *An Historical Journal of the Campaigns in North-America, for the Years, 1757, 1758, 1759, and 1760*, 2 vols. (London, 1769), *ESTC* t092827.

255. Capt. Philip Pittman, *The Present State of the European Settlements on the Missisippi* [*sic*]*; with a Geographical Description of that River* (London, 1770), with plates, *ESTC* t105647. Possibly the CLS expected a further illustrative supplement also.

256. William Cave, *The Lives, Acts and Matyrdoms, of the Holy Apostles of our Saviour* (Wolverhampton, [?1770]), *ESTC* t171591, a new edition of *Antiquitates Apostolicæ* (London, 1702).

257. George Lyttelton, *The History of the Life of King Henry the Second,* issued in full in 4 vols., but with staged publishing history; as noted above, n. 155.

258. James Lee, *An Introduction to Botany . . . Extracted from the Works of Dr Linnæus* (London, 1760), *ESTC* t081054, and a 2d ed., 1765 (*ESTC* t081053).

259. Probably *A Description of A New Chart of History* (London, 1767), *ESTC* n028393, and 2d ed., 1770 (*ESTC* t031658). See also below, n. 335.

260. The books must have arrived too late for inclusion in the 1772 *Catalogue*, appendix, and were probably all lost in the 1778 fire.

261. The secretary confirms that he has written and sent the bill (QM, 6 Oct. 1773, J, fol. 154). The brigantine *Expedition*, Capt. Michael Dove, sailed for London on 15 Aug.; *SCG*, 16 Aug. 1773.

262. A year earlier, at the QM of 1 July 1772, the chief justice had proposed that the Library Room be insured to the value of £1,000, and the committee was charged with accomplishing this at 1 percent if possible, and if not to write to the bookseller to see if he could get it done in England "upon best terms" (J, fol. 145). At the CM of 5 Aug. 1772 the prolonged question of obtaining insurance on the library and its books through an insurance broker is resolved "and Ordered that the Secretary do write the Bookseller to

get the same done in England agreeable to the Order of the Society at the last meeting thereof" (C, fols. 88–89).

263. Apparently from the 1753 London edition of Charles Nicolas Cochin, *Observations upon the Antiquities of the Town of Herculaneum* (*ESTC* t101272), which had 42 plates.

264. Unlisted in the 1811 *Catalogue*. The set could have been destroyed in 1778 fire. See above, nn. 125, 181, 203.

265. The letter repeats almost exactly the resolution that the "Society takes greatly amiss his Neglect of the Order . . . " (QM, 7 July 1773, J, fol. 153). The *Statutes at Large* in 8 vols. 4to listed in the 1811 *Catalogue*, p. 82; *State Trials* in 5 vols. 2°, p. 81. Eight volumes of *State Trials* were announced as having arrived at the AM of 4 Jan. 1780 (J, fol. 193). No copies of either survive in the library.

266. See below, n. 337.

267. At the QM of 6 July 1774 the secretary "informed the Society that it was not owing to the neglect of the Bookseller that no books had arrived for sometime past, but to his own occasioned in some degree by his device of rectifying the orders for the Books agreed to be sent for some of which he found were already in the library whilst others were twice ordered; that he had now got all the orders compleat and shoud write to the Bookseller at large immediately after this meeting" (J, fol. 162).

268. See above, nn. 125, 181, 203, 264.

269. See above, nn. 126, 159, 195, 265.

270. Probably Thomas Shirley, merchant, plantation owner, and slave-trader, member of the library since 1766.

271. The *Encyclopédie*. At the QM of 7 July 1773, it had been "Ordered that the Secretary do write to the Bookseller to subscribe at the Booksellers who advertises the Encyclopediæ in England whose name Mr Wells will inform the Secretary" (J, fol. 153). Other instructions (and reprimands) for the bookseller from this QM were sent in letter 29 (above).

272. Ship *Briton,* Alexander Urquhart, arrived Charleston from London on 19 July; *SCG,* 25 July 1774.

273. Bernard Picart, ed., *The Religious Ceremonies and Customs of the Several Nations of the Known World,* 3 vols. (London, 1731), *ESTC* t149011, and a seven-volume edition (London, 1733–1739), *ESTC* t137604.

274. *The Architecture of M. Vitruvius Pollio: Translated from the Original Latin, by W. Newton, Architect* (London, 1771), ESTC t022369.

275. Nathaniel Hooke, *The Roman History, from the Building of Rome to the Ruin of the Commonwealth,* vol. 4 (London, 1771), *ESTC* t071735 (earlier vols. in 4° ed.: 1738, 1745, 1764).

276. *The Designs of Inigo Jones,* 2 vols. (London, 1770), *ESTC* t116215.

277. Charles Rollin, *The Method of Teaching and Studying the Belles Lettres,* 4 vols. (London, 1770), *ESTC* t136386 (1st ed. in English, 1734).

278. *Philosophical Transactions of the Royal Society* (began publication in 1665; see *ESTC* t154206).

279. *The Works of M. Voltaire,* 25 vols. (London, 1761–1765), *ESTC* t052773.

280. Benjamin Stillingfleet, *Principles and Power of Harmony* (London, 1771), *ESTC* t113613.

281. *Medical Observations and Inquiries: By a Society of Physicians in London* (London, 1757), *ESTC* t105087; 4th ed., 1771 (*ESTC* t105087).

282. Comte Louis-Antoine de Bougainville, *A Voyage Round the World* (London, 1772), *ESTC* t082890.

283. Request for the *Annual Register* (first published in 1758, *ESTC* t154262) had begun in Oct. 1764 (see above, n. 73), and these were now a regular order.

284. James Ussher, *An Introduction to the Theory of the Human Mind* (London, 1771), *ESTC* t114173.

285. Thomas Pennant, *A Tour in Scotland* (Chester, 1771), *ESTC* t143680, and 2d ed., London, 1771 (*ESTC* t148761).

286. Thomas Pennant, *The British Zoology* (London, 1766), *ESTC* t154286, and four-volume edition, London, 1768–1770 (*ESTC* t148771).

287. Thomas Pennant, *Synopsis of Quadrupeds* (Chester, 1771), *ESTC* t051037.

288. Charles Burney, *The Present State of Music in France and Italy* (London, 1771), *ESTC* t116496.

289. William Boyce, *Cathedral Music: Being a Collection in Score of the Most Valuable and Useful Compositions for that Service*, 3 vols. (London, 1760–1773), *ESTC* t164552.

290. John Huddlestone Wynne, *A General History of the British Empire in America*, 2 vols. (London, 1770), *ESTC* t145445.

291. Sir John Dalrymple, *Memoirs of Great Britain and Ireland* (Edinburgh, 1771), *ESTC* t145644; 1st London ed., 1771 (*ESTC* t145647).

292. Henri-Louis Duhamel du Monceau, *The Elements of Agriculture*, 2 vols. (London, 1764), *ESTC* t130245.

293. Probably Sir William Chambers, *A Dissertation on Oriental Gardening* (London, 1772), *ESTC* t001897.

294. Pierre Augustin Guys, *A Sentimental Journey through Greece*, 3 vols. (London, 1772), *ESTC* t110207; listed in the MSS CLS inventory catalogue of 1785, J, fol. 84.

295. Georges Louis Leclerc, comte de Buffon, *The Natural History of the Horse* (London, 1762), *ESTC* t141047; listed as "Buffon's Nat. Hist.," in MSS CLS inventory catalogue of 1785, J, fol. 84 (a six-volume edition was also published 1775–1776, *ESTC* n019486).

296. Peter Kalm, *Travels into North America* (Warrington, 1770–1771), *ESTC* t123563; and two-volume London 2d ed., 1772 (*ESTC* t123553).

297. Not identified.

298. Probably an earlier version of [Hutchins], *A Topographical Description of Virginia, Pennsylvania, Maryland, and North Carolina . . . Containing P. Kennedy's Journal up the Illinois River, and a . . . List of the Different Nations and Tribes of Indians* (London, 1778), *ESTC* t067632.

299. Probably James Paine, *Plans, Elevations . . . Public and Private, Temples and Other Garden Buildings* (London, 1767), 2°, 74 plates (*ESTC* t135969).

300. John Rutty (Ruthy) published various treastises, notably *A Methodical Analysis of Mineral Waters* (London, 1757), *ESTC* t077193. The most recent reissue of Alexander

Sutherland was *Experimental Essays on the Virtues of the Bath and Bristol Waters,* 3d ed. (London, 1772), ESTC n031561.

301. George Edwards, *A Natural History of Birds,* 2 vols. (London, 1743–1747), *ESTC* t144870, with later editions.

302. Charles Cameron, *The Baths of the Romans Explained and Illustrated* (London, 1772), *ESTC* t021409.

303. Not identified.

304. David MacBride, *A Methodical Introduction to the Theory and Practice of Physic* (London and Edinburgh, 1772), *ESTC* t056402.

305. Colin Milne, *Institutes of Botany . . . translated from the Lectures of the Celebrated Charles von Linné* (London, 1771–1772; separate parts), *ESTC* t080796; an edition listed as "The Litchfield Translation of Linnaeus," J, p. 84, MSS CLS inventory catalogue of 1785.

306. Thomas Wildman, *A Treatise on the Management of Bees* (London, 1768), *ESTC* t101490 (2d ed., 1770, *ESTC* t122962).

307. John Guillim, *A Display of Heraldry,* 6th ed. (London, 1724), *ESTC* t140947, with an abridgment in 2 vols., London, 1755, *ESTC* t122962.

308. Edward Ives, *A Voyage from England to India, in the Year MDCCCIV* (London, 1773), *ESTC* t012210.

309. John Zephaniah Holwell, *India Tracts: By Mr Holwell, and Friends,* 2d ed. (London, 1764), *ESTC* t009067 (3d ed., 1774).

310. Thomas Leland, *The History of Ireland from the Invasion of Henry II,* 3 vols. (London, 1773), *ESTC* t135878.

311. *An Universal History, from the Earliest Account of Time to the Present . . . Compiled from Original Authors,* 7 vols. (London, 1736–1744), *ESTC* n036177. Originally published in parts. In 1752 *Proposals* were issued for republishing the whole, *ESTC* t153781.

312. Benjamin Kennicott issued *Proposals for Preparing for the Press the Various Readings Collected from the Hebrew MSS of the Old Testament* in London in 1770 (*ESTC* t148159), but the first volume of *Vetus Testamentum Hebraicum* was not published until 1776 and the second volume not until 1780.

313. Richard Price, *Observations on Reversionary Payments* (London, 1771), *ESTC* t012982 (under Parker), with a 3d ed. by 1773, *ESTC* t012984.

314. Richard Grey, *Memoria technica; or, A New Method of Artificial Memory* (London, 1730), *ESTC* t124078, with 4th ed., 1756, *ESTC* t108562.

315. Solomon Lowe, *Mnemonics Delineated in a Small Compass and Easy Method* (?London, 1737), *ESTC* t113653.

316. Apart from annual editions of the pocket *London Guide,* the obvious choice would have been John Rocque, *A Plan of London, with all the New Streets, Lanes, Roads, etc.,* first published in 1746 and with a recent edition in 1769. It offered great detail on a 1:12,200 scale.

317. D. Drury, *Illustrations of Natural History* (London, 1770), *ESTC* t144818 (with 2 further volumes by 1780).

318. Probably James Murray, *Eikon Basilke, or the Character of Eglon, King of Moab, and his Ministry* (Newcastle, 1773), *ESTC* t192674

319. This must be *A Supplement to the Essay on General History,* 2 vols. (London, 1764), *ESTC* t150354 (*The General History and State of Europe, from the Time of Charlemain to Charles V,* 5 vols. [London, 1754–1757], *ESTC* t137606).

320. Claude François Xavier, abbé Millot, *Elements of the History of England,* 4 vols. (London, 1771), *ESTC* t108852; "All Milots' Works" listed in MSS CLS inventory catalogue of 1785, J, fol. 84.

321. "The Secretary laid before the Soc. a Letter from the Bookseller offering to supply the Society with Pamphlets and Fugitive pieces, as usual, and to wait for peace." The secretary was ordered to write to accept and "return thanks for his Offer" (AM, 4 Jan. 1780, J, fol. 192).

322. AM, 4 Jan. 1780, with thanks recorded to the late secretary "being about to leave the Town" (J, fol. 191). John McCall, Jr., was to be secretary until the last meeting of 1787 (and librarian from July 1783; see below, n. 325). His father was a Charleston merchant (hence, the "Jr."), who died Dec. 1773; "Records Kept by Colonel Isaac Hayne," p. 170; *PHL,* 3:282. McCall, Jr., was also city treasurer (*Charleston Directory,* 1790), and clerk to the South Carolina Society; *Supplement to the State Gazette,* 18 Nov. 1784.

323. *Charles Town Packet,* brigantine of 60 tons, was a captured, renamed, French ship, registered in 1762, Olsberg, "Ship Registers," p. 210. Samuel Hill, Ship *Charlestown Packet,* entered inwards from London on 10 July (*SCG,* 12 July 1783) and cleared out for London on 15 Aug. (*SCG,* 16 Aug. 1783).

324. There is no CLS journal record of such a direction for the anniversary of Jan. 1783 or the quarterly meetings of 5 Feb. and 2 July 1783.

325. McCall was elected librarian on 2 July 1783 (J, fol. 196).

326. Ship *Peggy,* John Scott, entered from London on 29 Dec.; *SCG,* 30 Dec., 1783.

327. At the AM of 13 Jan. 1784, Nicoll was confirmed as bookseller and a bill of £13.13s.4d. ordered for him (J, fol. 200).

328. See below, n. 329.

329. Samuel Ball, Ship *Britannia,* cleared out for London on 19 Feb.; *SCG,* 19 Feb. 1784.

330. Alexander Garden (c.1730–1791), botanist and FRS 1773. Native of Aberdeenshire, he was M.D. of Edinburgh and professor of King's College, New York, before returning to Charleston in 1755. As a Loyalist, he departed finally for London in 1783.

331. Confirmed as bookseller at the AM of 11 Jan. 1785 (J, fol. 206).

332. Ship *Hunter,* Tho. Jay, entered in on 4 Nov. and cleared out for London on 24 Jan. 1785; *South Carolina State Gazette and General Advertiser* (hereafter *SCSG*), 4 Nov. 1784, 25 Jan. 1785

333. "Yesterday came into the Roads the Britannia Capt. Ball, from London, full of passengers," and note also of arrival of the *City of Charleston,* Capt. Hill; *SCSG,* 6 Dec. 1784, with both ships reported as entered, 7 Dec. in *SCSG,* 8 Dec. 1784.

334. Unidentified.

335. *A Description of a Chart of Biography* (Warrington, 1764), *ESTC* t184197, with the most recent of many editions, London, 1785 (*ESTC* t032350), the accompaniment to Priestley's one-sheet *Chart of Biography* (London, 1765); see also above, n. 259.

336. John Dawson Sr., planter, 2 East Bay; Nathaniel Russell, merchant, 16 East Bay; Elizer, *Directory for 1803,* pp. 14, 50. Nathaniel Russell (1738–1820), born in Bristol, Rhode

Island, arrived in Charleston in 1765 as commercial agent. He married, in 1788, Sarah, the daughter of William Hopton (1712–1786; a frequent attender at CLS meetings from at least 1759), and the brother of John Hopton (see below, n. 511). Russell resigned from the South Carolina legislature in 1798; *CGDA,* 7 Dec. 1798. In 1809 John Hopton contacted his brother-in-law when asked by the CLS to remonstrate with Lackington, Allen in London (see below, letter 112).

337. William Greenwood and his nephew William Higginson, who had come from Manchester, were partners with John Beswicke (and owners together of the Ship *America;* see above, n. 61), and William Greenwood was the richest London Carolina trader after Crokatt; see Rogers, *Evolution of a Federalist,* p. 75 n. 78. On the eve of the Revolution, the partnership was the largest in the Carolina trade; *PHL,* 1:96. William Greenwood, merchant, and William Greenwood, Jr., gentleman, are listed in the *Charleston Directory,* 1796. For the Higginson victory in reclaiming dues after the war, see Rogers, *Evolution of a Federalist,* pp. 250–51.

338. Ship *Eleanor,* C. Henderson, from London, entered in 20 Jan.; *SCSG,* 21 Jan. 1785.

339. Thomas Holcroft, *Noble Peasant: A Comic Opera in Three Acts* (London, 1784), *ESTC* t005521.

340. The *Lightning* (*sic*), Capt. Burton, arrived 23 Jan. from London: "she sailed from thence the 9 of November and from Plymouth the 1st of December" and "the ship Briton, Capt. Angus & the ship Sally —— [*sic*] arrived also yesterday in 52 days from the Downs"; *SCSG,* 24 Jan. 1785.

341. At the AM of 10 Jan. 1786, Charles Dilly is listed as the elected bookseller; no procedure or discussion is recorded (J, fol. 210). Robert Smith (also a signatory to letter 17a, above) was born in Norfolk and emigrated in 1757 to serve first as assistant minister, and then within months as rector of St. Philip's, Charleston. He was admitted to the CLS in Apr. 1763. He returned to Britain in 1768, to Charleston in 1770, and then was exiled to Philadelphia in 1780, returning to Charleston three years later. In 1795 he was elected bishop of the Episcopal Church in South Carolina. He died in 1801.

342. No record survives of this.

343. Wells is now in London. As a Loyalist he returned to Britain during the Revolution and apparently set up shop in Salisbury Court off Fleet St. (letter from Daniel Chaime to "Robert Wells of Salisbury-Court Square Bookseller and Stationer," 29 Sept. 1778, Edinburgh, National Library of Scotland, MS Ch. 3970).

344. At the QM of 4 Oct. 1786, "the Secretary laid before the Society a Letter from Charles Dilly of London, Bookseller, also one from William Nicoll, which being read; the Society referred the same to the special Committee, and they are directed to report thereon next Meeting" (J, fol. 213). Considered at the AM of 9 Jan. 1787, the Dilly letter is referred to the next meeting (J, fol. 214). At the QM of 4 Apr. 1787, "Mr Charles Dilly having declined the proposals of this Society as their Bookseller . . . the Society therefore agreed to dismiss Mr Dilly," confirmed, together with election of Wells, at the AM of 8 Jan. 1788 (J, fols. 215, 219).

345. The most recent London edition was *Opera inedite in prosa, e in verso di Niccolo Macchiavelli,* 3 vols. (London, 1777), *ESTC* n022037; but an edition in English was

probably desired, for which the most recent was *The Works of Nicholas Machiavel,* 2d ed., 4 vols. (London, 1775), *ESTC* n091220.

346. Vicesimus Knox, *Essays Moral and Literary,* 2 vols. (London, 1778–1789), *ESTC* t122387; the most recent edition was the 11th, in 2 vols., 1787 (*ESTC* n009472).

347. John Scott, *Digests of the General Highway and Turnpike Laws . . . Also an Appendix on the Construction and Preservation of Roads* (London, 1778), *ESTC* t084548; like Knox, above, a Dilly publication.

348. John Gillies, *The History of Ancient Greece, its Colonies and Conquests,* 2 vols. (London, 1786), *ESTC* t099924; 2d ed., 4 vols., 1787 (*ESTC* n007591).

349. McCall served as secretary for the next four years. See above, nn. 322, 325.

350. Edward Nairne, instrument maker of Cornhill, opposite the Royal Exchange, London, trading since 1748 and in partnership with Thomas Blunt.

351. Jesse Ramsden (1735–1800), FRS 1786, gained early fame with his New Universal Equatoreal, patented 1774. In 1790 he was "Mathematical, optical and philosophical instrument-maker, near the Little Theatre, in St James's, Haymarket" (pamphlet advertisement, *ESTC* n003005). *DNB* remarks that "the demand from all parts of Europe for his incomparable instruments was greater than could be satisfied by the constant labour of sixty workmen."

352. This statement and the mention of the £80 bill, for which there is no record of dispatch in 1788, suggests a missing letter in the copybook.

353. *ESTC* lists 72 English editions of works by Sallust, published 1701–1789.

354. John Boydell, *A Catalogue of the Pictures in the Shakespeare Gallery* (London, 1789), *ESTC* t129413, and 1790 version (*ESTC* t076467). The catalogues proclaim an intention to issue 18 numbers, each comprising 4 or 5 large prints of 24 x 19″ or 16 x 24″ at 3 guineas per number. Wells is unclear whether the library requires these larger prints, usually for framing, or small prints with the text offered at 2 guineas each number (see below n. 408), or both. The library opted for both, together with gilt frames and glass at still greater expense. Copies of later and continuing proposals, including *Shakespeare: The Substance of the Original Proposals for Publishing, by Subscription, A Collection of Large and Capital Prints* (1794), are still held by the CLS today (A.Pm.ser 4.v.20.no.7; and A.Pm.ser 1.v.11.no 1).

355. Ship *Olive Branch* from Baltimore entered in 9 Feb., *CGDA,* 9 Feb. 1790.

356. The *Briton* arrived 12 Jan. from London after a passage of 7 weeks, with notable passengers also listed in *CG,* 12 Jan. 1790.

357. Son of Philip Prioleau, a major importer, c.1736–1746, Stuart O. Stumpf, "South Carolina Importers of General Merchandise, 1735–1765," *SCHM* 84 (1983), 1–10, entry no. 106. As secretary and librarian, he advertised the AM for 1 pm, Tuesday, 12 Jan.; *CG,* 9 Jan. 1790. See also below, n. 394.

358. See above, n. 351.

359. George Adams, the younger (1750–1795), mathematical instrument maker to the king, prolific author on instruments and elementary science, and son of George Adams, the elder (see above, n. 63).

360. This is done in early 1793 (see below, letter 55).

361. William Blamyer was secretary, correspondent, and librarian in years between 1791 and 1797, residing 77 Church St.; *Charleston Directory,* 1794.

362. Charles Goodwin, formerly of Charleston, now part of Messrs Goodwin & Co, No 25, Park Street, Southwark (see below, letter 48).

363. David Ramsay (1749–1815), physician, historian, and sometime vice president of the CLS, arrived in Charleston in 1773 (and exiled to St. Augustine, Florida, 1780–1781). Among many works, he wrote *The History of the Revolution of South-Carolina* (1785), *The History of the American Revolution* (1790), and *History of South Carolina* (1809). Ramsay was a customer of Stockdale, having been introduced to the bookseller by his father-in-law, Henry Laurens. He also bought books from Stockdale on account of the South Carolina Senate of which he was president, 1792–1796.

364. John Stockdale (1749–1814), a native and reputedly blacksmith of Cumberland, was porter to John Almon from about 1774, on whose retirement in 1781 he set up at 181 opposite Burlington House, Piccadilly, as a rival to Almon's successor, Debrett. He was a notorious operator, noted "for his eccentricity of manners and coarseness of conduct"; Maxted, *London Book Trades,* p. 215. In 1768 Almon brought out Dickinson's *Letters for a Farmer in Pennsylvania* (see above, nn. 164, 190) in 1764 Almon had published *The Rights of British Colonies Asserted and Proved* and in 1776 he signed the English edition of Paine's *Common Sense.* The American connection continued with his employee Stockdale, a friend of Wilkes and a supporter of parliamentary reform and colonial causes. In 1781 Henry Laurens lodged with Stockdale on his release from the Tower, and other distinguished American guests included John Adams in 1783 and Jefferson in 1786; Stockdale, "John Stockdale of Piccadilly." See above, plate 8.

365. Ship *Olive Branch,* Westoll, for London, cleared out 21 Nov.; *CGDA,* 21 Nov. 1791.

366. For Charles Cotesworth Pinckney see below, n. 370.

367. Cleared out for London 23 Jan.; *CGDA,* 23 Jan. 1792.

368. Henry M. Bird, Robert Bird, and Benjamin Savage (the latter the son of John Savage, merchant of Charleston and in 1773 first president of the Charles Town Chamber of Commerce, before fleeing to London) were a leading firm in the Anglo-Carolinian commercial trade of the period. From at least 1790 the firm was located at Bury Court, close to St. Mary Axe (see above plate 5). The partners were major subscribers to the South Carolina state debt in 1790, and DeSaussure did business with Bird, Savage, and Bird for 30 years. The firm failed after the peace of Amiens, stopped payments in Feb. 1803, and was declared bankrupt 5 months later; see Rogers, *Evolution of a Federalist,* pp. 99, 203, 273–75, 355. John Savage, a Jew born in Bermuda, accumulated one of the largest fortunes in the Carolinas in partnership with Gabriel Manigault, and organized the Charles Town Chamber of Commerce to "adjust disputes relating to trade and navigation"; George C. Rogers, Jr., "The Charleston Tea Party: The Significance of December 3 1773," *SCHM* 75 (1974): 161.

369. Arthur St. Clair (1736–1812), governor of the Northwest Territory, 1787–1802. As commander of the Federal Army, he suffered a humiliating defeat by an Indian army on the banks of the Wabash, 4 Nov. 1791. A committee of the House of Representatives was set up to investigate.

370. General Charles Cotesworth Pinckney (1746–1825) served as president of the CLS 1792–1797 and 1798–1807. He was Federalist vice presidential candidate in 1800 and presidential candidate in 1804 and 1808. He is listed as planter of 1 East Bay, Elizer, *Directory for 1803*, p. 46. See also above, between letters 43 and 44.

371. See above, n. 368.

372. John Tunno, merchant, 6 Old Jewry, *Kent's Directory,* 1801. Tunno, a Loyalist, was banished to London exile after refusing to take the state oath in 1777, returned to Charleston during the British occupation (and is listed with his brother Adam in the 1782 *Directory*), returned to London in 1782, and was denied permission to return to Charleston in 1783 (confirmed in 1784). Adam, however, did return and became a citizen in 1784, thereafter acting as his brother's agent; see Geraldine M. Meroney, "William Bull's First Exile from South Carolina of 1777–1781," *SCHM* 80 (1979): 94 n. 12; Rogers, *Evolution of a Federalist,* p. 103; and below, n. 463.

373. See above, n. 362.

374. John Neufville (1727–1804), with his brother Edward, was in partnership with William Anderson and was a ship-owning merchant (see above, n. 209). He was appointed to the CLS committee at the QM of 3 Oct. 1759 (J, fol. 14). He was treasurer from 1764. A vestryman and churchwarden of St. Philips, Neufville remained in Charleston as commissioner of the Colonial Treasury in 1775 and was subsequently exiled to St. Augustine in 1780; Edward settled in Bristol; *PHL,* 1:243 n. 6, 244, 2:212 n. 9.

375. Ship *Laurens,* Marston, cleared out 4 Feb., *CGDA,* 4 Feb. 1792.

376. The *Hanbury,* McNeil, from London entered in at Charleston 29 Feb., *CGDA,* 29 Feb. 1792.

377. Ship *Laurens,* Marston, entered in 25 June, *CGDA,* 25 June 1792. Marston is therefore the carrier "by return," with the original later to arrive than the copy.

378. *Britannia,* Redman, from London, entered in 19 June, *CGDA,* 19 June 1792.

379. *Britannia,* Redman, cleared out for "Cowes & a Market" 12 July, *CGDA,* 12 July 1792.

380. Ship *Westberry,* Maslin, cleared out for Bristol 26 Aug., *CGDA,* 24 Aug. 1792.

381. Letter therefore sent with copy of letter 50 (above).

382. *Julius Pringle,* Callahan, entered in from London 17 Dec., *CGDA,* 17 Dec. 1792. John Julius Pringle was attorney general of South Carolina living at 93 Tradd Street, Charleston, and president of the Charleston Library Society from 1812.

383. *Gentleman's Magazine* began publication 1731. It had been a standing order for the CLS since at least letter 6 (above).

384. Samuel Buck, *Buck's Antiquities; or, Venerable Remains of above Four Hundred Castles, Monasteries, Palaces &c. &c. in England and Wales,* 3 vols. (London, 1774), *ESTC* t139229.

385. *The Scripture-Dictionary; or, Guide to the Holy Scriptures,* 2 vols. (Aberdeen: James Chalmers & Co., 1771), *ESTC* t176583.

386. The recent three-volume edition was William Camden, *Britannia: or, A Chorographical Description of the Flourishing Kingdoms of England, Scotland, and Ireland and the Islands Adjacent* (London, 1789), *ESTC* n015693.

387. Francis Grose, *The Antiquities of England and Wales,* 6 vols. (London, 1773–1787), *ESTC* t147669; *The Antiquities of Ireland,* 2 vols. (London, 1791, 1794),

ESTC t147219; *The Antiquities of Scotland,* 2 vols. (London, 1789, 1791), *ESTC* t141301.

388. John Latham, *A General Synopsis of Birds,* published in parts since 1781, *ESTC* t146461.

389. Thomas Pennant was a prolific author; Samuel Ireland, *A Picturesque Tour Through Holland, Brabant, and Part of France,* 2 vols. (London, 1790), *ESTC* t139136; William Gilpin, *Remarks on Forest Scenery and Other Woodland Views,* 2 vols. (London, 1791), *ESTC* t098991.

390. John Hunter, *An Historical Journal of the Transactions at Port Jackson and Norfolk Island, and the Discoveries that have been made in New South Wales* (London: Printed for John Stockdale, 1 Jan. 1793), *ESTC* t137599.

391. Bryan Edwards, *The History, Civil and Commercial, of the British Colonies in the West Indies,* 2 vols. (London: Printed for John Stockdale, 1793), *ESTC* t137074.

392. Philadelphia and New York editions of *The Life of Dr Benjamin Franklin* were published in 1794.

393. Details of the anniversary meetings after 1791 and before 1815 are unknown because no journal records survive between those dates (and no committee minutes after 1790 and before the restyled book committee minutes from 1849).

394. The Legare family had been leading Carolinian importers since the 1750s, Stumpf, "South Carolina Importers," no. 160, 188, 280 (Thomas, Daniel). Samuel Legare was on the CLS committee in the late 1780s. Legare and Theus, merchants are listed at 101 Church St., in the *Charleston Directory,* 1790; and Legare, Theus, and Prioleau, merchants, at 131 Broad St. in the *Charleston Directory,* 1794. Samuel Legare also managed the affairs of Nathaniel Russell during his extraordinary four months afloat in Charleston harbor in 1783–1784 awaiting permission to reenter the city; Rogers, *Evolution of a Federalist,* p. 104.

395. Bernard Beekman, surveyor, 109 East Bay, *Charleston Directory,* 1794; Col. Beekman, East Bay, *Charleston Directory,* 1796. He does not appear at the meetings recorded in the journal surviving from 1815.

396. Ship *Carolina Planter,* White, cleared out for London 4 Mar., *CGDA,* 4 Mar. 1793

397. *Major Pinckney,* Grice, cleared out for London 12 Mar., *CGDA,* 12 Mar. 1793.

398. *Federalist,* Pratt, cleared out for London 7 May, *CGDA,* 7 May 1793.

399. *Caroline,* Hilton, from London, entered in 24 Sept., *CGDA,* 24 Sept. 1793.

400. Arrival unrecorded, although the ship *Henricus IV,* Capt. Haskell, "spoke with the Ship Fame, of Bristol, from Jamaica, all well"; *CGDA,* 19 Dec. 1793.

401. Departure unrecorded, but brigantine *Lively,* Bunker, had returned to Charleston from London 31 Jan., *CGDA,* 31 Jan. 1794.

402. Departure unrecorded.

403. Ship *Ruby,* Atkin [*sic*], entered in from Madeira 12 Mar., *CGDA,* 12 Mar. 1793. Departure unrecorded.

404. A xebec, a small vessel with three masts, often associated with Mediterranean pirates.

405. The usual method of framing involved the pasting of the print on a canvas stretcher.

406. Ship *Major Pinckney,* Grice, from London, entered in 7 May, *CGDA,* 7 May 1794.

407. The fifth number included prints of the *Merry Wives of Windsor, Winter's Tale, and Titus Andronicus;* see plate 16 above.

408. A number of smaller prints, also illustrating Shakespearian scenes, were issued in each "number" (or in parallel numbers) of the Boydell series, in addition to the four or five main 24 x 16 or 19" prints. They were separately priced; the smaller prints and text costing an extra 2 guineas.

409. Ship *Federalist,* Pratt, cleared out for London 5 Nov., *CGDA,* 5 Nov. 1794.

410. Ship *Minerva,* Payne, cleared out for Bristol 25 Nov., *CGDA,* 25 Nov. 1794.

411. Brigantine *Romulus,* Wallace, from London, entered in 10 Apr., *CGDA,* 10 Apr. 1795.

412. No copies of the *CGDA* or *South Carolina State Gazette* have survived for July–Sept. 1795.

413. David Ogilvy (d. 1812) & Son, booksellers, of 315 High Holborn; Ogilvy was partnered by Speare, c. 1787–1797, and ran the "London and Westminster Circulating Library."

414. Surviving at the CLS is the pamphlet *Shakespeare: Substance of the Original Proposals . . . A Collection of Large and Capital Prints* marked "No. 6 published — No. 7 in January."

415. George Adams, *Lectures on Natural and Experimental Philosophy,* 5 vols. (London, 1794), *ESTC* t088417 (see also above, n. 359).

416. Ralph Izard (1741–1804) had returned to South Carolina from London and Paris in 1780, and by 1790 he commanded the second largest total acreage of plantations in the state. In 1789 he became South Carolina's first U.S. senator. The family possessed a major library, begun in the late seventeenth century; see Robert F. Neville and Katherine H. Bielsky, "The Izard Library," *SCHM* 91 (1990): 149–69.

417. That is, sent with the letterpress, and if bound, bound into their proper position to illustrate the text.

418. Sir James Edward Smith, *Icones pictæ plantarum rariorum* (London, 1790–1793), with 3 fasciculi of "Icones pictæ" and 75 plates, *ESTC* t036968.

419. John Price, merchant of 50 Finsbury Square, London, listed in the *Post Office Annual Directory,* 1802. He was the tenant of Lackington, Allen, and Co. See below, letter 88.

420. Thomas Mullett & Co., merchants of 11 Broad St. Buildings, listed in *Post Office Annual Directory,* 1802.

421. See above, n. 372.

422. Ship details have not been recovered: Charleston newspapers have not survived for these months. They are also missing for the relevant weeks for letters 73, 74, and 78 (below).

423. Ship *Roebuck,* Wilson, cleared out for Liverpool 15 Mar., *CGDA,* 15 Mar. 1796.

424. Ship *Washington,* Wardell, cleared out for London 24 Mar., *CGDA,* 24 Mar. 1796.

425. See above, n. 372.

426. Peter and John Dollond, opticians, 59 St. Paul's Churchyard, *Kent's Directory,* 1801. John, the son of Peter, had issued catalogues of instruments with his father since at least 1785; Tessa Murdoch, *The Quiet Conquest: The Huguenots 1685 to 1985* (London: Museum of London, 1985), opposite p. 132. See also above n. 91.

427. Ship *South-Carolina*, Gillender, cleared out for London 19 Nov., *CGDA*, 19 Nov. 1796.

428. Ship *Federalist*, Pratt, listed as "arrived" (and bringing in newspapers up to 3 Jan.) from London 7 Mar., after 60 days passage; *CGDA*, 8 Mar. 1797.

429. It was reported in *CGDA* of 10 Feb. 1797 that "Captain Pratt of the Ship Federalist writes from London that he expected to sail for this port between the 20th and 30th of Dec. if he was not prevented by a hard frost that was then setting"; and the *Ruby* arrives, *CGDA*, 8 Feb. 1797, reporting that the *Pacific* was to have sailed from London about 10 days after the *Ruby*. Actual arrival is lost.

430. Humphry Repton, *Sketches and Hints on Landscape Gardening* (London, [1794]), *ESTC* t073696.

431. Not obviously identifiable, but the CLS might have been thinking of Legrand, *Fabliaux or Tales, Abridged from French Manuscripts of the XIIth and XIIIth Centuries* (London, 1796), *ESTC* t200705 (1st ed., 1786).

432. Joseph Peace, attorney-at-law, listed at 110 Tradd St. in the 1782 *Charleston Directory*. Partner of Langdon Cheves from 1802; see also below, n. 442.

433. *Pacific*, Kennedy, cleared out for London 27 June, *CGDA*, 27 June 1798.

434. *Julius Pringle*, Miller, cleared out for London 30 July, *CGDA*, 30 July 1798.

435. *Pacific*, Kennedy, from London, is reported as off the Bar, *CGDA*, 31 Dec. 1798.

436. Hugh Bethune & Co., merchants, 7 Circus, Minories, *Kent's Directory*, 1801.

437. Lackington, Allen, & Co., of Finsbury Square, were managers of and successors to a flourishing if infamous bookshop. From the opening of his first shop in 1774, James Lackington (1746–1815) was the first bookseller to sell for cash only, appalling those offering credit—and higher prices. In 1793 Lackington opened his huge book emporium, the "Temple of the Muses" in Finsbury Square. Over a million books were said to be displayed and the bookselling business "carried on in its most extended and varied branches, viz. the purchase and publication of manuscripts, the purchase of libraries, and the sale of all kinds of new and old books, both wholesale and retail, printing, bookbinding, etc"; R. Ackermann, *Repositary of Arts, Literature, Commerce, Manufacture, Fashion and Politics*, 1st ser., 1 (1809), 251. In 1793 Robert Allen bought a quarter of the business, and in 1798 James Lackington retired in favor of his cousin George. The Temple of the Muses continued business under various partnerships until, at its later Pall Mall site, it was destroyed by fire in 1841.

438. Edwin Gairdner, merchant, resided at 72 East Bay; Elizer, *Directory for 1803*, p. 21. Mentioned also in Mabel L. Webber, "Inscriptions from the Independent or Congregational (Circular) Church Yard," *SCHM* 29 (1928): 149.

439. Simpson & Davison, merchants, 5 Warnford-court, Throgmorton St., *Post Office Annual Directory*, 1802.

440. Between 1803 and 1822 it was listed as the Carolina and Honduras Coffee House. See also above, n. 153.

441. John Davidson, CLS librarian, 1797–1813, listed in the *Charleston Directory*, 1802, as residing 5 Society St.

442. Joseph Peace was "a respectable attorney and collector" (John Hammond Moore, ed., "The Abiel Abbot Journals," *SCHM* 68 [1967]: 130). Peace took Judge Langdon

Cheves in partnership from 1802, as listed in that year's *Charleston Directory* at State House Square. Both had Scots ancestry. See also above n. 432.

443. Arrives Charleston 7 Apr., after a passage of 57 days; *CGDA,* 8 Apr. 1802.

444. Apparently to replace volumes listed in the 1770 *Catalogue* as 8^{vo-} nos. 288 and 289, *Paradise Lost,* 1741 ed., and *Paradise Regained,* 1727 ed.

445. 1811 *Catalogue,* p. 138. Probably to replace the Bacon "(frater Rogeri) opus majus," London 1733, listed as 2° no. 24 in 1770 *Catalogue.*

446. John Sharpe, ed., *The British Classics,* 24 vols. (London, 1803–1810). A prospectus was issued in 1803. The volumes are unlisted in the 1811 *Catalogue.*

447. 1811 *Catalogue,* p. 39; and still held by the library, Charles Linné and William Truron, *A General System of Nature,* 2 vols. (vol. 1 and vol. 4 lettered on spine) (London, 1802). See also above, nn. 232, 258, 305.

448. 1811 *Catalogue,* p. 61, lists "Pallas's Travels in the Russian Empire"; a copy with magnificent colored plates survives in the library, P. S. Pallas, *Travels through the Southern Provinces of the Russian Empire, in the Years 1793 and 1794,* 2 vols. (London, 1802–1803), lettered on the front cover rather than on the spine and retaining the pressmark inside cover, which is probably from the Lackington shop. The book was proposed by J. B. Holmes; CLS accessions 1798–1805, fol. 24.

449. 1811 *Catalogue* (p. 24) lists John Charnock's *Biographia navalis,* 8^{vo-} 6 vols. It no longer survives in the library. The book was proposed by R. Dewar; CLS accessions 1798–1805, fol. 21.

450. No record of Lovell's port entry appears in surviving newspapers.

451. See above, n. 419.

452. The CLS had used Price to broker bills of exchange in payment to Bird, Savage and Bird since Aug. 1795 (see above, letter 70), and the connection might suggest a further reason for the selection of Lackington, Allen in succession to Bird, Savage and Bird.

453. 1811 *Catalogue* (p. 134) lists "Philosophical Transactions at Large," 91 vols. 4to.

454. CLS currently holds Vivant Denon, *Travels in Upper and Lower Egypt,* 2 vols. (London, 1803).

455. Jean Jacques Barthelemy, *Travels in Italy, by Abbé Barthelemy, in a Series of Letters written to Count Caylus* (London, 1802). No longer at CLS.

456. Not listed in 1811 *Catalogue* and not now at CLS.

457. BL and CUL collections include annual Lackington, Allen catalogues 1787–1789, 1792–1794, 1796–1811, 1814, and 1817–1820. In 1787 copies could be bought at six other bookshops in London and Westminster, but also at Vowell's in Cambridge and Palmer's or Merrick's in Oxford; *Second Part of Lackington's Catalogue for 1787,* p. 1. The second volume of the 1792 *Catalogue* lists in addition to four London outlets, bookseller-agents at Cambridge, Oxford, Sherborne, Bath, Coventry, Bury, Plymouth, Norwich, Bristol, Newcastle, and Edinburgh. In 1801 the business was still growing with 21,868 entries in the annual (516 pp.) catalogue. The 1815 *Catalogue* contained 28,769 entries.

458. *The Brothers,* Capt. Rising, arrives at Charleston 29 Apr. 1803, having left New York 6 days before; *CGDA,* 30 Apr. 1803. *The Brothers* is registered on 20 Jan. 1802 as owned by John Rising and of 246 tons; PRO, BT 111/1, Ships Registers, 1786–1802, B C.22.

459. See above, n. 458.

460. *Polly,* Capt. Hancock, bound for London, cleared out of the Custom House, Charleston, *CGDA,* 5 Mar. 1803.

461. Clearing out apparently not recorded in the *CGDA.*

462. See above, n. 419.

463. Tunno and Loughnan, merchants of 3 New Court, Swithins Lane, London, listed in the *Post Office Annual Directory* (1802) and *Holden's Triennial Directory,* 2 vols., 4th ed. (1808), vol. 2. In *Kent's Directory* of 1801, Tunno is listed separately at 6 Old Jewry (see above, n. 372); and by *Kent's Directory* of 1816 Tunno and Loughnan ("madeira merchant") are listed separately. Elizer, *Directory for 1803,* p. 58, lists 4 Tunnos, including merchants Tunno and Price.

464. Ship *Maria,* Chisholm, bound for Liverpool, cleared out of the Customhouse, Charleston 2 May, *CGDA,* 2 May 1803.

465. Ship *Isabella,* Green, bound for London, cleared out of the Customhouse, Charleston 10 May, *CGDA* 10 May 1803.

466. See above, letter 91.

467. Ship *Cleopatra,* Davenport, arrived Charleston after a passage of 60 days, 21 Sept. 1803; *CGDA,* 22 Sept. 1803.

468. Sir Joseph Banks (1743–1820), president of the Royal Society 1778–1820, botanist and benefactor of the British Museum. His London house and great library were in Soho Square.

469. As the *Cleopatra* entered into port 21 Sept. (see above, n. 467) it must be assumed that unloading and delivery of the books took at least a week.

470. Ship *Two Friends,* Capt. McNeill (*sic*), bound for London, cleared the Customhouse, Charleston, *CGDA,* 30 Jan. 1804. Neil McNeil, sea captain of 21 King Street, Elizer, *Directory for 1803,* p. 39 (the *Directory's* spelling of McNeil is adopted in these notes).

471. Mackmurdo & Hickes, merchants, 2 Bread-street Cheapside, *Post Office Annual Directory* 1802.

472. McNeil returns to Charleston 25 June 1804 after a passage of 49 days; he clears out again for London 26 July 1804; *CGDA* reports both dates.

473. 25 June 1804, as above, n. 472.

474. Brigantine *George Washington,* Parrott, arrived Charleston after a 76–day passage from London, *CGDA,* 17 Oct. 1804

475. Given the recorded passage of 49 days to Charleston, McNeil must have left London 7 May 1804. He had left Charleston for London 30 Jan. An above-average passage of 65 days would have seen McNeil in London in the first week of Apr., giving a London docking period of 3–4 weeks.

476. John Charnock, *An History of Marine Architecture,* 3 vols. (London, 1800–1802), *ESTC* t011210, with a printed prospectus issued in 1796, *ESTC* t011211.

477. William Roscoe, *The Life and Pontificate of Leo the Tenth,* 4 vols. (Liverpool, 1805).

478. In fact, a confusion in the original order. Ann Radcliffe, *A Sicilian Romance,* 2 vols. (London, 1790), *ESTC* t062068, was translated into French in 1798 by Moylin Fleury as *Julia; ou, les souterrains du château de Mazzini.*

479. Charles Plumier, *Filicetum Americanum, seu filicum, polypodiorum adiantorum etc.*, had been published separately in folio in Paris in 1703 with a sumptuous 222 engraved plates (BL 452.h.1), and also as *Traité des fougères de l'Amerique* (Paris, 1705). Apparently this could not be obtained separately from his other works, *Description de plantes de l'Amerique*, (1693), *Nova plantarum americanarum genera* (1703), and the folio *Plantarum Americanarum fasciculus primus/decimus* (1755–1760).

480. This order is probably sent on McNeil's ship again. The *Two Friends*, but under Livingston, not McNeil, cleared for London *CGDA*, 24 Dec. 1804.

481. Thomas and William Earle & Co., merchants of Hanover St., Liverpool, listed in *Holden's Triennial Directory*, 4th ed., 2 vols. (1808), vol. 2.

482. As detailed below, McNeil was later captured by privateers and ship, captain, and cargo sent to Jamaica. The shipment is probably described (after its long delayed arrival) among the 101 titles listed in the *Supplement. 1st October 1806* (no other title page) to the 1806 *Catalogue*.

483. When recorded in the later invoice copy (letter 106) this is reproduced as £175.0.11.

484. *CGDA*, 29 Aug. 1805, noted "Ship St. Andrews, Pratt, was to sail from London for this port, on 20 July." The St. Andrews arrives in Charleston after a passage of 53 days, *CGDA*, 21 Sept. 1805: "Capt. Pratt, August 10th, was boarded by his Britannic Majesty's ship Amazon, Capt Parker, late one of Lord Nelson's squadron, last from Gibraltar, which was then supposed to be off Corunna. The Amazon treated us with the utmost politeness, and detained us only a few moments."

485. "Non-Military Journal, or Observations made in Egypt" listed in 1811 *Catalogue* under "Voyages and Travels, 4to," p. 61.

486. By this time the full history of McNeil's ill-fated voyage was well known in Charleston. On 7 June 1805 the *CGDA* and the *CC* reported the capture of the *Two Friends* by a French privateer, *l'Emerance*, a few miles from port, after a passage of 42 days from London. Five gentlemen and some crew were allowed to board a pilot boat to Charleston, but the cook, two boys, and McNeil (and the cargo) were taken to Jamaica, "the reason given . . . that Capt McNeil was not furnished with a certificate from the American Consul in London, stating that the cargo was American property." More details are given in the introduction above. The *Two Friends* arrived at Kingston, Jamaica, 9 July, news of this reaching Charleston three weeks later (*CGDA*, 30 July 1805), and finally arrived at Charleston from Kingston, Jamaica, 13 Oct., after an escorted passage of 31 days (*CGDA*, 14 Oct. 1805). The ship was accompanied into port by HM Sloop of War, *Peterell*, Capt. Lambden, "one of the convoy of the Jamaica fleet which left Jamaica early September." As the two ships split off to enter Charleston, the *Peterell* was attacked by a French privateer, the *Superb*, with a crew of 116 men, and "off our bar for some days past."

487. This is probably Thomas Holcroft, *Travels from Hamburg through Westphalia, Holland, and the Netherlands to Paris*, 2 vols. (London, 1804), rather than his earlier *Travels through Germany . . .*, 2 vols. (1796–1797).

488. The Shoolbreds were a leading London-Carolina merchant firm (CLS, Shoolbred business letter book, 1793–1796). James Shoolbred (d. 1847), son of John Shoolbred of

London, was appointed consul to Charleston, moving there c. 1790, and in 1793 married the daughter of Thomas Middleton. *Kent's Directory* of 1808 lists Shoolbred and Williams, merchants of 63 Mark Lane, London, although *Holden's Directory* of the same year gives 86 Mark Lane. The firm does not appear in *Kent's Directory* of 1816. A Shoolbred family is listed in the Charleston 1810 census.

489. Bird, Savage, and Bird had been declared bankrupt in June 1803 (see above, n. 368).

490. Thomas Thomson, *A System of Chemistry,* 4 vols. (Edinburgh, 1802) was published in a 2d ed. in 1804 (demand brought a 3d in 1807). Thomson's *New System of Chemistry* in one volume had, however, been published in Philadelphia in 1800 (*ESTC*w011507).

491. Lt. Col. John Macdonald, *Rules and Regulations for the Field Exercise and Manoeuvres of the French Infantry Translated from the French,* 2 vols. (London, 1803) (original edition 1791).

492. Ship *Wanderer,* Haswell, arrived from London 1 Sept. 1806, after a passage of 50 days, conveying newspapers to 5 July, *CGDA,* 1 Sept. 1806.

493. The *Two Friends* is used again; Capt. Livingston cleared for London 19 Jan., *CGDA* report in *CGDA,* 19 Jan. 1807.

494. John Haslett and Co., merchants, 1 Champney's Wharf, Charleston *Directory* 1796; John Haslet, merchant, Blake's Wharf, *Charleston Directory* 1801.

495. William Lee (*sic*) is listed as a flour dealer, 61 Strand St., Liverpool, in *Holden's Directory* (1808).

496. The *Two Friends,* Livingston, was reported as having passed Deal on Apr. 14 (*CGDA* 6 June 1807) and arrived at Charleston after a passage of 52 days, with Neil NcNeil goods, *CGDA,* 10 June 1807.

497. Thomas Holcroft, *The Theatrical Recorder,* 2 vols. (London, 1805–1806).

498. [William Curtis], *The Botanical Magazine; or, Flower-garden Displayed,* 14 vols. (London, 1787–1800). It was continued as *Curtis's Botanical Magazine* from 1800 to reach eventually 90 vols. It is unlisted in the 1811 *Catalogue* but a manuscript note in the copy of the *Catalogue* belonging to Thomas Bee Jr. suggests that certain periodicals were omitted.

499. Published in 1771 by Almon, Woodfall's three volumes were published in 1812, but the request here appears to be for the two-volume edition of 1806 (also an Edinburgh edition of 1808).

500. William Clark's *Travels in the Interior Parts of America* (London, 1805) and *Discoveries Made in Exploring the Missouri River and Washita* (Washington, 1806) were followed by a volume titled *A Journal of the Voyages of a Corps of Discovery* (London, 1807).

501. Henricus Stephanus [Henri Estienne le Grand], *Thesaurus Græcæ Linguæ,* was first published in 1572. A London edition was published in 1816. The Stephanus Latin thesaurus is listed in the 1811 *Catalogue,* p. 102, but not the Greek thesaurus. An undated note in another CLS manuscript book also reports on deliberations here; see below, n. 507.

502. But cf. this figure in the original copy, letter 101 above.

503. William Johnson (1771–1834), judge of the South Carolina Court of Common Pleas until 1804 when appointed by Jefferson as associate justice of the U.S. Supreme Court;

a founder of the South Carolina College at Columbia 1801–1802; see Daniel Walker Hollis, *South Carolina College*, vol. 1 of *University of South Carolina*, 2 vols. (Columbia: University of South Carolina Press, 1951–1956), pp. 22–26.

504. According to letter 109 (below), in the *Caledonia*. Ship *Caledonian* (*sic*), Henderson, cleared the Customhouse, Charleston, 14 Nov., bound for Liverpool, *CGDA*, 14 Nov. 1807.

505. Thomas Henry Hindley, London-Carolina merchant, was in partnership with James Gregorie (see below, n. 520) and took his naturalization oath 6 July 1807; Hemperley, "Federal Naturalization Oaths," p. 184. Hindley's wife "the daughter of a Professor" arrived from London in Feb. 1809; Library of Congress, Izard Papers, Margaret I. Manigault to Alice D. Izard, 26 Feb. 1809 (I am grateful to Robert Leath for this reference).

506. The firm is not listed in the Liverpool section of *Holden's Directory* (1808), but appears as Richard and Arnold Latham, 3 George's Dock Gates North, in *Gore's Liverpool Directory* (1821), p. 147, and as Harrison and Leatham (*sic*), merchants, at the same address in *Baines's Lancashire Directory* (1825), p. 394.

507. An undated note in the CLS miscellaneous book marked as "Accessions 1798–1805" reports, "Referr'd to the Committee the propriety of importing the Thesaurus of Stephens, Scapula Greek Lexicon and Constantine's Lexicon. The last edition of the latter book is, perhaps, not to be had, but others, differing not essentially, are frequently offered for sale. Hederic's Greek Lexicon, the only one belonging to the Society [Hederici Lexicon, 1811 *Catalogue*], is little more than a School book."

508. See above, n. 504.

509. *Montezuma*, Smith, arrived from London after a passage of 45 days, 29 Sept. 1808, and "by this we received our regular files of London papers up to 31st July," *CGDA*, 30 Sept. 1808. *Montezuma* had been used as a slave ship; Capt. Ives was bringing in 343 slaves from Africa when captured by a French privateer in August 1805, *CGDA*, 6 Sept. 1805.

510. Henry William DeSaussure (1763–1839), native of Beaufort, S.C., imprisoned for his part (as a seventeen-year-old) in the defense of Charleston against the British forces. He was appointed director of the Mint in Washington, D.C., in 1794, but returned to Charleston a year later and was elected to the Chancery Bench in 1808. He served as president of the CLS, 1807–1812. His father, Daniel DeSaussure, was partner in the leading merchant house of Smiths, DeSaussure, and Darrell.

511. John Hopton (1748–1831), son of William Hopton (1712–1786), partner with Robert William Powell (his brother-in-law) in one of the largest importing and slave-importing firms. He was also uncle to James Gregorie (see below, n. 520) and brother-in-law of Nathaniel Russell (see above, n. 336). In *Holden's Directory* of 1808 he is listed as merchant, 1 Angel Court, Throgmorton St., London.

512. Philip & Gardner were merchants in the slave trade (advertisement, *CG*, 14 Oct. 1805).

513. Hopton, the natural choice for advice in London, replies not to the president of the CLS but to his own brother-in-law Russell (see above, n. 336). Russell, self-made

merchant, Loyalist, and attorney to Lt. Gov. William Bull, native of the Carolinas, served Bull and administered his estate in his first 45–month exile; Meroney, "William Bull's First Exile,"p. 93; see also Bull, *Oligarchs in Colonial and Revolutionary Charleston,* and below, n. 520.

514. N[athaniel] Goldingham, merchant of 59 Old Broad St., as listed in *Kent's Directory* of 1808 and 1813 (but not in *Kent's Directory* of 1801 or the *Post Office Annual Directory* of 1802). Introduced by letter 114 (below).

515. Hopkins, Gray, and Glover, ship and insurance brokers of "3 and 4 upstairs," Kings-Arms Passage, 'Change Alley, as listed in *Kent's Directory,* 1808.

516. Hopton is listed as merchant in *Holden's Directory* of 1808, but not in *Kent's Directory* of 1813.

517. Thomas Roper, planter of 4 East Bay, *Charleston Directory,* 1790, listed as "Intendant," 75 East Bay, *Charleston Directory,* 1801, and as "late Intendant," 71 East Bay St., *Charleston Directory,* 1802. Roper is not listed as attending any of the meetings to the end of 1790 when the record of the journal begun in 1759 terminates, but he is listed regularly when at meetings at the beginning of the next surviving journal from 1815.

518. See below, n. 519.

519. Ship *Hamilton Moore,* Bosquet, arrived from London after a passage of 45 days with "Goods (nearly full)," *CGDA,* 17 Nov. 1809, adding "Captain le Bosquet sailed from the Downs 1st of October with a Convoy and several American ships." The newspaper report (unusually) also lists certain cargoes for receipt, including one for "J. Davidson."

520. James Gregorie (1777–1852), native of Edinburgh, son of a Virginia colonist, and established in Charleston as "Export Merchant"; Flora Belle Surles, *Anne King Gregorie* (Columbia, S.C.: privately printed by R. L. Bryan and Co., 1968), pp. 7–9. Gregorie was nephew of John Hopton and Nathaniel Russell (see above, n. 513). As noted at the end of this letter, the bill of exchange was transmitted via the firm's shipment; cf. Gregorie and Hindley cargo, below, n. 522.

521. Ship *Neutrality,* Miller, anchors at Five-Fathom-Hole after a passage of 70 days from London (and 57 from the Downs) with "a full cargo of goods" including many for Capt. McNeil, *Charleston Courier* (hereafter *CC*), 27 Oct. 1810. The report added that "she has experienced nothing but violent gales on her passage," giving details from the log.

522. *Isabella,* McNeil, had arrived in Charleston with the cargo of Hindley and Gregorie from London after a 58–day passage, *CC,* 27 Oct. 1810 (with the *Neutrality;* see above, n. 521); and cleared out again for London, with McNeil as captain and Hindley and Gregorie as main shippers, *CC,* 23 Jan. 1811 (the date of the letter).

BIBLIOGRAPHY

Charleston Library Society Manuscripts

MSS 29, CLS "Accessions 1798–1805" (the title is misleading)

CLS borrowing ledger, 1811–1814

CLS committee minute book, 1759–1780, 1785–1791

CLS journal book, 1759–1780, 1783–1790 ("Journall of the Proceedings of the Charles Town Library Society 1759")

CLS journal, 1815–1841

CLS letter book, 1758–1811 ("Copy Book of Letters")

CLS "Financial Records," receipt books (1758–1769), 1770–1789

Charleston Library Society Catalogues and Rules (in chronological order):

Rules of the Society for Erecting a Library, and Raising a Fund for an Academy at Charles-Town in South-Carolina. Charlestown: Peter Timothy, 1750.

A Catalogue of the Books Belonging to the Charles-Town Library Society, in Charles-Town, South-Carolina. London: W. Strahan, 1750.

The Rules and By-Laws of the Charleston Library Society: Together with the Act of the General Assembly of South-Carolina for Incorporating the Society. Charlestown: Robert Wells, 1762.

A Catalogue of Books, belonging to the Incorporated Charlestown Library Society. Charlestown: Robert Wells, 1770.

The Rules and By-Laws of the Charlestown Library Society. . . . 3d ed. Charlestown: Robert Wells, 1770.

A Catalogue of Books, given and devised by John Mackenzie Esquire, to the Charlestown Library Society. Charlestown: Robert Wells, 1772.

Appendix to the Catalogue of Books, belonging to the Incorporated Charlestown Library Society. Charlestown: Robert Wells, 1772.

The Rules and By-Laws of the Charleston Library Society. . . . 4th ed. Charleston: Nathan Childs, 1785.

The Rules and Bye-Laws of the Charleston Library Society. . . . 5th ed. Charleston: W. P. Young, 1805.

Catalogue of Books belonging to the Charleston Library Society . . . May 1806. Charleston: W. P. Young, 1806.

Supplement, 1st October 1806. Charleston, 1806.

A Catalogue of Books belonging to the Charleston Library Society . . . January 1811. Charleston: W. P. Young, 1811.

Supplementary Catalogue of Books belonging to the Charleston Library Society which have been purchased since January 1811. Charleston: J. Hoff, 1816.

A Catalogue of Books belonging to the Charleston Library Society. Charleston, 1826.

Manuscripts

American Antiquarian Society, Worcester, Mass.
    Condy Account Book, 1758–1770
    AAS Broadside Collection
American Philosophical Society, Philadelphia
    David Hall Papers and Hall letter book
Boston Public Library
    ** G.164.2, "Boydell's Shakespeare Subscribers Signatures" (1792)
British Library, London
    Add MSS 38,169, Woodfall accounts
    Add MSS 48,800
    M 1077, Archives of the Royal Literary Fund, 1790–1918
Charleston County Records
    Probate Court, Inventories, 1748–1751
Duke University, Rare Book, Manuscript, and Special Collections Library
    Charles Cotesworth Pinckney Papers, bills and receipts, 1788–1819
    John Rutledge, Jr., Papers, "Journal 1788"
Historical Society of Pennsylvania, Philadelphia
    James Logan letter books
James Duncan and Stephen Phillips Libraries, Peabody Essex Museum, Salem, Mass.
    Salem Athenaeum Records, 1760–1889, box 1, vol. 1
    Treasurer's book, 1761–1810
    MS 56, series I, Social Library Records, box 1, rules and regulations (1760)
    MS 161, Cabot Family Papers, box 2
John Murray Archives, Albemarle St., London
    John Murray I, account ledger 1, 1768–1780
    Letter books 1–12, 1765–1802
    Day books, 1768–1773, 1776, 1975–1797
Lambeth Palace Library, London
    Society for the Propagation for the Gospel in Foreign Parts (SPG) Papers, vols. x, xvi, xvi,
        xxxvi
Library Company of Philadelphia
    LCP minute books, 1 (1731–1768), 2 (1768–1785), 3 (1785–1794), 4 (1794–1816), 5
        (1816–1832)
    LCP box files of additional correspondence, invoices, and photocopies of letters held at
        the Historical Society of Pennsylvania
Massachusetts Historical Society, Boston
    Henry Knox Papers, 1719–1825, 56 vols.
    Suffolk Court Files, 89428; and Records of Superior Court of Judicature, 30
    Usher letter book, with surviving invoices, 1679–1685
New York Public Library
    Joseph Johnson letter book (also in facsimile at the British Library)
New York Society Library

NYSL first minute book (1754–1772)

Second minute book (1773–1832)

Keep Papers

North Carolina Collection, Wilson Library, University of North Carolina, Chapel Hill

Printed catalogues of Thomas Bray libraries, with annotations and insertions

Public Record Office, Kew, London

ADM 7/413–501, Muster Books, 1741–1759, 1772–1804

CO 5/377, South Carolina, Original Correspondence, 1764–1765

CO 5/848–851, Massachusetts Shipping Returns, 1686–1719

CO 5/510–11, South Carolina Shipping Returns, 1736–1764, and 1746–65 (in fact, 1764–1767)

CO 5/1228, New York Shipping Returns, 1755–1765 (in fact, 1755 and 1763–1764)

CUST 3, Ledgers of Imports and Exports, 1697–1780

CUST 11, Ledgers of Exports of Foreign and Colonial Merchandise, 1809–1899

CUST 14, Ledgers of Imports and Exports, Scotland, 1755–1827

CUST 15/1–140, Ledgers of Imports and Exports, Ireland, 1698–1829

E 190, Exchequer Series of Port Books

Scottish Record Office, Edinburgh

E504/22/3, 5, 12, Customs Ledgers

South Carolina Department of Archives and History, Columbia

Recorded Instruments, Inventories of Estates, 1736–1776

Records of the Secretary of State, vol. 73

Records of the Public Treasurers of South Carolina, 1725–1776, journal A (1735–1748) and journal B (1748–1776)

South Caroliniana Library and Archives, University of South Carolina, Columbia

Charles Cotesworth Pinckney Papers, 1779–1829

Manigault Papers

Alexander Keith commonplace book

Southern Historical Collection and Manuscripts Department, Wilson Library, University of North Carolina, Chapel Hill

Peace Papers

Rutledge Papers

Tracy W. McGregor Library, University of Virginia

Daybook of William Hunter (1750–1752)

Daybook of Joseph Royle (1764–1766)

Thomas Cooper Library, Special Collections, University of South Carolina, Columbia

Charles Pinckney's Library

Printed Primary Sources

Newspapers

American Weekly Mercury, 1728

Baltimore Daily Repository, 1793

Boston News-Letter, 1705

Charleston Courier

Charleston Gazette and Daily Advertiser

City Gazette, Charleston, 1790

City Gazette and Daily Advertiser, Baltimore, 1790

General Evening Post, London, 1798

London Chronicle, 1775

Morning Chronicle and London Advertiser, 1784

New York Gazette, 1764

Political and Commercial Register, 1805

Poulson's American Daily Advertiser, 1805

St. James's Chronicle, London, 1790

South Carolina Gazette

South Carolina State Gazette and General Advertiser

Supplement to the State Gazette, 1784

Books Printed before 1826

Ackermann, R. *Repositary of Arts, Literature, Commerce, Manufacture, Fashion and Politics.* 1st ser., 1. London, 1809.

Adams, George. *Micrographia Illustrata; or, the Knowledge of the Microscope Explain'd.* London: G. Adams, 1746.

———. *A Treatise Describing and Explaining the Construction and Use of Celestial and Terrestrial Globes.* London: G. Adams, 1766.

Baines, Edward. *Lancashire Directory.* 2 vols. Liverpool: W. Wales, 1825.

Beccaria, Cesare. *An Essay on Crimes and Punishments, Translated from the Italian; with a Commentary, attributed to Mons. de Voltaire, translated from the French.* London: J. Almon, 1767.

Boerhaave, Herman. *A New Method of Chemistry.* 2 vols. London: J. Osborn and T. Longman, 1721.

Bosc [Boscq], Jacques du. *The Accomplish'd Woman.* 2 vols. London: J. Watts and B. Dodd, 1753.

Bristol Education Society. *An Alphabetical Catalogue of all the Books in the Library belonging to the Bristol Education Society.* Bristol: Bristol Education Society, 1795.

Bristol Library Society. *A Catalogue of the Books Belonging to the Bristol-Library Society.* Bristol: Bristol, 1790.

Catesby, Mark. *The Natural History of Carolina, Florida, and the Bahama Islands.* 2 vols. London: W. Innys, R. Manby, et al., 1731–1743.

Census for 1820. Washington, D.C.: Gales and Seaton, 1820.

Charleston Directory, 1782, 1790, 1794, 1796.

Colden, Cadwallader. *History of the Five Indian Nations of Canada.* London: T. Osborne, 1747.

Dell, Henry. *The Booksellers: A Poem.* London: Henry Dell, 1766.

Douglass, William. *A Discourse Concerning the Currencies of the British Plantations in America.* Boston: S. Kneeland and T. Green, 1740.

Elizer, Eleazer. *A Directory for 1803: Containing; The Names of All the House-Keepers and Traders in the City of Charleston.* Charleston: W. P. Young, 1803.

Foster, Michael. *A Report of Some Proceedings on the Commission of Oyer and Terminer and Gaol Delivery for the Trial of the Rebels in the Year 1746 . . . and of other Crown Cases.* London: J. Worrall, B. Tovey, et al., 1762.

Gibson, Edmund. *Two Letters of the Lord Bishop of London.* London: [printed by Joseph Downing], 1727.

Gore's Liverpool Directory. Liverpool: J. Gore, 1821.

Granger, William. *New Wonderful Museum and Entertaining Magazine.* London: R. S. Kirby, 1802–1808.

Hales, Stephen. *Statical Essays.* 3d ed. 2 vols. London: W. Innys, R. Manby, and T. Woodward. 1738. [Including the 1st vol. originally published as *Vegetable Statics* in 1727.]

———. *A Description of Ventilators.* London: W. Innys, R. Manby, and T. Woodward, 1743.

Hewat, Alexander. *An Historical Account of the Rise and Progress of the Colonies of South Carolina and Georgia.* 2 vols. London: Alexander Donaldson, 1779.

Hill, Thomas [John]. *Young Secretary's Guide.* London: H. Rhodes, 1703.

Holden's Triennial Directory. 4th ed. 2 vols. London: W. Holden, 1808.

Kent's Directory. London: Causton, 1801, 1808, 1813.

Lackington, James. *The Confessions of J. Lackington, Late Bookseller, at the Temple of the Muses, In a Series of Letters to a Friend.* London: J. Lackington and R. Edwards, 1804.

———. *Memoirs of the Forty-Five First Years of the Life of James Lackington.* London, J. Lackington, 1791.

———. Annual catalogues, 1787–1789, 1792–1794, 1796–1811, 1814, and 1817–1820. London: J. Lackington.

Lambert, John. *Travels Through Lower Canada, and the United States of North America, in the Years 1806, 1807, and 1808.* 3 vols. London: Richard Phillips, 1810.

Lawson, John. *A New Voyage to Carolina.* London, 1709.

Library Company of Baltimore. *A Catalogue of the Books, &c Belonging to the Library Company of Baltimore to which are prefixed, the Bye-Laws of the Company and an Alphabetical List of the Members.* Baltimore: Library Company of Baltimore, 1797.

London Directory. London: H. Kent, 1763.

A London Directory, or Alphabetical Arrangement. London: H. Lowndes, 1797.

Milligan, Dr. [George Milligen-Johnston]. *A Short Description of the Province of South Carolina . . . In the Year 1763.* London: J. Hinton, 1770. British Library copy with marginal annotation dated 1775.

Nichols, John. *Literary Anecdotes of the Eighteenth Century.* 9 vols. London: Nichols, Son & Bentley, 1812–1815. Reprint, New York: Kraus, 1966.

The Post Office Annual Directory. London: T. Maiden, 1802.

Ramsay, David. *History of South Carolina, from its First Settlement in 1670 to the Year 1808.* 2 vols. Charleston: David Longworth, 1809.

Shecut, J. L. E. W. *Shecut's Medical and Philosophical Essays. Containing: 1st Topographical, Historical and Other Sketches of the City of Charleston.* Charleston: J. L. E. W. Shecut, 1819.

Smith, William Loughton. *The Numbers of the Phocion: Which were originally published in the Charleston Courier, in 1806, on the subject of neutral rights.* Charleston: Courier Office, 1806.

Smith, Josiah. *Mr Smith's Sermon Occasioned by the late Terrible Fire in Charlestown, South-Carolina, November 18, 1740.* [Boston]: Eleazor Phillips, 1741.

Tempest, P[ierce]. *Iconologia: Or, Moral Emblems, by Caesar Ripa.* London: B. Motte, 1709.

Trott, Nicholas. *The Laws of the Province of South-Carolina.* Charleston: Lewis Timothy, 1736.

Wolcot, John. *Tristia; Or, The Sorrows of Peter . . . By P. Pindar, Esq.* London: Walker, 1806.

Books Printed after 1826 and Web Sites

Adams, Henry. *History of the United States of America during the First Administration of Thomas Jefferson.* 9 vols. London: G. P. Putnam's Sons; and New York: Charles Scribner's Sons, 1891–1892.

Alston, Robin. "Library History Database." [1997 and Dec. 1998.] http://www.r-alston.-dircon.co.uk/contents.htm, incorporating Keith Manley's Library Database.

Amory, Hugh, and David D. Hall, eds. *The Colonial Book in the Atlantic World.* Vol. 1 of *A History of the Book in America.* New York: Cambridge University Press, 1999.

Anderson, Benedict. *Imagined Communities: Reflections on the Origin and Spread of Nationalism.* London: Verso, 1983.

Bailyn, Bernard, and Lotte Bailyn. *Massachusetts Shipping 1697–1714: A Statistical Study.* Cambridge, Mass.: Harvard University Press, 1959.

Barrow, Thomas C. *Trade and Empire: The British Customs Service in Colonial America, 1660–1775.* Cambridge, Mass.: Harvard University Press, 1967.

Berkeley, Edmund, and Dorothy Smith Berkeley. *Dr. Alexander Garden of Charles Town.* Chapel Hill: University of North Carolina Press, 1969.

Bocock, Robert. *Consumption.* London: Routledge, 1993.

Bond, W. H. *Thomas Hollis of Lincoln's Inn: A Whig and His Books.* Cambridge: University Press, 1990.

Bowes, Frederick P. *The Culture of Early Charleston.* Chapel Hill: University of North Carolina Press, 1942.

Breen, T. H. *Tobacco Culture: The Mentality of the Great Tidewater Planters on the Eve of the Revolution.* Princeton: Princeton University Press, 1985.

Bridenbaugh, Carl. *Cities in Revolt: Urban Life in America, 1743–1776.* New York: Alfred A. Knopf, 1955.

Brock, Leslie V. *The Currency of the American Colonies 1700–1764: A Study in Colonial Finance and Imperial Relations.* New York: Arno Press, 1975.

Brown, H. Glenn Brown, and Maude O. Brown. *A Directory of the Book-Arts and Book Trade in Philadelphia to 1820, Including Printers and Engravers.* New York: New York Public Library, 1950.

Brown, Olivia, comp. *The Whipple Museum of Science: Catalogue 7, Microscopes.* Cambridge: Whipple Museum, 1986.

Brown, Richard D. *Knowledge Is Power: The Diffusion of Information in Early America, 1700–1865.* New York: Oxford University Press, 1989.

Bruntjen, Sven H. A. *John Boydell, 1719–1804: A Study of Art Patronage and Publishing in Georgian London.* New York and London: Garland, 1985.

Bull, Kinloch, Jr. *The Oligarchs in Colonial and Revolutionary Charleston: Lieutenant Governor William Bull II and His Family.* Columbia: University of South Carolina Press, 1991.

Bullock, Steven C. *Revolutionary Brotherhood: Freemasonry and the Transformation of the American Social Order, 1730–1840.* Chapel Hill and London: University of North Carolina, 1996.

Bushman, Richard L. *The Refinement of America: Persons, Houses, Cities.* New York: Alfred A. Knopf, 1992.

Calhoun, Craig, ed. *Habermas and the Public Sphere.* Cambridge, Mass., and London: MIT Press, 1992.

Carson, Barbara G. *Ambitious Appetites: Dining, Behavior, and Patterns of Consumption in Federal Washington.* Washington, D.C.: American Institute of Architects Press, 1990.

Carson, Cary, Ronald Hoffman, and Peter J. Albert, eds. *Of Consuming Interests: The Style of Life in the Eighteenth Century.* Charlottesville and London: University Press of Virginia, 1994.

Catalogue of the Books Belonging to the Savannah Library Society: Instituted in the Year 1809 and Re-organized in the Year 1838. Savannah: Thomas Purse, 1839.

Chaplin, Joyce E. *An Anxious Pursuit: Agricultural Innovation and Modernity in the Lower South, 1730–1815.* Chapel Hill and London: University of North Carolina Press, 1993.

Charleston Library Society. *Report of the Committee of the Charleston Library Society.* Charleston, 1853.

Clark, J. C. D. *The Language of Liberty 1660–1832: Political Discourse and Social Dynamics in the Anglo-American World.* Cambridge: Cambridge University Press, 1994.

Clarke, Erskine. *Our Southern Zion: A History of Calvinism in the South Carolina Low Country, 1690–1990.* Tuscaloosa: University of Alabama Press, 1996.

Clarke, Francis G. *The American Ship-Master's Guide and Commercial Assistant.* Boston: Allen, 1850.

Clayton, Timothy. *The English Print 1688–1802.* New Haven and London: Yale University Press, 1997.

Clowse, Converse D. *Measuring Charleston's Overseas Commerce, 1717–1767.* Washington, D.C.: University Press of America, 1981.

Cochrane, J. A. *Dr Johnson's Printer: The Life of William Strahan.* London: Routledge and Kegan Paul, 1964.

Cohen, Anthony P. *The Symbolic Construction of Community.* London and New York: Routledge, 1985.

Cohen, Hennig. *The South Carolina Gazette 1732–1775.* Columbia: University of South Carolina Press, 1953.

Cohen, I. B. *Some Early Tools of American Science.* Cambridge, Mass.: Harvard University Press, 1950.

Coker, P. C. *Charleston's Maritime Heritage.* Charleston: Cokercraft, 1987.

Cordasco, Francesco. *Junius: A Bibliography of the Letters of Junius with a Checklist of Junian Scholarship and Related Studies.* Fairview, N.J., and London: Junius-Vaughn Press, 1986.

Curwen, Henry. *A History of Booksellers: The Old and the New.* London: Chatto and Windus, 1874.

Darnton, Robert. *The Forbidden Best-Sellers of Pre-Revolutionary France.* New York and London: W. W. Norton, 1995.

Davidson, Cathy N. *Revolution and the Word: The Rise of the Novel in America.* New York and Oxford: Oxford University Press, 1986.

Davis, Donald G., Jr., and John Mark Tucker. *American Library History: A Comprehensive Guide to the Literature.* Santa Barbara, Calif., and Oxford: ABC-CLIO, 1989.

Davis, Ralph. *The Rise of the Atlantic Economies.* London: Weidenfeld and Nicolson, 1973.

Davis, Richard Beale. *A Colonial Southern Bookshelf: Reading in the Eighteenth Century.* Athens: University of Georgia Press, 1979.

———. *Intellectual Life in the Colonial South 1585–1763.* 3 vols. Knoxville: University of Tennessee Press, 1978.

Earnest, Ernest P. *John and William Bartram, Botanists and Explorers.* Philadelphia: University of Pennsylvania Press, 1940.

Easterby, J. H. *A History of the College of Charleston Founded 1770.* Charleston, 1935.

———. *History of the St. Andrew's Society of Charleston.* Charleston: St. Andrew's Society, 1919.

Edgar, Walter B., and N. Louise Bailey, eds. *The Commons House of Assembly 1692–1775.* Vol. 2 of *Biographical Directory of the South Carolina House of Representatives.* Columbia: University of South Carolina Press, 1977.

Edgar, Walter B., ed. *The Letterbook of Robert Pringle.* 2 vols. Columbia: University of South Carolina Press, 1972.

Fliegelman, Jay. *Declaring Independence: Jefferson, Natural Language, and the Culture of Performance.* Stanford: Stanford University Press, 1993.

Ford, Edward. *David Rittenhouse: Astronomer-Patriot, 1732–1796.* Philadelphia: University of Pennsylvania Press, 1946.

Ford, Worthington Chauncey. *The Boston Book Market 1679–1700.* Boston: Club of Odd Volumes, 1917.

Friedman, Winifred H. *Boydell's Shakespeare Gallery.* New York and London: Garland, 1976.

Geertz, Clifford. *The Interpretation of Cultures.* London: Hutchinson, 1975.

Gongaware, George J. *The History of the German Friendly Society of Charleston, South Carolina, 1766–1916.* Richmond, Va.: Garett and Massie, 1935.

Goodman, Dena. *The Republic of Letters: A Cultural History of the French Enlightenment.* Ithaca, N.Y., and London: Cornell University Press, 1994.

Greenblatt, Stephen. *Marvelous Possessions: The Wonder of the New World.* Oxford: Clarendon Press, 1991.

Greene, Evarts B., and Virginia D. Harrington. *American Population before the Federal Census of 1790.* New York: Columbia University Press, 1932.

Greene, Jack P. *Imperatives, Behaviors, and Identities: Essays in Early American Cultural History.* Charlottesville and London: University Press of Virginia, 1992.

———. *The Quest for Power: The Lower Houses of Assembly in the Southern Royal Colonies, 1689–1763.* Chapel Hill: University of North Carolina Press, 1963.

Gummere, Richard M. *The American Colonial Mind and the Classical Tradition*. Cambridge, Mass.: Harvard University Press, 1963.

Habermas, Jurgen. *The Structural Transformation of the Public Sphere*. Trans. T. Burger and F. Lawrence. Cambridge, Mass.: MIT Press, 1989.

Hamer, Philip M., et al., eds. *The Papers of Henry Laurens*. 13 vols. Columbia: University of South Carolina Press, 1968–.

Hancock, David. *Citizens of the World: London Merchants and the Integration of the British Atlantic Community, 1735–1785*. Cambridge: Cambridge University Press, 1995.

Harlan, Robert Dale. *William Strahan: Eighteenth-Century London Printer and Publisher*. Ann Arbor, Mich.: Ann Arbor Publications, 1960.

Hayes, Kevin J. *A Colonial Woman's Bookshelf*. Knoxville: University of Tennessee Press, 1996.

———. *The Library of William Byrd of Westover*. Madison: Madison House, 1997.

Henretta, James A. *The Evolution of American Society, 1700–1815: An Interdisciplinary Analysis*. Lexington, Mass.: D. C. Heath, 1973.

Hindle, Brooke. *David Rittenhouse*. Princeton: Princeton University Press, 1964.

Hofstadter, Richard. *Anti-Intellectualism in American Life*. New York: Jonathan Cape, 1963.

Hollis, Daniel Walker. *South Carolina College*. Vol. 1 of *University of South Carolina*. 2 vols. Columbia: University of South Carolina Press, 1951–1956.

Howsam, Leslie. *Cheap Bibles: Nineteenth-Century Publishing and the British and Foreign Bible Society*. Cambridge: Cambridge University Press, 1991.

Hughes, Barbara. *Catalog of the Scientific Apparatus at the College of Charleston: 1800–1940*. Charleston: College of Charleston Library Associates, 1980.

Isaac, Rhys. *The Transformation of Virginia, 1740–1790*. Chapel Hill: University of North Carolina Press, 1982.

Johnson, Herbert A. *Imported Eighteenth-Century Law Treatises in American Libraries 1700–1799*. Knoxville: University of Tennessee Press, 1978.

Keep, Austin Baxter. *History of the New York Society Library*. New York: New York Society Library, 1908.

Klein, Lawrence E. *Shaftesbury and the Culture of Politeness: Moral Discourse and Cultural Politics in Early Eighteenth-Century England*. Cambridge: Cambridge University Press, 1994.

Klein, Rachel N. *Unification of a Slave State: The Rise of the Planter Class in the South Carolina Backcountry 1760–1808*. Chapel Hill: University of North Carolina Press, 1990.

Knight, Charles. *Shadows of the Old Booksellers*. London: Bell & Daldy, 1865.

Labaree, Leonard W., et al., eds. *The Papers of Benjamin Franklin*. 31 vols. New Haven: Yale University Press, 1959–1995.

Laugher, Charles T. *Thomas Bray's Grand Design: Libraries of the Church of England in America, 1695–1785*. Chicago: American Library Association, 1973.

Lee, Martyn J. *Consumer Culture Reborn: The Cultural Politics of Consumption*. London: Routledge, 1993.

Lemoine, Henry, and Douglas C. McMurtrie, eds. *Present State of Printing and Bookselling in America, 1796*. Chicago: privately printed, 1929.

Lillywhite, Bryant. *London Coffee Houses: A Reference Book of Coffee Houses of the Seventeenth, Eighteenth and Nineteenth Centuries*. London: G. Allen & Unwin, 1963.

Lonn, Ella. *The Colonial Agents of the Southern Colonies.* Chapel Hill, 1945.

Looby, Christopher. *Voicing America: Language, Literary Form, and the Origins of the United States.* Chicago and London: University of Chicago Press, 1996.

Lounsbury, Carl R. *From Statehouse to Courthouse: An Architectural History of South Carolina's First State House and Charleston County Court House.* Columbia: University of South Carolina Press, 2001.

Marston, E. *Sketches of Booksellers of Other Days.* London: S. Low, Marston, 1901.

[Mather]. "The Mather Papers." *Collections of the Massachusetts Historical Society,* 4th ser., 8 (1868).

Maxted, Ian. *The London Book Trades, 1775–1800: A Preliminary Checklist of Members.* Folkestone, Kent: Dawson, 1977.

Maxwell, W. Harold, comp. *A Bibliography of English Law to 1650.* London: Sweet and Maxwell, 1925.

McCombs, Charles F., ed. *Letter-Book of Mary Stead Pinckney, November 14th 1796 to August 29th 1797.* New York: Grolier Club, 1946.

McCorison, Marcus A., ed. *The 1764 Catalogue of the Redwood Library Company at Newport, Rhode Island.* New Haven and London: Yale University Press, 1965.

McCowen, George Smith, Jr. *The British Occupation of Charleston, 1780–82.* Columbia: University of South Carolina Press, 1972.

McCusker, John J. *Money and Exchange in Europe and America, 1600–1775: A Handbook.* Chapel Hill: University of North Carolina Press, 1978.

———, and Russell R. Menard. *The Economy of British America 1607–1789.* Chapel Hill and London: University of North Carolina Press, 1985.

Merrens, H. Roy, ed. *The Colonial South Carolina Scene: Contemporary Views 1697–1774.* Columbia: University of South Carolina Press, 1977.

Milburn, John R. *Adams of Fleet Street, Instrument Makers to King George: The History of a London Business, 1735–1830.* Aldershot, Hants.: Ashgate, 2000.

———. *Benjamin Martin: Author, Instrument-Maker, and "Country Showman."* Leyden: Noordhoff International, 1976.

Mitchell, Arthur. *The History of the Hibernian Society of Charleston, South Carolina, 1799–1981.* Charleston: Hibernian Society, [1985].

Moore, Caroline T. *Abstracts of the Wills of the State of South Carolina, 1740–1760.* Columbia, S.C.: C. T. Moore, 1964.

Morgan, Richard Parker. *A Preliminary Bibliography of South Carolina, 1731–1800.* Clemson, S.C.: Clemson University, [1966?].

Morison, Samuel Eliot. *The Maritime History of Massachusetts 1783–1860.* 4th ed. Cambridge, Mass.: Riverside Press, 1961.

Multhauf, Robert P. *Catalogue of Instruments and Models in the Possession of the American Philosophical Society.* Philadelphia: American Philosophical Society, 1961.

Murdoch, Tessa. *The Quiet Conquest: The Huguenots 1685 to 1985.* London: Museum of London, 1985.

Nadelhaft, Jerome J. *The Disorders of War: The Revolution in South Carolina.* Orono, Maine: University of Maine at Orono Press, 1981.

Namier, L. B. *England in the Age of the American Revolution.* London: Macmillan, 1930.

Nesbitt, Alexander. *History of the Family of Nisbet or Nesbitt in Scotland and Ireland.* Torquay: privately printed by A. Iredale, 1898.

Nettels, Curtis P. *The Money Supply of the American Colonies before 1720.* Madison, Wisc.: Curtis Putnam, 1934; reprint, New York: Sentry Press, 1964.

The New York Society Library: History, Charter and By-Laws. New York: NYSL, 1985.

Paston, George [pseud.]. *Little Memoirs of the Eighteenth Century.* London and New York: E. P. Dutton, 1901.

Petigru, James L. *Oration delivered before the Charleston Library Society at its First Centennial Anniversary June 13 1848.* Charleston: J. B. Nixon, printer, 1848.

Petit, James Percival. *South Carolina and the Sea: Day by Day toward Five Centuries 1492–1976 AD.* 2 vols. Charleston: Maritime and Ports Activities Committee of the States Ports Authority, 1976.

Pinckney, Elise, ed. *The Letterbook of Eliza Lucas Pinckney 1739–1762.* Chapel Hill: University of North Carolina Press, 1972; Columbia: University of South Carolina Press, 1997.

Pocock, J. G. A. *The Machiavellian Moment: Florentine Political Thought and the Atlantic Republican Tradition.* Princeton: Princeton University Press, 1975.

———, ed. *The Political Works of James Harrington.* Cambridge: Cambridge University Press, 1977.

Pointon, Marcia. *Hanging the Head: Portraiture and Social Formation in Eighteenth-Century England.* New Haven and London: Yale University Press, 1993.

Porter, Roy, et al., eds. *Science and Profit in 18th-Century London.* Cambridge: Whipple Museum, 1985.

Pratt, Anne Stokely. *Isaac Watts and His Gifts of Books to Yale College.* New Haven: Yale University Library, 1938.

Price, Jacob M. *Joshua Johnson's Letterbook, 1771–1774: Letters from a Merchant in London to His Partners in Maryland.* London: London Record Society, 1979.

Raven, James. *British Fiction 1750–1770: A Chronological Check-List of Prose Fiction Printed in Britain and Ireland.* Newark, London, and Toronto: Associated University Presses, 1987.

———. *Judging New Wealth: Popular Publishing and Responses to Commerce in England, 1750–1800.* Oxford: Oxford University Press, 1992.

Ravenel, Harriott Horry. *Eliza Pinckney.* New York: Charles Scribner's Sons, 1896.

Rees, Thomas, and John Britton. *Reminiscences of Literary London from 1779 to 1853.* London: Suckling & Galloway, 1896.

Remer, Rosalind. *Printers and Men of Capital: Philadelphia Book Publishers in the New Republic.* Philadelphia: University of Pennsylvania Press, 1996.

Rivington, Septimus. *The Publishing Family of Rivington.* London: Rivingtons, 1919.

———. *The Publishing House of Rivington.* London: Percival Rivington, 1894.

Robbins, Caroline. *The Eighteenth-Century Commonwealthman: Studies in the Transmission, Development, and Circumstance of English Liberal Thought from the Restoration of Charles II until the War with the Thirteen Colonies.* Cambridge, Mass.: Harvard University Press, 1959.

Rogers, George C., Jr. *Evolution of a Federalist: William Loughton Smith of Charleston, 1758–1812.* Columbia: University of South Carolina Press, 1962.

————. *Charleston in the Age of the Pinckneys.* Norman: University of Oklahoma Press, 1969; Columbia: University of South Carolina Press, 1980.

Sanders, Albert E., and William D. Anderson, Jr. *Natural History Investigations in South Carolina from Colonial Times to the Present.* Columbia: University of South Carolina Press, 1999.

Scott, James C. *Domination and the Arts of Resistance.* New Haven and London: Yale University Press, 1990.

Shepherd, James F., and Gary M. Walton. *Shipping, Maritime Trade, and the Economic Development of Colonial North America.* Cambridge: Cambridge University Press, 1972.

Shera, Jesse H. *Foundations of the Public Library in New England.* Chicago: University of Chicago Press, 1949.

Shields, David S. *Oracles of Empire: Poetry, Politics, and Commerce in British America, 1690–1750.* Chicago and London: University of Chicago Press, 1990.

————. *Civil Tongues and Polite Letters in British America.* Chapel Hill and London: University of North Carolina Press, 1997.

Simmons, R. C. *British Imprints Relating to North America 1621–1760.* London: British Library, 1996.

Sirmans, M. Eugene. *Colonial South Carolina: A Political History 1663–1763.* Chapel Hill: University of North Carolina Press, 1966.

Smith, Murphy D. *A Museum: The History of the Cabinet of Curiosities of the American Philosophical Society.* Philadelphia: American Philosophical Society, 1996.

Solomon, Harry M. *The Rise of Robert Dodsley: Creating the New Age of Print.* Carbondale and Edwardsville: Southern Illinois University Press, 1996.

Sosin, Jack M. *Agents and Merchants: British Colonial Policy and the Origins of the American Revolution, 1763–1775.* Lincoln, Neb.: University of Nebraska Press, 1965.

Spruill, Julia Cherry. *Women's Life and Work in the Southern Colonies.* Chapel Hill: University of North Carolina Press, 1938.

Starr, Rebecca. *A School for Politics: Commercial Lobbying and Political Culture in Early South Carolina.* Baltimore and London: Johns Hopkins University Press, 1998.

Stearns, Raymond Phineas. *Science in the British Colonies of America.* Urbana, Chicago and London: University of Illinois Press, 1970.

Steele, Ian K. *The English Atlantic 1675–1740: An Exploration of Communication and Community.* New York and Oxford: Oxford University Press, 1986.

Stokes, Roy, ed. *Esdaile's Manual of Bibliography.* London: George Allen and Unwin, 1967.

Stoler, Ann Laura, and Frederick Cooper, eds. *Tensions of Empire: Colonial Cultures in a Bourgeois World.* Berkeley, Los Angeles, and London: University of California Press, 1997.

Surles, Flora Belle. *Anne King Gregorie.* Columbia: privately printed by R. L. Bryan & Co., 1968.

Sutherland, Stella H. *Population Distribution in Colonial America.* New York: AMS Press, 1966.

Tapley, Harriet Silvester. *Salem Imprints 1768–1825: A History of the First Fifty Years of Printing in Salem, Massachusetts.* Salem, Mass.: Essex Institute, 1927.

Tebbel, John. *A History of Book Publishing in the United States.* 3 vols. New York and London: R. R. Bowker, 1972–1978.

Thomas, E. S. *Reminiscences of the Last Six-Five Years, Commencing with the Battle of Lexington.* 2 vols. Hartford, Conn: Case, Tiffany, and Burnham, 1840.

Thomas, Isaiah. *The History of Printing in America.* 2d ed. 2 vols. Albany, N.Y.: J. Munsell, 1874, also ed. Marcus McCorison (New York: Weathervane Books, 1970).

Thomas, M. Halsey, ed. *The Diary of Samuel Sewall 1674–1729.* 2 vols. New York: Farrar, Straus and Giroux, 1973.

Thompson, H. P. *Thomas Bray.* London: SPCK, 1954.

Thorne, Samuel E., trans. and ed. *Bracton on the Laws and Customs of England.* 5 vols. Cambridge, Mass.: Belknap Press, 1968.

Tierney, James E., ed. *The Correspondence of Robert Dodsley, 1733–1764.* Cambridge: Cambridge University Press, 1988.

Tinling, Marion, ed. *The Correspondence of the Three William Byrds of Westover, Virginia, 1684–1776.* 2 vols. Charlottesville: University Press of Virginia, 1977.

Turner, G. L'E. *The Great Age of the Microscope: The Collection of the Royal Microscopical Society through 150 years.* Bristol: Hilger, 1989.

———, and D. J. Bryden, eds. *A Classified Bibliography on the History of Scientific Instruments.* Oxford: International Union of the History and Philosophy of Science, Scientific Instrument Commission, 1997.

VerSteeg, Clarence L. *Origins of a Southern Mosaic: Studies of Early Carolina and Georgia.* Athens: University of Georgia Press, 1975.

Wallace, David D. *The History of South Carolina.* 4 vols. New York: American Historical Society, 1934.

Walsh, Richard, ed. *The Writings of Christopher Gadsden, 1746–1805.* Columbia: University of South Carolina Press, 1968.

Walton, Gary M., and James F. Shepherd. *The Economic Rise of Early America.* Cambridge: Cambridge University Press, 1979.

Waring, Joseph Ioor. *A History of Medicine in South Carolina, 1670–1825.* Columbia: South Carolina Medical Association, 1964.

Warner, Michael. *Letters of the Republic: Publication and the Public Sphere in Eighteenth-Century America.* Cambridge, Mass.: Harvard University Press, 1990.

Waterhouse, Richard. *A New World Gentry: The Making of a Merchant and Planter Class in South Carolina, 1670–1770.* New York and London: Garland, 1989.

Waters, Ivor. *The Unfortunate Valentine Morris.* Chepstow, Monmouthshire: Chepstow Society, 1964.

Weir, Robert M. *Colonial South Carolina: A History.* Millwood, N.Y.: KTO Press, 1983.

Wertenbaker, Thomas J. *The Golden Age of Colonial Culture.* New York: New York University Press, 1949.

Weston, Plowden C. J., ed. *Documents Connected with the History of South Carolina.* London: privately printed, 1856.

Wheatland, David. *The Apparatus of Science at Harvard, 1765–1800.* Cambridge, Mass.: Harvard University Press, 1968.

Wiggin, Cynthia B. *Salem Athenaeum: A Short History.* Salem: Forest River, 1971.

Wilson, John H., and Gary S. Wilson. *Early South Carolina Newspapers Database Reports: South Carolina Gazette 1732–.* Charleston: South Carolina Historical Society, 1995–.

Winans, Robert D. *A Descriptive Checklist of Book Catalogues Separately Printed in America 1693–1800.* Worcester, Mass.: American Antiquarian Society, 1981.

Winthrop Papers. 6 vols. Boston: Massachusetts Historical Society, 1929–1992.

Wolf, Edwin, II. *The Book Culture of a Colonial American City: Philadelphia Books, Bookmen, and Booksellers.* Oxford: Clarendon Press, 1988.

———. *The Library of James Logan of Philadelphia 1674–1751.* Philadelphia: Library Company of Philadelphia, 1974.

———, et al. *"At the Instance of Benjamin Franklin": A Brief History of the Library Company of Philadelphia.* 2d ed. Philadelphia: Library Company of Philadelphia, 1995.

Wood, Peter H. *Black Majority: Negroes in Colonial South Carolina from 1670 through the Stono Rebellion.* New York: Alfred A. Knopf, 1974.

Wright, Louis B. *The Cultural Life of the American Colonies, 1607–1763.* New York: Harper & Brothers, 1957.

Wright, Thomas Goddard. *Literary Culture in Early New England 1620–1730.* New Haven: Yale University Press, 1920.

Wroth, Lawrence C. *The Colonial Printer.* Portland, Me.: Southworth-Anthoensen, 1938; 2d ed., Charlottesville, Va.: Dominion Books, 1964.

———. *William Parks: Printer and Journalist of England and Colonial America.* Richmond: William Parks Club, 1926.

Zachs, William. *The First John Murray and the Late Eighteenth-Century London Book Trade.* Oxford: British Academy and Oxford University Press, 1998.

Zahniser, Marvin R. *Charles Cotesworth Pinckney: Founding Father.* Chapel Hill: University of North Carolina Press, 1967.

Articles and Essays

Alden, John E. "John Mein, Publisher: An Essay in Bibliographical Detection." *Papers of the Bibliographical Society of America* 36 (1942): 199–214.

Bedini, S. A. "Of 'Science and Liberty': The Scientific Instruments of King's College and Eighteenth Century Columbia College in New York." *Annals of Science* 50 (1993): 201–27.

Botein, Stephen. "The Anglo-American Book Trade before 1776: Personnel and Strategies," in William L. Joyce et al., eds., *Printing and Society in Early America,* pp. 48–82. Worcester, Mass.: American Antiquarian Society, 1983.

Brack, O. M., Jr. "The Ledgers of William Strahan," in D. B. Smith, ed., *Editing Eighteenth-Century Texts,* pp. 59–77. Toronto: University of Toronto Press, 1968.

Breen, T. H. "'Baubles of Britain': The American and Consumer Revolutions of the Eighteenth Centuries." *Past and Present* 119 (1988): 73–104.

———. "An Age of Goods: The Anglicization of Colonial America, 1690–1776." *Journal of British Studies* 25 (1986): 467–99.

Bushman, Richard L. "American High-Style and Vernacular Culture," in Jack P. Greene and J. R. Pole, eds., *Colonial British America: Essays in the New History of the Early Modern Era*, pp. 345–83. Baltimore and London: Johns Hopkins University Press, 1984.

Butterfield, L. H. "The American Interests of the Firm of E. & C. Dilly." *Papers of the Bibliographical Society of America* 45 (1951): 283–332.

Calhoun, Jeanne A., et al. "The Geographic Spread of Charleston's Mercantile Community, 1732–1767." *SCHM* 86 (1985): 182–220.

Chaldecott, J. A. "The Zograscope or Optical Diagonal Machine." *Annals of Science* 9 (1953): 315–22.

Chapman, Allan. "Scientific Instruments and Industrial Innovation: The Achievement of Jesse Ramsden," in R. G. W. Anderson et al., eds., *Making Instruments Count: Essays on Historical Scientific Instruments Presented to Gerard L'Estrange Turner*, pp. 418–30. Aldershot: Variorum, 1993.

Chaunu, Huguette, and Pierre Chaunu. "Économie Atlantique, Économie Mondiale (1504–1650): Problèmes de fait et de méthode." *Journal of World History* 1 (1953): 91–104. Translation in Peter Earle, ed., *Essays in European History, 1500–1800*, pp. 113–26. Oxford: Oxford University Press, 1974.

Christy, Miller. "Samuel Dale (1659?-1739), of Braintree, Botanist, and the Dale Family: Some Genealogy and Some Patriots." *Essex Naturalist* 19 (1918–1921): 49–69.

Clive, John, and Bernard Bailyn "England's Cultural Provinces: Scotland and America." *William and Mary Quarterly*, 3d ser., 11 (1954): 200–213.

Crary, Catherine Snell. "The Tory and the Spy: The Double Life of James Rivington." *William and Mary Quarterly*, 3rd ser., 16 (1959): 61–72.

French, Hannah D. "Early American Bookbinding by Hand 1636–1820," in Hellmut Lehmann-Haupt, ed., *Bookbinding in America: Three Essays*, pp. 3–127. Portland, Maine: Southwold-Anthoensen, 1941.

Gauci, Perry. "The City as Exchange: Merchant Culture 1660–1720," in *Centre for Metropolitan History: Annual Report 1997–8*, pp. 60–65. London: University of London Institute for Historical Research, 1999.

Gould, Christopher. "Robert Wells, Colonial Charleston Printer." *SCHM* 79 (1978): 23–49.

Greenburg, Alan M. "'A Splendid Establishment . . . Charmingly Arranged': 18th and 19th Century Observers of the Charleston Library Society." *South Carolina Librarian* 24, no. 2 (Fall 1980): 5–10.

Gregorie, Anne King. "The First Decade of the Charleston Library Society." *Proceedings of the South Carolina Historical Association* 5 (1935): 3–10.

Harlan, Robert D. "David Hall's Bookshop and Its British Sources of Supply," in David Kaser, ed., *Books in America's Past: Essays Honoring Rudolph H. Gjelsness*, 2–25. Charlottesville: Bibliographical Society of the University of Virginia, 1966.

———. "William Strahan's American Book Trade, 1744–76." *Library Quarterly* 31 (1961): 235–44.

Hemperley, Marion R. "Federal Naturalization Oaths, Charleston, S.C., 1790–1860." *SCHM* 66 (1965): 183–92.

Higgins, W. Robert. "The South Carolina Revolutionary Debt and Its Holders, 1776–1780." *SCHM* 72 (1971): 15–29.

Hillman, E. Haviland. "The Brisbanes." *SCHM* 14 (1913): 115–33.

Howe, Mark A. DeWolfe, ed. "Journal of Josiah Quincy, Junior, 1773." *Proceedings of the Massachusetts Historical Society* 49 (1916). 424–81.

Hunt, Arnold. "Bibliotheca Heberiana," in Robin Myers and Michael Harris, eds., *Antiquaries, Book Collectors and Circles of Learning*, pp. 83–112. Winchester and New Castle, Del.: St. Paul's Bibliographies and Oak Knoll Press, 1996.

Jackson, Harvey H. "Hugh Bryan and the Evangelical Movement in Colonial South Carolina." *William and Mary Quarterly* 43 (1986): 594–614.

Jervey, Ellen Heyward. "Items from a South Carolina Almanac." *SCHM* 32 (1931): 73–80.

John, A. H. "The London Assurance Company and the Marine Insurance Market of the Eighteenth Century." *Economica,* n.s., 25 (1958): 126–41.

Johnson, Herbert A. "The Constitutional Thought of William Johnson." *SCHM* 88 (1989): 132–45.

Kaldenbach, C. J. "Perspective Views." *Print Quarterly* 2 (1985): 86–104.

Kaplanoff, Mark D. "Charles Pinckney and the American Republican Tradition," in Michael O'Brien and David Moltke-Hansen, eds., *Intellectual Life in Antebellum Charleston*, pp. 85–122. Knoxville: University of Tennessee Press, 1986.

———. "How Federalist Was South Carolina in 1787–88?" in David R. Chesnutt and Clyde N. Wilson, eds., *The Meaning of South Carolina History: Essays in Honor of George C. Rogers, Jr.,* pp. 67–103. Columbia: University of South Carolina Press, 1991.

Kaufman, Paul. "The Community Library: A Chapter in English Social History." *Transactions of the American Philosophical Society,* n.s., vol. 57, pt. 7 (1967).

Kinane, Vincent. "'Literary Food' for the American Market: Patrick Byrne's Exports to Mathew Carey," *Proceedings of the American Antiquarian Society* 104 (1995), 315–22.

Korey, Marie Elena. "Three Early Philadelphia Book Collectors." *American Book Collector,* n.s., 2, no. 6 (Nov.–Dec. 1981): 2–13.

Landon, Richard G. "Small Profits Do Great Things: James Lackington and Eighteenth-Century Bookselling." *Studies in Eighteenth-Century Culture* 5 (1976): 387–99.

Lethwaite, Susan. "The Pre-Trial Examination in Upper Canada," in Greg T. Smith et al., eds., *Criminal Justice in the Old World and the New: Essays in Honour of J. M. Beattie,* pp. 85–103. Toronto: Centre for Criminology, University of Toronto, 1998.

[Logan, William.] "William Logan's Journal of a Journey to Georgia, 1745." *Pennsylvania Magazine of History and Biography* 36 (1912): 1–16, 162–86.

Martin, Sidney Walter, ed. "Ebenezer Kellogg's Visit to Charleston, 1817." *SCHM* 49 (1948): 1–14.

Mazyck, W. G. "The Charleston Museum, Its Genesis and Development." *Year Book, City of Charleston, 1907,* 13–36.

McConnell, Anita. "From Craft Workshop to Big Business: The London Scientific Instrument Trade's Response to Increasing Demand, 1750–1820." *London Journal* 19 (1994): 36–53.

McCusker, John. "The Business Press in England before 1775." *Library,* 6th ser., 8 (1986): 205–31.

McDougall, Warren. "Scottish Books for America in the Mid 18th Century," in Robin Myers and Harris, Michael Harris, eds., *Spreading the Word: The Distribution Networks of Print 1550–1850*, pp. 21–46. Winchester and Detroit: St. Paul's Bibliographies, 1990.

McMurtrie, Douglas C. "A Bibliography of South Carolina Imprints, 1731–1740" *SCHM* 34 (1933): 117–37.

———. "The First Decade of Printing in the Royal Province of South Carolina." *Library*, 4th ser., 13 (1933): 425–52.

Merrens, H. Roy. "A View of Coastal South Carolina in 1778: The Journal of Ebenezer Hazard." *SCHM* 73 (1972): 177–93.

Meroney, Geraldine M. "William Bull's First Exile from South Carolina of 1777–1781." *SCHM* 80 (1979), 91–104.

Millburn, John R. "The Office of Ordnance and the Instrument-Making Trade in the Mid-Eighteenth Century." *Annals of Science* 45 (1988): 221–93.

Mohl, Raymond A. "'The Grand Fabric of Republicanism': A Scotsman Describes South Carolina 1810–1811." *SCHM* 71 (1970): 170–88.

Moltke-Hansen, David. "The Expansion of Intellectual Life: A Prospectus," in Michael O'Brien and David Moltke-Hansen, eds., *Intellectual Life in Antebellum Charleston*, pp. 3–44. Knoxville: University of Tennessee Press, 1986.

———. "Protecting Interests, Maintaining Rights, Emulating Ancestors: US Constitution Bicentennial Reflections on the Problem of South Carolina, 1787–1860." *SCHM* 89 (1988): 160–82.

Morton, Alan Q., ed. *Science Lecturing in the Eighteenth Century: A Special Issue, British Journal for the History of Science* 28 (1995).

Nash, R. C. "South Carolina and the Atlantic Economy in the Late Seventeenth and Eighteenth Centuries." *Economic History Review*, 2d ser., 45 (1992): 677–702.

———. "Trade and Business in Eighteenth-Century South Carolina: The Career of John Guerard, Merchant and Planter." *SCHM* 96 (1995): 6–29.

Neville, Robert F., and Katherine H. Bielsky. "The Izard Library." *SCHM* 91 (1990): 149–69.

Olsberg, R. Nicholas. "Ship Registers in the South Carolina Archives." *SCHM* 74 (1973): 189–299.

Parks, Stephen. "George Berkeley, Sir Richard Steele, and the Ladies Library." *Scriblerian* 8 (1980): 1–2.

Pearson, Edward. "'Planters Full of Money': The Self-Fashioning of the Eighteenth-Century South Carolina Elite," in Jack P. Greene, Randy Sparks, and Rosemary Brana-Shute, eds., *Money, Trade and Power: The Evolution of Colonial South Carolina's Plantation Society*, pp. 299–321. Columbia: University of South Carolina Press, 2001.

Pennington, Edgar Legaré. "Beginnings of the Library in Charles Town, South Carolina." *Proceedings of the American Antiquarian Society*, n.s., 44 (1935): 159–87.

———. "The Reverend Thomas Morritt and the Free School." *SCHM* 32 (1931): 34–45.

Piazzi, Prof., of Palermo. "Account of the Life and Labours of the late Mr Ramsden." *Philosophical Magazine* 16 (1803): 253–62.

"Pope and Woodfall," and "Woodfall's Ledger, 1734–1747." *Notes and Queries* 11 (1855): 377–78, 418–20, 1765–71.

Purchas, Samuel. "A Discourse of the Diversity of Letters . . . ," in *Hakluytus Posthumus, or Purchas His Pilgrimes,* 1: 485–504. 20 vols. Glasgow: James MacLehose and Sons, 1905.

Raven, James. "From Promotion to Proscription: Arrangements for Reading and Eighteenth-Century Libraries," in James Raven, Helen Small, Naomi Tadmor, eds., *The Practice and Representation of Reading in England,* pp. 175–201. Cambridge: Cambridge University Press, 1996.

———. "New Reading Histories, Print Culture, and the Identification of Change: The Case of Eighteenth-Century England." *Social History* 23 (1998): 268–87.

———. "The Representation of Philanthropy and Reading in the Eighteenth-Century Library." *Libraries and Culture* 31, no. 2 (Spring 1996): 492–510.

———. "Selling One's Life: James Lackington, Eighteenth-Century Booksellers, and the Design of Autobiography," in O. M. Brack, Jr., ed., *Writers, Books, and Trade: An Eighteenth-Century English Miscellany for William B. Todd,* pp. 1–23. New York: AMS Press, 1994.

———. "Sent to the Wilderness: Mission Literature in Colonial North America," in James Raven, ed., *Free Print and Non-Commercial Publishing Since 1700,* pp. 135–61. Aldershot, Hants., and Burlington, Vt.: Ashgate, 2000.

"Records Kept by Colonel Isaac Hayne." *SCHM* 10 (1909): 145–70, 220–35.

Reid, Nina. "Loyalism and the 'Philosophic Spirit' in the Scientific Correspondence of Dr Alexander Garden." *SCHM* 92 (1991): 5–14.

Reilly, Elizabeth Carroll. "The Wages of Piety: The Boston Book Trade of Jeremy Condy," in William L. Joyce et al., eds., *Printing and Society in Early America,* pp. 83–131. Worcester, Mass.: American Antiquarian Society, 1983.

Reinke, Edgar C. "A Classical Debate of the Charleston, South Carolina, Library Society." *Papers of the Bibliographical Society of America* 61 (1967): 83–99.

Rogers, George C., Jr. "The Charleston Tea Party: The Significance of December 3, 1773." *SCHM* 75 (1974): 153–62.

Rugheimer, Virginia, and Guy A. Cardwell, Jr. "The Charleston Library Society." *South Atlantic Bulletin,* vol. 8, no. 2 (Oct. 1942): 4–5.

———. "Charleston Library Society." *Southeastern Librarian* 5 (1955): 137–40, 154.

[Sewall.] *The Letter-Book of Samuel Sewall. Collections of the Massachusetts Historical Society,* 6th ser., vols. 1–2 (1886, 1888).

———. "The Diary of Samuel Sewall, 1674–1729." *Collections of the Massachusetts Historical Society,* 5th ser., vol. 6, pt. 2 (1879).

Shammas, Carole. "Consumer Behavior in Colonial America." *Social Science History* 6 (1982): 67–86.

Sherman, Stuart C. "The Library Company of Baltimore, 1795–1854." *Maryland Historical Magazine* 39 (1944): 6–24.

Spain, Frances L. "Libraries of South Carolina: Their Origins and Early History, 1700–1830." *Library Quarterly* 16 (1947): 28–42.

Spawn, William. "The Evolution of American Binding Styles in the Eighteenth Century," in John Dooley and James Tanis, eds., *Bookbinding in America 1680–1910,* pp. 29–36. Bryn Mawr, Penn.: Bryn Mawr College Library, 1983.

Stiverson, Cynthia Z., and Gregory A. Stiverson. "The Colonial Retail Book Trade: Availability and Affordability of Reading Material in Mid-Eighteenth-Century Virginia," in William L. Joyce et al., eds., *Printing and Society in Early America,* pp. 132–73. Worcester, Mass.: American Antiquarian Society, 1983.

Stockdale, Eric. "John Stockdale of Piccadilly: Publisher to John Adams and Thomas Jefferson," in Robin Myers and Michael Harris, eds., *Author/Publisher Relations during the Eighteenth and Nineteenth Centuries,* pp. 63–87. Oxford: Oxford Polytechnic Press, 1983.

Stoney, Samuel G., ed. "The Great Fire of 1778 Seen through Contemporary Letters." *SCHM* 64 (1963): 23–26.

Stumpf, Stuart O. "South Carolina Importers of General Merchandise, 1735–1765." *SCHM* 84 (1983): 1–10.

Sutherland, John. "The Book Trade Crash of 1826." *Library,* 6th ser., 9 (1987): 148–61.

Swam, E. G. "Brothers of the Spade: Correspondence of Peter Collinson, of London, and of John Custis, of Williamsburg, Virginia, 1734–1746." *Proceedings of the American Antiquarian Society* 58 (1948): 15–190.

Swift, Katherine. "Bibliotheca Sunderlandiana: The Making of an Eighteenth-Century Library," in Robin Myers and Michael Harris, eds., *Bibliophily,* pp. 63–89. Cambridge and Alexandria, Va.: Chadwyck-Healey, 1986.

Warner, Michael. "The Public Sphere and the Cultural Mediation of Print," in William S. Solomon and Robert W. McChesney, eds., *Ruthless Criticism: New Perspectives in U.S. Communications History,* Minneapolis: University of Minnesota Press, 1993.

Webber, Mabel L. "Extracts from the Journal of Mrs Ann Manigault 1754–1781." *SCHM* 20 (1919): 57–63, 128–41, 204–12, 254–59.

———. "Inscriptions from the Independent or Congregational (Circular) Church Yard (contd.)." *SCHM* 29 (1928): 133–50.

Webster, Pelatiah. "Journal of a Visit to Charleston, 1765," in H. Roy Merrens, ed., *The Colonial South Carolina Scene: Contemporary Views 1697–1774,* pp. 218–26. Columbia: University of South Carolina Press, 1977.

Weir, Robert M. "'The Harmony We Were Famous For': An Interpretation of Pre-Revolutionary South Carolina Politics." *William and Mary Quarterly* 26 (1969): 473–501.

———. "The Role of the Newspaper Press in the Southern Colonies on the Eve of the Revolution: An Interpretation," in Bernard Bailyn and John Hench, eds., *The Press and the American Revolution,* pp. 99–150. Worcester, Mass.: American Antiquarian Society, 1980.

Wheeler, Joseph Towne. "Thomas Bray and the Maryland Parochial Libraries." *Maryland Historical Magazine* 34 (1939): 246–65.

Winans, Robert B. "Bibliography and the Cultural Historian: Notes on the Eighteenth-Century Novel," in William L. Joyce et al., eds., *Printing and Society in Early America,* pp. 83–131. Worcester, Mass.: American Antiquarian Society, 1983.

Winton, Calhoun. "The Colonial South Carolina Book Trade." *Proof: The Yearbook of American Bibliographical and Textual Studies* 2 (1972): 71–87.

Wolf, Edwin, II. "James Logan's Correspondence with William Reading, Librarian of Sion College," in Hellmut Lehmann-Haupt, ed., *Homage to a Bookman: Essays on Manuscripts, Books and Printing,* pp. 209–19. Berlin: Mann Verlag, 1967.

———. "The Library of Edward Lloyd IV of Wye House." *Winterthur Portfolio* 5 (1969): 87–121.

Zachs, William. "'An Illiterate Fellow of a Bookseller': John Murray and His Authors, 1768–1793," in Robin Myers and Michael Harris, eds., *A Genius for Letters: Booksellers and Bookselling from the 16th to the 20th Century,* pp. 123–43. Winchester and New Castle, Del.: Oak Knoll, 1996.

Unpublished Works

Edgar, Walter Bellingrath. "The Libraries of Colonial South Carolina." Ph.D. diss., University of South Carolina, 1969.

Houlette, W. D. "Plantation and Parish Libraries in the Old South." Ph.D. diss., University of Iowa, 1933.

Kaplanoff, Mark D. "Making the South Solid: Politics and the Structure of Society in South Carolina, 1790–1815." Ph.D. diss., University of Cambridge, 1979.

McDougall, Warren. "Charles Elliot's Book Adventures in America 1777–1790, and the Trouble with Thomas Dobson." Unpublished paper, 1997.

Moltke-Hansen, David. "The Empire of Scotsman Robert Wells, Loyalist South Carolina Printer-Publisher." M.A. thesis, University of South Carolina, 1984.

Reilly, Elizabeth Carroll. "Common and Learned Readers: Shared and Separate Spheres in Mid-Eighteenth-Century New England." Ph.D. diss., Boston University, 1996.

Spain, Frances L. "Libraries of South Carolina: Their Origins and Early History, 1700–1830." Ph.D. diss., University of Chicago, 1944.

Spearman, R. Alan. "The Johnston Library at Hayes Plantation: The Character of the Eighteenth-Century Library and Its Evolution in the First Half of the Nineteenth Century." M.A. thesis, University of North Carolina, 1988.

Walters, Alice Nell. "Tools of Enlightenment: The Material Culture of Science in 18th-Century England." Ph.D. diss., University of California–Berkeley, 1992.

Wenner, Evelyn Wingate. "George Steevens and the Boydell Shakespeare." Ph.D. diss., George Washington University, 1952.

INDEX

Page numbers to references within the annotated Letter Book are italicized. The contents of appendixes and tables are not indexed.

A Muse in Livery (Robert Dodsley), 93

Aberdeen, 38

Abridgment of the Laws of the United States (William Graydon), 212

academies of science, 48

Academy of Fine Arts, Charleston, 198

Accomplish'd Woman (Jacques du Boscq), 202

account books, 110

Account of some Experiments and Observations on Tar-water (Stephen Hales), 172

Account of the Weather and Diseases of South Carolina (Chalmers), 171

achromatic telescope, 176. *See also* telescopes

Ackermann, Rudolph, 100

Ackers, Charles, 90

Adair, James, 31

Adams, George, the elder, 172–73, 174, 175–76, 179, *245, 248*

Adams, George, the younger, 129, 178, 179, 181–82; and CLS telescope saga, *279, 280, 291, 292, 296, 301;* and death, *303; Essay on Vision, 274;* and Writtenhouse, 177–79

Adams, Hannah, 212

Adams, Henry, 77

Adams, John, 161, 212

Admiralty Court, 206

Adventure (ship), *246*

Adventurer (John Hawkesworth), 199, *265*

Advice to People in General (Samuel Auguste David Tissot), *252*

Aertsen, William, and Co., 213

Africa (ship), *248*

Agricultural Society, Charleston, 76

Ainsworth, Robert, *241*

air guns, 173

air pumps, 166, 173, 174, 180, *294*

Alberti, Leon Baptista, 32

Alfred (William Soranzo), 201

algerines, *294. See also* xebeques

Algonquin, 162–63

Allen, Robert, 99. *See also* Lackington, Allen

Allen's *Alarm,* 153

alligator, 149

almanacs, 214

Almon, John, 93, 97, 145

Almoran and Hamet, 203

Alston, Charles, 223

Alstorphius and Van Hemert, 128, *298, 299, 300, 304*

Amelia (Henry Fielding), 32, 199

America (ship), *255*

America: and economic crisis of 1790s, 129–30; and political grievances, 107; publications relating to, 193. *See also* revolution

American Atlas (Thomas Jefferys), 212

American Biography (Jeremy Belknap), 212

American Citizen's Sure Guide, 212

American Consul, 205

American Encyclopedia, 212, 213

American Ornithology (Alexander Wilson), 212

American Philosophical Society, 23, 166, 178

American Philosophical Transactions, 212

American Revolution of South Carolina (David Ramsay), 212

American Tale (Walter Kennedy), 201

American Universal Geography, 212

Amsterdam, 128, *298, 304;* booksellers in, 10

Analogy of Religion (Bishop Joseph Butler), 162

Ancient History (Charles Rollin), 35

Ancient History (William Stukeley), 161

Anderson, Adam, 163, 221, *247*

Anderson, Hugh, 35

Andrews, William, 192

Anglia Judaica (De Blossiers Tovey), 154, 247

Anglican Church, 18, 28, 191; high church, 192. *See also* Episcopalians

Angoulême china factory, 71

Annapolis County, Maryland, 23

Annotations upon the Holy Bible (Matthew Poole), 153

Annual Register, 93, *247, 269, 272*

Annuities and Reversions (Thomas Simpson), 155

"Annuities" (Richard Price), *270*

Antigua, 5, 11

Anti-Lucretius (Melchior de Polignac), 190

antiquarian book market, 107. *See also* Charleston Library Society, rare books

Antiquarian Society of Charleston, 77

Antique Paintings of Herculaneum, 162

Antiquities (Francis Grose), 161, *289*

Antiquities (Samuel Buck), *289*

Antiquity of Stone-Heng (Inigo Jones), 161

Apollo Belvedere (or Belvidere), 63, 78, 198

Apology (Mordecai), 192

Apology for the Apostolic Order (John Henry Hobart), 192

Apology for the True Christian Divinity (Robert Barclay), 163

Appeal to Common Reason and Candour for Reviewing the Liturgy, 162

Apthorp, Charles W., 241

Arbuthnot, John, 162

Architecture hydraulique (Bernard Forest de Belidor), 82

Arnott, Capt. Thomas, *263*

Arrowsmith's maps, 212

Art of Cookery (Hannah Glasse), 202

Art of Making Common Salt (William Brownrigg), 164

Arthur Mervyn (Charles Brockden Brown), 212

Arthur, Capt. George, *259*

Arthur, King, 156

Arthur, Prince, 78

Ash, John, 216

Ashley Plantation, 167

Ashley River, 74

Asia, literature of, 188–89

Asiatic Researches (Sir William Jones), 188

Askew, John, 10

Assheton, Ralph, 161

astronomical quadrants. *See* quadrants

Astronomy (Roger Long), 182

astronomy, 174

Atkins and Weston, 33

Atkins, Capt., *294, 295*

Atkins, Charles, estates confiscated, 69

Atlantic, changes in shipping, 13; ideas of Atlantic history, 13–14

Atterbury, Francis, 192

Atterbury, Francis, *Works of,* 192
Ayeen Akbery or Institutes of the Emperor Akber, 189
Azores, 11

Baburye's book of rates, 265
back numbers, orders for, 106–7
Backhouse's tavern, 174
Bacon, Francis, Works of, 312
Bage, Robert, 203
Bahar Danush, 189
Bailey and Waller, booksellers, 213
Bailyn, Bernard, 8
Baker, Henry, 175
Bakman, Samuel, *302, 304*
Balguy, John, 162
Ball, John, 171
Ball, Capt. Samuel, 39, 103, 116, *246, 260, 261, 265, 272, 273, 274;* bag of, *261;* seized, 147
Baltimore, 21
Baltimore Evening Post, 207
Baltimore Library Company, 99, 199–200, 210–11; catalogues, 151, 186; membership, 68; number of volumes, 81; rules of, 56; and shipment loss, 204–5
Bance-Island (ship), *243*
Bank of England, 121, 126, 127
Bank of the United States, 117, *280*
Bank of the United States, Charleston, 63
bankruptcies, 177
Banks, Sir Joseph, *317*
Baptists, 7, 21
Barbadoes, 13, 147
Barbary pirates, 22
Barclay, David, Jr., 82
Barclay, Robert, 163
Baretti, Giuseppe Marco Antonio, *264*
Barge Yard, Bucklersbury, 127
Barker Church, John, 196

Barkley, John, 87
Barlow, Joel, 212
Barnes, Capt. John, 127, *244, 245*
barometers, 174, 177, *252, 256*
Baron, Alexander, 38, 65, 170–71
Baronagium genealogicum 'Peerage' (Joseph Edmondson), *252, 260, 263, 267, 269*
Barracoa, 206
barter, 124
Barthélemy, Jean Jacques, *314*
Baskerville's Bible, 241
Bath, England, 100
Baths of the Romans (Charles Cameron), 162, *270*
Baumgarten, Siegmund Jakob, *243*
Beatson, Alexander, 188
Beattie, James, *265*
Beaufain (ship), *259*
Beaufort, S.C., 202
Beccaria [Bonesana], Cesare, 155, 158, 188, 214, *264;* works of, *266*
Bee, Thomas, 82, 95, 160, 179, *277, 279*
Beekman, Benjamin, *291*
bees, 164
Beggar's Opera (John Gay), 199
Belidor, Bernard Forest de, 82
Belknap, Jeremy, 212
Belsham, Thomas, 192
Bengal, 188, 196, 189
Bentley, Richard, 190
Berenger de Beaufain, Hector, 49
Beresford, Richard, 69
Berkeley, George, 82, 202
Berkeley, Sir William, 6
Berlin Decree, 22, 209
Bermuda, 97
Besse, Joseph, 163
Best, William, 215
Beswicke, John, 126

Beswicke-Greenwood-Higginson partnership, 127

Bethune, Hugh and Co., *309*

Betsy Thoughtless (Eliza Haywood), 32

Bible Society of Charleston, 76, 191

Bibles, 6, 11, 12, 43, 147, 152, 191; Algonquin (John Eliot), 162–63; imports of, 32; Kennicott's, *270;* patent, 117

bibliophiles. *See* book collectors

Biddle, Owen, 212

Bielfeld, Jacob Friedrich von, *264, 266*

bill brokers, 128

bill-brokers, and family ties, 103

bills of entry, *237*

bills of exchange. *See* bills of transfer

bills of lading, 133, *261, 272, 273, 274, 275, 293, 295, 297, 301, 303, 304, 305, 306, 308, 309, 314, 320, 335, 339*

bills of transfer (and of exchange), 99, 121, 124–26, 140, 145, 224, *237, 238, 239, 240, 241, 242, 245, 247, 249, 250, 256, 259, 262, 263, 267, 268, 274, 280, 282, 285, 286, 291, 292, 307, 310, 311, 313, 315, 316, 317, 318, 320, 321, 323, 325, 326, 327, 328, 329, 330, 331, 331, 332, 337, 338, 341;* bill-drawing, 128; and difficulties, *298;* periods of sight, 125–26, *265;* protesting of, 130, *302;* purchase of, 128; wider acceptance of, 130. *See also* bill brokers

binders, American, 7. *See also* bookbinding

Biographia Britannica, 155, *243, 247*

Biographical History of England (James Granger), *260*

Bion, Nicolas, 182

Birch, Dr. Thomas, 126, 146, 173, 220

Birchin Lane, Cornhill, 127, 145, *310*

Bird, Henry M., 97. *See also* Bird, Savage, and Bird

Bird, Robert, 97. *See also* Bird, Savage, and Bird

Bird, Savage, and Bird, merchants (Henry M. Bird, Benjamin Savage, and Robert Bird), 86, 88, 97, 99, 101, 108, 115, 117, 128, 129, 130, 133, 136, 147, 181, 197, 199, 224, *281, 282, 283, 285, 286, 322, 323, 325, 326, 328, 332;* and American vessels, 206–7; appointed by CLS, 98; as superior to booksellers, *288;* continuing CLS letters and accounts of, *288–309, 311;* failure of 99; and interest charges, 121; and insurance, 132, *287;* and periodicals, 112

Birt, Samuel, 87, 119

Bishopsgate Within, London, 127

Blackburne, Francis, 192

Blackstone, Sir William, 159, 160, 188, *252*

Blackwell, Thomas, *247*

Blair, Capt. —, *293*

Blamyer, William, 181, *280, 281, 284, 285, 288*

Blandford, HMS, 148, *239*

Blandy, Miss, trial of, 154

Blayney, Benjamin, 193

Blunt, Thomas, *278*

Blythe, Thomas, 72; his tavern as CLS meeting place, 61

Boadicia (Richard Glover), read by Eliza Pinckney, 70

Boerhaave, Hermann, 172

Bohun, Edmund, 167

Bolingbroke, Henry St. John, first Viscount, 154

bond holding, 59

book advertising, in Charleston, 32

book agents, 4, 8, 9, 10, 85, 105; and colonial agents, 135; use of London agents, 35, 113. *See also* book collectors book binding, types of, 110; in Charleston, 33, 213; local, 7; trade bindings, 110. *See also* book lettering

book catalogues. *See* book trade

book collecting, 47; in colonies, 10

book collectors, as book agents, 10; S.C. gentlemen as, 35

book history, xviii

book importation. *See* book transit

book lettering 88, 110, *245, 254, 273*

Book of Common Prayer, 152

Book of Martyrs (John Foxe), 191

book of rates, 265

book orders, 5; length of passage and time taken to complete, 135–44; process of, 106; prospectuses, 9; sellers' and merchants' commission, 98, 129, 215, *283, 286, 288, 296, 300, 301, 308, 309, 324, 327, 328, 332, 334, 336, 337, 340;* size and frequency of, 135. *See also* book trade; book transit; booksellers

book reprinting in America, 157–58. *See also* publication

book trade, across the Atlantic, 3, 6; and transatlantic book ordering procedure 102–14; advertising of new publications, 9; American coastal, 224–25; auctioneers' catalogues, 87, 151; auctions, 7, 31, 32, *270;* books difficult to find, 194; British, 47; catalogues 6, 9, 98, 151; colonial demand, 7, 28, 225–26; and commercial changes, 224; and cultural links, 226; discounts, 92; exports, 155; import of books, 31, 85; import of books on medicines, 171; imported print, range of, 32; imports and seasonality, 147; in Boston, 87; in Charleston, 31, 33, 35–36, 82, 84, 204, 213–15; incidentals in overseas ordering, 115; information about

books, 9, 105; institutional demand, 8, 225; invoices, 133; kinship ties with CLS, 98; latest publications from London, 209; London book export market and specialisms, 33, 112–13; London book export trade, social dimension of, 225; London sites of, 18; and medicines, 31; relations, 104; and declining religious market, 7; structure of, 224–25; unsalables, 87, 89, 92; unsolicited orders, 108. *See also* book agents; book transit; books; transatlantic book trade

book transit, arrivals in Carolina, 153; Byrne's delivery times, 141; by captain's cabin, 13, 146, *241, 247, 258;* captain's-bag references, 115; cargoes nearly go missing, 146; cargoes lost, 149, *308;* cargo procedures and packing, 144–45, 146–47; costs and charges, 115, 116; financing of, 9–10; imports, 7, 32; imports from London continue, 215; imports to America and trade changes, 225–26; imports to Charleston, 31–32, 204; interest charges for delay, 116; invoicing of, 140; loss of consignments at sea, 130–31, 147–48, 204; packing, 133, 146–47; sea passages, length of, 136–44; ships loading and book collecting and packing times, 144; and shipping duty, 115; and shipping improvements, 13. *See also* ships; book agents; book trade; books

bookbinding, 110; concerns about, 111, *260, 262, 264, 320;* sewed or in boards, 110

book-burning, 153

books, subjects of: architectural and design, 164–65; building and architecture; 152; classics, 89, *250, 252;* commerce, 163;

books (*continued*)
conveyancing manuals, 155; domestic advice, 164; etiquette, 165; historical, 152, 153, 161–62, 163; horticultural, 152, 164, 169; husbandry, 152; Indian and Asian travels, 193; Indian law and commercial manuals, 189; law, 4, 6, 30, 49, 77, 87, 105, 155–60, 163, 190, 212; mathematics, 153; medical, 214, 152, 153; music, 152; politics and philosophy, 152; practical learning, 163; reference, 163; religion, 153; scientific, 190; theological, 152; voyages and travel, 153, 203. *See also* Bibles; novels; poetry; "polemical divinity"; prayer-books; psalm books; psalters; school and cheap books; sermons
books, advancing demand for fiction, 199–203; lag between publication and reception, 18; manufacturing, 164; rhetoric, 152; out of print, *265, 319;* second-hand, *250;* and status, 8. See *also* publication
booksellers, 3, 35, 204, 213–15; and antiquarian books, 160–61; apology by, *240;* bills, transit of, *255;* and book searches, 222; business visits to America, 96; collection and dispatch of overseas orders, 97; commercial ploys, 194; credit terms, 117–19; debts to, 120; discounts, 119; dismissed by CLS, 56, 88, 89, 91, 94, 95, 96, 97, *249, 250–51, 253–54, 256, 262, 263, 275, 276, 277, 330, 332–33, 334, 337;* attempted dismissal of, *253–54;* difficulty in collecting orders, 109; elections to the CLS, 87–89, 90–101, *240, 246–47, 248, 250, 251, 256, 257, 275, 276, 277;* European, 109; exporting from London, 87; gifts to and from, 104; in London,

3; in London and difficulties with American trade, 224, *333–34;* in London and their business papers, 86; in New York, 210; great diversity of in London, 90; judgment of, 89, 104, 106, 107, *273;* knowledge of the sea, 131; lending services, 222; newspaper puffs, 194; orders to, 89; and overseas customers, 7, 109; pricing agreements, 119–20; reprimanded by *CLS, 239, 249, 250, 251, 253, 254, 265, 274, 329;* requiring return of loaned books, 35; respectability of, 89, 104; and ship timetables, 135; and shipping information, 145; wealth of, 90. *See also* book orders; book trade; book transit; Charleston booksellers
bookshops, as news centres, 145
Boone, Thomas, Governor, 18, 22, 61, 157
Bosomworth, Harvey and Smith and Co., 60
Bosquet, Capt. John le, *336, 337*
Bostock, Peter, 39
Boston, 7, 9, 13, 21, 103, 109, 110, 116, 131, 134, 135, 141, 147, 163, 166, 212, 224; booksellers, 210; and the Court of Jurisdiction, 120; harbor, 12; literary clubs, 51; printing, 215
Boswell, James, 96
Botanical Dictionary (Richard Bradley), 167
Botanical Magazine, 194, *324*
Botany (James Lee), 169
botany, 10, 166
Botein, Stephen, 7, 120
Botterell, Capt. John, *246*
Bougainville, Comte Louis-Antoine de, *269*
Boughton, Charles, 189
Boulter, Robert, 7
Boulton, Matthew, 196
Bourdieu, Pierre, 14

Bowen, T. B., 83

Bowes, Frederick, 79

Bowyer, William, 90

Boyce, William, *269*

Boyd, William, 207

Boydell, John and Josiah, 99, 194–98, *298, 299; Catalogue,* 197; prints, 108, 194–98, 208; series medal, 196–97; "Shakspeare" prints and series, 78, 195–98, 204, *279, 294, 308, 309;* shipment captured, *308;* Shakespeare Gallery, 195

Boyle, Charles, 190

Bracton. *See* Bratton, Henry de

Bradford, William III, 92

Bradley, Richard, 164, 167

Bradley's maps, 212

Brailsford family, 46

Brailsford, Edward, 38

Brailsford, Morton, 37

Brailsford, Samuel, 37, 60; as state bond-holder, 60

Braintree, Essex, 162

Bratton (or Bracton), Henry de, 156, 160, 161, 186, *252*

Bray Associates, 81–82

Bray, Thomas, 34, 42, 81–82; and SPG Charleston library, 153

Bremar, Francis, 33

Brewton, Miles, 69, 169, *253*

Brisbane family, 38, 90, 103; estate on Ashley River, 56

Brisbane, James, 76, 226; banishment and confiscation, 69

Brisbane, Robert, 37, 92, 124–25, *237, 238, 239*

Brisbane, W. & J., firm of 124–25, *237, 238*

Bristol, 43, 100, 148, *242, 249, 257;* book exports, 33; port, 12; slave trade, 128

Bristol Education Society, catalogue, 195

Bristol Library Society, 81, 196

Bristol Packet (brigantine), *242*

Britannia (William Camden), 158, *289*

Britannia (ship), *272, 273, 281, 282, 283, 285, 286, 287, 289, 297*

British and Foreign Bible Society, 193

British Classics, 312

British Library, St. Pancras, London, 175

British Magazine (Tobias Smollett), *240, 247, 255, 263*

British Museum, London, 3

British Zoology (Thomas Pennant), 170, *269*

Briton (ship), 233, *274, 279*

Broad Street, Charleston, 95

Brooke, Henry, 200, 203

Broom Hall, Goose Creek, S.C., 77

Brothers (ship), *314, 315*

Brown, Charles Brockden, 212

Brown, Christopher, 109

Brown, John, 162, *265*

Browne, Patrick, 169

Brownrigg, William, 164

Bruce, David, 214

Brunswick, duchess of, 196

Bryan, Hugh and Jonathan, 46

Buchanan, George, 158

Buck, Samuel, *289*

Bucklersbury, London, 126

Builders Companion (William Jones), *248*

Builder's Companion (William Pain), 164–165

Bull, William, 20, 25, 61, 65, 75, 168, 169, 171, 172; book collection of, 223; father's house, 167; as ubiquarian, 50

Bulloch, James, 35

Burder, George, 193

Burke, Aedanus, 69, 157

Burke, Edmund, 93, 155

Burkitt, William, 153

Burlamaqui, Jean Jacques, 154–55, 158, *265*

Burlington, earl of, 82

Burlington House, London, 96

Burman, Caspar, 190, *243*

Burn, Richard, 155, *265*

Burnet, Gilbert, 191

Burney, Charles, *269*

Burney, Frances, 200, 203

Burrows, William, 37; and son, 65

Burton, Robert, 197

Bury Court, London, 88

Bury, England, 100

Bush Lane, Cannon Street, London, 126

Bushman, Richard L., 15, 16

Bute, earl of, 103

Butler, Capt. —, *309*

Butler, John, 92, *238, 240*

Butler, Bishop Joseph, 162

Butler, Sarah, *287*

Byrd, William II, 147, 161, 163

Byrne, Patrick, 141

Cabot, Joseph, 11

Cadell, Thomas, 87

Cadiz, 12

Cæsar, Julius, 42, 154, 189

Caledonia (ship), *329*

Caledonian and Hibernian societies, 22

Callahan, Capt., *287, 288, 289*

Cambridge, 100, *313;* Emmanuel College library, 196; King's College library, 196; university, 160, 183

Cambridge, Massachusetts, 163

Camden, William, 158, *289*

camera obscura (solar), 175, 180, *245, 248*

Cameron, Charles, 162, *270*

Campaigns in North-America (Capt. John Knox), *266*

Campbell, Colen, *317*

Canary Islands, 11

Cannon, Daniel, 62

captain's cabin. *See* book transit

captain's-bag. *See* book transit

Carey, Matthew, 115; delivery times, 141

cargoes. *See* book transit

Caribbean 11, 12, 17, 23; sugar route, 135

Carne and Wilson, firm of, 222

Carne, Samuel, 31, 171; banishment and confiscation, 69

Carolina Coffee House, 127, 145, *258, 310*

Carolina Planter (ship), *291, 292*

Carolina Walk, Royal Exchange, London, 127

Carolinas. *See* South Carolina

Caroline (ship), *293*

Carter, G. (author of *Essay on the Yellow Fever),* 215

Carwithen, William, 61, 73, 76, 78, 106

Carwithin, Mrs., 73

Catesby, Mark, 167, 169, 175, *262*

Cathedral Music (William Boyce), *269*

Catholic. *See* Roman Catholicism

Cato, 35

Catullus, 190

Cave, William, *266*

Caw, Drs. David, Lewis, and Thomas, 170

Cay, John, *258*

Celestina, 200

Chalmers, James, 162, *289*

Chalmers, Dr. Lionel, 18, 65, 160, 170, 171, 173

Chambaud, Lewis, *264*

Chambers, Sir William, 165, *269*

Champney's Street, Charleston, 86

Chaplin, Joyce, 164

Chapman, George (translator), 189

Chapman's Companion, 214

Charles Davenant, Works of, 266

Charles Rollin, 35

Charles Rollin, The Method of Teaching and Studying the Belles Lettres, 269

Charles Town Packet (brigantine), *250, 271*

Charles Town. *See* Charleston

Charleston:
—ambitious community, 19
—architecture, 19
—booksellers of, 27–36, 204, 214, 216
—booksellers rarely supply CLS, 82
—and British and European links, 226
—British reoccupation of, 81, 88, 95, 171, 226, *271*
—buildings and the "West Indian" look, 164
—change of name, *273*
—cheap printing and prints, 30
—circulating libraries, 76–77, 201, 215, 222
—civic culture, 27, 79–80
—commodification and refinement, 228
—and competition, 33
—debate about civility, 79
—defense of slavery, 23
—dissenters in, 34
—early cultural history of, 26
—early libraries, 34–35
—Episcopal Church of St. Michael, 63
—fires of 1740, 1778 and 1787, 21
—first state house, 20
—and French sympathies, 226
—gardens, 169
—general merchants as book importers, 135
—general societies, 50
—and house design, 164
—imperial and European connections, 226
—importing booksellers, 32–33
—inadequacy of, 35–36
—isolation of, 219
—jail, 63
—links with northern ports, 17
—libraries and prints, 194
—literary culture of, 33–34, 204
—local book supply, 84
—local plays, 201
—freemasons, 38
—meteorological recordings, 170
—new wealth in, 46–47
—planter aristocracy, 23
—and pleasure, 228
—politics, 22
—population, 20–21
—port and importation, 21
—port of, 137
—printed books, 201
—printers in, 27–36, 204, 214, 216
—and printing, 213–15
—private libraries, 34–35
—processions, 52, 80
—radicalism in, 127
—religious publications, 30
—and religious tolerance, 162
—sale of slaves, 41
—and scientific instruments, 173
—Scots community and connections, 103
—sense of self-importance, 16–17
—ship owners, 207
—social emulation of Europe, 77
—social structure, 25
—societies and female membership, 202
—and theological controversy, 191
—and vulgarity, 227
—wealth holding, 24
—wealth of, 23
—widows carrying on business, 70
—women and book ownership, 203

Charleston (*continued*)

—women and reading, 201

—and women's education, 203

See also South Carolina

Charleston Academy. *See* Charleston College

Charleston Chamber of Commerce, Rules of, 51

Charleston (Charles Town) Chamber of Commerce, 98

Charleston College, 86; projected, 45, 77

Charleston Courier, 205, 207

Charleston Courthouse, as home to CLS, 58, 62–63

Charleston Exchange, 62

Charleston Faculty of Physic, 170

Charleston Fellowship Society, 51

Charleston Gazette, 205

Charleston Library Society *Catalogues,* 3–4, 80–81, 91, 105, 150–152, 153, 154, 159, 162, 163, 164, 169, 176, 177, 182, 184, 186, 188, 189, 198, 199, 201, 203, 211, 212, 215, 223; confusions in, 190, *268–69;* design of, 151; format categories, 54; printed 54; subject divisions, 186

Charleston Library Society librarian, 31, 62, *267;* as cataloguer, 55; duties of, 76, 171, *268;* salary, 54, 76

Charleston Library Society members: arrears of, 56; balloting of, 59, *277;* banished by British, 69; certificates, 44; composition of, 159–60; dismissal of, 56; disputes about orders, 105; doctors, 170–71; early membership, 38–39; election of, 53, 67, 68; entry fees, 72; estates confiscated, 69; families, 39; fines for nonattendance, 54; fines for books, 55; fines for service refusal, 56;

lawyers, 159–60; list of founder members, 38; Loyalism of, 226; membership applications by, 71; membership rejections, 72; membership Scottish links, 38; membership totals, 68; membership, per household, 69, 71; non-attendance fines, 54; non-payment of dues, 72; numbers in 1750, table 1, 40; personal libraries of, 223; political divisions among, 69, 157; *poor attendance by, 245;* purchase of shares by, 72, 73; recording problems of, 38; share transfers by, 68, 72–73; social composition, 220; social profile, 67–71, 74–75; stock disposal by, 69; wives of, 70–71

Charleston Library Society:

—accessions records, 150, 152

—accounts, 115, *254*

—advertisement of 1750, 39

—agents, 129

—agrarian science and domestic horticulture, 163–64

—American book suppliers, 210

—American editions 212, 213

—American publications not held, 212

—American stock, *284, 285, 286, 287*

—anniversary and quarterly meetings, 53, 234, *243, 249*

—antique books of, 160

—arrival of books, 150, 152

—attempt to found a college, 220

—average cost per title, 211

—belles lettres, 193, 199–203

—Bibles, 162–63

—bills of exchange, 124

—binding and lettering requirements, 8, 108, 113, *241, 247, 273*

—biography and history, 184, 186

—bond holding rules of, 59

—bonds and security, 59–60, *277*
—book circulation records, 71
—book fines, 55
—book lists, 154
—book ordering difficulties, 150
—book orders, 103, 154
—book storage, permanent building, 61–64
—book supply, 221–22
—book trade with London, 85
—bookseller appointment letters, 88
—booksellers' incompetence, 209
—borrowing from, 200–201, 202–3, 214
—borrowing rules, 55
—botanical and related natural history, horticultural and agricultural books, 168–69
—and British occupation, 158, 226, *271*
—budget, 179
—building, *267*
—camera obscura, 175, 180, *245, 248*
—capital lent to treasury, 60
—capital stock, 45, 58–59
—certificates, design of, 44
—and civility, 14
—and civilization, 219;
—civilizing mission, 44–45
—classical literature, 184, 186, 189–90, 199, 214
—collecting policy, 186
—as colonial assembly's reading room, 158
—colored prints, 194
—and commercial lending libraries, 222
—committee and book ordering, 150–51, 152

—committee meetings, *240, 241*
—committee membership, attraction, 59
—committee quorum, 53–54
—committees, 39, 221
—composition of, 218
—concern over overdue books, 56
—contribution to scientific learning, 182–83
—copy book of letters, historical value of, 233–35
—costs of instruments, 179
—countermanding of orders, 205, *254, 255, 262, 318, 319*
—country membership, 38, 55, 56, 67
—Courthouse rooms, 172, 198
—credit difficulties, 120–21, 128, 130, *277, 280*
—credit to booksellers, 114, 117–18
—cultural activity, 227
—curios collection, 64–66
—design of, 219
—difficulty with orders in London, 109
—dinners, 57–58
—dispatch of books to members, 56
—distinction between share and membership, 73
—dividends, 117
—and domestic libraries, 222
—donation of books to, 82–83
—election of booksellers, 87–89, 90–101
—election of president, 67
—embarrassment over light reading, *292, 310*
—emulation of learned societies, 221
—exclusive membership, 71
—exhibition and experiments in electricity, 172, 174

Charleston Library Society (*continued*)
—expenditure on books, 83
—extraordinary meetings, 53, 177, 178
—failure of book suppliers, 224
—and failures, 220–21
—female membership and use, 69–71
—feminization of, 202–3, 214, 220
—financial accounts, 234
—fines for service refusal, 56
—fire of 1778, 62, 77, 81, 88, 95,
    152, 171, 180, 182, 186, 214, *270*
—fire of 1778 and rebuilding of collec-
    tion, 221
—foreign language books, 186
—foundation of, 3, 37–38, 41–43
—founder officers, 37
—founding declaration, 42, 68
—founding instrument, 46
—French books, *318, 319*
—fund for a professorship of mathe-
    matical and natural philosophy, 83
—funds lent out at interest, 116, *262*
—general instructions to booksellers,
    106, 107–8, 110, 146, *247, 248,*
    249, 250, 251, 257, 258, 261, 262,
    277
—general meetings, 53, 150
—and gentility, 228
—globes, 174–75, 179, *263*
—high price of imports, 211
—history and travel books, 193
—holdings and changes, 150–203
—hospitality, 78
—imaginative literature, 184, 186
—increasing exclusiveness, 67–70
—indebtedness, 120–21
—Indian and Bengali literature,
    188–89
—inelastic funds, 126
—inquorate meetings, 57

—insurance, 131
—insurance on collection, 81
—intellectual centre, 26
—and intellectual community,
    218–20, 226–29
—interest liabilities, 121
—interest on its bonds, 81
—interrupted by war, 95
—invoices and billing, 113
—invoices from London, 115
—journal, 3
—and *Junius,* 188, *324*
—labeling instructions, 110
—labeling, shipping, and packing
    requirements, 8
—law and politics books, 184, 186
—letter book and recording practice,
    233–34
—letter book, transcription and gaps,
    234
—letters, 3
—letters, misaddressed, 88
—letters, language of, 104
—letters, style and language, 102
—letters, time of writing, 140–4
—library room and layout, 186
—library room in courthouse, 226
—local book supply, 84
—and local booksellers, *246*
—local donations, 81
—local printing, 202
—loss of spirit, 56–57
—low attendance at, 220
—Manigault rooms, 172
—manuscripts catalogue, 193, *274*
—masculine interests, 201–2
—material collection, 27
—mathematical, optical, and other
    scientific instruments, 173–75
—medical books, 171

—meeting attendance, 56

—meeting places, 60–61

—meeting times, 58

—microscope (and solar miscroscope), 173–76, 179, 181, *245, 248, 284, 291*

—military books, 186

—minute book, 3

—mission of, 49, 50, 58

—modern literature, 186–88, 214–15

—moneylending by, 221

—monthly periodicals, 221

—museum projected, 168

—natural curiosities, described, 78

—natural history and scientific interests, 166–83

—natural history cabinet/museum, 63, 220, *301*

—natural history committee, 174

—natural history prints, *301, 306*

—natural science texts, 199

—neo-Latin compositions, 190

—new books, proposals for, 150–51, *268–69, 270*

—number of volumes, 81

—notes errors in accounting, 113

—novels and imaginative literature, 165, 198–202, 220, *310, 311*

—officers, 53

—opening hours, 54

—ordering and literary tensions, 111

—ordering processes, 222

—orders, multiple copies as precaution, 131

—organization, 53–57

—orreries and planetariums, 177–78

—overdue books, 154

—payments to London booksellers, 115–126

—and Philadelphia book merchants, 225

—plays, 186, 201

—poetry, 186

—and "polemical divinity," 153

—and polite society, 227

—political controversialism, 157, 188

—as a political focus, 219

—poor spirit of, 93

—popularity of the holdings, 154

—precautions against fire, *267*

—preferred format of books ordered, 108

—president's duties, 53, 71

—presidents, 75

—print collection, 194–98, 209

—as a "private community," 228

—proceedings, 53–4

—professor of mathematics and of natural and experimental philosophy, 174

—proposed college, 15

—protested bill charges, 130

—and public science, 220

—publications on science, 166

—purchase of instruments, 174

—purchases locally considered, 93

—purchasing policy, 150–51, 152

—purchasing records, 213

—quarterly Committee, 53–4

—quarterly meetings (general meetings), 53–4, 71–72, 216

—rare books, 193–94, 223, *289, 324*

—ratification of library, 37

—reading/library room, 60

—reference books, 201–2, 223

—reflecting religious and ethnic diversity, 37–38

—religious books, 162–63, 191–93

Charleston Library Society (*continued*)
—religious holdings, 184, 186
—rules, 3, 41, 53, 57, 64, 71, 88, 104, 173, 174, *268, 276;* preamble of, 43; printing of, 41
—science books, 170
—scientific and mathematical instruments, 166, 173–83, *292*
—scientific apparatus, 64, 83
—scientific experiment, 172
—scrutinizes accounts, 113–14
—seals, 43–44, 49
—secretaries, role of, 233
—secretary remunerated, 76
—secretary-correspondents, 76
—and sermon writing and classical language composition, 202
—servants collect books, 71
—sizes and costs of incoming consignments, 115–17, 121–32
—and sociability, 15, 228–29
—and social and political power, 227
—spending on books, 154
—and Statehouse, 186
—theological volumes, 186
—thermometer, 177
—total book purchases, 81
—tourist visits to, 20, 56–57, 62, 63, 78, 186, 194, 195, 198
—trade and commerce books, 186
—transaction costs, 121–32
—transatlantic credit of, 109
—travel literature, 186
—unordered books sent, 106
—viewing prints, 176
—wealth of, 38, *286,* 59, 81, 117, 216–17
—and women, 220
—and women readers, 202–3
—as a working resource, 202
See also book lettering and bookbinding; telescopes; and Charleston Library Society, *Catalogues,* librarian, and members
Charleston Literary and Philosophical Society, 65
Charleston Museum, 65, 76, *301*
Charleston Statehouse, 63. *See also* Charleston Courthouse; Charleston Library Society, courthouse rooms
Charleston subscription publication, 30
Charles-Town (ship), 127, *245*
Charlestown Packet (ship), *271*
Charlotte Temple, 212
Charlotte, Queen, 192, 196
Charming Sally, 264
Charnock, John, *312, 319*
chart of biography, *274*
charts for merchants and seafarers, 152
Chaucer, 199
Cheesman, Capt. Christopher, 103, *244*
Chelsea, 164
Chequer Yard, London, 127
Cherokee, 75
Chesapeake, 11, 12, 135
Chester, book exports from, 33
Chetham's Library, Manchester, 196
Chislehurst, 94
Chisolm, Capt. —, *309, 316*
Chisolm, Colin, 212
Chiswell, Richard, 7, 10
Christ Church College, Oxford, 75
Christian's Theology (George Pretyman Tomline), 193
Chrysal or the Adventures of a Guinea (Charles Johnstone), 199, *265–66*
church and state, separation of, 192
churches, as loan agencies, 59
Churchill, Charles, *252*

Cicero, 105, 189

circulating libraries, 95, 98; catalogues of, 151

Civil Law in Its Natural Order (Jean Domat), 154

civilization as transportable, 218

Clark, William, 171, 193

Clarke, John (translator), 189

"Clarke's Maritime Discoveries," 193, *324*

Clarkson, Thomas, 215

class and exclusivity, 16–17

classical literature, *254;* authors, 223; CLS debate, *249;* controversy in Charleston, 105–6; ordering by CLS, 47

Clayton, John, 223

Cleland, John, 70

Cleland, John, of Charleston, 49

Clementine, 265

Cleopatra (ship), 136, 144, 225, *317*

Clerk, Hugh and Robert, 32

Clerk's Manual, 155

Clive, John, 8

Cobb, James, 201

Cockburn, Patrick, 162

cockets, 133, 144

Codex juris ecclesiastici Anglicani (Edmund Gibson), 162, *252*

coffee houses, 129, 145

Cohen, Anthony P., xviii, xix

coins, 166

Coke 158, 159

Colcock, John 65, 76, 95, 96, 113, 121, 126, 233, *255, 257, 258, 262, 263, 265, 267, 268, 269;* resigns as secretary, *271,* death of, 104, *272*

Colden, Cadwallader, 148, 172

Colden, David, 172

Colebrooke, Sir George, 127

Collection of Poems by Several Hands (Robert Dodsley), 93, 199, *252*

Collection of Psalms and Hymns, 30

College and Academy of Philadelphia, 178

College of Charleston, 45, 77, 182, 183

College of New-Jersey. *See* Princeton

College of William and Mary, 82, 120

Collins [Colins], Samuel, 153

Collinson, Peter, 4, 10, 169, 219

Colloquies (Erasmus), 190

colonial agents, 11. *See also* book agents

Columbia, S.C., 202, 206, 213; Assembly moves to, 158; as new South Carolina capital, 63

Columbiad (Joel Barlow), 212

Columbian Magazine, 212

Commentaries (Caesar), 189

Commentaries (Sir William Blackstone), 159, 188, *252*

Commercial Grammar (William Guthrie), 163

commission. *See* book orders

Committee of Merchants, London, 218

Common Law, abuses of, 156

Common Sense (Thomas Paine), 214

"Commonwealth" discourse, 157

communities, of conscience, 15; construction of, xviii, 14–18; imagined, 227; intimacy of, 103; perceptions of, 218, 219

compass, 174; pocket, *288;* gunner's, *303*

Compendious History of the Church (Louis Ellies du Pin), 162

Compendium of Anatomy (Lorenz Heister), 171

Compendium of Latin Grammar (Thomas Mills), 190

Compendium of Latin Syntax (Thomas Mills), 190

Compendium of the Law of Nations on Privateers, Captures and Re-Captures (Georg Friedrich de Martens), 189

Compleat Arbitrator, 155

Compleat Housewife (Eliza Smith), 202–3

Complete History of England (Tobias Smollett), 247

comte de Buffon, Georges Louis Leclerc, *270, 292*

Condy, Jeremiah [Jeremy], 7, 11, 85, 87, 111, 119, 132; uses navy, 148

Confessional (Francis Blackburne), 192

Confessions (James Lackington), 100

congregationalist, 21

Congreve, William, Works of, 265

Constitutional Convention [federal] in Philadelphia, 157

Constitutional Convention of Pennsylvania, 179

constitutional rights, 158

Construction and Principal Uses of Mathematical Instruments (Nicolas Bion), 182

consumption, history of, 8, 14. *See also* Charleston; South Carolina; North America

contractors for American British forces, 126

convoys, 134, 148–49, 206; petition about, 149; duty, *336*

Cookson, Joseph, 249

Coombes, Capt. William, 145, 149, *245, 256*

Cooper, John, 37, 61, 218

Cooper, Dr. Thomas, 167

Cooper, Thomas and Mary, 89

Copley medal, 170

Coram, Thomas, 43

Corbett, Charles and Charles, booksellers, 87

Corbett, Thomas, 102

Cornelia, HMS, 144

Cornelius Nepos, 105, 189

correspondence, transatlantic, 172

Corrie, Capt. —, 204, *244, 245*

Corry, John, 212

Cosslett, Charles, 65

Costa, Isaac de, 32

cotton, 19, 20, 168

Cotton, Sir Robert, 160, *264*

country ideology, 18

Country Justice (Michael Dalton), 155

Course of Experimental Philosophy (John Desaguliers), 172

Course of Lectures on Elocution (Thomas Sheridan), 165, *265*

"*Court Calendar,*" *252, 262*

Court of Lieutenancy, London, 91

courtesy books, 152

Coventry, England, 100

Coventry, Francis, 32

Cowan, Andrew, 32, 135, 204

Cowes, Isle of Wight, 242

Cox, Thomas Campbell, 213

Craftsman, The, 222

Crawford, Bellamy, 69

Crawford, Daniel, 49, 75, 223

credit, 109, 114, 117–19; and colonial currencies, 121–24; difficulties, 11, 120–21, 128, 130, *277, 280;* and payment methods, 115; terms, 117; and troubled money markets, 128

Creech, Thomas, 190

Criterion: or, Miracles Examined (Bishop John Douglas), 192

Critical History of the Old Testament (Richard Simon), 192

Critical Review, 33, 111, *241, 243, 247, 255. See also* periodicals

critical reviews. *See Critical Review; Monthly Review;* periodicals

Crokatt, James, 51, 103, 126, 127, 158, 163, *237, 238, 239;* as Indian trader and colony Agent, 38; family estates confiscated, 69

Cronstedt, Axel Frederik, 170, *265*

Crouch, Charles, 33, 84

Crowfield Plantation, 222

"Crown Law" (Sir Michael Foster), 159

Cuba, 205

Cuff, John, 173

Cumberland, England, 97

Cumberland, Henry Frederick, duke of, 265

Cummings, Penhallow, R.N., 148

Cunningham, Timothy, 163, *265*

Curling, Alexander(?), *261*

Curling, Capt. Daniel, 234, *259, 261*

Curll, Edmund, 89

currency. *See* credit

Curwen, Henry, 99

custom house, 144; at Charleston, 207; procedures and duties, 215, *332*

customs duties, 133, *320*

"D. of C." (Henry Frederick, Duke of Cumberland), *265*

Dacier, M., 190, *266*

Dale, Samuel, 162, 167, 169

Dale, Dr. Thomas, 49, 126, 146, 162, 170, 172, 214, 220

Dalrymple, Sir John, *269*

Dalton, Michael, 155

"dambargo." *See* Nonimportation, Embargo, and Nonintercourse Acts

dancing, 165

Danzig, 196

Darby, Pennsylvania, Library Company of, 3

Dart, John, 34, 72, 73

Dashwood, Capt. —, 132

Davenport, Capt. —, *317*

Davidson, John, 76, 171, 207, 208, 209, 210, 211, 214, *334, 337;* letters to and from Lackington, Allen, *310–29, 333–34, 335–41*

Davis, James, 29

Davis, Richard Beale, 152–53, 162, 222

Dawson, John, *274*

de Bracton. *See* Bratton, Henry, de

De jure maritimo e navali (Charles Malloy), 156

De laudibus legum Angliæ (Sir John Fortescue), 156, *252*

De legibus et consuetudinibus Angliæ (Henry de Bratton), 160

de rerum Natura (Lucretius), 190

Deal, England, 136, 141

Deas brothers, 46; and estate, 56

Debates in the House of Commons (Anchitel Grey), *248*

Debrett, John, 97

Decline and Fall of the Roman Empire (Edward Gibbon), 90, 193, *274*

Defence of the Constitutions of Government of the United States of America (John Adams), 212

Defoe, Daniel, 199

deism, 191–92

Dell, Henry, 91, 105

Delphin (or Dauphin) editions, 190

Deluc, Jean André, 82, 192

Demosthenes, 154, *252*

Deneslone, J., 125, *237*

Denon, Vivant, *313–14*

Desaguliers, John, 172

DeSaussure, Henry William, 76, 98, 210, 215, 218, *330, 335*

Description de plantes de l'Amerique (Charles Plumier), 170

Description of Ventilators (Stephen Hales), 172

Dewar, Robert, 69

Diana (ship), *329*

Dickinson, John, *258*

"Dictionaricum Botainical," 167

Dictionary by Samuel Johnson, 93

Dictionary of the Holy Bible (John Brown), 162

Dictionary of Trade and Commerce (Malachy Postlethwayt), 11

Digests of the General Highway and Turnpike Laws (John Scott), *277*

Dillon, Mr., 72; his tavern, as CLS meeting place, 57, 61

Dilly, Charles, 88, 96, 109, 128, 146, *277;* elected CLS bookseller, *275, 276;* firm of (with brother Edward), 5, 87, 145; resigned and dismissed by CLS, *277*

Dilly, Edward, 96; firm of (with brother Charles), 5, 87, 145

Dio Chrysostom (Gilbert Wakefield), 190

Discourses Concerning Government (Algernon Sidney), *265*

Discoveries Made in Exploring the Missouri River and Washita (William Clark), 193

Display of Heraldry (John Guillim), 161, 270

dissenters, in Charleston, 34

Dissertation on Asia (Sir William Jones), 188

Dissertation on Oriental Gardening (Sir William Chambers), 165

Dissertation on the Means of Preserving Health (David Ramsay), 214

Dissertation upon Oratory (William Best), 215

Divine Legation of Moses (William Warburton), 35

divinity. *See* "polemical divinity"

Dobson, Thomas, 212

Dodsley, James, 88, 93, 94, 95, 113, 118, 120, 141, 176, *249, 250, 251, 254, 258, 260;* dismissed as CLS bookseller 94, *249, 250–51;* elected CLS bookseller, 94, *248*

Dodsley, Robert, 6, 90, 93–94, 146, 199, *248, 252;* death of, *248;* elected CLS bookseller, 93, 94, *246;* firm of (with brother James), 87

dollar, 124. See *also* credit

Dollond (or Dolland), John, 176–77, *303*

Dollond (or Dolland), Peter, 176, 181, 182, *248*

Dolphin (ship), *257*

Dolphin, HMS, 149, *242*

Domat, Jean, 154

Donaldson, Alexander, 6

Dott, Daniel, 72, *73, 76*

Douglas, Bishop John, 192

Douglas, Sir Robert, *250*

Douxsaint, Paul, 37

Dove, Capt. Michael, *267*

Downs, 12

Dr. Musgrave's Reply (Samuel Musgrave), *261*

drawing instruments, 174

Drayton, John, 30, 214

Drayton, Judge William, 63

Drayton, William, 83

Droit de Gens (Emmerich de Vattel), 155, *258*

Drury, D., *270*

Dryden, John, *312*

du Boscq, Jacques, 202

du Monceau. *See* Duhamel du Monceau

du Pin, Louis Ellies, 162

Dublin, 141; publications from, 34

Duhamel du Monceau, Henri-Louis, 164, *269*

Dummer, Jeremiah, 82

Duncan, Mrs., 203

Dunlop, J. B., 78

DuPre, Jean, of St. James, Goose Creek, 70

Durham and Wilson, firm of, 87, 146,

242; elected CLS bookseller, 93, *240.*
See also Durham, Thomas; Durham and
Wilson, firm of

Durham, Thomas, 88. *See also* Wilson,
David; Durham and Wilson, firm of

Duties of the Female Sex (Thomas
Gisborne), 203

duties on paper, *312, 321*

Dyche, Thomas, his spelling books and
New Testaments, 33

Eagles, Thomas, 196

Earle, Thomas and William and Co., 128,
321

East Harding Street, London, 91

East-Bay, Charleston, 169

Eastern religion, philosophy, and literature,
192

Ecclesiastical History, Antient and Modern
(John Lawrence Mosheim), *258*

economic volatility in the 1790s, 132

Eden, Thomas and Co., 99

Eden: or, A Compleat Body of Gardening
(John Hill), *262*

Edgar, Walter, 153, 156, 184, 189, 202, 223

Edgeworth, Maria, 71, 203

Edinburgh, 13, 33, 100, 171, 204; merchants, 32, 128; press, 6; university
library, 196

Edinburgh Magazine, 103

Edmondson, Joseph, *252, 260, 263, 267,
269. See also* Harley, Robert

Education of Daughters (François de Salignac de la Mothe Fénelon), 203

Edwards, Bryan, 290

Edwards, George, 170, *270*

Edwards, John, and Co. 33

Egyptian hieroglyphs, as library emblems,
44

Egyptian mummies, 166

Eikon Basilke, 270

Eleanor (ship), *274*

electricity, apparatus 166, 180; essay about,
172; machines 173, 174

Elementa chemie (Hermann Boerhaave),
172

Elements of Agriculture (Henri-Louis
Duhamel du Monceau), 164, *269*

Elements of the Civil Law (John Taylor),
154, 247

Elements of the History of England (Claude
François Xavier, abbé Millot), *270*

*Elements of the Theory and Practice of Chym-
istry* (Pierre Joseph Macquer), 172

Elements of Universal Erudition (Jacob
Friedrich von Bielfeld), *264, 266*

Elevations (James Paine), 164

Eliot, John, 162–63

Elizabeth (ship), 148, *245*

Ellen (Maria Edgeworth), 71

Elliot, Charles, 204

Elliot Street, Charleston, 213

Elliott, Barnard, 71

Elliott, Juliet, 71

Elliott, William, 50

Ellis, John, 167, 169, 173, 219

Ellis, Thomas and William, 32

Emerance (privateer), 205, 206

Emmanuel College library, Cambridge, 196

empire, idea of, 13–14

Encyclopaedia Britannica, American edition,
212

Encyclopédie, 47, 155, *269*

encyclopaedia, *312;* purchase of, 82. *See
also Encyclopédie*

English Channel, 12, 13, 141, 149, 204

English Civil War, influence of, 157

English Grammar (Henry Osborne), 214

English Grammar (Robert Lowth), 93

enlightenment, iconography of, 44

Enquiry into the Beauties of Painting (Daniel Webb), *243*

Enquiry into the Truth and Certainty of the Mosaic Deluge (Patrick Cockburn), 162

Episcopalians, 21, 191, 192. *See also* Anglican Church

Erasmus, Desiderius, 190

Essay on Crimes and Punishments (Cesare Beccaria), 214, *264, 266*

Essay on Electricity (George Adams), 172–73

Essay on Fevers (Lionel Chalmers), 171

Essay on General History (François Marie Arouet de Voltaire), *270*

Essay on the History of Civil Society (Adam Ferguson), *259*

Essay on the Nature and Immutability of Truth (James Beattie), *265*

Essay on the Vital and Other Involuntary Motions of Animals (Robert Whytt), 223

Essay on Vision (George Adams, the younger), *274*

Essay Towards a System of Mineralogy (Axel Frederik Cronstedt), *265*

Essays and Observations (of Edinburgh), 167

Essays Moral and Literary (Vicesimus Knox), *277*

Essays on Human Understanding (John Locke), 156

Essays upon Several Subjects of Literature and Morality (Nicolas C. J. Trublet), *243*

estates confiscated, 69

ESTC (*English Short-Title Catalogue*), 154

Etonians, 190

evangelicalism, 18, 192; and religious debates, 226

Exact Abridgement of the Records of the Tower of London (Sir Robert Cotton), *264*

Exchange, London. *See* Royal Exchange

Experimental Essays on the Virtues of the Bath and Bristol Waters (Alexander Sutherland), *270*

Explanatory Notes and Practical Observations on the New Testament (William Burkitt), 153

Exposition of the XXXIX Articles (Gilbert Burnet), 191

Fables (John Gay), 199

Faerie Queene (Edmund Spenser), 199

Fagnan, Marie-Antoinette, 198

Fairlawn plantation, S.C., 74

Falkland Islands, *265*

Falmouth, England, 12, 13, 134

False Shame or the American Orphan in Germany (August Friedrich von Kotzebue), 201

Fame (ship), *293, 296*

Fariau, Francis, 62

Farmers Dictionary, 312

Farmer's Register, 207

Farqhar, Capt. —, *302*

Farquharson, John, 180

Fayssoux, Dr. Peter, 65, 72, 171

Federalist (ship), *292, 298, 305*

Federalist party, 75, 207, 209; leadership, 19

Fellowship Society, Charleston, 50; as state bond-holder, 60

Fénelon, François de Salignac de la Mothe, 203

Ferdinand Count Fathom (Tobias Smollett), 199

Ferguson, Adam, 163, *259*

fiction. *See* books

Fielding, Henry, 32, 198, 199

Filicetum Americanum (Charles Plumier), 169

fines. *See* Charleston Library Society members

Finsbury Square, London, 99, 129

Fleet Street, London, 18

Fleta seu commentarius juris Anglicani, 160, 161, *252*

Fletcher, James (junior), 88, 89, 92, 94–95, 106, 107, 108, 110, 113, 114, 118, 120, 121, 134, 135, 140, 156, 160, 177; *249, 250, 252, 254, 256, 258, 259, 260, 261;* dismissed 95, *253–54, 256, 262, 263;* attempted dismissal, *253–55;* elected, 94, *251;* and James senior, 94; and James Rivington, 31

Fleury, Moylin, 222

Flora Carolinaeensis (John Shecut), 215

Flora Caroliniana (Thomas Walter), 169

Flora Virginica (John Clayton), 223

flour, 20

Foedera (Thomas Rymer), *259*

Fool of Quality (Henry Brooke), 200

Fordyce, Dr. James, 202

Forest Scenery (William Gilpin), *289*

formularies for justices of the peace, 155

Forrest, John, 128, *265*

Fortescue, Sir John 156, 158, 186, *252*

fossils, 166

Foster, Sir Michael, 159, 188

Fothergill, John, 171

Fox, Charles James, 196

Fox, George, 163

Foxe, John, 191

Francis, Philip, *245*

Frankfurt fairs, 9

Franklin, Benjamin, 4, 26, 28, 47–48, 90, 151, 166; and daughter, 202; *Life of, 290*

Franklin Library of Charleston, 77

Franklin's Head, Broad Street, Charleston, 213

Franks, Moses, 117

Frauds of Romish Monks, 153

Frederician Code, *263*

Free and Candid Disquisitions Relating to the Church of England (John Jones), 191

Free School, Charleston, 34, 61

Freemasons, 38, 213; lodges, 52; Grand Lodge, Charleston, 50, 213

freight expenses, 115, 116; *311, 312, 320, 334, 336, 340*

French Dictionary (Lewis Chambaud), *264*

Freneau and Paine, firm of, 213

Friendly Brothers of Ireland, 50

Friendly Sons of St. Patrick, 22, 50

Friendship (ship), 147

fugitive pieces, *272*

Full and Clear Reply to Doct. Thomas Dale (James Kirkpatrick), 214

Fuseli, Henry, 195

Gadsden, Christopher, 18, 22, 61, 168; banished, 69; and classics, 105–6, 220; and the Gadsden debate, 156–57

Gadsden, Thomas, 35

Gairdner, Edwin and Co., *310, 311, 331*

Gallini, Giovani, 165, *252, 262*

Garden, Alexander, botanist, 18, 25, 27, 38, 82, 108, 147, 149, 166, 167, 169, 172, 173, 175, 183, 219, 221, 223; banishment and deprivations, 69; book collection of, 223; in London, *273;* and Otranto estate, 56; and specimens, 39

Garden, Alexander, senior, 90

Garden, Rev. Alexander, commissary, 25, 46, 213; library of, 77

Gardener's Dictionary (Philip Miller), 164, 167

gardenia, 167

Garnett, John, *338, 340*

Gates, Rev. Dr., 86, 109, 135, 145

Gay, John, 199

gazetteer, *252*

Gazetteer (Jedidiah Morse), 212

Gedde, John, 164

Geertz, Clifford, xviii

genealogy, 152

Genera animalium (Linnaeus), 170

General Assembly of South Carolina, 213

General Collection of Treatys (Samuel Whatley), 105, 163

General Evening Post, 218

General History of the British Empire in America (John Huddlestone Wynne), 193, *269*

General Synopsis of Birds (John Latham), *289*

General Treatise of Husbandry (Richard Bradley), 164

Genet, Edmond Charles Édouard, 226

Geneva, 221

Genlis, Stéphanie Felicité, comtesse de, 200

"genteel collection of publick and private buildings," *270*

Gentleman and Lady Instructed, 202

Gentleman's Magazine, 111, 168, *240, 247, 255, 289*

Gentlemens and Builders Companion (William Jones), *164*

Gentoo Code of Laws, 189

geographical and chronological tables, *266*

Geographical, Historical, and Commercial Grammar (William Guthrie), *265*

geological specimens, 166

geometry, 174

George III, 175, 179, 188, 196 ,226

George, Prince of Wales, 196

George Washington (brigantine), *319, 320*

Georgetown, Winyah, 70

German Friendly Society, Charleston, 50, 58; as state bond-holder, 60

Gerrish, Samuel, 87

Gervais, John Lewis, *249*

Gibbes, William, 62

Gibbes, Rev., 198

Gibbon, Edward, 90, 193, *274;* Gibbon's Roman History, 95

Gibson, Edmund, Bishop of London, 45–46, 162, *252*

Gifford, Samuel, 77, 201

Gilbert, Sir Geoffrey, 155

Gill, William, and Wright, Thomas, firm of, 87, 120, 130

Gillies, John, *277*

Gilpin, William, *289*

Gisborne, Thomas, 203

Glasgow, 11, 33; port of, 12, 13

Glass, Thomas, 171

Glasse, Hannah, 202

Glen, James, Governor of South Carolina, 25–26

globes, 70, 173, 174–75, 177, 179, *252, 256, 263*

Glossarium archaiologicum (Sir Henry Spelman), 160, *252*

Glover, Richard, read by Eliza Pinckney, 70

Goldingham, Nathaniel, 121, 134, 147, 215–16, *332, 333, 334, 335, 336, 337, 338, 339, 340, 341*

Goldsmith, Oliver, 200

Goodwin, Charles, 129, 181, *280, 282, 283, 284;* and Co., *284, 291, 292*

Goose Creek, S.C., 35, 55–56, 70

Gordon, Capt. James, *254, 256*

Gordon, John, 54, 72; his tavern as CLS meeting place, 61

governors of South Carolina, as CLS presidents, 75; council of, 158

Gracie, Archibald, *338*

Gradus ad Parnassum, 190

Grafton, Augustus Henry Fitzroy, duke of, 188

Grainger. See Granger

grammars, 153

Grammatical Institutes (John Ash), 216

Granger, James, *260*

Gravesande, Willem, 172

Gravesend, England, 141, 205

Gray, Charles Gray, M.P., 64

Gray, Thomas, 93

Graydon, William, 212

Great Tower Street, London, 127

Greek, 189–90

Greek thesaurus, *324, 328*

Green, Capt. —, 132, *316*

Greene, Jack P., 79

Greenock, Scotland, 204

Greenwood, William, 127, *274;* and Higginson and Co., 126, 127–28, *274*

Gregg, John, 169

Gregorie, Anne King, 83

Grey, Anchitel, *248*

Grey, Richard, *270*

Grice, Capt. —, *296*

Griffiths, Ralph, 90, 112

Griggs, Isaac, 183

Grimball, Thomas, 60, 65

Grimké, Judge John Faucheraud, 81, 160, *270;* as state bond-holder, 60; his book collection, 152

Grindlay, James, 38, 159

Grose, Francis, 161, *289*

Grotius, Hugo, 158, 159, 188

Guadalope, 205

Guardian, The, 35

Guicciardini, Francesco, 82

Guildhall, London, 194

Guillim, John, 161, *270*

Gulf Stream, 12

Gunn (or Gun), Capt. Henry, *261, 263*

Guthrie, William, 163, *265*

Guy, Thomas, 89

Guys, Pierre Augustin, *269*

Habermas, Jürgen, 14, 15–16, 52; and communities of conscience, 228

Hakewill, William, 156, 186

Hale, Capt. —, 145

Hale, Sir Matthew, 159

Hales, Stephen, 82, 172

Halesia, 172

Halfpenny, William and John, 165

Hall, David, 7, 9, 86, 87, 90, 92, 111, 117, 118, 120, 146, 151

Hall, Hercules, 59

Hall, Bishop Joseph, 153

Hall, William, 59

Hall, Capt. William, 66

Halley's comet, 174, 180

Hamilton Moore (ship), *336, 337, 338, 339*

Hamilton, Alexander, 196

Hamilton, James, *309*

Hanbury (ship), *284*

Hanbury and Gosling, firm of, 127

Hanbury and Lloyd, firm of, 127

Hancock, Thomas, 118, 120

Harlan, Robert, 135

Harleian MSS catalogue, 162

Harley, Robert, Lord Oxford, 118, *263*

Harriet Stuart (Charlotte Lennox), 199

Harrington, James, 156, 157, 188

Harris, Benjamin, 10

Harris, James, *265*

Harrison, R. and A., and Latham, firm of, 128, *328, 330, 331*

Harrison, Thomas and James, 90

Harvard College, 82, 166, 177; library, 63; library catalogues, 151

Haslet, John and Co., *324*

Hastings, Warren, 196

Havana, 208, *327*

Hawkesworth, John, 199, *265*

Hawkins, William, 159

Hayes, Kevin, 163, 203, 222

Hayward, Eliza, 32, 199

Hazard, Ebenezer, 71, 212

Headlam, Capt. Thomas, *246*

Heart of Oak (ship), *261*

Hebrew Orphan Society, Charleston, 50

Heister, Lorenz, 171

Helps to Composition or 600 Skeletons of Sermons (Claude and Charles Simeon), 193

Henderson, Capt. —, *329*

Henderson, Capt. C., *274*

Henderson, William, 61, 82

Henry Laurens (ship), 234; as "Laurence," *283*

Henry VI, 156

heraldry, 152

Herbemont, Dubroca of, 215

Herculaneum, paintings, *267*

Hermes or a Philosophical Inquiry Concerning Universal Grammar (James Harris), *265*

Herodotus, 105

Herriot, Capt. Benjamin, *242*

Heylyn (or Heylen), John, 105, *252*

Heywood, Henry, 202

Hibernian Society, Charleston, 50

Higgins, Capt. George, *254*

Higginson, William, 127–28, *274*

High Holborn, London, 98

Hill, —, author of *The Young Secretary,* 125

Hill, John, 173, *262*

Hill, Capt. Samuel, *271, 274*

Hilton, Capt., *293*

Hindley and Gregorie, firm of, *338, 341*

Hindley, Thomas Henry, *328*

Historical [Journal] of New South Wales (John Hunter), *290*

Historical and Chronological Deductions of the Origin of Commerce (Adam Anderson), 163, *247*

Historical Collections (Ebenezer Hazard), 212

Historical Society of Pennsylvania, Philadelphia, 4

histories. *See* books: subjects of

History and Antiquities of Harwich and Dovercourt (Samuel Dale),162, 167

History and Present State of Electricity (Joseph Priestley), 155, *265*

History of Ancient Greece (John Gillies), *277*

History of Civil Society (Adam Ferguson), 163

History of Cornelia (Sarah Scott), 198

History of Cornelia, 154

History of England (abbé Millot), 161

History of England (Oliver Goldsmith), 200

History of England (Paul de Rapin), 31

History of his Own Times (Gilbert Burnet), 191

History of Insects (John Swammerdam), *265*

History of Ireland (Thomas Leland), 161, *270*

History of King Henry the Second (George Lyttleton), 161, *258, 260*

History of Massachusetts-Bay (Thomas Hutchinson), 193, *258*

History of Military Transactions in Hindostan (Robert Orme), 188

History of New-York (William Smith), 212

History of South Carolina (David Ramsay), 167–68, 212

History of South Carolina (William Drayton), 83

History of the Church of Christ (Joseph and Isaac Milner), 192

History of the First Discovery and Settlement of Virginia (William Stith), 212

History of the Life of King Henry the Second by Lyttelton, *266*

History of the Quakers (William Sewel), 163

History of the Rebellion and Civil-War in Ireland (Ferdinando Warner), *252, 262*

History of the Reign of the Emperor Charles V (William Robertson), 193, 200, 221, *259*

History of the Rise, Progress, and Accomplishment of the Abolition of the African Slave-Trade (Thomas Clarkson), 215

History of the Rise, Progress, and Termination of the American Revolution (Mercy Otis Warren), 212

History of the Royal Society (Thomas Birch), 173

History of the Wars in Italy (Francesco Guicciardini), 82

History of the West Indies (Bryan Edwards), *290*

Hoadly, Bishop Benjamin, 192

Hobart, John Henry, 192

Hobbes, Thomas, 153

Hogarth Moralized, 266

Hogarth, William, prints of, 77

Holcroft, Thomas, 194, 209, 213, *322, 323, 324*

Holden, Samuel, 82

Hollis, Thomas, 82

Holwell, John Zephaniah, *270*

Homer, 189

honey, 164

Hooke, Nathaniel, 161, *258, 269*

Hooke, Robert, 182

Hooker, Richard, 49, 152

Hope, Lord, 82

Hopkins, Grey (or Gray), and Glover, firm of, 207, *327*

Hopkins, Mr., 60

Hopkins, Samuel, 59

Hopkinson, Thomas, 126

Hopton, John, 210, 215–16, *330, 332, 333, 335, 337, 338;* estates confiscated, 69

Hopton, William, plea rejected, 56

Horace, v, 105, 189, 190, 218, 222

Horne, Thomas Hartwell, 192

Horry, Peter, 31, 135

Horse-Hoing Husbandry (Jethro Tull), 164

Hort, William, 76

House of Commons, *Journals,* 158, 159, *261, 263*

House of Commons, Westminster: debating practice, 57

Howes, Edward, 10

Huddlestone Wynne, John, 193

Hueston, Samuel, 85

Hugh Trevor (Thomas Holcroft), 213

Huguenots, 21

Hume, David, 192

Hume, John, 57

Hunter (brigantine), 206

Hunter (ship), *274*

Hunter, John, *290*

Hunter, William, 87, 119

hurricanes, 21

Hutchins, [Th.?], 193, *270*

Hutchinson, Thomas, 193

Hutchinsonian Devotions (William Andrews), 192

Huygens, Christian, 178

hygrometer, 177, *252*

Hymns (Isaac Watts), 153

Icon Basilicon, 270

Icones pictæ plantarum rariorum (James Edward Smith), 194, *301*

Iconologia (Caesar Ripa), 49

Illinois (— Hutchins), 270

Illustrations of Natural History (D. Drury), 270

imagined community, 227

immigration, 19

import of books. *See* book trade

imprints, post-dating of, 105

improvement, 221

Independence; or Which Do You Like Best, the Peer or the Farmer (William Ioor), 201

Independent Meeting House of Charleston, 52

India Tracts (John Zephaniah Holwell), 270

India, 188, 193; wars in, 22

Indian and Asian travels, 193

Indian Antiquities, 188

Indian law and commercial manuals, 189

Indian pink, 166, 167

indigo, 19, 20, 70, 163, 168, 214

Inglis, Capt. —, *309*

Inigo Jones, Designs of, 269

Inns of Court, London, 127, 160, 159; colonial students at, 79

Innys, William, 10

Inquiry into the Principles of Political Œconomy (Sir James Steuart), *259*

Institute of Hindoo Laws (William Jones), 189

Institutes (Sir Edward Coke), 159

Institutes of Botany (Colin Milne), *270. See also* Linneaus

Institutes of Entomology (Linneaus), 170

Institutes of the Laws of England (Thomas Wood), 159

instruments. *See* scientific instruments

insurance, 127, 131, 215, *237, 243, 245, 267, 269, 292, 294, 297, 301, 303, 310, 311, 320, 321, 335, 337, 340;* and duty charges, 208; rates 131–32; transatlantic, 131; underwriters, 208,

309, 323, 324, 325, 326, 327, 328, 331, 332

interest charges, 11, 115, 117, *337, 340*

Interpretation of the New Testament (John Heylyn), 105, *252*

Introduction to Botany (James Lee), 170, *266*

Introduction to the Theory and Practice of Physic (David MacBride), *270*

Introduction to the Theory of the Human Mind (James Ussher), *269*

Introduction to the True Astronomy (John Keill), 182

inventories. *See* library inventories

invoicing. *See* book transit

Ioor, William, 201

Ireland, 11

Ireland, Samuel, 289

Irish Society, Charleston, 50

Isabella (ship), *316, 341*

Isaeus, 223

Italian Dictionary (Giuseppe Marco Antonio Baretti), *264*

Itinerant Observations in America in the *London Magazine,* 46

Itinerarium curiosum (William Stukeley), 162

Ive, John, 10

Ives, Edward, *270*

Izard family estate, 56

Izard, Elizabeth Stead, 71

Izard, Henry, 160; library of, 222

Izard, Ralph, 35, 71, 76, 168, 203, *301;* library of 222; state bond-holder, 60

Jacksonburgh, S.C., *272*

Jamaica, 13, 168, 206, 208; sale of CLS books at, 206, 207, *322, 323, 324, 325, 327*

Jay, Capt. Thomas, *274*

Jefferson, Thomas, 22, 161, 207

Jefferys, Thomas, 212

Jeremiah and the Lamentations, 193

Jews, 21, 97

Joannis Lelandi antiquarii de rebus Britanni-cis collectanae, 266

Johnson, Joseph, 6

Johnson, Dr. Samuel, 90, 93; Johnson's *Dictionary,* 90

Johnson, Judge William, 172, 174, 200, 206, *326*

Johnston, Robert, 69

Johnstone, Charles, 199

Jones and Fisher, merchants, *241*

Jones, Inigo, 161

Jones, John, 191

Jones, Sir William, 188, 189

Jones, William, architectural writer, 164

Jordan, Capt. George, *254, 256, 263*

Joseph Andrews (Henry Fielding), 198

Josephus, 32

Journal of the Voyages of a Corps of Discovery (William Clark), 193

Journals (George Fox), 163

Journals [of the United States Congress], 212

Journals of the House of Commons, 108–9, 158, *270*

Journals of the House of Lords, 155

Julia; ou, les souterrains de Mazzini, 222

Julius Pringle (ship), 137, *287, 289, 295, 308*

Justice of the Peace, and Parish Officer (Richard Burn), 155, *265*

Justin, 105, 189

Kalm, Peter, 193, *270*

Kanor (Marie-Antoinette Fagnan), 198

Kaplanoff, Mark, 24

Keill, John, 182

Keith, Rev. Alexander, rector of Prince George Winyaw, 44

Kellogg, Arnold, 196

Kellogg, Ebenezer, 63, 78, 186, 198

Kennedy, Capt. —, 103, *305, 308*

Kennedy, James, 200

Kennedy, Walter, 201

Kennicott, Benjamin, *270*

Kerr, Capt., 103, *281, 285, 287*

Kerr's Animal Kingdom, 292, 293

Kilburne, Richard, 156

Kilpatrick, trans., *252*

King, Isaac, 127

King, Richard, bookseller of Charleston, 33, 84

King's Bench, London, 90, 156, 159

King's College library, Cambridge, 196

King's College, New York, library of, 43

King's Printing Office, London, 91

Kingston, Jamaica, 206

Kirk and Lukens, firm of, 128, *298, 300, 302, 303, 304, 307*

Kirkpatrick, James, 214

Kit-Cat Club, London, 51

Knapton, John and Paul, 89

Knight, Charles, 100, 211

knowledge, practical, 47

Knox, Henry, 7, 9, 104, 109, 110, 116, 117, 119–20, 131; bill settlement dispute, 130; debt to Longman, 120; delivery times of, 141; turn-round voyages of, 134

Knox, Capt. John, *266*

Knox, Vicesimus, *277*

Kotzebue, August Friedrich von, 201

Kynaston, Samuel, 31

Lackington, Allen, and Co., 5, 88, 99–101, 115, 129, 134, 145, 146, 152, 173, 177, 188, 199, 201, 205, 206, 207,

Lackington, Allen, and Co. (*continued*) 209, 215, 216, 222, 224; appointed, *310;* and arbitration of retrieved shipment, *325–26;* and binding, 111; and books' passage, 136, 140, 141; catalogue of new publications, *314;* catalogues, 100, *323;* defense of conduct, *333–34, 335;* dismissal of, *330, 332–33, 334, 337;* elected CLS bookseller, 99; end of service to CLS, 210–11, 215–16; invoices, 208; letters from and to CLS, *310–32 333–34, 335–36;* and periodicals, 112, *335;* specialisms of, 112–13; supplies, 211

Lackington, George, 100, 120. *See also* Lackington, Allen, and Co.

Lackington, James, 93, 99, 100, 173. *See also* Lackington, Allen, and Co.

Ladies Diary, 202

Ladies Library (George Berkeley), 202

Lady's Magazine, 203

Lambert, John, 78, 194, 195

Lane, William, 90

Langford, Nicholas, 33, 82, 84, 85, 112, 159

Langley, Betty, 164

Larger Treatise Concerning Tithes (Sir Henry Spelman), 159

Laslie (or Lasley), Capt. John, *256, 266*

Latham, John, *289*

latin, 189–90; dictionary, *241;* verse composition, 190

Lauderdale, earl of, 189

Laura: An American Novel, 201

Laurens, Henry, 35, 39, 47, 67, 82, 87, 148, 160, 163, 169, 221; as a mason, 50

Laurens, John, 20, 82, 160, 164

law books, 4, 6, 30, 49, 77, 87, 105, 155–60, 163, 190; American, 212

law codes, Russian, *266*

Law of Bills of Exchange (Timothy Cunningham), *265*

Law of Evidence (Sir Geoffrey Gilbert), 155

Law of Nature and Nations (Samuel Pufendorf), 159

Law-Dictionary (Timothy Cunningham), *265*

Laws of Bills of Exchange (Timothy Cunningham), 163

"Laws of Several Provinces of America," 252, *262*

Laws of the Province of South-Carolina, 30

Laws of Trade, *266*

Lawson, John, 167, 169, *262*

Lawyer: An American Novel, 201

leather binding, 110

Lectures on Natural and Experimental Philosophy (George Adams), *301*

Lee (or Lees), William, 128

Lee, James, 169, 170, *266*

Lee[s], William, *324*

Leefe, Benjamin, *309*

legal literature. *See* law books

Legare, Benjamin, banished, 69. *See also* Legare, Theus and Prioleau

Legare, Theus, and Prioleau, merchants, *291, 292*

Legrande's Tours through the Auvergne, 305

Leibniz, Gottfried Wilhelm, 46

Leiden, 170, 172, 178

Leigh, Egerton, as a mason, 50

Leigh, Grandmaster Peter, 50

Leith, 6, 32

Leland, John, 192, *266*

Leland, Thomas, 161, *270*

Lemoine, Henry, 225

Lennox, Charlotte, 199

Leo X, Pope, 222, *319, 322*

Leslie, Charles, 191

Letter from the Cocoa Tree (Philip Francis), *245*

Letters Written during a Tour (John Drayton), 214

letters concerning overseas trade in books, 10. *See also* Charleston Library Society

Letters from a Farmer in Pennsylvania (John Dickinson), *258, 262*

Letters of Junius, 188, *324*

letters of marque, 148, 205. *See also* privateers

Leverett and Cox, Boston, 224

Lewis, Matthew, 83, 215

Liberty (ship), *266*

Liberty in Louisiana (James Workman), 201

libraries, American, 217; bequests of, 49; and book collections of colonial South Carolina, 153; and borrowing records, 200; building, 47; in Charleston, 35; colonial domestic, 158–59; commercial circulating libraries, 8, 35; and continuing London trade, 217; and demand for books, 8; design of, 48; in eighteenth-century England, 48; European models of, 48, 64; for sale in Charleston, 77; mission statements, 42–43; moral purpose of, 9; and new orders for fiction, 199–200; parochial, cataloguing of, 34; private, 34–35; private colonial, 161; proprietary, 8; scientific and natural history collections, 64–65; sociability of, 15, 47; in South Carolina, 34–35, 48–49, 223; subscription libraries in England, 48. *See also* library catalogues; library inventories; library societies

library catalogues, design of 151; and subject divisions, 186

library companies. *See* library societies

Library Company of Baltimore. *See* Baltimore Library Company

Library Company of Bridgetown at Mount Holly, N.J., 51

Library Company of Burlington, N.J., catalogue, 151

Library Company of Philadelphia, 3, 4, 8, 9, 10, 26, 47, 99, 126, 159, 166, 169, 173, 217; and book agents, 85, 89; and book requests from members, 150; catalogues, 151; curiosities, 64–65; female shareholding and usage, 69–70; foundation articles, 41–42; housed, 64; membership fee, 72; membership records, 38; number of volumes, 81; scientific instruments, 64; seal of, 44

library inventories in South Carolina, 34–35, 48–49, 153, 173, 184, 202; and classics, 189

library societies, 3, 5, 26; and booksellers' general instructions, 107; in England, 48; foundation of, 218; mission of, 45. *See also* Baltimore Library Company; Bristol Library Society; Charleston Library Society; Darby, Philadelphia, Library Company of; Franklin Library; Library Company of Philadelphia; New York Society Library; Philogrammatican Library; Redwood Library Company; Salem Social Library; Savannah Library Society; social library, idea of; Union Library Company

Lieberkühn, Johann Nathanael, 175

Life of Nadir Shah (Sir William Jones), 188

Lightening (ship), *274*

lighthouses, 13

Lining, Dr. John, 25, 48–49, 166, 167, 170, 172, 183, 223; as a mason, 50

Linnaeus, 46, 149, 167, 169, 170, 219, 223, *270, 292, 293, 312*

Linné, Carl von. *See* Linnaeus

Linnean Society of London, 169

Lintot, Bernard, 89

Literary and Philosophical Society of South-Carolina, 77, 168

literary categories, 153

Literary Magazine and British Review, 203

literary societies, 16

literary tastes in South, 162

literature, social ambit of, 46–47; and sociability, 227

Little New Street, London, 90

liturgy, 191

Lively (American brigantine), *293, 295, 296*

Liverpool Library, 8

Liverpool, 134, *302, 338, 339;* merchants and brokers of, 128, *321, 324, 328, 338;* port of, 12; ships from, 134; and the slave trade, 128

Lives, Acts and Matyrdoms, of the Holy Apostles of our Saviour (William Cave), *266*

Lives of the Poets (Samuel Johnson), 96

Livingston, Capt. —, 140

Livingston, Freer, Legare, and Co., 59

Livy, 105, 189

lizards, 149

Lloyd, Edward, of Wye, Maryland, 105, 197; and family, 99; and library, 158

Lloyd's List, 131; *237*

Lloyd's Register, 131

Locke, John, 154, 156, 157, 186; *Works of,* 156; read by Eliza Pinckney, 70

Logan, Colonel George, 38

Logan, James, 8, 10, 11, 89, 147, 161

Logan, William, 37

Loganian Library, Philadelphia, catalogue, 151

London, 4, 93. *See also* booksellers; book-trade; merchants

London Chronicle, 93, 218

London Magazine, 11, 111, 112, *240, 247, 255, 260*

London Missionary Society, 193

Long, Roger, 182

Longinus, 154

Longman, Thomas, and Co., 9, 87, 104, 109, 116, 119–20, 130, 131, 146; and delivery times, 141

Love, Solomon, *270*

Lovell, Capt. —, *311, 312*

Lowndes, Thomas (of Charleston), 200

Lowth, Robert, 93, *252*

loyalism, 17, 19, 69, 107, 120, 146; and compensation, 226; and cultural ties, 157; and exile, 98

Lucian, 190

Lucretia (ship), 132

Lucretius, 190

Ludlam, Rev. Richard, 35

luxury goods, 8

Lyttelton, George, 161, *266*

Lyttelton, William Henry, 75, 82

MacBride, David, *270*

Macchiavelli, Niccolo, Works of, 277

Mackenzie, John, 35, 81, 156; collection of, 81; and bequest to CLS, 77, *270*

Mackmurdo, Hickes & Co., merchants, *318, 331*

Mackrell, Capt. Thomas, *261, 263*

Maclean, Charles, 189

Macquer, Pierre Joseph, 172

Madeira, 11

magazines, 13, 107, 110, *237, 238, 239, 240, 241, 243, 247, 250, 253, 254, 255, 256, 261, 262, 264, 269, 272, 273, 274, 276, 277, 279, 307;* delay in receipt of, 146. *See also* periodicals; reviews

magic lanthorn, *245*

magistrates, 155

mail-services, 12

Maitland, Capt. Richard, *263*

Major Pinckney (ship), *291, 292, 296*

Malebranche, Nicolas, 70

Mallard, Capt. John, *245*

Malloy, Charles, 156

Malone, Edmund, 195, 196

Manigault family, 23, 27, 35

Manigault, Ann, 70, 174

Manigault, Gabriel, 61, 70, 75, 98, 102, 113, 126, 127, 180, 200, 221, 228, *246;* and Kinloch Court building, 180; as state bond-holder, 60; as ubiquarian, 50

Manigault, Joseph, 98

Manigault, Peter, 87, 102, 160, 180; value of library, 35; telescope of, 180

Mannheim library, 64

Manning, William, 97, 98

Mansell St., Goodman's Fields, London, 126

Mansfield, England, 93

Mansion House, London, 194

map of city of London, *270*

maps, *330*

Margaretta: An American Novel, 201

Maria (ship), *309, 316*

Marine Dictionary (Charnock), *312, 319*

marine insurance, 131

"Maritime Discoveries" by Clarke, 193, *324*

Markell. *See* Mackrell

Marlowe, Capt. Benjamin, *242*

Marshal, Capt. John, *242*

Marshall, John, 212

Marston, Capt. —, *285*

Marston, Edward, 34

Martens, Georg Friedrich de, 189

Martin, Benjamin, 177, 178, 182; *252*

Martin, Josiah, 10

"Martin's" Hogarth Moralized [published by Trusler], *266*

Martyn, Edward, *242*

Mary (ship), *254, 297, 299*

Maryland, bills of credit, 124

Mason, Capt. —, 134

Mason, George, 218

Mason, William, 58, 94, 106, 135, *248, 249, 250, 251, 252, 255;* admitted member, 57

masons. *See* freemasons

Massachusetts, 26; bills of credit, 124; paper mills, 6

Mathematical Elements of Natural Philosophy (Willem Gravesande), 172

mathematical instruments, 174, 177, *252, 256, 293, 295. See also* scientific instruments

mathematics, 174. *See also* books, subjects of

Mather, Cotton, 10

Mather, Increase, 10

Maurice, Thomas, 188

Mazyck, Isaac, 50

Mazyck, William, 73

McCall, Hext, 160

McCall, John Jr., 39, 41, 96, 104, 233, *273, 274, 275, 276, 277;* as CLS librarian and secretary, 39; becomes secretary, *271, 272*

McCauley, Alexander, 37, 38

McCauley, Mrs., 73

McKie, Patrick, 38

McLeod, Donnom and Mazyck, and Co., 59

McNeil, Capt. Neil, 205, *284, 297, 318, 319, 320, 321, 341;* and loss of shipment, 205–7, *322, 327*

Meadows, William, 10

Medical Dissertation (William Clark), 171

Medical Observations and Inquiries (John Fothergill), 171

Medical Observations and Inquiries: By a Society of Physicians in London, 269

Medical Society of Charleston, 211

Medical Society of South Carolina, 57, 63, 171

medicine, 170–71. *See also* books, subjects of

Mein, John, 120, 135

Memoirs (Maximilien de Béthune, duc de Sully), 200

Memoirs (James Lackington), 100, 173

Memoirs of Great Britain and Ireland (Sir John Dalrymple), *269*

Memoirs of Major Robert Rogers, 31

Memoirs of Richelieu, 200

Memoirs of the Court of Augustus (Thomas Blackwell), *247*

Memoria Technica (Richard Grey), *270*

merchants, as booksellers to CLS, 98–99; copy books of, 233; in the Carolinas, 127; kinship bonds, 98, 103, 145; libraries of, 163; merchant houses in London, 160

Mermaid (ship), *261*

Merrick, Oxford, 100

Methodical Analysis of Mineral Waters (John Rutty [Ruthy]), *270*

Mexico, 12

Meyer, Philip, 59, *274*

Michael, Andrew, Chevalier Ramsay, *248*

Michaelangelo, 194

Michie, James, 35, 49, 223; library of, 77

Michie, William, *241*

Micrographia (Robert Hooke), 182

Micrographia Illustrata (George Adams), 175–76

micrometer, 177, *245, 248, 252, 262, 279, 284. See also* scientific instruments

Microscope Made Easy (Henry Baker), 175

microscopes, 173, 174, 175, 176, 179, *245, 248, 291;* repair of, 181, *284. See also* scientific instruments

Middle Row, Holborn, London, 98

Middle Temple, 160. *See also* Inns of Court

Middleton, Conyers, 259

Middleton, Emma Philadelphia, 203

Middleton, Henry, 168

Middleton, Lorton and Hope and Co., 59

Middleton, Thomas, 37; as assembly member, 51; as state bond-holder, 60

Middleton, William, library of, 222

Midwifery (William Smellie), 222

Mildred, Daniel, 82

Mill Hill, London, 169

Millar, Andrew, 87

Miller, Capt. Asa, *339, 340*

Miller, John, 85

Miller, Philip, 164, 167

Miller, Robert, of Williamsburg, 9, 103, 104, 109, 116, 131, 132, 136, 144, 145; delivery times, 141

Miller, William, 103

Milligen, George, 82

Milligen-Johnston, George, 20; visit to CLS, 56–57

Millot, Claude François Xavier, abbé, 161, *270*

Mills, Thomas, 190

Milne, Colin, *270. See also* Linnaeus

Milner, Joseph and Isaac, 192

Milton, John, 157, 199; works of, *312*

Mineralogy (Axel Cronstedt), 170

Minerva (goddess), 43, 49; as classical image, 44

Minerva (ship), *263, 298*

mirror, concave, 176, 264, *266;* and stand, 275

Mirrour (Henry Dell), 105, *252*

Mirrour of Justices, 105, 156, 161, *262*

Miscellaneous Tracts (Conyers Middleton), *259*

missionary activity, 25, 46; and advice, 193

Mitchell, Capt. —, *243*

Mitchell, John, 171

Mnemonics Delineated (Solomon Love), *270*

Modern Chivalry, 212

Modern History of Hindostan (Thomas Maurice), 188

Modus tenendi parliamentum (William Hakewill), 156

molatto gentleman, 47

Moll Flanders (Daniel Defoe), 199

Monday Evening Club, Salem, 51

money. *See* credit

Monk, The (Matthew Lewis), 83, 215

Montagu, Lord Charles Greville, 75, *253*

Montesquieu, de Secondat, Charles, Baron de, 154, 156, *258, 262, 263*

Montezuma (ship), 141, *329, 333, 335*

Monthly Chronicle, 244

Monthly Magazine and American Review, 212

Monthly Review, 111, 112, *241, 243, 247, 255. See also* periodicals

Monthly Review Index, 243

monthly reviews. *See* periodicals

Moore, John, 83

Moral and Theological Tracts (John Balguy), 162

Morals (Seneca), 189

Mordecai (author of *Apology*), 192

Morgan, Charles, 95

Morning Chronicle, 104, 129

Morning Exercise Against Popery (Nicholas Vincent), 153

morocco binding, 110

Morritt, Rev. Thomas, 25, 34

Morse, Jedidiah, 212

Mosheim, John Lawrence, *258*

Moth, Capt. Hugh, *248*

Motte, Jacob, 72–73; as ubiquarian, 50; his back store, 32

Motte, Mrs., 69

Moultrie, John, 25, 167, 170

Moultrie, John, Jr., 171

Mount Sion Society, Charleston, 50

Muir, Capt. William, *241*

Muir, William, shipowner, 207

mules, 164

Mullet, Thomas, *302;* and Co., *303*

Murdock, William, 99

Murphy's *Tacitus,* 200

Murray, John I, 6, 9, 86, 103, 104, 109, 114, 116, 119, 120, 132, 135, 136, 145; business letters of, 86; and insurance, 131

Musæ Etonenses, 190

Museum of the Literary and Philosophical Society of South-Carolina, 77

Museum Rusticum et Commerciale, 248

museum-cabinets, 166

Musgrave, Samuel, *261*

Mylne. *See* Milne

Mynde, James, engraver of London, 44

Nadelhaft, Jerome J., 157

Nairne (or Narne), Edward, *278*

Nairne and Blunt, firm of, 180

Nancy (ship), *254, 256, 263*

Napoleonic wars, 204

Narrative of a Expedition (John Stedman), 215

Natural History of Birds (George Edwards), 170, *270*

Natural History of Birds (William Smellie), *292, 293*

Natural History of Carolina (Mark Catesby), 169, *262*

Natural History of Jamaica (Patrick Browne), 169

Natural History of the Horse (Georges Louis Leclerc, comte de Buffon), *270*

natural history, political implications of, 170

natural philosophical instruments. *See* scientific instruments

Naval Architecture, 319

naval convoys, 148–49

naval stores, 19

navigational aids, 13; printed aids, 152

negroes, importation of, 39; Christian conversion of, 46; representation of, 46. *See also* slaves

Nelson, William, 155, 156

Nesbitt, Arnold, Albert, and Alexander, 127

Netherlands, 76, 300

Neufville, John, 37, *283*

Neutrality (ship), *339, 340, 341*

New Abridgement and Critical Review of the State Trials (Thomas Salmon), *258*

New and Compendious System of Optics (Benjamin Martin), 177

New Broad St, London, 127

New Court, Swithins Lane, London, 146

New England, 111; and "codfish aristocracy," 8; logocentrism of, 17; merchants; 11; population of, 28; shipping routes, 13

New Hampshire Assembly, 11

New Jersey College. *See* Princeton

New System of Agriculture (John Laurence), 164

New Testament (Thomas Belsham), 192

New York, 6, 21, 93, 134, 141, 166, 196, 207, *242, 315, 338, 339;* booksellers in, 210; booktrade, 224; Federal Hall, 64; King's College, 43; harbour, 12; literary clubs, 51. See *also* New York Society Library

New York Packet (ship), *319*

New York Society Library, 5, 9, 10, 117, 256, 199; agents in London, 85; book delivery times, 144; bookplates, 43; bookplates and their scenes, 49, 75; catalogue, 151, 159; foundation of, 42; freight for, 116; housed in City-Hall, 64; and insurance, 131–32; membership fees, 72; number of volumes, 81; opening hours, 54

Newcastle, England, 100

Newcome, William, 193

Newfoundland, 11

Newmarket races, 92

news, from London and Europe, 225; of shipments, 136

newspapers, *237,* (or "papers," *238*), *319, 322;* advertisements, 6, 104; arrival of in Charleston, 194; newspapers and periodicals in London, 9

Newton, Isaac, 32

Newton, W., architect, *269*

Nichols, John, 91, 96, 129

Nickleson, John, 126

Nickleson [or Nickelson or Nicholson], Sarah, 127; and Co., 126, *246;* Nickleson-Shubrick partnership, 127

Nicoll (or Nicholl or Nicol), William, 87, 88, 89, 95–96, 104, 105, 106, 107–8, 109, 113, 114, 116, 120, 121, 125, 126, 134, 140, 141, 146, 177, 180, 180, 233, *257, 259, 260, 264, 265, 267, 268, 271, 272, 273, 274, 278, 279;* dismissed by CLS, 96, *275, 276, 277;* elected CLS bookseller, 95, *256, 257;* and insurance, 132; passage of books, 144

Nilous, Horapollo, 44

No Cross, No Crown (William Penn), 163

Noble Peasant (Thomas Holcroft), *274*

Noel, Nathaniel, 118

nonconformists, 21

Nonimportation, Embargo, and Nonintercourse Acts, 22, 209, 211; resolutions,
207

Non-Military Journal, 322

North America, and colonial book demand
increase in, 7, 225–26; colonial consumption levels, 8; colonial extension of
British and London society, 28; colonial
imports (general), 8; colonial political
authority, 14; libraries buying American
publications, 85

North Carolina, compared to South
Carolina, 227

North, Frederick, Lord, 188

Norwich, England, 100

notorial charges, 130, *300*

Nova plantarum americanarum genera
(Charles Plumier), 170

novels, 7, 152, 154, 188, 203; American
201, 212; imported, 32; relative low
price, 7; reprints of, 201

Nutt, John, 127

*Observations on the Impolicy of Recommenc-
ing the Importation of Slaves* (David
Ramsay), 214

Observations on the Nature of Civil Liberty
(Richard Price), 214

Oceana (James Harrington), 156

Ode to Shakespeare, 261

Ode to the Hero of Finsbury Square (Peter
Pindar), 100

*Office and Authority of the Justice of the
Peace* (William Nelson), 155, 156

Office of Ordnance, 175

Offices (Cicero), 189

Ogier & McKinney, 318

Ogilvy, David, 98; and sons, 98

Ogilvy (or Ogilvie) and Speare, firm of, 98,
99, *301, 304*

Old Broad St., London, 215

Old Jewry, London, 146

Oliphant (or Olyphant), Dr. David, 59,
171; banished, 69

Olive Branch (ship), *279, 281*

On Crimes And Punishments (Beccaria), 155

On the Management of Bees (John Gedde),
164

optical instruments, *248. See also* scientific
instruments

opticks, 174

Orations (Cicero), 189

Orders-in-Council, 209

Oriental Customs (George Burder), 193

Orme, Robert, 188

orreries (or planetariums), 177–79, 220

Osborne, Henry, 214

Osborne, Thomas, 7, 10, 87

Oswald, Richard, 126, *249*

Otranto estate, Goose Creek, S.C., 56

outports. *See* ports

Ovid, 105, 189

Oxford, 94, 100, *313;* university, 160, 183

Pacific (ship), 204, 208, *305, 308*

packages in ship cabins, 13, 146, *241, 247,
258*

packet boat service, 13

Pain, William, 164

Paine, James, 164

Paine, Thomas, 192, 212, 214

Palæographia (William Stukeley), 161

Paley, William, 191, *314*

Pall Mall, London, 93, 94, 195, *248, 249*

Pallas, P. S., *312*

Palmer, bookseller of Oxford, 100

Pamela (Samuel Richardson), read by Eliza Pinckney, 70

pamphlets, 13, *238, 239, 240, 243, 247, 251, 253, 254, 256, 257, 258, 260, 261, 264, 265, 269, 272, 274*

paper, duties on, *312, 321;* manufacture of, 6

Paper Mill, St. Paul's Churchyard, 95

Paradise Lost (John Milton), 199

Paradise Regained (John Milton), 199

Paris, 76, 126

Parks, William, 28, 87

Parnham, John, 76

Parrott, Capt. Enoch, *319, 320*

passages, by ship. *See* book transit

Paternoster Row, London, 18, 104, 110; and binders, 110

Paul's Wharf, 127

Pawley, Percival and George, 59

Peace of Amiens, 99

Peace of Paris, 107; commissioner for, 126

Peace, Joseph, *307, 308, 309;* no longer treasurer, *311*

Pearch, George, 11

Peckham, England, 169

Peerage of Scotland (Sir Robert Douglas), *250*

Peggy (ship), *272*

Penman, James and Edward, 204

Penn, John, 166

Penn, William, 163

Pennant, Thomas, 170, *269, 289*

Pennsylvania, 7, 147; assembly, 179; bills of credit, 124

Pennsylvania Coffee House, 145

Pensacola, 13

Peregrine Pickle (Tobias Smollett), 32

periodicals, 7, 11, 110, 111, *258;* and criticism, 112; and journals, 106; and monthly reviews, 221; ordered by American libraries, 49; reviews, 104, 193–94, *237, 239, 240, 241, 243, 247, 250, 253, 255, 262, 264, 269, 276, 277, 307;* reviews and new publications, 9

Perkins, Samuel, 50

Peronneau, Henry and Alexander, 31

Peronneau, Samuel, 31

Perrie, Mary, 70

Perry, Capt. John, *259*

Persian Letters (Charles, Baron de Montesquieu), 154, *258, 262*

Petronius, 189, 190

Petty, Sir William, 46

Phalaridis Epistolae (Charles Boyle), 190

Pharmacologia (Samuel Dale), 167

Phelp, Robert, 69

Phepoe, Thomas, 69

Philadelphia, 8, 9, 21, 84, 86, 87, 89, 90, 92, 111, 117, 134, 141, 145, 151, 166, 171, 177, 191, *338, 339;* booksellers in, 210, *287, 309, 334, 337, 338;* book-trade, 224; harbor, 12, 147; libraries, 3; literary clubs, 51; paper mills; 6; printing in, 30; publishing, 212. *See also* Library Company of Philadelphia; Loganian Library

Philip, Robert, 72

Phillips, Eleazer Jr., 28

Phillips, Eleazer, 28, 31, 32–33

Philogrammatican Library, Lebanon, Connecticut, 3

Philo-historic Society, Pennsylvania, 218

Philosophia Britannica (Benjamin Martin), 177

Philosophical Experiments (Stephen Hales), 172

Philosophical Principles of Natural and Revealed Religion (Andrew Michael, Chevalier Ramsay), *248*

Philosophical Transactions of the Royal Society, 173, 247, *269, 313, 314*

Philpott Lane, London, 126

physicians, as CLS members, 51

Physiological Essay on the Yellow Fever (G. Carter), 215

Picart, Bernard, 162, *269*

Piccadilly, London, 97, 100

Pillans, Dr. William, 223

Pinckney family, 23, 128

Pinckney, Charles Cotesworth (1746–1825), 62, 70, 71, 75–76, 84, 97, 128, 130, 160, 168, 191, 196, 197, 199, 200, 207, 218, *281, 282, 283, 284, 285, 286, 287, 288, 290, 291, 292, 293, 294, 305;* banished, 69; continuing letters to and from BSB, *296–304;* letter to Lackington, Allen, *310–11;* membership certificate, 44

Pinckney, Col. Charles (1731–82), 75, 157; as a mason, 50

Pinckney, Charles, Hon. (d. 1758), 21, 70, 75; as ubiquarian, 50

Pinckney, Charles, Jr. (1757–1824), 69, 75, *281;* banished, 69; library of, 222–23

Pinckney, Eliza Lucas, 46, 70, 163, 223

Pinckney, Mary Stead, 71

Pinckney, Thomas, 160; banished, 69

Pindar, Peter, 100

Pino, Hipólito San José Giral del, *264*

piracy. *See* privateers

pitch, 19

Pitt (ship), *242*

Pittman, Capt. Philip, 193, *266*

Plantarum Americanarum fasciculus (Charles Plumier), 1*70*

plantations, expansion of, 55–56; society, 19

Plato's Head, London, 93

plays, 108, *241, 247, 257, 260, 319*

Pleas of the Crown (Sir Matthew Hale and William Hawkins), 159

Pliny, elder and younger, 190

Plumier, Charles, 169; *Plumier's Ferns, 319*

Plutarch, 34; *Lives,* 70

Plymouth, England, 12, 100

Poems (John Gay), 199

poetry, 153

"polemical divinity," 18, 89, 162, 190, 227, *252, 257*

Polignac, Melchior de, 190

Political Letters (Cato), 35

Polly (ship), 294, 315

Polly (Snow *Polly,* ship), *259*

Polyaenus, 190

Pomona: or, The Fruit-Garden Illustrated (Batty Langley), 164

Pompey the Little (Francis Coventry), 32

Poole, Matthew, 147, 153

Pope, Alexander, 93, 189

Port-au-Prince, 149

Porteus, Beilby, 193

Portland (Snow *Portland,* ship), *254*

ports, 12, 13, 17, 137; American, closed by winter, 12; clearing and entry, 144–45; transatlantic ports and transport of books to English outports, 12–13

Portsmouth, England, parcels and passengers joining at, 12

Portuguese (marine), *295*

Post Office, 13; *London, 335*

Postlethwayt, Malachy, 11

Potts, Mr., *242*

poultry, 164

Poultry, London, 96

Powell, Thomas, 76

power of attorney, ineffective, 120

Powhatan (ship), *304*

Practical Justice of the Peace (Joseph Shaw), 155

Practical Justice of the Peace (William Simpson), *214*

Pratt, Capt. John, *305, 322*

prayerbooks, 6

Presbyterian church, Charleston, 191

Present State of Music in France and Italy (Charles Burney), *269*

Present State of the European Settlements on the Missisippi [*sic*] (Capt. Philip Pittman), 193, *266*

Preservation; or, The Hovel of the Rocks, 201

press licensing, 6

Pretyman Tomline, Sir George, 193

Price, John, 129, *313;* and Co., *302, 303, 315, 316, 331*

Price, Richard, 214, *270*

Price, Samuel, 76

Priestley, Joseph, 155, *259, 265, 266, 274*

Prince Edward (ship), *243*

Prince of Wales (ship), *249*

Princeton, 178; library catalogue, 151; orrery, 178–79

Principles and Power of Harmony (Benjamin Stillingfleet), *269*

Principles of Action in Matter (Cadwallader Colden), 172

Principles of Natural Law (Jean Jacques Burlamaqui), 154–55, *265*

Pringle, John Julius, 160

Pringle, Robert, 168

print culture, ideas about, 14–15

"printedness," idea of, 14

printers, colonial, 28

printing, costs of in America, 6; development of in London, 107; and publishing in America, 211

printing presses, 6

prints, 194; conveyed, 108; imported from the Continent, 194–95

Prioleau, Philip, *279;* banished, 69. *See also* Legare, Theus, and Prioleau

Prioleau, Samuel, 82; banished, 69

privateers, 12, 131, 135, 204, 205, *322;* and loss of American pride and commerce, 205–6; and privateering, 132, 147–49

promissory notes, 121. *See also* bills of transfer

Prospects of the Mississippi River, 266

Protestantism, 10

Provincial Library at Charles-Town, 34

psalm books, 33

psalters, 12

Public Acts, 212

Public Advertiser, 188

public securities. *See* Charleston Library Society and American stock

public sphere, idea of, 14

publication, by subscription, 30, 31; and reprints in America, 205, 210, 211

Pufendorf, Samuel, 159, 188

Purchas, Samuel, 42, 43

quadrants, 174, 177, *252, 254, 255, 256*

quakers (Society of Friends), 10, 81, 82, 85, 99; as book agents, 4; books of, 163

Queen Charlotte, 226

Quincy, Josiah, Jr, 26, 77–78, 227; visit to CLS, 62

Rabelais, 222

Racquet and Co., *278*

Radcliffe, Ann, 222, *319*

Rainier, Capt. John, *255, 259*

Rainier, Capt. Peter, *264*

Ramage, Mr., 72; his tavern as CLS meeting place, 61

Rambler, 154

Ramsay, Dr. David 20, 147, 167–68, 200, 212, 214, 220, *281, 301, 305, 306;* banished, 69; his publications, 30

Ramsay, Martha Laurens, 70

Ramsden, Jesse, 180, 181, *278, 279, 284, 291*

Ranger (ship), *311, 312*

Raper, Robert, 31

Rapin, Paul de, 32

Rattray, John, 35

Raynal, Abbé, 71

Read, James, 120

Reade, Samuel, 11

readers, and imagined community, 227

reading, colonial experience of, 227; educational and occupational, 152; women and, 70–71, 174, 201–3

Reading, William, 10

Real Christian's Hope in Death, 30

Reason, goddess of, 43

Recherches sur les modifications de l'atmosphère (Jean André Deluc), 82, 192

Recorder (Thomas Holcroft), *324*

Recovery (ship), *309*

Redwood Library Company, Newport, Rhode Island, 3, 5, 11, 218

reference works, 163

Reflections on the Causes of the Grandeur and Declension of the Romans ("Letters on the Roman Republick") (Charles, Baron de Montesquieu), *263*

Reflections on the Painting and Sculpture of the Greeks (Johann Joachim Winckelmann), 223

Religion of Nature Delineated (William Wollaston), 154, 192

religious books, 153

Religious Ceremonies and Customs of the Several Nations of the Known World (Bernard Picart), 162, *269*

religious exiles, 21

Religious Tract Society, 193

Remington, John, 76, 93, 125, 126, 175, 176, *242, 243, 245*

Reports (Sir John Strange), 102

Repton, Humphry, 305

Reuben and Rachel (Susanna Rowson), 215

Review of the History of England, 35

Review of the War in Mysore (James Salmond), 188

Review of the Works of the Royal Society (John Hill), 173

reviews. *See* periodicals

revolution, American, 3, 20, 84, 126, 127; and Loyalist zeal, 19; revolutionary cause in Philadelphia, 179; and revolutionary war, 68, 88, 95, 132, *272*

Revolutionary Congress [of South Carolina], 157

Reynolds, Sir Joshua, 91

Rhimer. *See* Rymer

Rhode Island, 215, 218. See *also* Redwood Library Company

rice, 12, 19, 20, 32, 98, 168

Rich, Capt. —, *294*

Richards, Capt. —, *304*

Richardson, Joseph, 87

Richardson, Samuel, 199; read by Eliza Pinckney, 70

Richmond, Virginia, 197

rights of Englishmen, 156, 160

Rights of War and Peace (Grotius), 159

Ripa, Caesar, 49

Rising, Capt. John, *314*

Rittenhouse, David, 177–79; and his orrery, 220

River Thames, depiction of, 112

Rivington and Fletcher, firm of, 92, *240;* elected as CLS bookseller, 92, *256*

Rivington, Charles, Sr., 91

Rivington, Charles II, 91

Rivington, F. C. & J., 216, *334, 336, 339*

Rivington, James, 7, 33, 92, 93, 94, 103, 113, 119, 121, 125, 146, 148, 177,

Rivington, James (*continued*)
  237, 238, 239, 240, 242; and John, 87,
  91; firm elected as CLS bookseller, 91
Rivington, John, 93, *241;* and James, 87,
  91; firm elected as CLS bookseller 91
Rivingtons, bookselling family of, 87,
  91–92
Robertson, William, 193, 200, 221, *259*
Roderick Random (Tobias Smollett), 199
Roebuck (ship), *302*
Rogers, George, 23, 157, 183
Rolle, Denys, *250*
Roman Catholicism, 21, 192
Roman History (Nathaniel Hooke), 161,
  258
*Roman History, from the Building of Rome to
  the Ruin of the Commonwealth*
  (Nathaniel Hooke), *269*
Roman law, 156
Romulus (brigantine), *299*
Roper, Thomas, *335*
Rosa or American Genius and Education, 201
Roscoe, William, 222, *319*
Rose and Crown, the Poultry, London, 96
Rose, Alexander, 69
Rossel, James Theodore, *249*
Rotterdam, 278
Roughead. *See* Ruffhead
Round Court, Strand, London, 93
Rowand, Robert, 55
Rowley, John, 178
Rowson, Susanna, 215
Royal Charlotte (ship), *244*
Royal College of Physicians, London, 169
Royal Exchange, London, 126, 127
Royal Literary Fund, 226
Royal Military Academy, 179
Royal Society for the Encouragement of
  Arts, Manufactures and Commerce, 167

Royal Society of Arts, 168
Royal Society, London, 48, 167, 169, 170,
  173, 181, 219
Ruby (ship), *294, 295, 304, 315*
Ruddiman, Thomas (as translator), 189
Rudiments of English Grammar (Joseph
  Priestley), *259*
Ruffhead, Owen, *258*
Rules for French Infantry, 323
rum books, 7, 92
Rush, Benjamin, 171, 212
Russell, Richard, 222
Russell, Nathaniel, 200, 215, *274, 332,
  333, 334,*
Rust, Capt. —, *306*
Rutledge family, 128
Rutledge, Andrew, 49, 62
Rutledge, John Jr., 160; European Tour
  by, 64
Rutty [Ruthy], John, 170, *270*
Rymer, Thomas, *259*

Sacheverell, Thomas, 37
Sadler, Catherine, xvii
Saint-Evremond, Works of, 263, 264
Sainte Domingue, 17, *214, 215;* declaration
  of independence, *214*
Salem Social Library, 51, 85, 119, 148
Salem, 11, 51, 132
Salkeld, William, 159
Sallust, 105, *279*
Sally (ship), *274, 294*
Salmon, Thomas, 35, *258*
Salmond, James, 188
salt, danger to books, *338*
Samuel Johnson, 96
Savage, Benjamin, 97, *288. See also* Bird,
  Savage, and Bird
Savage, John, 97–98

Savannah Library Society, 200; catalogue, 151; foundation and membership, 68; rules of, 64

Saxby, George, *253;* estates confiscated, 69

Say, C., 85

Scholar Arm'd, 192

school and cheap books, 110

schools, for slave children, 46

science and natural history, colonial interest in, 170–73; demonstrations and experiments, 166–67, 172–74

scientific academies, 173

scientific and botanical illustrations, 194

scientific and legal manuals, in Latin, 190

scientific communities, 172

scientific instruments, 64, 166–83, 206, *248, 252, 256, 282, 293, 295;* instrument workshops in London, 181–82

Scold, J., *268*

Scotland, 13, 117, 119; customs records of, 33; trade to Charleston, 32, 204. *See also* Scots

Scots, 22; trading diaspora of, 103; and Presbyterians, 153; and anti-Scots prejudices, 103. *See also* Scotland

Scots "Jews," 103

Scott, James, vendue master, 86, 103

Scott, Capt. John, *272*

Scott, John, author, *277*

Scott, John, bookseller, 33, 84

Scott, Jonathan, translator, 189

Scott, Sarah, 198

Scott, William, 73

Scripture chronological tables (John Brown), *265*

Scripture-Dictionary (James Chalmers), 162, *289*

sea captains, local, 133–34; and family ties, 103

sea passage, length of, 135; and turnround, 134. *See also* book transit

Seaman, George, 49, 194

Secker, Thomas, 191

second Charleston library society. *See* Franklin Library

secondhand books, *250*

sectarianism, 191–92, 214

Selden, John. *See Fleta seu commentarius juris Anglicani*

Select Batchelors Society, Charleston, 50

Seneca, 189

Sentimental Journey through Greece (Pierre Augustin Guys), *269*

Septuagint, *264*

serial publications. *See* periodicals

Sermons (Francis Atterbury), 192

Sermons (Thomas Secker), 191

Sermons (William Paley), 191

Sermons to Young Women (Dr. James Fordyce), 202

sermons, other religious writings, and scriptural scholarship, 162; printed in Charleston, 213

Servitude (Robert Dodsley), 93

Seven Sisters (brigantine), *302*

Seven Years' War, 22, 148

Sewall, Samuel, 10, 129, 134

Sewel, William, 163

Shaftesbury, Anthony Ashley Cooper, third earl of, 153

Shakespeare Gallery, London, 196, 197. See *also* Boydell

Shakespeare, William, 34, 80, 195, 222, *261, 312; Dramatic Works,* 198, 199; prints of, 99, 198. *See also* Boydell

Shaw and Le Blanc, firm of, *327*

Shaw, Capt. —, *304*

Shaw, Joseph, 155

Shecut, John, 30, 79, 216
sheepskin bindings, 110
Shenstone, William, Works of, 252
Sherb, Christopher, 168
Sherborne, England, 100
Sheridan, Thomas, 165, *265*
Shields, David, 51–52
shipping. *See* book transit; ships
ships, 133; across the ocean, 11, 109, 112; armed, 148–49; capture of, 132, 205, *308;* cargoes, 135; crew sizes, 131; delays, 116, 141; importance of American, *292;* insurance, 115, 116, 205; loading and clearing out, 141; news of, 133–34; ownership of, 103, 206–8; routes of, 135; and shipping improvements, 13; sinkings and seizures, 204, *244;* time in port, 144–45. *See also* book transit
Shirley, (?)Thomas, *269*
Shoolbred and Williams, firm of, *322*
Short Introduction to English Grammar (Robert Lowth), 252
Shubrick, Richard, 126–7; and Thomas, 126
Sicilian Romance (Ann Radcliffe), 222
Sidney (or Sydney), Algernon, 157, 188, *265*
Siege of Belgrade (James Cobb), 201
sight, periods of. *See* bills of transfer
sights. *See* telescopes
Simblett[s], Capt. Henry, *257, 259*
Simeon, Claude and Charles, 193
Simon, Richard, 192
Simons, Mr., 62
Simpson and Co., *300*
Simpson and Davison, merchants, *310, 311*
Simpson, James, *253*
Simpson, John and Co., *265. See also* Simpson and Co.

Simpson, Thomas, 155
Simpson, William, 214
Sinclair, John, 31, 37, 61; library of, 77
single microscope. *See* microscope
Sion College, England, 10
Sketches and Hints (Humphry Repton), *305*
slave trade, 45, 128; resumption of, 20. *See also* negroes; slaves
slaves, 4, 20, 46, 168; as pressmen, 41; classical names of, 47; consignments of, 39, 126; headrights of, 55–56; importers of, 45; school for, 46; and slave labor, 19; uprisings of, 25, 46. *See also* negroes; slave trade
Sloane, Sir Hans, 164, 168, 169
Smellie, William, 222, *292, 293*
Smith, Benjamin, 81, 158
Smith, D., 213
Smith, Eliza, 202
Smith, Capt. James, *241*
Smith, James Edward, 194, *301*
Smith, Josiah, 214
Smith, Julius, *271*
Smith, Dr. Robert (later Bishop), 86, 191, *253, 275*
Smith, William (Provost of New Jersey College/Princeton), 178
Smith, William, author, 212
Smollett, Tobias, 32, 199, *240, 247, 255, 263*
snakes, 149
sociability, 51–52, 228; and discursive institutions, 15–16
social library, idea of, 58
societies, as loan agencies, 59; dinners by, 58; female membership of, 69; preambles to rules of, 50–51. *See also* library societies
Society for Promoting Christian Knowledge [SPCK], 34, 42, 91

Society for the Propagation of the Gospel in Foreign Parts [SPG], 34, 88; bookplate of, 42–43; plan for a school at Charleston, 34; receives books, 34; as state bond-holder [listed as Society for the Propagation of Christian Knowledge], 60

Society of Antiquarians, London, 48, 194, *266*

Society of Apothecaries, London, 164

Society of Cincinnati, 76

Society of Friends. *See* Quakers

Soho mint, Birmingham, England, 196–97

solar microscope. *See* microscope

Solomon's Lodge of Masons, Charleston, 50

Soranzo, William, 201

South Carolina:
   —agriculture, 163–64
   —ancient political rights and liberties, 18
   —backcountry of, 17, 80; and its backwardness, 43
   —bees, 164
   —bills of credit, 144
   —bonds, 60
   —book collecting, 153
   —book shipment records, 204
   —books, entertainment, and education, 223
   —botany, 167–70
   —British connections, 226
   —British reoccupation of, 22
   —and Caribbean, 219
   —cash crops in, 19
   —cash economy of, 124
   —circulating libraries, 222
   —climate of, 21, 166, 170
   —colonial agents of, 103, 168
   —as commercial country, 47
   —constitution, 191; historical approaches to, 14–18
   —and country ideology, 17
   —culture of virtue in, 26
   —currency, 124
   —disease in, 166–67, 170
   —economy, 19–20, 22–23
   —elite culture of, 17–18
   —exceptionalism of, 80
   —factors, *267*
   —fauna and ornithology, 169
   —growth of, 20
   —intellectual life of, 152, 223
   —isolation of, 219
   —literary and scientific distinction of, 25, 33–34, 219–20
   —medical interests, 170–71
   —merchants of, 3
   —merchants in London, 126
   —natural disasters, 21
   —news and information, 133
   —planter aristocracy of, 23
   —politics, 157
   —population of, 20
   —prejudice against, 227
   —printers in, 28
   —private libraries in, 34–35, 156, 169, 222–23
   —and regional identity, 17
   —regulations, reports and special publications of local churches and societies, 214
   —religious conflict in, 21
   —Revolutionary Congress of, 157
   —and scientific instruments, 173
   —sectarianism in, 191–92
   —sense of self-importance, 16–17
   —social and intellectual life, 202–3

South Carolina (*continued*)
—state debt of, 98
—state laws and ordinances, 214
—state senators, 76
See *also* Carolina Coffee House;
Charleston; *South Carolina Gazette*
South Carolina (ship), *304, 306*
South Carolina Agricultural Society, 168
*South Carolina and American General
Gazette,* 41
South Carolina Assembly: grant for books,
34; ratifies library, 34
South Carolina Bank Building, as housing
CLS, 63
South Carolina College, 76, 183, 206, 207,
208; library of, 213, *326*
South Carolina Commons House of
Assembly, 18, 28, 157, 158; leaders of,
67; printer to, 213; and its library, 202
South Carolina Council, 157
South Carolina Gazette, 28, 31, 32, 33, 35,
61, 91, 92, 156, 157, 222; advertise-
ments in, 41, 77; on Charleston society,
56; and CLS foundation, 37; and CLS
public advertisements, 59, 65; and
debates about baptizing slaves, 46; list of
CLS founder members, 38; list of lost
books, 56; on processions, 52; and ship-
ping news, 133–34
South Carolina Library Society (mistaken
address for CLS), *296, 303. See also*
Charleston Library Society
South Carolina Society, 41; foundation of,
50
South Carolina State Assembly: resolutions
of, 214
South Carolina statehouse library, 158
South Carolina Supreme Court, 220
South Carolina Treasury, CLS loans to, 60
Southampton, England, 12

South-Carolina Laws (Nicholas Trott), 158
South-Carolina Society for Promoting and
Improving Agriculture, 214
"Southern cultural lag," 152, 222
Southwark, England, *284*
Spanish Dictionary (Hipólito San José Giral
del Pino), *264*
Spectator, 153; as model, 51
Spelman, Sir Henry, 159, 160, 161, 186,
252
Spencer, Mr., of London, 147
Spenser, Edmund, 199
Spirit of the Laws (Charles, Baron de
Montesquieu), 156
Sprat, Thomas, 173
St. Andrew (ship), *322*
St. Andrews, Charleston, 190
St. Andrew's Society, Charleston, 22, 50,
67, 171, 226; foundation of, 50;
preamble to rules of, 50–51
St. Augustine, 13, 22
St. Cecilia Society, Charleston, 50, 71, 202;
as state bond-holder, 60; foundation of
50; rules of, 51; women banned from, 69
St. Clair, General Arthur, *282*
St. David's Society, Charleston, 50
St. George's Society, Charleston, 50; as state
bond-holder, 60; foundation of, 50
St. Helena (ship), *257*
St. James, Goose Creek, S.C., 35; as state
bond-holder, 60
St. James's, Haymarket, London, 181
St. John Laird (ship), *287*
St. Mary Axe, London, 88
St. Patrick society (Friendly Sons of St.
Patrick), 22, 50
St. Paul's Church Yard, London, 94, 95,
109, 110, 177, 216, *334*
St. Paul's Cathedral, London, 91, 127
St. Peter's Hill, London, 127

St. Philip's, Charleston, 30, 44; rector of, 96

St. Stephen's parish, Charleston, 24

Stamp Act, repeal of, 188

Starr, Rebecca, 80

State Bank, Charleston, 213

State of Russia under the Present Czar (Capt. John Perry), *259*

State of the Nation, 260

State Papers (John Thurloe), 159

State Trials, 155, *252, 262*

Stationers' Company, London, 132

Stationers' Hall, London, 194

Statutes at Large (John Cay), 155, 158, *258*

Statutes at Large (Owen Ruffhead), *258*

Statutes at Large, 267

Stedman, John, 215

Steevens, George, 195

Steevens, Isaac Reed, 195

Stephanus, Henricus (Henri Estienne le Grand), 190; *324, 328*

Stephens, Capt. John, *243*

Sterne, Laurence 199, *250*

Steuart, Sir James, *259*

Steven (Greek thesaurus). *See* Stephanus

Stevenson, J., 125, *237*

Stewart, Matthew, *259, 262*

Steyning Lane, London, 91

Stith, William, 212

Stockdale, John, 5, 6, 88, 90, 99, 108, 109, 115, 118, 120, 129, 130, 132, 134, 141, 145, *281, 282, 284, 286, 287, 288, 290;* appointed CLS bookseller, 97; dismissed, 97, *286;* and book searches, *288–89;* and packing arrangements, 147

Stone, Edmund, 182

Stonehenge (William Stukeley), 162

Stono slave rebellion, 25, 46

Stradæ prolusiones, 190

Strahan, William, 7, 80–81, 87, 89, 90–91, 92, 93, 95, 113, 118, 119, 120, 234, *237, 238;* correspondence with Hall, 86, 103, 146; dismissed by CLS, 91; elected as CLS bookseller, 90; prints CLS catalogue, 54–55

Straits of Gibraltar, 132, *295*

Strange, Sir John, 102

Stratagems of War (Polyaenus), 190

Stuart, Francis, 194

Stuart, John 41; as a mason, 50

Stukeley, William, 161–62

Success (ship), 149, *246, 249*

Sufferings of the Quakers (Joseph Besse), 163

sugar ships, 12; and "sugar route," 11

Sully, by Maximilien de Béthune, duc de, 200

Sunderland, Charles Spencer, third earl of, 118

Supplement to the Encyclopaedia Britannica, 212

Supplement to the English Universal History (Siegmund Jakob Baumgarten), *243, 247*

Sutherland, Alexander, 170, *270*

Swallow (H.M. packet boat), *264*

Swammerdam, John, 170, *265*

Swift, Jonathan, Works of, 252, 262, 312

Synopsis criticorum (Matthew Poole), 147

Synopsis of Quadrupeds (Thomas Pennant), 170, *269*

System of Chemistry (Thomas Thomson), *323*

Systema naturae (Linnaeus), 46, *265*

Tables of Ancient Coins (John Arbuthnot), 162

Tacitus, 105, 190, 200

taler. *See* dollar

Tales (Maria Edgeworth), 71

Tales of an Old Tub, 154

taverns, 171, 174; as CLS meeting places, 72

Taylor, James, 33

Taylor, Jeremy, 202

Taylor, John, 154, 247

telescopes, 173, 174, 180–82, *252, 262, 263, 272, 292–93;* and CLS repair problems, 129, 181–82, 220, *273, 276, 277, 278, 279, 283, 284, 291;* sights, 177, *262*

Tempest, Pierce, 49

Temple Coffee House Botany Club, London, 167

Temple of the Muses, Finsbury Square, London, 99, 100. See *also* Lackington, James; Lackington, Allen, and Co.

Terence, 189

Tertullian, 190, *Works of,* 259

Tew, Thomas, 35

Thames, River, 12, 133; wharves of, 127

theology, 193; theological titles, 152

thermometers, 177, *252, 256. See also* scientific instruments

Thesaurus linguæ latinae lompendiarius (Robert Ainsworth), *241*

thesaurus, Greek and Latin, 190

Theus, James, *281, 286. See also* Legare, Theus, and Prioleau

Thomas Cooper Library, University of South Carolina, 222

Thomas, Ebenezer, 85, 204, 215

Thomas, Isaiah, 6, 33; on Robert Wells, 41

Thomas, John, 35

Thomas, Rev. Samuel Thomas of Charleston, 34

Thomlinson, Hanbury, Colebrooke and Nesbitt, firm 126, *241;* Bucklersbury premises, 127. *See also* Thomlinson, John

Thomlinson, John, 5, 11

Thomson, Thomas, *323*

Thrasi, Steven, 178

Throgmorton St, London, 127

Thurloe, John, 159

Tibbits, Capt. —, *329*

Tillotson, Archbishop John, 32, 152; *Sermons of,* 153

Timothée, Louis. *See* Timothy, Lewis

Timothy and Mason, firm of, 190

Timothy, Elizabeth, 28, 31

Timothy, Lewis, 28–30, 47

Timothy, Peter, 28, 37, 157, 202, 213

Tindal, Matthew, 153

Tissot, Samuel Auguste David, *252*

Titi Petronii arbitri satyricon, 243

tobacco, 135; and tobacco ships, 12

Todd, Mr., *312*

Tom Jones (Henry Fielding), 198

Tonson, Jacob, 89

Topographical Description of Virginia, Pennsylvania, Maryland, and North Carolina ([?]Th. Hutchins), 193

tortoises, 149

Tour in Scotland (Thomas Pennant), *269*

Tour Through Holland (Samuel Ireland), *289*

Tovey, De Blossiers, 154, 247

Town and Country Magazine, 11

Tracts, Physical and Mathematical (Matthew Stewart), *259, 262*

Tradd Street, Charleston, 41

Trade and Commerce (Adam Anderson), 221

trade publishers, 89

trade winds, 11–12

trade, to the Far East, 189; turbulence in, 127–28

tradesmen and kinship ties to CLS, 98

tragedies, 241, 247, 257

Traité des fougères de l'Amerique (Charles Plumier), 169–70

Tranquebar, East-Indies, 10

transaction costs, 114–16, 125–26

Transactions of the American Philosophical Society, 178

Transactions of the New York Society for the Promotion of Agriculture, 212

Transactions of the Royal Society, 166

transatlantic book trade, 3, 6, 102–5; difficulties of, 11; crossing difficulties of, seasonality, 12; crossings speeds, 12; shipping routes, 11–12; personal relations, 102. *See also* book trade; book transit; Charleston Library Society

transatlantic letters, 172; speed of, 11

transatlantic market, 87

transatlantic relationships, 16

travel books, 203

Travels (John Lawson), 169, *262*

Travels (Thomas Holcroft), 194, 209; and missing plates, *322, 323, 324*

Travels in Italy (Jean Jacques Barthelemy), *314*

Travels in the Interior Parts of America (William Clark), 193

Travels in Upper and Lower Egypt (Vivant Denon), *313–14*

Travels into North America (Peter Kalm), 193, 270

Travels through . . . the Russian Empire (P. S. Pallas), *312*

treaties, collections of, 266

Treatise of Artificial Magnets (John Mitchell), 171

Treatise of Fevers (John Ball), 171

Treatise of the Indian Americans, 31

Treatise on Hieroglyphics (Horapollo Nilous), 44

Treatise on the Art of Dancing (Giovani Gallini), 165, *252, 262*

Treatise on the Management of Bees (Thomas Wildman), 164; *270*

Trial (ship), *301*

Tristram Shandy (Laurence Sterne), 132, 199, *250*

Trott, Nicholas 30, 158

Trott, Sarah, widow of Nicholas, 35

Trublet, Nicolas C. J., l'Abbé, *243;* essays of, *244*

Truron, William, *312*

Tull, Jethro, 164

Tully's Head bookshop, London, 93

Tunno, John, 208, 209, *302, 303, 307, 325, 328;* and Loughnan, 146, *315, 316, 320, 327, 331;* Tunno's bag, 146, *282*

Turl, Oxford, 94

"turn-round" ship passages, 134, 135, 140, 205; as handicaps, 145; improvement in, 145

turpentine, 19

Twelve Commentaries on Fevers (Thomas Glass), 171

Two Brothers (ship), *306, 307*

Two Catechisms (Henry Heywood), 202

Two Friends (ship), 136, 140, 141, 205, *318, 323, 324, 326, 28;* and its seizure, 205–8, *323, 325, 327*

Two Treatises of Government (John Locke), 156

Tybee Island, Ga., 13

Tycho Brahe's Head, Fleet Street, London, 175

ubiquarians, 50

underwriting. *See* insurance

Union Library Company of Philadelphia, 3; catalogues of, 151

Union Library of Hatboro, Pennsylvania, 70

Union St., Charleston, *267*

unitarians, 192

United Provinces, interrupted commerce
with Britain, *300*

United States, federal courts, 127–28; seal
of, 44

Universal History, 32, 161, *245, 270*

Universal Magazine, 49, 111, 112, *240,
244, 247, 255*

Universal Review, 240

unsaleable books, 87, 89, 92. *See also* rum
books

Urquhart, Capt. Alexander, *269*

Usher, John, 10

Ussher, James, *269*

usuance, 125

Utrecht, professor of Hebrew at, 10

Valk, Jacob, 73, 74

Varnod, widow, 203

Vattel (or Vattell), Emmerich de, 155,
158, *258*

Vaughan, John, *309, 338*

Vegetable Staticks (Stephen Hales), 172

vendue. *See* auctions and book auctions

Venus de Medicis, 78

Viart, Jacob, 28

Vicary, Capt. —, *301*

Vie de Toussaint Louverture (Dubroca of
Herbemont), 215

View of South-Carolina (John Drayton), 30,
214

View of the War with Tippo Sultan (Alexander
Beatson), 188

Vincent, Nicholas, 153

vines, 168

Virgil, 105; read by Eliza Pinckney, 70

Virginia Coffee House, 145

Virginia resolutions 157

Virginia, 6, 79, 147; bills of credit, 124;
population of, 28; tobacco aristocracy,
17–18

Vitruvius Britannicus (Colen Campbell),
317

Vitruvius Pollio, 269

Voltaire, 155, *270; Works of, 269*

voluntary societies, 27

Votes of Parliament, 237

Vowell, bookseller of Cambridge, England,
100

Voyage from England to India (Edward Ives),
270

Voyage Round the World (Comte Louis-
Antoine de Bougainville), *269*

*Voyage to the Islands Madera, Barbados,
Niewas* (Sir Hans Sloane), 168

Wagner, John, 59

Wakefield, Gilbert, 190

Walcot, James, 153

Wallace, Capt. —, *299*

Waller, Thomas, 87

Walter, John, 59

Walter, Thomas, 169

Wanderer (ship), *323, 325, 326*

War of 1812, 4, 22, 148, 216

War of Independence, 81, 89, 148, 168

Warburton, William, 35

Ward, John, agent to NYSL, 10, 116,
131–32, *278*

Ward, Joshua, 60, *277*

Wardell, Capt. —, *302*

warfare: and foreign hostilities, 132,
325–26; disrupting trade, 13, 148,
329, 330

Warner, Ferdinando, *252, 262*

Warner, Michael, 227

Warren, Mercy Otis, 212

Warrington, England, 193

Washington (ship), *302*

Washington, D.C., 193

Washington, George, 70; biographies of, 212

Waterhouse, Richard, 67, 79, 80

Watkins, Adrian, 117

Watts, Isaac, 32, 82, 153

Wauchop, Capt. George, *264*

Webb, Daniel, *243*

Webb, George, 28

Webster, Pelatiah, 78

Wedgwood, Josiah, 196

Weems, Mason Locke, 212

Wells, Helena, 226

Wells, Robert, 33, 46, 77, 81, 84, 85, 88, 92, 96–97, 101, 103, 109, 129, 165, 180, 182, 196, 197, 214, 234, *253, 267, 279;* book advertisements, 151; bookshop in Charleston, 41; elected CLS bookseller, 97, *277;* estates confiscated, 69; and local book supply, 41; and loyalism, 226; as a mason, 50; printer of CLS rules, 53

Wesley, John and Charles, 30

West India merchants, 126

West Indian (ship), *309*

West Indies, 13, 19, 20, 226

Westberry (ship), *286*

Westminster, 100. *See also* House of Commons

Westminster Hall, 94–95

Westminster School, 160

Westover, Virginia, 163

Whatley, Samuel, 105, 163

White, Capt. John, *243*

White Lyon Court London, 91

White, Mr. Painter, 78

White, Thomas, 87

Whitefield, George, 46, 49, 153

Whitmarsh, Thomas, 28

Whitworth, Sir Charles, *266*

Whytt, Robert, 223

Wieland: An American Novel (Charles Brockden Brown), 201, 212

Wigg, Edward, 31, 167

Wildman, Thomas, 164, *270*

Wilkes, John, 97, 157

Williamsburg, Va., 87, 103, 119, 141

Williamson, John, 201

Williamson, William, 65

Wilson, Alexander, 212

Wilson, bookseller of Charleston, 33

Wilson, Capt. —, *302*

Wilson, Capt. James, *266*

Wilson, Capt. Roderick, *249*

Wilson, David, 88, 108, 113, 121, 125, 126, 141, 149, 176, *241, 242, 243, 244, 245, 246, 262;* elected as CLS bookseller, 93; and instruments, 175; and loss of order, 136–37. *See also* Durham, Thomas; Durham and Wilson, firm of

Wilson, James, 59

Winans, Robert, 87

Winckelmann, Johann Joachim, 223

wine, 168, 173

Wine Office Court, off Fleet Street, London, 90

Winthrop family, London books for, 10; papers of, 9

Winthrop, John, 147

Winthrop, Wait, 11

Winyaw (or Winyah), 44

Winyaw (ship), *304*

Winyaw Indico Society, 168; as state bondholder, 60

Witherspoon, John, 178

Wolf, Edwin, 155

Wollaston, William, 154, 192; as
    "Wolston," 153
women: banned from local societies, 69;
    book borrowing by, 200; and electrical
    experiments, 174, 180; and libraries, 16;
    as library members, advertised for, 8;
    merchants, 70; and reading, 70–71,
    174, 201–3, 220; and sociability, 16
Wood, George, 33, 76, 84, 201, 222
Wood, Thomas, 159
Woodfall, George, 188
Woodfall, Henry Sampson, 188
Woodmason, Charles, 32, 43
Woods and Dillwyn, firm of, 4, 85, 99
Woods, Samuel, 99. *See also* Woods and
    Dillwyn
Woodward, William W., 211, *334, 337*
Woolf, Capt. Ephraim, *244*
Workman, James, 201
World, The, 93
Wragg, family of, 25, 39, 46
Wragg, John, 69
Wragg, Joseph Jr., 37, 39; library of, 156
Wragg, Samuel Jr., 37, 39
Wragg, William, 157
Wright and Gill. *See* Gill and Wright

Wright, Alexander, 69
Wright, James, 159
Wright, Joseph, of Derby, 195
Wright, Thomas, 90
Wurtenburg, Duke of, 178
Wye, Maryland, 197
Wynne, John Huddlestone, *269*

xebeques, 132, *295*

Yale, 82, 166, 201; catalogues of the college
    library, 151; libraries of, 63
Yarmouth (schooner), 135
yellow fever, 21, 167
Yelverton, Sir Henry, 159
Young Carpenter's Assistant (Owen Biddle),
    212
Young Gentlemen and Ladys Philosophy
    (Benjamin Martin), *252*
Young Secretary (Hill), 125
Young, William Price, 85, 200, 212, 213,
    216

Zahniser, Marvin R., 84
Zeluco (John Moore), 83
Zoological System (Linnaeus), *292, 293*